For all the students, teachers and programmers who want to get professional programming methodology and advanced programming proficiency.

LEARN PROFESSIONAL PROGRAMMING IN .NET USING C#, VISUAL BASIC, AND ASP.NET

Adalat Khan

Library of Congress Control Number:		2018909718
ISBN:	Hardcover	978-1-9845-0153-0
	Softcover	978-1-9845-0154-7
	eBook	978-1-9845-0155-4

Print information available on the last page.

Rev. date: 08/25/2018

To order additional copies of this book, contact:
Xlibris
1-800-455-039
www.Xlibris.com.au
Orders@Xlibris.com.au
513543

Contents

In the name of ALLAH who is merciful and mighty

Dedication

I dedicate this effort to my beloved parents whose cordial prayers, guidance and encouragement helped me success in my goal.

Preface

First of all I am grateful to almighty Allah for granting the great chance of utilizing my knowledge and experience. No man or his knowledge is utterly perfect. Rather everybody in this world tries his best to attempt solving problems to the maximum extent. I have only tried my best to provide due guidance and step-wise solution of programming in .NET. The main purpose of writing this book is to provide professional programming logics and deep concepts of programming. This book covers the basic programming fundamentals, professional programming logics and deep concepts of programming in .NET such as the flow control statements in C# and Visual Basic, the basic programming techniques, procedures and procedural programming concepts, arrays, structures, delegates, Lambda Expression, Errors and Exceptions handling in .NET, Windows applications development, Console applications development, Object Oriented programming, the study of different Namespaces, Files and Streams handling in C# and Visual Basic programming languages, Introduction to Database and Database Management System, Database Programming, LINQ in .NET, Collections in .NET, Web Technologies in .NET, ASP.NET, the basic requirements of ASP.NET, Websites and Web applications development, MVC Web application development, Web Services, Web APIs. This book covered the above-mentioned topics in details in a very simple way. It also contains various advanced logical programs. Each topic in this book is explained with suitable programming examples. The programs in this book are error free and fully tested and executed using Microsoft Visual Studio.NET 2015 Enterprise Edition.

This book provides deep programming techniques and knowledge from beginning level to the higher level and it is efficient for all those students, teachers, and researchers who want to get professional programming logics and become professional programmers.

The Book Organization

This book contains 19 Chapters. Following is the details of the chapters:

Chapter # 1

This chapter explains the .NET Framework, the .NET Framework Class Library, Basic Class Library, Common Language Infrastructure, Common Intermediate Language, Common Language Specification, Common Type System, Virtual Execution System, Namespaces, Assembly, Microsoft Visual Studio.NET, Visual Studio.NET Application Projects, Console Applications, Windows Applications, the structure of C# program, the structure of Visual Basic.NET program, Basic Components of Windows Applications, Windows Forms, Control Objects, Events, Events Handlers, Application development in .NET.

Chapter # 2

This Chapter explains Variables, types of variables, Constants, the variables naming conventions, limitation of variables, memory representation of different types of variables, the Scope of variables, Expressions, Escape Sequences, Keywords, type Casting, Comments, Operators and its different types such as Arithmetic Operators, Arithmetic Assignment Operators, Compound Assignment Operators, Relational Operators, Logical Operators, Increment and Decrements Operators, the Prefix Increment and Decrement Operators, the Postfix Increment and Decrement Operators, Convention of Expression Solutions, the sizeof Operator, Conditional Operator.

Chapter # 3

This Chapter explains the flow control statements in .NET programming languages (C#, Visual Basic) such as the Sequence statements, the Selection statements i.e. "if statement", if-else statements, nested if-else statements, and switch statement, Iterative statements i.e. the Counted loops (for loop) and the Uncounted Loops (the while loop, and do-while loop), break statement, continue statement, goto statement, and foreach loop

Chapter # 4

This chapter explains Arrays, types of arrays, Arrays declarations, Arrays Initializations, Memory Representations of Arrays, Jagged arrays, Structures, declaration of Structures, declaration of Structure variables, memory representation of Structures, structure of arrays.

Chapter # 5

This Chapter explains Procedures, Benefits of Procedures, Parts of Procedures, Access Modifier, Return Type, Procedure Name, Parameter List, Types of Procedures, Methods, and Types of Methods in C#, Static Methods, Non-Static

Methods, Functions, Subroutines, and Naming Convention for Procedures, Variables Scopes and Lifetime.

Chapter # 6

This Chapter explains Object Oriented programming in details such as Classes, Declaration of Classes, Features of Classes, Constructors, Default Constructor, Parameterized Constructor, Copy Constructor, Static Constructor, Destructors, Objects, Declaration of Objects, Accessing Members of a Class, Encapsulation / Data Hiding, Inheritance, Accessibility, Types of Classes, Abstract Class, Sealed Class, Static Class, Interface, Polymorphism, Methods Overloading, Methods Overriding, Virtual Method, Operators Overloading, the types of access modifiers such as Private, Public, Protected, Internal, Internal Protected.

Chapter # 7

This Chapter explains characters, Strings and String classes in details.

Chapter # 8

This Chapter explains Exception and Errors handling.

Chapter # 9

This Chapter explains designing and building Windows applications.

Chapter # 10

This Chapter explains Database and Database Management System.

Chapter # 11

This Chapter explains Database application development in .NET.

Chapter # 12

This Chapter explains Delegates and Lambda expression in details.

Chapter # 13

This chapter explains Collections in .NET.

Chapter # 14

This chapter explains LINQ in .NET.

Chapter # 15

This Chapter explains Streams and Stream classes in .NET.

Chapter # 16
This Chapter explains Web Technologies in .NET.

Chapter # 17
This Chapter explains the basic fundamentals and requirements of ASP.NET.

Chapter # 18
This chapter explains Websites and Web applications development in ASP.NET.

Chapter # 19
This chapter explains Web Services in .NET.

Adalat Khan

July, 2018

CHAPTER 1

The .NET Framework and .NET Programming Languages

CHAPTER CONTENTS

- Computer Programming
- Types of Computer Programming
- Structure Programming
- Object Oriented Programming
- Programming Languages
- Types of Programming Languages
- Low Level Languages
- Machine Language
- Assembly Language
- High Level Languages
- Types of High Level Languages
- Translator
- Assembler
- Compiler
- Interpreter
- Data
- Types of Data
- Qualitative Data
- Quantitative Data
- Discreet Data
- Continuous Data
- Data Representation in Computer System
- Data of Programming Languages
- Numeric Data
- Alphabetic Data
- Alphanumeric Data
- Introduction to .NET Framework
- The .NET Framework Class Library
- Basic Class Library

- Common Language Infrastructure
- Common Intermediate Language
- Common Language Specification
- Common Type System
- Virtual Execution System
- Namespaces
- Fully Qualified Name of a Class
- User-defined Namespaces
- Built-in Library Namespaces in .NET
- Assembly
- Microsoft Visual Studio.NET
- Microsoft Visual Studio.NET Code Editor
- Microsoft Visual Studio.NET Debugger
- Microsoft Visual Studio.NET Designer
- Microsoft Visual Studio.NET Tools
- Properties Editor
- Solution Explorer
- Object Browser
- Team Explorer
- Server Explorer
- Visual Studio.NET Application Projects
- Console Application
- Windows Application
- Basic Components of Windows Applications
- Windows Forms
- Controls Objects
- Events
- Events Handlers
- Procedures Visual C# Programming Language
- Fundamentals of C# Programming Language
- Rules for writing C# Programs
- General Structure or Skeleton of C# Program
- Visual Basic.NET Programming Language
- Fundamentals of Visual Basic.NET
- General Structure or Skeleton of VB.NET Program
- Applications Development in .NET

Computer Programming

Computer programming is the process of designing, writing, testing, debugging, and maintaining the source code of a computer program that can be written in any computer programming language. Computer programming is a way of communication through which we send the set of instructions or statements to the computer system to perform specific operations or to solve a specific problem or algorithm. A computer program is a set of instructions or statements written in a sequence in any computer programming language that perform a specific task. When we write a program in any computer programming language, is called source code of the program. The source code of a program is normally in the form of human readable form. Computer system only understands machine language and it does not understand the source code of a program or human readable languages. The binary language or the language of zero and one is called machine language. When we write a computer program by any programming language, the translator of that programming language converts source code of the program into machine code and then converts into an executable file. The executable file is in the form of machine readable form or in binary form and it is ready for execution. The central processing unit of a computer system then executes the executable file or binary file of the computer program and performs a specific task or achieves a desire goal.

Types of Computer Programming

Computer programming is generally categorized into the following two types:

- Structure Programming
- Object Oriented Programming

Structure Programming

Structure Programming is a subset of procedural programming that enforces a logical structure on the program being written to make it more efficient and easier to understand and modify. It is sometimes known as modular programming. Structured programming normally uses a top-down design model, in which developers map out the overall program structure into separate subsections. Each subsection known as method, subroutine, or function which is depend on programming language and it is executed separately and performs a specific task. A defined subsection or set of similar subsections is coded in a separate module or sub module, which means that the code can be loaded into memory more efficiently and that modules can be reused in other programs. After a module has been tested individually, it is then integrated with other modules into the overall program structure.

Structure programming first suggested by corrado bohm and guiseppe jacopini. The two mathematicians demonstrated that any computer program could be written with just three structures such as decisions, sequences, and Iterations. Dijkstra developed the most common methodology through which developer separates programs into subsections that each has only one point of access and one point of exit. Almost any language can use structured programming techniques to avoid common drawback of unstructured languages. Certain programming languages such as Ada, Pascal, and dBase are designed with features that encourage or implement a logical program.

Object Oriented Programming

It is a programming methodology in which we define user-defined data types called objects. The fundamental concept behind object-oriented programming is to combine different data types and methods in a single entity called class. A class is the combination of different data types and methods. The data types of a class are called member data and methods of a class are called member methods. A class behaves like a separate program but it cannot execute independently without the support of another program. To execute a class, it must be called from another program or an application using an object of that class. An object of a class is a user-defined variable that is also called software bundle of variables and related methods that can be declared from a class and it is used to access the members of that class. The objects are declared in a program in which we want to use class. When an object is declared from a class then all the member data and member methods of that class are inherited in the declared object. Therefore, an object is the combination of member data and member methods of a class. This property of an object is called encapsulation. The data encapsulation and data hiding are the key terms in the description of object-oriented languages. An object-oriented programming is a technique that makes an object's data private or protected i.e. hidden and allow programmers to access and manipulate that data only through method call.

Programming Languages

Programming language is an artificial language designed to communicate with computer system. A programming language provides an interface and allows us to send instructions to the computer system to perform a specific task or to achieve a desire goal. The programming languages allow us to develop a set of instructions or statements that constitute a computer program. A computer program is a set of instructions or statements written in any programming language to achieve a specific task. The programming languages provide built-in libraries that contain a variety of different built-in objects such as variables, constants, operators, structures, decision statements, iteration statements, procedures, interfaces, delegates, threads, graphics objects, database connection objects and so on for different tasks and goals. When we design an application or a program using any programming language then we use the built-in objects of that programming language and achieve a desire result or a goal. We can also create user-defined objects in any programming language to achieve a specific task. Each programming language has its own procedures and structure to develop applications or programs.

When we write a program using any programming language, the translator of that programming language compile our program and perform different checks for errors. If there is any error in the program then the translator does not execute the program until we remove all errors from the program. Some programming languages indexed all the errors of a program in a list with some description. When we remove all errors and program becomes error free then the translator converts the program source code into machine language code. The source code of a program is always in human readable form and computer system understands only machine language and does not understand human readable languages. Therefore, the translator of a programming language converts source code of the program into machine language code which is called executable file. The executable file is always in the form of binary language form that is in the form of zero or one. The central processing unit of computer system then executes the executable file of the program and performs our desire goals.

Types of Programming Languages

Basically programming languages are divided into the following two types:

- Low Level Languages
- High Level Languages

Low Level Languages

The low-level computer programming languages are machine codes. Computer system cannot understand instructions given in the form of high-level languages or human languages but it can only understand and execute instructions given in the form of machine language. The binary language or the language of zero and one is called machine language. The low level programming languages directly interact with the computer hardware. Therefore, the low level programming languages require more experience and knowledge about computer hardware, CPU registers, and interrupt interfaces. A program written in a low level language requires small memory and executes very quickly as compare to a program written in a high level language because a program written in high level languages require more memory and executes slowly. The low level programming languages are divided into the following two types:

- Machine Language
- Assembly Language

Machine Language

It is a programming language in which the set of instructions or statements are written in the form of machine code. The machine language is also called binary language or the language of zero and one. The computer system only understands machine language or binary language. The machine language is represented inside in the computer by a string of binary digits (0 and 1). The symbol 0 stands for the absence of an electric pulse and 1 stands for the presence of an electric pulse. When the sequence of code or a set of instructions is given to the computer system using machine language, the computer system recognizes the codes and converts it in to electrical signals and executes directly without any translation. The machine language does not use any translator because the program or set of instructions are written in a machine language is already in the form of machine language or in binary form. When we give any instructions or set of instructions to the computer system in the form of machine language, the computer system directly executes the instructions very quickly without any translation. Therefore, machine language is a very fast language because no translator program is required for the central processing unit of computer system.

Assembly Language

A low-level programming language in which operation codes and operands are given in the form of alphanumeric symbols instead of 0's and 1's is called assembly language. In assembly language the set of symbols and letters combines with each other. In a simple word we can say that assembly language is the symbolic representation of machine code which also allows symbolic designation of memory locations. For example, ADD for addition, SUB for subtraction etc. The assembly language requires a translator to translate the assembly language code into machine language code because the assembly language code is not in the form of machine language but it is in the form of symbols. The translator of assembly language converts the assembly language code to machine code. The translator of assembly language is called assembler.

High Level Languages

High level languages are also called symbolic languages that use English words and Mathematical symbols for example, +, -, * /, >, <, <=, >= etc. They are very close to human languages. When we give the sequence of code or a set of instructions to computer system using any high level programming language, the high level programming language first converts the source code of the set of instructions into machine language code and then executed by the central processing unit and achieves the desire goals. The high level languages are actually designed to solve the particular problems of mathematics, general logical problems, general applications, and business accounts problems etc and therefore high level languages are called problem oriented languages. For example, the programming language COBOL (Common Business Oriented Language) is designed for business purposes, the programming language FORTRAN (Formula Translation) is designed for mathematical formula orientation and calculation and so on.

Types of High Level Languages

There are different types of high-level programming languages. The different high level programming languages are developed for different purposes and goals. Some of these programming languages are BASIC, C, C++, JAVA, COBOL, FOTRAN, Pascal, C#, Visual Basic, Oracle, and Prolog etc. These programming languages are similar with each other in some characteristics while in some other characteristics they are different from each other for example, the Oracle language is developed for the database designing and development, the Prolog is developed for logical problems such as to develop Robots, Expert system etc. The COBOL language is developed for business purposes, the BASIC and FORTRAN languages are developed for Algebraic formula processing, and C, C++, C#, Java and Visual Basic are designed for the general application programming.

Translator

It is a computer program that translates a program written in one language into an equivalent another language depending on the type of the translator. There are the following three types of translators:

- Assembler
- Compiler
- Interpreter

Assembler

It is a translator program that translates the source code a program written in assembly language into machine code.

Compiler

It is a translator program that translates the source code of a program written in a high-level language into machine language code. The machine language code is also called object code. When compiler translates the source code of a program into machine language code then it links the machine language code and creates an executable file. The executable file is then directly executed by the central processing unit of computer system. The compiler reads source code of a program and translates the whole program into machine language code at once. If there is any error occurs in the source program, the compiler prompts an error message and if there are more errors in the program, the compiler indexes all the errors in a list. When we remove errors from source code of the program then the compiler translates the source program into machine language code and creates an executable file. The executable file is then executed by the central processing unit at the same time.

The compiler first copies the whole program into memory and then directly executed by the central processing unit. Therefore, the compiler is very fast and directly executes the entire program at one time but it consumes more memory space because compiler copies the entire program into the memory. The debugging process is also very difficult in compiler because one error can produce many other unauthentic errors.

Interpreter

It is a translator program that translates the source code of a program written in a high-level language into machine language code. The interpreter translates the source code of a program into machine language code instruction by instruction or line by line and at the same time the central processing unit executes the program line by line. During translation if there is any error occurs in the source code of the program, the interpreter stops translation and displays the error report. When we remove the listed error then the interpreter starts translation again and translates rest of the program line by line. The interpreter is a slow process because it translates the program line by line. In interpreter the debugging process is very easy. Each line of code is analyzed and checked before being executed. The interpreter requires less memory space because interpreter loads one line in the memory at a time. When one line is checked, translated into machine code and successfully executed by the central processing unit then interpreter loads another line of the source code of program and on this way it executes the entire program.

Data

The collection of facts and figures about a particular task is called data. The particular task may be analysis, measurement, survey, research and so on. The facts and figures are always in the form of characters, symbols, alphabets, numbers, constants, text, graphs, diagrams, charts, pictures, images, audio/video clips, audio/video conferencing, questioners, interview questions, survey, observation, and analysis etc. The facts and figures are also called raw materials. In other words we can say that when we collect different raw materials or facts and figures about a particular object or task then the collected materials or facts and figures about that particular object or task is called data. For example, if we are doing a research on any animal then we study that animal deeply and collect different facts and figures or materials about that animal. These facts and figures or materials may be the animal weight, height, shape, body structure, color of the body, color of the eyes, sleeping hours, method of eating, behavior, activities, and attitude etc. The collection of all these facts and figures is called data about a specified animal. Similarly, if we are doing a survey on community health condition then we collect different facts and figures such as how many people are sick in a specified area, how many of them are male, how many of them are female and children, how many of them have critical condition and how many of them have small infection, how many of them are under treatment and how many of them are admitted into hospital and so on. The collection of all these facts and figures is called data about a specified disease.

Types of Data

The data is categorized into the following two general types:

- Qualitative Data
- Quantitative Data

Qualitative Data

It is the type of data that describes the quality of a specified object or a task. The qualitative data of an object or a task cannot be measured and counted but it can only be observed. The possible qualitative data of an object are color, shape or structure, texture, smells, location, gender, beauty, qualification, designation, physical appearance, thinking, behavior, physical fitness, knowledge, skills or experience, health condition, relationship and so on. For example, the knowledge, experience and skills of an employee, the taste of a mango, the texture of a leaf, the personal behavior and attitude of a person, the beauty, color, and smell of a flower, the gender, marital status, location, and nationality of a person and so on.

Quantitative Data

It is the type of data that describes the quantity of a specified object or a task. The quantitative data is numerical data that can be measured and counted. The possible quantitative data of an object are weight, height, length, depth, width, speed, time, body temperature, size, number of relatives, number of friends, marks, percentage, area, volume, costs or expenses, ages and so on. For example, marks, percentage, and CGPA of a student, monthly salary and bonus of an employee, the number of kids of a person, the numbers of teachers in a school, the number of legs of a dog, the number of players in a team and so on. The quantitative data is further divided in to the following two types:

- Discreet Data
- Continuous Data

Discreet Data

It is that type of quantitative data which we can count but cannot measure for example, the number of kids of a person, the marks and percentage of a student, the number of teachers in a school, the number of players in a team and so on.

Continuous Data

It is that type of quantitative data which we can measure but cannot count for example, height or weight of a person, speed of a car, and temperature of a body etc.

Data Representation in Computer System

The computer system is designed in such a way that it does not understand human readable languages or high level languages but it only understands and processes data in the form of machine code. The machine code is also called binary form of data or binary language. The binary language is a mathematical number system that contains only two digits or alphabets 0 and 1. These alphabets are also called bits. The computer system transfers and processes machine code or binary language in the form of electric signals. The bit 0 represents the absence of an electric pulse and the bit 1 represents the presence of an electric pulse. When we give data to a computer system in the form of human readable language or in the form of a high level language, the computer system converts that data into machine code or binary language and processes that data in the form of 0 and 1. A bit means binary digits and it represents the memory space of data. It is the smallest and the basic unit of data that have a single binary value either 0 or 1. The data is stored in the computer storage devices in the form of binary language that is in the form of 0 and 1. In a computer system and other telecommunication devices the data transfer rate is measured in the form of number of bits transferred in one second of time, for example if 500 bits are transferred in one second then we can say that the data transfer rate is 500 bits per second and so on. The other unit of data is called byte and it is bigger than bit. Eight bits memory space is equal to one byte.

Data of Programming Languages

We give data to a computer system by using a program written in any programming language. The data exist in different varieties of forms for example, in the form of characters, symbols, alphabets, numbers, constants, graphs, diagrams, charts, pictures, images, audio/video clips, audio/video conferencing, questioner, interview questions, survey, observation, and analysis etc. The programming languages take data in the form of numbers, letters and other special characters. According to computer programming languages the data can be divided into the following three types:

- Numeric Data
- Alphabetic Data
- Alphanumeric Data

Numeric Data

When data contains only decimal numbers from 0 to 9 and a decimal point notation then it is called numeric data. For example, 23, 90, 100, 12.13, 2.5, 100.5 and so on are numeric data. The numeric data is further divided into the following type:

- Integer Numeric Data
- Real Numeric Data

Integer Numeric Data

When numeric data contains only decimal numbers from 0 to 9 and does not contain any decimal point notation then the data is called integer numeric data. For example, 23, 90, 100 etc are integer numeric data.

Real Numeric Data

When numeric data contains decimal numbers from 0 to 9 along with a decimal point notation then the data is called real numeric data. For example, 12.13, 2.5, 100.5 etc are real numeric data.

Alphabetic Data

When data contains only English alphabets from capital A to capital Z or from small a to small z is called alphabetic data. For example "Asad", 'Sajad" etc are alphabetic data.

Alphanumeric Data

The alphanumeric data is also called text. When numeric data, alphabetic data, and some other special characters combine with each other then it forms alphanumeric data. For example, House#-13, Registration number = 577-ICIT-2003 etc.

Introduction to .NET Framework

The .NET Framework is a software framework developed by Microsoft that runs mostly on Microsoft Windows. It provides a multiple language environment for the development of different types of applications software. The .NET framework provides multiple language interoperability that means each language of the .NET framework can use the programming codes written in other language. The .NET framework provides a huge shared library for the .NET programming languages that is called .NET Framework Class Library (FCL). Each programming language of the .NET framework uses this shared library. The .NET framework also provides a common runtime environment which is called Common Language Runtime (CLR). The CLR is the execution engine or a Virtual Machine of .NET framework that provides different basic services and handles executions of the .NET programs. It is responsible for managing the execution of all programs of .NET programming languages. When CLR executes a program then during execution it manages all the basic requirements of execution for example, to allocate memory or automatic memory management, exceptions handling, Garbage collections, Threads managements and execution, code verification, compilation of the program, code access security, and other system services. The Framework Class Library (FCL) and the Common Language Runtime (CLR) are the two main components of the .NET Framework.

The .NET Framework Class Library

The .NET Framework Class Library (FCL) is one of the core components of Microsoft .NET Framework. It is a library of huge collections that contains reusable classes, interfaces and data types that can be used in a consistence manner across multiple languages to accomplish a range of common programming tasks. The .NET FCL is an object oriented class library and its contents are organized in a hierarchical tree structure and they are divided in different logical categories or groups according to the same functionality and nature. Each category of these contents is placed in a named container which is called a namespace. The namespaces are logical grouping of types for the purpose of identification. A namespace is a container inside in the FCL that contains specified contents of the FCL. The contents of some namespaces are further categorized into different sub namespaces according their same functionality and nature. Therefore, we can say that namespaces creates a hierarchical tree inside in the .NET FCL.

Basic Class Library

The Basic Class Library (BCL) is the foundation of Microsoft .NET Framework and it is part of .NET Framework Class Library (FCL). The BCL is available to all programming languages supported by .NET Framework and it provides the basic common classes that contain a larger number of common functions and features across all the .NET programming languages such as Data Type definition, Collections, file reading and writing (IO operations on files), Reflection, Assembly, Graphics representation, Database interaction, and XML documents manipulation.

Common Language Infrastructure

The Common Language Infrastructure (CLI) is a specification developed by Microsoft and standardized by European Computer Manufacturers Association ECMA that defines a single environment and multiple platform execution system for multiple high level programming languages. The different high level programming languages use a single environment and access the same resources. The CLI allows us to write programs in different high levels programming languages using a single environment. The programs written in different high level programming languages can be executed in different system environment or different operating systems using a common runtime program without rewrite those programs. The goal of CLI is to ensure the different types of high level programming languages to work on a single environment and to access a common class library or to share the .NET class library among different high level programming languages. The CLI provides a common intermediate language that stores the translated code of a program written in any high level .NET programming language into an assembly and then translated into machine code or native code and then executed by the central processing unit of computer system. The CLI also allows different programming languages to share their objects with each other. For example, an object written in one programming language can be access in another programming language. This facility of CLI is called Common Language Specification (CLS). The CLI has the following different components:

- Common Intermediate Language
- Common Language Specification
- Common Type System
- Virtual Execution System

Common Intermediate Language

This component of CLI is a lowest level human readable programming language that was formerly known as Microsoft Intermediate Language (MSIL) but after its standardization it is called Common Intermediate Language (CIL). It is an object oriented assembly programming language that works on stack based and it is executed by the virtual machine. When we write a program in any .NET high level programming language and when we compile that program then the compiler of that programming language translates the source code of the program into CIL code. When source code of a program is translated into CIL code then an assembly is created automatically and code of the CIL is stored into an assembly. The translated source code of a program into CIL code is called byte-code. The byte-code is then translated into machine code or native code and executed by the central processing unit of computer system or the byte-code is directly executed by the virtual machine.

Common Language Specification

This component of CLI ensures the multiple high level programming languages to work on a single environment and executes on multiple platform. The Common Language Specification (CLS) allows all the programming languages of .NET framework to access the same resources of the .NET framework. It provides a common interface or platform for several different programming languages that provide language interoperability. The language interoperability means each language of the .NET framework can use the programming codes written in other programming language.

Common Type System

This component of CLI provides a set of data types. The set of data types of CLI is a common set of data types for all the programming languages of the .NET framework that facilitates the cross language integration. The Common Type System (CTS) also ensure that objects written in one .NET programming language can interact with the objects of another .NET programming language. The set of data types can be value type or reference type. The value types are stored in the stack while the reference types are stored in the heap.

Virtual Execution System

This component of CLI provides an execution environment and a runtime engine for executing managed code of a program. When the compiler of a high level .NET programming language compiles the source code of a program into CIL code and stored into an assembly then the translated source code of a program into CIL code is called byte-code. The Virtual Execution System (VES) reads byte-code and uses a Just in Time (JIT) compiler and compiles byte-code into native machine code and then executed by the central processing unit of the computer system. This executing code is called managed code.

Namespaces

A namespace is an abstract container that provides context for the classes, interfaces, delegates, enumeration, structures, and value types. There are two types of namespaces such as built-in library namespaces and user-defined namespaces. The built-in library namespaces are already designed and placed in the .NET Framework Class Library. The .NET framework is the collection of huge amounts of classes, interfaces, delegates, enumerations, structures, and value types. The contents of the .NET framework are divided into different categories according to their similar functionality and nature such as Data Access, Common Types, Debugging, File Access, Security, Network Communication, Windows Applications, Web Applications, Console Applications, Database Applications, Graphics Applications and Animations, Web Services, XML Data etc. Each category of the .NET framework is placed in a separate named container which is called namespace. Each namespace has its own unique name and each namespace contains the same functionality classes, interfaces, delegates, enumerations, structures, and value types. These namespaces are called built-in namespaces and they are placed in the .NET Framework Class Library (FCL). Therefore, we can say that a namespace is an abstract container that contains logical groups of classes, interfaces, delegates, enumeration, structures, and value types of the same functionality and nature.

The contents of some namespaces are further categorized into different sub namespaces according to their similar functionality and nature. Simply we can say that a namespace also contain sub namespaces called child namespaces. The child namespaces may also contain sub namespaces called child-child namespaces and the child-child namespaces may also contain sub namespaces called child-child-child name spaces and so on. The child namespaces are inside in their parent or base namespaces and they create a hierarchical tree inside in the .NET Framework Class Library. In a single namespace no two classes have the same name but different namespaces can have the same name classes. The purpose of the namespaces is to avoid name collisions and conflicts. For example, if we have two classes with the same name but different functionality then we can place each class in a different namespace. A class in a namespace can be accessed by using the dot (.) operator as a delimiter between the class name and the namespace of that class.

Fully Qualified Name of a Class

A fully qualified name is a name that specifies a class, a structure, an interface, a delegate, an enumeration, a data type, an object, or a procedure in a hierarchical structure. A hierarchical structure is a structure that has multiple levels arranged in such a manner that each level is inside another level like a tree. The inside level of structure is always the child of the outside structure level and therefore it is called child structure and the outside structure level is called parent structure. The outermost level of a structure is called root level or parent level of the entire child levels declared inside in the different levels of that root or parent level.

Each level of the namespace is an abstract container that provides context for the classes, interfaces, delegates, enumerations, structures, and value types. The sub namespaces or child namespaces that are declared inside in the root or the parent namespace are called sub namespaces of level one, the sub namespaces or child namespaces that are declared inside in the sub namespaces of Level one are called sub namespaces of Level two, and the sub namespaces or child namespaces that are declared inside in the sub namespaces of Level two are called sub namespaces of Level three and so on. The following diagram shows the architecture or tree of namespaces:

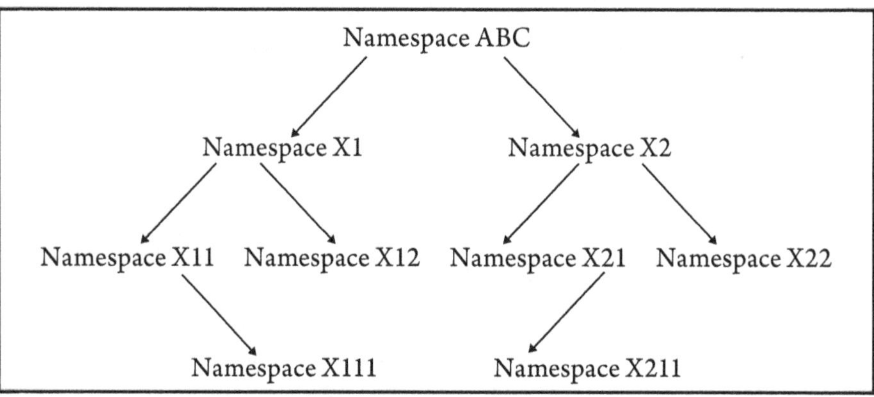

The above diagram shows the tree of namespaces. The Namespace ABC is the root namespace that has three levels of child namespaces. The first level of parent Namespace ABC contains two child namespaces that are Namespace X1 and Namespace X2 and they are declared inside in the root namespace ABC, the second level of parent Namespace ABC contains four child namespaces that are Namespace X11, Namespace X12, Namespace X21, Namespace X22 and they are declared inside in the first level of the child namespaces, and the third level of parent Namespace ABC contains two child namespaces that are Namespace X111 and the Namespace X211 and they are declared inside in the second level of child namespaces. The fully qualified name of a class is constructed by concatenating the names of all the namespaces that contain the type. For example, if a class is inside in the root namespace then the fully qualified name of that class will be constructed by concatenating the name of the parent namespace and the class name. Following is the general syntax for the fully qualified name of a class that is declared inside in the root namespace:

Parent_Namespace.Class_name

The above declaration shows that the class is declared inside the parent or the base namespace because only one namespace is concatenated with the class name. For example, if we want to access any class declared inside in the root or the parent Namespace ABC then we can use the following fully qualified name of that class:

ABC.Class_name

Similarly, if a class is declared inside in any level of the parent namespace then the fully qualified name for that class will be constructed by concatenating parent namespace and all its levels of child namespaces up to that level of child namespace where the class is declared. For example, if a class is declared inside in the first level child namespace then the fully qualified name for that class will be constructed by concatenating the parent namespace and its first level child namespace with the class name. Following is the general syntax for the fully qualified name of a class that is declared inside in the first level of any child namespace:

Parent_Namespace.Child_NamespaceLevel1.Class_name

The above declaration shows that the class is declared inside in the first level child namespace. Using the above namespace tree, if we want to access any class declared inside in the first level of any child namespace then we can use the following fully qualified name of that class:

ABC.X1.Class_name or ABC.X2.Class_name

If a class is declared inside in the second level of any child namespace then the fully qualified name for that class will be constructed by concatenated the parent namespace and its first two levels child namespaces that are level one child namespace and level two child namespace with the class name. Following is the general syntax for the fully qualified name of a class declared inside in the second level of any child namespace:

Parent_Namespace.Child_NamespaceLevel1.
Child_NamespaceLevel2.Class_name

The above declaration shows that the class is declared inside in the Level two child namespace because the parent class is concatenated with its first two Levels child namespaces that are Level one child namespace and Level two child namespace. Using the above namespace tree if we want to access a class that is declared inside in the second level of any child namespace then we can use the following fully qualified name of that class as:

ABC.X1.X11.Class_name or ABC.X1.X12.Class_name
ABC.X2.X21.Class_name or ABC.X2.X22.Class_name

Similarly, using the above namespace tree if we want to access a class that is declared inside in the third level of any child namespace then we can use the following fully qualified name of that class as:

ABC.X1.X11.X111.Class_name or ABC.X2.X21.X211.Class_name

The fully qualified name of a class contains the namespaces names and the class name concatenated with each other by using a dot operator between them. If we want to use any class or any other content of a namespace in our program then we have to use the fully qualified name of that class or content of the namespace. If we don't know the fully qualified name of a class or any other content of a namespace then we use directives to include the namespace of that class in the program. The directive is used to include a specified namespace in the program. The different .NET programming languages have different syntaxes to include namespaces in the programs. In C# the directive **"using"** is used to include a specified namespace in a program while in Visual Basic.NET the directive **"Imports"** is used to include a specified namespace in a program. Following are some important features of namespaces:

- A single namespace cannot have two classes with the same names. Namespaces avoid naming conflicts between classes, which have the same names. In an application we can use two classes with the same name provided by different namespaces.

- Namespaces help us to create logical groups of related classes and interfaces, which can be used by any language in the .NET Framework. The namespace keyword is used to declare a user-defined namespace scope. This namespace scope also organizes the code and gives us a way to create globally-unique types.
- Namespaces allow us to organize our own user defined classes so that they can be easily accessed in other applications.

User-defined namespaces

The namespaces also allows us to create user-defined namespaces to eliminate the naming conflicts between different codes developed at different locations. In user-defined namespaces we can define different classes, interfaces, structures, enumerations, delegates, and value types to organize our code and create globally unique type. When we create a namespace then we can use it in the future in all our programs or applications when we need. The .NET framework provides a keyword **namespace** that is used to declare user-defined namespaces. In C# and Visual Basic a keyword namespace is used to declare a namespace followed by name of the namespace. The name of a namespace is a user defined name and it can be any valid identifier. The members or elements of a namespace are declared inside in body of the namespace. In C#, body of a namespace is enclosed within curly braces while in Visual Basic body of a namespace is enclosed within two keywords **Namespace** and **End Namespace**. Following is the general declaration of namespaces:

Namespace Declaration in C#

namespace Namespace_Name
{
…………………………
Members of namespace
…………………………
}

Namespace Declaration in VB.NET
Namespace Namespace_Name …………………………

```
Members of namespace
…………………………
End Namespace
```

In the above declaration the **Namespace_name** is a user defined name of the namespace. The user-defined name can be any valid identifier. We cannot use any access modifiers with a namespace declaration. By default a namespaces has public access and we cannot change it. A namespace allows us to declare members or elements only as public or internal. We cannot declare a member or an element of a namespace as a private or a protected.

Built-in Library Namespaces in .NET

The .NET Framework provides different built-in namespaces that are declared in the .NET Framework Class Library. These namespaces provide different classes, interfaces, enumerations, delegates, structures, and data types for different types of applications development. The classes and other contents of these namespaces provide various types of built-in keywords, methods, and other different data types that are used to develop different applications such as Console applications, Windows Forms applications, Database applications, Graphics GDI applications, Files handling applications, Multithreaded applications, Web applications, ASP.NET web applications, Web Services applications, Class Library applications, Network handling applications, WPF applications, XML applications, Silverlight applications, WCF Services applications, Devices applications and so on. The namespaces are categorized according to these applications types because each application type has its own set of namespaces. In an application or in a program if we want to use any content of any namespace then the namespace of that content must be included at the top of the program or the fully qualified name of that content must be used in the application or program.

The Microsoft .NET Framework contains a huge amount of namespaces. These namespaces contain a root or a parent namespace and various types of sub namespaces or child namespaces. The sub namespaces or child namespaces are defined inside in the root or parent namespace and they make a hierarchical structure inside in the .NET Framework Class Library. The name of the root or parent namespace is called System namespace and it is defined inside in the .NET Framework that contains all the base classes and fundamental classes, interfaces, delegates, structures, enumerations, and defines various commonly used value and reference Data types, String values manipulation, Collections, various methods for Data types conversion, Events, Events handlers, Attributes, Exceptions, Garbage collections, various methods for Mathematical operations, Application Environment Management, the standard input output streams for Console applications and a huge amount of sub or child namespaces that are defined inside in different child levels of the System namespace. The sub or child namespaces of the System namespace are categorized into different groups of namespaces according to the application types. Following is the list and details of built-in namespaces declared in the .NET Framework Class Library:

Namespace	**Description**
System	This namespace is the root or parent namespace defined in the .NET Framework that contains all the base and fundamental classes, interfaces, delegates, structures, enumerations, and defines various commonly used value and reference Data types, String values manipulation, Collections, various methods for Data types conversion, Events, Events handlers, Attributes, Exceptions, Garbage collections, various methods for Mathematical operations, Application Environment Management, the standard input output streams for Console applications and a huge amount of sub namespaces or child namespaces that are defined inside in different child levels of the System namespace.
System.Windows.Forms System.Windows.Forms.Design System.Windows.Controls System.Windows.Data System.Windows.Navigation	These namespaces contains different classes that allow us to develop Windows applications. They provide Windows Forms and different Controls Objects. The Controls Objects are also called Windows Forms controls because they are related with the Windows Forms and basically they are

System.Windows.Resources System.Windows.Shapes System.Windows.Shell System.Windows.Threading System.Windows.Documents System.Windows.Converters System.Windows.Markup System.Windows.Media System. Windows.Media.Effects System.Windows.Ink System.Windows.Automation System.Windows.Annotations System.Windows.Input	used to design Windows Forms. The Controls Objects are used on Forms for different purposes such as some Controls Objects are used for input purposes that allow a user to input data to the application using input devices, some Controls Objects are used for output proposes that display or view the data or information, and some Controls Objects are used to arrange other controls on the Windows Form. These namespace also provide different dialog boxes that are used to perform different operations on the applications for example, to open or save the files, to change the style or text color, to set the page size, to use the print preview, and to print a file etc. Some classes of these namespaces provide Menus and Toolbars controls that can be used to design Menu bars, Status bars, and context Menus on Windows Form. They also provide layout, to control the arrangement of other Controls Objects on the Form surface.
System.Data System.Data.Common System.Data.OleDb System.Data.Odbc System.Data.ProviderBase System.Data.Sql System.Data.SqlClient System.Data.SqlTypes System.Data.Objects	These namespaces provide various classes for databases management and operations. The Classes of these namespaces are used to establish connection to different databases and perform different operations or commands on a database such as insert data in database, retrieve data from database, update or delete data from database. They provide different data providers such as OLEDB, ODBC, and

	data provider for Oracle. The classes of these namespaces represent ADO. NET architecture. The ADO stands for ActiveX Data Object and .NET means Microsoft .NET Framework. It is the modified form of old ADO and it is specially designed for the .NET framework. It is an object oriented set of libraries that allow us to interact with the data sources. The data source is a database but it can also be a text file, an excel spread sheet, or an XML file. The ADO.NET is a set of software components providing data access and data services based on disconnected dataset and XML. It provides different classes that are used to retrieve data, manipulate data, and update data in the database. It has the ability to work in a disconnected manner. It provides different data providers such as MS SQL Server, Oracle, OLEDB, Open Database Connectivity (ODBC), Access Driver, and ODBC for Oracle. The ADO. NET provides two basic components such Dataset and Data Provider. The DataSet represents disconnected data which is made up of DataTables and DataRelations. The Dataset contains a collection of one or more DataTables objects made up of rows and columns of data. The data provider provides Connection Object, Command Object, DataReader Object, and DataAdapter Object.

System.Drawing System.Drawing.Configuration System.Drawing.Design System.Drawing.Design2D System.Drawing.Imaging System.Drawing.Printing System.Drawing.Text	These namespaces are used to design Graphics Design Interface (GDI) applications. They allow us to design different graphics objects such as lines, circles, rectangles, ellipse, polygon, pies, paths, triangles, curves, bitmap images etc and provide different brushes used to fill the graphics shapes with specified colors. They also allow us to design the animated objects and use different fonts, and colors. They provide classes and enumerations for advanced two-dimensional and vector graphics designing such as hatch brushes, matrix that represents geometric transformation, and graphics paths.
System.IO System.IO.Compression System.IO.IsolatedStorage System.IO.MemoryMappedFiles	These namespaces provide various Classes and some Enumerations that are used to create, delete, and manipulate files and directories. They allow us to perform input and output operations on files and data streams.
System.IO.Pipes System.IO.Ports	The Classes of these namespaces provide both synchronous and asynchronous input and output operations on files. They also allow us to retrieve files or directories path information. A path is a string that provides the location of a file or a directory.
System.Threading	This namespace provides various Classes for Multithreaded application development.

System.Globalization	The classes of this namespace provide information about the culture and different regions such as information about the human speaking languages, the region or a country, and define various types of calendars such as Gregorian calendar, Hebrew calendar, Hijri calendar, Japanese calendar, Julian calendar, Korean calendar, Persian calendar, Taiwan calendar, and define different dates formats, numbers formats, and currencies etc.
System.Diagnostics System.Diagnostics.Contracts System.Diagnostics.Eventing System.Diagnostics.Tracing System.Diagnostics.Design	These namespaces provide classes that allow us to debug and trace the execution of an application. They allow us to interact with the system processes, events logs, and performance counters. These namespaces also allow us to perform different operations on the events log such as create and delete events logs, read, and write in the events logs and events sources on the network.
System.Net System.Net.Sockets Syste.Net.Security System.Net.Cache System.Net.Configuration System.Net.Mail System.Net.Mime System.Net.NetworkInformation System.Net.Http	These namespaces are used in Network programming and Network management software application development such as Chat Severs, Email Servers etc. The Classes of these namespaces allow us to interact with the network services and communicate over the network and internet. They allow us to develop such applications or programs that detect the network connection, establish network connection between devices, information about the network traffic and information about the network addresses. It also allows us to develop such applications or programs that send

	E-mail using a Simple Mail Transfer Protocol (SMTP) and transfers data using the Hypertext Transfer Protocol (HTTP) and File Transfer Protocol (FTP).
System.Web System.Web.Caching System.Web.ClientServices SystemWeb.Compilation System.Web.Configuration System.Web.DynamicData System.Web.Handlers System.Web.Hosting System.Web.Mail System.Web.Management System.Web.Profile System.Web.Query System.Web.Routing System.Web.Script System.Web.Security System.Web.SessionState System.Web.UI System.Web.Util	The System.Web namespace contains a number of child namespaces that allow us to develop the ASP.NET Web applications and allow us to set cookies, configure page caching, ASP.NET application configuration, and retrieve web server and web browser related information.
System.Web.Services System.Web.Services.Configuration System.Web.Services.Discovery System.Web.Services.Protocols	These namespaces are used to create XML Web services and components using ASP.NET that are published over the Internet.
System.Security System.Security.Permissions System.Security.Policy System.AccessControl System.Security.Cryptography System.Security.Authentication System.Security.Principal System.Security.Util	These namespaces are used for authentication, authorization, encryption, policies, and rights management.

System.Xml System.XML.Linq System.XML.Resolvers System.Xml.Schema System.Xml. Serialization System.Xml.XPath System.Xml.Xsl	These namespaces are used to create and access XML files.

Assembly

An assembly is a compiled code of the Common Language Infrastructure (CLI) which is used for the deployment, versioning, and security permissions. When we create an application using any .NET programming language and when the source code of that application is compiled, the compiler translates the source code into Common Intermediate Language (CIL) code. When source code of the program is translated into CIL code, an assembly is created automatically and the CIL code is stored in it. An assembly is a file that is automatically generated by the compiler when a .NET application is successfully compiled. It can be either a Dynamic Link Library or an executable file and it is generated only once for an application when first time an application is successfully compiled. When an assembly is generated for an application then during each subsequent compilation of that application the assembly is not created again but the existing assembly gets updated.
An Assembly contains Intermediate Language (IL) code, which is similar to Java byte code. In the .NET programming language, an assembly is a collection of different types and resources that forms a logical unit of functionality and in the .NET Framework all types are existed in assemblies. Therefore, we can say that an Assembly is the building block of the .NET Framework application. When an application is compiled then a Metadata is created with Microsoft Intermediate Language (MSIL) and stored in a file called Assembly Manifest. The assembly manifest is a file that contains information about the assembly name, the version number, the culture and language supported by assembly, a list of other assemblies that this assembly is referenced. The assembly manifest is used when we need to use classes from another assembly in our code. When we create a new application project using any .NET programming language, a separate file is created inside in the application project folder which is called AssemblyInfo file.

The AssemblyInfo file contains information about the assembly such as assembly title, assembly description, assembly configuration, assembly

Company, assembly product, assembly copyright, assembly trademark, and assembly culture. There are two types of assemblies such as private assembly and public or shared assembly. The assembly file which is located in the application folder is called private assembly because it is available only to a single application or program. A public or share assembly is an assembly that is allowed to be shared by more than one application. A share assembly must reside in Global Assembly Cache (GAC). The GAC allows us to share assemblies across different applications. The GAC is installed with the .NET Framework and its folder is located inside in the windows folder.

Microsoft Visual Studio.NET

Microsoft Visual Studio.NET is an Integrated Development Environment (IDE) designed by Microsoft Corporation. It provides a complete set of development tools for building of console and graphical user interface applications using the Windows forms and other graphical objects or controls objects of Windows Forms, ASP.NET Web applications, ASP.NET Web Services applications, XML Web services applications, Windows services applications, and Mobile applications. The Microsoft Visual Studio.NET is used to write the native code and managed code supported by Microsoft Windows. The Microsoft Visual Studio .NET is designed for the .NET framework. The .NET framework provides different features for Microsoft Visual Studio.NET, for example the Common Language Runtime (CLR), The Common Language Infrastructure (CLI), the .NET Framework Class library that contains a huge amount of classes, interfaces, delegates, enumerations, structures, and value types. Microsoft Visual Studio.NET provides different types of programming languages to work and run on the same visual environment and access the same resources of the .NET Framework. The most commonly used programming languages of Visual Studio.NET are Visual C#, Visual Basic.NET, Visual C++. NET, and ASP.NET. The .NET Framework also provides multiple language interoperability. The multiple language interoperability means each language of Microsoft Visual Studio.NET can use the programming codes written in other language. The programming languages of Visual Studio.NET use the common .NET Framework Class Library and designed different applications using the common Integrated Development Environment (IDE).

The .NET Framework provides Common Language Infrastructure (CLI) that ensures all the programming languages of Microsoft Visual Studio. NET to use the same common resources of the .NET Framework, for example the common .NET Framework Class Library, a single common

Integrated Development Environment (IDE), and a single common execution environment and so on. The CLI provides a common execution environment which is called Common Intermediate Language (CIL). A program written in any programming language of Visual Studio.NET is compiled by the compiler of that programming language and it is translated into CIL code (byte-code) and stores into an assembly. The CIL code is then translated into machine code and executed by the central processing unit of the computer system. Microsoft Visual Studio.NET provides different features for designing and development of software applications or programs. Following are the details of the features of Microsoft Visual Studio.NET:

- Microsoft Visual Studio.NET Code Editor
- Microsoft Visual Studio.NET Debugger
- Microsoft Visual Studio.NET Designer

Microsoft Visual Studio.NET Code Editor

The Code Editor is an area of Microsoft Visual Studio IDE that allows us to write the source codes of applications or programs. It is same like a text editor such as notepad or Microsoft Word document text editor. The Code Editor of Visual Studio is common to all the Visual Studio programming languages. The Code Editor of Microsoft Visual Studio provides the following features:

- IntelliSense System
- Syntax Highlighting
- Bookmarking
- Background Compilation

IntelliSense System

IntelliSense System is a feature of Microsoft Visual Studio.NET Code Editor that is also called Microsoft implementation of auto completion system. This system works like a sensor or detector and detects or senses when we write a program codes. When we try to write any built-in keyword, variable, function, method, class, structure, delegate, enumeration, thread, a flow control statement, and any other built-in statement in a Visual Studio.NET programming language then the IntelliSense System automatically detects and senses that built-in keyword or statement and completes it before we type the complete word. Therefore, this facility of Visual Studio saves our time and we can write a very large program in less time.

Syntax Highlighting

Syntax Highlighting is a feature of Microsoft Visual Studio.NET Code Editor that arranges all the built-in keywords and statements used in a program in different colors and fonts according to different categories of the keywords and statements. The same category keywords and statements are arranged in the same colors and fonts. This feature of Code Editor makes a program code very simple, user friendly, arranges in different categories that enable us to find out errors in the program very easily and quickly.

Bookmarking

Bookmarking is a feature of Microsoft Visual Studio.NET Code Editor that allows us to set bookmarks in our program code. A bookmark is a mark or a sign used to mark or specify a line, or a place in a program code to retrieve or navigate that line, or place later quickly.

Background Compilation

Background Compilation is a feature of Microsoft Visual Studio.NET Code Editor that provides background compilation of the program code. The Background Compilation compiles the program code on the same time when we are writing the code. When we are writing a program code then the Background Compilation of Code Editor compiles that code and provides feedback about the program code. For example, if we make any syntax or keyword mistakes then it underlines the incorrect syntax or keyword using a red line. The background compilation is not the program translation but it just compiles the program code to find out mistakes in our syntaxes and keywords.

Microsoft Visual Studio.NET Debugger

The Debugger of Visual Studio.NET is a computer program used to test and find errors in our applications or programs. When we write an application or a program using any Visual Studio.NET programming language then the Debugger of Visual Studio.NET tests the source code of the program and finds errors if occurred in the code. The Visual Studio.NET Debugger works both as a source level debugger and as a machine level debugger and supports both types of codes such as managed code and machine or native code. The Visual Studio.NET Debugger is a common debugger program that is used to debug a program or an application written in any Visual Studio.NET programming language. The Visual Studio.NET Debugger also allows us to set breakpoints to stop the debugging of the program at any specified point of the program execution. The breakpoints are normally used to analyze and check the execution process of the program code step by step or line by line and detect errors in the program codes. The breakpoints are also used with condition. We can use breakpoints and performs different conditions on breakpoints. When a program is executing and during execution if a certain condition is satisfied then it triggers breakpoints.

Microsoft Visual Studio.NET Designer

Microsoft Visual Studio.NET provides different types of designer tools that allow us to design different applications or programs using Designer. Microsoft Visual Studio.NET provides different designer tools such Windows Forms Designer, Web Designer, Class Designer, Data Designer, WPF Designer, Mapping Designer, and Silverlight Designer etc. Each Designer has its own environment for designing applications or programs. These designers are used to design different applications or programs such as Windows Forms applications, ASP.NET Web applications, Console applications, Class Library applications, Windows Control Library applications, Crystal Reports applications, and Device applications programs etc. Some designers such as Windows Forms Designer, WPF Designer, Web Designer etc provides Windows Forms and different Controls Objects while some other designers such as Console applications, Class Library applications do not provide Windows Forms and Controls Objects. A Windows Form is a container that has a visual graphical appearance and normally displays on the computer desktop. It is actually a visual frame or a container for the Controls Objects. Controls Objects are placed on Windows Forms and design Windows applications. Windows application starts from Windows Forms and it contains one or more Windows Forms. Control Objects are graphical controls that are used on the Windows Forms. Each Control Object provides an entry point and allows a user to interact with the application or program in a graphical user interface. Controls Objects are designed for Windows applications programs and they are categorized into different groups according to the same functionality and nature and placed in a toolbox.

A toolbox is a container that holds Controls Objects. Each Control Object is itself a class and they are placed inside in the namespace System.Windows. Forms. The groups of these Controls Objects are Commands controls, Containers controls, Menus and Toolbars controls, Data controls, Components controls, Printing controls, Dialog controls, and Crystal Reports controls. Each group of the Controls Objects has the same functionality controls. For example, Commands control group contains text and action related controls such as Command Buttons, Textboxes, Labels, Radio buttons, Check Boxes, Combo Boxes, and List Boxes etc similarly, the Container Control contain different types of controls that are used to group or arrange Windows Controls on the Form. These controls are Panel, FlowLayoutPanel, GroupBox, SplitContainer, and TabControl.

Microsoft Visual Studio.NET Tools

The Microsoft Visual Studio.NET IDE provides the following important tools for the developers:

- Properties Editor
- Solution Explorer
- Object Browser
- Team Explorer
- Server Explorer

Properties Editor

Properties Editor is a small window that contains all the properties and list of events of a selected object such as Form control or any other Form Control object. The Properties window is used to perform various operations on the selected object such as to give a name or rename the existing name of the selected object, to change the size, the background or the foreground color of the selected object, to change the location, position or icon of the selected object and to make the selected object enabled/disabled or visible/invisible etc. The Properties window is located in the **View** menu of the Microsoft Visual Studio.NET. We can also open the Properties window by pressing F4 from the keyboard while the Visual Studio project is opened.

Solution Explorer

Solution Explorer is a small window that contains the application files. It organized the application files into a tree view structure and grouped all the same files in the same place. The Solution Explorer allows us to manage our project and all its related files for example, rename the existing solution, rename the project name, add new project or remove an existing project, rename an existing file, add new file or remove an existing file, add and remove project references etc. When we open a new project then the Solution Explorer arranges all the related files of that project in a tree view structure and makes the project name as a root node or parent node of all the other related files. If we add more projects in a Solution Explorer then it arranges all the projects separately and makes separate root node for all the projects. The Solution Explorer window is located in the **View** menu of Microsoft Visual Studio.NET. We can also open the Solution Explorer window by pressing Ctrl+Alt+L from the keyboard while the Visual Studio project is opened.

Object Browser

The Object Browser is a window that displays all the symbols such as the .NET Framework and COM components, value types, namespaces, various types of libraries, interfaces, enumerations, and classes etc and it allows us to locate and examine the entire symbols for further details. For example if we want to know further details about any class, interfaces, enumeration, methods, event, property, and value type etc then we use Object Browser. The Object Browser contains three pans such as Objects pane that is located on the left side, a Members pane that is located on the upper right side, and a Description pane that is located on the lower right side. In the Objects pane all the symbols are displayed in a hierarchical structure. When we click on any symbol then its contents are displayed on the upper right pane and when we click on any content then its description and syntax is displayed on the lower right pane. The Object Browser window is located in the **View** menu of Microsoft Visual Studio.NET. We can also open the Object Browser window by pressing Ctrl+Alt+J from the keyboard while the Visual Studio project is opened.

Team Explorer

The Team Explorer is a small window that allows us to manage our project and share our efforts with the project team members. It is actually an interface between the project team members. If we develop a project by more developers then we use the Team Explorer window to distribute work among all the team members. The developers also coordinate their efforts with other team members. The Team Explorer window is located in the **View** menu of Microsoft Visual Studio.NET. We can also open the Team Explorer window by pressing Ctrl+\, Ctrl+m from the keyboard while the Visual Studio project is opened.

Server Explorer

The Server Explorer window allows us to manage the database connections, log on to the servers and explore different services and database files. It displays all the contents such as database files, and servers etc in a tree view structure and allow us to explore the files. The Servers node contains the list of servers and allows us to explore the contents such as Event Logs, Management Classes, and Services etc. It also contains SharePoint Connections and Windows Azure Web Sites.

Visual Studio.NET Application Projects

A project is a development interface provided by Microsoft Visual Studio.NET for the development of various applications in .NET programming languages such as Console applications, Windows applications, Web applications, WPF applications, Class Library, Windows Services, and Web Services etc. When we want to develop an application or program then the first step is to open a new project in a specified .NET programming language. When we open a new project then it contains various raw materials for our new application. The raw materials contain the source code files that allow us to write the application code, the resource files that hold all the application icons, the references files that hold the external files such as namespaces and the links of other application relying on our new application, the destination path where we want to save our project, the build and release information and paths, and some other settings.

Console Applications

Console application is a programming environment in Microsoft Visual Studio. NET that provides a Text-based User Interface (TUI) to develop computer programs or applications in different .NET programming languages. It is also called Character User Interface. Console Application does not provide Graphical User Interface environment as well as graphical user controls. It uses the command prompt to get data or input from the user and displays output of the program or application on the command prompt window. The command prompt is automatically linked with the Console Applications. When we write a program and run it from Microsoft Visual Studio.NET code editor interface then the command prompt automatically launches and displays output of the program written in any .NET programming language. The Console Application program is always executed from a single fixed point that is called main execution point or general execution point of the program.

It only allows us to connect with the program or application using a single entry point. Console Applications uses standard Input/output devices for data entry or display. The key source of data entry of Console Application is only a keyboard. The user can use only a keyboard to send data to the Console Application program. Therefore, Console Application provides a single entry point and a single execution point which is called main entry point and main execution point of the application or program. The single main entry point and execution point of the program is actually a procedure which is called driver method or driver subroutine of the program. In Console application the execution of the program always starts from this procedure or method. The name of this procedure is always fixed and its name is **main.** It is built-in name for this procedure or method and it cannot be changed. The main procedure or method is declared inside in the general Class or general Module of the Console Application.

The program structure of the Console Application is different in different .NET programming languages. In C# the structure of Console Application contains at least one namespace, one class, and main procedure or method while in Visual Basic.NET the structure of Console Application contains at least one Module and main procedure or subroutine.
The Console application is a very fast and easy application environment of Microsoft Visual Studio.NET and normally it is used for the learning purposes of .NET programming languages because it is easy, simple and involves no graphical Controls Objects and complex environment. Therefore, it is recommended for all who want to learn the basic concepts, statements or syntaxes of any .NET programming languages then the Console application is very easy approach for them to learn the .NET programming languages.

Windows Applications

Windows application is a programming environment in Microsoft Visual Studio.NET that provides Graphical User Interface (GUI) for applications development. The GUI of Windows application is a visual programming environment that provides different tools and features to develop interactive software applications. Unlike Console application windows application provides multiple entry points and multiple execution points because windows application uses different tools and features such as windows Forms and Controls Objects that provide multiple user interfaces at multiple points of an application. The multiple entry points mean that a windows application takes input from the user at multiple points using Controls Objects and view data or information at the same GUI. For example, a windows application contains one or more window Forms, one or more Controls Objects such as command buttons, text boxes, check boxes, radio buttons, combo boxes, lists etc. Each Control Object is an entry point for the user. The multiple execution points means that a windows application provides multiple execution paths for the application. For example, in a windows application there is no single fixed main procedure or method like Console application but unlike Console application, a windows application is event driven application that contains a series of procedures. These procedures contain block of codes or statements of the application and they are called events handlers because each procedure is executed by a particular event. The execution of a windows application depends on these procedures or events handlers. When a procedure or events handler is executed then it executes the block of codes and performs a specific task but the main difference between Console application and Windows application is that when we run a Console application, the compiler always starts execution from the main procedure of the Console application automatically and executes the entire program without any event while in Windows application the procedures cannot be executed automatically because they require different events to execute. Windows application takes input from the user using almost all the input devices such as keyboard, mouse, scanner, Barcode reader, and Finger prints reader etc.

Basic Components of Windows Applications

Windows applications provide some core components that are used to design and develop windows applications. Following is the details of some important components:

- Windows Forms
- Controls Objects
- Events
- Events Handlers

Windows Forms

A Windows Form is a graphical Application Programming Interface (API) provided by Microsoft Visual Studio.NET for different .NET programming languages to develop different visual and graphical user interfaces. The Windows application always starts from a Windows Form. A Windows Form is a rectangular container that has a visual graphical appearance and normally displays on the computer desktop. A Windows Form is actually the representation of a Window and it is used in Windows applications that provide user interface and allow users to interact with the application. The Windows Form takes input or information from the user and displays the output or information to the user on the same interface. The Windows application is made up from one or more Windows Forms. The Windows Forms are actually visual rectangular frames or containers for the Control Objects. The Control Objects are used to design the Windows Forms according to the application specification. The Windows Forms hold Control Objects and provide different layouts to arrange the Control Objects in different formats according to the programmers or developers settings. The area of a Windows Form that holds the Control Objects is called client area or container area of the Windows Form. The Control Objects are graphical controls that are also called Windows Forms Control Objects. The Control Objects are used on the Windows Forms to allow a user to interact with the application. The Control Objects provide different interfaces which allow a user to input data or information to the application, view, or display data or information.

A Windows Form is a class in the .NET Framework and it is defined in the System.Windows.Forms namespace. The Form class represents a Window within an application and it provides different types of Windows Forms such as Single Document Interface (SDI) Windows Forms, Multiple Document Interface (MDI) Windows Forms, and Modal Windows Forms. The modal Windows Forms are special types of Windows Forms that are called Dialog Boxes. A Dialog Box is a special type of a Windows Form in Windows application that allows a user to communicate with the application. It prompts and allows a user to perform a command or sends a response to the application. It asks a question from the user and requires an acknowledgment from the user about a particular task that whether the application processed that particular task or not. It also sends information or progress report to the user and also alerts for the error report when occurs during the application execution or when a user input the wrong or irrelevant information or data to the application.

The Multiple Document Interface (MDI) is the collections of different types of Windows Forms that contain Parent Windows Form and child Windows Forms. The Windows Form class provides different sets of properties, methods, and events that provide different operations or tasks for different purposes. The properties can be set during the program designing time and also can be set during run time of the application. The properties of a Windows Form are used to change the characteristics or state of the Windows Forms such as to change and set the size of the Form, change the Form Title, change the Form background color, change the Form Icon, change the Form style, change the Form border style, change or set the default display location of the Form, change the fore Color of all the Control Objects placed on the Form, change the mouse cursor shape while moving over the Form, change the font style of all the Control Objects placed on the Form and so on.

Control Objects

Control Objects are graphical Objects provided by .NET for Windows Forms designing. Control Objects provide different interfaces and allow users to interact with the application. The Control Objects are also called Windows Forms Control Objects because they are used on the Windows Forms. The Windows Forms are containers or interfaces for the Control Objects. The Control Objects are placed on Windows Forms and design a Windows application. Control Objects are placed on a Windows Form for particular purposes and they are placed on a Windows Form to design it according to the application specification. Control Objects provide multiple entry points and multiple execution points for Windows application and allow users to interact with the application at multiple points. There are different types of Control Objects provided by Microsoft .NET Framework. Some of these Control Objects are used on Windows Forms for input and output purposes which allow users to enter data or information to the application and display data or information on the same interfaces, some Control Objects are used to arrange other Control Objects on the surface of a Windows Form which are called Container Control Objects, some Control Objects are used to create Menus, Toolbars, Pop-up Menus, and Task bar on Windows Form, some Control Objects are used to display the Windows standard Modals Dialog Boxes, and some Control Objects are used to provide different services to the users such as Event Log services, Directory entry service, error provider services, Messages Queue services, Processes services, File System Watcher services, Service Controller services, Timer service and so on.

Events

An event is a signal or an action in Windows application that occurs when a particular external factor, source, or an operation occurs. The external factors, sources, or operations are usually performed by the users using the input devices such as keyboard, mouse, barcode readers, and finger print devices etc.

The events are also performed by sensors devices, and timers. The sensors are hardware devices attached to some Windows application for different purposes such as security, checking, matching or comparing objects, and recognition of an object etc. When a user operates a keyboard or a mouse, it triggers different events for example, when a user presses any key from the keyboard, the keyboard key Press event occurs similarly, if a user presses the mouse button, the mouse click event occurs and so on. The sensor receives a signal or an input from the environment and responds to the Windows application and executes a particular event handler. There are some other factors, sources, or operations involved in Windows applications that triggers different events such as Threads execution, Messages from other application or from the same application, or when a specified condition is satisfied in the application, or when a Windows Form is loaded into the memory, the form Load event occurs similarly, when a Windows form is resized, the resize event occurs and so on.

Events are the keys of the execution of events handlers. When an event occurs, it informs the application that something has been occurred or changed in the application and calls a particular event handler and executes the block of codes or statements written in the body of that event handler.

Events Handlers

A Windows application is made up of one or more Windows Forms and one or more Control Objects. The Windows Forms and Control Objects provide various procedures which are called events handlers. An event handler is a small block of codes or statements of the application which is executed to perform a specific task. Each event handler requires an event to execute the block of codes or statements of the application. Events are the keys of execution of events handlers. When an event occurs, it informs the application that something has been occurred or changed in the application and calls a particular event handler and executes the block of codes or statements written in the body of that event handler. Windows application contains a series of different events handlers which are executed in a sequence. The program codes of Windows application is always written in various events handlers. Each event handler has its own purpose and it is related to a particular event. When a particular event occurs, it executes the related event handler.

Procedures

A procedure is a named block of statements or code enclosed by a declaration statement that can be executed independently to perform a specific task. The declaration statement of a procedure is a block that contains starting point and ending point of the procedure. The block of statements or code must be placed inside in the declaration statement of the procedure. Each procedure may contain the same nature or the same functionality block of statements or codes. A Procedure has two types such as Events Handlers and user defined Procedures. An event handler is a procedure that contains a small block of codes or statements of the application and when it is executed then it performs a specific task. An Event Handler is executed by an Event. A user-defined Procedure is also a small block of codes or statements that is executed to perform a specific task but the main difference is that an Event Handler is executed when an event occurs in the application while a user-defined procedure is executed manually from a calling point or calling code. A user-defined procedure cannot execute automatically without calling code or calling point. When a user-define procedure is executed then it may also return a value to the calling point or calling code. For more details about Procedures please read the chapter "Procedural Programming in .NET".

Visual C# Programming Language

Microsoft Visual C# is an object oriented high level programming language designed by Microsoft Corporation. It is part of the Microsoft Visual Studio programming languages and based on the .NET framework. The C# programming language is a general purpose programming language used to develop various types of applications and programs such as Console applications, Windows Forms applications, ASP.NET Web applications, Class Library applications, WPF applications, Silverlight applications etc. The C# programming language is designed by combining the features of C++, and Java programming languages. The program syntax of C# is very near to Java and C++ programming languages but due to some extra features of C#, its program structure is different from Java, and C++ programming languages. The C# programming language uses the common library and the Common Intermediate Language of the .NET framework to compile their programs.

Fundamentals of C# Programming Language

Following are some fundamentals of C# programming language:

1. Each program of C# programming language starts from a class which is called general class or program class. The general class or program class is also called driver class of C# program because it contains a method which is called driver method. The driver method is used to execute the C# program. The name of the driver method is always **main** because it is the built-in name of the driver method. The C# program always starts execution from this driver method and without this driver class a C# program cannot be executed. By default each program of C# programming language is enclosed inside in a namespace declaration. The namespace is a container for the C# program that holds other contents of the program. The other contents of C# program may be classes, interfaces, delegates, enumerations, structures, and value types etc. By default the namespace name is the program name but we can also give any name to the namespace according to our choice. The using of namespace scope is optional because we can also write a C# program without the using of namespace scope but it is a very good approach to write a C# program inside in the body of the namespace because it removes the naming conflicts of same name classes, interfaces, structures etc in different applications.
2. C# programming language does not support global variables and global methods because C# program starts from a class therefore, all the variables and methods must be declared inside in the class body.
3. C# programming language is an object oriented programming language. Its classes can be implemented number of interfaces but it does not support multiple inheritance.
4. C# programming language supports operator overloading like C++ programming language.
5. In C# programming language a Boolean variable does not return 0 or 1. It always returns True or False.
6. The C# programming language does not support unsafe type casting for example, from Boolean to integer, from enumeration to integer etc.
7. In C# programming language all the value type variables are initialized to zero and reference type variables are initialized to null.
8. In C# programming language the array indexing starts from zero.
9. In C# programming language the managed memory cannot be freed explicitly because it is garbage collected.

10. In C# programming language we cannot declare a variable with a keyword WithEvent like Visual Basic.
11. In C# programming language the string concatenation can be done using the arithmetic addition sign +.
12. In C# program body of a method (procedure) is always enclosed within curly braces.
13. C# programming language supports only structured error handling and does not support unstructured error handling.
14. C# programming language supports both single line and multiple line comments like C++ programming language.
15. C# programming language supports Auto XML documentation.
16. C# programming language supports automatic memory management.
17. C# programming language supports pointers.

Rules for writing C# Programs

The following rules must be kept in the mind while you are writing a C# program:

1. Each executable statement of a C# program must be terminated with a semicolon. There are two types of statements in programming languages such as executable statements and non-executable statements. Executable statements are executed to perform specific tasks while non-executable statements do not execute by themselves but they are used to execute another statement or block of statements therefore, they are called non-executable statements. The examples of non-executable statements are flow control statements such as if condition, for loop, while loop, and foreach loop because they do not execute by itself but they are used to execute another statement or block of statements. Therefore, semicolons are not placed after the flow control statements and other non-executable statements.
2. The block of statements must be enclosed within curly braces. For example, all the flow control statements (if condition, for loop, while loop, do-while loop, foreach loop) of C# programming language by default execute a single statement because the scope of these flow control statements is limited to only one statement. If we want to execute more statements or block of statements then we must enclosed the block of statements within curly braces.
3. The square brackets are used to declare arrays and access the indexes of arrays in C# programming language.

4. In C# programming language a single equal sign is used for all types of assignments while double equal signs are used in case of value comparisons. For example, if we want to compare two values using any decision statement or conditional statement then we must use the double equal signs between the compare values.
5. The C# programming language is a case-sensitive programming language and its all keywords are in lower case. Therefore, we cannot write built-in statements or keywords of C# in capital letters. In C# programming language if we declare two same name variables, one is in lower case and another one is in capital or upper case then the C# compiler considers them two different variables.
6. In C# programming language all built-in statements, keywords, methods, classes, structures, threads, delegates, value types and all other built-in contents are placed inside in different namespaces according to their functionalities and natures. Therefore, if we want to use any keyword, statement, or any other built-in content in our program then we must include the namespace of that keyword and statement at the top of the program.

General Structure or Skeleton of C# Program

The C# programming language provides various types of applications such as Console Applications, Windows Forms Applications, ASP.NET Web Applications, WPF Applications, and Windows Service Applications etc. Each application type has its own structure but usually a C# application contains three blocks such as namespace block, class block, and procedure or method block. The namespace block is the outermost block of a C# application and all other blocks or contents of the application are declared inside in the namespace block. Therefore, namespace is a container for the C# application that holds other contents of the application. The other contents of the C# application may be classes, interfaces, delegates, structures, enumerations, and value types etc. By default the namespace name is the application name but we can give any name to the namespace. The second block of the C# application is the class block. The class block is declared inside in the namespace block and it is called main class or application class. The main or application class contains one or more procedures or methods and other contents. Each procedure is an entry point and an execution point of the application. When we run a C# application then the compiler always starts execution of the application from a specified procedure or method. The various application types of C# programming language depend on different .NET framework versions and different Visual Studio.NET environments. Following are some useful application types of the C# programming language:

- Console Applications
- Windows Forms Applications
- ASP.NET Web Applications
- WPF Applications
- Windows Service Applications

Console Applications

In Console Application a C# program contains at least one namespace, one class, and one procedure or method block. The first or the outermost block is the namespace block, the second or middle block is the class block, and the third or innermost block is procedure or method block. The method of the program is a built-in method and it is called driver method of the program because it executes a C# program and it is a single entry and single execution point of the C# program. The name of the driver method in Console application is always fixed and its name is main. It is built-in name of the driver method and we cannot change it. The program code or the block of statements is always placed inside in the body of the main method. The main method is declared inside in the main or general class body. Therefore, a class in which the main method is declared is also called driver class of the program. When we run a Console Application then C# compiler always starts execution of the program from the driver or main method. Following is the general structure or skeleton of a C# program in Console Application:

```
namespace Namespace_name
{
class Class_name
{
public static void main(string[] args)
{
…………………………………………..
This is the main Method or driver method of the program. The program
code or Block of statements is written here.
…………………………………………..
}
}
}
```

The above structure or skeleton of the C# program contains one namespace, one class, and one method and there are three blocks or scopes. In the above structure the driver or main method is declared with three extra keywords such as public, static, and void. These three keywords are generally used with a method, class, and a structure etc to provide information about that method, class or a structure. The first keyword public is an access modifier that is used to define a scope for the method, class or a structure. The scope means access limitation. For example, when we declare a method, a class or a structure with public modifier then we can access that method, class or structure from anywhere of the program similarly, if we declare a method, a class or a structure with private modifier then we can't access that method, class, or structure outside that block where we defined it. Furthermore if we declare a method with protected modifier then we can only access that method inside in that class, module, or structure block where we defined it and we cannot access outside from that scope or block. By default the driver or main method of the C# program in Console Application is public that means we can call it from anywhere in the program. The second keyword static means that this method does not belongs to any instance of a class. When we declare a method with the static keyword then it makes the method accessible without an instance of the program. By default the driver or main method of Console application is static. If we declare the driver or main method of the Console Application as a non-static method then it requires an instance of the program. The third keyword is void that means nothing to return. When we declare a method with the keyword void then that method does not return any value.

Windows Forms Applications

In windows Forms application a C# program contains at least one namespace, one class, and at least one procedure or method block. The namespace block is the outermost block of a C# program and it is a container for other contents of the program. The second outermost block or middle block of the program is the class block that is called main class or application class and its name is **Form1**. This is the default name of the class in windows Forms application and it implements the main and general Form class. The main and general Form class represents a window or a dialog box that makes up an application's user interface. A windows Forms application provides at least one Form such as Form1 but we can also add more Forms. When we add another Form to a windows Forms application then its name is Form2 and so on. The Form1, and Form2 etc are the default names of the Form classes but we can also give any user-defined name to a windows Form. The third block of C# program is a procedure or method block. The procedure or method block is usually event handler and its name contains two parts, first part is the name of the Form class either the Form default name such as Form1 or any other user-defined name and second part of the event handler is a specified event of windows Forms application. The method block is always inside in the main or application class block. The main or application class block contains one or more procedures or methods and other contents. Each procedure is an entry point and an execution point of the application. Following is the general structure or skeleton of the C# program in windows Forms application:

```
namespace namespace_name
{
public partial class Form1 : Form
{
public Form1()
{
InitializeComponent();
}
private void Form1_Load(object sender, EventArgs e)
{
..............................
Body of the procedure or event handler. The program code or block of
statements is written here.
..............................
}
}
}
```

The above structure of the C# program contains three blocks such as namespace block, class block, and method block. The first block starts from the line **namespace namespace_name**. In this line the **namespace_name** indicates user-defined name of the namespace. Its default name is the program name but we can give any name to the namespace. The second block starts from the line **public partial class Form1:Form**. In this line the word **Form1** indicates the class name and it is implemented from the main and general Form class. Form1 is the default name of the Form class and we can give any user-defined name to it. The third block of the program starts from the line **private void Form1_Load(object sender, EventArgs e)**. In this line the word **Form1_Load** indicates the name of the method or event handler and it takes two parameters such as **object sender** and **EventArgs e**. The first parameter

sender indicates the sender object and the second parameter **EventArgs** indicates an event. As previously we discussed that an event handler is a small block of codes that is executed to perform a specific task. The name of an event handler contains two parts. The first part indicates the class name and the second part indicates an event. The first part of the Form1_Load event handler is Form1 that indicates the form class Form1 and the second part of the Form1_Load is Load that indicates the Form1 class Load event. It means that the event handler **Form1_Load** will be executed if the Form1 class Load event occurs.

Since in the .NET framework programming languages all the classes, interfaces, delegates, structures, enumeration, and value types are placed in different namespaces therefore, a C# program requires a specified namespace that is to be included at the top of the program before the namespace scope declaration in both the Console and Windows application environment. To include a namespace in a C# program a keyword **using** is used. Following is the general syntax to include a namespace in a C# program:

using Namespace_name;

Visual Basic.NET Programming Language

Microsoft Visual Basic.NET is an object oriented high level programming language designed by Microsoft Corporation and it is shortly called VB.NET. It is a part of Microsoft Visual Studio programming languages and based on the .NET framework. The VB.NET programming language is the modified form of Visual Basic 6 in which different new features are included. The new and the most important feature of the VB.NET is object oriented programming feature. This feature of Visual Basic enables it to become part of the .NET programming languages. The VB.NET is a general purpose programming language used to develop various types of applications and programs such as Console applications, Windows Forms applications, ASP.NET Web applications, Class Library applications, WPF applications, Silverlight applications etc. The VB.NET uses the common library and the Common Intermediate Language of the .NET framework to compile their programs. The program syntax and structure of VB.NET is very different from the C# program syntax and structure.

Fundamentals of Visual Basic.NET

Following are some basic fundamentals and rules for writing programs in VB.NET programming language and comparison with the C# programming language:

1. The VB.NET programming language is not a case-sensitive programming language and it accepts any built-in keyword or statement either in small letters, or in capital letters. Therefore, we can write the built-in statements or keywords of VB.NET either in small, or in capital letters. We can also write the built-in keywords or statements in mixed case (small and capital letters combination). When we write any built-in keyword or statement then the VB.NET compiler automatically adjust the case of that keyword and statement. In VB.NET programming language if we declare two same name variables, one is in lower case and the second one is in capital case then the VB.NET compiler always consider these two same name variables as a single repeated variable and the compiler gives an error message that a repeated single variable is not allowed. The C# programming language is a case sensitive language and all the keywords and statements of C# programming language are in small letters.
2. All the keywords and statements in VB.NET are in capitalized form. When we write any built-in library keyword or statement of VB.NET programming language in capital letters or in small letters then the VB.NET automatically converts that keyword or statement in capitalized form. The C# programming language does not convert the letters case.
3. In VB.NET we can declare a variable with the WithEvent keyword but in C# programming language we cannot declare a variable with WithEvent.
4. In VB.NET a single equal (=) sign is used for assignment as well as for values comparison while in C# programming language the double equal (==) signs are used for the comparison.
5. In VB.NET the string concatenation can be performed using the ampersand (&) sign while in C# programming language the string concatenation can be performed using the arithmetic addition sign (+).
6. The VB.NET statements do not terminate with semicolon while each executable statement of C# programming language must be terminated with a semicolon. The VB.NET programming language does not support semicolon.

7. The block of statements in VB.NET does not need to enclose within curly braces because VB.NET does not support the using of curly braces. In C# programming language the block of statements must be enclosed within curly braces.
8. The block of statements in VB.NET is always enclosed within the built-in block of VB.NET. In VB.NET all the statements are in the form of pairs like HTML tags which contains the starting statement and ending statement for example, procedures, If statements, If-else statements, select case statements, classes, structures, delegates, enumeration and so on are always ended with the End statement similarly, the for loop is ended with the Next statement, the while loop is ended with the End While statement etc. Therefore the block of statements in VB.NET is always enclosed within the built-in block of VB.NET.
9. In VB.NET programming language the array indexing starts from zero like C# programming language.
10. VB.NET programming language supports dynamic arrays. A dynamic array allows us to increase its size after its declaration during run time. The keyword ReDim is used to redefine the size of an array in VB.NET programming language. The C# programming language does not support Redim keyword.
11. In VB.NET the variables can be declared using a keyword **Dim**. The Dim keyword means dimension.
12. The VB.NET keywords and statements are more user friendly than the keywords and statements of C# programming language because most of the keywords and statements of VB.NET are in the form of human readable language words. For example, in C# for AND operation a keyword **&** is used twice, and for OR operation a keyword | is used twice while in VB.NET for AND operation a keyword **And** is used instead of & and for OR operation a keyword **Or** is used instead of | keyword which are more user friendly and human readable keywords.
13. VB.NET programming language supports both types of error handling such as structured error handling and unstructured error handling while C# only support structured error handling and does not support unstructured error handling.
14. VB.NET programming language provides With.....End With block that defines a series of statements related to a specified object without using the name of that object again and again. The C# programming language does not support this block and don't have any equivalent for this block.

15. VB.NET programming language only supports single line comments and does not support multiple line comments while C# programming language supports both types of comments.
16. The VB.NET statements are continued using the underscore character while the C# statements are continue until the semicolon. A semicolon terminates the statement of C# programming language.
17. VB.NET does not support the auto XML documentation while C# supports the auto XML documentation.
18. VB.NET does not support automatic memory management while C# programming language supports automatic memory management.
19. VB.NET programming language supports implicit type conversion and it is performed automatically by default while in C# programming language the conversion is performed explicitly by casts and also by using the conversion methods.
20. In VB.NET the array size and elements are specifies using small parentheses while in C# the array size and elements are specifies using the square brackets.

General Structure or Skeleton of VB.NET Program

The VB.NET programming language also provides various types of applications like C# programming language such as Console Applications, Windows Forms Applications, ASP.NET Web Applications, WPF Applications, Class Library Applications, and Silverlight Applications etc. Each application type has its own structure but usually VB.NET application contains two blocks such as class block and a procedure block. The first or outer block of a VB.NET application is a class block that is also called main class or general class of the application. The second block of VB.NET application is the procedure block that is also called subroutine block. A subroutine is a procedure or an event handler that controls or executes the VB.NET application. A VB.NET application has one or more subroutines. Each subroutine has an entry point and an execution point of the application. When we run a VB.NET application then the compiler always starts execution of the application from a specified subroutine. The various application types of VB.NET programming language depend on different .NET framework versions and different Visual Studio.NET environments. Following are some useful application types of VB.NET programming language:

- Console Applications
- Windows Forms Applications

- ASP.NET Web Applications
- WPF Applications

Console Application

In Console application the VB.NET program contains one Module block, and one procedure block. The Module block is the first or outer block and it is also called main Module or general Module of the VB.NET program. The procedure block is the second or inner block of the VB.NET program and it is also called subroutine. The subroutine block is a built-in block of VB.NET program that is called driver subroutine. The name of the driver subroutine in Console Application is always fixed and its name is main. This is the built-in name of the driver subroutine in VB.NET program and we cannot change this name. The driver subroutine always declared inside in the main or general Module of the VB.NET program. Therefore, a VB.NET Console application contains at least two blocks such as Module block and subroutine block. The Module block is a container that holds other contents of the application. The program code or the block of statements is always placed inside in the body of the main subroutine. In Console application each program of VB.NET has a single entry point and a single execution point of the program. Following is the general syntax of VB.NET program structure or skeleton in Console application:

```
Module Module1

Sub Main()
.........................
This is body of the VB.NET program
.........................

End Sub

End Module
```

Windows Form Application

In windows Forms application a VB.NET program contains at least one class, and at least one procedure or subroutine block. The first or outer block is the class block and the second or inner block is a procedure or subroutine block. The class block is a container for the program that is called main or general class of the application and its name is **Form1** by default. This is the default name of the class in windows Forms application and it implements the main and general Form class. The Form class represents a window or a dialog box that makes up an application's user interface. A windows Forms application provides at least one Form such as Form1 but we can also add more Forms. When we add another Form to a windows Forms application then its name is Form2 and so on. The Form1, and Form2 etc are the default names of the Form classes but we can also give any user-defined name to a windows Form. The procedure or subroutine block is actually an event handler and its name contains two parts, first part is the name of the Form class either the Form default name such as Form1 or any other user-defined name and second part of the event handler is a specified event of windows Forms application. The subroutine block is always inside in the main or application class block. The main or application class block contains one or more procedures or subroutines and other contents. Each procedure or subroutine is an entry point and an execution point of the application. Following is the general structure or skeleton of the VB.NET program in windows Forms application:

```
Public Class Form1

Private Sub Form1_Load(sender As System.Object, e As System.EventArgs)
Handles MyBase.Load
..............................

Body of the procedure or event handler. The program code or block of
statements is written here.
..............................

End Sub

End Class
```

The above structure of the VB.NET program contains two blocks such as class block, and subroutine block. The first block starts from the line **Public Class Form1**. In this line the word **Form1** indicates the class name and it is implemented from the main and general Form class. Form1 is the default name of the Form class and we can give any user-defined name to it. The second block of the program starts from the line **Private Sub Form1_Load(sender As System.Object, e As System.EventArgs)**. In this line the word **Form1_Load** indicates name of the subroutine or event handler and it takes two parameters such as **System.Object** and **System.EventArgs e**. The first parameter System. Object indicates the sender object and the second parameter System.EventArgs indicates an event. The first part of the Form1_Load event handler is Form1 that indicates the form class Form1 and second part of the Form1_Load is Load that indicates the Form1 class Load event. It means that the event handler **Form1_Load** will be executed if the Form1 class Load event occurs.

Applications Development in .NET

The .NET Framework provides an interface for many programming languages to work on the same platform and to use the common .NET Framework Class Library. The .NET Framework also allows us to write an application in one .NET Framework programming language and convert it into another .NET Framework programming language codes. Each programming language of the .NET Framework provides its own building structure and a methodology for the development of applications. The development process of an application in the .NET programming languages is called a project. A project is a planning, organizing, methodology and a process for the development of applications. Microsoft Visual Studio.NET is a software development tool designed by Microsoft Corporation that is used to develop various kinds of software applications in the .NET framework such as Console applications, Windows Forms applications, Class Library, ASP.NET Web applications, WPF applications, and Silverlight applications etc. Each application type has its own project type. To develop an application using one of the .NET Framework programming languages such as Visual C# or Visual Basic.NET, a new project is created using Microsoft Visual Studio.NET environment. A new Project can be created using different versions of Microsoft Visual Studio.NET. The project creation process in all the Visual Studio.NET versions are almost the same. The following steps demonstrate a new project in Visual Studio.NET:

1. Open Microsoft Visual Studio.NET Professional.
2. Select **File** Menu of Visual Studio.NET Professional and click **New** option from the File menu and then click Project.

When we click the Project option then it displays a New Project dialog box that contains different Projects types. The New Project dialog box contains three pans or columns. The Left side Pane displays the list of Microsoft Visual Studio.NET Programming languages, the middle or the center pane displays all the Projects types of a selected Programming language and the right side pane displays a brief description of the selected project type. To develop an application, the first step is to select a programming language from the left side pane and then select the Project type from the center Pane of the New Project dialog box. When we select programming language and Project type from the New Project dialog box then Microsoft Visual Studio.NET creates a folder for the new application Project. The default name of the new application Project is the name of the Project type but we can give any name to the new application Project. The New Project dialog box also contains two textboxes. The first textbox takes a user-defined name for the application Project and the second textbox takes a location string for the new application Project. A location string is a specified path where we want to store our new project. Following is the snapshot of Microsoft Visual Studio.NET 2013 Professional New Project dialog box:

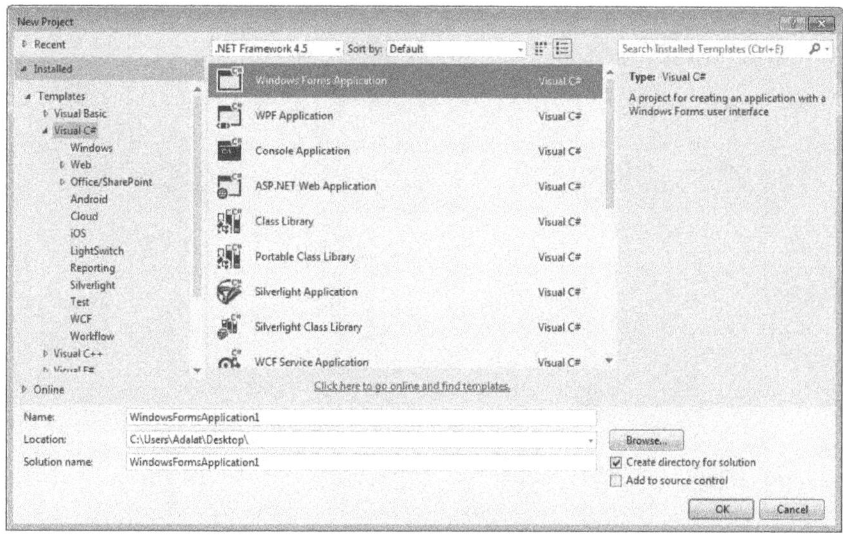

When we click on OK button then Microsoft Visual Studio.NET creates a folder for the new application Project and saves the new application Project in the created folder and also places all the necessary files and other resources in the created folder. The application Project folder contains different sub folders and files and they depend on different programming languages of the .NET Framework. For example, the application project folder of C# programming language contains Project file, Windows Forms, and three sub folders such as Properties, obj, and bin. The Project file extension of the C# programming language is always .csProj. The properties sub folder contains Setting, Resources, and AssemblyInfo files. The obj sub folder contains the resources files, the Cache files, and an executable file of the application and the bin sub folder contain an executable file of the application and a Manifest file that contains information about the Assembly. The application project folder of VB.NET programming language contains Project file, Windows Forms, and three sub folders such as obj, My Project, and bin. The Project file extension of VB.NET programming language is always .vbProj. The sub folder obj contains the resources files, the cache files, the XML document file and an executable file of the application. The bin sub folder contains a Manifest file that contains information about assembly, an XML file, and an executable file of the application and my project sub folder contains Setting file, Resources files, and application files.

CHAPTER 2

Variables, Constants and Basic Elements

CHAPTER CONTENTS

- Variables
- Data Types
- Primitive Data Types
- Primitive Data types in .NET Framework
- Non-Primitive Data Types
- Declaration of Variables
- Initialization of Variables
- The Variables Naming Conventions
- Limitation of Variables (data types ranges) in .NET
- Memory Representation of Data Types
- Constants and its Declaration
- Operators
- Arithmetic Operators
- Arithmetic Assignment Operators
- Relational Operators
- Logical Operators
- Examples of Logical Operators
- Increment and Decrement Operators
- Types of Increment and Decrement Operators
- Prefix Increment/Decrement Operators
- Postfix Increment/Decrement Operators
- Compound Assignment Operators
- The sizeof Operator
- Conditional Operator
- Expressions
- Expression Precedence
- Comments
- Typecasting
- Why we use Typecasting?

- ➢ The Convert Class
- ➢ Escape Sequences
- ➢ Keywords

Variables

A variable is an identifier that indicates a storage location in computer memory and it is used to reference the data stored at a memory location. The memory is logically divided into various cells called memory locations. A memory location is capable of storing data. Each memory location has a physical address that is called memory address. A memory address is a unique physical address that uniquely identifies a memory location. A computer program works on the basis of some input and output that takes input data from a user and sends to the memory and retrieves data from the memory and sends back to the user. A computer program uses memory addresses to execute machine code, store data in a memory location, and retrieve data from memory location using variables. A variable is a user-defined name or an identifier of a specified memory location that is used to send data to that memory location and retrieve data from it. Furthermore, we can say that a variable is a data traveler between a computer program and a computer memory location.

The computer programming languages provide a mechanism that is called variables declaration. The variables declaration is a process that is used to declare variables. When a variable is declared, a memory space or memory location is reserved for it in the memory and a memory address is assigned to it. Each variable has its own separate memory location and each memory location has its own memory address. The size of the memory location depends on the variable type because each type of variable has its own data size. There are different types of data such as integer data, real data, and alphabetic data or character data etc. Each type of data has its own variable type and each type of data occupies a specific amount of space in the computer memory. Each variable has a single memory location that can store only a single data at a time. When we input data to a variable, it stores that data into its specified memory location. A variable is called variable because its data or value changes time to time for example, if a variable currently has a data and we input new data to it then it overwrites the current data and holds the new input data in the memory location. Therefore, the data stored by a variable is temporary and each time when we input new data to a variable, it overwrites the previous data and holds the last input data in the memory location. The memory location of a variable is a temporary location and it is created when we declare a variable. When a variable is terminated then the memory location of that variable is also terminated.

A real life example of a variable is a glass containing water. In this case the glass is a variable and water is data or information. The contents of glass may change time to time because sometime it may contains water, sometime milk, and sometime it may contain other liquids etc. A glass can hold a single content at a time.

Data Type

Data Type means the type of data that a variable can store. The data is basically categorized into three basic types such as integer data, real or floating point data, and alphabetic or character data. The Data types are used to declare variables for temporarily data storage in memory. Each data type is used to declare a variable for a specific type of data for example, an integer variable can store integer data, a real or floating point variable can store real or floating point data, and a character or string variable can store alphabetic or character data. Therefore, if a program uses an integer data, the variable will be declared of type integer similarly, if a program uses a character data then the variable will be declared of type character and so on. When a variable is declared, a memory space is reserved to it. The memory space is reserved on the basis of a variable data type because each data type occupies different amount of memory space. The memory spaces are reserved temporarily during run time of a program. When a program is terminated then all the variables of that program are undeclared and their associated memory spaces are released. The data in a memory is represented in the form of bits. A bit is the smallest unit of data that is called binary digit and a group of bits is called bytes. The memory space of one byte is equal to eight bits. The variables are declared before usage. The Data types are usually categorized into the following two types:

- Primitive Data Types
- Non-Primitive Data Types

Primitive Data Types

Primitive data types are predefined data types defined in the built-in library of a programming language and they are used to declare variables for specific types of data. The primitive data types are already structured and all the specifications are defined in advanced such as the data type nature, the data type range i.e. the minimum and maximum range of data, and the amount of memory space to be reserved in the computer memory etc. The data type specifications are predefined for each data type and they are not changeable. For example, when a variable is declared from any data type, a specific amount of memory space is reserved for it in computer memory and the minimum and maximum ranges of data is defined. The .NET Framework provides a set of primitive data types that are used to declare variables such as integer data type, single or float data type, long integer data type, double data type, long double data type, string data type, byte data type, date and time data type, Boolean data type etc. Furthermore, the primitive data types are predefined data types that are used to declare variables. The variables are declared to store data. Each variable can store a specific type of data for example, to store integer data, an integer variable is declared similarly, to store a string data, a string variable is declared etc.

Primitive Data Types in .NET Framework

The .NET framework built-in library provides a common set of primitive data types for variables declaration. Each primitive data type is used to declare a variable for a specific type of data. The .NET framework set of primitive data types is common to the .NET framework programming languages such as C#, VB.NET, and C++.NET. Each programming language of the .NET framework provides its own set of data types and also supports the common set of primitive data types of the .NET Framework. Following is the list of .NET framework primitive data types supported by C# and VB.NET programming languages:

Data Types in C#	Data Types in VB.NET	Description
int	Integer	This data type is called integer data type and it is used to declare integer variables. The variables of this data type can store both the positive and negative integer values.

uint	UInteger	This data type is called unsigned integer data type. The unsigned means no sign. This data type is used to declare unsigned integer variables. The unsigned integer variables only can store the positive integer value. An integer variable can store both the positive and negative value and it reserves one bit memory space for the value sign either + sign or – sign. When we use the unsigned keyword with the int data type then the unsigned keyword does not reserve one bit memory space for a sign but it uses all the bits of int for the value. Therefore, an unsigned variable does not store negative values.
byte	Byte	This data type is an unsigned integer data type and it is used to declare unsigned integer variables. The unsigned integer variables can store only positive values and they cannot store negative values.
sbyte	SByte	This data type is a signed integer data type and it is used to declare signed integer variables. The signed integer variables can store both the positive and negative values.
short	Short	This data type is called short integer data type that is used to declare short integer variables. The short integer variables can store both the positive and negative integer values. It is similar to the integer data type but its value range is half of the integer data type.
ushort	UShort	This data type is called unsigned short integer data type and it is used to declare unsigned short integer variables. The unsigned short integer variables only can store the positive integer value.

long	Long	This data type is called long integer data type. The long integer data type is used to declare long integer variables. A long integer variable is same as an integer variable that can store both the positive and negative integer data but the main difference is that the size of a long integer variable is double than the size of an integer variable.
ulong	ULong	This data type is called unsigned long integer data type. It is used to declare unsigned long integer variables. An unsigned long integer variable only can store the positive integer data.
float	Single	This data type is called float data type that is used to declare float variables. A float variable is used to store a real data or a floating point data.
double	Double	This data type is used to declare double variables. A double variable is same as a float or a single variable that is used to store a real value or a floating point value but the main difference is that the size of a double variable is double than a float or a single variable.
decimal	Decimal	This data type is used to declare decimal variables.
char	Char	This data type is called character data type that is used to declare character variables. A character variable is used to store a character data.
string	String	This data type is used to declare string variables.
datetime	DateTime	This data type is used declare Date and Time variables.

bool	Boolean	This data type is used to declare Boolean variables. A Boolean variable takes a Boolean value either true or false.
object	Object	This data type is used to declare objects. It can store any type of value.

Non-primitive Data Types

Non-primitive data types are reference types and they are usually associated with a group of data. The non-primitive data types are actually derived from primitive data types and each non-primitive data type is the combination of two or more primitive data types. The non-primitive data types are used in structures, and classes and they allows us to declare instances. When an instance of a non-primitive data type is declared, a memory space is assigned to it. The memory space of a non-primitive data type is on the basis of a group of primitive data types that grouped in a structure or in a class.

Declaration of Variables

Variable declaration is a mechanism that allocates a space or location in the computer memory and allows us to give a user-defined name to that allocated memory location. When a name is assigned to the allocated memory space then it is called variable. Therefore, variables declaration is a process that allows us to reserve memory spaces or memory locations for temporarily storage of data. Variables are usually declared from the data types. Each type of data has its own variable type. The declaration process reserve memory space and tells the compiler about the variable name, the variable type, the variable scope, and the variable size. The computer programming languages provide various data types that are used to declare the different nature and the different sizes variables in the memory for example, integer variables for integer data, real or floating point variables for real or floating point data, and characters or strings variables for alphabetic or character data etc. Each data type occupies a specific amount of space in the memory. When a variable is declared in the memory, a memory space is allocated to it on the basis of variable type and a unique address is assigned to it that is called memory address. A memory address is an identifier for a variable that is used to identify that variable in the memory and track the data.

Variables can be declared anywhere in the program but usually they depend on the scope and accessibility because a computer program has different scope levels and a single program may contain various blocks, functions, and modules. If a variable is declared within a block then it is local to that block and it cannot be accessed outside the block similarly, if a variable is declared within a function then it is local to that function and it cannot be accessed outside that function. If a variable is declared at the top of the program outside all the functions or procedures then that variable is global to all the functions or procedures and it can be accessed inside all functions or procedures of the program. The accessibility and scope of variables also depends on the access modifiers. The access modifiers will be covered later in this chapter. Following is the general declarations of variables in C# and VB.NET:

Declaration of Variables in C#
Datatype_name <Variables_list>;
Declaration of Variables in VB.NET
Dim <Variables_list> As Datatype_name

In the above declaration the **Datatype_name** indicates the name of a data type and **Variables_list** indicates the list of variables we want to declare. The variables list may contain one or more variables and they are separated by comma for example, if we declare two or more same type variables then they are listed in a line and they are separated by putting comma between them. In VB.NET declaration, the word **Dim** means dimension which is a keyword in Visual Basic programming language and it is used to declare variables. The following declaration demonstrates the declaration of variables list:

Declaration of Variables in C#
Datatype_name <variable1, variable2, ———variable_n>;
Declaration of Variables in VB.NET
Dim <variable1, variable2, ———variable_n> As Datatype_name

The following declaration demonstrates how to declare an integer variable in C# and VB.NET programming languages:

Declaration of integer Variable in C#	**Declaration of integer Variable in VB.NET**
int variable_name; For example int x;	Dim Variable_name As Integer For example Dim x As Integer

In the above declaration, x is a user-defined name of the declared variable and its type is integer similarly, to declare floating point and character variables, the following declarations are used:

Declaration in C#	Declaration in VB.NET
float Variable-name; char Variable_name; For example float y; char z;	Dim Variable_name As Double Dim Variable_name As Char For example Dim y As Double Dim z As Char

In the above declaration a floating point variable y is declared from data type float and a character variable z is declared from data type char. If we want to declare multiple variables of the same data type then all the variable names are listed on the front of that data type separated by commas:

Declaration in C#	Declaration in VB.NET
int x, y, z; float x1, y1, z1; char ch1, ch2, ch3;	Dim x, y, z As Integer Dim x1, y1, z1 As Double Dim ch1, ch2, ch3 As Char

The C# programming language is a case sensitive programming language while VB.NET is not a case sensitive language. Therefore, if two variables of the same name but in different cases are declared such as one variable is in capital letters and another variable is in small letters then they are valid and they will work properly in C# programming language but they are invalid and will not work in VB.NET programming language. Consider the following example:

Declaration of Variables in C#	Declaration of Variables in VB.NET
int X, x; //valid and working	Dim X, x As Integer 'invalid

The above declaration declares two variables of the same name, one is in small letter x and another one is in capital letter X. They are valid and do not identical in C# but they are invalid in VB.NET because C# is a case sensitive language and cannot understand the two identical letters written in small and in capital form and VB.NET is not a case sensitive programming language and always considers the same letters as identical written in small and in capital form.

Variables Initialization

The process that assigns values or data to variables is called variables initialization. A variable can either be initialized at the time of the declaration or after the declaration anywhere in the program. A value is assigned to a variable by using an equal or assignment operator. The assignment operator is used between the variable and the value. The variable is used on the left side of the assignment operator and the value is used on the right side of the assignment operator. The following example declares an integer variable and initializes it with value 23:

Variables Initialization in C#

int x = 23;
 	
The above statement is equivalent to the following statements:
int x;
x = 23;

Variables Initialization in VB.NET
Dim x As Integer = 23 The above statement is equivalent to the following statements: Dim x As Integer x = 23

We can also declare and initialize multiple variables of the same or different type on the same line separated by commas. In C# variables initialization, we must put semicolon between the two different types of variables while no need to put semicolon between the same types of variables. See the following example:

Variables Initialization in C#
int s = 5, t = 7, w = 8, p = 9; int x = 2, y = 4, z = 5; float a = 2.3f, b = 5.6, c = 6.2;
Variables Initialization in VB.NET
Dim x As Integer = 2, y As Integer = 4, z As Double = 23.5

Variables Naming Conventions

The Naming Conventions are some fundamental rules for choosing the user-defined names of variables in computer programming languages. The variable name is also called an Identifier. An identifier is a user-defined name given to a variable, array, procedure, structure, enumeration, object, and a class. A valid variable name or an identifier is a sequence of one or more letters, digits or underscore characters. To give names to variables the following fundamental rules should be kept in the mind:

- Each variable must have a valid name.
- The Blank spaces, punctuation marks, or symbols cannot become part of an identifier.
- Only letters, digits, and single underscore characters are allowed in identifier.
- A variable identifier always begins with a letter or with an underscore character.
- A Variable identifier can contain two successive underscore characters anywhere.
- A variable identifier cannot start with a digit i.e. the first character of an identifier must not be a digit for example, the identifiers 2ad and 3xy are not valid for variables.
- The variable identifier cannot match any reserved keyword of the .NET languages.
- In a single block no two variables can have the same identical name.
- Both the capital and small letters are allowed in variables identifiers but they depend on the programming language nature. For example C# is a case sensitive while VB is not a case sensitive language. If we declare two variables of the same names in C# language in such a way that one variable is in capital letters and another variables is in small letters then C# programming language considers these two same name variables as two different variables while VB programming language considers these two same names variables as a single repeating variable.
- We can give any name to a variable but always we should give a meaningful name. For example if we want to find an average of the student marks then a variable that holds the average must be "avg" or "average". These two names are more descriptive than using the variable names "xyz123" or axd21 etc for average.

Limitation of Variables (data types ranges) in .NET

The limitation of variables means maximum and minimum ranges of variables for values. Each variable stores positive and negative value. The maximum range means limitation for the positive value and the minimum range means limitation for the negative value. Each variable has a maximum and a minimum range for value. A variable only can store a value that is equal or less than the maximum range and equal or greater than the minimum range of that variable and it cannot store a value that is greater than its maximum range and smaller than its minimum range. When a variable is declared, a memory space is allocated to it in the form of bits. A bit is a memory unit representing a single binary digit 0 or 1. The variables maximum and minimum ranges are shown in the following table:

C# Data Types	VB.NET Data Types	Space in Bytes	Value Range
byte	Byte	1	0 to 255
sbyte	SByte	1	-128 to 127
short	Short	2	-32768 to 32767
ushort	UShort	2	0 to 65535
int	Integer	4	-2147483648 to 2147483647
uint	UInteger	4	0 to 4294967295
long	Long	8	-9223372036854775808 to 9223372036854775807
ulong	ULong	8	0 to 18446744073709551615
float	Single	4	±1.5e−45 to ±3.4e38 (Precision:7 digits)
double	Double	8	±5.0e−324 to ±1.7e308 (Precision:15-16 digits)
decimal	Decimal	16	(-7.9 x 1028 to 7.9 x 1028) / (100 to 28) (Precision:28-29 digits)
char	Char	2	

string	String	Size varies	
datetime	DateTime	8	
bool	Boolean	1 and 4 respectively	
object	Object	Size varies	

Memory Representation of Data Types

When a variable is declared, a memory space is allocated to it in the computer memory. The allocated memory space is in the form of bits. A bit is the smallest unit of data and its other unit is called byte. One byte memory space is equal to eight bits. When a memory space is allocated to a variable then computer assigns an address to that memory location. Each memory location has its own memory address. Each variable has a minimum and maximum range for values. Therefore, a variable cannot store a value greater than the maximum range and smaller than the minimum rage of that variable. The general formula that represents the minimum range of a variable is **-2^n-1** and the general formula that represents the maximum range of a variable is **2^n-1**. Here n represents the total number of bits allocated in the memory for example, in C# and VB.NET programming languages an integer variable takes 4 bytes memory space so n = 32 bits, similarly a long variable takes 8 bytes memory space so n = 64 bits.

Constant Variables

A variable that holds its value throughout the program execution and does not change or lost its value during the entire execution then the variable is called constant variable and its value is called constant value. The constant value of a variable is also called literal. In many mathematical applications the numerical constants and scientific formula constants are used, for example the value of is always equal to 3.14, the value of gravitational acceleration g is always equal to 9.8, and the total number of days in a non-leap year is always 365 etc. These values are called constant values and the variables that hold these constant values are called constant variables. A constant variable can be declared by using a keyword **const** precede the data type of the variable and it is initialized with a value at the time of declaration. Following is the general syntax of constant variable declaration:

C# Declaration
const Datatype_name <Variable_name = Value>;
VB.NET Declaration
Const Variable_name As Datatype_name = Value

In the above declaration the **Datatype_name** indicates the data type of the variable, the **Variable_name** indicates the name of the variable, the **const** is a keyword that is used to declare a constant variable, and **Value** is an expression involving only constant quantities that gives to the variable. In VB.NET a constant variable can be declared by using a keyword **Const** and a keyword Dim does not use in the declaration of a constant variable. Following are some examples of constant variables:

Constant Variables declaration in C#
const float x = 3.14; const float y = 9.8;
Constant Variables declaration in VB.NET
Const y As Double = 3.14 Const z As Double = 9.8

Constant Values Suffixes

The C# programming language provides some notations that are used to represent the exact types of the constant values. These notations are called suffixes. A constant value or literal can be of any data type such as an integer constant, a real or a floating point constant, a character constant, a string constant, a Boolean constant etc. The C# compiler by default treats some type of constant values or literals as some other type for example, when we initialize a float or a decimal variable by assigning a constant value then the C# compiler generates an error message because by default C# compiler treats constant values of float and decimal variables as double. Therefore, to represent the constant values of a specified data type, the suffix of that data type is used. The suffixes are used with the constant values as postfix. The C# programming language provides the following different suffixes for different types of constants values or literals:

Literal Type	Suffix	Description
long	L or l	When a constant value is assigned to a long variable then by default the C# compiler treat it as integer value therefore, to represent a long integer constant value, the suffix capital L or small l is used with the constant value. For example, the constant value 10 is an integer by default but the constant value 10L is a double.
float	F or f	When a floating point constant value is assigned to a float variable then by default the C# compiler treat it as double value and generates an error message because we are trying to assign a double value to a float variable therefore, to remove the compiler error and to represent a float constant value, the suffix capital F or small f is used. For example, the constant value 2.5 is a double by default but the constant value 2.5F or 2.5f is a float.
decimal	M or m	When a floating point constant value is assigned to a decimal variable then by default the C# compiler treat it as double and generates a compiler error because we are trying to assign a double value to a decimal variable therefore, to remove the compiler error and to represent a decimal constant value, the suffix capital M or small m is used. For example, the constant value 2.5 is a double by default but the constant value 2.5M or 2.5m is a decimal.
double	D or d	When a floating point constant value is assigned to a float or a double variable then by default the C# compiler treat it as double therefore, when we assign a constant value to a double variable then no need to use any suffix. The C# programming language also provides a suffix capital D or small d that represents
		a double constant value. For example, if we want to represent an integer value or a floating point value as double then we use the suffix D or d such as 2.5D, 2.5d, or 4D and 4d etc are double constant values.

Operators

Operator is a special symbol that indicates a certain action or operation when used with one or two operands. An operand is a constant value or a variable while an operation is an action performed on one or two operands either to modify the value held by one or both of the operands, or to produce a new value by combining the existing values of the operands. Therefore, an operation is performed using at least one symbol and one value. The symbol is called an operator and a value is called an operand. When an operator is used between the two or more variables or constants then it forms an expression and when it is used between the two or more expressions then it forms a complex expression. The operators are categorized into the following different types:

- Arithmetic Operators
- Arithmetic Assignment Operators
- Relational Operators
- Logical Operators
- Increment and Decrement Operators
- Compound Assignment Operators
- The sizeof Operator
- Conditional Operator

Arithmetic Operators

Mathematical operators are called arithmetic operators such as +, -, *, / etc. When a mathematical operator is used with one or two operands then it performs a specified operation. The basic arithmetic operations are addition, subtraction, multiplication and division but arithmetic operators also provide some advanced operations such as percentages calculations, square roots, exponentiation, and logarithmic functions. Arithmetic operation is performed according to an order of the operators. Each arithmetic operator has its own priority. The C# and Visual Basic programming languages support the following different types of arithmetic operators:

Operators	Descriptions
+	It used for addition.
-	It is used for subtraction.
*	It is used for multiplication.

/	It is used for division.
%	It is used to hold the remainder or modulus.

Arithmetic operators can be used with a single or two operands. When an operator is used with a single operand then it is called Unary operator and when it is used between the two operands then it is called Binary operator. Following are the examples of Unary and Binary operators:

c+, x++, ++x Unary Operators
x + y, 2 + 3, x + z Binary Operators

Arithmetic Assignment Operator

In C# and Visual Basic the equal sign (=) is used for the arithmetic assignment operator. This operator is used to assign a constant value or value of an expression to a variable or one variable to another variable. The arithmetic assignment operator is used between the source and the target operands and it always assigns value of the right side operand to the left side operand. Therefore, the assignment is always done from right side of the arithmetic assignment operator to the left side of the arithmetic assignment operator. Following are the examples of arithmetic assignment operator:

C# Assignment	VB.NET Assignment
Salary = 10; Percentage = 96.45;	Salary = 10 Percentage = 96.45

In the above example, we assigned an integer value 10 to a variable **Salary** and a real value 96.45 to a variable **Percentage.** If we want to assign a single constant value or a single variable to more than one variable at the same time then we can use the following assignment statement:

a = b = c = d = 10; C# Assignment
a= b = c = d = 10 Visual Basic Assignment

In the above assignment statements we assigned a constant value 10 to four variables a, b, c, and d. It means that variables a, b, c, and d are equal to 10. These types of assignments are called multiple arithmetic assignments. In case of multiple arithmetic assignments, the data type of all the variables must be the same.

Relational Operators

Relational operators are used to perform comparison between the two constants, variables, and expressions. Each relational operator has two operands one on each side and each operand may be a single variable, expression or a single constant. When a relational operator performs comparison then it returns a Boolean value. A Boolean value is either **true** or **false**. If a comparison is true then it returns true and if it is false then it returns false. The relational operators are also called comparison operators. The C# and VB.NET programming languages provide the following relational operators:

Operator	Description
==	This operator is the combination of two equal signs and it is called Equal To operator. It has two operands one on each side and it is used to check whether values of the two operands are equal or not. If both values are equal then it returns true otherwise, it returns false. This operator is used only in C# and VB.NET does not support this operator for equality.
=	This operator is called Equal To operator. It has two operands one on each side and it is used to check whether values of the two operands are equal or not. If both the values are equal then it returns true otherwise, it returns false. This operator is used only in VB.NET and C# does not support it for equality.
>	This operator is called Greater than operator. It has two operands one on each side and it is used to check whether the left side operand is greater than the right side operand or not. If the left side operand is greater than the right side operand then it returns true otherwise, it returns false. It is used in C# as well as in VB.NET.
<	This operator is called Less than operator. It has two operands one on each side and it is used to check whether the left side operand is less than the right side operand or not. If the left side operand is less than the right side operand then it returns true otherwise, it returns false. It is used in C# as well as in VB.NET.
>=	This operator is called Greater or Equal To operator and it is used to check whether the left side operand is greater or equal to the right side operand or not. It is used in C# as well as in VB.NET.

<=	This operator is called Less or Equal To operator and it is used to check whether the left side operand is less or equal to the right side operand or not. It is used in C# as well as in VB.NET
! =	This operator is called Not Equal To operator and it is used in C# to perform comparison for not equal operation. It has two operands one on each side and checks whether values of both the operands are equal or not. If values of both the operands are not equal then it returns true otherwise it returns false.
< >	This operator is called Not Equal To operator and it is used in VB.NET to perform comparison for not equal operation. It has two operands one on each side and checks whether values of both the operands are equal or not. If values of both the operands are not equal then it returns true otherwise it returns false.

Consider the following example of relational operators:

C# Example	**VB.NET Example**
x = 2; y = 3;	x = 2 y = 3

In the above example we declared two variables x and y initialized with values 2 and 3 respectively. The value of variable x is less than the value of variable y. If we want to show this comparison in C# and VB.NET then the following statement is used:

y > x

Similarly, if we want to show the smaller value between x and y then the following statement is used:

x < y

Now consider the following example of equal operator:

C# Example	**VB.NET Example**
x = 2; y = 2;	x = 2 y = 2

The above example declares two variables x and y initialize with value 2. Since the values of both variables are equal therefore, we can write this statement by using the equal operator as bellow:

C# Example	VB.NET Example
x == y;	x = y

Logical Operators

Logical Operators are used to combine two or more sets of relational comparison or conditions within a single condition. A logical operator has two operands one on each side and each operand of logical operator is considered a condition that can be evaluated to a true or false value. Each operand of logical operator returns a Boolean value either true or false. The logical operator then uses the result of both the operands and determines the overall result of the condition. The logical operators work same as conjunctions in English grammar that connect two words together. The C# and VB.NET programming languages provide the following types of logical operators:

Operators		Description
C#	VB	
&&	And	This operator is called AND operator and it is used for AND operation. When two relational comparisons or conditions are combined with each other by AND operator then the whole condition is considered true if results of both the operands are true. If result of one of the operand is false then the whole condition is false.
||	Or	This operator is called OR operator and it is used for OR operation. When two relational comparisons or conditions are combined with each other by OR operator then the whole condition is considered true if result of one of the operand is true.
!	Not	This operator is called NOT operator and it is used for the NOT operation. This operator is used to reverse the status of the relational comparisons or conditions. For example, if a relational comparison or condition returns true then this operator converts it to false and if the result is false then it converts it to true.

Examples of Logical Operators

Suppose we have three integer variables x, y, and z initialized with values 3, 2, and 1 respectively as below:

C# Example	VB.NET Example

x = 3;
y = 2;
z = 1;
	x = 3
	y = 2
	z = 1

In the above declaration the value of variable x is greater than the value of variable y and the value of variable z. We can write this statement by using logical operator as bellow:

C# Example	VB.NET Example
(x > y) && (x > z)	(x > y) And (x > z)

In the above expression the AND logical operator has two operands one on each side. The first operand is (x > y) and the second operand is (x > z). Since in the above expression both the operands (x > y) and (x > z) are true therefore, the whole condition is true and it will returns true. Now consider the following example:

C# Example	VB.NET Example

x = 3;
y = 2;
z = 5;
 	
(x > y) || (x > z)
	x = 3
	y = 2
	z = 5
	
	(x > y) Or (x > z)

In the above expression the OR logical operator has two operands one on each side. The first operand is (x > y) and the second operand is (x > z). Each operand is itself a relational condition or comparison. Since in the above expression the first operand is true that is (x > y) therefore, the whole condition is true.

Increment and Decrement Operators

The increment and decrement operators are unary operators that add or subtract one from their operands respectively. They are used with single operands either left or right side. The double plus sign (++) is called increment operator and it is used to increment the value of its operand by 1 while the double minus sign (--) is called decrement operator and it is used to decrement the value of its operand by 1. The C# programming language supports both increment and decrement operators in the form of (++) and (--) respectively but VB.NET does not support the increment and decrement operators in the form of (++) and (--). The VB.NET replaces the increment operator (++) by (+=1) and the decrement operator (--) by (-=1).

Types of Increment and Decrement Operators

The Increment and Decrement operators are further divided into the following two types:

- Prefix Increment/Decrement Operators
- Postfix Increment/Decrement Operators

Prefix Increment/Decrement Operators

When an increment (++) or decrement (--) operator is used before or at the left side of an operand then it is called prefix increment or prefix decrement operator. In prefix increment the increment operator (++) is used while in prefix decrement the decrement operator (--) is used at the left side of an operand. The prefix increment or prefix decrement operator first increments or decrements the current value of an operand then the incremented or decremented value is used.

Postfix Increment/Decrement Operators

When an increment (++) or decrement (--) operator is used after or at the right side of an operand then it is called postfix increment or postfix decrement operator. The postfix increment or postfix decrement operator first use the value of operand then it increments or decrements the value by 1.

Program # 1

Write a program that demonstrates the using of Prefix Increment and Prefix Decrement Operators.
C# Program

```
using System;
class MainClass
{
static void Main(string[] args)
{
int x = 10;
++x; //Increment x by 1
++x; //Increment x by 1
++x; //Increment x by 1
--x; //Decrement x by 1
--x; //Decrement x by 1
--x; //Decrement x by 1

Console.WriteLine(x);
Console.WriteLine("Press any key to exit program");
Console.ReadKey();
}
}
```

The above program declares one variable x and initializes it with a value 10. The program first increments the value of variable x three times and it becomes 13 then it decrements the value of variable x three times and it becomes 10. Therefore, the last value of variable x is 10.

Program # 2

Write a program that demonstrates the using of Postfix Increment and Postfix Decrement Operators.
C# Program

```
using System;
class MainClass
{
```

```
static void Main(string[] args)
{
int x = 10;
x++; //Increment x by 1
x++; //Increment x by 1
x++; //Increment x by 1
x--; //Decrement x by 1
x--; //Decrement x by 1
Console.WriteLine(x);
Console.WriteLine("Press any key to exit program");
Console.ReadKey();
}
}
```

Visual Basic Program

```
Module Module1

Sub Main()

Dim x As Integer = 10

x += 1 'Increment x by 1
x += 1 'Increment x by 1
x += 1 'Increment x by 1
x -= 1 'Decrement x by 1
x -= 1 'Decrement x by 1

Console.WriteLine(x)

Console.WriteLine("Press any key to exit program")
Console.ReadKey()
End Sub

End Module
```

The above program declares a variable x and initializes it with a value 10. The program then increments the value of variable x three times and it becomes 13 then it decrements the value of variable x two times and it becomes 11 therefore, the final value of variable x is 11.

Compound Assignment Operators

When an assignment operator is combined with another type of operator then it is called compound assignment operator. A compound assignment operator modifies the value of an operand by performing an operation on the value currently stored in that variable. It performs two tasks. For example if it is combined with the arithmetic operators then first it performs mathematical operation then assigns the calculated value to the left side operand. A compound assignment operator is also used to reduce the repeating variables in case of value assignment in an expression. In a program when the same variable appeared on both sides of the arithmetic assignment operator then the compound assignment operator is used to reduce the repeating variables. Consider the following example:

C# Example	VB.NET Example
cost = cost + 10;	cost = cost + 10

The above expression increments the value of variable **cost** by 10 and assigns it back to variable **cost**. Since the same variable "cost" appears on both sides of the arithmetic assignment operator therefore, compound assignment operator is used to reduce the repeating variable **cost**.

C# Example	VB.NET Example
cost += 10;	cost += 10

Similarly to subtract 10 from variable **cost**, the following compound assignment operator is used:

C# Example	VB.NET Example
cost -= 10;	cost -= 10

The other types of compound assignment operators are *=, /=, >>=, <<=, &=, |=, ^= and %= etc.

The sizeof operator

It is a unary operator used to return the size of a data type in bytes. It takes a data type as argument and returns the allocated memory space of that data type in bytes. The sizeof operator helps in memory allocation for data structures. If we develop an application that involves dynamic memory allocation then the sizeof operator is widely use to find the allocated memory space of a variable. It can be used to the value type and cannot be used to the reference type. The sizeof operator is used in C# language and Visual Basic language does not support this operator. Following is the general syntax of sizeof operator:

return_type sizeof (data_type);

In the above syntax the **return_type** indicates the return value of sizeof operator. The return value of sizeof operator is always an integer value. The argument **data_type** indicates a data type name. Following is the programming example of sizeof operator:

Program # 3

```
using System;

class MainClass
{
static void Main(string[] args)
{
Console.WriteLine("Number of bytes of int data type = " +
                    sizeof(int));
Console.WriteLine("Number of bytes of float data type = " +
                    sizeof(float));
Console.WriteLine("Number of bytes of double data type = " +
                    sizeof(double));
Console.WriteLine("Number of bytes of char data type = " +
                    sizeof(char));

Console.WriteLine("Press any key to exit program");
Console.ReadKey();
}
}
```

Conditional Operator

Conditional Operator is denoted by a question mark (?). This operator is a ternary operator that requires three operands. The first operand is a conditional expression to be placed before the conditional operator or at the left side of the conditional operator. The second and third operands may be any expressions or statements to be placed after the conditional operator or at the right side of the conditional operator. The second and third operands are distinguished by using a full colon (**:**) between them. The conditional operator is used if we want to perform a decision or a relational comparison between the two or more values or variables. It evaluates the first operand or the conditional expression and returns a Boolean value either, true or false. If the conditional expression is true then it returns **true** and evaluates or returns the second operand and ignores the third operand. If the conditional expression is false then it returns **false** and evaluates or returns the third operand and ignores the second operand. Following is the general syntax of conditional operator:

Return_value = Conditional_Expression ? Expression1: Expression2;

In the above syntax the **Conditional_Expression** indicates the first operand. The **Expression1** and **Expression2** are the second and third operands respectively. The **Return_value** is a variable that hold the return value of the conditional operator. If the first operand Conditional_Expression returns true then the conditional operator evaluates or returns the second operand Expression1 and ignores the third operand Expression2. If the first operand returns false then the conditional operator evaluates or returns the third operand Expression2 and ignores the second operand Expression1. Following are the programming examples of conditional operator:

Program # 4

Write a program that finds either a given integer number is positive or negative.

```
using System;

class myExample
{
static void Main(string[] args)
{
int x;
string z;
Console.WriteLine("Enter any number=");
x = System.Convert.ToInt32(Console.ReadLine());
```

```
z = (x >= 0) ? "Positive" : "Negative";
Console.WriteLine("The number is = " + z);

Console.WriteLine("Press any key to exit program");
Console.ReadKey();
}
}
```

Program # 5

Write a program that finds the greatest value between the two integer numbers using the conditional operator.

```
using System;

class myExample
{

public static void Main(string[] args)
{
int x, y, greater;

Console.WriteLine("Enter the first number=");
x = System.Convert.ToInt32(Console.ReadLine());
Console.WriteLine("Enter the second number=");
y = System.Convert.ToInt32(Console.ReadLine());

greater = (x > y) ? x : y;
Console.WriteLine("The greater number is = " + greater);

Console.WriteLine("Press any key to exit program");
Console.ReadKey();
}
}
```

Program # 6

Write a program that finds the greatest value among the three integer numbers using the conditional operator.

```
using System;
class myExample
{
public static void Main(string[] args)
{
int x, y, z, greatest;

Console.WriteLine("Enter the first number=");
x = System.Convert.ToInt32(Console.ReadLine());
Console.WriteLine("Enter the second number=");
y = System.Convert.ToInt32(Console.ReadLine());
Console.WriteLine("Enter the third number=");
z = System.Convert.ToInt32(Console.ReadLine());

greatest = (x > y && x > z) ? x : (y > x && y > z) ? y : z;
Console.WriteLine("The greatest number is = " + greatest);

Console.WriteLine("Press any key to exit program");
Console.ReadKey();
}
}
```

Expressions

When one or more operators are combined with one or more operands then it is called an expression. The operators are special symbols that represent particular actions or operation and operands are variables, or constant values. An operator performs an action or operation when used with one or two operands. The operation of an operator either modifies the value of one or both of the operands, or to produce a new value by combining the existing values of the operands. Therefore, an operation is performed using at least one operator and at least one operand. Following is an example of expression:

$$x + y$$

In the above expression x and y are operands and the symbol + is an arithmetic operator. The expression may also be complex and sometime a single operand of an expression further contains multiple operands and operators and it is itself an expression. Therefore, when two or more simple expressions are combined with each other then it forms a complex expression. Following is an example of complex expression:

(x + y) * z

In the above expression (x + y) is the first operand of the arithmetic operator * and z is the second operand of the arithmetic operator *. The first operand (x + y) is itself an expression that further contains two operators x and y and one operator +.

Expression Precedence

Expression precedence means how to evaluate an expression. A simple expression is very easy to evaluate but to evaluate a complex expression some mathematical rules must be followed. According to mathematical rules each operator has its own priority. If we evaluate a complex expression then the operator with the highest priority will be evaluated first, the operator with the second highest priority will be evaluated second, and on this way the entire expression will be evaluated. In a complex expression two operators always share a single operand for example, consider the following expression:

2 + 3 * 4

The above expression contains three operands 2, 3, 4 and two operators + and *. In this expression the operators + and * share single operand 3. Therefore, logically the above expression has two parts such as 2 + 3 and 3 * 4. It is not clear which part of the expression is evaluated first either 2 + 3 or 3 * 4. According to mathematical rules if two operators share the same operand then the operator with the highest priority will be evaluated first. For example the above expression 2 + 3 * 4 is treated as 2 + (3 * 4) which means that 3 * 4 will be evaluated first because multiplication has the higher precedence or higher priority than addition. Following is the list of operators and their precedence:

Precedence	operators	Type	Evaluation
Highest 1st	() [] . new typeof	Unary	Left to Right
2nd	! ~ ++ --	Unary	Left to Right
3rd	* / %	Binary	Left to Right

<table>
<tr><td>4th</td><td>+ -</td><td>Binary</td><td>Left to Right</td></tr>
<tr><td>5th</td><td>> < >= <=</td><td>Binary</td><td>Left to Right</td></tr>
<tr><td>6th</td><td>== !=</td><td>Binary</td><td>Left to Right</td></tr>
<tr><td>7th</td><td>&</td><td>Binary</td><td>Left to Right</td></tr>
<tr><td>8th</td><td>^</td><td>Binary</td><td>Left to Right</td></tr>
<tr><td>9th</td><td>|</td><td>Binary</td><td>Left to Right</td></tr>
<tr><td>10th</td><td>&&</td><td>Binary</td><td>Left to Right</td></tr>
<tr><td>11th</td><td>||</td><td>Binary</td><td>Left to Right</td></tr>
<tr><td>12th</td><td>?:</td><td>Ternary</td><td>Right to Left</td></tr>
<tr><td>13th
Lowest</td><td>= *= /= %= += -=
&= ^= |= <<= >>=</td><td>Binary</td><td>Right to Left</td></tr>
</table>

Expression Evaluation Rules

To evaluate a complex expressions the following rules and priority of operators should be considered:

1. An expression is always evaluated from left side to the right side.
2. The highest precedence operator will be evaluated first, the second highest precedence operator will be evaluated second and on this way the entire expression will be evaluated for example, the expression 2 + 3 - 4 will be evaluated as (2 + 3) – 4 because + and – have the same priority similarly, the expression 2 + 3 * 4 will be evaluated as 2 + (3 * 4) because multiplication has the highest priority than the addition.
3. If two operators with the same precedence share a single same operand then the left side operator or the first coming operator will be evaluated first.
4. The conditional operator (?:) and all the assignment operators will be evaluated from right side to the left side because they are right associative operators. For example the expression 2 = 3 = 4 will be evaluated as 2 = (3 = 4).
5. We can also control the order of precedence by using parentheses for example, in expression 2 + 3 * 4, the multiplication will be evaluated first then the addition will be evaluated because multiplication has the highest priority than the addition but if we use parentheses such as (2 + 3) * 4 then the addition (2 + 3) will be evaluated first because we

enclosed it within parentheses and parentheses have highest priority than the multiplication.

Comments

Comment is a message that explains what is going on at what point in a program. Comments are extra information about the source code of a program and they are used to summarize the program codes and to explain briefly the programmer thoughts or purpose of the specific part or code of a program. Comments are a very useful way to remind ourselves or to explain for other programmers what the specific block or line of codes, or what a particular part of a program code is for. For example, when we are designing a program that contains some logical, technical, or difficult tasks and we want to explain the solution process or methods of the logical or technical tasks to make the program more descriptive for the future and for other programmers to understand the program code and purpose of the specific logical or technical block of codes more easily. The compilers and interpreters of programming languages always ignore the comments lines because they are not executable lines and statements.

The C# programming language provides two types of comments such as single line comments and multiple lines comments. The single line comments start with double forward slashes // while multiple lines comments are placed inside in a pair of /* and */ statements. The statement /* indicates the start point of the comments and the statement */ indicates the ending point of the comments. The Visual Basic programming language only provides a single line comments that start with an apostrophe punctuation mark (') and it does not support multiple line comments.

Program # 7

Write a program that demonstrates the uses of comments.
C# Program

```
using System;
class MainClass
{
static void Main(string[] args)
{

// A single line comments
```

```
/* Multiple lines comments
........... ..................................
................................................*/

Console.WriteLine("Press any key to exit program");
Console.ReadKey();
}
}
```

VB.NET Program

```
Module Module1

Sub Main()

'A single line comments
Console.WriteLine("Press any key to exit program")
Console.ReadKey()
End Sub

End Module
```

Type Conversion

Type Conversion is a process that is used to convert or change the type of one data type into another data type. This process is usually used when we assign the value of one type of a variable into another type of variable for example, to assign an integer value to a long or short integer variable similarly, to assign a double value to a single or float variable etc. The Type Conversion process is divided into the following two types:

- Implicit Type Conversion
- Explicit Type Conversion

Implicit Type Conversion

This type of conversion is also called automatic type conversion and it is performed by the compiler automatically. This conversion does not require any special syntax, built-in keyword, or method but it is performed by the compiler automatically using the assignment operator. The assignment operator is used between the source data type and the target data type. The data type we want to convert is called source data type and it is placed on the right side of the assignment operator and the data type to which we want to convert the source data type is called target data type and it is placed on the left side of the assignment operator. The implicit type conversion is a type safe conversion and no data is lost during the conversion process. This type of conversion is usually performed between the same nature data types from smaller capacity data type to larger capacity data type such as from short integer data type to integer data type, from integer data type to long data type, from single or float data type to double data type, from double data type to long double data type etc. The implicit conversion is possible only if value of the source variable can fit into the target variable without being changed (truncated or rounded off). For example, a long integer variable can store any value of an integer variable of type int because a long variable is larger than an int variable. The capacity or the memory space of a long integer variable is 8 bytes and the capacity or the memory space of an int variable is 4 bytes similarly, a double variable can store any value of a single or float variable because double variable is larger than single or float variable. The memory space of a double variable is 8 bytes and the memory space of a single or float variable is 4 bytes. The following programming example shows implicit type conversion from smaller capacity data types to larger capacity data types:

C# Example

```
int Integer_Value = 25;        //Declare and initialize an int variable
long Long_Value;               //Declare a long int variable

//Assign the value of int variable into long variable
Long_Value = Integer_Value;
```

```
float Float_Value = 2.5f;      //Declare and initialize a float variable
double Double_Value;           //Declare a double variable

//Assign the value of float variable into double variable
Double_Value = Float_Value;
```

The above programming example converts the value of an integer data type variable I**nteger_Value** into a long integer data type variable L**ong_Value** and the value of a float data type variable **Float_Value** into a double data type variable D**ouble_Value** implicitly. Since, the above example converts the smaller capacity data type variables into the larger capacity data type variables, therefore the conversions are successful and 100% safe.

The Implicit type conversion is not possible from a larger capacity data type to a smaller capacity data type even if both the data types have the same nature for example, conversion from integer data type to short integer data type, from long integer data type to integer data type, from double data type to single or float data type, from long double data type to double data type or float data type etc. These types of implicit conversions are not possible because the value of a larger capacity data type variable cannot be assigned to a smaller capacity data type variable even if the data types of both the variables have the same nature and store the same nature data. The following programming example shows implicit type conversion from larger capacity data type variables to smaller capacity data type variables:

C# Example

```
long Long_Value = 25;        //Declare and initialize a long int variable
int Integer_Value;           //Declare an int variable

//Assign the value of long variable into int variable
Integer_Value = Long_Value;

//Declare and initialize a double variable
double Double_Value = 2.5;
float Float_Value;           //Declare a float variable

//Assign the value of double variable into float variable
Float_Value = Double_Value ;
```

The above programming example converts the value of a long integer data type variable **Long_Value** into an integer data type variable **Integer_Value** and the value of a double data type variable **Double_Value** into a float data type variable **Float_Value** implicitly. Since, the above programming example converts the larger capacity data type variables into smaller capacity data type variables therefore the above conversions are not possible implicitly.

Explicit Type Conversion

Explicit Type Conversion is a type of conversion that is used to convert the value of one data type into another data type manually. This type of conversion is possible from smaller capacity data type variables to larger capacity data type variables and also from larger capacity data type variables to smaller capacity data type variables. The explicit type conversion is not performed by the compiler automatically but it requires a special type of operation that is called type casting operation. The type casting operation converts the value of one data type into another data type manually.

Typecasting

Typecasting is a process that is used to change the type of a variable from its declared type to a new type temporarily. This process is usually used in such cases when we want to assign an expression to a variable or the value of one type of variable to another type of variable. A variable that we cast its value is called source variable and a variable to which we assign the casted value is called target variable. The typecasting process first change the type of a source variable into the type of a target variable and then assign the casted value of a source variable to a target variable. In typecasting operation the data type of the target variable is used enclosed within small braces. Following is the general syntax of typecasting:

Target_Variable = (Datatype_Name) Expression;
Target_Variable = (Datatype_Name) Source_Variable;

The first syntax is used to cast the value of an expression to a variable and the second syntax is used to cast the value of one variable to another variable. In the above declaration the **Target_Variable** indicates the name of a target variable, the S**ource_Variable** indicates the name of a source variable, and the D**atatype_Name** indicates the data type of a target variable. The Datatype_Name explicitly converts the type of the source variable into the type of the target variable and assign the converted value into target variable using an assignment operator. The explicit conversion will be performed only if the Datatype_Name is similar to the data type of the target variable. For example, if the target variable is an integer then the integer data type is used for typecasting similarly, if the target variable is a float then a float data type is used for typecasting operation etc.

Why we use Typecasting?

When we divide two integer values then it always return an integer result. If the division of two integer values produces a float or real value then it returns only the integer part of the result and ignores the float or real part. For example, consider the following example:

```
int x = 5, y = 2;
float z;
z = x / y;
```

In the above declaration the expression x/y produces a float or real result 2.5 because the value of variable x is 5 and the value of variable y is 2. The expression divides the value of x on the value of y and assigns the resultant value to variable z. Since both the value of x and y are integer therefore, the expression only assigns the integer part 2 to variable z and ignores the float or real part .5. Similarly in an expression if the value of numerator is less than the value of denominator then the result will always be 0. For example, consider the following expression as:

```
x = 2;
y = 3;
z = x / y;
```

The above expression x/y produces the resultant value 0.666 but it only assigns the integer part 0 to variable z and ignores the float or real part .666. Therefore, in an expression if both the numerator and denominator are integers then it always return the integer part of the resultant value and ignore the float or real part. In such cases we cannot get the accurate and actual result. The typecasting operation is used to return the accurate and actual result from the expression. To use the typecasting operation on the above expression, the float data type is used before the expression because the target variable z is a float variable. So the above expression will be:

```
z = (float) x / y;
```

Now the above expression produces the accurate result 0.666 and returns the complete result 0.666 to variable z. The above typecasting operation is called automatic typecasting of data types. It is a simple typecasting that can be applied on a simple variable or expressions for temporary conversion. Following is the programming example of typecasting:

Program # 8

C# program without typecasting

using System;
 	
class MainClass
{
static void Main(string[] args)
{
int x, y;
float z;
x = 2; y = 3;
z = x / y;
Console.WriteLine("The Value of z = "+ z);
 	
Console.WriteLine("Press any key to exit program");
Console.ReadKey();
}
}
 	
The output of this program would be: 0

C# program using typecasting

using System;
 	
class MainClass
{
static void Main(string[] args)
{
int x, y;
x = 2; y = 3;
float z;
z = (float) x / y;
Console.WriteLine("The Value of z = "+ z);
Console.WriteLine("Press any key to exit program");
Console.ReadKey();
}
}
The output of this program would be: 0.666

The Convert Class

The Convert class is used to convert one base data type to another base data type. It supports the conversion of almost all types of base data types for example, an Integer data type to a String data type, a String data type to an Integer data type, a String data type to a Single or a Double data type, a DateTime data type to a String data type, a Sting data type to a DateTime data type and so on. The Convert class supports Boolean, Char, Byte, SByte, Int16, UInt32, Int64, UInt16, UInt32, UInt64, Single, Double, Decimal, DateTime, and String data types. The conversions of some base data types are not possible for example the conversion of a Char data type to a Boolean, Char data type to a Single, Char data type to a Double, Char data type to a Decimal, and Char data type to a DateTime is not possible and vise versa similarly, the DateTime data type can only be converted into a String data type and it cannot be converted into other types of base data types. Following is the general declaration of Convert Class:

The C# Declaration
public static class Convert
The Visual Basic.NET Declaration
public NotInheritable Class Convert

The Methods of Convert Class

The Convert class provides a set of methods used to convert one base data type to another base data type. It provides a separate method for each conversion type. Each method of the Convert class takes a source data type as a parameter and returns its equivalent target data type. Following is the list and details of the Convert Class methods:

ToBoolean	ToByte	ToChar	ToDateTime
ToDecimal	ToDouble	ToInt16	ToInt32
ToIn64	ToSByte	ToSingle	ToString
ToUInt16	ToUInt32	ToUInt64	ChangeType

ToBoolean() Method

This method is used to convert a specified data type value to its equivalent Boolean value. Following is the general declaration of this method:

C# Declaration
public static bool ToBoolean(DataType)
Visual Basic.NET Declaration
public shared Function ToBoolean(DataType) As Boolean

In the above declaration, the **DataType** is a parameter of the ToBoolean() method that indicates a source data type value to be converted into Boolean data type. This parameter takes a data type value such as Byte, Decimal, Single, Double, Int16, Int32, Int64, SByte, Object, String, UInt16, UInt32, or UInt64 and converts it into its equivalent Boolean data type value. The conversion of Char and DateTime data type is not supported by this method.

ToByte() Method

This method is used to convert a specified data type value to its equivalent Byte value. Following is the general declaration of this method:

C# Declaration
public static byte ToByte(DataType)
Visual Basic.NET Declaration
public shared Function ToByte(DataType) As Byte

In the above declaration, the **DataType** is a parameter of the ToByte() method that indicates a source data type value to be converted into Byte data type. This parameter takes a data type value such as Boolean, Decimal, Single, Double, Int16, Int32, Int64, SByte, Object, String, UInt16, UInt32, or UInt64 and converts it into its equivalent Byte data type value. The conversion of DateTime data type is not supported by this method.

ToChar() Method

This method is used to convert a specified data type value to its equivalent Character value. Following is the general declaration of this method:

C# Declaration
public static char ToChar(DataType)
Visual Basic.NET Declaration
public shared Function ToChar(DataType) As Char

In the above declaration, the **DataType** is a parameter of the ToChar() method that indicates a source data type value to be converted into Char data type. This parameter takes a data type value such as Byte, Int16, Int32, Int64, SByte, Object, String, UInt16, UInt32, or UInt64 and converts it into its equivalent Char data type value. The conversion of Boolean, Single, Double, Decimal and DateTime is not supported by this method.

ToDateTime() Method

This method is used to convert a specified string value into its equivalent DateTime value. Following is the general declaration of this method:

C# Declaration
public static DateTime ToDateTime(DataType)
Visual Basic.NET Declaration
public shared Function ToDateTime(DataType) As DateTime

In the above declaration, the **DataType** is a parameter of the ToDateTime() method that indicates a string data type value to be converted into DateTime value. This parameter takes a string value and converts it into its equivalent DateTime value. The conversion of other data type values such as Boolean, Byte, Int16, Int32, Int64, SByte, Object, UInt16, UInt32, and UInt64 is not supported by this method.

ToDecimal() Method

This method is used to convert a specified data type value to its equivalent Decimal value. Following is the general declaration of this method:

C# Declaration
public static decimal ToDecimal(DataType)

Visual Basic.NET Declaration
public shared Function ToDecimal(DataType) As Decimal

In the above declaration, the **DataType** is a parameter of the ToDecimal() method that indicates a source data type value to be converted into Decimal data type. This parameter takes a data type value such as Boolean, Byte, Int16, Int32, Int64, SByte, Object, String, UInt16, UInt32, orUInt64 etc and converts it into Decimal data type value. The conversion of Char and DateTime data type values into Decimal data type is not supported by ToDecimal() method.

ToDouble() Method

This method is used to convert a specified data type value to its equivalent Double value. Following is the general declaration of this method:

C# Declaration
public static double ToDouble(DataType)
Visual Basic.NET Declaration
public shared Function ToDouble(DataType) As Double

In the above declaration, the **DataType** is a parameter of the ToDouble() method that indicates a source data type value to be converted into Double data type. This parameter takes a data type value such as Boolean, Byte, Int16, Int32, Int64, SByte, Object, String, UInt16, UInt32, or UInt64 and converts it into Double data type value. The conversion of Char and DateTime data type values into Double data type is not supported by ToDouble() method.

ToIn16() Method

This method is used to convert a specified data type value to its equivalent Int16 value. Following is the general declaration of this method:

C# Declaration
public static Int16 ToInt16(DataType)
Visual Basic.NET Declaration
public shared Function ToInt16(DataType) As Int16

In the above declaration, the **DataType** is a parameter of the ToInt16() method that indicates a source data value to be converted into Int16 data type. This parameter takes a data type value such as Boolean, Byte, Int32, Int64, SByte, Object, String, Char, UInt16, UInt32, or UInt64 and converts it into Int16 data type value. The conversion of DateTime data type value into Int16 data type is not supported by ToInt16() method.

ToSByte() Method

This method is used to convert a specified data type value to its equivalent SByte value. Following is the general declaration of this method:

C# Declaration
public static sbyte ToSByte(DataType)
Visual Basic.NET Declaration
public shared Function ToSByte(DataType) As SByte

In the above declaration, the **DataType** is a parameter of the ToSByte() method that indicates a source data type value to be converted into SByte data type. This parameter takes a data type value such as Boolean, Byte, Int16, Int32, Int64, Object, String, Char, UInt16, UInt32, or UInt64 and converts it into SByte data type value. The conversion of DateTime data type value into SByte data type is not supported by ToSByte() method.

ToSingle() Method

This method is used to convert a specified data type value to its equivalent Single value. Following is the general declaration of this method:

C# Declaration
public static single ToSingle(DataType)
Visual Basic.NET Declaration
public shared Function ToSingle(DataType) As Single

In the above declaration, the **DataType** is a parameter of the ToSingle() method that indicates a source data type value to be converted into Single data type. This parameter takes a data type value such as Boolean, Byte, Int16, Int32, Int64, SByte, Object, String, UInt16, UInt32, or UInt64 and converts it into

Single data type value. The conversion of Char and DateTime data type values into Single data type is not supported by ToSingle() method.

ToString() Method

This method is used to convert a specified data type value to its equivalent String value. Following is the general declaration of this method:

C# Declaration
public static string ToString(DataType)
Visual Basic.NET Declaration
public shared Function ToString(DataType) As String

In the above declaration, the **DataType** is a parameter of the ToString() method that indicates a source data type value to be converted into String data type. This parameter takes a data type value such as Boolean, Byte, Int16, Int32, Int64, SByte, Object, String, Char, UInt16, UInt32, UInt64, or DateTime and converts it into String data type value.

ToUInt16() Method

This method is used to convert a specified data type value to its equivalent Unsigned Int16 value. Following is the general declaration of this method:

C# Declaration
public static UInt16 ToUInt16(DataType)
Visual Basic.NET Declaration
public shared Function ToUInt16(DataType) As UInt16

In the above declaration, the **DataType** is a parameter of the ToUInt16() method that indicates a source data type value to be converted into UInt16 data type. This parameter takes a data type value such as Boolean, Byte, Int32, Int64, SByte, Object, String, Char, UInt32, or UInt64 and converts it into UInt16 data type value. The conversion of DateTime data type value into UInt16 data type is not supported by the ToUInt16() method.

ChangeType() Method

The ChangeType() method is a general purpose method that is used to convert any data type value into any other data type. Following is the general declaration of this method:

C# Declaration
public static Object ChangeType(Object Value, Type ConversionType)
VB.NET Declaration
public shared Function ChangeType(Value As Object, ConversionType As Type) As Object

This method takes two parameters. The first parameter is **Value** of type Object that indicates a source data type value to be converted into target data type value. The second parameter is **ConversionType** of type Type that indicates a target data type to which the source data type value to be converted.

Escape Sequences

Escape Sequences are used to define different special characters in a string output. The escape sequences are categorized into two types such as printable escape sequences and non-printable escape sequences. The printable escape sequences are used to define or print a specified special character within a string lateral for example, to define a null character in a string, to define a back slash character in a string, or to define single quotes or double quotes in a string. The non-printable escape sequences are also called control sequences and they are used to organize the output of a program on the display screen. The non-printable escape sequences do not print anything physically on the screen but they are used to perform actions on the control and display the output of a program in a specified format. For example, they are used to move the control back, to move the control one tab forward, or transfer the control to the new line etc. Therefore, the non-printable escape sequences provide facility to display the output of a program in a specified organized form. The escape sequences are denoted by a back slash followed by a specified character and they are usually used with the output object or output statement. Following is the list of escape sequences used in C# programming languages:

Escape Sequence	Description
\a	It is used to produce an alarm or alert.
\b	It is used to move the control one space back.
\f	It is used for form feed.
\n	It is used to transfer the control to the new line.
\t	It is used to leave 8 spaces or horizontal Tab.
\r	It is used for carriage return.
\v	It is used for vertical tab.
\0	It is used to print a Null character.
\\	It is used to print a backslash.
\’	It is used to print a single quote.
\”	It is used to print double quotes.

Program # 9

Write a C# program that demonstrates the uses of escape sequences

```
using System;

class MainClass
{
static void Main(string[] args)
{
Console.WriteLine(“Hello\n Welcome to \”.NET\””);

Console.WriteLine(“Press any key to exit program”);
Console.ReadKey();
}
}
```

This program will display the following output:
Hello
Welcome to “.NET”

The above program uses two escape sequences (**\n**) and (\”). The program first prints Hello on the screen then the first escape sequence \n transferees the program control to the new line and prints the remaining string i.e. Welcome to ".NET" on the new line. The second escape sequence \" encloses a string i.e. .NET within double quotes such as ".NET".

Keywords

A computer programming language has a set of built-in words called keywords. The keywords are commands or statements and they are defined in a computer programming language for specific tasks. The meaning and the function of each keyword is understandable for the compiler of a programming language in which they are defined. Each keyword of a programming language has a meaningful name and each keyword has its own task or purpose. For example, all the data types of a programming language are keywords and they are used to declare variables such as int, float, char, long int, double etc similarly, the decision statements and the iteration statements of a programming language are keywords such as the if statement, the if else statement, the switch statement, the for loop, the while loop, and the do-while loop etc. We cannot give the name of any keyword to variable, an object, an array, a structure, a class, a function etc because a keyword name is reserved only to that keyword.

CHAPTER 3

Flow Control Statements in .NET

CHAPTER CONTENTS

- Flow Control Statements
- Sequence Statements
- Selection Statements
- If Statement
- If-else Statement
- Nested If-else Statement
- Switch Statement
- Iterative Statements
- Start Expression
- Test Expression
- Counter Expression
- Types of the Loops
- Counted Loops
- for Loop
- Declaration of for Loop in C#
- Declaration of for Loop in VB.NET
- Uncounted Loops
- while Loop
- while Loop as a Counted Loop
- do-while Loop
- do-while Loop in C#
- do-while Loop in VB.NET
- do-until Loop in VB.NET
- Why we use do-while Loop?
- Nested Loops
- The break Statement
- The continue Statement
- The goto Statement
- Limitations of goto Statement
- The foreach Loop

Flow Control Statements

The flow of a program is a way through which a program is executing. The flow control statements provide different mechanisms that control the flow of a program during the program execution. They perform different actions on the program statements for example, make a decision among different values, constants, and variables etc, ignore a specified statement or block of statements during a program execution, or repeat a single statement or block of statements up to a specified number of times. The flow control statements also allow us to group individual statements into a single logical unit to control their execution in such a way that either a single statement is evaluated or all the statements are evaluated on the basis of certain conditions. The control statements are categorizes into the following three types:

- Sequence Statements
- Selection Statements
- Iterative Statements

Sequence Statements

It is the default control structure of programming languages that executes the statements of a program in a linear way one after another without any check or condition. For example, it starts execution of a program from the first line and executes each line one by one and on this way it executes the entire statements of a program.

Selection Statements

Selection statements are the program flow control statements that allow us to choose one or more statements among different statements of a program. They are conditional statements and they perform different decisions or conditions among different statements and execute a specified single statement or group of statements and ignore rest of the statements. They provide multiple execution paths in which they execute one execution path at a time according to the condition. The selection statements are categorized into the following two types:

- If Statement
- Switch Statement

if Statement

The if statement is used to check the relationship among different values, variables, statements and expressions using the relational operators and makes a decision about which statement to be executed based on the result of that decision. It uses relational operators for decision and performs relational comparison among different values, variables, and expressions. If result of the relational operators is true then it returns true and executes a statement or group of statements and if result of the relational operators is false then it returns false and ignores a statement or group of statements. A statement or group of statements are the body of the "if statement". In C# the body of if statement is enclosed within curly braces while in Visual Basic the body of if statement is enclosed within **If** and **End If** statements. The condition includes any relational comparison and must be enclosed within small parentheses. Following is the general syntax of "if statement":

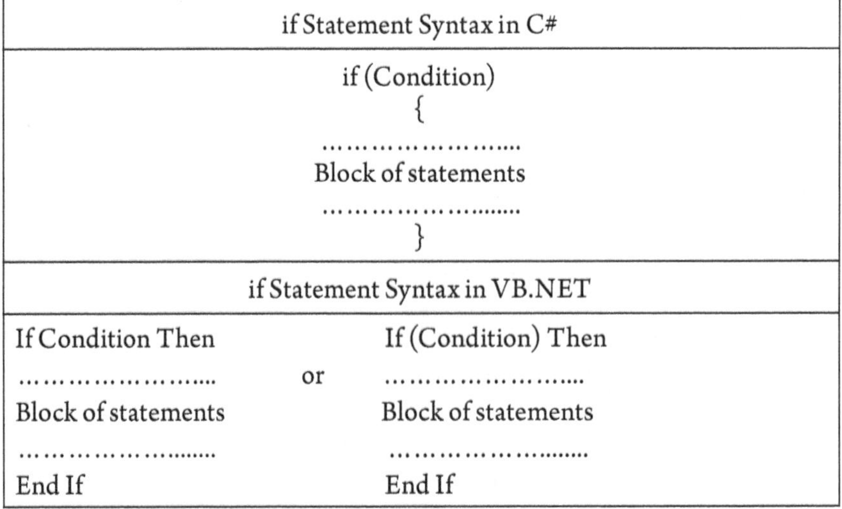

if Statement Syntax in C#		

if (Condition)
{
……………………..
Block of statements
……………………..
}		

if Statement Syntax in VB.NET		

If Condition Then
……………………..
Block of statements
……………………..
End If
	or	If (Condition) Then
		……………………..
		Block of statements
		……………………..
		End If

In the above declaration the **Condition** indicates a condition or a relational expression of the "if statement", the **Then** is a keyword used only in Visual Basic after the condition, and the "**Block of Statements**" indicates body of if statement. In C# the condition or relational expression is always enclosed within small braces while in Visual Basic the condition or the relational expression braces are optional. The body of "if statement" is a single statement or a group of statements. If body of "if statement" contains a group of statements then they are enclosed within curly braces because the scope of "if statement" is limited to only one statement. Therefore, if a group of statements is used without enclosing within curly braces then the "if statement" will only execute the first statement and will ignore rest of the statements. The above declaration of "if statement" is used if we perform a simple decision. In case of multiple or complex decision between different values, variables, constants, and expression the if-else and nested if-else statements are used.

if-else Statement

The if-else statement is similar to "if statement" but the main difference is that the if-else statement contains one condition and two blocks of statements. It executes one block of statements at a time and ignores another block. If the condition of if-else statement is true then it executes the first block of statements and ignores the second block of statement similarly, if the condition of if-else statement is false then it executes the second block of statements and ignores the first block of statements. The first block of statements is placed before the "else" and the second block of statements is placed after the "else". Following are the general syntaxes of "if-else" statement:

if-else Statement in C#
Syntax-1

if (Condition)
Statement-1;
else
Statement-2;

Syntax-2

if (Condition)
{
Statement-1;
Statement-2; The First Block
……………
Statement-n;
}
else
{
Statement-1;

<table>
<tr><td>Statement-2;
…………… The Second Block
Statement-n;
}</td></tr>
<tr><td>if-else Statement in VB.NET</td></tr>
<tr><td>Syntax-1

If Condition Then
Statement-1
else
Statement-2
End If

Syntax-2

If Condition Then
Statement-1;
Statement-2; The First Block
……………...
Statement-n;
Else
Statement-1;
Statement-2;
…………… The Second Block
Statement-n;
End If</td></tr>
</table>

Nested if-else Statement

If we use one if-else statement within the body of another if-else statement then it is called nested if-else statement. The nested if-else statement is used to perform a multiple or complex decision between the two or more values, variables, constants, and expressions. A nested if-else statement may contain two or more if-else statements. If it contains two if-else statements then the first if-else statement is called outer if-else statement and the second if-else statement is called inner if-else statement similarly, if it contains more than two if-else statements then the first if-else statement is called outer if-else statement, the second if-else statement is called first inner if-else statement, the second if-else statement is called the second inner if-else statement and so on. If the outer if-else statement becomes false then the control goes to the first inner if-else statement. If the first inner if-else statement becomes false then control goes to the second inner if-else statement and so on. Following is the general syntax of nested if-else statement:

The nested if-else Statement in C#	

if (Condition-1)
{
Statement-1;
Statement-2;
……………...
Statement-n;
}
	The First Block

else
if (Condtion-2)
{
Statement-1;
Statement-2;
……………
Statement-n;
}
	The Second Block

else
if (Condition-n)
{
Statement-1;
Statement-2;
……………
Statement-n;
}
	The first n^{th} Block

else
{
Statement-1;
Statement-2;
……………
Statement-n;
}
	The second n^{th} Block

The nested if-else Statement in VB.NET	
First Syntax	
If Condition-1 Then	
Statement-1	
Statement-2	The First Block
…………….	
Statement-n	
Else	
If Condition-2 Then	
Statement-1	
Statement-2	
……………	The Second Block
Statement-n	
Else	
If Condition-n Then	
Statement-1	
Statement-2	
……………	The first n^{th} Block
Statement-n	
Else	
Statement-1	
Statement-2	
……………	The second n^{th} Block
Statement-n	
End If	
End If	
End If	
Second Syntax	
If Condition-1 Then	
Statement-1	
Statement-2	The First Block
…………….	
Statement-n	
ElseIf Condition-2 Then	
Statement-1	
Statement-2	

....	The Second Block
Statement-n	
ElseIf Condition-3 Then	
Statement-1	
Statement-2	
....	The first n^{th} Block
Statement-n	
Else	
Statement-1	
Statement-2	
....	The second n^{th} Block
Statement-n;	
End If	

In nested if-else statement, the compiler first checks Condition-1. If Condition-1 is true then executes the first block of statements and ignores the remaining conditions. If Condition-1 is false then the compiler checks Condition-2. If Condition-2 is true then compiler executes the second block of statements and ignores the remaining conditions. If Condition-2 is false then compiler checks the third condition and on this way the compiler checks the entire if-else statements of a nested if-else statement.

The if-else statement is a better approach and it is better than the simple if statement because in case of simple if statement, if we have two or more nested if statements without else statements, the compiler first checks all the conditions then executes body of the true condition but in case of if-else statements, if we have two or more nested if-else statements then compiler checks the first condition. If first condition is true then control executes body of the first condition and ignores the remaining conditions. If second condition is true then compiler executes body of the second condition and ignores the remaining conditions and so on. Therefore, the if-else statement saves the compiler processing time.

Program # 1

Write a program that checks whether a given integer number is positive or negative.

C# Program

```using System;```
 	
class MainClass
{
static void Main(string[] args)
{
int x;
 	
Console.WriteLine("Enter any integer number");
x = System.Convert.ToInt32(Console.ReadLine());
if (x >= 0)
Console.WriteLine("The number is positive");
else
Console.WriteLine("The number is Negative");
 	
Console.WriteLine("Press any key to exit program");
Console.ReadKey();
}
}

```
C# Program

using System;

class MainClass
{
static void Main(string[] args)
{
int x;

Console.WriteLine("Enter any integer number");
x = System.Convert.ToInt32(Console.ReadLine());
if (x >= 0)
Console.WriteLine("The number is positive");
else
Console.WriteLine("The number is Negative");

Console.WriteLine("Press any key to exit program");
Console.ReadKey();
}
}
```

```
Visual Basic Program

Module Module1

Sub Main()

Dim x As Integer

Console.WriteLine("Enter any integer number=")
x = System.Convert.ToInt32(Console.ReadLine())
If x >= 0 Then
Console.WriteLine("The number is positive")
Else
Console.WriteLine("The number is negative")
End If
Console.WriteLine("Press any key to exit program")
Console.ReadKey()
End Sub

End Module
```

Program # 2

Write a program that checks whether a given number is even or odd.
C# Program

```
using System;

class MainClass
{
static void Main(string[] args)
{
int x;

Console.WriteLine("Enter any number");
x = System.Convert.ToInt32(Console.ReadLine());
if (x % 2 == 0)
Console.WriteLine("The number is Even");
else
Console.WriteLine("The number is Odd");

Console.WriteLine("Press any key to exit program");
Console.ReadLine();
}
}
```

VB.NET Program

```
Module Module1

Sub Main()

Dim x As Integer

Console.WriteLine("Enter any number=")
x = System.Convert.ToInt32(Console.ReadLine())
If (x Mod 2) = 0 Then
Console.WriteLine("The number is Even")
Else
Console.WriteLine("The number is Odd")
End If
```

```
Console.WriteLine("Press any key to exit program")
Console.ReadKey()
End Sub

End Module
```

Program # 3

Write a program that inputs three integer numbers and finds the greatest number among them.
C# Program

```
using System;

class MainClass
{
static void Main(string[] args)
{
int a, b, c;

Console.WriteLine("Enter the first number");
a = System.Convert.ToInt32(Console.ReadLine());
Console.WriteLine("Enter the second number");
b = System.Convert.ToInt32(Console.ReadLine());
Console.WriteLine("Enter the third number");
c = System.Convert.ToInt32(Console.ReadLine());

if (a > b && a > c)
Console.WriteLine("The number a is greater");
else
if (b > a && b > c)
Console.WriteLine("The number b is greater");

else
Console.WriteLine("The number c is greater");
Console.WriteLine("Press any key to exit program");
Console.ReadLine();
}
}
```

Visual Basic Program

Module Module1
 	
Sub Main()
 	
Dim a, b, c As Integer
 	
Console.WriteLine("Enter the first number=")
a = System.Convert.ToInt32(Console.ReadLine())
Console.WriteLine("Enter the second number=")
b = System.Convert.ToInt32(Console.ReadLine())
Console.WriteLine("Enter the third number=")
c = System.Convert.ToInt32(Console.ReadLine())
 	
If (a > b And a > c) Then
Console.WriteLine("The number a is greater")
ElseIf (b > a And b > c) Then
Console.WriteLine("The number b is greater")
Else
Console.WriteLine("The number c is greater")
End If
 	
Console.WriteLine("Press any key to exit program")
Console.ReadKey()
End Sub
 	
End Module

Switch Statement

The switch statement is a flow control statement that gives us multiple choices to transfer control to a specified statement or block of statements. It performs a decision among different statements and executes a single statement or a block of statements at a time and ignores the remaining statements of the program. The switch statement is used when multiple choices are given and one choice is to be selected at a time therefore, it is also called multiple choices statement. It divides a program in different parts. Each part is called case. Each case contains a single statement or block of statements and it has a unique value that identifies the case. The case value may be a numeric, a character, a special character, or a string. If a case value is a character, a special character, or a string then it must be enclosed within double quotes and if it is a numeric value then the double quotes is not used. The switch statement takes one parameter that is called Expression. The parameter Expression is a value, a variable, or a relational comparison and it is the controller of the switch statement that controls the entire cases of the switch statement. This parameter takes input value from a user and executes a case that matches with the input value. The switch statement selects a single case at a time according to the input value and executes all the statements in the body of that case. A switch statement also contains a case that does not have any value and it is called default case. If a user input a value that does not match with any case of the switch statement then switch statement executes the default case. The default case executes the user defined message or any block of statements. If the parameter Expression is a relational comparison then the value of each case depends on the return value of the relational comparison.

In C# the switch statement is called switch-case statement while in Visual Basic the switch statement is called Select-Case statement. In C# a keyword **break** is used at the end of each case of the switch statement that terminates the current active or running case after its execution and sends the control back to the switch Expression. In Visual Basic the keyword break is not used. The Visual Basic programming language automatically terminates the case after its execution and sends the control back to the Select-Case Expression. Following is the general declaration of the switch-case and Select-Case statements:

The declaration of switch-case Statement in C#
switch(Expression) { case “Value-1”: The block of Statements-1; break; case “Value-2”: The block of Statements-2; break; case “Value-3”: The block of Statements-3; break; ....

.... case “Value-n”: The block of Statements-n; break; default: The default block of Statements; break; }
The declaration of Select-Case Statement in Visual Basic
Select Case [Expression] Case “Value-1” The block of Statements-1 Case “Value-2” The block of Statements-2 Case “Value-3” The block of Statements-3 .... Case “Value-n” The block of Statements-n Case Else The default block of Statements End Select

The parameter **Expression** indicates the expression of the switch and Select Case statements that takes input choice from a user. It can be a value, a variable, or a relational comparison. The case value from Value-1 to Value-n depends on the parameter Expression. The Expression executes one case or choice at a time and it depends on the user input value. In C# a full colon (:) is used after each case value while in Visual Basic the full colon is not used. In C# the name of the default case is default but in Visual Basic the name of the default case is Case Else. Following are the programming examples of switch-case and Select-Case statements:

Program # 4

Write a program that adds, subtracts, multiplies and divides two integer values using the switch statement.
C# Program

```
using System;

class MainClass
{
public static void Main(string[] args)
{
int x, y;
string opt;

Console.WriteLine("Enter the first number = ");
x = System.Convert.ToInt32(Console.ReadLine());
Console.WriteLine("Enter the second number = ");
y = System.Convert.ToInt32(Console.ReadLine());
Console.WriteLine("Enter any arithmetic operator =");
opt = Console.ReadLine();

switch(opt)
{
case "+":
Console.WriteLine("The sum of x and y ="+ (x + y));
break;
case "-":
Console.WriteLine("The subtraction of x and y ="+ (x - y));
break;
case "*":
Console.WriteLine("The multiplication of x and y ="+ (x * y));
break;
case "/":
Console.WriteLine("The division of x and y ="+ (x / y));
break;
default:
Console.WriteLine("You entered the wrong operator");
break;
}
Console.WriteLine("Press any key to terminate the program");
```

Console.ReadKey(); } }
VB.NET Program
Module Module1 Sub Main() Dim x, y As Integer Dim opt As Char Console.WriteLine("Enter the first number = ") x = System.Convert.ToInt32(Console.ReadLine()) Console.WriteLine("Enter the second number = ") y = System.Convert.ToInt32(Console.ReadLine()) Console.WriteLine("Enter any arithmetic operator =") opt = Console.ReadLine() Select Case opt Case "+" Console.WriteLine("The sum of x and y = " & x + y) Case "-" Console.WriteLine("The subtraction of x and y = " & x - y) Case "*" Console.WriteLine("The multiplication of x and y = " & x * y) Case "/" Console.WriteLine("The division of x and y = " & x / y) Case Else Console.WriteLine("You entered the wrong operator") End Select Console.WriteLine("Press any key to exit program") Console.ReadKey() End Sub End Module

Program # 5

Write a program that checks an integer value either it is a positive, negative or zero.

C# Program

```
using System;

class MainClass
{
public static void Main(string[] args)
{
int n;

Console.WriteLine("Enter any integer value = ");
n = System.Convert.ToInt32(Console.ReadLine());

switch((n == 0) ? 0 : (n > 0) ? 1:2)
{
case 0:
Console.WriteLine("The number is zero");
break;
case 1:
Console.WriteLine("The number is positive");
break;
case 2:
Console.WriteLine("The number is negative");
break;
}
Console.WriteLine("Press any key to terminate the program");
Console.ReadKey();
}
}
```

Program #6

Write a program that checks whether a character is an alphabetic, a numeric or any other special character using the switch statement.

C# Program

using System;
 	
class MainClass
{
public static void Main(string[] args)
{
char ch;
 	
Console.WriteLine(“Enter any character = “);
ch = System.Convert.ToChar(Console.ReadLine());
 	
switch((ch >= 65 && ch <= 90 || ch >= 97 && ch <= 122) ? “CL” : (ch >= 48 && ch <= 57) ? “NV” : “SC”)
{
case “CL”:
Console.WriteLine(“You entered English alphabet”);
break;
case “NV”:
Console.WriteLine(“You entered numeric value”);
break;
case “SC”:
Console.WriteLine(“You entered a special character”);
break;
}
Console.WriteLine(“Press any key to terminate the program”);
Console.ReadKey();
}
}

Iterative Statements

Iteration is a process that repeats a single statement or a block of statements in a program until a specified condition becomes true. The Iterative statements are the flow control statements used for the iteration process that repeats a given series of statements or commands until specified conditions are met. When a program is written and in a program if some commands or statement needs repetition or multiple executions then they are placed in the body of an Iterative statement and the limit of the iteration is specified. The iterative statements are also called loops. An iterative statement or loop uses a variable called index variable. The index variable of a loop is an integer variable that initializes the loop and set the limit or the last value of the iteration. An iterative statement or loop has the following three parts:

- Start Expression
- Test Expression
- Counter Expression

Start Expression

The start expression indicates the initial or starting position of a loop. It is an assignment statement that initializes a loop with any starting value. A loop always starts execution from this part. It usually assigns the loop starting value to the index variable but it can also be any legal expression. When a loop starts execution then this part of the loop executes only once at first time and never execute again. Therefore, the Start Expression is the initialization point of a loop that initializes a loop with a specified integer value. The Start Expression can be written as:

Index_Variable = Starting_Value;

Test Expression

The Test Expression is a condition part of a loop that evaluates the loop condition. The loop condition is usually a relational condition that returns a Boolean value either true or false. The Test Expression checks the condition during each trip of a loop and compares the return value of the relational condition. If the return value is true then body of the loop executes and if the return value is false then body of the loop terminates and the program control transfers to the next step or next line of the program.

Counter Expression

The Counter Expression is the counter part of a loop that counts the number of executions or iterations of a loop during execution. It sets the loop index variable as a counter that increments or decrements the total number of iterations of the loop. If the Start Expression of a loop is smaller than the Test Expression then Counter Expression increments the counter and if the Start Expression of a loop is greater than the Test Expression then Counter Expression decrements the counter and counts the number of iterations of the loop. The Counter Expression always executes after each trip of a loop and increment or decrement the counter variable and matches the incremented or decremented value with the Test Expression or condition of the loop. If the counter value is in the range of the Test Expression then the loop executes next iteration otherwise, the loop terminates and the program control transfers to the next step or next line of the program.

Types of Loops

The loops are basically categorized into the following two types:

- Counted Loops
- Uncounted Loops

Counted Loops

If the starting position and ending position or values of the Start Expression and Test Expression of a loop are known then the loop is called counted loop. The counted loop is used if we repeat a single statement or block of statements and we know the starting position from where we want to start the loop and ending position to where we want to repeat the loop for example, to display ten integer values on the screen, to display any message or data on the screen five times etc. If we display 10 integer values on the screen from 1 to 10 then in this case the starting position or the Start Expression of the loop will be 1 and the ending position or the Test Expression of the loop will be 10. The most programming languages provide a loop statement called **for Loop.** The "for loop" is used as a counted loop.

The for Loop

This loop is used to repeat a single statement or block of statements again and again until a specified condition is met or satisfied. It is always used in such cases when the starting position and ending position of a loop are known. It has three parts or parameters. The first part is Start Expression that is used to initialize the loop index variable. The second part is Test Expression that is used to check the loop condition. The Test Expression part is actually a condition that returns true or false value. If the return value is true then body of the loop executes otherwise body of the loop terminates and the program control transfers to the new line of the program. The third part is Counter

Expression that is used as a counter and counts the number of iterations or trips of a loop by incremented or decremented the loop index variable. The block of statements is placed within the body of the loop. When a single statement or block of statements is placed within the body of for loop, it iterates or repeats that statement or block of statements until a specified condition of the Test Expression is met or satisfied.

The for loop usually uses a numeric variable that is called loop index variable. The Start Expression part of the for loop initializes the loop index variable by any specified value that is called initial value or start position of the loop. The loop always starts iterations or executions from Start Expression part. The Test Expression part fixes a final value to the loop index variable. The third part of the loop is Counter Expression that increments or decrements the initial value of the loop index variable during each iteration of the loop and the loop is terminated when value of the index variable reaches to its final value. In C# and Visual Basic the keyword **for** is used for the activity of counted loop.

Declaration of for Loop in C#

In C# programming language, the for loop has three parts or parameters enclosed within a pair of small braces and they are distinguished from each other by using commas. The parts of for loop are Start Expression, Test Expression, and Count Expression. Following is the general syntax of for loop in C# programming language:

```
for (Start_Expression; Test_Expression; Count_Expression)
{
………………
Body of the loop
………………
Block of statements or code is written here
………………
}
```

The **Start_Expression** is the first part of the loop that specifies the initial value of the loop index variable. It initializes the loop index variable by assigning any specified value. The **Test_Expression** is the second part of the loop that specifies a condition or final value of the loop index variable. It uses a relational condition and returns a Boolean value either true or false. If Boolean value is true then loop executes a statement or block of statements otherwise, the loop terminates and transfers the control to the next step or next line of the program. The **Counter_Expression** is the third part of the loop that increments or decrements the loop index variable by a specified value and counts the number of iterations or executions of the loop. In C# the area between the two curly braces {} is body of the loop. If a loop executes a single statement then the curly braces can be avoided. Since, for loop is not an executable statement but it executes another statement or a block of statements therefore, in C# a semicolon is not written after the loop. If a semicolon is used after the for loop then it will only display the last value of the index variable.

Declaration of for Loop in VB.NET

In VB.NET programming language, the for loop is called For-Next loop. The For-Next loop has three parts such as Start Expression, Test Expression and Counter Expression. The body of the For-Next loop is enclosed within the keywords For and Next. Following is the general syntax of For-Next loop:

```
For Start_Expression To Test_Expression [Step ± Counter_Expression]
..............................
Body of the loop
..............................
Block of statements or code is written here
..............................
Next [Variable]
```

The **Start_Expression** is the first part of the loop that indicates the initial value of the loop index variable. It initializes the loop index variable by assigning any specified value. The **Test_Expression** is the second part of the loop that indicates the final value of the loop index variable or condition of the loop. The **Counter_Expression** is the third part of the loop that increments or decrements the loop index variable by a specified step value and counts the number of iterations or executions of the loop. The **Step** is a keyword that is used with the loop **Counter_Expression** part and it specifies the step value of increment or decrement. It is optional and can be omitted. If we omit the step value then the Counter_Expression increments or decrements the loop index variable by 1. The **Next** is a keyword that generates the next iteration of the loop. It is placed at the end of the repeating statements. It uses the loop index variable. When loop completes the first iteration and control reaches to the **Next** keyword, the **Next** keyword returns back the control and requests the Counter_Expression part to generate the next iteration of the loop. The Counter_Expression part then increments or decrements the index variable by any specified step value and generates the next iteration of the loop. This process continues until the final value of the index variable or condition of the loop is met or satisfied. Following are the programming examples of for loops in C# and VB.NET:

Program # 7

Write a program that displays 10 natural numbers from 1 to 10 using for loop.
C# Program

using System;
 	
class MainClass
{
public static void Main(string[] args)
{
int i;
for(i = 1; i <= 10; i = i + 1)
{
Console.WriteLine(i);
}
Console.WriteLine("Press any key to terminate the program");
Console.ReadKey();
}
}

VB.NET Program
Module Module1 Sub Main() Dim i As Integer For i = 1 To 10 Step 1 Console.WriteLine(i) Next i

```
Console.WriteLine("Press any key to exit program")
Console.ReadKey()
End Sub

End Module
```

The above program declares one integer variable **i** as a loop index variable that controls the iterations of the loop. The initial value of the loop index variable i is 1 that specifies the Start Expression and the final or last value of the loop is 10 that specify the Test Expression. The Test Expression first compares the current value of variable i with the final value and determines whether they or equals or not. In first step or first iteration, the value of i is 1 and final value is 10. The Test Expression is (i<=10). Since in first step the condition is true because 1 is less than 10 therefore, the current value of variable i will be printed on the screen. The Count Expression part of the loop (i = i + 1) then increments variable i by 1. Now the new value of variable i is 2. The Test Expression again checks the condition (i<=10) and compares the current value of variable i with the final value. Since, the condition is remains true because 2 is less than 10 then 2 will be printed on new line of the screen. The Count Expression (i = i + 1) increments variable i by 1 during each iteration of the loop and print the value of variable i until the value of variable i becomes 11. When the value of variable i becomes 11 then the loop will terminate because 11 is not less than 10.

Program # 8

Write a program that displays first five even numbers from 0 to 10 using for loop.
C# Program

```
using System;

class MainClass
{
public static void Main(string[] args)
{
int i;
for(i = 0; i <= 10; i = i + 2)
{
Console.WriteLine(i);
```

```
}
Console.WriteLine("Press any key to terminate the program");
Console.ReadKey();
}
}
```

VB.NET Program

```
Module Module1

Sub Main()

Dim i As Integer

For i = 0 To 10 Step 2
Console.WriteLine(i)
Next i

Console.WriteLine("Press any key to exit program")
Console.ReadKey()
End Sub

End Module
```

The above program declares one integer variable **i** as a loop index variable that controls the iterations of the loop. The initial value of the loop index variable i is 0 that specifies the Start Expression and the final or last value of the loop is 10 that specify the Test Expression. The Test Expression first compares the current value of variable i with the final value and determines whether they or equals or not. In first step or first iteration, the value of i is 0 and final value is 10. The Test Expression is (i<=10). Since in first step the condition is true because 0 is less than 10 therefore, the current value of variable i will be printed on the screen. The Count Expression part of the loop (i = i + 2) then increments variable i by 2. Now the new value of variable i is 2. The Test Expression again checks the condition (i<=10) and compares the current value of variable i with the final value. Since, the condition is remains true because 2 is less than 10 then 2 will be printed on new line of the screen. The Count Expression (i = i + 2) increments variable i by 2 during each iteration of the loop and print the value of variable i until the value of variable i becomes 12. When the value of variable i becomes 12 then the loop will terminate because 12 is not less or equal to 10.

Uncounted Loops

If the starting position and ending position or values of the Start Expression and Test Expression of a loop are unknown then the loop is called uncounted loop. The uncounted loop is used if we repeat a single statement or a block of statements and we do not know the starting position from where to start the loop and ending position to where to repeat the loop for example, if we write a program that reads characters from the keyboard and the characters reading continue until zero is pressed or any other specified value that is fixed in the loop condition or Test Expression. When a specified fixed condition value is pressed from the keyboard then the loop terminates and the program control transfers from body of the loop to the next step or next line of the program. In this case we do not know the starting position of the loop because we can enter any character from the keyboard. The ending position is also unknown because this program may terminate at the first iteration if we enter a specified fixed condition value at the first iteration of the loop, the program may also continue to the second iteration, third iteration or it may continue up to infinite iterations. These types of programs are not possible using the counted loops therefore, the uncounted loops are used. The uncounted loops have dual nature because they also can be used as counted loops. In C# the examples of uncounted loops are **while loop** and **do-while loop** and in VB.NET the examples of uncounted loops are **While...End While** loop and **Do...While** or **Do...Until** loop.

while loop

The "while loop" is used when we do not know the starting position and ending position of the repeating statements. It has dual nature or functionality that can be used as an uncounted loop and also can be used as a counted loop like "for loop". If "while loop" is used as an uncounted loop then it only contains the Test Expression part that is used as a condition of the loop and other two parts of the loop are not used. It iterates or executes body of the loop as long as the Test Expression or condition is true. In C# and VB.NET a keyword **while** is used for while loop but the declaration syntaxes are different. In C# body of the loop is enclosed within curly braces {} and in VB.NET body of the loop is enclosed between the **While** and **End While** statements. As an uncounted loop the "while loop" has the following general syntaxes in C# and VB.NET:

The while Loop Syntax in C#

while (Test_Expression)
{
……………………………
 	
Body of the loop
……………………………
Block of statements or code is written here
}

The while Loop Syntax in VB.NET
While Test_Expression …………………………… Body of the loop …………………………… Block of statements or code is written here End While

The **Test_Expression** indicates condition of the loop. It is usually a relational condition that returns a Boolean value either true or false. If the returned value is true, body of the loop will execute and if the returned value is false, body of the loop will terminate and the program control will transfer from body of the loop to the next step or next line of the program. In C# the **Test_Expression** is always enclosed within small braces () but in VB.NET the braces are optional and can be omitted. Following is the programming example of while loop used as uncounted loop:

Program # 9

Write a program that reads characters from the keyboard until we press zero. When we press zero then the program will terminate.
C# program
using System; class MainClass {

```
static void Main(string[] args)
{
char ch;
Console.WriteLine("Enter any character");
ch = System.Convert.ToChar(Console.ReadLine());
while (ch != 48)
{
Console.WriteLine("You entered = " + ch);
Console.WriteLine("Enter any character");
ch = System.Convert.ToChar(Console.ReadLine());
}

Console.WriteLine("Press any key to exit program");
Console.ReadKey();
}
}
```

VB.NET Program

```
Module Module1

Sub Main()

Dim ch As Char

Console.WriteLine("Enter any character = ")
ch = Console.ReadLine()

While Asc(ch) <> 48

Console.WriteLine("You entered = " & ch)
Console.WriteLine("Enter any character = ")
ch = Console.ReadLine()

End While
Console.WriteLine("Enter any number to exit program")
Console.ReadKey()
End Sub
End Module
```

The above program reads characters from the keyboard and displays on the screen continuously until zero is entered. When zero is entered from the keyboard, the program will terminate and the program control will transfer from body of the loop. In the C# program the Test Expression or condition is (ch ! = 48). In this condition 48 is the ASCII code of 0. When we enter a character from the keyboard, the Test Expression compares its ASCII code with 48. If ASCII code of the entered character is 48, the program will be terminated because in this case the condition of the while loop will true. In the VB.NET program the condition is Asc(ch) <> 48. In this condition the **Asc** is a built-in function that takes any character as a parameter and returns the ASCII code of that character as an integer value. When we enter any character from the keyboard, the Asc function returns its ASCII code. The Test Expression then compares the Ascii code of the entered character with the condition 48. If the condition is true, the loop will be terminated.

The above program is a good example of uncounted while loop because in this program we don't know the starting position and ending position of the character reading process. We can enter any character at any iteration of the loop. If we enter 0 at the first iteration of the loop, the loop will be terminated at the first iteration similarly, if we enter 0 at the second iteration, the loop will be terminated at the second iteration and so on. If we do not enter zero, the loop will be reading characters and will be displayed on the screen and the characters reading process will continue until we enter zero.

while Loop as a Counted Loop

while loop can also be used as a counted loop like "for loop". If while loop is used as a counted loop then it contains three parts like for loop such as Start Expression, Test Expression, and Count Expression. The first part Start Expression initializes the loop index variable by assigning any specified value. The second part Test Expression fixes a condition or assigns a final value to the loop index variable. The third part Counter Expression is counter of the loop that increments or decrements the loop index variable and counts the number of iterations. As a counted loop "while loop" has the following general syntaxes in C# and VB.NET:

The while Loop Syntax in C#

Start_Expression;
while (Test_Expression)
{
……………………………..
Body of the loop
……………………………......
Count_Expression;
}

The while Loop Syntax in Visual Basic
Start_Expression While Test_Expression …………………………….. Body of the loop ……………………………...... Count_Expression End While

The **Start_Expression** indicates the start position of the loop that initializes the loop index variable by a specified value. The **Test_Expression** is the second part of the loop that indicates the final value of the loop index variable. The **Counter_Expression** is the third part of the loop that increments or decrements the loop index variable and counts the number of iterations. Following are the programming examples of while loop used as counted loop:

Program # 10

Write a program that displays the first 10 natural numbers using while loop.
C# Program
using System; class MainClass {

static void Main(string[] args)
{
int x;
 	
x = 1;
while (x<=10)
{
Console.WriteLine(x);
x = x + 1;
}
Console.WriteLine("Press any key to exit program");
Console.ReadKey();
}
}

VB.NET Program
Module Module1 Sub Main() Dim x As Integer x = 1 While x <= 10 Console.WriteLine(x) x = x + 1 End While Console.WriteLine("Enter any number to exit program") Console.ReadKey() End Sub End Module

The above program declares a loop index variable x that controls the loop. The initial value of the loop index variable x is 1 and final value of the loop is 10. The Test Expression part of the loop is (x <= 10) that checks the condition. Since, the condition is true because the initial value of x is 1 and final value of the loop is 10 therefore, 1 will be displayed on the screen. The Count Expression part is (x = x + 1) that increments variable x by 1. Now the value of variable x is 2. The Test Expression part again checks the condition. The condition is remains true because (2<=10) then 2 will be printed on the new line of the screen. The Count Expression part increment the value of variable x and this process continues until the value of variable x becomes 11. When the value of variable x becomes 11 then the loop will be terminated and the program control will be transferred from body of the loop.

do-while Loop

The do-while loop works same as while loop but the main difference is that while loop first checks the condition or Test Expression then executes body of the loop but do-while loop first executes body of the loop then checks the loop condition or Test Expression because in do-while loop the body is placed before the condition or Test Expression part. The do-while loop first executes body of the loop then the Counter Expression part generates the second iteration of the loop by incremented or decremented the loop index variable and checks the condition or Test Expression. If the condition is true then it executes body of the loop second time and this process continues until the condition or the Test Expression becomes false. If the condition or Test Expression becomes false then loop terminates and the program control transfers from body of the loop. In do-while loop body of the loop always comes before the condition or Test Expression and it is called post-test loop. Therefore, do-while loop executes body of the loop at least one time even if the condition of the loop is false. The do-while loop is used if we repeat a single statement or a block of statements at least one time even if the condition of the loop is false.

Declaration of do-while Loop in C#

In C# the do-while loop starts from a keyword **do** and ends with a keyword **while**. The body of do-while loop is between the keywords **do** and **while** enclosed within curly braces. If body of the loop contains a single statement then the curly braces becomes optional and can be omitted. Since in C# each executable statement ends with a semicolon therefore, a semicolon is used after the do-while loop because unlike other types of loops the do-while loop is an executable statements and it executes body of the loop at least one time even if the condition is false. Following is the general syntax of do-while loop in C#:

The do-while Loop Syntax in C#

Start_Expression;
do
{
…………………………..
Body of the loop
…………………………….
Count_Expression;
}
while(Test_Expression);

Following are the programming examples of the do-while loop in C# programming language:

Program # 11

Write a program that prints the first 10 natural numbers on the screen using the do-while loop.
C# Program

```
using System;

class MainClass
{
public static void Main(string[] args)
{

int x;
x = 1;
do
{
Console.WriteLine(x);
x = x + 1;
}
while (x <= 10);

Console.WriteLine("Press any key to terminate the program");
Console.ReadKey();
```

```
}
}
```

Program # 12

Write a program that reads characters from the keyboard continuously until we entered zero 0.

C# Program

```
sing System;

class MainClass
{
static void Main(string[] args)
{

char ch;

Console.WriteLine("Enter any character");
ch = System.Convert.ToChar(Console.ReadLine());
do
{
Console.WriteLine("You entered = " + ch);
Console.WriteLine("Enter any character");
ch = System.Convert.ToChar(Console.ReadLine());
}
while (ch != 48);
Console.WriteLine("Press any key to exit program");
Console.ReadKey();
}
```

Program # 13

Write a program that executes body of the do-while loop at least one time even if the condition is false at the first iteration.

C# Program

```
using System;

class MainClass
```

```
{
static void Main(string[] args)
{

int x;
x =11;

do
{
Console.WriteLine(x);
x = x + 1;
}
while (x <= 10);

Console.WriteLine("Press any key to exit program");
Console.ReadKey();
}
}
```

The output of the above program will be 11. The initial value of variable x is 11 and final value is 10. The condition is already false at the first iteration because the Test Expression of the loop is (11<=10) that is already false but do-while loop first executes body of the loop then checks the condition therefore, it executes body at least one time even if the condition is false.

Declaration of do-while Loop in VB.NET

In VB.NET the "Do-While" loop has dual functionality that can be used as Do-While loop and as while loop. The VB.NET allows us to place body of the Do-While loop before or after the condition or Text Expression. If we place body of the Do-While loop after the condition or Test Expression then first it checks condition or Test Expression then executes body of the loop and it will work same as while loop. In this case the Do-While loop is called Pre-test Do-While loop because in this case it first checks the condition or Test Expression then executes body of the loop. If we place body of the Do-While loop before the condition or the Test Expression then first it executes body of the loop then checks the condition and it will work as Do-While loop. In this case the Do-While loop is called Post-test Do-While loop because in this case it first executes body of the loop then checks the condition or Test Expression. The

VB.NET provides three keyword **Do, While**, and **Loop** for do-while loop. Following are the two general syntaxes of Do-While loop in VB.NET:

The do-while Loop Syntaxes in VB.NET	
Syntax # 1	Syntax # 2
Start_Expression Do While (Test_Expression) .... Body of the loop .... Count_Expression Loop	Start_Expression Do .... Body of the loop .... Count_Expression Loop While (Test_Expression)

In syntax# 1 the Do-While loop works same as while loop because in this syntax body of the loop comes after the condition or Test Expression. In Syntax# 2 the Do-While loop works same as the actual Do-While loop because in this syntax body of the loop comes before the condition or Test Expression. Following are the programming examples of Do-While loop:

Program # 14

Write a program that prints the first 10 natural numbers on the screen using the do-while loop.
VB.NET Program
Using Post-test do-while Loop

```
Module Module1

Sub Main()

Dim x As Integer

x = 1
Do

Console.WriteLine(x)
x = x + 1
Loop While (x <= 10)
```

```
Console.WriteLine("Press any key to exit program")
Console.ReadKey()
End Sub

End Module
```

Using Pre-test Do-While Loop

```
Module Module1

Sub Main()

Dim x As Integer

x = 1
Do While (x <= 10)
Console.WriteLine(x)
x = x + 1
Loop

Console.WriteLine("Press any key to exit program")
Console.ReadKey()
End Sub

End Module
```

Program # 15

Write a program that executes body of the Do-While loop at least one time if the loop condition is false at the first iteration.

VB.NET Program

```
Module Module1

Sub Main()

Dim x As Integer
x = 11
```

```
Do
Console.WriteLine(x)
x = x + 1
Loop While x <= 10

Console.WriteLine("Enter any number to exit program")
Console.ReadKey()
End Sub

End Module
```

The output of the above program will be 11. The initial value of variable x is 11 and final value is 10. The condition is already false at the first iteration because the Test Expression of the loop is (11<=10) that is already false but do-while loop first executes body of the loop then checks the condition therefore, it executes body at least one time even if the condition is false.

Do-Until Loop in VB.NET

The Do-Until loop is similar to the Do-While loop but the main difference is that the Do-While loop iterates body of the loop until the Test Expression or condition becomes false and Do-Until loop iterates body of the loop until the Test Expression or condition of the loop becomes true. Therefore, the Do-Until loop is the opposite form of the Do-While loop. The Do-Until loop iterates body of loop as long as the condition false and it terminates iterations when the Test Expression or condition becomes true. For example, if starting value of the loop index variable x is 1 and final value of the loop index variable x is 10 then the Start Expression of the Do-Until loop will be "x = 1" and the Test Expression or condition will be "x = 10". It means that the Do-Until loop will iterates body of the loop until the index variable x is equal to ten. The VB.NET provides three keywords **Do, Until,** and **Loop** for the Do-Until loop. The following two are the general syntaxes of Do-Until loop:

Syntax # 1	**Syntax # 2**
Start_Expression Do Until (Test_Expression) ……………………………..	Start_Expression Do ……………………………..

Body of the loop	Body of the loop
....	....
Count_Expression	Count_Expression
Loop	Loop Until (Test_Expression)

The syntax#1is used for the Pre-test Do-Until loop and syntax# 2 is used for the Post-test Do-Until loop.

Why we use do-while Loop?

The do-while loop plays an important role because sometime in some applications or programs, we execute a piece of code or statement once and on the basis of that execution we decide whether to execute that code repeatedly or not. In such situations we use do-while loop. The best example of using the do-while loop is games programming. Almost all games provide at least one active life to each user when a user starts a game. When a user starts a game, it assigns an active life and allows that user to play the game and get more lives after each specified successful task of the game. When a user completed a specified task of the game, the game program assigns another active life to that user and increases the game session time for the current user. When a user did not complete a specified task or did not find any specified object of the game in a specified time specified by the game program then the user lost one life and the game program decrease the user session time.

The Nested Loops

When we use one loop inside in the body of another loop then it is called nested loop and this process is called nesting of loops. In a nested loop the first loop is called outer loop and the second loop is called inner loop. The inner loop is placed in the body of the outer loop. The outer loop is also called driver or main loop because it repeats the inner loop again and again until the condition of the outer loop becomes false. Each iteration or trip of the outer loop executes the inner loop completely. For example, when the outer loop starts first iteration, the inner loop executes completely similarly, when the outer loop starts the second iteration, the inner loop executes completely and this process continue until the outer loop becomes false. When the condition of the outer loop becomes false then the entire nested loop terminates. We can also nest more than two loops and we can nest all types of loops for example, nested for loops, nested while loops, and nested do-while loops. Following is the general syntax of nested loops:

```
Loop1
{
Loop2
{
Loop3
{
……………..
……………..
Loop-n
{
Body of Loop-n
}
Body of Loop3
}
Body of Loop2
}
Body of Loop1
}
```

For example, to nest two for loops, the following syntax can be used.

```
for(Start_Expression1; Test_Expression1; Count_Expression1)
{
for(Start_Expression2; Test_Expression2; Count_Expression2)
{
Body of inner loop
}
Body of outer loop
}
```

The following programming example demonstrates the nested for loop in details:

Program # 16

<table>
<tr><td colspan="2">Write a program that demonstrates the nested for loop</td></tr>
<tr><td>

```
using System;

class MainClass
{
static void Main(string[] args)
{
int i, j;
for (i = 1; i <= 3; i++)
{
for (j = 1; j <= 3; j++)
{
Console.WriteLine(i + " " + j);
}
}

Console.WriteLine("Press any key to exit program");
Console.ReadKey();
}
}
```

</td><td>

Output

```
i   j
1   1
1   2
1   3
2   1
2   2
2   3
3   1
3   2
3   3
```

</td></tr>
</table>

The output of the above program shows that each iteration or trip of the outer loop executes the entire inner loop.

The break Statement

The break statement is used to terminate the execution of a loop or a case in the switch statement. It is usually used with the conditional statements and when a specified condition becomes true, the break statement terminates the execution of the currently running loop and transfers the program control to the next block or next statement of the program following the loop. In case of nested loops it terminates execution of the innermost loop. The switch statement contains one or more cases. Each case is terminated by the break statement because when a specified case is terminated, the program control transfers to the next case of the switch statement. Therefore, to prevent execution of the next coming case in the switch statement, the break statement is used at the end of each case. Following is the programming example of break statement:

Program # 17

```
using System;

class MainClass
{
static void Main(string[] args)
{
int x;

for (x = 1; x <= 10; x = x + 1)
{
if (x == 5)
break;
else
Console.WriteLine(x);
}

Console.WriteLine("Press any key to exit program");
Console.ReadKey();
}
}
```

The above program declares for loop and displays integer values. The index variable of the loop is x. The initial value of the loop index variable is 1 and its final value is 10. The conditional statement is used that checks the value of the loop index variable with the condition during each iteration or trip of the loop. When loop starts iteration, it displays values from 1 to 4 and ignores values from 5 to 10 because the values from 1 to 4 are not matched with the value of the conditional statement. When value of the loop index variable becomes 5 then it stops iterations and terminates body of the loop because in body of the conditional statement the break statement is used that terminates the loop and transfers the program control from body of the loop to the next line of the program.

The continue Statement

The continue statement is used to skip a specified iteration or trip of a loop specified by the conditional statement. The continue statement is used in the body of the loop with the conditional statement. The conditional statement specifies a particular value of the loop index variable for continue statement. When loop starts iteration, the conditional statement compares the value of the loop index variable with the condition. If value of the loop index variable is matched with the condition, the continue statement skips that value and starts execution of the next iteration or next trip of the loop. Following is programming example of continue statement:

Program # 18

```
using System;

class MainClass
{
static void Main(string[] args)
{
int x;

for (x = 1; x <= 10; x = x + 1)
{
if (x == 5)
continue;
else
Console.WriteLine(x);
}

Console.WriteLine("Press any key to exit program");
Console.ReadKey();
}
}
```

The output of the above program is 1 2 3 4 6 7 8 9 10. The program uses for loop that prints integer values. The loop index variable is x. The initial value of the loop index variable is 1 and its final value is 10. The conditional statement is used that checks the value of the loop index variable with the condition during each iteration or trip of the loop. When loop starts iterations, it displays values from 1 to 4. When loop starts the fifth iteration then the condition of the conditional statement becomes true that is (x==5), the continue statement then skips the execution of the current iteration and skips value 5 and starts execution of the next iteration of the loop. The loop then executes the next iterations and displays values from 6 to 10.

Program # 19

<table>
<tr><td colspan="2">Write a program that skips the similar values of a nested loop and prints the remaining dissimilar values.</td></tr>
<tr><td><pre>using System;

class MainClass
{
static void Main(string[] args)
{
int i, j;

for (i = 1; i <= 3; i++)
{
for (j = 1; j <= 3; j++)

{
if (i == j)
continue;
else
Console.WriteLine(i + " " + j);
}
}

Console.WriteLine("Press any key to exit program");
Console.ReadKey();
}
}</pre></td><td>Output
i j
1 2
1 3
2 1
2 3
3 1
3 2</td></tr>
</table>

The above program uses nested for loop. The index variable of the outer loop is i and index variable of the inner loop is j. The initial value of both variables is 1 and the final value is 3. The program displays the dissimilar combinations of the loop variables i and j and skips the similar combinations such as (1, 1), (2, 2), and (3, 3) because the conditional statement checks each combination of the loops and if the value of variable i is equal to the value of variable j, the continue statement skips that combination and starts the next iteration of the inner loop. The continue statement only skips the iteration of the inner loop because it is in the body of the inner loop.

The goto Statement

The goto statement is used to transfer the program control from the current position to a specified position specified by a label statement. The goto statement allows us to stop the execution of the current block, statement, method, or a portion of a program and transfer the program control to a specified block, statement, method, or portion during run time of a program. The goto statement requires a labeled statement. A label is a valid identifier followed by a semi colon. Each goto statement has a label body that references the goto statement by using the name of that label. To transfer the program control from the current position to a specified position, the goto statement is used in the current position of the program followed by a label name and the label body is placed in the target position of the program where the program control is to be transferred. When a program is executing and during execution if the program control reaches to the goto statement, the program control leaves the current position and jumps to the target position that is specified by a label. Following is the general syntax of goto statement:

```
Program line1...............
Program line2...............
Program line3...............

goto Identifier;

Program line5..............
Program line6..............
Program line7..............

Label Identifier:

Program line9..............
Program line10..............
```

In the above syntax the **identifier** is the name of a label. The name of the label can be any numeric value, character value, or a string. The identifier of goto statement and the identifier of the Label must be the same. In the above syntax we have ten lines program. In the program we want to transfer the program control from line 4 to line 8 So, when we execute this program and during execution when the program control reaches to line 4, the program control will be transferred from line 4 to line 8 and will skips the lines from line 5 to line 7 and will start execution of the program from line 9 and will execute rest of the program after line 9.

The limitations of goto Statement

The goto statement cannot work in some cases and cannot transfer program control from some places of a program. Following are the details of some cases where the goto statement cannot transfer the program control:

- The goto statement cannot transfer program control from finally block of Try....Catch as well as from the class definition.
- The goto statement cannot transfer program control inside in the mid of any block but it always transfers program control to the start position of the block because some time a block needs initialization of variables and initialization is always placed in the top position of the block therefore, if goto statement starts execution of a block from mid or from any other onward position then the block will not execute successfully and it will produce compiler error.
- The goto statement cannot transfer program control inside a class definition.
- A single goto statement must have a label but multiple goto statements can access a single label. It means that each label must have a unique name because in a program two identical labels cannot be used but multiple goto statements can be used followed by a same label name.

The following programming example demonstrates the using of goto statement:

Program # 20

```
using System;

class MainClass
{
static void Main(string[] args)
```

```
{
int n;
Pos:
Console.WriteLine ("Enter any positive integer number =");
n = System .Convert.ToInt32(Console .ReadLine());
if (n < 0)
goto Pos;
else
Console.WriteLine("You entered a positive number");

Console.WriteLine("Press any key to exit program");
Console.ReadKey();
}
}
```

The above program reads an integer positive value from the keyboard. When an integer value is entered, it checks that value whether it is positive or negative. If the value is positive then the program will prompt a message that "You entered a positive number" and it will terminate otherwise, if the value is negative then the goto statement will transfer the program control before the entry point of the program by using a label **Pos** and the program will start again from the beginning and asks for the integer value.

The foreach Loop

The foreach loop is used to retrieve elements from a collection or an array. It uses a variable like other loops that takes elements from a collection or an array in a sequence one by one. Unlike other loops it does not contain three parts such as initialization or Start Expression, condition or Test Expression, and Counter Expression. The foreach loop starts iteration from the first element of a collection or an array and retrieves elements one by one until the last element is retrieved. During each iteration or trip, it retrieves a single element from a collection or an array and stores it in the loop variable. If a collection is an integer collection, the loop variable must be an integer variable, similarly if a collection is a string collection, the loop variable must be a string variable and so on. Following is the general declaration of the foreach loop:

Declaration in C#
foreach(Variable_Name in Collection)
Declaration in VB.NET
For Each Variable_Name In Collection

In the above declaration the parameter **Variable_Name** indicates the foreach loop variable that retrieves elements and **Collection** indicates the name of a collection or an array from which we want to retrieve elements.

Program # 21

Write a program that retrieves elements from an array using foreach loop.

```
using System;

namespace foreachLoop
{
class MainClass
{
static void Main(string[] args)
{
int[] Arr = new int[] {7, 1, 2, 3, 5, 8, 13};
foreach (int i in Arr)
{
System.Console.WriteLine(i);
}
System.Console.Write("Press any key to exit program");
System.Console.ReadKey();
}
}
}
```

VB.NET Program

```
Module Module1
Sub Main(ByVal args As String())
Dim Arr As Integer() = New Integer() {7, 1, 2, 3, 5, 8, 13}
Dim i As Integer
For Each i In Arr
System.Console.WriteLine(i)
```

```
Next
System.Console.Write("Press any key to exit program")
System.Console.ReadKey()
End Sub
End Module
```

CHAPTER 4

Arrays and Structure

CHAPTER CONTENTS

Arrays

An array is the collection of different values of the same data type stored in contiguous memory locations and it is represented by a single name. An array can be declared from any data type like an ordinary variable but the main difference is that an ordinary variable only can store a single value at a time while an array contains one or more memory locations that can store one or more values of the same data type at the same time. Each memory location of an array behaves like an ordinary variable that store a single value at a time. The values of an array are called elements. When an array is declared as integer type then it can store only integer values similarly, when an array is declared as string type then it can store only string values and so on. Therefore, we can say that an array is a single named variable that contains one or more contiguous memory locations and stores one or more different values of the same data type. Each memory location of an array is capable of storing only one value at a time like an ordinary variable. The memory locations of an array depend on its size specified at the time of the declaration.

Each memory location of an array has its own memory address and they are distinguished from each other by a subscript or index. An Index is a number starts from zero that differentiates one element of an array from another element.

Why we use Arrays?

When an ordinary variable is declared then it can store only a single value at a time. If we want to store more than one value then we need to declare more variables i.e. individual variable for each value. Suppose if we want to add 10 integer values then first we have to store these values in the memory therefore, to store 10 values in the memory we can follow the following two approaches:

1. We have to declare 10 individual variables and store 10 values in computer memory using 10 variables.
2. We have to declare an array of size 10 and store 10 values in computer memory using array.

We can use both approaches to store values in computer memory but second approach is the best because if we need to add 100, 1000, or more values then it is very difficult to declare 1000 or more individual variables and also it is very difficult to give unique name to each variable because in a program no two variables can have identical names so, it is also very difficult to find out 1000, or more different identifiers or names to declare these variables. To declare such amount of variables it will take a lot of time and will increase size of the program. It is also very difficult to handle such amount of variables and the program will become more ambiguous.

Therefore, to remove the drawbacks of ordinary variables we declare an array to store more values in a single entity under a single name. An array provides a separate room or a separate memory location for each value. Each memory location of an array has the same memory space and each value or element of an array occupies the same amount of memory space for example, when we declare an integer array of size 10 then 40 bytes memory space will be reserved for it because it is the collection of 10 integer memory locations or integer variables and each integer variable occupies 4 bytes memory space in .NET, so 10 * 4 = 40 bytes similarly, if we declare a floating point array of size 10 as double type then 80 bytes memory space will be reserved for it because in this case it is the collection of 10 double variables and each double variable occupies 8 bytes memory space, so 10 * 8 = 80 bytes.

When an array is declared then computer assigns a memory address to it. The memory address is usually assigned to the starting index of array that is called base address. The index number of an array always starts from 0. The element of index 0 is the first element of an array, the element of index 1 is the second element of an array, and the element of index 2 is the third element of an array and so on.

An array can have one or more dimensions. A dimension is a direction in which we can vary the specification of an array's elements. The dimensions of an array are specified at the time of its declaration.

Types of Arrays

According to dimensions there are the following two types of arrays:

1. Single Dimensional Arrays
2. Multiple Dimensional Arrays

Single Dimensional Arrays

A single dimensional array has one dimension that contains multiple columns and a single row and it stores elements in a linear form. Each element of a single dimensional array has a single index number. A single dimensional array is similar to a set in mathematics but the main difference is that a set contains unique values while an array may store unique or repeating values of the same data type. For example a single dimensional array is used to store the number of days of a year, names of the months, names of the students in a class and so on. Following is the general declaration of a single or one dimensional array:

C# Declaration
Datatype_name[] Array_name = new Datatype_name[Array_size];
VB.NET Declaration
Dim Array_name (Array_size) As Datatype_name

In the above declaration the **Datatype_name** indicates data type of an array, the **Array_name** indicates name of an array, and the **Array_size** indicates size of an array. Following is the declaration of an integer array:

C# Declaration	VB.NET Declaration
int[] num = new int[10];	Dim num(10) As Integer

The above declaration declares an integer array **num** for 10 integer values. The size of an array is defined according to the number of values we want to store similarly, to store floating point or real values in an array, a real type array is declared. Following is declaration of an array that stores floating point or real values:

C# Declaration	VB.NET Declaration
double[] num = new double[12];	Dim num(12) As Double

The above declaration declares a double type array **num** for 12 floating point or real values.

Initialization of Single Dimensional Arrays

Initialization is a process that provides data or values to an array. A single dimensional array can be initialized by using the following different ways:

C# Initialization
Syntax # 1
int[] num = new int[10] {1, 2, 3, 4, 5, 6, 7, 8, 9, 10};
Syntax # 2
int[] num = new int[] {1, 2, 3, 4, 5, 6, 7, 8, 9, 10, 11, 12, 13};
Syntax # 3

int[] num = new int [5];
num[0]=2;
num[1]=4;
num[2]=1;
num[3]=6;
num[4]=3;

VB.NET Initialization
Syntax # 1
Dim num() As Integer = {1, 2, 3, 4, 5, 6, 7, 8, 9, 10, 11, 12, 13}

Syntax # 2
Dim num(5) As Integer num(0) = 1 num(1) = 2 num(2) = 3 num(3) = 4 num(4) = 5

The C# programming language allows us to initialize an array using the above three different syntaxes. The first syntax of C# is a fixed syntax that allows us to fix the size of an array and provide values according to its size for example, in the first syntax of C#, the array size is fixed to 10 that only can store 10 values. In the second syntax of C# the array size is not defined but it is initialized with 13 values so its size becomes 13. In the second syntax the array is also called unlimited array because it has no fixed size but it can be initialized with any number of values. The third syntax of C# is an important syntax and it is used to initialize an array during run time of the program. In the third syntax, the values are assigned to its subscripts or index number. To assign values to an array during runtime of a program, a loop is used to assign values to each index of an array. Since the index number of one dimensional array starts from zero therefore, the loop index variable also starts from zero and assigns the first input value to index number 0, the second input value to index number 1, and the third input value to index number 3 and so on.

In the first syntax of VB.NET, the array size is not defined but it is initialized with 13 values so its size becomes 13. In the first syntax of VB.NET the array is also called unlimited array because it has no fixed size but it can be initialized with any number of values. VB.NET does not support to initialize the fixed size array like the first syntax of C#. To initialize a fixed size array in VB.NET, only the second syntax of VB.NET is used.

The character and string arrays can be initialized by the following different ways:

Array initialization in C#
Character Array Initialization: char[] chr = new char[5] {'a', 'b', 'c', 'd', 'e'};

```
or
char[] chr = new char[] {'a', 'b', 'c', 'd', 'e', 'f', 'g'};

String Array Initialization:
    string [] str = new string [3] {"C Sharp", "Visual Basic", "Java"};
    or
    string [] str = new string [] {"C Sharp", "Visual Basic", "Java"};
    or
    string[] str = new string[3];
    str[0] = "C Sharp";
    str[1] = "Visual Basic";
    str[2] = "Java";
```

The above example initializes a character array **chr** and a string array **str** respectively. To initialize a character array in C#, each character value must be enclosed within single quotes and to initialize a string array, each string value must be enclosed within double quotes. The VB.NET programming language also supports character and string arrays like C# but in VB.NET the values of both the character and string arrays are enclosed within double quotes. VB.NET does not support initialization of character arrays with single quotes.

Program # 1

Write a program that stores 5 elements in an array and displays them on the screen.
C# Program

```
using System;

class MainClass
{
static void Main()
{
int [] num = new int [5];
num[0] = 1;
num[1] = 2;
num[2] = 3;
num[3] = 4;
num[4] = 5;
```

```
Console.WriteLine(num[0]);
Console.WriteLine(num[1]);
Console.WriteLine(num[2]);
Console.WriteLine(num[3]);
Console.WriteLine(num[4]);

Console.WriteLine("Press any key to exit program");
Console.ReadKey();
}
}
```

VB.NET Program

```
Module Module1

Sub Main()

Dim num(5) As Integer
num(0) = 1
num(1) = 2
num(2) = 3
num(3) = 4
num(4) = 5

Console.WriteLine(num(0))
Console.WriteLine(num(1))
Console.WriteLine(num(2))
Console.WriteLine(num(3))
Console.WriteLine(num(4))

Console.WriteLine("Press any key to exit program")
Console.ReadKey()
End Sub

End Module
```

Multiple Dimensional Arrays

A multiple dimensional array contains multiple rows and multiple columns and it store data in the form of rows and columns like a table. There are different types of multiple dimensional arrays for example, two dimensional, three dimensional, and more than three dimensional. If an array has two dimensions then it is called two-dimensional array similarly, if an array has three dimensions then it is called three-dimensional array. A Two-dimensional array contains the number of rows and columns and it stores values or elements in the form of rows and columns like matrices in mathematics. Each element of a two dimensional array has an index number. Each index number has two values. The first value of an index indicates the row position and second value of an index indicates the column position of an element. If a two-dimensional array has two rows and two columns then it is called 2x2 array similarly, if a two-dimensional array has three rows and three columns then it is called 3x3 array and so on. To access a value or an element of a two-dimensional array, the row and the column position of that element is specified. Two-dimensional arrays are used if we want to store multiple related data for example, the number of students of each class in a school, the number of students of a class and their marks in each subject, and the number of employees of each department in an organization etc. Following is the general declaration of two-dimensional arrays:

C# Declaration
Datatype_name[,] Array_name = new Datatype_name[Rows, Column];
VB.NET Declaration
First Method: Dim Array_name (Rows, Column) As Datatype_name Second Method Dim Array_name (,) As Datatype_name = {Initialization}

In the above declaration the **Datatype_name** indicates data type of a two-dimensional array, the **Array_name** indicates name of an array, **Rows** indicates the number of rows, and **Column** indicates the number of columns in a two-dimensional array. Following is the declaration of a 2x2 integer array:

C# Declaration	VB.NET Declaration
int[,] num = new int[2, 2];	Dim num(2, 2) As Integer

The above declaration declares a 2x2 integer array **num** that contains two rows and two columns. A 2x2 array can store four elements. Similarly, following is the declaration of a 3x3 integer array:

C# Declaration	VB.NET Declaration
int[,] num = new int[3, 3];	Dim num(3, 3) As Integer

The above declaration declares a 3x3 integer array **num** that contains three rows and three columns. A 3x3 array can store nine elements.

Initialization of Two-dimensional Arrays

A two-dimensional array can be initialized by the following different ways:

Array initialization in C#

First Method:

```
int[,] num = new int[2, 2] {{1, 2}, {3, 4}};
```

Second Method:

```
int[,] num = new int[2, 2];
num[0, 0] = 1;
num[0, 1] = 2;
num[1, 0] = 3;
num[1, 1] = 4;
```

Array initialization in VB.NET

First Method:

```
Dim num(,) As Integer = {{1, 2}, {3, 4}}
```

Second Method:

```
Dim num(2, 2) As Integer
num(0, 0) = 1
num(0, 1) = 2
num(1, 0) = 3
num(1, 1) = 4
```

Program # 2

Write a program that reads a 3x3 array and display all elements on the screen.
C# Program

```
using System;

class MainClass
{
static void Main(string[] args)
{
int[,] num = new int[3,3];
num[0, 0] = 1;
num[0, 1] = 2;
num[0, 2] = 3;
num[1, 0] = 4;
num[1, 1] = 5;
num[1, 2] = 6;
num[2, 0] = 7;
num[2, 1] = 8;
num[2, 2] = 9;

Console.WriteLine(num[0, 0]);
Console.WriteLine(num[0, 1]);
Console.WriteLine(num[0, 2]);
Console.WriteLine(num[1, 0]);
Console.WriteLine(num[1, 1]);
Console.WriteLine(num[1, 2]);
Console.WriteLine(num[2, 0]);
Console.WriteLine(num[2, 1]);
Console.WriteLine(num[2, 2]);

Console.WriteLine("Press any key to exit program");
Console.ReadKey();
}
}
```

VB.NET Program
Module Module1 Sub Main() Dim num(3, 3) As Integer num(0, 0) = 1 num(0, 1) = 2 num(0, 2) = 3 num(1, 0) = 4 num(1, 1) = 5 num(1, 2) = 6 num(2, 0) = 7 num(2, 1) = 8 num(2, 2) = 9 Console.WriteLine(num(0, 0)) Console.WriteLine(num(0, 1)) Console.WriteLine(num(0, 2)) Console.WriteLine(num(1, 0)) Console.WriteLine(num(1, 1)) Console.WriteLine(num(1, 2)) Console.WriteLine(num(2, 0)) Console.WriteLine(num(2, 1)) Console.WriteLine(num(2, 2)) Console.WriteLine("Press any key to exit program") Console.ReadKey() End Sub End Module

Jagged Arrays

Jagged array is a type of array who's each element is itself a separate array. When different arrays are combined with each other under a single entity or name then it is called jagged array. A jagged array is also called an array of arrays. Each element of a jagged array can be of different sizes and dimensions. A jagged array is used when we have data or information that makes two dimensional shapes but not rectangular for example, if we want to store the yearly calendar data in an array then we will use jagged array because a single year contains twelve months and each month further contains number of days. Since each month has different number of days therefore the calendar data does not make a proper rectangular shape. Following is the general declaration of a jagged array:

Jagged Array Declaration in C#
Data_Type[][] Array_name = new Data_Type[Size][];
Jagged Array Declaration in VB.NET
Dim Array_name As Data_Type()() = New Data_Type (Size)() {}

The above declaration declares a single dimensional jagged array. The **Data_type** indicates data type of jagged array, the **Array_name** indicates the name of a jagged array, and **Size** indicates size or the number of elements of a jagged array. Since each element of a jagged array is itself a separate array therefore, we must declare all the elements of a jagged array before use. Following is the general declaration of elements of a jagged array:

Declaration in C#

```
//Declare a jagged array
int[][] MyArray = new int[5][];

//Declare the elements of jagged array
MyArray[0] = new int[10];
MyArray[1] = new int[4];
MyArray[2] = new int[6];
MyArray[3] = new int[7];
MyArray[4] = new int[3];
```

Declaration in VB.NET

```
//Declare a jagged array
Dim MyArray As Integer()() = New Integer(4)() {}

//Declare the elements of jagged array
MyArray(0) = New Integer(9)
MyArray(1) = New Integer(3)
```

```
MyArray(2) = New Integer(5)
MyArray(3) = New Integer(6)
MyArray(4) = New Integer(2)
```

The above declaration declares an integer jagged array. The array name is **MyArray** and it contains five elements. Each element is itself a separate single dimensional integer array. The first element is an array of 10 elements, the second element is an array of 4 elements, the third element is an array of 6 elements, the fourth element is an array of 7 elements, and the fifth element is an array of 3 elements.

Initialization of Jagged Array

Since each element of a Jagged array is itself a separate array therefore, all the elements of a Jagged array should be initialized. To initialize the elements of a Jagged array, each element is separately initialized by assigning proper values according to the size of that element or array. The elements of a Jagged array can be initialized by the following way:

Jagged Array Initialization in C#

```
//Declare a jagged array
int[][] MyArray = new int[5][];

//Declare the elements of jagged array
MyArray[0] = new int[10];
MyArray[1] = new int[4];
MyArray[2] = new int[6];
MyArray[3] = new int[7];
MyArray[4] = new int[3];

//Initialize the elements of Jagged Array
MyArray[0] = new int[10] {1, 3, 5, 7, 9, 2, 4, 6, 8, 10};
MyArray[1] = new int[4] {2, 4, 6, 8};
MyArray[2] = new int[6] {2, 4, 6, 1, 3, 9};
MyArray[3] = new int[7] {2, 4, 6, 8, 5, 1, 3};
MyArray[4] = new int[3] {2, 4, 6};
```

Jagged Array Initialization in VB.NET

/Declare a jagged array
Dim MyArray As Integer()() = New Integer(4)() {}
 	
//Declare the elements of jagged array
MyArray(0) = New Integer(9)
MyArray(1) = New Integer(3)
MyArray(2) = New Integer(5)
MyArray(3) = New Integer(6)
MyArray(4) = New Integer(2)
 	
Initialize the elements of Jagged Array
MyArray(0) = New Integer(9) {1, 3, 5, 7, 9, 2, 4, 6, 8, 10}
MyArray(1) = New Integer(3) {2, 4, 6, 8}
MyArray(2) = New Integer(5) {2, 4, 6, 1, 3, 9}
'MyArray(3) = New Integer(6) {2, 4, 6, 8, 5, 1, 3}
MyArray(4) = New Integer(2) {2, 4, 6}

Program # 3

Write a program that displays the elements of a jagged array.
C# Program

namespace JaggedArrayTest
{
class JaggedArrayTest
{
static void Main(string[] args)
{
//Declare a Jagged array of five elements
int[][] MyArray = new int[5][];
 	
//Initialize the elements of Jagged Array
MyArray[0] = new int[5] {1, 3, 5, 7, 9};
MyArray[1] = new int[4] {2, 4, 6, 8};
MyArray[2] = new int[3] {2, 4, 6};
MyArray[3] = new int[7] {2, 4, 6, 8, 5, 1, 3};
MyArray[4] = new int[6] {2, 4, 6, 8, 10, 12};

```
//Display the elements of jagged Array
for (int i = 0; i < MyArray.Length; i++)
{
for (int j = 0; j < MyArray[i].Length; j++)
{
System.Console.Write(MyArray[i][j] + " ");
}
System.Console.WriteLine();
}
System.Console.WriteLine("Press any key to exit");
System.Console.ReadKey();
}
}
}
```

VB.NET Program

```
Module Module1

Sub Main(ByVal args As String())

'Declare a Jagged array of five elements
Dim MyArray As Integer()() = New Integer(4)() {}

'Initialize the elements of the Jagged Array
MyArray(0) = New Integer(4) {1, 3, 5, 7, 9}
MyArray(1) = New Integer(3) {2, 4, 6, 8}
MyArray(2) = New Integer(2) {2, 4, 6}
MyArray(3) = New Integer(6) {2, 4, 6, 8, 5, 1, 3}
MyArray(4) = New Integer(5) {2, 4, 6, 8, 10, 12}

'Display the elements of Jagged Array
For i As Integer = 0 To MyArray.Length - 1
For j As Integer = 0 To MyArray(i).Length - 1
System.Console.Write(MyArray(i)(j) & " ")
Next

System.Console.WriteLine()
```

```
Next

System.Console.WriteLine("Press any key to exit")
System.Console.ReadKey()

End Sub
End Module
```

Structures

A structure is the collection of heterogeneous data that is used to store multiple related data such as a data that contains multiple attributes of different data types. For example, students record in a school that contains student name, roll number, class grade, total marks, percentage etc, the employee records in each department of an organization that contains employee name, department, position, employee scale etc. Each attribute of data has its own data type for example, in students records the student name is a string data, roll number is an integer data, class grade is an integer data, total marks is an integer data, and percentage is a real or float data. Therefore, a structure collects two or more different data types under a single entity and the whole structure is represented by a single name. Each data type of a structure is called member data. A structure is also called value type data type and it allows us to declare structure variables. A structure variable is similar to ordinary variables but the main difference is that a structure variable is the combination of two or more ordinary variables. A structure may also contain methods or functions called member methods or member functions. A structure variable is used to pass data to the structure and access its member data and member functions. A single structure variable can store and access only a single record.

Structures support constructors, member functions, operators, fields, properties, enumeration, and constants like classes. The members of a structure can have different access levels such as private members and public members etc. A structure can also implements interfaces and can have constructors like classes but the main difference between classes and structures is that a structure variable is a value type that directly contains data of the structure and a class variable is a reference type that contains a reference to the data. Structures only support parameterized constructors and they do not support the default constructors (parameter less constructors). Structures use stack allocation and classes use heap allocation. The members of a structure are public by default while the class variables and constants are private by default and other class members are public by default. We cannot declare an empty structure but we can declare an empty class. Structures cannot be inherited from other structures while classes are inheritable and they can be inherited from other classes. A structure does not require a constructor while a class requires at least one constructor.

Why we use Structures?

As we know that an array is the collection of homogenous data type that can store only data of the same data type and it cannot store multiple related data or a data that contains multiple attributes of different data types for example, in some cases we deal a single object that have multiple attributes of multiple data types such as an object name, object type, object quality, object status, object quantity and so on. Therefore, structures are used to store the multiple attributes of an object for example, students records in a school that contains multiple attributes, the employee records in each department of an organization that contains multiple attributes etc. To store such a related data of different data types, we can use one of the following two approaches:

1. Declare individual arrays for each attribute of a student record for example, one array for the students names, second array for the students addresses, third array for the students marks, fourth array for the students percentages, and fifth array for the students contact numbers etc.
2. Declare a single structure to store the entire student record.

The second approach is the best because if an object have 50 or more attributes then it is very difficult to declare 50 or more individual arrays for each attribute and the program will also become more difficult to handle because the declaration of such amount of arrays will increase length of the program. Therefore, a single structure is declared to store the multiple attributes of an object.

Declaration of structures

In C# a structure is declared using a **struct** keyword. The member data or elements of a structure are declared within a pair of curly braces {} while in VB.NET a structure is declared using s **structure** keyword and the member data or elements of a structure are declared within **Structure** and **End Structure** statements. Structures are usually declared at the top of the program but they can also be declared anywhere in the program. When structures are declared at the top of the program then they are called global structures. A global structure can be accessed anywhere in the program. When a structure is declared within the body of any function or any block then the structure is called local structure. A local structure is local to the function or block where it is declared. We cannot access a local structure outside that function or block where it is declared. Following is the general declaration of structure:

Structure Declaration in C#

[modifiers] struct Structure_name
{
Data_type member_data_1;
Data_type member_data_2;
-------------------------------- 	
Data_type member_data_n;
}

Structure Declaration in VB.NET
[modifiers] Structure Structure_name Data_type member_data_1; Data_type member_data_2;
-------------------------------- Data_type member_data_n; End Structure

In the above declaration the **modifiers** indicates access modifiers such as private and public etc. The **struct** and **Structure** are keywords used to declare a structure in C# and in VB.NET respectively. The **Structure_name** indicates a user defined name of the structure.

Declaration of Structure Variables

When a structure is declared then it becomes a new data type and allows us to declare variables. A structure variable is used to pass data to the structure and access its member data and member functions. In C# the structure variables can be declared in two ways such as using the new operator and without using the new operator. When a structure variable is declared without using the new operator then it does not call constructor automatically and when a structure variable is declared using the new operator with parameters then it call the appropriate constructor automatically. In VB.NET the structure variables can be declared using the Dim and new operator. Unlike classes, structures can be instantiated without using the new operator. When structure variables are declared without using the new operator then the fields will remain unassigned and the object cannot be used until all of the fields are initialized.

When a structure variable is declared then a separate memory location is reserved for it and it stores data in that associated memory location. Therefore, when two or more structure variables are declared then a separate memory location is reserved for each variable. Each structure variable store data in its own associated memory location and one variable does not affect on the data of another variable for example, no two structure variables can update or overwrite their data. A structure variable can store only a single record. For example, if we want to store a single record then a single structure variable will be declared similarly, if we want to store two records then two structure variables will be declared and so on. Structure variables can be declared by the following way:

Declaration in C#
Declaration without new Operator: Structure_name Variable-1, Variable-2, Variable-3, -------, Variable-n; Declaration with new Operator: Structure_name Variable_name = new Structure_name (Parameter_list);
Declaration in VB.NET
Declaration without New Operator: Dim Variable-1, Variable-2, Variable-3, -------, Variable-n As Structure_name
Declaration with New Operator: Dim Variable-1, Variable-2, Variable-3, -------, Variable-n As New Structure_name

In the above declaration the **Structure_name** indicates the name of a structure and the **Parameter_list** indicates the number of parameters of a specified constructor we want to call. Following is a simple structure that stores the record of students:

Declaration in C#

public struct students
{
public string Name; //Students Name
public int Rno; //Students Roll Number
public int Marks; //Student Marks
public float Percentage; //Students Percentage
}

Declaration in VB.NET
Public Structure Students Dim Name As String 'Student Name Dim Rno As Integer 'Student Roll Number Dim Marks As Integer 'Student Marks Dim Percentage As Single 'Student Percentage End Structure

The above declaration declares a structure **students** that contains four attributes such as student name, roll number, marks, and percentage. To assign values to the structure member data, the structure variables are used.

Initialization of Structure Member Data

Initialization is a process that provides data to the member data of a structure. The member data of a structure cannot be initialized inside in the structure body because the entire structure is considered as a single data type and member data are the parts of a structure. The member data of a structure can only be initialized outside of the structure body using structure variables. The member data of a structure can be accessed using the dot (.) operator. The dot operator (.) is used between the structure variable name and the structure data member name. Following is the general syntax to initialize the structure member data:

Initialization in C#
Structure_variable . Structure_member = Value;
Initialization in VB.NET
Structure_variable . Structure_member_name = Value

In the above declaration the **Structure_variable** indicates the name of a structure variable, the **Structure_member** indicates the name of a member data we want to initialize, and **Value** indicates the value we are assigning to the member data. The following programming example demonstrates structure in details:

Program # 4

Write a program that declares a structure and store the records of two students.
C# Program

```
using System;

class MainClass
{
public struct Students
{
public string Name;
public int Rno;
public int Marks;
public float Percentage;
}
static void Main(string[] args)
{
Students Std1, Std2;

Std1.Name = "Mr. Asad Khan";
Std1.Rno = 1;
Std1.Marks = 678;
Std1.Percentage = 82.5f;

Std2.Name = "Mr. Zahid Aslam";
Std2.Rno = 2;
Std2.Marks = 718;
Std2.Percentage = 86.5f;

Console.WriteLine("Student Name = " + Std1.Name);
Console.WriteLine("Student Roll Number = " + Std1.Rno);
```

```
Console.WriteLine("Student Marks = " + Std1.Marks);
Console.WriteLine("Student Percentage = " + Std1.Percentage);

Console.WriteLine("Student Name = " + Std2.Name);
Console.WriteLine("Student Roll Number = " + Std2.Rno);
Console.WriteLine("Student Marks = " + Std2.Marks);
Console.WriteLine("Student Percentage = " + Std2.Percentage);

Console.WriteLine("Press any key to exit program");
Console.ReadKey();
}
}
```

VB.NET Program

```
Module Module1
Public Structure Students
Dim Name As String
Dim Rno As Integer
Dim Marks As Integer
Dim Percentage As Single
End Structure

Sub Main()

Dim Std1, Std2 As New Students

Std1.Name = "Mr. Asad Khan"
Std1.Rno = 1
Std1.Marks = 678
Std1.Percentage = 82.5

Std2.Name = "Mr. Zahid Aslam"
Std2.Rno = 2
Std2.Marks = 718
Std2.Percentage = 86.5

Console.WriteLine("Student Name = " & Std1.Name)
Console.WriteLine("Student Roll Number = " & Std1. Rno)
```

```
Console.WriteLine("Student Marks = " & Std1.Marks)
Console.WriteLine("Student Percentage = " & Std1.Percentage)

Console.WriteLine("Student Name = " & Std2.Name)
Console.WriteLine("Student Roll Number = " & Std2.Rno)
Console.WriteLine("Student Marks = " & Std2.Marks)
Console.WriteLine("Student Percentage = " & Std2.Percentage)

Console.WriteLine("Press any key to exit program")
Console.ReadKey()

End Sub
End Module
```

In the above program, two structure variables Std1 and Std2 are declared to store the data or record of students. Each structure variable store a single record therefore, the above program only can store the record of two students. Similarly, to store the record of three students, three structure variables will be declared and so on. Furthermore, we can say that if we have hundreds or thousands of records then we have to declare hundreds or thousands of structure variables. The declaration of such amounts of variables is very difficult because it will increase length of the program, the program will become ambiguous and it will consume more time. Therefore, to reduce this drawback, an array of structure is used.

Array of Structure

Array of structure is used to store the data or record of more objects or entities. It is the collection of two or more structure variables under a single name. The entire array of structure is represented by a single name. An array of structure is similar to ordinary arrays but the main difference is that each index of an array of structure contains all members of a structure and each index stores a single record in a structure. When an array of structure is declared then a separate memory location is assigned to each index. Therefore, each index of an array of structure stores record in a separate memory location. Following is the general declaration of array of structure:

Array of Structure declaration in C#
Structure_name[] Array_name = new Structure_name [Array_size];
Array of Structure declaration in VB.NET
Dim Array_name(Array_size) As Structure_name

In the above declaration the **Structure_name** indicates the name of a structure, the **Array_name** indicates the name of an array, and the **Array_size** indicates the size of an array of structure. The following programs store the record of students using array of structure:

Program # 5

Write a program that declare an array of structure and store the records of three students.
C# Program

```
sing System;

class MainClass
{
public struct Students
{
public string Name;
public int Rno;
public int Marks;
public float Percentage;
}

static void Main(string[] args)
{
uStudents[] Std = new Students [3];

Std[0].Name = "Mr. Asad Khan";
Std[0].Rno = 1;
Std[0].Marks = 678;
Std[0].Percentage = 82.5f;

Std[1].Name = "Mr. Zahid Aslam";
```

```
Std[1].Rno = 2;
Std[1].Marks = 718;
Std[1].Percentage = 86.5f;

Std[2].Name = "Mr. Shahid Akhtar";
Std[2].Rno = 3;
Std[2].Marks = 750;
Std[2].Percentage = 87.2f;

Console.WriteLine("Student Name = " + Std[0].Name);
Console.WriteLine("Student Roll Number = " + Std[0].Rno);
Console.WriteLine("Student Marks = " + Std[0].Marks);
Console.WriteLine("Student Percentage = " + Std[0].Percentage);

Console.WriteLine("Student Name = " + Std[1].Name);
Console.WriteLine("Student Roll Number = " + Std[1].Rno);
Console.WriteLine("Student Marks = " + Std[1].Marks);
Console.WriteLine("Student Percentage = " + Std[1].Percentage);

Console.WriteLine("Student Name = " + Std[2].Name);
Console.WriteLine("Student Roll Number = " + Std[2].Rno);
Console.WriteLine("Student Marks = " + Std[2].Marks);
Console.WriteLine("Student Percentage = " + Std[2].Percentage);

Console.WriteLine("Press any key to exit program");
Console.ReadKey();
}
}
```

VB.NET Program

```
Module Module1

Public Structure Students
Dim Name As String
Dim Rno As Integer
Dim Marks As Integer
Dim Percentage As Single
```

```
End Structure

Sub Main()

Dim Std(3) As Students

Std(0).Name = "Mr. Asad Khan"
Std(0).Rno = 1
Std(0).Marks = 678
Std(0).Percentage = 82.5

Std(1).Name = "Mr. Zahid Aslam"
Std(1).Rno = 2
Std(1).Marks = 718
Std(1).Percentage = 86.5

Std(2).Name = "Mr. Shahid Akhtar"
Std(2).Rno = 3
Std(2).Marks = 750
Std(2).Percentage = 87.2

Console.WriteLine("Student Name = " & Std(0).Name)
Console.WriteLine("Student Roll Number = " & Std(0).Rno)
Console.WriteLine("Student Marks = " & Std(0).Marks)
Console.WriteLine("Student Percentage = " & Std(0).Percentage)

Console.WriteLine("Student Name = " & Std(1).Name)
Console.WriteLine("Student Roll Number = " & Std(1).Rno)
Console.WriteLine("Student Marks = " & Std(1).Marks)
Console.WriteLine("Student Percentage = " & Std(1).Percentage)

Console.WriteLine("Student Name = " & Std(2).Name)
Console.WriteLine("Student Roll Number = " & Std(2).Rno)
Console.WriteLine("Student Marks = " & Std(2).Marks)
Console.WriteLine("Student Percentage = " & Std(2).Percentage)

Console.WriteLine("Press any key to exit program")
```

```
Console.ReadKey()

End Sub
End Module
```

Memory Representation of Structure

When a structure variable is declared then a memory space is assigned to it. The size of the assigned memory space depends on the members of a structure. If members of a structure increase then the size of the structure variables increase. For example, if a structure contains two integer variables then its variable will occupy 8 bytes memory space because an integer variable occupies 4 bytes memory space similarly, if a structure contains three integer variables then its variable will occupy 12 bytes memory space. Consider the following simple structure declaration:

```
public struct Test
{
public int x;
public double y;
}
```

The above declaration declares a structure that contains two member data. The first member data is an integer variable x and the second member data is a double variable y. The integer variable occupies 4 bytes memory space and double variable occupies 8 bytes memory space therefore, when a structure variable is declared from the above structure, it will occupy 12 bytes memory space.

CHAPTER 5

Procedural and Modular Programming in .NET

CHAPTER CONTENTS

Procedures

Procedural programming languages are based on the concept of units, modules, and scopes. A procedural program is composed of one or more units or modules. These units or modules are either user defined or provided in a built-in code library. Each module is composed of one or more procedures. A procedure is a named block of statements or code enclosed by a declaration statement that can be executed independently to perform a specific task. The declaration statement of a procedure is a block that contains starting point and ending point of procedure. The block of statements or code is placed inside in the declaration statement of a procedure. Each procedure may contain the same nature or the same functionality block of statements or code. A procedure is executed when it is invoked or called. A procedure can be invoked or called from various places within a program. When a procedure is executed, it returns the program control back to the calling point or calling code.

A large program is divided into a set of small and more manageable sections or parts called sub-procedures or subprograms. Each sub-procedure or subprogram performs a defined function while the combined action of sub-procedures or subprograms makes a complete program.

Why divide a program in procedures?

A single program may contain one or more tasks and sometime it may contains large amount of tasks and it reaches to hundreds or thousands of lines that is very difficult to read the entire program line by line. A very large program may also contain repeated tasks that increases the size of program and consumes the processor processing time because in this case processor executes the same repeated code again and again.

A large program is divided into small sections or parts (procedures) according to different tasks and functionality of the program codes. For example, if we write a program that needs to accept, calculate, and display data then it contains three different tasks. Therefore, we can divide this program into three small parts and create three sub-procedures or subprograms that accept, calculate, and display data respectively. Similarly, a database program contains different tasks such as insert new record, update record, delete record, search record, and display record etc. Each task of a database program is different and it needs a separate procedure. Therefore, a separate procedure is created for each task that insert, update, delete, search and display record respectively.

We can also divide a large program into small sections or parts (procedures) according to the repeating tasks for example, if we are writing a program and at some different locations the program needs to calculate the greatest number among three different numbers. Suppose, if a program needs this calculation at five different places and we write the code of this calculation in all the five places then we will repeat the same code. Therefore, a single procedure is declared that calculate the greatest number among three different numbers and it is invoked from anywhere in the program when needed.

Benefits of Procedures

Procedures have the following benefits:

- Procedures divide a large program into a set of small and more manageable sections or parts that make the program easy to read, understand and maintain.
- Procedures categorize a single program into more small sections or parts according to the repeating tasks that make the program size shorter and save the processor processing time as well as the programmer time.
- Procedures allow us to break a program into discrete logical units, each of which can be debugged more easily. For example, in a large program if any logical error occurs then it is very difficult to detect that error because when a program is executing, the compiler only detects syntactical errors and it does not detect logical errors of a program. To detect logical errors of a large program, the entire program is checked line by line but it is very difficult because sometime a program has large amount of tasks and it may contain hundreds or thousands of lines. Therefore, if we divide a large program into different procedures according to different tasks of a program code then we can easily find out the logical errors.
- All procedures can access and update the same global data anywhere in the program.
- When a procedure successfully executed, it always returns the program control to the calling point of program.
- We can invoke or call a single procedure from different places of a program and can execute one or more times.
- Procedures used in one program can act as building blocks for other programs, usually with little or no modification.

Parts of Procedures

A procedure has the following parts:

- Access Modifier
- Return Type
- Procedure Name
- Parameter List

Access Modifier

Access modifier specifies the access level of a procedure. Access level is a scope or limitation of a procedure that tells us whether a procedure can be invoked from a specified location in a program or not. The .NET provides different access modifiers such as public, private, protected, and internal. A procedure has one access modifier at a time. When a procedure is declared with public modifier, it can be accessed from anywhere in the program similarly, if a procedure is declared with private modifier, it cannot be accessed outside that block where it is declared, and if a procedure is declared with protected modifier then it can be accessed inside in that class, module, or structure where it is declared. A procedure is Public by default and it can be accessed from anywhere in a program.

Return Type

Return type indicates the return value of a procedure. When a procedure is invoked, the program control transfers to the body of that procedure and procedure starts execution. When a procedure is successfully executed, the program control returns back to the calling code or calling point of the program. It also returns a value to the calling code. The return value of a procedure depends on the procedure type.

Procedure Name

This part of a procedure indicates the name of a procedure. It is a user-defined name that should be meaningful according to the nature and functionality of the block of statements or code placed in the body of a procedure. For example, if a block of code is written that calculates the greatest value among three different integer numbers then the procedure name should be **GreatestValue** similarly, if a block of code is written that calculates the sum of two numbers then the procedure name should be **CalculateSum** etc.

Parameter List

This part of a procedure indicates the number of parameters that a procedure have. A parameter is a variable enclosed in parenthesis that holds and carry data or information from calling point to the procedure definition. Therefore, parameters are the way of communication between the procedure call and the procedure definition (procedure body). If a procedure takes more parameters then they are separated by using commas. Each parameter sends a single value at a time.

Types of Procedures

The type of procedures is based on programming languages. The different types of programming languages have different names for procedures. For example, in C# procedures are called methods and in Visual Basic procedures are called Functions and Subroutines. Following is the details of methods, functions, and subroutines:

- Methods
- Functions
- Subroutines

Methods

A method is a procedure used in C# programming language. It is a block of statements or code that is executed to perform a specific task. The block of statements or code is enclosed within curly braces {}. The first curly brace indicates the starting point of a method and the second curly brace indicates the ending point of a method. Each method has a user-defined name. A method can be invoked or called from anywhere in a program. When a method is invoked, the program control transfers to the method body and the method starts execution. When a method is executed, the program control returns back to the calling code. The calling code is a location from where the method is invoked. A single method can be called from different places in a program.

A method takes zero, one or more parameters. The parameters carry data from calling point to the method body. Each parameter is a variable, constant, or an expression. The parameters are enclosed within small parenthesis and they are separated by comma. Each parameter carries a single value at a time. If a method does not carry data or information then it has blank parenthesis without parameters. A method can return a single value to the calling point with the **return** statement. The return value of a method is normally a calculated value of the method. If a method does not return any value then its return type is declared void. To declare the return type of a method as a void a keyword **void** is used after the modifier and before the name of a method. The **return** statement is also used to terminate a method by force at any point during its execution. When a method is executing and if the program control reaches to the return statement then the method is terminated and return statement transfers the program control back to the calling point. The return value of a method needs a variable in the calling point of the program to catch the return value. The C# programming language only supports methods inside in the body of a class or a structure. The methods in C# always called member methods of a C# class or a structure. In C# we cannot declare methods outside body of a class or a structure. Following is the general declaration of methods in C# programming language:

Method Declaration in C#

[modifier] Return_value Method_name ([Parameter_list]);
{
……………………………………..
Block of Statements or body
……………………………………..
}

In the above declaration, the **[modifier]** indicates access level of a method. The **Return_value** indicates the return type of a method. It is a variable, constant or an expression. If a method does not return any value then its return type is void. The keyword void means nothing to return. The **Method_name** indicates the name of a method and the **Parameter_list** indicates the number of parameters that a method have.

Types of Methods in C#

The C# programming Language provides the following two types of methods:

- Static Methods
- Non-Static Methods

Static Methods

When we declare a method with the keyword static is called static method. A static method can be accessed using the name of the class without instance variable. A static method can be declared in both the static and in non-static classes. For example if we have a class XYZ and we declared a static method MyMethod in this class then we can directly access the method MyMethod using the class name XYZ without declaring instance variable of the class XYZ.

The main method of C# program is always static. Following is the programming example of static method:

Program # 1

Write a program that calls a static method

```
using System;

namespace ConsoleApplication1
{
class XYZ
  {
public static void MyMethod()
    {
      Console.WriteLine("Hello from Static Method");
    }
  }
  class Program
  {
    static void Main(string[] args)
      {
      XYZ.MyMethod();

      Console.ReadKey();
    }
  }
}
```

Non-Static Method

When a method is declared without the using of static keyword then it is called non-static method. A non-static method cannot be accessed directly without the instance variable of the class where it is declared.

Functions

A function is a procedure used in Visual Basic programming language. It is a block of statements or code that is executed to perform a specific task. The block of statements or code is enclosed within a set of **Function** and **End Function** declaration statements. The Function and End Function are the two keywords that indicate starting point and ending point of a Function respectively. Each Function has its own user defined name. A Function can be invoked or called from anywhere in a program. When a Function is invoked, the program control transfers to the Function body and the Function starts execution. When a Function is executed, the program control returns back to the calling code. The calling code is a location from where the Function is invoked. A single Function can be called from different places in a program.

A Function takes zero, one or more parameters. The parameters carry data from calling point to the Function body. Each parameter is a variable, constant, or an expression. The parameters are enclosed within small parenthesis and they are separated by comma. Each parameter carries a single value at a time. If a Function does not carry data or information then it has blank parenthesis without parameters. A Function can return a single value to the calling point with the **return** statement. The return value of a Function is normally a calculated value of the Function. If a Function does not return any value then its return type is declared void. To declare the return type of a Function as void, a keyword **void** is used after the modifier and before the name of a Function. The **return** statement is also used to terminate a Function by force at any point during its execution. When a Function is executing and if the program control reaches to the return statement then the Function is terminated and return statement transfers the program control back to the calling point. The return value of a function needs a variable in the calling point of program to catch the return value. Following is the general declaration of a Function:

Function Declaration in Visual Basic
[modifier] Function Function_name ([Parameter_list]) As Return_value …………………………………….. Block of Statements or body …………………………………….. End Function

In the above declaration, the [**modifier**] indicates access level of a Function. It is Public by default that can be called from anywhere in the program, the keyword **Function** indicates Function, and the [**Parameter_list**] indicates the number of parameters of a Function.

Subroutines

A subroutine is a procedure used in Visual Basic programming language that contains a block of statements or code and it is executed to perform a specific task. The block of statements is enclosed by the **Sub** and **End Sub** declaration statements. A subroutine can be invoked from anywhere in the program like a function. When a subroutine is invoked, the program control transfers to the subroutine body and subroutine starts execution. When a subroutine is executed, the program control returns back to the calling code. A subroutine takes zero, one or more parameters. The parameters carry data from calling point to the subroutine body. Each parameter is a variable, constant, or an expression. The parameters are enclosed within small parenthesis and they are separated by comma. Each parameter carries a single value at a time. When a subroutine is executed successfully and the program control reaches to the End Sub statement then it returns the program control back to the calling point. A subroutine is similar to a function but the main difference is that a subroutine cannot return any value to the calling point of the program. A subroutine cannot be defined in modules, classes, and structures. Following is the general declaration of subroutine procedure:

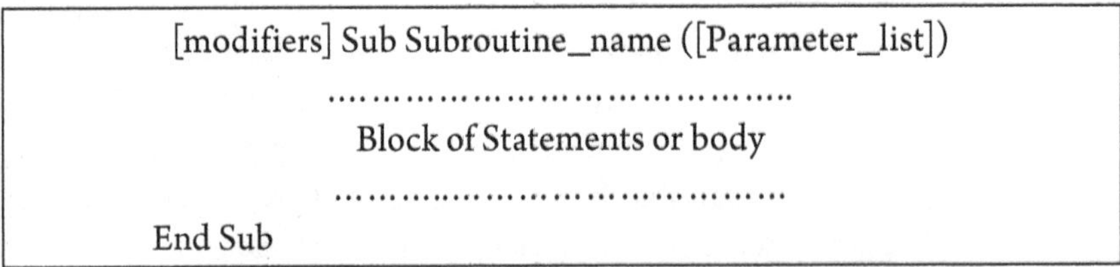

```
[modifiers] Sub Subroutine_name ([Parameter_list])
        ........................................
        Block of Statements or body
        ........................................
End Sub
```

In the above declaration, the [**modifier**] indicates access level of the subroutine procedure. A subroutine is public by default that can be called from anywhere in the program. The **Sub** is a keyword that indicates the subroutine procedure, the **Subroutine_name** is a user defined name of the subroutine procedure, and the [**Parameter_list**] indicates the number of parameters of subroutine. All the event handlers in Visual Basic are coded as subroutines procedures. The Visual Basic language also provides a facility to terminate a subroutine at any point before successfully execution by using a Visual Basic statement **Exit Sub**. The Exit Sub is a statement used to exit a subroutine at any point.

Naming Convention of Procedures

The following rules should be kept in the minds while declaring procedures (Methods, Functions, and Subroutines):

- In a program no two procedures have the same identical names.
- In a single program if two procedures have the same identical names then their parameters should be different.
- A procedure name always starts with an alphabetic letter or an underscore character and cannot start with any numeric value. After the first letter, the numeric values and additional underscore characters can be used.
- No special symbols other than an underscore can be allowed in a procedure name.
- The name of a procedure should be meaningful and short to the point. For example, if a procedure calculates the greatest value between the two integer values then the name of the procedure should be **greatest_Number()** etc.

Variables Scopes and Lifetime

A procedure can have multiple levels or scopes and it can be defined in three different locations in a program such as within classes, structures and modules. The level of a procedure depends on the definition. The data of a procedure also shows various levels or scopes. When a procedure is defined independently outside any other procedure then its variables and data are local to this procedure only and they cannot be used outside its body similarly, the variables and data of another procedure cannot be used inside in this procedure. When a procedure is defined inside another procedure then it is called inner procedure and the procedure where it is defined is called outer procedure. The outer procedure is called higher scope procedure and the inner procedure is called lower scope procedure. The higher scope procedure cannot access data of the lower scope procedure and the lower scope procedure can access the data of the higher scope procedure because the lower scope procedure is defined inside in the body of the higher scope procedure. Therefore, the variables and data of the higher scope procedure are global to the lower scope procedure.

Variables scope and life time

According to scope and life time variables are categorized into the following two types:

- Local Variables
- Global Variables

Local Variables

When a variable is declared inside any procedure or block then it is called local variable. The scope of a local variable is local to that procedure or block where it is declared. A local variable cannot be accessed outside that procedure or block where it is declared. When the program control transfers to a procedure or a block then all the local variables of that procedure or block become active and when the program control returns from body of the procedure or block then all the local variables of that procedure or block becomes undeclared and loss their values. Following is the programming example of Local Variables:

Program # 2

C# Program

```
using System;

namespace LocalVariables
{
class MainClass
{
static void Main(string[] args)
{
int x = 2; {
int y = 5;
Console.Write("The value of y = " + y);
Console.Write("\n");
}
Console.Write("The value of x = " + x);
Console.Write("\n");
//Call the method LocalVariablesTest()
LocalVariablesTest();
System.Console.Write("Press any key to exit program");
System.Console.ReadKey();
}

static void LocalVariablesTest()
{
int z = 3;
Console.Write("The value of z = "+ z);
```

```
Console.Write("\n");
z = z + 1;
}
}
}
```

The above program declared three integer variables x, y, and z. Variable x is declared inside in the main() method, variable y is declared in a separate block inside in the main() method, and variable z is declared inside in a separate method LocalVariablesTest(). Variable x is local to the main() method that can be accessed inside in the entire main() method, variable y is local to its block where it is declared and it cannot be accessed outside its local block even it cannot be accessed inside in the main() method outside its local block because variable y is declared inside in a separate block. Variable z is local to the method LocalVariablesTest() and it cannot be accessed outside it.

Global Variables

When a variable is declared outside all the procedures or blocks then it is called global variable. A global variable is normally declared at the top of the program outside all the procedures and blocks and it is visible to all the procedures and blocks. The lifetime of a global variable is throughout the program execution. When a program is executing, the global variables of that program are active and keep their last modified values. When a program is terminated, the global variables of that program are undeclared and lose their values. Following is the programming example of Global Variables:

Program # 3

C# Program

```
using System;

namespace LocalVariables
{

class MainClass
{
```

```
static int x = 5;

static void Main(string[] args)
{
Console.Write("The value of x = " + x);
Console.Write("\n");

//Call the method LocalVariablesTest()
LocalVariablesTest();
System.Console.Write("Press any key to exit program");
System.Console.ReadKey();
}

static void LocalVariablesTest()
{
Console.Write("The value of x = " + x);
Console.Write("\n");
}
}
}
```

The above program declared an integer variable x inside in the main class of the program outside all the methods. Therefore, it is global to all the methods and blocks inside in the main class because it is declared outside all the methods. Therefore, the scope of the variable x is global to all the methods and it can be accessed anywhere in the program.

CHAPTER 6

Object Oriented Programming in .NET

CHAPTER CONTENTS

- Object Oriented Programming
- Classes
- Private
- Public
- Protected
- Internal
- Internal Protected
- Declaration of Classes
- Features of Classes
- Constructors
- Default Constructor
- Parameterized Constructor
- Copy Constructor
- Static Constructor
- Destructors
- Objects
- Declaration of Objects
- Accessing Members of a Class
- Encapsulation / Data Hiding
- Inheritance
- Public Inheritance
- Protected Inheritance
- Private Inheritance
- Single Inheritance
- Hierarchical Inheritance
- Multilevel Inheritance
- Accessing Child Class Members using Base Class
- Accessibility
- Types of Classes
- Abstract Class

- Sealed Class
- Static Class
- Interface
- Polymorphism
- Static or Compile-time Polymorphism
- Dynamic or Runtime Polymorphism
- Methods Overloading
- Methods Overriding
- Virtual Method
- Method Hiding
- Operators Overloading
- The operator Method
- Types of Operators Overloading
- Unary Operators Overloading
- Binary Operators Overloading

Object Oriented Programming

Object oriented programming is programming methodology that allows us to define user-defined data types called object oriented data types. The object oriented data types are similar to ordinary data types but the main difference is that an ordinary data type is used to declare a variable that holds a single value of a specified data type for example, to store an integer value, an integer variable is declared similarly, to store a double value, a double type variable is declared and so on. On the other hand an object oriented data type is the combination of different ordinary data types and procedures or methods that is called class. A class is an object oriented data type that contains one or more ordinary variables and one or more procedures or methods. The ordinary variables of a class are called member data and methods of a class are called member methods. A class allows us to declare variables are called objects. When an object is declared from a class, all the member data and member methods of that class are inherited into the declared object. A single object of a class can access all the member data and member methods of the class at the same time.

Classes

A class is a user-defined data type and it is a blueprint or a user-defined template that is used to declare variables called objects. The fundamental concepts behind a class is that it combines two or more ordinary variables of the same or different types and two or more procedures or methods into a single entity and the whole class is represented by a single name. A single program can have one or more classes and in a single program each class has its own unique name. The name of a class is a user-defined name that follows the C# programming variables naming convention. Therefore, a class is a container that allows us to declare one or more ordinary variables of the same or different types and one or more procedures or methods. When ordinary variables and methods are declared in a class then they become members of that class. The ordinary variables of a class are called member data and methods of a class are called member methods. When members of a class are declared then they are combined into a single entity under a single name and become a data type that is called object oriented data type. A class allows us to declare variables called objects. When an object is declared from a class, all the member data and member methods of that class are inherited into the declared object. A single object of a class can access all the member data and member methods of that class at the same time. Each member of a class (member data and member method) has its own access level. The access level of a member is the accessibility level or scope that specifies how and where a member of a class will be used. The .NET provides different keywords called access modifiers or access specifiers. These keywords are used to define the access level or scope of the members of a class. Following is the details of access modifiers:

- Private
- Public
- Protected
- Internal
- Internal Protected

Private

When member of a class is declared as private then the scope of that member is local to the class where it is declared and it cannot be accessed outside from body of that class. The private members only can be accessed inside in a class where they are declared and they cannot be accessed outside from body of that class. By default all the members of a class are private. If we do not use any access modifier with a member data or member method then the accessibility level of that member will be private by default.

Public

The public Access Modifier is called global access modifier that provides a global scope to a class members. When a member of a class is declared as public then that member is accessible within all the classes of a program. Therefore, the scope of a public member is global for the entire program and it can be accessed anywhere in the program.

Protected

The protected access modifier is similar to private access modifier but the main difference is that when a member is declared as private, it cannot be accessed outside from that class where it is declared but when a member is declared as a protected then it can be accessed inside in the class where it is declared as well as in all its derived or child classes. Therefore, a protected member can be accessed inside in the local class as well as in all its derived or child classes but it cannot be accessed outside from the local class as well as from all its derived classes.

Internal

The Internal members of a class are visible within files in the same assembly for example if a class member is declared as internal then it can be accessed only inside in the same assembly.

Internal Protected

If a class member is declared as internal protected then it is visible within the containing assembly and in the descendent of the current class.

Declaration of Classes

The C# programming language provides a built-in keyword **class** that is used to declare classes. The class declaration always starts with the keyword **class** followed by a user-defined name of the class and a pair of curly braces. The first curly brace is the starting point of a class and the second curly brace is the ending point of a class. The user-defined name is a valid identifier that follows the C# variables naming convention. The body of a class is enclosed within the starting and ending curly braces. Following is the general declaration of a class:

```
<access-modifier> class <class-name>
{
//Member Data Declaration
<access-modifier> <data-type> variable-1;
<access-modifier> <data-type> variable-2;
……………………………………………….
……………………………………………….
<access- modifier > <data-type> variable-n;

//Member Methods Declaration
<access- modifier > <return-type> method-1(parameter-list)
{……….}
<access- modifier > <return-type> method-2(parameter-list)
{……….}
……………………………………………….
……………………………………………….
<access- modifier > <return-type> method-n(parameter-list)
{……….}
}
```

In the above declaration the **<class-name>** indicates a user-defined name of a class. The user-defined name of a class is a valid identifier that follows the variable naming convention of C# programming language. Each member of a class has its own access modifier that defines the access level or scope of a member. Following is an example of a simple class:

```
class ClassExample
{
//Declare the member data
private int x;
public double y;

//Declare a member Method
public void myMtd()
{
Console.WriteLine("Welcome to Object Oriented Programming");
}
}
```

The above declaration declares a class **ClassExample** that contains one member method myMtd() and two member data x and y. The first member data x is an integer variable and its access level is private, the second member data y is a double variable and its access level is public.

Features of Classes

The C# classes provide the following features:

- Constructor
- Destructor
- Objects
- Encapsulation / Data Hiding
- Inheritance
- Polymorphism
- Method Overloading
- Method Overriding
- Operator Overloading

Constructor

It is a member method of a class that has the same name as the class name. A constructor is used to declare and initialize the data members of a class. When an object of a class is declared, the constructor of that class invokes automatically and initializes all the member data. It is a member method of a class like ordinary method but the main difference is that a constructor is used to declare and initialize member data of a class and it does not return value. Therefore, the return type is not specified for a constructor. If we specify the return type then it generates an error. A constructor cannot be declared as a virtual or static and cannot be declared as a const, volatile, or const volatile. There are the following types of constructors:

- Default Constructor
- Parameterized Constructor
- Copy Constructor
- Static Constructor

Default Constructor

This type of constructor is also called parameter less constructor that has no parameters. The default constructor invokes automatically when a parameter less object of that class is declared. The default constructor is usually used to provide initial values to the class data members.

Parameterized Constructor

This type of constructor has one or more parameters and it invokes automatically when an object is declared with the same parameters list for example, if a constructor has one parameter then it will be invoked if an object is declared with one parameter similarly, if a constructor has two parameters then it will be invoked if an object is declared with two parameters and so on. Following is an example of the default and parameterized constructors:

```
Class ClassExample
{
public ClassExample ()
{
Console.WriteLine("Parameter less Constructor");
}
public ClassExample(int x)
{
Console.WriteLine("Parameterized Constructor");
}
}
```

The above declaration declares a class that contains two constructors. The first constructor is a parameter less or default constructor that has no parameters. The second constructor is a parameterized constructor that has one integer parameter. When a parameter less object is declared then the default or first constructor will be invoked and when an object is declared with one parameter then the second or parameterized constructor will be invoked.

Copy Constructor

This type of constructor is used to declare an object from an existing object of a class. The copy constructor makes a duplicate copy of an existing object and creates a new object of the same type and the same nature. To declare a new object from an existing object of a class, the existing object is passed to the parameter of the constructor of that class.

Static Constructor

A static constructor is used to initialize the class static members. It cannot be called explicitly with the new object but it is called when the class is first referenced. A static constructor has the following some limitations:

- A static constructor must be parameter-less.
- A static constructor can't be overloaded.
- A static constructor does not have any modifier.

In the following example, the Customer class has a static constructor that initializes the static member and it is called when the class is referenced in the Main () method:

Program # 1

Write a program that demonstrates the using of static constructor

```
using System;
namespace ProgramNamespace
{
class Customer
{
//Declare the class Member Variable
static private int x;
//Declare a Constructor to initialize the class static data member
static customer()
{
x = 10;
}

//Declare a method to display the value of the static data member
static public void DisplayInfo()
{
Console.WriteLine(x);
}
```

```
//Declare the Main method of the program
static void Main(string[] args)
{
//Call the method to display the value of the static data member
Customer.DisplayInfo();
}
}
}
```

Destructor

A destructor is a member method of a class that is invoked automatically when an object of a class is destroyed. It is usually used to release the previous allocated dynamic memory, release other resources previously allocated to a process, and release the database connections etc. The name of a destructor is the same as that of the class name with a prefix tilde symbol (~) and it neither returns a value nor takes any parameter. Following are some characteristics of a destructor:

- The name of a destructor is the same as that of the class name with a prefix tilde ~ symbol.
- A destructor does not take parameters unlike constructors.
- A destructor has no return type like a constructor.
- A single class has only a single destructor.
- A destructor cannot be overloaded because it does not take any parameters.

Program # 2

Write a program that demonstrates the using of destructor

```
using System;

namespace ClassExample
{
class DestructorExample
{
public DestructorExample()
{
Console.WriteLine("Welcome to OOP");
```

```
}

~DestructorExample()
{
Console.WriteLine("Object is being released");
}

class ProgramClass
{
static void Main(string[] args)
{
DestructorExample ObjDestDemo = new DestructorExample();

Console.ReadKey();
}
}
}
}
```

Objects

An object is a user-defined variable that is declared from a class. It is similar to ordinary variables but the main difference is that an ordinary variable can store a single value at a time and it is declared for a single type value while an object is a variable that bundled one or more ordinary variables and one or more methods and it is declared from a class. When an object is declared from a class then all the member data and member methods of that class are inherited into the declared object and a memory location is created for it. The memory location of an object represents the complete structure of a class in the memory. When two or more objects are declared from a class then for each object a separate memory location is created and each memory location represents the complete structure of a class. Therefore, an object is a source that is used to access the member data and member methods of a class. The class member data and member methods are always hidden from rest of the program and they cannot be accessed without an object of that class.

Declaration of Objects

When a class is declared, it becomes a user-defined data type and allows us to declare objects. An object can be declared from a class by using the name of a class followed by an object name or list of objects separated by commas. Following is the general declaration of an object:

<class-name> <object-name> = new <class-name>;

The **<class-name>** specifies the name of a class from which it is to be declared and **<object-name>** specifies the name of an object to be declared from a class. The object name is a user-defined name and it is a valid identifier that follows the C# language variables naming convention. When more objects are declared from a class, they are written in a list separated by comma. When an object is declared, a memory location is created for it in the memory. The memory location of an object represents the complete structure of a class and each member data of a class has its own separate memory location in it. Therefore, when a memory location is created for an object then that memory location is further divided according to the member data of a class.

Accessing members of a Class

The dot operator is used to access members of a class. The dot operator is used between the object name and the class member name. Following is the general syntax to access the class members:

<object-name>. <member-data>
<object-name>. <member-method>

In the above declaration, the **<object-name>** specifies the name of an object, the **<member-data>** specifies the member data of a class to be accessed, and **<member-method>** specifies the name of a member method to be accessed from a class. The dot operator links the object name with the class member name.

Program # 3

Write a program that demonstrates the using of default and parameterized constructors.

```
using System;

namespace ClassExample
```

```
{
class ConstExample
{

public ConstExample()
{
Console.WriteLine("Welcome to OOP");
}

public ConstExample(int x)
{
Console.WriteLine(x);
}

class ProgramClass
{
static void Main(string[] args)
{
ConstExample objConstDemo = new ConstExample();
ConstExample objConstDemo1 = new ConstExample(3);
Console.ReadKey();
}
}
}
}
```

The above program declares a class **ConstExample** that contains two constructors. The first constructor is a default constructor that does not take any parameter and the second constructor takes a single integer parameter. In the main method of the program two objects are declared ObjConstDemo and ObjConstDemo1. The first object is a parameter-less object that invokes the parameter-less constructor and the second object has a single parameter that invokes parameterized constructor ConstExample(int x) and displays the value of variable x.

Program # 4

Write a program that adds two integer values

```
using System;
namespace ClassExample
```

```
{
class AddValues
{
private int x, y;

//Declare a constructor that initialize the class member data
public AddValues()
{
x = 5;
y = 3;
}

//Display the sum of x and y
public void Display()
{
Console.WriteLine(x+y);
}

class ProgramClass
{
static void Main(string[] args)
{
AddValues objAddValues = new AddValues();

//Call the method Display
objAddValues.Display();
Console.ReadKey();
}
}
}
}
```

The above program declares a class **AddValues** that contains two member data or variables x and y, one parameter-less constructor and one member method Display(). The variables are initialized with the values 5 and 3 respectively by constructor of the class. The member method Display() is used to add and display the result of the variables x and y. In the main method of the program an object **objAddValues** is declared that invokes the member method Display().

Encapsulation/Data Hiding

This feature of a class describes the ability of an object to hide the data and methods from rest of the program. When an object is declared from a class, it bundled all the member data and member method of that class. The combination of member data and member method of a class into a single object is called data encapsulation or data hiding. The data of a class can be hidden by using **private** and **protected** access modifiers with the class member data and member method.

Inheritance

It is a process in which new classes are derived from the existing classes. The existing classes are called base classes, parent classes, or super classes and new classes are called derived classes, subclasses, or child classes. When a new class is derived from an existing class, all the members (member data and member method) of that class are inherited into the derived or child class. A child class can access the member data and member methods of the base or parent class. The accessibility of the parent class members depends on the access modifiers. Each member of a class is declared with a specific access modifier such as private, public, and protected. Each access modifier has its own scope and access level. When a new class is derived from an existing class, the derived or child class can access all the public and protected members of the parent class and cannot access the private members of the parent class. The private members are local to the class where they are declared and they cannot access outside from that class.

A new class can be derived from one or more existing classes. When a new class is derived from one existing class then this type of inheritance is called single inheritance and when a new class is derived from more than one existing classes then this type of inheritance is called multiple inheritance. When a new class is derived from an existing class then all the members (member data and member methods) of the existing class are inherited into the new or derived class except constructors, destructor, overloaded operators, and friend method of the existing class. The constructors, destructor, overloaded operators, and friend method of a base or parent class do not inherit into the derived or child class. To derive new classes from existing classes, the following general syntax is used:

class <child-class> : access-modifier <parent-class>

In the above declaration, the **<child-class>** specifies a derived or child class name, the **access-modifier** specifies an access modifier such as private, public, and protected, and **<parent-class>** specifies an existing class or base class name. A new class is derived from an existing class with an access-modifier. An access-modifier is used to control the access level of the existing or parent class members.

Types of Inheritance according to Access Level

When a new class is derived from an existing or parent class, an access modifier is used to control the access level or accessibility of the base or parent class members. Each access modifier performs restrictions on a child class or derived class. If an access modifier is not used then the private access modifier is used by default that does not inherit members of the base or parent class into the child or derived class. Following are the types of inheritance according to access level:

- Public Inheritance
- Protected Inheritance
- Private Inheritance

Public Inheritance

When a new class is derived from a public base or parent class, the public members of the base class becomes public members of the derived or child class, the protected members of the base class become protected members of the derived or child class, and private members of the base class do not inherit in the derived or child class. Following is the general declaration of public inheritance:

class <Derived-Class> : public <Base-Class>

Protected Inheritance

When a new class is derived from a protected base class, the public and protected members of the base class become protected members of the derived or child class and private members of the base class do not inherit in the derived or child class. Following is the general declaration of protected inheritance:

class <Derived-Class> : protected <Base-Class>

Private Inheritance

When a new class is derived from a private base class, the public and protected members of the base class become the private members of the derived or child class and private members do not inherit in the derived or child class. Following is the general declaration of private inheritance:

class <Derived-Class> : private <Base-Class>

Program # 5

Write a program that demonstrates inheritance.

```
using System;

namespace Inheritance
{
public class A
{
public void mtdA()
{
Console.WriteLine("Member Method of Class A");}
}

public class B : A
{
public void mtdB()
{
Console.WriteLine("Member Method of Class B");
}
}

class Program
{
static void Main(string[] args)
{
A Obj1 = new A();
B Obj2 = new B();

Obj1.mtdA();
```

```
Obj2.mtdA();
Obj2.mtdB();
Console.ReadKey();
}
}
}
```

The above program declared two classes A and B. Class A is parent or base class and class B is derived or child class and it is derived from class A. In the main method of program two objects obj1, and obj2 are declared. The first object obj1 is declared from class A and the second object obj2 is declared from class B. The object obj1 only can access the member method of class A i.e. mtdA() and cannot access the member method of class B i.e. mtdB(). The object obj2 can access the member method of class A as well as the member method of class B because class B is a child class of class A and the member method mtdA() is a public member method of class A and it is inherited in class B.

Types of Inheritance according to Hierarchy

When new classes are further derived from existing child classes then this process is called inheritance hierarchy. The inheritance hierarchy makes different levels of classes and it behaves like a tree. Each level can have one or more classes. The first level of classes is called base level or parent level and other levels are called child levels. The first child level is derived from the base level and it is called child level classes of the base level, the second child level is derived from the first child level and it is called child-child level classes of the base level, the third child level is derived from the second child level and it is called child-child-child level classes of the base level and on this way the new child classes can be derived from the last child level classes. On the basis of hierarchy, inheritance is divided into the following types:

- Single Inheritance
- Hierarchical Inheritance
- Multilevel Inheritance

Single Inheritance

When a new class is derived from a single existing class then this type of inheritance is called single inheritance. In single inheritance a child class has a single parent class. Following is the general declaration of single inheritance:

```
class child-class : access-modifier parent-class
```

Hierarchical Inheritance

When two or more new classes are derived from a single existing class then this type of inheritance is called hierarchical inheritance. In this type of inheritance a parent class has more than one child classes. Following is the general form of hierarchical inheritance:

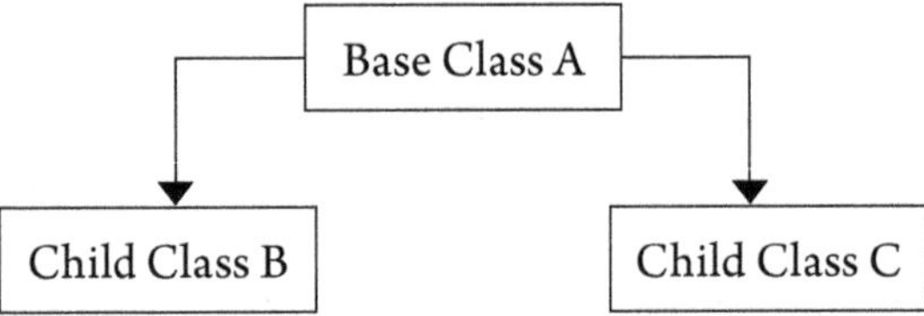

The above diagram contains three classes, A, B, and C. Class A is parent class and the other two classes B and C are child classes which are derived from class A.

Multilevel Inheritance

When a child class becomes parent of another class then this type of inheritance is called multilevel inheritance. Following is the general form of multilevel inheritance:

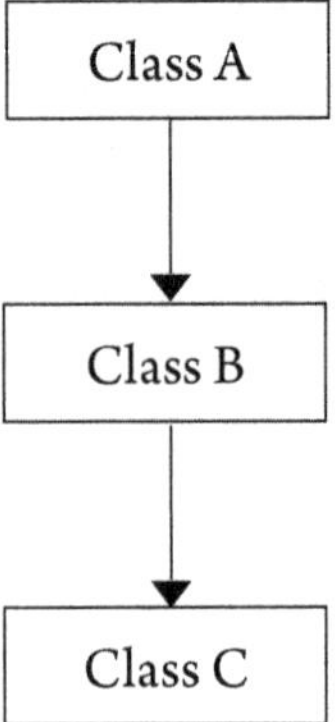

The above diagram contains three classes, A, B, and C. Class A is a parent class that has a child class B and child class B further has a child class C.

Accessing Child Class members using Base Class

The objects of the base class cannot access the members of the derived or child class because when a class is derived, all members of the base class inherit into the derived or child class but members of the derived or child class do not inherit into the base or parent class therefore, an object of the base class only can access a member method of a derived or child class that have the same name method with the base class and it is declared as a virtual in the base class.

Accessibility

Accessibility is a programming technique that is used to set the accessibility level of class members to outside assemblies or derived types. The following table describes the accessibility of class members:

Keyword	Description
Public	If a class member is declared as public then it is visible in the current assembly as well as in the referencing assembly. There is no accessibility restriction on public members.
private	If a class member is declared as private then it is visible only inside in the current class. The class members are private by default.
protected	If a class member is declared as protected then it is visible inside in the current class as well as in the inherited or derived classes.
Internal	If a class member is declared as internal then is visible only in the current project assembly.
Internal protected	If a class member is declared as Internal Protected then it is visible in the current assembly as well as in the inherited or derived classes.

Following is the programming example of private, public, and protected class members:

Program # 6

```
using System;
namespace ConsoleApplication1
```

```
{
class Parent
{
private int x;
public float y;
protected String z;
}
class Child : Parent
{
protected void VariablesInitialization()
{
x = 2;                          //Error because variable is private
y = 3.2f;                       //No error because it is public
z = "Object Oriented";          //No error because it is protected
}
}

class Program
{
static void Main(string[] args)
{
Child obj;
obj = new Child();

obj.VariablesInitialization();  //Error because it is protected
obj.x = 3;                      //Error because it is private
obj.y = 5.7f;                   //No error because it is public
obj.z = "Object Oriented";      //Error because it is protected
Console.ReadKey();
}
}
}
```

The above program declares three variables x, y, and z in the parent class. Variable x is integer and its accessibility level is private, variable y is float and its accessibility level is public, and variable z is String and its accessibility level is protected. In the child class these variables are initialized. Variable y and z are initialized successfully but variable x produces an error because the accessibility level of variable x is private and private members cannot be accessed outside from a class where it is declared. In the main method of the program an object is declared from the child class and accessed variable x, y, z and child class method VariablesInitialization(). The child class object successfully accessed only variable y because variable y is public and public member is accessible anywhere in the program, variable x is private and a private member cannot be accessed outside from a class where it is declared, variable z and method VariablesInitialization() are protected and protected members cannot be accessed outside from the inherited classes.

Types of Classes

Following are different types of classes:

- Abstract Class
- Sealed Class
- Static Class

Abstract Class

An abstract class is a general class that provides a complete prototype of a class but it does not allow us to create its objects. It is declared with a keyword abstract. An abstract class contains member methods and they are declared with abstract keyword. The member methods of an abstract class are called abstract member methods. An abstract member method can contain signatures but it cannot contain body or implementation. The declaration of an abstract member method contains method name and signatures followed by semicolon without body block and it must be overridden in any non-abstract derived class. Therefore, an abstract class is a class that is declared as a base class for inheritance and it must be inherited by declaring derived or child classes. The derived or child classes must implement all the abstract methods of an abstract class. Following is the programming example of abstract class:

Program # 7

```
using System;
namespace InheritanceExample
{
public abstract class MyAbstractClass
```

```
{
public abstract void MyAbstractMethod();
}
public class AbstractImplement : MyAbstractClass
{
public override void MyAbstractMethod()
{
Console.WriteLine("Abstract class method");
}
}
class ProgramClass
{
static void Main(string[] args)
{
AbstractImplement obj = new AbstractImplement();
obj.MyAbstractMethod();
Console.ReadKey();
}
}
}
```

In the above program we declared an abstract class MyAbstractClass with an abstract method MyAbstractMethod() that does not have implementation here in the abstract class but it is implemented in the derived class AbstractImplement.

Sealed Class

It is a class which is declared with the keyword sealed. A sealed class is declared to define the inheritance level of a class. The keyword sealed makes a class fixed and prevents it from further derivation. A sealed class can be a derived or child class of another class but it cannot be a base or parent class of another class. A sealed class cannot be marked as an abstract class.

Static Class

When a class is declared with a keyword static is called static class. The static keyword is usually used with the declaration of variables, objects, methods, and classes. When a variable is declared with a static keyword is called static variable, when a method is declared with a static keyword is called static method, and when a class is declared with a static keyword is called static class. When we declare a static class then it cannot be instantiated and we cannot declare instance variables from it. A static class is usually the same as non-static class but the main difference is that a static class has no constructors and we cannot declare instance variables from it. A static class has no constructors and compiler does not create a parameter less constructor by default. A static class only contains static members and it does not contain non-static members. The members of a static class can be accessed using the class name itself without instance variables. The static classes are totally abstract but we cannot use the abstract modifier with static classes. The static classes only can be inherited from Object class and they cannot be inherited from any other classes because they are abstract and sealed.

Interface

An interface is similar to classes but it has no implementation. It can contain member methods, properties, events, or indexer. The members of an interface contains only the declaration without implementation and they just provide prototypes or signatures details. The members of an interface are implicitly public and abstract and they must be implemented in the derived or inherited classes. Interfaces are used to implement multiple inheritance because C# does not provide multiple inheritance directly. Following is the difference between interfaces and abstract classes:

- An Interface cannot contain any implementation but an Abstract class can contain some implementations.
- An Interface can only inherit other Interfaces but Abstract classes can inherit from other classes as well as from Interfaces.
- An Interface cannot contain Constructors and Destructor but an Abstract class can contain Constructors and Destructors.
- An Interface don not contain fields but an Abstract class contains fields.

The best option between abstract classes and interfaces is interfaces because the derived or child classes of an Interface can also be inherited from another type and interfaces are easier as compared to abstract classes. Following is the programming example of an Interface:

Program # 8

```
using System;

namespace ConsoleApplication1
{
//Interface declaration
public interface xyz
{
void methodA();
void methodB();
}
//Interface implementation
class test : xyz
{
public void methodA()
{
Console.WriteLine("methodA");
}
public void methodB()
{
Console.WriteLine("methodB");
}
}
class program
{
static void Main(string[] args)
{
test obj = new test();
obj.methodA();
obj.methodB();

Console.ReadKey();
}
}
}
```

The following programming example demonstrates, how to inherit an Interface from other Interfaces:

Program # 9

```
using System;
namespace ConsoleApplication1
{
// Interface declaration
public interface xyz
{
void methodA();
void methodB();
}
//Child Interface inherited from Interface xyz
public interface abc : xyz
{
void methodC();
}

//Interface implementation
class test : xyz
{
public void methodA()
{
Console.WriteLine("methodA");
}
public void methodB()
{
Console.WriteLine("methodB");
}
public void methodC()
{
Console.WriteLine("methodC");
}
}
class program
{
static void Main(string[] args)
{
test obj = new test();
obj.methodA();
```

```
obj.methodB();
obj.methodC();
Console.ReadKey();
}
}
}
```

Polymorphism

Polymorphism is a programming technique in which a single thing has multiple forms or multiple shapes for example a variable, a method, an object, or an operator etc. In polymorphism a single object has many forms or shapes and it performs multiple operations for example in case of inheritance when the base or parent class reference is used to refer to a child class object similarly, a single method behaves differently in multiple forms such as in case of method overloading or method overriding. In polymorphism an operator is also used to perform different operations such as in case of operator overloading in which the natural functionality of an operator is changed and it is used for other purpose or task. For example, the natural functionality of the plus + operator is addition, the natural functionality of the minus – operator is subtraction and the natural functionality of the equal = operator is equality of the two values. When the natural functionality of an operator is changed and it is used for another purpose then this process is called operator overloading. Polymorphism is achieved by different techniques such as method overloading, operator overloading, and method overriding. Polymorphism has the following two types:

- Static or Compile-time Polymorphism
- Dynamic or Runtime Polymorphism

Static or Compile-time Polymorphism

In this type of polymorphism the decision is made at the compile-time. The example of this type of polymorphism is method overloading. The method overloading is a concept where a class can have more than one method with the same name and different parameters. In Static or Compile-time polymorphism the compiler knows which overloaded method is to be called. The compiler checks the type and the number of parameters passed to the method and decides which method is to be called at compile-time. This type of polymorphism is also called early binding.

Dynamic or Run-time Polymorphism

In this type of polymorphism the decision is made at run-time. The example of this type of polymorphism is method overriding. Method overriding allows us to have methods in the base and in the derived classes with the same name and the same parameters. This type of polymorphism can point to any derived class from the base class object at runtime that shows the ability of runtime binding or late binding. Following is the example of run-time Polymorphism:

Program # 10

Write a program that demonstrates Run-time Polymorphism

```
using System;
class Parent
{
public void Show()
{
Console.WriteLine("Parent.Show() method ");
}
}
class Child : Parent
{
public void Show()
{
Console.WriteLine("Child.Show() method");
}
}
class OverridingExample
{
static void Main()
{
Parent var; //Declare a reference of the Parent class
var = new Parent();
var.Show();
var = new Child();
```

```
var.Show();
}
}
```

In the above program var is a reference variable of the Patent class that has two statuses either refer to the object of the Parent class or object of the Child class therefore, this dual nature of the variable is called run-time polymorphism.

Method Overloading

When two or more methods with the same name and different parameters are used then this process is called method overloading. Following is the programming example of Method Overloading:

Program # 11

Write a program that demonstrates method overloading.

```
using System;

namespace ConsoleApplication1
{
public class MethodOverloading
{
public void Addition(float x, float y)
{
float result = x + y;
Console.WriteLine("Add two Float values = "+ result);
}
public void Addition(int x, int y)
{
int result = x + y;
Console.WriteLine("Add two Integer values = "+ result);
}
}
class ProgramClass
{
static void Main(string[] args)
```

```
{
MethodOverloading obj = new MethodOverloading();
obj.Addition(2.5f, 3.8f);
obj.Addition(3, 7);
Console.ReadKey();
}
}
}
```

Method Overriding

When the same name and the same signatures member methods are declared in both the parent and a child class then the member method of the child class always overrides the member method of the base class and an object of the child class only can access the member method of the child class and ignores the same name member method of the parent class. For example, if we have two classes A and B in which class A is parent and class B is child class and a same name method with the same parameters is declared in both the classes A and B. Now if we declare an object from the child class B, the member method of the child class B will be invoked and the same name member method in the parent class A will be overridden and cannot not be accessed using the object of the child class B similarly, if we declare an object from the parent class A then it can access the member method of class A and cannot access the member methods of the child class B. This feature is called method overriding. Method overriding is achieved by using two keywords virtual and override. The virtual keyword is used with a member method of the base class and the override keyword is used with a member method of the child class. Consider the following programming example:

Program # 12

```
using System;
class Parent
{
public virtual void Show()
{
Console.WriteLine("Parent.Show() method ");
}
}
```

```
class Child : Parent
{
public override void Show()
{
Console.WriteLine("Child.Show() method");
}
}
class OverridingExample
{
static void Main()
{
Child obj;
obj = new Child();
obj.Show();
}
}
```

Virtual Keyword

The virtual keyword is used to modify a method, property, indexer, or an event declaration and allow it to be overridden in a derived class.

Virtual Method

A member method of a class that is overridden in a derived class is called virtual method. A virtual method is usually declared in the base or parent class with a keyword virtual. The idea behind a virtual method is to redefine the implementation of the base class method in the derived class as required. If a method is virtual in the base class, it needs the override keyword in the derived class. By default all the member methods of a class are non-virtual. The non-virtual methods cannot be overridden. The virtual keyword cannot be used with the static, abstract, private or override modifiers. In Java programming language all the member methods of a class are virtual by default unless we use the final keyword. The final keyword is used to prevent a method from overriding. The C# programming language uses the strategy of C++ programming language where all the member methods are not virtual by default but we use the virtual keyword with a method if we want to override it in the derived classes.

Methods Hiding

If a method with the same name and same signature is declared in both the base and child classes and the virtual and override keywords are not used then the derived class version of that method hides the base class version. Usually we override methods rather than hide them. If we do not use the virtual and override keywords with the same name methods in inheritance classes then the .NET gives warning message that the child class method hides the inherited member method of the base class.

Operator Overloading

Operator overloading is a mechanism which is used to change the natural implementation or functionality of an operator and use an operator for other user-defined purpose or task. The .NET Framework provides various types of operators which have pre-defined implementation or functionality. Each operator has its own implementation and each operator is used for a specific purpose or task. For example, the plus + operator is used to add two numeric values, the minus – operator is used to subtract two numeric values, the equal = operator is used for the equality of two values, and the operators ++ and -- are used to increment and decrement a numeric variable by 1 respectively, the operators (==, >=, <=, !=, >, <) are called relational operators and they are used for comparison. All these implementations of operators are the natural implementations or functionalities of operators. When these natural implementations or functionalities of operators are changed and they are used for other purposes is called operator overloading. Following is the list of operators that shows which operator can be overloaded and which operator cannot be overloaded:

<table>
<tr><th>Operator</th><th>Description</th><th>Overloaded</th></tr>
<tr><td>+, -, !, ~, ++, --, true, false</td><td>Unary</td><td>Yes</td></tr>
<tr><td>+, -, *, /, %, &, |, ^, <<, >></td><td>Binary</td><td>Yes</td></tr>
<tr><td>==, !=, <, >, <=, >=</td><td>Relational Operators</td><td>Yes</td></tr>
<tr><td>|, &, ^, >>, <<</td><td>Bitwise Operators</td><td>Yes</td></tr>
<tr><td>+=, -=, *=, /=, %=, &=, |=, ^=, <<=, >>=</td><td>Compound Assignment Operators</td><td>No</td></tr>
<tr><td>&&, ||</td><td>Logical Operators</td><td>No</td></tr>
</table>

=, ?:	Equal and Conditional operators	No
typeof, sizeof	typeof and sizeof operators	No
[]	Array index operator	No
new, is, as	Operators	No
()	Conversion operator	No

The operator Method

The operator method is a built-in method or function that is used to overload operators. This method is used to overload operators in C# and VB.NET. The operator method contains a keyword operator, return type and a list of parameters. It is declared in a class and it is used as a member method of the class like other member methods. It has a return type and takes parameters. It is used to overload both the unary and binary operators. The operator which is to be overloaded is placed between the operator keyword and the parameters list of the operator method. Following is the general declaration of the operator method or operator function:

C# Declaration
public static Return_type operator Operator_Symbol (Parameters)
VB.NET Declaration
Public Shared Operator Operator_Symbol (Parameters) As Return_type

In the above declaration, the **Return_type** indicates return type of the operator method, the **operator** is a keyword, the **Operator_Symbol** indicates a symbol of an operator to be overloaded, and the **Parameters** indicates the list of parameters to be passed to the operator method. The operator method can be called or invoked using an object of the enclosing class. The operator method must be public and static.

Types of Operators Overloading

The operator overloading is divided into the following two types:

- Unary Operators Overloading
- Binary Operators Overloading

Unary Operators Overloading

When an operator is used with a single operand is called unary operator. A unary operator is used with a single operand either left side or right side. When it is used with the left side of an operand is called prefix unary operator and when it is used with the right side of an operand is called postfix unary operator. Following are the examples of unary operators:

+x, -x, ++x, --x, x++, x--

To overload unary operators, the operator method is declared with a single parameter. The parameter of the operator method must be the same type as that of the enclosing class. The following programming example demonstrates the unary operator overloading:

Program # 13

Write a program that overloads the unary plus + operator

```
using System;
namespace ConsoleApplication1
{
class unaryOpt
{
int x;
public unaryOpt(int a)
{
x = a;
}
public void display()
{
Console.WriteLine(x);
}
public static unaryOpt operator +(unaryOpt x1)
{
x1.x = +x1.x;
return x1;
}
}
class program
```

```
{
public static void Main()
{
unaryOpt obj1 = new unaryOpt(10);
obj1.display();

Console.ReadKey();
}
}
}
```

The above program displays the output 10

Program # 14

Write a program that overloads the unary plus + operator with increment by 1

```
using System;
namespace ConsoleApplication1
{
class unaryOpt
{
int x;

public unaryOpt(int a)
{
x = a;
}
public void display()
{
Console.WriteLine(x);
}
public static unaryOpt operator +(unaryOpt x1)
{
x1.x = ++x1.x;
return x1;
}
}
class program
```

```
{
public static void Main()
{
unaryOpt obj1 = new unaryOpt(10);
obj1.display();

unaryOpt obj2 = +obj1;
obj2.display();

unaryOpt obj3 = +obj2;
obj3.display();

Console.ReadKey();
}
}
}
```

The above program displays the output 10, 11, 12

Binary Operators Overloading

When an operator is used with two operands is called binary operator. A binary operator is always used between the two operands, one on each side of the operator. Following are the examples of binary operators:

x + y, x – y, x * y, x / y, x == y, x >= y, x <= y, x += y

To overload binary operators, the operator method is declared with two parameters. The type of the first parameter must be the same as that of the enclosing class and type of the second parameter can be of any type. The following programming example demonstrates the binary operator overloading:

Write a program that overload the binary plus + operator

```
sing System;

namespace ConsoleApplication1
{
class equation
```

```
{
int x,y;
upublic equation()

{
}
public equation(int x1, int y1)
{
x = x1;
y = y1;
}
public static equation operator +(equation obj1, equation obj2)
{
equation obj3 = new equation();
obj3.x = obj1.x + obj2.x;
obj3.y = obj1.y + obj2.y;
return obj3;
}
public void show()
{
Console.Write(x + "x");
Console.Write("+");
Console.Write(y + "y");
Console.WriteLine();
}
}
class program
{
public static void Main()
{
equation x, y, z;
x = new equation(3, 2);
y = new equation(4, 1);
z = x + y;
Console.Write("x = ");
x.show();
Console.Write("y = ");
y.show();
```

```
Console.Write("z = ");
z.show();

Console.ReadKey();
}
}
}
```

The above program adds two equations using binary plus operator overloading. The object obj1 reads the first equation value i.e. the value of x and y and object obj2 reads the second equation value i.e. the value of x and y. The operator member method adds the first equation with the second equation and returns the resultant equation to the object obj3 by using the following statement:

obj3 = obj1 + obj2;

In the above statement obj1 is added with obj2 and result is assigned to obj3. When this statement is executed, it calls the operator member method that overloads the plus operator. The operator member method adds two given equations and returns the resultant equation to object obj3. The object obj1 contains the first equation, the object obj2 contains the second equation and object obj3 contains the resultant equation of obj1 and obj2.

CHAPTER 7

Characters, Strings, String Classes and Date/ Time handling in .NET

CHAPTER CONTENTS

- Introduction to Characters
- Characters Encoding
- ASCII Codes System
- Non-printable ASCII Characters Table
- Printable ASCII Characters Table
- Introduction to Strings
- String Class in .NET
- Constructors of String Class
- Properties of String Class
- Length Property
- Chars Property
- Methods of String Class
- Copy Method
- CopyTo Method
- Join Method
- Split Method
- Insert Method
- Remove Method
- Replace Method
- Composite Formatting Feature
- Format Method
- PadRight and PadLeft Methods
- ToLower and ToUpper Methods
- Trim Method
- TrimStart and TrimEnd Methods
- Clone Method
- StartsWith and EndsWith Methods
- IndexOf Method
- LastIndexOf Method

- ToString Method
- ToCharArray Method
- SubString Method
- Contains Method
- Equals Method
- GetType Method
- IsNullOrEmpty Method
- IsNullOrWhiteSpace Method
- Drawbacks of String Class
- StringBuilder Class

Introduction to Characters

In computer technology a character is a unit of information that roughly contains a grapheme. A grapheme is the set of units of a writing system (a letter or combination of letters) that represents a phoneme such as an alphabet or a symbol in the written form of a natural language. Furthermore, a character is a letter, number, space, punctuation mark, or a symbol used in writing, printing or typed on a computer for example, English alphabets capital letters from A to Z or small letters from a to z, numerical digits from 0 to 9, punctuation marks such as ".", "{}", "[]", "!", "?", "\", "/", "-", etc and whitespaces.

Each character requires one byte or eight bits of memory space for example if we store a single character in a computer memory, it requires one byte or eight bits of memory space such as the word "science" consists of seven characters so it takes 7 bytes of memory space. The list of characters that can be typed is defined by the ASCII set of characters.

Characters Encoding

It is a process that converts a sequence of characters into some other format. This process consists of different specified codes used to pair each character from a given form such as from letter, number, word, phrase, or gesture to another specialized form in order to facilitate the transmission of data through telecommunication networks or storage of text in computers. There are different encoding systems are used to encode characters. The common and important encoding system is ASCII codes system.

ASCII Codes System

The word ASCII stands for American Standard Code for Information Interchange. It is a characters encoding system that represents characters in numerical form or it is the numerical representation of characters. The ASCII codes system is used to represent text in computers and in other telecommunication devices that use text. According to the ASCII codes system each and every character (letter, number, and punctuation symbol) has a corresponding numeric value that is called ASCII code. The ASCII codes system consists of 128 ASCII codes or numeric values from 0 to 127 decimal. The first 32 from 0 to 31 and the last numeric value 127 represent non-printing control characters that effect how text and space is processed, and the remaining 95 ASCII codes or numeric values from 32 to 126 represent printable characters. For example according to this system the English capital letter 'A' has numeric value 65, the small English letter 'a' has numeric value 97, and number 0 has numeric value 48, the Delete key has numeric value 127 and so on. Following is the complete tables of non-printable and printable ASCII codes:

Non-printable ASCII Characters Table

ASCII Code	Non-printable Character	Description
0	NUL	Null Character
1	SOH	Start of Header
2	STX	Start of Text
3	ETX	End of Text
4	EOT	End of Transmission
5	ENQ	Enquiry
6	ACK	Acknowledgment
7	BEL	Bell
8	BS	Backspace
9	HT	Horizontal Tab
10	LF	Line Feed
11	VT	Vertical Tab
12	FF	Form Feed

13	CR	Carriage Return
14	SO	Shift Out
15	SI	Shift In
16	DLE	Data link Escape
17	DC1	Device Control1
18	DC2	Device Control2
19	DC3	Device Control3
20	DC4	Device Control4
21	NAK	Negative Acknowledgment
22	SYN	Synchronous Idle
23	ETB	End of Transmission Block
24	CAN	Cancel
25	EM	End of Medium
26	SUB	Substitute
27	ESC	Escape
28	FS	File Separator
29	GS	Group Separator
30	RS	Record Separator
31	US	Unit Separator
127	DEL	DEL

Printable ASCII Characters Table

ASCII Code	Keyboard Character	ASCII Code	Keyboard Character
32	Spacebar	33	!
34		35	#
36	$	37	%
38	&	39	
40	(	41	)
42	*	43	+

44	,	45	-
46	.	47	/
48	0	49	1
50	2	51	3
52	4	53	5
54	6	55	7
56	8	57	9
58	:	59	;
60	<	61	=
62	>	63	?
64	@	65	A
66	B	67	C
68	D	69	E
70	F	71	G
72	H	73	I
74	J	75	K
76	L	77	M
78	N	79	O
80	P	81	Q
82	R	83	S
84	T	85	U
86	V	87	W
88	X	89	Y
90	Z	91	[
92	\	93	]
94	^	95	_
96	`	97	a
98	b	99	c
100	d	101	e
102	f	103	g

104	h	105	i
106	j	107	k
108	l	109	m
110	n	111	o
112	p	113	q
114	r	115	s
116	t	117	u
118	v	119	w
120	x	121	y
122	z	123	{
124	|	125	}
126	~		

Introduction to Strings

A string is a finite sequential collection of Unicode characters. It is typically used to represent Text. Each Unicode character in a string is defined by a Unicode scalar value also called Unicode code point or numeric value of Unicode character. Each code point is encoded using UTF-16 encoding and the numeric value of each element of the encoding is represented by a **Char**. The collection of **Char** objects forms a string. A single **Char** usually represents a single code point and numeric value of the Char equals to code point. A string is generally a data type in various programming languages and is often implemented as a byte or word array that stores a sequence of elements. Each element of an array is the collection of characters. A string may also denote more general array data types and other sequential data types and structures.

When a string is created, its value is always fixed and it cannot be modified, therefore it is called static string. Different methods are used to modify a string. The Methods that appear to modify a String return a new String containing the modification. The .NET framework class library provides a special class that is used to perform different operations on strings. This class is called **String** Class. The String Class provides different methods for string modification. In object-oriented programming languages string methods are often implemented as properties and methods of string objects. In functional and list-based programming languages a string is represented as a list of character codes, therefore all list-manipulation procedures could be considered string methods. However such programming languages may implement a subset of explicit string-specific methods as well. A String characters can be accessed using the index position of a **Char**. An index is a non negative numeric value starting from the first position in the string that is always zero.

String Class in .NET

String class is used to represent a string in a series of Unicode characters. It provides different constructors, properties and methods. Constructors are used to declare and initialize string instances. The methods of string class are used to perform different operations on strings such as to compare two strings, to search a specified single character or a substring in a string, to replace a single character or a specified set of characters in a string with new characters, to remove a single character or a specified set of characters from a string, to insert new characters in a string, to convert a string from upper case into lowercase and from lowercase into upper case, to concatenate one or more strings with each other etc. When an instance of string class is declared and it is initialized with a string value then the value is called immutable value. The immutable value means read-only or fixed value, therefore when an instance of string class is initialized with a string value, it cannot be changed or updated but it is always the same. The methods of the string class do not modify the current instance of a string but they create a new instance of the string class and return the modified values to the new instance of the string for example, if a specified set of characters are replaced in the current instance of a string with a new specified set of characters or a substring using the string class method, it creates a new instance of the string class and returns the modified value of the current instance of the string class to the newly created instance of the string similarly, if a specified single character or a set of characters are removed from current instance of the string class using the string class method, it creates a new instance of the string class and returns the modified value to the newly created instance of the string class and value of the current instance of the string class is remain the same.

Constructor of String Class

Constructor of a class is used to declare and initialize the class instances. String class provides an overloaded list of constructors. Each overloaded form of string class constructor is used to declare and initialize instances of the string class in different way. Following is the details of some important overloaded forms of string class constructor supported by the .NET Framework:

- String(Char[])
- String(Char, Int32)
- String(Char[], Int32, Int32)

String(Char[])

This constructor is used to declare and initialize a new instance of the string class from an array of Unicode characters. It takes a single parameter of characters type array. To create an instance of the string class using this constructor, an array of characters is declared and it is assigned to this constructor as parameter. When a character array is assigned to this constructor as parameters, it create a new instance of the string class and copies all the characters from characters array into the new instance of the string class. Following is its general declaration:

C# Declaration
public String(char[] charactersArray)
Visual Basic.NET Declaration
Public Sub New (charactersArray As Char())

In the above declaration, the parameter **charactersArray** indicates characters array. Following is the programming example of this constructor:

Program # 1

Write a program that declares and initializes a new instance of the String Class from a specified Unicode characters array.

C# Program

```
using System;

namespace MyNamespace
{
class MyProgramClass
{
static void Main(string[] args)
{
```

```
//Declare an array of characters
char[] charactersArray = {'A', 'D', 'A', 'L', 'A', 'T'};

//Declare and initialize a new string from characters array
String myString = new String(charactersArray);

//Display the new created string
Console.WriteLine("The new String is = " + myString);

Console.WriteLine("Press any key to exit program");
Console.ReadKey();
}
}
}
```

VB.NET Program

```
Module Module1
Sub Main()

'Declare an array of characters
Dim charactersArray As Char() = {"A", "D", "A", "L", "A", "T"}

'Declare and initialize a new string from characters array
Dim myString As String = New String(charactersArray)

'Display the new created string
Console.WriteLine("The new String is = " + myString)

Console.WriteLine("Press any key to exit program")
Console.ReadKey()
End Sub
End Module
```

The above program declares and initializes a new instance of the string class from a specified array of Unicode characters that contains six characters such as (A, D, A, L, A, T) and assigned it to the string class constructor String(charactersArray) as parameter. The string class constructor then joins the entire characters of array and declares a new instance of the string class and initializes it with the string value ADALAT.

String(Char, Int32)

This constructor is used to declare and initialize a new instance of the string class from a single specified Unicode character that is repeated zero, one, or more specified number of times. It takes two parameters. The first parameter is a Char type parameter that indicates a specified single Unicode character, the second parameter is an Int32 type parameter that indicates number of repetition of the character to be repeated. Following is its general declaration:

C# Declaration
public String(char singleCharcter, int count)
VB.NET Declaration
Public Sub New (singleCharacter As Char, count As Integer)

In the above declaration, the first parameter **singleCharacter** indicates a single Unicode character and second parameter **count** indicates the number of times we want to repeat a specified single Unicode character that is specified in the first parameter. Following is the programming example of this type of constructor:

Program # 2

Write a program that declares and initializes a new instance of the String Class from a specified single Unicode character and repeats it five times.

C# Program

```
using System;
namespace MyNamespace
{
class MyProgramClass
{
static void Main(string[] args)
{
//Declare a single character
char singleCharacter = 'A';

//Declare and initialize a new string from single character
String myString = new String(singleCharacter, 5);
```

```
//Display the new created string Console.WriteLine("The new String is =
" + myString);

Console.WriteLine("Press any key to exit program");
Console.ReadKey();
}
}
}
```

VB.NET Program

```
Module Module1
Sub Main()

'Declare a single character
Dim singleCharacter As Char = "A"
'Declare and initialize a new string from single character
Dim myString As String = New String(singleCharacter, 5)

'Display the new created string
Console.WriteLine("The new String is = " + myString)

Console.WriteLine("Press any key to exit program")
Console.ReadKey()
End Sub
End Module
```

The above program declares and initializes a new instance of the string class from a specified single Unicode character and it is repeated five times. The character is 'A' and it is repeated five times then the output string is AAAAA.

String(Char[], Int32, Int32)

This constructor is used to declare and initialize a new instance of the string class from a specified array of Unicode characters between the two index positions. This constructor is same as the first constructor String(Char[]) but the main difference is that the first constructor String(Char[]) declares and initializes a new instance of the string class from the entire elements of a specified characters array and this constructor declares and initializes a new instance of the string class from specified elements between the two index positions of characters array. This constructor takes three parameters. The first parameter is an array of Unicode characters, the second parameter is an integer value that indicates the start index position from which we want to start, and third parameter is an integer parameter that indicates the length or the number of characters we want to copy from characters array. Following is its general declaration:

C# Declaration
public String(char[] charactersArray, int startIndex, int length)
VB.NET Declaration
Public Sub New (charactersArray As Char(), startIndex As Integer, length As Integer)

In the above declaration of constructor, the first parameter **charactersArray** indicates an array of Unicode characters, the second parameter **startIndex** is an integer type parameter that indicates the starting index position of characters array from which we want to start the copy operation of characters, and third parameter **length** is an integer type parameter that indicates the length or the number of characters we want to copy from characters array to the new instance of the string class. Following is the programming example of this type of constructor:

Program # 3

Write a program that declares and initializes a new instance of the String class from an array of Unicode characters between the two specified index positions.
C# Program

```
using System;

namespace MyNamespace
{
class MyProgramClass
{
```

```
static void Main(string[] args)
{
//Declare an array of characters
char[] charactersArray = {'A', 'D', 'A', 'L', 'A', 'T'};

//Declare and initialize a new string from characters array
String myString = new String(charactersArray, 2, 3);
//Display the new created string
Console.WriteLine("The new String is = " + myString);

Console.WriteLine("Press any key to exit program");
Console.ReadKey();
}
}
}
```

VB.NET Program

```
Module Module1
Sub Main()

'Declare an array of characters
Dim charactersArray As Char() = {"A", "D", "A", "L", "A", "T"}

'Declare and initialize a new string from characters array
Dim myString As String = New String(charactersArray, 2, 3)

'Display the new created string
Console.WriteLine("The new String is = " + myString)

Console.WriteLine("Press any key to exit program")
Console.ReadKey()
End Sub
End Module
```

The above program declares an array of characters charactersArray that contains six characters (A, D, A, L, A, T) and assigned it to the first parameter of the constructor String(Char[], Int32, Int32) and assigned 2 and 3 to its second and third parameters respectively. The constructor String(charactersArray, 2, 3) then starts the characters copy operation from index position 2 and copies

3 characters and declares a new instance of the string class that contains the string value ALA.

Properties of String Class

String class provides the following two properties:

- Length
- Chars

The Length Property

This property is used to find the number of characters or length of a string and returns it as an integer value. Following is its general syntax:

C# Syntax
public int Length;
VB.NET Syntax
Public ReadOnly Property Length As Integer

The Chars Property

This property is used to find a specified character in a given string. It returns the Char object that indicates a character at a specified position in a given string. This property takes an integer parameter that indicates a specified index of a given string and returns the character of that index. Following is its general syntax:

C# Syntax
public char Chars [int Index];
VB.NET Syntax
Public ReadOnly Property Chars (Index As Integer) As Char

In the above syntax, the **Index** indicates the index position of a specified character in a given string.

Methods of String Class

The string class provides various methods which are used to perform different operations on the string. The methods of String class are static methods therefore no instance variable is required to declare from the String class but all the methods can be accessed directly with the class name String. Following is the list and details of the string class methods:

Compare	CompareTo	Concat
Copy	CopyTo	Join
Split	Insert	Remove
Replace	Format	PadRight
PadLeft	ToLower	ToUpper
Trim	TrimStart	TrimEnd
Clone	StartsWith	EndsWith
IndexOf	IndexOfAny	LastIndexOf
LastIndexOfAny	ToString	ToCharArray
SubString	Contains	Equals
GetType	IsNullOrEmpty	IsNullOrWhiteSpace

Compare Method

This method is used to compare two specified strings and decides whether they are equal or not. It is also used to compare a small part or substring of one specified string with a small part or substring of another specified string. When it compares two specified strings or two substrings, it returns an integer value. The return value can be zero, less than zero, or greater than zero. If both the strings are equal, the return value is 0, if first string is greater than second string, the return value is greater than zero, and if first string is less than second string, the return value is less than zero. This method is an overloaded member method of string class and it provides various overloaded forms. Following is the details of some important overloaded forms of the Compare method:

- Compare(String, String)
- Compare(String, String, Boolean)
- Compare(String, Int32, String, Int32, Int32)
- Compare(String, Int32, String, Int32, Int32, Boolean)

Compare(String, String)

This overloaded form of the Compare method is used to compare two specified strings. It takes two parameters of String type that indicates two strings to be compared. It is a case sensitive that also checks the characters case sensitivity of both the strings. For example, if both the strings are same but one string is in small letters and another string is in capital letters or if some characters of the second string are in small letters and some characters are in capital letters then it returns a non-zero value that indicates both the strings are not same. Following is its general declaration:

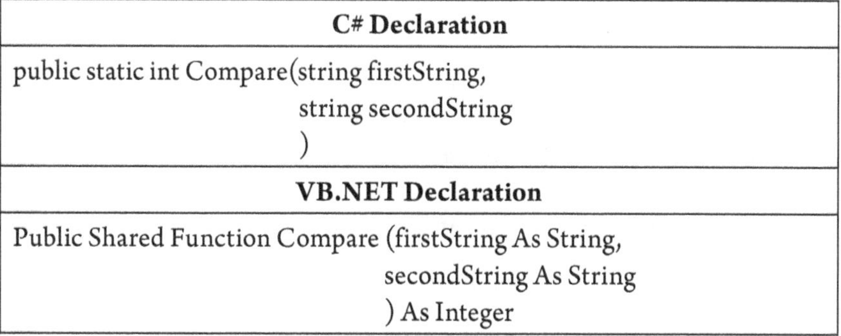

C# Declaration

```
public static int Compare(string firstString,
                          string secondString
                          )
```

VB.NET Declaration

```
Public Shared Function Compare (firstString As String,
                                secondString As String
                                ) As Integer
```

In the above declaration, the first parameter **firstString** indicates first string, and second parameter **secondString** indicates second string.

Compare(String, String, Boolean)

This overloaded form of the Compare method is used to compare two specified strings without case sensitivity of both the strings. It checks each character of the first string with each character of the second string and ignores the case sensitivity of each character in both the strings. It also allows us to enable and disable the case sensitivity of characters. If the case sensitivity of characters is enable then it checks the characters case sensitivity otherwise, it ignores the characters case sensitivity. It takes three parameters. The first and second parameters are String type and the third parameter is a Boolean value either true or false. If the third parameter is set to true value then it ignores the case sensitivity of both the strings and if the third parameter is set to false value then it checks the case sensitivity of both the string values. Therefore, this overloaded form of the compare method has two functionalities. Following is its general declaration:

C# Declaration
public static int Compare(string firstString, string secondString, bool caseSensitivity)
VB.NET Declaration
Public Shared Function Compare (firstString As String, secondString As String, caseSensitivity As Boolean) As Integer

In the above declaration, the parameter **firstString** indicates the first string, the parameter **secondString** indicates the second string, and the parameter **caseSensitivity** indicates the Boolean value either true or false.

Compare(String, Int32, String, Int32, Int32)

This overloaded form of the Compare method is used to compare a small part or substring of one specified string with a small part or substring of another specified string. It takes five parameters. The first parameter is a string parameter that indicates a string to be compared its substring, the second parameter is an integer value that indicates the starting index position of the substring within the first specified string, the third parameter is a string parameter that indicates the second specified string to be compared its substring with the substring of the first specified string, the fourth parameter is an integer value that indicates the starting index position of the substring within the second specified string, and fifth parameter is an integer value that indicates the number of characters or lengths of the substrings within the first and second specified strings. Following is its general declaration:

C# Declaration
public static int Compare(string firstString, int firstIndex, string secondString, int secondIndex, int lengthOfSubstring)

VB.NET Declaration
Public Shared Function Compare (firstString As String, firstIndex As Integer, secondString As String, secondIndex As Integer, lengthOfSubstring As Integer) As Integer

Compare(String, Int32, String, Int32, Int32, Boolean)

This overloaded form of the Compare method is used to compare a small part or substring of one specified string with a small part or substring of another specified string without case sensitivity. It takes six parameters. The first parameter is a string parameter that indicates a string to be compared its substring, the second parameter is an integer value that indicates the starting index position of the substring within the first specified string, the third parameter is a string parameter that indicates the second specified string to be compared its substring with the substring of the first specified string, the fourth parameter is an integer value that indicates the starting index position of the substring within the second specified string, the fifth parameter is an integer value that indicates the number of characters or lengths of the substrings within the first and second specified strings, and the sixth parameter is a Boolean value that indicates the case sensitivity checks of both the substrings within the first and the second specified strings. This parameter takes a Boolean value either true or false. When it is set to true, the Compare method ignores the case sensitivity of both the substrings and if it is set to false, the Compare method does not ignore the case sensitivity of both the substrings and compares the two substrings with the case sensitivity. Following is its general declaration:

C# Declaration
public static int Compare(string firstString, int firstIndex, string secondString, int secondIndex, int lengthOfSubstring, bool caseSensitivity)

VB.NET Declaration
Public Shared Function Compare (firstString As String, firstIndex As Integer, secondString As String, secondIndex As Integer, lengthOfSubstring As Integer, caseSensitivity As Boolean) As Integer

Program # 4

Write a program that compares two strings.

C# Program

```
using System;
namespace MyNamespace
{
class MyClass
{
static void Main(string[] args)
{
string String1 = "ABC";
string String2 = "XYZ";
int Result;
Result = String.Compare(String1, String2);
Console.WriteLine("First Result = " + Result.ToString());
String2 = "ABC";
Result = String.Compare(String1, String2);
Console.WriteLine("Second Result = " + Result.ToString());
String1 = "XYZ";
String2 = "ABC";
Result = String.Compare(String1, String2);
Console.WriteLine("Third Result = " + Result.ToString());

Console.WriteLine("Press any key to exit program");
Console.ReadKey();

}
}
}
```

VB.NET Program

```
Module Module1

Sub Main()
Dim String1 As String = "ABC"
Dim String2 As String = "XYZ"
Dim Result As Integer
Result = String.Compare(String1, String2)
Console.WriteLine("First Result = " & Result.ToString())
String2 = "ABC"
Result = String.Compare(String1, String2)
Console.WriteLine("Second Result = " & Result.ToString())
String1 = "XYZ"
String2 = "ABC"
Result = String.Compare(String1, String2)
Console.WriteLine("Third Result = " & Result.ToString())

Console.WriteLine("Press any key to exit program")
Console.ReadKey()
End Sub

End Module
```

CompareTo Method

This method is an instance method that is used to compare strings or objects. It compares the current instance of a string with a specified string or object. When it compares two strings, it returns an integer value. The return value can be zero, less than zero, or greater than zero. If both the strings are equals, the return value is 0, if first string is greater than second string, the return value is greater than zero, and if first string is less than second string, the return value is less than zero. Following is its general declaration:

C# Declaration

```
public int CompareTo(string specifiedString);

public int CompareTo(Object specifiedObject)
```

VB.NET Declaration
Public Function CompareTo (specifiedString As String) As Integer Public Function CompareTo (specifiedObject As Object) As Integer

The CompareTo method uses the current string or object as a prefix and the specified string or object as a parameter. The following programming example demonstrates the CompareTo method.

Program # 5

Write a program that compares two strings using the CompareTo method.

C# Program

```
using System;
namespace MyNamespace
{
class MyClass
{
static void Main(string[] args)
{
string String1 = "ABC";
string String2 = "ABC";
int Result;
Result = String1.CompareTo(String2);
Console.WriteLine("Result = " + Result.ToString());

Console.WriteLine("Press any key to exit program");
Console.ReadKey();
}
}
}
```

VB.NET Program

```
Module Module1

Sub Main()
```

```
Dim String1 As String = "ABC"
Dim String2 As String = "ABC"
Dim Result As Integer
Result = String1.CompareTo(String2)
Console.WriteLine("Result = " & Result.ToString())

Console.WriteLine("Press any key to exit program")
Console.ReadKey()
End Sub

End Module
```

The output of the above program would be 0 because both the strings are equals.

Concat Method

This method is used to concatenate two or more strings or the string representation of objects and return a new single concatenated string. It is also used to concatenate the elements of a string array or string representation of elements of an object array. When it concatenates two or more strings or string representation of objects or the elements of an array, it returns a new single concatenated string to the new instance of the string class. This method is an overloaded member method of the string class and it provides various overloaded forms. Following are some important overloaded forms of the Concat method:

- Concat(String, String)
- Concat(String, String, String)
- Concat(String, String, String, String)
- Concat(String[])
- Concat(Object, Object)
- Concat(Object, Object, Object)
- Concat(Object, Object, Object, Object)
- Concat(Object[])

The first, second, and third overloaded forms of the Concat method are used to concatenate two, three, and four specified strings respectively. The first overloaded form Concat(String, String) is used to concatenate two specified strings, the second overloaded form Concat(String, String, String) is used to concatenate three specified strings, and the third overloaded form Concat(String, String, String, String) is used to concatenate four specified strings. The fourth overloaded form Concat(String[]) is used to concatenate the elements of a string array and return a new single concatenated string of array elements. The fifth, sixth, and seventh overloaded forms of Concat method are used to concatenate the string representation of two, three, and four objects respectively. The fifth overloaded form Concat(Object, Object) is used to concatenate the string representation of two specified objects, the sixth overloaded form Concat(Object, Object, Object) is used to concatenate the string representations of three specified objects, and the seventh overloaded form Concat(Object, Object, Object, Object) is used to concatenate the string representation of four specified objects. The eight overloaded form Concat(Object[]) is used to concatenate the string representation of elements of an object array. Following is theire general declarations:

C# Declaration

public static string Concat(string string1, string string2);
 	
public static string Concat(string string1, string string2,
string string3);
 	
public static string Concat(string string1, string string2,
string string3, string string4);
 	
public static string Concat(Object object1, Object object2);
 	
public static string Concat(Object object1, Object object2,
Object object3);
 	
public static string Concat(Object object1, Object object2,
Object object3, Object object4);

VB.NET Declaration
Public Shared Function Concat (string1 As String, string2 As String) As String Public Shared Function Concat (string1 As String, string2 As String, string3 As String) As String

```
Public Shared Function Concat (string1 As String, string2 As
                              String, string3 As String,
                              string4 As String) As String

public static string Concat(params string[] values)

Public Shared Function Concat (object1 As Object, object2 As
                              Object) As String

Public Shared Function Concat (object1 As Object, object2 As
                              Object, object3 As Object)
                              As String

Public Shared Function Concat (object1 As Object, object2 As
                              Object, object3 As Object,
                              object4 As Object) As String

Public Shared Function Concat (ParamArray values As String()
                              ) As String
```

Since each overloaded form of the Concat method returns a new single concatenated string value to the new instance of the string class therefore, a new instance of the string class is declared to receive the return string value of the Concat method.

Program # 6

Write a program that cancatenates two strings and objects.
C# Program

```
using System;
namespace MyNamespace
{
class MyClass
{
static void Main(string[] args)
{
//To Cancatenate two Strings
```

```
string String1 = "ABC";
string String2 = "XYZ";
string NewString;
NewString = string.Concat(String1, String2);
Console.WriteLine(NewString);

//To Cancatenate two Objects
object Object1 = "ABC";
object Object2 = "XYZ";
NewString = string.Concat(Object1, Object2);
Console.WriteLine(NewString);

Console.WriteLine("Press any key to exit program");
Console.ReadKey();
}
}
}
```

VB.NET Program

```
Module Module1

Sub Main()
'To Cancatenate two Strings
Dim String1 As String = "ABC"
Dim String2 As String = "XYZ"
Dim NewString As String
NewString = String.Concat(String1, String2)
Console.WriteLine(NewString)

'To Cancatenate two Objects
Dim Object1 As Object = "ABC"
Dim Object2 As Object = "XYZ"
NewString = String.Concat(Object1, Object2)
Console.WriteLine(NewString)
Console.WriteLine("Press any key to exit program")
Console.ReadKey()
End Sub

End Module
```

Program # 7

Write a program that cancatenates an array of strings.
C# Program

```
using System;
namespace MyNamespace
{
class MyClass
{
static void Main(string[] args)
{

//Declare an Array of String
string[] StringsArray = new string[6];

//Initialize the String Array
StringsArray[0] = "abc";
StringsArray[1] = "def";
StringsArray[2] = "ghi";
StringsArray[3] = "jkl";
StringsArray[4] = "mno";
StringsArray[5] = "pqr";

string ResultStringl;
ResultString = string.Concat(StringsArray);
Console.WriteLine(ResultString);

Console.WriteLine("Press any key to exit program");
Console.ReadKey();
}
}
}
```

Copy Method

This method is used to make a duplicate copy of a specified string and returns it to the new instance of the string class. It takes a single string parameter that specifies a string value. Following is its general declaration:

C# Declaration
public static string Copy(string inputString);
VB.NET Declaration
Public Shared Function Copy (inputString As String) As String

In the above declaration, the parameter **inputString** indicates a string we want to make its duplicate copy.

Program # 8

Write a program that creates a duplicate copy of a specified string

C# Program

```
using System;
namespace MyNamespace
{
class MyClass
{
static void Main(string[] args)
{
string String1 = null;
string String2 = null;
String1 = "ABC";
String2 = string.Copy(String1);
Console.WriteLine("String2 = " + String2);

Console.WriteLine("Press any key to exit program");
Console.ReadKey();
}
}
}
```

VB.NET Program

```
Module Module1

Sub Main()

Dim String1 As String, String2 As String
```

```
String1 = "ABC"
String2 = String.Copy(String1)
Console.WriteLine("String2 = " & String2)

Console.WriteLine("Press any key to exit program")
Console.ReadKey()
End Sub

End Module
```

CopyTo Method

This method is used to copy the number of characters from a given string into an array of characters. It copies a specified number of characters from a specified position in a given string into a specified position in an array of characters. This method takes four parameters. The first parameter is an integer value that specifies the starting index position of character in a specified string, the second parameter is a string array that specifies the destination array in which the number of characters are to be copied, the third parameter is an integer value that specifies the starting index position in the destination array from where the copy operation is to be started, and the fourth parameter is an integer value that specifies the number of characters are to be copied from a specifies string into the destination array. Following is its general declaration:

C# Declaration

```
public void CopyTo(int stringIndex,
                   char[] destinationArray,
                   int destinationArrayIndex,
                   int numberOfCharacters);
```

VB.NET Declaration

```
Public Sub CopyTo (stringIndex As Integer,
                   destinationArray As Char(),
                   destinationArrayIndex As Integer,
                   numberOfCharacters As Integer)
```

Program # 9

Write a program that copies the number of characters from a string into a specified position in an array.
C# Program

```
using System;
namespace MyNamespace
{
class MyClass
{
static void Main(string[] args)
{
//Declare a String
string MyString = "Programming";

//Declare an Array of characters
char[] MyStringArray = new char[23];

//Initialize the string array MyStringArray
MyStringArray[0] = 'T';
MyStringArray[1] = 'h';
MyStringArray[2] = 'e';
MyStringArray[3] = ' ';

//Copy contents of the MyString variable into MyStringArray
MyString.CopyTo(0, MyStringArray, 4, MyString.Length);

//Insert characters into MyStringArray after the CopyTo method
MyStringArray[15] = ' ';
MyStringArray[17] = 'S';
MyStringArray[18] = 'k';
MyStringArray[19] = 'i';
MyStringArray[20] = 'l';
MyStringArray[21] = 'l';

//Display the contents of the MyString Array
Console.WriteLine(MyStringArray);
```

```
Console.WriteLine("Press any key to exit program");
Console.ReadKey();
}
}
}
```

VB.NET Program

```
Module Module1

Sub Main()

'Declare a String
Dim MyString As String = "Programming"

'Declare an Array of Characters
Dim MyStringArray(22) As Char

'Initialize the string array MyStringArray
MyStringArray(0) = "T"
MyStringArray(1) = "h"
MyStringArray(2) = "e"
MyStringArray(3) = ""

'Copy contents of the MyString variable into MyStringArray
MyString.CopyTo(0, MyStringArray, 4, MyString.Length)

'Display the contents of the MyString Array
MyStringArray(15) = ""
MyStringArray(17) = "S"
MyStringArray(18) = "k"
MyStringArray(19) = "i"
MyStringArray(20) = "l"
MyStringArray(21) = "l"

'Display the contents of the MyString Array
Console.WriteLine(MyStringArray)

Console.WriteLine("Press any key to exit program")
```

```
Console.ReadKey()
End Sub

End Module
```

The above program would display the output "The Programming Skill". Initially three characters T, h, and e are assigned into the first three indexes of MyStringArray then the value of the string variable MyString is assigned and then five characters i.e. S, k, i, l, l are assigned into the last five indexes of array MyStringArray.

Join Method

This method is used to concatenate the entire elements or some specified elements of a string array or a collection and inserts a string separator between each element. When it concatenates the elements of an array or a collection, it returns a single concatenated string value to the new instance of the String class. For example, if the elements of a string array are "Morning", "Afternoon", "Evening", "Night" and the string separator is a comma "," then it concatenates these elements and returns a single concatenated string of these elements as Morning,Afternoon,Evening,Night. The Join method is an overloaded member method of the String class and it provides the following types of overloaded forms:

- Join(String, String[])
- Join(String, String[], Int32, Int32)
- Join(String, Object[])

Join(String, String[])

This overloaded form of Join method is used to concatenate the elements of a string array and returns a single concatenated string to the new instance of the String class. It takes two parameters. The first parameter is a string parameter that specifies a separator to be used between the elements of array, and second parameter specifies a string array. Following is its general declaration:

C# Declaration

```
public static string Join(string separator,
                          string[] stringArray);
```

VB.NET Declaration
Public Shared Function Join (separator As String, stringArray As String()) As String

Program # 10

Write a program that concatenates the elements of a string array and inserts a string separator between each element.

C# Program

```
using System;

namespace MyNamespace
{
class MyClass
{
static void Main(string[] args)
{
//Declare a string array having four elements
string[] StringArray = new string[4];

//Initialize the string array with the string values
StringArray[0] = "Morning";
StringArray[1] = "Afternoon";
StringArray[2] = "Evening";
StringArray[3] = "Night";

string ConcatenatedString ;
ConcatenatedString = string.Join(",", StringArray);
Console.WriteLine("The String = " + ConcatenatedString);

Console.WriteLine("Enter any key to exit program");
Console.ReadKey();
}
}
}
```

VB.NET Program

```
Module Module1

Sub Main()
'Declare a string array having four elements
Dim StringArray(4) As String

'Initialize the string array with the string values
StringArray(0) = "Morning"
StringArray(1) = "Afternoon"
StringArray(2) = "Evening"
StringArray(3) = "Night"

Dim ConcatenatedString As String
ConcatenatedString = String.Join(",", StringArray)
Console.WriteLine("The String = " + ConcatenatedString)

Console.WriteLine("Enter any key to exit program")
Console.ReadKey()
End Sub

End Module
```

Join(String, String[], Int32, Int32)

This overloaded form of Join method is used to concatenate specified number of elements of a string array and returns a single concatenated string to the new instance of the String class. It takes four parameters. The first parameter is a string parameter that specifies a separator to be used between each element, the second parameter is a string array, the third parameter is an integer parameter that specifies the starting index position from which the characters concatenation operation is to be started in string array, and fourth parameter is an integer parameter that specifies the number of characters to be joined or concatenated. For example, if elements of a string array are "Morning", Afternoon", "Evening", "Night" and a string separator is comma "," then the declaration of the Join method join(String, String[], 0, 2) concatenates only the first two elements from index position 0 to index position 1 and returns a concatenated string as Morning,Afternoon, similarly, the declaration of Join method Join(String, String[], 1, 2) concatenates the second and third elements of the string array and returns a concatenated string as AfterNoon,Evening. Following is the general declaration of this overloaded form of Join method:

C# Declaration
public static string Join(string separator, string[] stringArray, int startIndexPosition, int numberOfElements);
VB.NET Declaration
Public Shared Function Join (separator As String, stringArray As String(), startIndexPosition As Integer, numberOfElements As Integer) As String

Program # 11

Write a program that concatenates specified number of elements of a string array and returns a single concatenated string.
C# Program

```
using System;

namespace MyNamespace
{
class MyClass
{
static void Main(string[] args)
{
//Declare a string array having four elements
string[] StringArray = new string[4];

//Initialize the string array with the string values
StringArray[0] = "Morning";
StringArray[1] = "Afternoon";
StringArray[2] = "Evening";
StringArray[3] = "Night";
```

```
string ConcatenatedString ;
ConcatenatedString = string.Join(",", StringArray, 0, 2);
Console.WriteLine("The String = " + ConcatenatedString);
Console.WriteLine("Enter any key to exit program");
Console.ReadKey();
}
}
}
```

VB.NET Program

```
Module Module1

Sub Main()
'Declare a string array having four elements
Dim StringArray(4) As String

'Initialize the string array with the string values
StringArray(0) = "Morning"
StringArray(1) = "Afternoon"
StringArray(2) = "Evening"
StringArray(3) = "Night"

Dim ConcatenatedString As String
ConcatenatedString = String.Join(",", StringArray, 0, 2)
Console.WriteLine("The String = " + ConcatenatedString)

Console.WriteLine("Enter any key to exit program")
Console.ReadKey()
End Sub

End Module
```

The above program concatenates the first and second elements of the String array StringArray and displays the concatenated string of the first and second element as Morning,Afternoon and ignores rest of the elements.

Join(String, Object[])

This overloaded form of Join method is used to concatenate the elements of a collection or an object array and returns a single concatenated string to the new instance of the String class. It takes two parameters. The first parameter is a String parameter that specifies a separator to be used between each element of the collection or an object array, and second parameter specifies a collection or an object array. For example, if elements of the collection or an object array are "Morning", "Afternoon", "Evening", "Night" and a string separator is comma "," then the declaration of the Join method join(String, Object[]) concatenates these elements and returns a single concatenated string of these elements as Morning,Afternoon,Evening,Night. Following is the general declaration of this overloaded form of Join method:

C# Declaration
public static string Join(string separator, Object[] objectArray);
VB.NET Declaration
Public Shared Function Join (separator As String, objectArray As String()) As String

The Split Method

This method is used to split or divide a long string into small parts using a specified separator or delimiter. A separator or delimiter is one or more characters that separate the text strings. The large string is separated using a specified single or a set of characters. The common delimiters are commas (,), full colon (:), semicolon (;), full stop (.), quotes (", '), braces ({}), pipes (|), and slashes (/ \) etc. The delimiters are always used in almost all computer applications for example, when we specify the path of any folder or a file, the back slash (\) delimiter is used to separate the directories and filenames for example, the path "C:\Documents and the Settings\Adalat.Khan\My Documents\New folder\Visual Basic.NET Book" contains one full colon and five back slashes similarly, when the Disk Operating System (DOS) specifying the file path, the backslash (\) is used as a delimiter that separates the directories and filenames. Furthermore, when a program stores a large amount of data, it may use a delimiter to separate each of the data values. For example, the string "I like:Programming" has a full colon as its delimiter similarly, the string "Gold|Smith" has a pipe as its delimiter. When this method splits a long string into small parts, it returns the string split parts into an array of String. The Split method is an overloaded member method of the String class and it provides the following overloaded forms:

- Split(Char[])
- Split(Char[], Int32)

Split(Char[])

This overloaded form of Split method is used to split a string into small parts using a specified single character or a list of characters as separator or delimiter. It takes a single parameter of type character array that specifies the delimiter. When it splits a string into small parts, it returns the split parts into an array of string. Therefore, an array of string is declared to receive the split parts of the string. For example, if we have a string such as **www.myweb.com** and we want to split it into three parts such as www, myweb, and com then in this case the delimiter is a single character dot (.) similarly, if we have a string **Morning,Afternoon:Evening;Night** and we want to split it into four parts such as Morning, Afternoon, Evening, and Night then in this case the delimiter contains three characters i.e. comma (,), full colon (:) and semi colon (;). When we do not specify the parameter of this overloaded form then by default it uses a white space character as a separator or delimiter and split a string according to the white space character. Following is the general declaration of this overloaded form of Split method:

C# Declaration
public string[] Split(char[] delimiter)
VB.NET Declaration
Public Function Split (delimiter As Char()) As String()

Program # 12

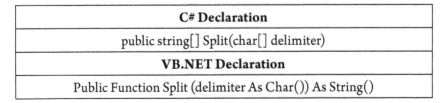

Write a program that splits a string into small parts using a specified single character as delimiter or separator.
C# Program
using System; namespace MyNamespace { class MyClass { static void Main(string[] args)

```
{
//Declare a source string we want to split in parts using delimiter
string MyString = "www.myweb.com";

//Declare a string array that stores the separated parts of the string //
MyString
string[] StringArray;

//Declare a character array that stores the delimiter character
char[] CharArray = {'.'};

//Call the Split method to split the string MyString
StringArray = MyString.Split(CharArray);

//Retrieves the separated parts of the string from StringArray
foreach (string str in StringArray)
{
if (!string.IsNullOrEmpty(str.Trim()))
{
Console.WriteLine(str);
}
}
Console.WriteLine("Press any key to exit program");
Console.ReadKey();
}
}
}
```

VB.NET Program

```
Module Module1

Sub Main()
'Declare a source string we want to split in parts using delimiter
Dim MyString As String = "www.myweb.com"

'Declare a string array that stores the separated parts of the string
'MyString
Dim StringArray As String()
```

```
'Declare a character array that stores the delimiter character
Dim CharArray As Char() = {"."}

'Call the Split method to split the string MyString
StringArray = MyString.Split(CharArray)

'Retrieves the separated parts of the string from StringArray
For Each str As String In StringArray
If Not String.IsNullOrEmpty(str.Trim()) Then
Console.WriteLine(str)
End If
Next
Console.WriteLine("Press any key to exit program")
Console.ReadKey()
End Sub

End Module
```

Program # 13

Write a program that splits a string into small parts using multiple characters as delimiter or separator.

C# Program

```
using System;

namespace MyNamespace
{
class MyClass
{
static void Main(string[] args)
{
//Declare a source string we want to split in parts using delimiter
string MyString = "Morning,Afternoon:Evening;Night";

//Declare a string array that stores the separated parts of the string
//MyString
string[] StringArray;
```

```
//Declare a character array that stores the delimiter characters char[]
CharArray = {‘,’, ‘:’, ‘;’};

//Call the Split method to split the string MyString
StringArray = MyString.Split(CharArray);

//Retrieves the separated parts of the string from StringArray
foreach (string str in StringArray)
{
if (!string.IsNullOrEmpty(str.Trim()))
{
Console.WriteLine(str);
}
}
Console.WriteLine(“Press any key to exit program”);
Console.ReadKey();
}
}
}
```

VB.NET Program

```
Module Module1

Sub Main()
‘Declare a source string we want to split in parts using delimiter
Dim MyString As String = “Morning,Afternoon:Evening;Night”

‘Declare a string array that stores the separated parts of the string
‘MyString
Dim StringArray As String()

‘Declare a character array that stores the delimiter characters
Dim CharArray As Char() = {“,”, “:”, “;”}

‘Call the Split method to split the string MyString
StringArray = MyString.Split(CharArray)

‘Retrieves the separated parts of the string from StringArray
```

```
For Each str As String In StringArray
If Not String.IsNullOrEmpty(str.Trim()) Then
Console.WriteLine(str)
End If
Next

Console.WriteLine("Press any key to exit program")
Console.ReadKey()
End Sub

End Module
```

We can also use the string delimiter as a list of characters without using of characters array. When a delimiter is used as a list of characters instead of characters array, all the delimiter characters are used in the parameter of Split method as a list separated by commas and enclosed each character in quotes either in single quotes or in double quotes. In C# programming language each character is enclosed in single quotes while in VB.NET programming language each character is enclosed in double codes and after each character or at least one character, a constant c is also used as a postfix. Following is the programming example:

Program # 14

C# Program

```
using System;

namespace MyNamespace
{
class MyClass
{
static void Main(string[] args)
{
//Declare a source string we want to split in parts using delimiter
string MyString = "Morning,Afternoon:Evening;Night";

//Declare a string array that stores the separated parts of the string
//MyString
```

```
string[] StringArray;

//Call the Split method to split the string MyString
StringArray = MyString.Split(',', ':', ';');

//Retrieves the separated parts of the string from StringArray
foreach (string str in StringArray)
{
if (!string.IsNullOrEmpty(str.Trim()))
{
Console.WriteLine(str);
}
}
Console.WriteLine("Press any key to exit program");
Console.ReadKey();
}
}
}
```

VB.NET Program

```
Module Module1

Sub Main()
'Declare a source string we want to split in parts using delimiter
Dim MyString As String = "Morning,Afternoon:Evening;Night"

'Declare a string array that stores the separated parts of the string
'MyString
Dim StringArray As String()

'Call the Split method to split the string MyString
StringArray = MyString.Split(","c, ":"c, ";"c)

'Retrieves the separated parts of the string from StringArray
For Each str As String In StringArray
If Not String.IsNullOrEmpty(str.Trim()) Then
Console.WriteLine(str)
End If
Next
```

```
Console.WriteLine("Press any key to exit program")
Console.ReadKey()
End Sub

End Module
```

Split(Char[], Int32)

This overloaded form of Split method is used to split a string into small parts using a specified single character or a list of characters as separator or delimiter. It allows us to split a string according to the specified number of parts or substrings. It takes two parameters. The first parameter is a character array that specifies a single character or a list of characters to be used as delimiter, and the second parameter is an integer parameter that specifies the number of parts or substring of a long string that is to be splited. Following is the general declaration of this overloaded form of Split method:

C# Declaration
public string[] Split(char[] delimiter, int count)
VB.NET Declaration
Public Function Split (delimiter As Char(), count As Integer) As String()

Following is the programming example of this overloaded form of Split method:

Program # 15

C# Example

```
using System;

namespace MyNamespace
{
class MyClass
{
static void Main(string[] args)
{
//Declare a target string we want to split in parts
```

```
string MyString = "one,two:three,four;five,six";

//Declare a character array that contains the delimiter
char[] Delimiter = {',', ':', ';'};

//Declare a string array that stores the small parts of the target //string
string[] StringArray;

//Call the Split method to split the string in two parts
StringArray = MyString.Split(Delimiter, 2);
//Retrieves the separated parts of the string from StringArray
foreach (string str in StringArray)
{
Console.WriteLine(str);
}
Console.WriteLine();

//Call the Split method to split the string in three parts
StringArray = MyString.Split(Delimiter, 3);
//Retrieves the separated parts of the string from StringArray
foreach (string str in StringArray)
{
Console.WriteLine(str);
}
Console.WriteLine();

//Call the Split method to split the string in 6 parts
StringArray = MyString.Split(Delimiter, 6);
//Retrieves the separated parts of the string from StringArray
foreach (string str in StringArray)
{
Console.WriteLine(str);
}
Console.WriteLine("Press any key to exit program");
Console.ReadKey();
}
}
}
```

Insert Method

This method is used to insert a single character or a substring at a specified index position in the current instance of a string and returns a new modified string value. It starts the insertion operation from a specified index position and inserts the number of characters or a substring in the current instance of a string. When it inserts a single character or a substring, it returns a new modified string value to the new instance of the String class. Therefore, a new instance of the String class is declared to receive the return string value. This method takes two parameters. The first parameter is an integer parameter that specifies the starting index position of characters in the current instance of a string from where the insertion operation is to be started and second parameter is a string parameter that indicates a single character or a substring to be inserted in the current instance of a string. Following is the general declaration of this method:

C# Declaration
public string Insert(int startIndex, string substring)
VB.NET Declaration
Public Function Insert (startIndex As Integer, substring As String) As String

Program # 16

Write a program that inserts the number of characters or a substring in a given string.

C# Example

```
using System;

namespace MyNamespace
{
class MyClass
{
static void Main(string[] args)
{
//Declare the target string in which we want to insert a set of //characters or substring
string MyTargetString = "I Like Programming";
```

```
//Declare the Substring we want to insert in the Target String string
substring = "C Sharp ";

string resultString;
resultString = MyTargetString.Insert(7, substring);
Console.WriteLine(resultString.ToString());

Console.WriteLine("Press any key to exit program");
Console.ReadKey();
}
}
}
```

The above program inserts a substring "C Sharp " in the string "I Like Programming" at the index position 7 therefore, the program will display "I Like C Sharp Programming". The program starts insertion operation from index position 7 and inserts total eight characters including the white space character at the end of the substring. The white space character is inserted at the end of the substring to create a single space between the C sharp and the last word Programming.

Remove Method

This method is used to remove a set of characters or a substring from the current instance of a string and returns a new modified string value to the new instance of the String class. It starts the remove operation from a specified index position and removes specified number of characters. If length of the substring or number of characters does not specified then it removes the number of characters or a substring from a specified starting index position to the end of the string. This method is an overloaded member method of the String class and it provides the following two overloaded forms:

- Remove(Int32)
- Remove(Int32, Int32)

Remove(Int32)

This overloaded form of Remove method is used to remove a set of characters or a substring from the current instance of a string and returns a new modified string value to the new instance of the String class. It removes a set of characters or a substring from a specified index position to the end of the string. It takes a single integer parameter that specifies the starting index position of a set of characters or a substring to be removed from the string. Following is the general declaration of this overloaded form of Remove method:

C# Declaration
public string Remove(int startIndex)
VB.NET Declaration
Public Function Remove(startIndex As Integer) As String

Remove(Int32, Int32)

This overloaded form of Remove method is used to remove a set of characters or a substring from the current instance of a string and returns a new modified string to the new instance of the String class. It removes a set of characters or a substring between the two index positions of a string. It starts the remove operation from the first specified index position and remove a set of characters or a substring until the second specified index position is reached. It takes two integer parameters. The first parameter specifies the starting index position of a set of characters or a substring to be removed from a string and the second parameter specifies the number of characters or the length of a substring to be removed from a string. Following is the general declaration of this overloaded form of Remove method:

C# Declaration
public string Remove(int startIndex, int numberOfCharacters)
VB.NET Declaration
Public Function Remove (startIndex As Integer, numberOfCharacters As Integer) As String

Program # 17

Write a program that removes a specified set of characters or a substring from a string.
C# Example
using System; namespace MyNamespace

```
{
class MyClass
{
static void Main(string[] args)
{
//Declare a target string from which we want to remove specified
//characters
string MyTargetString = "I Like C Sharp Programming";

//Declare a string variable ResultString that receives the modified //string
string ResultString;

//Call the function Remove to remove specified characters
ResultString = MyTargetString.Remove(7, 8);
Console.WriteLine("New String= " + ResultString);

Console.WriteLine("Press any key to exit program");
Console.ReadKey();
}
}
}
```

VB.NET Example

```
Module Module1

Sub Main()

'Declare a target string from which we want to remove specified 'characters
Dim MyTargetString As String = "I Like C Sharp Programming"

'Declare a string variable ResultString that receives the modified 'string
Dim ResultString As String

'Call the function Remove to remove specified characters
ResultString = MyTargetString.Remove(7, 8)
Console.WriteLine("New String= " & ResultString)

Console.WriteLine("Press any key to exit program")
```

```
Console.ReadKey()
End Sub

End Module
```

The above program removes a substring “C Sharp ” from the target string “I Like C Sharp Programming”. In the program, the Remove method is used with two parameters. The value of the first parameter is 7 that specifies the starting index position of the set of characters or substring to be removed and value of the second parameter is 8 that specifies the number of characters or length of the substring to be removed from the target string. In the target string “I Like C Sharp Programming”, the substring “C Sharp ” starts from the index position 7 and length of the substring “C Sharp ” is 8 characters including white space character at the end of the word C Sharp. Therefore, the program removes the substring “C Sharp” from the target string “I Like C Sharp Programming” and displays the output “I Like Programming”.

Program # 18

Write a program that removes the number of characters from a string starting from a specified index position to the end of the string.

C# Example

```
using System;
namespace MyNamespace
{
class MyClass
{
static void Main(string[] args)
{
string MyTargetString = “I Like C Sharp Programming”;
string ResultString;
ResultString = MyTargetString.Remove(7);
Console.WriteLine(“New String= “ + ResultString);

Console.WriteLine(“Press any key to exit program”);
Console.ReadKey();
}
}
}
```

The above program uses Remove method with one parameter. The value of the parameter is 7 that specifies the starting index position of the number of character or substring to be removed therefore, the above program removes the number of characters from the target string starting from the index position 7 to the end of the target string and display "I Like" instead of "I Like C Sharp Programming".

Replace Method

This method is used to replace all occurrences of a single specified Unicode character or a substring in the current instance of a string with a new specified Unicode character or a substring and returns a new modified string value to the new instance of the String class. The Replace method is an overloaded member method of the String class and it provides the following two overloaded forms:

- Replace(Char, Char)
- Replace(String, String)

Replace(Char, Char)

This overloaded form of Replace method is used to replace all the occurrences of a single specified Unicode character in the current instance of a string with a new specified Unicode character and returns a new modified string value to the new instance of the String class. It takes two character parameters. The first parameter specifies a Unicode character to be replaced with a new Unicode character and second parameter specifies a Unicode code character that replaces all the occurrences of a character in the current string. Following is the general declaration of this overloaded form of Replace method:

C# Declaration
public string Replace(char currentCharacter, char newCharacter)
VB.NET Declaration
Public Function Replace (currentCharacter As Char, newCharacter As Char) As String

Replace(String, String)

This overloaded form of Replace method is used to replace all the occurrences of a specified substring in the current instance of a string with a new specified substring and returns a new modified string to the new instance of the String class. It takes two string parameters. The first parameter specifies a substring to be replaced with a new substring and second parameter specifies a new substring that replaces all the occurrences of the current substring in the target string. Following is the general declaration of this overloaded form of Replace method:

C# Declaration
public string Replace(string currentSubstring, string newSubstring)
VB.NET Declaration
Public Function Replace (currentSubstring As String, newSubstring As String) As String

Program # 19

Write a program that replaces all the occurrences of a single specified character in a string with a new single character.
C# Program

```
using System;

namespace myNamespace
{
class myClass
{
static void Main(string[] args)
{
//Declare a target string
string myTargetString = “ABCADBBA”;
string newString;
newString = myTargetString.Replace(“A”, “X”);
Console.WriteLine(“The Current String = “ + myTargetString);
Console.WriteLine(“The New String =” + newString);

Console.WriteLine(“Press any key to exit program”);

Console.ReadKey();
}
}
}
```

VB.NET Program

```
Module Module1

Sub Main()
'Declare a target string
Dim myTargetString As String = "ABCADBBA"
Dim newString As String
newString = myTargetString.Replace("A", "X")
Console.WriteLine("The Current String = " & myTargetString)
Console.WriteLine("The New String = " & newString)

Console.WriteLine("Press any key to exit program")
Console.ReadKey()
End Sub

End Module
```

The above program declares a target string "ABCADBBA" and replaces a character A with a new character X. Therefore, the program replaces all the occurrences of the character A with a new character X and will display the output "XBCXDBBX".

Program # 20

Write a program that replaces all the occurrences of a specified substring in a target string with a new specified substring.

C# Program

```
using System;

namespace myNamespace
{
class myClass
{
static void Main(string[] args)
{
//Declare a target string
string myTargetString = "The C Sharp is a Programming
                        Language. The C Sharp Programming
```

```
                    Language is a Good Programming
                    Language";

string newString;
newString = myTargetString.Replace("C Sharp", "VB.NET");
Console.WriteLine("The Current String = " + myTargetString);
Console.WriteLine("The New String ="+ newString);

Console.WriteLine("Press any key to exit program");
Console.ReadKey();
}
}
}
```

VB.NET Program

```
Module Module1

Sub Main()
'Declare a target string
Dim myTargetString As String = "The C Sharp is a Programming
                          Language. The C Sharp Programming
                          Language is a Good Programming
                          Language"

Dim newString As String
newString = myTargetString.Replace("C Sharp", "VB.NET")
Console.WriteLine("The Current String = " & myTargetString)
Console.WriteLine("The New String = " & newString)

Console.WriteLine("Press any key to exit program")
Console.ReadKey()
End Sub

End Module
```

The above program declares a target string "The C Sharp is a Programming Language. The C Sharp Programming Language is a Good Programming Language" and replaces the substring "C Sharp" with a new substring "VB. NET". Therefore, the program will display the output "The VB.NET is a

Programming Language. The VB.NET Programming Language is a Good Programming Language".

Composite Formatting Feature

The Composite Formatting Feature is a special feature used in various methods that format the strings. It is used to insert a list of objects in a target string and returns a single formatted string. The list of objects to be inserted in the target string may be a single or more objects and each object may be of any type of variable, or a constant value and they are separated by comma. It takes a target string and a list of objects as parameter. The target string is also called Composite Format String or Target Template String. The Composite Format String or the Target Template String contains a single item or a list of items called format items. The format items are also called place holders. Each format item or place holder has a unique index number. The index number of the format item or place holder starts from zero. The index number of the first format item or place holder is zero, the index number of the second format item or place holder is one, and the index number of the third format item or place holder is two and so on. Each index of the format item or place holder is enclosed in a pair of braces {} as {index}. For example the first format item or place holder can be written as {0}, the second format item or place holder can be written as {1}, the third format item or place holder can be written as {2} and so on.

Each format item or place holder corresponds to an object in the list. The Composite Formatting Feature returns a new string where each format item or place holder is replaced by the string representation of the corresponding object in the list. The Composite Formatting Feature replaces each format item or place holder with the string representation of the corresponding object in the list and also format each object in the list by using various Format Controls with the index number of the format items or place holders. The format item or place holder at index number zero inserts and formats the first object of the list, the format item or place holder at index number 1 inserts and formats the second object of the list and so on. The multiple format items or place holders can also refer the same object in the list by specifying the same object multiple times in the list. The Composite Formatting Feature is supported by various methods such as Format(), ToString(), Consol.Write(), Console.WriteLine(), Debug.WriteLine(), StreamWriter.Write(), StreamWriter.WriteLine(), TextWriter.Write(), TextWriter.WriteLine() etc. Each method that supports the Composite Formatting Feature is used to format a target string by inserting a list of objects and returns a new formatted string.

Format Controls

The Format Controls are constants used with the format item or place holder of the target template string and format the corresponding objects in the list to be inserted in the target template string. The Format Controls are used with the index number of the format items or place holders inside in the braces concatenated with full colon such as {IndexNumber:FormatControl}. There are different types of Format Controls such as Numeric Format Controls that are used to format the numeric values, Date/Time Format Controls that are used to format the date and time values etc. Following is the details of the Format Controls:

- Numeric Format Controls
- Date/Time Format Controls

Numeric Format Controls

Numeric Format Controls are used to perform different format operations on numeric values for example, to display the currency sign or the percentage sign with the numeric values, to display the numeric values in scientific format, to fix the decimal point and the number of digits after the decimal point, to fix the number of digits of a numeric value for example, if a numeric value is fixed to five digits then it always displays that numeric value in the format of five digits. If a numeric value is less than the fixed number of digits then it displays extra zeros with the numeric value as prefix. Following is the list of some useful Numeric Format Controls:

Control	Type	Description
C or c	Currency	This Format Control is used to display the currency sign with a number as prefix. For example the output of the {0:C} of 432.00 is $432.00.
D or d	Decimal	This Format Control is used to display a number in a decimal form with the optional padding for example, the output of the {0:D} of 1234 is 1234, the output of the {0:D6} of 1234 is 001234, the output of the {0:D7} of 1234 is 0001234 and so on.

E or e	Exponential	This Format Control is used to display a number in scientific form with the optional value for fractional part for example, the output of the {0:E} of 1234.32 is 1.23432E+003, the output of the {0:E1} of 1234.32 is 1.2E+003, the output of the {0:E2} of 1234.32 is 1.23E+003, the output of the {0:E4} of 1234.32 is 1.2343E+003, the output of the {0:E5} of 1234.32 is 1.23432E+003, and the output of the {0:E8} of 1234.32 is 1.23432000E+003 and so on.
F or f	Fixed point	This Format Control is used to display a number including the specified number of decimal digits. It fixes the decimal point in a number and displays the specified number
		of digits after the decimal point for example, the output of the {0:F} of 12345 is 12345.00, the output of the {0:F1} of 12345 is 12345.0, the output of the {0:F2} of 12345 is 12345.00, the output of the {0:F3} of 12345 is 12345.000 and so on.
N or n	Number	This Format Control is used to fix the decimal point in a number and display the specified number of digits after the decimal point and insert the comas and display a number in a group of three digits form for example the output of the {0:N} of 123456789.12 is 123,456,789.12, the output of the {"0:N1"} of 123456789.12 is 123,456,789.1, the output of the {"0:N5"} of 123456789.12 is 123,456,789.12000 and so on.
X or x	Hexadecimal	This Format Control is used to convert a numeric value into hexadecimal form for example, the output of the {0:X} of 432 is 1B0.

0	Zero Padding	This Format Control is used to fix the number of digits of a numeric value and displays extra zeros if a numeric value is less than the fixed number of digits. For example the output of the {0:0000} of 1234 is 1234, the output of the {0:00000} of 1234 is 01234, the output of the {0:000000} of 1234 is 001234, the output of the {0:000000.00} of 1234 is 001234.00 and so on.
%	Percentage	This Format Control is used to multiply a numeric value by 100 and appends a percentage sign to it for example the output of the {0:00.00%} of .432 is 43.20%.

Date/Time Format Controls

The Date/Time Format Controls are used to format the date and time values and perform different operations on it for example, to display a long date that contains the date and time, to display a short date that contains only date, to display only a day, a month, or a year etc. Following is the list of some useful Date/Time Format Controls:

Control	Description
D	This Format Control is used to convert the date/time object into a long date pattern string. The long date pattern string contains only a long date in the form of "dddd, dd MMMM yyyy". For example, the output of the {0:D} of 12/9/2013 is Monday, December 09, 2013.
d	This Format Control is used to convert the date/time object into a short date pattern string. The short date pattern string contains only a short date in the form of "MM/dd/yyyy". For example, the output of the {0:d} of 12/9/2013 is 12/9/2013.
T	This Format Control is used to convert the date/time object into a long time pattern string. The long time pattern string contains only a long time in the form of "HH:mm:ss". For example, the output of the {0:T} of 12/9/2013 is 12:00:00 AM.

t	This Format Control is used to convert the dater/time object into a short time pattern string. The short time pattern string contains only a short time in the form of "HH:mm". For example, the output of the {0:t} of 12/9/2013 is 12:00 AM.
F	This Format Control is used to convert the date/time object into full date/time pattern string. The full date/time pattern string contains a long date in the form of "D" and long time in the form of "T". For example, the output of the {0:F} of 12/9/2013 is Monday, December 09, 2013 12:00:00 AM.
f	This Format Control is used to convert the date/time object into full date/time pattern string. The full date/time pattern string contains a long date in the form of "D" and a short time in the form of "t". For example, the output of the {0:f} of 12/9/2013 is Monday, December 09, 2013 12:00 AM.
G	This Format Control is used to convert the date/time object into a general date/time pattern string. The general date/time pattern string contains a short date in the form of "d" and a long time in the form of "T". For example, the output of the {0:G} of 12/9/2013 is 12/9/2013 12:00:00 AM.
g	This Format Control is used to convert the date/time object into a general date/time pattern string. In this case the general date/time pattern string contains a short date in the form of "d" and a short time in the form of "t". For example the output of the {0:g} of 12/9/2013 is 12/9/2013 12:00 AM.
M or m	This Format Control is used to convert the date/time object into month/day pattern string. The month/day pattern string contains only a month and a day in the form of "MMMM dd". For example, the output of the {0:M} of 12/9/2013 is December 09.
Y or y	This Format Control is used to convert the date/time object into year/month pattern string. The year/month pattern string contains only a year and a month in the form of "yyyy MMMM". For example, the output of the {0:Y} of 12/9/2013 is December 2013.
R or r	This Format Control is used to convert the date/time object into a standard date/time pattern string. In this case the standard date/time pattern string contains the standard GMT date and time in the form of "ddd, dd MMM yyyy HH:mm:ss GMT". For example, the output of the {0:R} of 12/9/2013 is Mon, 09 Dec 2013 00:00:00 GMT.

dd	This Format Control is used to convert the date/time object into the day of the month pattern string. The day of the month pattern string contains the day of a month from 1 through 31. For example, the output of the {0:dd} of 12/9/2013 is 09.
ddd	This Format Control is used to convert the date/time object into the day of the week pattern string. The day of the week pattern string contains the day of a week in short form from Sat through Fri. For example, the output of the {0:ddd} of 12/9/2013 is Mon.
dddd	This Format Control is used to convert the date/time object into the day of the week pattern string. The day of the week pattern string contains the day of a week in full form from Saturday through Friday. For example, the output of the {0:dddd} of 12/9/2013 is Monday.

Format Method

This method is used to insert a list of objects in a target string and returns a single formatted string. The list of objects to be inserted in the target string may be a single or more objects and each object may be of any type of variable, or a constant value and they are separated by comma. It takes a target string and a list of objects as parameter. The Format method is an overloaded member method of the String class and it provides the following overloaded forms:

- Format(String, Object)
- Format(String, Object, Object)
- Format(String, Object, Object, Object)
- Format(String, Object[])

Format(String, Object)

This overloaded form of Format method is used to insert a string representation of an object in a format item or place holder of the Target Template String and returns a single formatted string. It takes two parameters. The first parameter is a String parameter that specifies the Target Template String in which the string representation of an object is to be inserted and second parameter is an Object type parameter that specifies the string representation of an object to be inserted in the format item or place holder of the Target Template String. Following is its general declaration:

C# Declarations
public static string Format(string templateString, Object singleObject)
VB.NET Declarations
Public Shared Function Format (templateString As String, singleObject As Object) As String

Format(String, Object, Object)

This overloaded form of Format method is used to insert the string representations of two specified objects in the format items or place holders of the Target Template String and returns a single formatted string. It takes three parameters. The first parameter is a String parameter that specifies the Target Template String, the second and third parameters are Object type parameters that specify the string representations of two specified objects respectively to be inserted in the format items or place holders of the Target Template String. Following is its general declaration:

C# Declarations
public static string Format(string templateString, Object firstObject, Object secondObject)
VB.NET Declarations
Public Shared Function Format (templateString As String, firstObject As Object, secondObject As Object) As String

Format(String, Object, Object, Object)

This overloaded form of Format method is used to insert the string representations of three specified objects in the format items or place holders of the Target Template String and returns a single formatted string. It takes four parameters. The first parameter is a String parameter that specifies the Target Template String, the second, third, and fourth parameters are Object type parameters that specify the string representations of three specified objects respectively to be inserted in the format items or place holders of the Target Template String. Following is its general declaration:

C# Declarations
public static string Format(string templateString, Object firstObject, Object secondObject, Object thirdObject)
VB.NET Declarations
Public Shared Function Format (templateString As String, firstObject As Object, secondObject As Object, thirdObject As Object) As String

Format(String, Object[])

This overloaded form of Format method is used to insert the string representations of corresponding objects of a specified array in the format items or place holders of the Target Template String and returns a single formatted string. It takes two parameters. The first parameter is a String parameter that specifies the Target Template String in which the string representation of a corresponding object is to be inserted, and second parameter is an Object type array that contains a single object or more objects to be inserted in the format items or place holders of the Target Template String. Following is its general declaration:

C# Declarations
public static string Format(string templateString, params Object[] objectArray)
VB.NET Declarations
Public Shared Function Format (templateString As String, ParamArray objectArray As Object()) As String

Program # 21

Write a program that formats and inserts a specified number of objects in the format items or place holders of a target template string and returns a new single formatted string.
C# Program

```
using System;

namespace myNamespace
{
class myClass
{
static void Main(string[] args)
{
string str1 = "VB.NET programming";
string str2 = "C Sharp programming";
DateTime dt = new DateTime(2017, 1, 1);
string formattedString;
formattedString = String.Format("I like {0} but using {1} from
                    {2:d}", Str1, Str2, dt);
Console.WriteLine("The Formatted String = " + formattedString);

Console.WriteLine("Press any key to exit program");
Console.ReadKey();
}
}
}
```

ViB.NET Program

```
Module Module1

Sub Main()

Dim str1 As String = "VB.NET programming"
Dim str2 As String = "C Sharp programming"
Dim dt As New DateTime(2017, 1, 1)
Dim formattedString As String
formattedString = String.Format("I like {0} but using {1} from
```

```
{2:d}", Str1, Str2, dt)
Console.WriteLine("The Formatted String = " & formattedString)

Console.WriteLine("Press any key to exit program")
Console.ReadKey()
End Sub

End Module
```

The above program inserts the value of variable str1 in the place holder {0}, the value of variable str2 in the place holder {1} and the value of variable dt in the place holder {2} and displays a single formatted and concatenated string "I like VB.NET programming but using C Sharp programming from 1/1/2017".

Program # 22

Write a program that formats and inserts the string representations of corresponding objects of an array in the format items or place holders of the target template string and returns a new formatted string.

C# Program

```
using System;

public class BookInfo
{
public String bookName;
public String bookAuthorName;
public int bookNumberOfPages;
public DateTime bookPublicationYear;

public BookInfo(String name, String authorName,
                int numberOfPages,
                DateTime publicationYear)
{
bookName = name;
bookAuthorName = authorName;
bookNumberOfPages = numberOfPages;
bookPublicationYear = publicationYear;
}
```

```
}

public class MyProgramClass
{
public static void Main()
{

//Declare and initialize the publication date
DateTime dt = new DateTime(2017, 8,9);
//Declare an object of the class BookInfo and pass the book //information
to the class BookInfo
BookInfo bookObj = new BookInfo(" C# Programming",
                                "Adalat Khan", 1250, dt);

//Declare an array of objects to be formatted and insert in a //template string
object[] formatObjectsList = new object[4];

//Initialize the Objects array with the class data
formatObjectsList[0] = bookObj.bookName;
formatObjectsList[1] = bookObj.bookAuthorName;
formatObjectsList[2] = bookObj.bookNumberOfPages;
formatObjectsList[3] = bookObj.bookPublicationYear;

String resultString;

//Call the Format method to insert the string representations of //
corresponding elements of objects array in the target template //string
resultString = String.Format("My book name is {0} written by
                    {1} and it contains {2} pages
                    published in {3:d}",
                    formatObjectsList);

Console.WriteLine(resultString);

Console.WriteLine("Press any key to exit program");
Console.ReadKey();
}
}
```

VB.NET Program

```
Module Module1

Public Class BookInfo

Public bookName As String
Public bookAuthorName As String
Public bookNumberOfPages As Integer
Public bookPublicationYear As DateTime

Public Sub New(name As String, authorName As String,
                  numberOfPages As Integer,
                  publicationYear As DateTime)

bookName = name
bookAuthorName = authorName
bookNumberOfPages = numberOfPages
bookPublicationYear = publicationYear
End Sub
End Class

Sub Main()

Dim dt As New DateTime(2017, 8, 9)
Dim bookObj As New BookInfo("C# Programming",
                                  "Adalat Khan", 1250, dt)

Dim formatObjectsList As Object() = New Object(3) {}

'Initialize the Objects array with the class data
formatObjectsList(0) = bookObj.bookName
formatObjectsList(1) = bookObj.bookAuthorName
formatObjectsList(2) = bookObj.bookNumberOfPages
formatObjectsList(3) = bookObj.bookPublicationYear
Dim resultString As String
resultString = String.Format("My book name is {0} written by
                              {1} and it contains {2} pages
```

```
                              published in {3:d}",
                              formatObjectsList)

Console.WriteLine(resultString)

Console.WriteLine("Press any key to exit program")
Console.ReadKey()
End Sub
End Module
```

The above program declares a class BookInfo that stores information about the books using member data. The information contains the book name, the author name, the number of pages in a book, and the publication year of a book and these information are stored in the member data of the class BookInfo i.e. bookName, bookAuthorName, bookNumberOfPages, and bookPublicationYear. The main method of the program declares an object **bookObj** of the class BookInfo that sends information about a book to the class BookInfo and initializes the class member data using the constructor of the class BookInfo. The main method of the program also declares an array of objects **formatObjectsList** that stores the data of the class BookInfo. The size of object array is 4 and it stores the book name in index zero, the author name in index 1, the number of pages in index 2, and the publication year in index 3. The main aim of the above program is to insert the elements of an object array in the corresponding format items or place holders of the target template string. The main method of the above program used the Format method with two parameters. The first parameter is a user-defined target template string i.e. "My book name is {0} written by {1} and it contains {2} pages published in {3:d}" and second parameter of the Format method is objects array. Therefore, the Format method of the above program inserts the elements of an object array in the corresponding format items or place holders enclosed in the braces {}. The Format method inserts the object of index 0 i.e. the bookObj.bookName in the format item or place holder {0}, the object of index 1 i.e. the bookObj.bookAuthorName in the format item or place holder {1), the object of index 2 i.e. the bookObj.bookNumberOfPages in the format item or place holder {2}, the object of index 3 i.e. the bookObj.bookPublicationYear in the format item or place holder {3) and displays the following formatted output:

My book name is C# Programming written by Adalat Khan and it contains 1250 pages published in 9/8/2017.

PadRight Method

This method is used to align a string to the left by padding blank spaces or a specified Unicode character on the right or at the end of the string. When it aligns a string to the left, it returns a new string of a specified length in which the end of the current string is padded with blank spaces or a specified Unicode character to the end of the string. The PadRight method is an overloaded method of the String class and it provides the following two overloaded forms:

- PadRight(Int32)
- PadRight(Int32, Char)

PadRight(Int32)

This overloaded form of PadRight method is used to align a string to the left by padding blank spaces on the right or at the end of the string. It takes a single integer parameter that specifies the width or length of the string plus any additional padded blank space characters. When it aligns a string to the left, it returns a new string of a specified length in which the end of the current string is padded with blank spaces. It has the following general declaration:

C# Declaration
public string PadRight(int Width)
VB.NET Declaration
Public Function PadRight (Width As Integer) As String

In the above declaration, the parameter **Width** specifies the width or length of the original string plus any additional padded blank space characters.

PadRight(Int32, Char)

This overloaded form of PadRight method is used to align a string to the left by padding a specified Unicode character on the right or at the end of the string. It takes two parameters. The first parameter is an integer parameter that indicates the width or length of the string plus any additional padded specified Unicode character on the right or at the end of the string. The second parameter is a character parameter that indicates a specified Unicode character to be padded on the right or at the end of the string. It has the following general declaration:

C# Declaration
public string PadRight(int TotalWidth, char PaddingChar)
VB.NET Declaration
Public Function PadRight (TotalWidth As Integer, PaddingChar As Char) As String

In the above declaration, the parameter **Width** specifies the width or length of the original string, and parameter **PaddingChar** specifies a specified Unicode character to be padded on the right or at the end of the string.

Program # 23

Write a program that aligns a string to the left by padding white space characters on the right or at the end of the string.

C# Program

```
using System;

namespace MyNamespace
{
class MyClass
{
static void Main(string[] args)
{
string MyString;
MyString = "C Sharp Programming";
string NewString;

NewString = MyString.PadRight(19);
Console.WriteLine(NewString);

NewString = MyString.PadRight(5);
Console.WriteLine(NewString);

NewString = MyString.PadRight(24);
Console.Write(NewString);
```

```
Console.WriteLine("VB.NET Programming");

Console.WriteLine("Press any key to exit program");
Console.ReadKey();
}
}
}
```

VB.NET Program

```
Module Module1

Sub Main()

Dim MyString As String
MyString = "C Sharp Programming"
Dim NewString As String

NewString = MyString.PadRight(19)
Console.WriteLine(NewString)
NewString = MyString.PadRight(5)
Console.WriteLine(NewString)

NewString = MyString.PadRight(24)
Console.Write(NewString)
Console.WriteLine("VB.NET Programming")

Console.WriteLine("Press any key to exit program")
Console.ReadKey()
End Sub

End Module
```

The above program produces the following output:

```
C Sharp Programming
C Sharp Programming
C Sharp Programming          VB.NET Programming
```

The width or length of the original string is 19 characters. In first call of the PadRight method, the value of the parameter Width is 19 which is equal to the original string, in second call of the PadRight method, the value of the parameter Width is 5 which is less than the original string and in third call of the PadRight method, the value of the parameter Width is 24 which is five characters greater than the original string. The first call of the PadRight method returns a new instance of the string identical to the original string, the second call of the PadRight method returns a reference to the original or existence string, and third call of the PadRight method return a new instance of the string identical to the original string and aligns the new instance of the string to the left by padding five white space characters to the right or at the end of the string.

Program # 24

Write a program that aligns a string to the left by padding a specified Unicode character on the right or at the end of the string.
C# Program

```
using System;

namespace MyNamespace
{
class MyClass
{
static void Main(string[] args)
{
string MyString;
MyString = "C Sharp Programming";
string NewString;

NewString = MyString.PadRight(24, '*');
Console.WriteLine(NewString);

Console.WriteLine("Press any key to exit program");
Console.ReadKey();
}
}
}
```

VB.NET Program

```
Module Module1

Sub Main()

Dim MyString As String
MyString = "C Sharp Programming" 'The original String
Dim NewString As String              'New instance of the String
NewString = MyString.PadRight(24, "*")
Console.WriteLine(NewString)

Console.WriteLine("Press any key to exit program")
Console.ReadKey()
End Sub

End Module
```

The above program aligns the string "C Sharp Programming" to the left by padding five asterisks characters to the right or at the end of the string.

PadLeft Method

This method is used to align a string to the right by padding white spaces or a specified Unicode character on the left or at the beginning of the string. When it aligns a string to the right, it returns a new string of a specified length in which the beginning of the string is padded with blank spaces or a specified Unicode character. The PadLeft method is an overloaded method of the String class and it provides the following two overloaded forms:

- PadLeft(Int32)
- PadLeft(Int32, Char)

PadLeft(Int32)

This overloaded form of PadLeft method is used to align a string to the right by padding blank spaces on the left or at the beginning of the string. It takes an integer parameter that specifies the width or length of the string plus any additional padded blank space characters. When it aligns a string to the right, it returns a new string of a specified length in which the beginning of the string is padded with blank spaces. It has the following general declaration:

C# Declaration
public string PadLeft(int Width)
VB.NET Declaration
Public Function PadLeft (Width As Integer) As String

In the above declaration, the parameter **Width** specifies the width or length of the string plus any additional padding characters. If value of the parameter Width is less than length of the original or existing string, the PadLeft method returns a reference to the original or existing string, if value of the parameter Width is equal to the length of the original or existing string, the PadLeft method returns a new instance of the string identical to the original or existing string, and if value of the parameter Width is greater than length of the original or existing string, the PadLeft method returns a new instance of the string identical to the original or existing string and aligns the new instance of the string to the right by padding white space characters on the left or at the beginning of the new instance of the string according to the size we specified.

PadLeft(Int32, Char)

This overloaded form of PadLeft method is used to align a string to the right by padding a specified Unicode character on the left or at the beginning of the string. It takes two parameters. The first parameter is an integer parameter that specifies the width or length of the string plus any additional padded Unicode character on the left or at the beginning of the string. The second parameter is a character parameter that indicates a specified Unicode character to be padded on the left or at the beginning of the string. This overloaded form has the following general declaration:

C# Declaration
public string PadLeft(int Width, char PaddingChar)
VB.NET Declaration
Public Function PadLeft (Width As Integer, PaddingChar As Char) As String

In the above declaration, the parameter **Width** specifies the width or length of the original string, and parameter **PaddingChar** specifies a specified Unicode character to be padded on the left or at the beginning of the string.

Program # 25

Write a program that aligns a string to the right by padding a specified Unicode character on the left or at the beginning of the string.

C# Program

```
using System;

namespace MyNamespace
{
class MyClass
{
static void Main(string[] args)
{
string MyString;
MyString = "C Sharp Programming"; //The original String
string NewString;

NewString = MyString.PadLeft(24, '*');
Console.WriteLine(NewString);

Console.WriteLine("Press any key to exit program");
Console.ReadKey();
}
}
}
```

VB.NET Program

```
Module Module1

Sub Main()
Dim MyString As String
MyString = "C Sharp Programming" 'The original String
Dim NewString As String
```

```
NewString = MyString.PadLeft(24, "*")
Console.WriteLine(NewString)

Console.WriteLine("Press any key to exit program")
Console.ReadKey()
End Sub

End Module
```

The above program aligns the string "C Sharp Programming" to the right by padding five asterisk characters on the left or at the beginning of the string and produces the following output:

*****C Sharp Programming

ToUpper and ToLower Methods

These methods are used to convert the current instance of a string into uppercase and lowercase characters string respectively. The ToUpper method converts the current instance of a string in upper case characters string and the ToLower method converts the current instance of a string in lower case characters string. When they convert the current instance of a string into upper case or lower case, they return new strings in which all the characters of the current instances are converted into upper case and lower case respectively. Following are the general declarations of these methods:

C# Declaration
public string ToUpper() public string ToLower()
VB.NET Declaration
Public Function ToUpper As String Public Function ToLower As String

Program # 26

Write a program that converts a string into upper case and lower case characters string.

C# Program

```
using System;

namespace MyNamespace
{
class MyClass
{
static void Main(string[] args)
{
string smallString = "abcdefghijkl";
string capitalString = "ABCDEFGHIJKL";
string newString = null;

newString = smallString.ToUpper();
Console.WriteLine("Converted to Uppercase = " + newString);

newString = capitalString.ToLower();
Console.WriteLine("Converted to Lowercase = " + newString);

Console.WriteLine("Press any key to exit program");
Console.ReadKey();
}
}
}
```

VB.NET Program

```
Module Module1

Sub Main()

Dim smallString As String = "abcdefghijkl"
Dim capitalString As String = "ABCDEFGHIJKL"
Dim newString As String

newString = smallString.ToUpper()
```

```
Console.WriteLine("Converted to Uppercase = " & newString)

newString = capitalString.ToLower()
Console.WriteLine("Converted to Lowercase = " & newString)

Console.WriteLine("Press any key to exit program")
Console.ReadKey()
End Sub

End Module
```

Trim Method

This method is used to remove white space characters from the beginning and the end of the current instance of a string or all the occurrences of a set of characters specified in an array of characters from the beginning and the end of the current instance of a string and return a new modified string. It does not modify the current instance of a string but it returns a new string in which all the white space characters or all the occurrences of a set of characters specified in an array of characters are removed from the beginning and the end of the current instance of a string. This method is an overloaded member method of the String class and it provides the following two overloaded forms:

- Trim()
- Trim(Char[])

Trim()

This overloaded form of Trim method is used to remove all the white space characters from the beginning and the end of the current instance of a string and returns a new modified string. Following is the general declaration of this overloaded form of Trim method:

C# Declaration
public string Trim()
VB.NET Declaration
Public Function Trim As String

Trim(Char[])

This overloaded form of Trim method is used to remove all the occurrences of a set of characters specified in an array of characters from the beginning and the end of the current instance of a string and return a new modified string. It takes a single parameter that specifies a character array. Following is its general declaration:

C# Declaration
public string Trim(params char[] trimChars)
VB.NET Declaration
Public Function Trim (ParamArray trimChars As Char()) As String

In the above declaration, the parameter **trimChars** specifies an array of characters in which a single character or a set of characters to be specified we want to remove from the beginning and the end of the current instance of a string.

Program # 27

Write a program that removes a set of specified characters from the beginning and the end of the current instance of a string.
C# Program

```
using System;

namespace MyNamespace
{
class MyClass
{
static void Main(string[] args)
{
string myString
myString = " **.*I Like C Sharp Programming**,*.* ";

char[] characterssToTrim = {' ', '*', '.', ','};

string resultString = myString.Trim(characterssToTrim);
```

```
Console.WriteLine(resultString);

Console.WriteLine("Press any key to exit program");
Console.ReadKey();
}
}
}
```

VB.NET Program

```
Module Module1

Sub Main()

Dim myString As String
myString = " **.*I Like C Sharp Programming**,*.*"

Dim characterssToTrim() As Char = {" ", "*", ".", ","}
Dim resultString As String
resultString = myString.Trim(characterssToTrim)
Console.WriteLine(resultString)

Console.WriteLine("Press any key to exit program")
Console.ReadKey()
End Sub

End Module
```

The above program removes extra spaces, asterisks characters, coma character and dot characters from the beginning and the end of the string myString and displays the following output:

"I Like C Sharp Programming".

TrimStart and TrimEnd Methods

The TrimStart and TrimEnd methods are used to remove all the occurrences of a set of characters specified in an array of characters from the beginning and the end of the current instance of a string respectively. The TrimStart method removes all the occurrences of a set of characters specified in an array of characters from the beginning of a string and the TrimEnd method removes all the occurrences of a set of characters specified in an array of characters from the end of the string. The functionality of the Trim method is actually divided into TrimStart and TrimEnd methods because the Trim method is used if a set of specified characters to be removed from the beginning and the end of a string. If we want to remove a set of specified characters only from one side either from the beginning or from the end of a string then the TrimStart or the TrimEnd method is used. If we remove all the occurrences of a set of specified characters from the beginning of a string then the TrimStart method is used and if we want to remove all the occurrences of a set of specified characters from the end of a string then the TrimEnd method is used. Following is the general declarations of the TrimStart and TrimEnd methods:

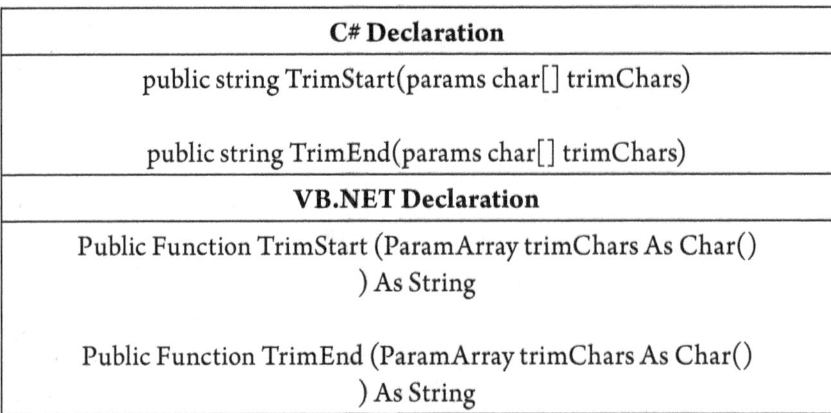

C# Declaration
public string TrimStart(params char[] trimChars) public string TrimEnd(params char[] trimChars)
VB.NET Declaration
Public Function TrimStart (ParamArray trimChars As Char()) As String Public Function TrimEnd (ParamArray trimChars As Char()) As String

The TrimStart and TrimEnd methods take a single parameter **trimChars** that indicates an array of characters we want to remove from the beginning and the end of the current instance of a string.

Program # 28

Write a program that removes a set of specified characters from the beginning and the end of a string using the TrimStart and the TrimEnd methods.
C# Program

```
using System;

namespace MyNamespace
{
class MyClass
```

```
{
static void Main(string[] args)
{
string myString ;
myString = "* **.*I Like C Sharp Programming**,*.* *";

//Declare an array of characters that contain a set of specified //characters
we want to remove from the beginning and the end of //a string
char[] charactersToTrim = {' ', '*', '.', ','};

string resultTrimStart, resultTrimEnd;

//Call the TrimStart method
resultTrimStart = myString.TrimStart(charactersToTrim);

//Call the StringEnd method
resultTrimEnd = myString.TrimEnd(charactersToTrim);

Console.WriteLine("The TrimStart = " + resultTrimStart);
Console.WriteLine("The Trim End = " + resultTrimEnd);

Console.WriteLine("Press any key to exit program");
Console.ReadKey();
}
}
}
```

VB.NET Program

```
Module Module1

Sub Main()

Dim myString As String
myString = "* **.*I Like C Sharp Programming**,*.* *"

Dim charactersToTrim() As Char = {" ", "*", ".", ","}

Dim resultTrimStart, resultTrimEnd As String
```

```
'Call the TrimStart method
resultTrimStart = myString.TrimStart(charactersToTrim)

'Call the TrimEnd method
resultTrimEnd = myString.TrimEnd(charactersToTrim)

Console.WriteLine("The TrimStart = " & resultTrimStart)
Console.WriteLine("The Trim End = " & resultTrimEnd)

Console.WriteLine("Press any key to exit program")
Console.ReadKey()
End Sub

End Module
```

The above program displays the following output:

The TrimStart = I Like C Sharp Programming**,*.* *
The TrimEnd = * **.*I Like C Sharp Programming

Clone Method

This method is used to create a duplicate copy of the current instance of a string object and returns a reference of the current instance of a string in the form of an object. Following is the general declaration of this method:

C# Declaration
public Object Clone();
VB.NET Declaration
Public Function Clone As Object

Program # 29

Write a program that creates clone of a current string.
C# Program

```
using System;

namespace MyNamespace
```

```
{
class MyClass
{
static void Main(string[] args)
{
string myString = "ABCD";

//Create a duplicate string object from the current string MyString
object stringObject = myString.Clone();
Console.WriteLine("String Clone = " + stringObject.ToString());

Console.WriteLine("Press any key to exit program");
Console.ReadKey();
}
}
}
```

VB.NET Program

```
Module Module1

Sub Main()

'Declare a string
Dim myString As String = "ABCD"

'Create a duplicate string object from the current string MyString
Dim stringObject As Object = myString.Clone()
Console.WriteLine("String Clone = " & stringObject.ToString())

Console.WriteLine("Press any key to exit program")
Console.ReadKey()
End Sub

End Module
```

StartsWith Method

This method is used to compare a specified substring with the beginning of the current instance of a string and determines whether a specified substring matches with the beginning of the current instance of a string or not. When it matches a specified substring with the beginning of the current instance of a string, it returns a Boolean value either true or false. If a specified substring matches or equal to the beginning of the current instance of a string then it returns true otherwise it returns false. Following is the general declaration of this method:

C# Declaration
public bool StartsWith(string strValue)
VB.NET Declaration
Public Function StartsWith (strValue As String) As Boolean

This method takes a single String parameter that indicates a substring to be compared with the beginning of the current instance of a string.

EndsWith Method

This method is used to compare a specified substring with the end of the current instance of a string and determines whether a specified substring matches with the end of the current instance of a string or not. When it matches a specified substring with the end of the current instance of a string, it returns a Boolean value either true or false. If a specified substring matches or equal to the end of the current instance of the string then it returns true otherwise it returns false. Following is the general declaration of this method:

C# Declaration
public bool EndsWith(string strValue)
VB.NET Declaration
Public Function EndsWith (strValue As String) As Boolean

This method takes a single String parameter that indicates a substring to be compared with the end of the current instance of a string.

Program # 30

Write a program that compares a specified substring with the beginning and the end of the current instance of a string.

C# Program

```
using System;

namespace MyNamespace
{
class MyClass
{
static void Main(string[] args)
{
string myString = "I like programming";

//Call two user-defined methods
startsWidthTest(myString);
endsWidthTest(myString);

Console.WriteLine("Press any key to exit program");
Console.ReadKey();
}
public static void startsWidthTest(string str)
{
bool find;
find = str.StartsWith("I like");
if (find == true)
Console.WriteLine("The string begins from substring I like");
else
Console.WriteLine("The substring is not matched");
}
public static void endsWidthTest(string str)
{
bool find;
find = str.EndsWith("programming");
if (find == true)
Console.WriteLine("The string end at a substring programming");
else
Console.WriteLine("The substring is not matched");
}
}
}
```

VB.NET Program

```
Module Module1

Sub Main()

Dim myString As String = "I like programming"

'Call two user-defined subroutines
startsWidthTest(myString)
endsWidthTest(myString)

Console.WriteLine("Press any key to exit program")
Console.ReadKey()
End Sub

Public Sub startsWidthTest(ByVal str As String)
Dim find As Boolean
find = str.StartsWith("I like")
If find = True Then
Console.WriteLine("The string begins from substring I like")
Else
Console.WriteLine("The substring is not matched")
End If
End Sub
Public Sub endsWidthTest(ByVal str As String)
Dim find As Boolean
find = str.EndsWith("programming")
If find = True Then
Console.WriteLine("The string end at a substring programming")
Else
Console.WriteLine("The substring is not matched")
End If
End Sub
End Module
```

IndexOf Method

This method is used to search the first occurrence of a specified Unicode character or a substring in the current instance of a string. It starts search process from first character or index position 0 of the current instance of a string and searches the first occurrence of a specified Unicode character or a substring. When it finds a specified Unicode character or a substring in the current instance of a string, it returns its index position. When it does not find a specified Unicode character or a substring, it returns -1. This method is an overloaded method of the String class and it provides the following different overloaded forms:

- IndexOf(Char)
- IndexOf(String)
- IndexOf(Char, Int32)
- IndexOf(String, Int32)

IndexOf(Char)

This overloaded form of IndexOf method is used to search the first occurrence of a specified Unicode character in the current instance of a string. When it finds the first occurrence of a specified Unicode character, it returns its index position otherwise, it returns -1. It takes a character parameter that indicates a specified character to be searched in the current instance of a string. Following is its general declaration:

C# Declaration
public int IndexOf(char searchChr)
VB.NET Declaration
Public Function IndexOf (searchChr As Char) As Integer

IndexOf(String)

This overloaded form of IndexOf method is used to search the first occurrence of a specified substring in the current instance of a string. When it finds the first occurrence of a specified substring, it returns its index position otherwise, it returns -1. It returns the index position of the first character of the target substring. It takes a String parameter that specifies a substring to be searched in the current instance of a string. Following is its general declaration:

C# Declaration
public int IndexOf(string substringStr)

VB.NET Declaration
Public Function IndexOf (substringStr As String) As Integer

Program # 31

Write a program that returns index position of the first occurrence of a specified character and first occurrence a specified substring from a given string.

C# Program

```
using System;

namespace MyNamespace
{
class MyClass
{
static void Main(string[] args)
{
string myString = "I like programming and like C#, like VB";

int index;

//find a character "i" in the string myString
index = myString.IndexOf("i");
Console.WriteLine("The character i is at index {0}", index);

//find a substring "like" in the string myString
index = myString.IndexOf("like");
Console.WriteLine("The substring starts from index {0}", index);

Console.WriteLine("Press any key to exit program");
Console.ReadKey();
}
}
}
```

VB.NET Program

```
Module Module1

Sub Main()
```

```
Dim myString As String
myString = "I like programming and like C#, like VB"

Dim index As Integer

'find a character "i" in the string myString
index = myString.IndexOf("i")
Console.WriteLine("The character i is at index {0}", index)
'find a substring "like" in the string myString
index = myString.IndexOf("like")
Console.WriteLine("The substring starts from index {0}", index)

Console.WriteLine("Press any key to exit program")
Console.ReadKey()
End Sub
End Module
```

The above program declared a target string "I like programming and like C#, like VB". The program used the IndexOf method two times. The first IndexOf method finds the index position of the first occurrence of character "i" and second IndexOf method finds the index position of the first occurrence of substring "like" and it returns index position of the first character of substring "like". Since first occurrence of character "i" is fourth character of the target string and its index position is 3 and first occurrence of substring "like" starts from index position 2 therefore, the above program produces the following output:

The character i is at index 3
The substring starts from index 2

IndexOf(Char, Int32)

This overloaded form of IndexOf method is used to search the first occurrence of a specified Unicode character in the current instance of a string. It works same as the first overloaded form IndexOf(Char) but the main difference is that the first overloaded form searches the first occurrence of a specified Unicode character in the current instance of a string and starts search process from the first character or index position 0 but this overloaded form of IndexOf method searches a specified Unicode character in the current instance of a string and starts search process from a specified index position. Following is its general declaration:

C# Declaration
public int IndexOf(char searchChr, int startIndex)
VB.NET Declaration
Public Function IndexOf (searchChr As Char, startIndex As Integer) As Integer

This overloaded form of IndexOf method takes two parameters. The first parameter is a character parameter that specifies a Unicode character to be searched in the current instance of a string and second parameter is an integer parameter that specifies the index position in the current instance of a string from which search process is to be started.

IndexOf(String, Int32)

This overloaded form of IndexOf method is used to search the first occurrence of a specified substring in the current instance of a string. This overloaded form works same as the second overloaded form of the IndexOf method i.e. the IndexOf(String) but the main difference is that the second overloaded form searches the first occurrence of a specified substring in the current instance of a string and starts search process from first character or index position 0 of the current instance of a string but this overloaded form of IndexOf method searches a specified substring in the current instance of a string and starts search process from a specified index position. Following is its general declaration:

C# Declaration
public int IndexOf(String searchStr, int startIndex)
VB.NET Declaration
Public Function IndexOf (searchStr As String, startIndex As Integer) As Integer

This overloaded form of IndexOf method takes two parameters. The first parameter is a string value that specifies a substring to be searched in the current instance of a string and second parameter is an integer value that specifies the index position in the current instance of a string from which search process is to be started.

Program # 32

Write a program that returns index position of the first occurrence of a specified character and first occurrence of a specified substring and starts search process from a specified index position of the current instance of a string.
C# Program

```
using System;

namespace MyNamespace
{
class MyClass
{
static void Main(string[] args)
{
string myString = "I like programming and like C#, like VB";

int index;

//find a character i in the string myString
index = myString.IndexOf("i", 4);
Console.WriteLine("The character i is at index {0}", index);

//find a substring like in the string myString
index = myString.IndexOf("like", 3);
Console.WriteLine("The substring starts from index {0}", index);

Console.WriteLine("Press any key to exit program");
Console.ReadKey();
}
}
}
```

VB.NET Program

```
Module Module1

Sub Main()

Dim myString As String
```

```
myString = "I like programming and like C#, like VB"

Dim index As Integer

'find a character "i" in the string myString
index = myString.IndexOf("i", 4)
Console.WriteLine("The character i is at index {0}", index)

'find a substring "like" in the string myString
index = myString.IndexOf("like", 3)
Console.WriteLine("The substring starts from index {0}", index)

Console.WriteLine("Press any key to exit program")
Console.ReadKey()
End Sub
End Module
```

The above program declared a target string "I like programming and like C#, like VB" and used the IndexOf method two times. The first IndexOf method finds the index position of the first occurrence of character "i" and second IndexOf method finds index position of the first occurrence of substring "like" and it returns index position of the first character of substring "like". The first IndexOf method starts search operation from index position 4 and second IndexOf method starts search operation from index position 3. Since first occurrence of character "i" is the fourth character of target string but search operation starts from index position 4 so, it returns index position 15 because from index position 4 to end of the target string the first occurrence of character "i" occurs at index position 15 and starting index position of the first occurrence of substring "like" starts from index position 23 because from index position 3 to end of the target string the first occurrence of substring "like" starts from index position 23 so, it returns index position 23 and above program produces the following output:

```
The character i is at index 15
The substring starts from index 23
```

LastIndexOf Method

This method is used to search the last occurrence of a specified Unicode character or a substring in the current instance of a string. It starts search process from last character or from last index position and goes backward towards the first character or index position 0 and searches a specified Unicode character or a substring in the current instance of a string. When it finds a specified Unicode character or a substring in the current instance of a string, it returns the index position of the last occurrence of a specified Unicode character or a substring from left side to the right side or from index position 0 to the last index position. If it does not find a specified Unicode character or a substring then it returns -1. This method works same as IndexOf method but the main difference is that IndexOf method searches the first occurrence of a specified Unicode character or a substring in the current instance of a string and starts search process from left side to the right side or from index position 0 to the last index position in the current instance of a string and LastIndexOf method searches the last occurrence of a specified Unicode character or a substring in the current instance of a string from left side to the right side or from index position 0 to the last index position in the current instance of a string. This method is an overloaded method of the String class and it provides the following different overloaded forms:

- LastIndexOf(Char)
- LastIndexOf(String)
- LastIndexOf(Char, Int32)
- LastIndexOf(String, Int32)

LastIndexOf(Char)

This overloaded form of LastIndexOf method is used to search last occurrence of a specified Unicode character in the current instance of a string. When it finds the last occurrence of a specified Unicode character in the current instance of a string, it returns its index position otherwise, it returns -1. It takes a character parameter that specifies a Unicode character to be searched in the current instance of a string. Following is its general declaration:

C# Declaration
public int LastIndexOf(char searchChr)
VB.NET Declaration
Public Function LastIndexOf (searchChr As Char) As Integer

LastIndexOf(String)

This overloaded form of LastIndexOf method is used to search last occurrence of a specified substring in the current instance of a string. When it finds the last occurrence of a specified substring, it returns its starting index position otherwise, it returns -1. It takes a string parameter that specifies a substring to be searched in the current instance of a string. Following is its general declaration:

C# Declaration
public int LastIndexOf(string substringStr)
VB.NET Declaration
Public Function LastIndexOf (substringStr As String) As Integer

Program # 33

Write a program that returns index position of the last occurrence of a specified character and last occurrence of a specified substring from current instance of a string.

C# Program

```
using System;

namespace MyNamespace
{
class MyClass
{
static void Main(string[] args)
{
string myString = "I like programming and like C#, like VB";

int index;

//find a character "i" in the string myString
index = myString.LastIndexOf("i");
Console.WriteLine("The character i is at index {0}", index);

//find a substring "like" in the string myString
index = myString.LastIndexOf("like");
```

```
Console.WriteLine("The substring starts from index {0}", index);

Console.WriteLine("Press any key to exit program");
Console.ReadKey();
}
}
}
```

VB.NET Program

```
Module Module1

Sub Main()

'Declare a string
Dim myString As String
myString = "I like programming and like C#, like VB"

Dim index As Integer

'find a character "i" in the string myString
index = myString.LastIndexOf("i")
Console.WriteLine("The character i is at index {0}", index)

'find a substring "like" in the string myString
index = myString.LastIndexOf("like")
Console.WriteLine("The substring starts from index {0}", index)

Console.WriteLine("Press any key to exit program")
Console.ReadKey()
End Sub
End Module
```

The above program declared a target string "I like programming and like C#, like VB" and used the LastIndexOf method two times. The first LastIndexOf method finds index position of the last occurrence of character "i" and second LastIndexOf method finds index position of the last occurrence of substring "like" and it returns index position of the first character of substring "like". Since last occurrence of character "i" from left side to the right side is thirty fourth 34 character of the target string and its index position is 33 and last occurrence of substring "like" starts from index position 32 therefore, the above program produces the following output:

The character i is at index 33
The substring starts from index 32

LastIndexOf(Char, Int32)

This overloaded form of LastIndexOf method is used to search last occurrence of a specified Unicode character in the current instance of a string. It searches a specified Unicode character and starts search process from a specified index position and goes backward towards the first character or index position 0. It takes two parameters. The first parameter is a character parameter that specifies a Unicode character to be searched in the current instance of a string and second parameter is an integer parameter that specifies index position of the current instance of a string from which the search process is to be started. Following is its general declaration:

C# Declaration
public int LastIndexOf(char searchChr, int startIndex)
VB.NET Declaration
Public Function LastIndexOf (searchChr As Char, startIndex As Integer) As Integer

LastIndexOf(String, Int32)

This overloaded form of LastIndexOf method is used to search last occurrence of a specified substring in the current instance of a string. It searches a specified substring and starts search process from a specified index position and goes backward towards the first character or index position 0. It takes two parameters. The first parameter is a string parameter that specifies a substring to be searched in the current instance of a string and second parameter is an integer parameter that specifies index position of the current instance of a string from which the search process is to be started. Following is its general declaration:

C# Declaration
public int LastIndexOf(String searchStr, int startIndex)

VB.NET Declaration
Public Function LastIndexOf (searchStr As String, startIndex As Integer) As Integer

Program # 34

Write a program that returns the index position of the last occurrence of a specified character and the last occurrence of a specified substring and starts search process from a specified index position of the current instance of a string.

C# Program

```
using System;

namespace MyNamespace
{
class MyClass
{
static void Main(string[] args)
{
string myString = "I like programming and like C#, like VB";

int index;

//Find a character i in the string myString
index = myString.LastIndexOf("i", 23);
Console.WriteLine("The character i is at index {0}", index);

//Find a substring like in the string myString
index = myString.LastIndexOf("like", 29);
Console.WriteLine("The substring starts from index {0}", index);

Console.WriteLine("Press any key to exit program");
Console.ReadKey();
}
}
}
```

VB.NET Program

```
Module Module1

Sub Main()

Dim myString As String
myString = "I like programming and like C#, like VB"

Dim index As Integer

'find a character "i" in the string myString
index = myString.LastIndexOf("i", 23)
Console.WriteLine("The character i is at index {0}", index)

'find a substring "like" in the string myString
index = myString.LastIndexOf("like", 29)
Console.WriteLine("The substring starts from index {0}", index)

Console.WriteLine("Press any key to exit program")
Console.ReadKey()
End Sub
End Module
```

The above program declared a target string "I like programming and like C#, like VB" and used the LastIndexOf method two times. The first LastIndexOf method finds the index position of the last occurrence of character "i" and second LastIndexOf method finds the index position of the last occurrence of substring "like" and it returns the index position of the first character of substring "like". The first LastIndexOf method starts search operation from index position 23 and second LastIndexOf method starts search operation from index position 29. Since last occurrence of character "i" is the thirty fourth 34 character of target string but search operation starts from index position 23 so, it returns index position 15 because from index position 23 to beginning of the target string, the last occurrence of character "i" from left side to the right side occurs at index position 15 and the starting index position of first occurrence of substring "like" starts from index position 23 because from index position 29 to beginning of the target string, the last occurrence of substring "like" from left side to the right starts from index position 23 so, it returns index position 23 and above program produces the following output:

The character i is at index 15
The substring starts from index 23

ToString Method

This method is used to convert an object of any specified type to its equivalent string representation. The ToString method is defined in the Object class while all classes and structures are based on Object class, therefore when we define an object or a variable of any specified type then it automatically inherits the ToString method. Following is its general declaration:

C# Declaration
public override string ToString()
VB.NET Declaration
Public Overrides Function ToString As String

Program # 35

Write a program that converts different variables to their equivalent string representations and assigned to the string variable.
C# Program

```
using System;

public class MyProgramClass
{
public static void Main()
{
int intVar = 3;                         //An Integer variable
short shortVar =1;                      //A Short variable
byte byteVar = 2;                       //A Byte variable
long longVar = 20;                      //A Long variable
decimal decimalVar = 2.3M;              //A Decimal variable
double doubleVar = 3.5;                 //A Double variable
float floatVar = 1.3F;                  //A Float variable
bool booleanVar = true;                 //A Boolean variable
object objectVar = new object();        //An Object variable
string stringVar;                       //A String variable
```

```
stringVar = intVar.ToString();
Console.WriteLine(stringVar);          //Output "3"
stringVar = shortVar.ToString();
Console.WriteLine(stringVar);          //Output "1"
stringVar = byteVar.ToString();
Console.WriteLine(stringVar);          //Output "2"
stringVar = longVar.ToString();
Console.WriteLine(stringVar);          //Output "20"
stringVar = decimalVar.ToString();
Console.WriteLine(stringVar);          //Output "2.3"
stringVar = doubleVar.ToString();
Console.WriteLine(stringVar);          //Output "3.5"
stringVar = floatVar.ToString();
Console.WriteLine(stringVar);          //Output "1.3"
stringVar = booleanVar.ToString();
Console.WriteLine(stringVar);          //Output "true"
stringVar = objectVar.ToString();
Console.WriteLine(stringVar);          //Output "System.Object"

Console.WriteLine("Press any key to exit program");
Console.ReadKey();
}
}
```

VB.NET Program

```
Module Module1

Sub Main()
Dim intVar As Integer = 3              'An Integer variable
Dim shortVar As Short = 1              'A Short variable
Dim byteVar As Byte = 2                'A Byte variable
Dim longVar As Long = 20               'A Long variable
Dim decimalVar As Decimal = 2.3        'A Decimal variable
Dim doubleVar As Double = 3.5          'A Double variable
Dim floatVar As Single = 1.3           'A Float variable
Dim booleanVar As Boolean = True       'A Boolean variable
Dim objectVar As New Object()          'An Object variable
Dim stringVar As String                'A String variable
```

```
stringVar = intVar.ToString()
Console.WriteLine(stringVar)
stringVar = shortVar.ToString()
Console.WriteLine(stringVar)
stringVar = byteVar.ToString()
Console.WriteLine(stringVar)
stringVar = longVar.ToString()
Console.WriteLine(stringVar)
stringVar = decimalVar.ToString()
Console.WriteLine(stringVar)
stringVar = doubleVar.ToString()
Console.WriteLine(stringVar)
stringVar = floatVar.ToString()
Console.WriteLine(stringVar)
stringVar = booleanVar.ToString()
Console.WriteLine(stringVar)
stringVar = objectVar.ToString()
Console.WriteLine(stringVar)

Console.WriteLine("Press any key to exit program")
Console.ReadKey()
End Sub

End Module
```

ToCharArray Method

This method is used to convert the current instance of a string into a Unicode characters array. It allows us to access each character of a string individually. It converts a complete string or a specified set of characters or a substring into an array of Unicode characters. When it converts a string or a specified set of characters, it returns an array of Unicode characters that contains the converted string or a specified substring. This method is an overloaded method of the String class and it provides the following two overloaded forms:

- ToCharArray()
- ToCharArray(Int32, Int32)

ToCharArray()

This overloaded form of ToCharArray method is used to convert the current instance of a string into an array of Unicode characters. It does not take any parameter. Following is its general declaration:

C# Declaration
public char[] ToCharArray()
VB.NET Declaration
Public Function ToCharArray () As Char()

ToCharArray(Int32, Int32)

This overloaded form of ToCharArray method is used to convert a set of specified characters or a substring into an array of Unicode characters. It takes two integer parameters. The first parameter specifies the starting index position of the current instance of a string from which the characters copy peration is to be started and second parameter specifies the number of characters or the length of a specified substring to be copied into an array of Unicode characters. Following is its general declaration:

C# Declaration
public char[] ToCharArray(int startIndex, int length)
VB.NET Declaration
Public Function ToCharArray (startIndex As Integer, length As Integer) As Char()

Program # 36

Write a program that converts a string into an array of Unicode characters.
C# Program

```
using System;

namespace MyNamespace
{
class MyProgramClass
{
```

```
static void Main(string[] args)
{
string myString = "I like Programming";
char[] charArray;

//Call the ToCharArray method and converts the string
charArray = myString.ToCharArray();

//Display the characters array charArray
for (int i = 0; i < charArray.Length; i = i + 1)
{
Console.Write("The character at index {0} = ", i);
Console.WriteLine(charArray[i]);
}
Console.WriteLine("Press any key to exit program");
Console.ReadKey();
}
}
}
```

VB.NET Program

```
Module Module1
Sub Main()

Dim myString As String = "I like Programming"
Dim charArray As Char()

'Call the ToCharArray method and convert the string myString
charArray = myString.ToCharArray()

'Display the characters array charArray
For i As Integer = 0 To charArray.Length- 1
Console.Write("The character at index {0} = ", i)
Console.WriteLine(charArray(i))
Next i

Console.WriteLine("Press any key to exit program")
Console.ReadKey()
End Sub
End Module
```

Program # 37

Write a program that converts a set of specified characters of a string to an array of characters from index position 2 to index position 5.

C# Program

```
using System;

namespace MyNamespace
{
class MyProgramClass
{
static void Main(string[] args)
{
string myString = "I like Programming";
char[] charArray;

//Call the ToCharArray method and converts 4 characters
charArray = myString.ToCharArray(2, 4);

//Display the characters array charArray
for (int i = 0; i < charArray.Length; i = i + 1)
{
Console.Write("The character at index {0} = ", i);
Console.WriteLine(charArray[i]);
}
Console.WriteLine("Press any key to exit program");
Console.ReadKey();
}
}
}
```

VB.NET Program

```
Module Module1
Sub Main()

Dim myString As String = "I like Programming"
Dim charArray As Char()

charArray = myString.ToCharArray(2, 4)
```

```
'Display the characters array charArray
For i As Integer = 0 To charArray.Length - 1
Console.Write("The character at index {0} = ", i)
Console.WriteLine(charArray(i))
Next i

Console.WriteLine("Press any key to exit program")
Console.ReadKey()
End Sub
End Module
```

SubString Method

This method is used to retrieve a specified substring from the current instance of a string. It starts the retrieving of a substring from a specified index position and continues to the end of the string. It is also used to retrieve a substring from a specified index position and retrieves the number of characters of a specified length. It is an overloaded member method of the String class and it provides the following two overloaded forms:

- Substring(Int32)
- Substring(Int32, Int32)

Substring(Int32)

This overloaded form of Substring method is used to retrieve a substring from a specified index position to the end of a string. It takes a single integer parameter that specifies the starting index position of a substring to be retrieved from a string. Following is its general declaration:

C# Declaration
public string Substring(int startIndex)
VB.NET Declaration
Public Function Substring (startIndex As Integer) As String

Substring(Int32, Int32)

This overloaded form of Substring method is used to retrieve a substring between the two specified index positions of a string. It starts the retrieving of a substring from a specified index position and retrieves the number of characters or a substring of a specified length. It takes two integer parameters. The first parameter specifies the starting index position from which the retrieving of a substring is to be started and second parameter specifies the number of characters or the length of a substring to be retrieved. Following is its general declaration:

C# Declaration
public string Substring(int startIndex, int length)
VB.NET Declaration
Public Function Substring (startIndex As Integer, length As Integer) As String

Program # 38

Write a program that retrieves a specified substring from a specified index position to the end of a string and between the two specified index positions from the current instance of a string.
C# Program

```
using System;

namespace MyNamespace
{
class MyClass
{
static void Main(string[] args)
{
//Declare a string
string myString = "I like C Sharp programming";

string subStr;

subStr = myString.Substring(7);
Console.WriteLine("The Substring = " + subStr);

subStr = myString.Substring(7, 7);
Console.WriteLine("The Substring = " + subStr);
```

```
Console.WriteLine("Press any key to exit program");
Console.ReadKey();
}
}
}
```

VB.NET Program

```
Module Module1

Sub Main()

'Declare a string
Dim myString As String
myString = "I like C Sharp programming"

Dim subStr As String

subStr = myString.Substring(7)
Console.WriteLine("The Substring = " & subStr)

subStr = myString.Substring(7, 7)
Console.WriteLine("The Substring = " & subStr)

Console.WriteLine("Press any key to exit program")
Console.ReadKey()
End Sub
End Module
```

The above program used two overloaded forms of Substring method. The first overloaded form retrieves a substring from index position 7 to the end of the string myString and second overloaded form of Substring method retrieves a substring starts from index position seven and retrieves seven characters or substring. The above program produces the following output:

```
The Substring = C Sharp programming
The Substring = C Sharp
```

Contains Method

This method is used to search a specified substring in the current instance of a string. It returns a Boolean value either true of false. If a specified substring exists in the current instance of a string then it returns true otherwise it returns false. It starts search process from first character of the string and searches the entire string. It is a case-sensitive method that compares only the same case substring. This method takes a string parameter that specifies a substring to be searched in the current instance of a string. Following is the general declaration of this method:

C# Declaration
public bool Contains(string searchStr)
VB.NET Declaration
Public Function Contains (searchStr As String) As Boolean

Program # 39

Write a program that searches a specified substring in the current instance of a string.

C# Program

```
using System;

namespace MyNamespace
{
class MyProgramClass
{
static void Main(string[] args)
{
string myString = "I like C Sharp programming";

bool find;
find = myString.Contains("C Sharp");
if(find == true)
Console.WriteLine("The substring found in the string");
else
Console.WriteLine("The substring not found in the string");
```

```
Console.WriteLine("Press any key to exit program");
Console.ReadKey();
}
}
}
```

VB.NET Program

```
Module Module1

Sub Main()

Dim myString As String
myString = "I like C Sharp programming"

Dim find As Boolean
find = myString.Contains("C Sharp")
If find = True Then
Console.WriteLine("The substring found in the string")
Else
Console.WriteLine("The substring not found in the string")
End If

Console.WriteLine("Press any key to exit program")
Console.ReadKey()
End Sub
End Module
```

Equals Method

This method is used to determine whether value of a specified string or string object is equal to value of the current instance of a string or string object or values of the two specified strings or objects are equal. It returns a Boolean value either true or false. If value of a specified string or string object is equal to value of the current instance of a string or object, it returns true otherwise, it returns false. By default this method is case-sensitive method that compares values of the same case strings and objects but it can also be made as case-insensitive using the culture-insensitivity rules. This method is an overloaded member method of the String class and it provides the following overloaded forms:

- Equals(Object)
- Equals(String)
- Equals(String, String)
- Equals(String, String, StringComparison)

The first overloaded form of Equals method Equals(Object) determines whether the value of a specified string object is equal to value of the current instance of a string object, the second overloaded form Equals(String) determines whether value of a specified string is equal to the value of the current instance of a string, the third overloaded form Equals(String, String) determines whether values of the two specified strings are equal or not, and the fourth overloaded form Equals(String, String, StringComparison) determines whether values of the two specified strings are equal or not using the culture rules. Following is the general declarations of the Equals method:

C# Declarations
public override bool Equals(Object obj) public bool Equals(string strValue) public static bool Equals(string strValue1, string strValue2) public static bool Equals(string strValue1, string strValue2, StringComparison comparisonType)
VB.NET Declarations
Public Overrides Function Equals (obj As Object) As Boolean Public Function Equals (strValue As String) As Boolean Public Shared Function Equals (strValue1 As String, strValue2 As String) As Boolean Public Shared Function Equals (strValue1 As String, strValue2 As String, comparisonType As StringComparison) As Boolean

The first declaration takes an Object parameter **obj** that specifies an object, the second declaration takes a single String parameter **strValue** that specifies a string object, the third declaration takes two String parameters **strValue1** and **strValue2** that specify two strings to be compared with each other, and the fourth declaration takes three parameters. The first and second parameters **strValue1** and **strValue2** specify two string objects to be compared with each other, and third parameter comparisonType is a StringComparison type parameter that specifies the culture, case, and sort rules used in the comparison.

Program # 40

Write a program that checks value of a string object with value of the current instance of a string whether they are equal or not and also checks values of the two string objects with each other whether they are equal or not.
C# Program

```
using System;

namespace MyNamespace
{
class MyProgramClass
{
static void Main(string[] args)
{
//Declare strings and string object
string myString = "C Sharp Programming";
object obj = "C Sharp Programming";
string myString2 = "C Sharp Programming";

bool find;

//Compare a string object with the current instance of the string
find = myString.Equals(obj);
if (find == true)
Console.WriteLine("The string is equal to the object");
else
Console.WriteLine("The string is not equal to the object");

//Compare the two string objects with each other
```

```
find = string.Equals(myString, myString2);
if (find == true)
Console.WriteLine("Both strings are equal");
else
Console.WriteLine("The strings are not equal");

Console.WriteLine("Press any key to exit program");
Console.ReadKey();
}
}
}
```

VB.NET Program

```
Module Module1
Sub Main()

'Declare strings and string object
Dim myString As String = "C Sharp Programming"
Dim obj As Object = "C Sharp Programming"
Dim myString2 As String = "C Sharp Programming"

Dim find As Boolean
'Compare a string object with the current instance of the string
find = myString.Equals(obj)
If find = True Then
Console.WriteLine("The string is equal to the object")
Else
Console.WriteLine("The string is not equal to the object")
End If

'Compare the two string objects with each other
find = String.Equals(myString, myString2)
If find = True Then
Console.WriteLine("Both strings are equal")
Else
Console.WriteLine("The strings are not equal")
End If

Console.WriteLine("Press any key to exit program")
```

```
Console.ReadKey()
End Sub
End Module
```

The above program produces the following output:

The string is equal to the object
Both strings are equal

GetType Method

This method is used to get the type of the current instance. The current instance may be an object of a class or a variable of any data type. This method is inherited from Object class and it works same as TypeOf operator but the main difference is that the TypeOf operator is generally used when we know the type of an object or a variable and if we want to inspect or compare objects or variables with each other while GetType method is used when we do not know the type of an object of a class or a variable and we want to determine the exact type of that specified object or variable. The second difference is that the TypeOf operator gets resolved at compile time while GetType method gets resolved at runtime of the program. Furthermore, the TypeOf operator works with exact types and it does not work with instances or objects while GetType method works with the instances or objects and it is used when we do not know the type of any object or variable. The TypeOf operator takes the name of any class or any data type such as int, float, double, char, string, byte etc and returns the actual type of that class or data type as **System.Type** while GetType method uses the current object name or a variable name and returns the type of that object or variable. Following is the general declaration of the GetType method:

C# Declaration
public Type GetType()
VB.NET Declaration
Public Function GetType As Type

Program # 41

Write a program that returns the type of the current object or variable.
C# Program

```
using System;

class A          //Declare an empty Class A
{
}
class B : A      //Declare an empty Class B inherited from Class A
{
}
class C : B      //Declare an empty Class C inherited from Class B
{
}
class MainProgramClass
{
static void Main()
{
A objA = new A();              //Declare an Object of Class A
A objB = new B();              //Declare an Object of Class B
A objC = new C();              //Declare an Object of Class C
int x = 2;                     //Declare an Integer Variable
float y = 3;                   //Declare a Float Variable
string str = "My String";      //Declare a String Variable

//Get the types of the above Objects and Variables
Console.WriteLine("The type of objA = " + objA.GetType());
Console.WriteLine("The type of objB = " + objB.GetType());
Console.WriteLine("The type of objC = " + objC.GetType());
Console.WriteLine("The type of x = " + x.GetType());
Console.WriteLine("The type of y = " + y.GetType());
Console.WriteLine("The type of str = " + str.GetType());

Console.WriteLine("Press any key to exit program");
Console.ReadKey();
}
}
```

VB.NET Program
Class A 'Declare an empty Class A End Class Class B Inherits A 'Declare an empty Class B inherited from Class A End Class Class C Inherits B 'Declare an empty Class C inherited from Class B End Class Module Module1 Sub Main() Dim objA As New A() 'Declare an Object of Class A Dim objB As A = New B() 'Declare an Object of Class B Dim objC As A = New C() 'Declare an Object of Class C Dim x As Integer = 2 'Declare an Integer Variable Dim y As Single = 3 'Declare a Float Variable 'Declare a String Variable Dim str As String = "My String" 'Get the types of the above Objects and Variables Console.WriteLine("The type of objA = " & Convert.ToString(objA.GetType())) Console.WriteLine("The type of objB = " & Convert.ToString(objB.GetType())) Console.WriteLine("The type of objC = " & Convert.ToString(objC.GetType())) Console.WriteLine("The type of x = " & Convert.ToString(x.GetType())) Console.WriteLine("The type of y = " & Convert.ToString(y.GetType())) Console.WriteLine("The type of str = " & Convert.ToString(str.GetType())) Console.WriteLine("Press any key to exit program")

```
Console.ReadKey()
End Sub

End Module
```

IsNullOrEmpty Method

This method is used to check whether a specified string is null or empty string. It takes a string value as parameter and checks whether it is null or empty string. This method returns a Boolean value either true or false. If a specified string is null or empty then it returns true otherwise, it returns false. Following is the general declaration of this method:

C# Declaration
public static bool IsNullOrEmpty(string strValue)
VB.NET Declaration
Public Shared Function IsNullOrEmpty (strValue As String) As Boolean

Program # 42

Write a program that checks a string whether it is null, or empty string using the IsNullOrEmpty method.

C# Program

```
using System;

class MainProgramClass
{
public static void Main()
{
string str1 = "I like programming";
string str2 = "";
string str3 = null;

Console.WriteLine("The String str1 {0}", stringTest(str1));
Console.WriteLine("The String str2 {0}", stringTest(str2));
```

```
Console.WriteLine("The String str3 {0}", stringTest(str3));

Console.WriteLine("Press any key to exit program");
Console.ReadKey();
}

public static string stringTest(string s)
{
bool x;
x = string.IsNullOrEmpty(s);
if (x == true)

return "is null or empty";
else
return "is not null and not empty";
}
}
```

VB.NET Program

```
Module Module1
Sub Main()
Dim str1 As String = "I like programming"
Dim str2 As String = ""
Dim str3 As String = Nothing

Console.WriteLine("The String str1 {0}", stringTest(str1))
Console.WriteLine("The String str2 {0}", stringTest(str2))
Console.WriteLine("The String str3 {0}", stringTest(str3))

Console.WriteLine("Press any key to exit program")
Console.ReadKey()
End Sub

Public Function stringTest(ByVal s As String) As String
Dim x As Boolean
x = String.IsNullOrEmpty(s)
If x = True Then

Return "is null or empty"
```

```
Else
Return "is not null and not empty"
End If
End Function
End Module
```

The above program produces the following output:

The String str1 is not null and not empty
The String str2 is null or empty
The String str3 is null or empty

IsNullOrWhiteSpace Method

This method is used to check whether a specified string is null, empty or it contains only white space characters. It takes a string value as parameter and checks whether it is null, empty, or it contains one or more white space characters. This method returns a Boolean value either true or false. If a specified string is null, empty, or it contains one or more white space characters then it returns true otherwise, it returns false. Following is the general declaration of this method:

C# Declaration
public static bool IsNullOrWhiteSpace(string strValue)
VB.NET Declaration
Public Shared Function IsNullOrWhiteSpace (strValue As String) As Boolean

Program # 43

Write a program that checks a string whether it is a null, an empty string, or it only contains whitespaces using the string method IsNullOrWhiteSpace.
C# Program

```
using System;

class MainProgramClass
{
public static void Main()
```

```
{
string str1 = "I like programming";
string str2 = "";
string str3 = null;
string str4 = " ";

Console.WriteLine("The String str1 {0}", stringTest(str1));
Console.WriteLine("The String str2 {0}", stringTest(str2));
Console.WriteLine("The String str3 {0}", stringTest(str3));
Console.WriteLine("The String str4 {0}", stringTest(str4));

Console.WriteLine("Press any key to exit program");
Console.ReadKey();
}

public static string stringTest(string s)
{
bool x;
x = string.IsNullOrWhiteSpace(s);
if (x == true)

return "is null, empty, or White Spaces";
else
return "is not null and not empty";
}
}
```

VB.NET Program

```
Module Module1
Sub Main()
Dim str1 As String = "I like programming"
Dim str2 As String = ""
Dim str3 As String = Nothing
Dim str4 As String = ""

Console.WriteLine("The String str1 {0}", stringTest(str1))
Console.WriteLine("The String str2 {0}", stringTest(str2))
Console.WriteLine("The String str3 {0}", stringTest(str3))
Console.WriteLine("The String str4 {0}", stringTest(str4))
```

```
Console.WriteLine("Press any key to exit program")
Console.ReadKey()
End Sub

Public Function stringTest(ByVal s As String) As String
Dim x As Boolean
x = String.IsNullOrWhiteSpace(s)
If x = True Then

Return "is null, empty, or White Spaces"
Else
Return " is not null and not empty"
End If
End Function

End Module
```

The above program displays the following output:

The String str1 is not null and not empty
The String str2 is null, empty, or White Spaces
The String str3 is null, empty, or White Spaces
The String str4 is null, empty, or White Spaces

Drawbacks of String Class

The main drawback of String class is that an instance of the String class is immutable that means read-only or unchangeable. When an instance of the String class is declared and initialized with a string value, it cannot be changed during the program execution due to the immutability nature of the String class. When a modification operation is performed on an instance of the String class by any String class method, a new instance of the String class is created and the modified value of the current instance is returned to the new instance of the String class and current instance is always the same as before modification operation. Therefore, each modification operation on the current instance of String class requires a new allocation of memory space for the new created instance of the String class. If a single modification operation is performed on the current instance of the String class ten times or more times then each time a separate instance is created in the memory and creates a new instance of the String class in a separate memory location that wastes the memory space and performance of the application might be decreased due to memory consumptions. When we are using long string values, the String class is not recommended to handle and manage the long string values because it decreases the performance and efficiency of the whole application due to the huge amount of memory consumption.

The .NET Framework provides another Class for string declaration and manipulation that is called StringBuilder Class. The StringBuilder Class is used to remove the drawbacks of the String class. The instance of the StringBuilder class is the same as an instance of the String class but the main difference is that an instance of the String class is immutable that means read-only or unchangeable while an instance of the StringBuilder class is mutable that means read-write or changeable. When an instance of the stringBuilder class is used and any modification operation is performed on the current instance of the StringBuilder class, the modification actually occurs in the current instance of the StringBuilder class and new instance does not create during the modification operation therefore, during each modification of the current instance of StringBuilder class a new instance does not create in the memory but modification operation always occurs in the current instance of the StringBuilder class and it does not require extra memory space that might be increased the performance of the application as compare to the String class. Therefore, for efficiency and performance the StringBuilder class is a best choice for long string declaration and manipulation instead of String class.

StringBuilder Class

The StringBuilder class is used to declare and initialize the mutable instances of strings. The mutable instances mean read-write or changeable. When an instance of StringBuilder class is declared, it is read-write or changeable and all modification operations performed by StringBuilder class methods always modify the current instance of StringBuilder class and new instance of StringBuilder class do not create. The StringBuilder class does not require extra memory space during any modification operation because when we declare and initialize an instance of the StringBuilder class and if we perform any modification operation, the modification always occurs in the current instance of StringBuilder class and new instance do not create during any modification operation because the value of StringBuilder class is mutable. Therefore, the efficiency and performance of StringBuilder class is faster than the String class. The StringBuilder class is recommended when we are using a very long string values. The StringBuilder class is located in the System.Text namespace and it cannot be inherited. The namespace System.Text must be imported in the application before the using of StringBuilder class.

Constructor of StringBuilder Class

The constructor of StringBuilder class is used to declare and initialize its instances. It provides the following constructors:

- StringBuilder()
- StringBuilder(Int32)
- StringBuilder(String)
- StringBuilder(Int32, Int32)
- StringBuilder(String, Int32)
- StringBuilder(String, Int32, Int32, Int32)

StringBuilder()

This is the default constructor of StringBuilder class that requires no parameters and it is used to declare and initialize instances of the StringBuilder class that contains empty strings. When it declares an instance, its capacity is set to the implementation-specific default capacity. Following is the general declaration of this constructor:

C# Declaration
public StringBuilder() For example: StringBuilder myInstance = new StringBuilder();
VB.NET Declaration
Public Sub New For example: Dim myInstance As New StringBuilder

StringBuilder(Int32)

This constructor is used to declare and initialize an instance of the StringBuilder class using a specified capacity or length. It takes an integer parameter that specifies the length of a string. Following is the general declaration of this constructor:

C# Declaration
public StringBuilder(int length) For example: int length = 100; StringBuilder myInstance = new StringBuilder(length);
VB.NET Declaration
Public Sub New (length As Integer) For example: Dim length As Integer = 100 Dim myInstance As New StringBuilder(length)

StringBuilder(String)

This constructor is used to declare and initialize an instance of the StringBuilder class using a specified string value. It takes a string parameter that specifies a string value. The specified string value is an initial or starting value of this instance of the StringBuilder class. Following is the general declaration of this constructor:

C# Declaration
public StringBuilder(string stringValue) For Example: string initialString= "Initial string value"; StringBuilder myInstance = new StringBuilder(initialString);
VB.NET Declaration
Public Sub New (stringValue As String) For example: Dim initialString As String = "Initial string value" Dim myInstance As New StringBuilder(initialString)

StringBuilder(Int32, Int32)

This constructor is used to declare and initialize an instance of the StringBuilder class by specifying the initial and final lengths or sizes of the string value. This constructor takes two integer parameters. The first parameter specifies the starting length or size of the string value and second parameter specifies the maximum length or size of the string value. The value of the first parameter is assigned to the Capacity property and value of the second parameter is assigned to the maxLength property of the StringBuilder class. The length or size of the first parameter is a starting or initial length and the number of characters or length of the string value may exceed the length or size of the first parameter and it can be extended to the maximum length or size of the string value specified in the second parameter. If the number of characters or length of the string value exceeds the length or size value of the first parameter then the StringBuilder object allocates additional memory to store the extra characters and if its value is zero then the implementation-specific default capacity is used. The second parameter defines the maximum length or size of the string value and the number of characters or length of the string value cannot exceed the length or size value of the second parameter because it is the exact final length or size of the string value. If number of characters or length of the string value exceeds the length or size value of the second parameter, the StringBuilder object does not allocate additional memory but it throws an exception. Following is the general declaration of this constructor of the StringBuilder Class:

C# Declaration

public StringBuilder(int initialLength, int finalLength)
 	
For example:
int initialLength = 255;
int finalLength = 1024;
StringBuilder myInstance = new StringBuilder(initialLength,
finalLength);

VB.NET Declaration
Public Sub New (initialLength As Integer, finalLength As Integer) For example: Dim initialLength As Integer = 255 Dim finalLength As Integer = 1024 Dim myInstance As New StringBuilder(initialLength, finalLength)

StringBuilder(String, Int32)

This constructor is used to declare and initialize an instance of the StringBuilder Class by a specified string value with a specified length. It takes two parameters. The first parameter is a string parameter that specifies an initial string value and second parameter is an integer parameter that specifies length or size of the string value. The second parameter defines the maximum length or size of the string value. The value of second parameter can be increased when the number of characters of string value is increased or exceeded. The value of the second parameter is assigned to the Capacity property of the StringBuilder class. If number of characters or length of the string value exceeds from length or size value of the second parameter, the StringBuilder object allocates additional memory to store extra characters of the string value. If length or size of string value is zero, the implementation-specific default capacity is used. Following is the general declaration of this constructor of StringBuilder class:

C# Declaration
public StringBuilder(string stringValue, int length) For Example: string stringValue = "Initial string value"; int length = 255; StringBuilder myInstance = new StringBuilder(stringValue, length);
VB.NET Declaration
Public Sub New (stringValue As String, length As Integer) For example: Dim stringValue As String = "Initial string value " Dim length As Integer = 255 Dim myInstance As New StringBuilder(stringValue, length)

StringBuilder(String, Int32, Int32, Int32)

This constructor is used to declare and initialize an instance of the StringBuilder class by a specified substring with specified length for example, if we have a long string value and we want to initialize a new instance of the StringBuilder class from a substring value between the two index positions of the long string. This constructor takes four parameters. The first parameter is a string parameter that specifies a long string value from which a specified substring value is selected between the two index positions, the second parameter is an integer parameter that specifies the starting index position of the substring value to be selected from the long string, the third parameter is an integer parameter that specifies the number of characters or length of the substring value, and fourth parameter is an integer parameter that specifies the starting or initial size of the new instance of the StringBuilder class. Following is the general declaration of this constructor of StringBuilder class:

C# Declaration

public StringBuilder(string stringValue,
                    int startIndex,
                    int substringLength,
                    int length)
 	
For example:
string stringValue = "Initial string value";
int startIndex = 0;
int substringLength = 5;
int length = 10;
StringBuilder myInstance = new StringBuilder(stringValue,
                    startIndex,
                    substringLength,
                    length);

VB.NET Declaration

Public Sub New (stringValue As String, startIndex As Integer,
                    substringLength As Integer,
                    length As Integer)
 	
For example:
Dim stringValue As String = "Initial string value"
Dim startIndex As Integer = 0
Dim substringLength As Integer = 5
Dim length As Integer = 10
Dim myInstance As New StringBuilder(stringValue,
                    startIndex,
                    substringLength,
                    length)

Methods of StringBuilder Class

The StringBuilder class provides the following methods:

Method	Description
Append	This method is used to append information or one or more characters to the end of the current instance of StringBuilder.
AppendFormat	This method is used to replaces a format specifier passed in a string with formatted text.
AppendLine	This method is used to insert the default line terminator at the end of the current instance of the StringBuilder.
Insert	This method is used to insert a string or object into specified index of the current instance of StringBuilder. The instance of the StringBuilder class starts from index 0 therefore, the value should be provided on zero index bases.
Remove	This method is used to remove a specified number of characters from the current instance of StringBuilder. It takes two integer parameters. The first parameter specifies the index position in the current instance of the StringBuilder and second parameter specifies the number of characters to be removed from current instance of the StringBuilder.
Replace	This method is used to replace a specified character at a specified index.
Clear	This method is used to remove all characters from the current instance of StringBuilder.

Program # 44

Write a program that appends a substring to the end of the current instance of the StringBuilder.
C# Program

```
using System;
using System.Text;
```

```
namespace StringBuilderClassExample
{
class Program
{
static void Main(string[] args)
{
StringBuilder str = new StringBuilder("I Like C#");

str.Append(" Programming");
Console.WriteLine(str);

Console.ReadKey();
}
}
}
```

The above program produces the following output:

I Like C# Programming

Program # 45

Write a program that appends a line terminator to the current instance of the StringBuilder.
C# Program

```
using System;
using System.Text;

namespace StringBuilderClassExample
{
class Program
{
static void Main(string[] args)
{
string[] LanguagesList = {"C++", "C#", "Java"};

StringBuilder str = new StringBuilder(
"Following are my favourate Languages:").AppendLine();
```

```
foreach (string item in LanguagesList)
{
str.Append(item).AppendLine();
}
Console.WriteLine(str);

Console.ReadKey();
}
}
}
```

The above program produces the following output:

Following are my favorite Languages:
C++
C#
Java

Program # 46

Write a program that removes a specified number of characters from the current instance of StringBuilder.
C# Program

```
using System;
using System.Text;

namespace StringBuilderClassExample
{
class Program
{
static void Main(string[] args)
{
StringBuilder str;
str = new StringBuilder("I Don't Like C# Programming");
str.Remove(1, 6); //Remove six characters starting from index 1

Console.WriteLine(str);
```

```
Console.ReadKey();
}
}
}
```

The above program produces the following output

I Like C# Programming

Program # 47

Write a program that inserts a substring to the current instance of the StringBuilder.
C# Program

```
using System;
using System.Text;

namespace StringBuilderClassExample
{
class Program
{
static void Main(string[] args)
{

StringBuilder str = new StringBuilder("I Like Programming");

str.Insert(2, "C# ");

Console.WriteLine(str);

Console.ReadKey();
}
}
}
```

The above program inserts C# after two characters from start of the string.

Program # 48

Write a program that replaces specified number of characters to the new specified number of characters in the current instance of the StringBuilder.
C# Program

```
using System;
using System.Text;

namespace StringBuilderClassExample
{
class Program
{
static void Main(string[] args)
{
StringBuilder str = new StringBuilder("I Like C# Programming");

str.Replace("C#", "VB.NET");

Console.WriteLine(str);

Console.ReadKey();
}
}
}
```

The above program replaces the word C# with VB.NET and produces the following output:

I Like VB.NET Programming

CHAPTER 8

Errors and Exceptions handling in .NET

CHAPTER CONTENTS

- Exception
- Exception Handling
- General Overview of Errors
- Syntactical Errors
- Run Time Errors
- Semantic Errors
- Logical Errors
- Exception Handling Techniques
- Exception Oriented Block
- Exception Handler Block
- Finally Block
- Exception Handling in VB.NET
- Throwing Exceptions
- Exception Class

Exception

An unusual event that occurs in a program and causes either abnormal termination of a program or generates inaccurate result is called exception. It is an object that allows us to transmit information about an error from one place of a program to another place. It usually transmits information from the place where an error occurs to the place where the error is handling.

Exception Handling

The set of some precautionary measures or mechanism that take in order to control and handle the exceptions is called Exception Handling. It is a predefined mechanism provided by programming languages that allows us to catch and handle exceptions and errors when occurs in a program. The methods or block where the errors are handled is called exception handler.

General overview of Errors

Errors are usually categorized into the following four types:

- Syntactical Errors
- Run time Errors
- Logical Errors
- Semantic Errors

Syntactical Errors

These types of errors are called compile time errors and they are detected during the compilation of a program. Syntactical errors occurs when we change the programming language rules, general syntaxes or declaration of keywords, statements, built-in methods, or constant values for example, in C# programming language a keyword **int** is used to declare integer variables. If we use a complete word integer instead of **int** keyword then it will generate a syntactical error. For example, consider the following declaration of integer variable:

```
int x;
integer x;
```

The first declaration "int x" is correct according to C# programming language and the second declaration "integer x" is incorrect because the word integer is not the keyword of C# programming language for integer variables declaration. Therefore, the second declaration produces syntactical error during compile time of the program. Similarly, if we change the basic rules of C# programming language then it also generates syntactical errors during compile time of the program. Consider the following C# statement:

```
if (a is greater than b)
Console.WriteLine("a is greater");
```

The above declaration of "if statement" is incorrect according to C# programming language and it will produce syntactical error when we compile.

Run time Errors

These types of errors are detected when a program is running after its compilation. The run time errors cannot be detected during the program compilation but they are detected if we remove all the syntactical errors from a program and we run it for execution. There are some other factors that involve in the generation of run time errors. Following is the details of some common factors that involve in the generation of run time errors:

- Elimination of Driver Method
- Division by Zero
- Array out of Bound

Elimination of Driver Method

When we skip the main() method of a program then it generates run time error. The main() method is the driver method that starts the execution of a C# program. When we run a C# program, the compiler always starts execution from the main() method. If compiler does not find the main() method then it generates an error and the program execution fails. Consider the following C# programming example:

```
using System;
namespace Example
{
class Program
{
static void message(string[] args)
{
Console.WriteLine("Hello");
}
}
}
```

The above program has no syntactical errors but when we run this program then it generates run time error and displays error message that "undefined method "main" in module" or "unresolved external symbol _main referenced in method" and the program execution fails.

Division by Zero

When a program is performing some mathematical calculations and during calculation when division by zero occurs then it generates division by zero error and the program execution terminates abnormally. The following program generates division by zero error:

Program # 1

```
using System;
namespace Example
{
class Program
{
static void Main(string[] args)
{
int x = 3;
int y = 0;
int Result;
Result = x / y;
Console.WriteLine(Result);
}
}
}
```

The above program declares two integer variables x and y. The variable x is initialized with value 3 and variable y is initialized with value 0. The program is correct syntactically according to C# programming language and there is no compile time error but when we run this program then it generates run time error because it divides 3 by 0. The program encounters the error message "Attempted to divide by zero".

Array out of Bounds (Subscript)

When we use subscript or an index of an array which is greater than its maximum size then it generates a run time error "Array out of Bounds". The following program generates an error array out of bound:

Program # 2

```
using System;

namespace ArrayExample
{
class Program
{
```

```
static void Main(string[] args)
{
int[] num = new int[5];
num[0] = 1;
num[1] = 2;
num[2] = 3;
num[3] = 4;
num[4] = 5;

Console.WriteLine(num[5]);
Console.ReadKey();
}
}
}
```

The above program declares an integer array of size 5 and it initializes it with five integer values. The program tries to display the value of index position 5. Since the maximum size of array is 5 and index of array always starts from 0 therefore, the last index of array is 4. The program will generate a run time error "Index was outside the bounds of the array".

Logical Errors

These types of errors are related to our personal logics and programming skill and they occur when we use incomplete or inaccurate programming logic for a particular task. The logical errors do not detect during compile time as well as during runtime of a program. Logical errors do not affect the program execution but they produce irrelevant result.

Detection of Logical Errors

Logical errors are related to personal logic and programming skill and they are not detected by the compiler. If a program does not produce accurate result then it may contain logical errors. The logical errors can only be detected manually. To detect logical errors, the entire program is reviewed from top to bottom line by line and finds the location of the error. The detection of logical errors is easy in a small program but it is very difficult to detect logical errors in a large program because the exact location of the error is unknown. The revision of a large program is very difficult and time consuming. Therefore, logical errors can be removed easily if the program is divided into small methods. If a small method is created for each task or activity of a program then it is very easy to find out logical errors.

Semantic errors

When incorrect data types are used for variables declaration then compiler produces errors. These types of errors are called semantic errors. The compiler does not detect semantic errors but the program produces irrelevant result.

Exception Handling Mechanism

The C# programming language provides three blocks for exception handling mechanism. These blocks are try block, catch block and finally block. The try block is associated with the catch and finally blocks and it requires one or more catch blocks or a finally block or both at the same time. The try block is called exception oriented block and catch block is called exception handler block. The exception oriented block is a block of codes where errors are generated and the exception handler block is a block of codes where errors are handled and managed. When an error occurs in a program, the Exception Handling Mechanism transfers the program control from try block to catch block and handle and manage the error. Following is the details of Exception Oriented Block, Exception Handler Block, and finally block:

- Exception Oriented Block
- Exception Handler Block
- Finally Block

Exception Oriented Block

It is a block of small piece of codes that may cause errors. The exception oriented block starts with a keyword **try** followed by curly braces. The piece of codes that may cause error is placed in the body of try block between the curly braces. Following is the general syntax of this block:

```
Try
{
…………………
Body of the try block.
The piece of program codes that may cause error is placed here
…………………
}
```

Example of Exception Oriented or try Block

When two numeric values are divided with each other then sometime it may produce error for example, if the denominator is zero then it produces "divide by zero error". The following program demonstrates the exception oriented or try block in details:

Program # 3

```
using System;

namespace Example
{
class Program
{
static void Main(string[] args)
{
int x = 3;
int y = 0;
int Result;
try
{
Result = x / y;
}
Console.WriteLine(Result);
}
}
}
```

In the above program the try block contains a piece of codes that divides two values in which the value of the denominator is 0. Therefore, it produces "divide by zero error". When an error occurs, the try block transmits it to the exception handler block or catch block for handling and managing. The exception handler block then provides user-defined information to the user about that error.

Exception Handler Block

It is a block of codes where exceptions are handled and managed. When exception oriented or try block produces an error then exception handler block receives that error and produces appropriate message about the error. The exception handler block starts with a keyword **catch** followed by curly braces.

The body of this block is located between the two curly braces. The catch block is similar to a method and it takes a single parameter that is associated with the error. When catch block caught an error from try block then body of the catch block is executed. If a try block does not produce any error then the associated catch block is ignored. Following is the general syntax of catch block:

```
catch(Exception)
{
........................
Body of catch block
........................
}
```

The parameter **Exception** specifies an object of the Exception class. The Exception class represents errors that occur during an application execution. The following program demonstrates the try and catch blocks in details:

Program # 4

```
using System;

namespace Example
{
class Program
{
static void Main(string[] args)
{
int x = 3;
int y = 0;
int Result;

try
{
Result = x / y;
Console.WriteLine(Result);
}
catch (Exception e)
{
Console.WriteLine("Division by zero has occurred");
```

```
}
Console.ReadKey();
}
}
}
```

The above program divides two integer values. Since the denominator is zero therefore, the try block produces an error and transmits it to the catch block. The catch block receives the error and displays the message that "Division by zero has occurred".

Finally Block

This block is used if a block of statements or code is executed in all cases. The finally block is executed in all cases and it does not matter the exceptions occur or not. Usually it is used to clean up the resources which are previously allocated such as variables allocation, database connections, close files streams etc. When the program control leaves a try block, the finally block starts execution. Following is the general syntax of finally block:

```
Finally
{
.....................
Body of finally block.
A piece of a program code that we want to execute ................
}
```

Exception Handling in VB.NET

Visual Basic also provides Try, Catch, and Finally blocks but the main difference between Visual Basic and C# is that in Visual Basic the Catch and Finally blocks are inside in the body of the Try block therefore, Visual Basic wrapped up Catch block and Finally block into the body of the Try block. Following is its general declaration:

```
Try

Block of Statements

Catch-1 [exception [As type]] [When expression]
```

```
Catch-Statements-1
Exit Try

Catch-2 [exception [As type]] [When expression]
Catch-Statements-2
[Exit Try]
...
Catch-n [exception [As type]] [When expression]
Catch-Statements-n
Exit Try

Finally
Finally-Statements
End Try
```

Program

```
Module Module1

Sub Main()

Dim x As Integer = 3
Dim y As Integer = 0
Dim Result As Integer

Try
Result = x / y
Console.WriteLine(Result)

Catch ex As Exception
Console.WriteLine("Division by zero has occurred")

End Try

Console.ReadKey()

End Sub
End Module
```

The above program divides two integer values. Since the denominator is zero therefore, the try block produces an error and transmits it to the catch block. The catch block receives the error and displays the message that "Division by zero has occurred".

Throwing Exceptions

In exception handling mechanism, the Try and Catch blocks handles the exceptions which occurred automatically in an application due to unexpected events such as division by zero, array out of bound, insufficient memory allocation, out of range exception, type mismatch, Input/output exceptions etc but if we want to produce exceptions manually with our own defined message to the user then we use conditional exception handling mechanism. The conditional exception handling mechanism throws exceptions manually when a specified condition becomes true. For example, if we create an application or program that reads only positive numbers and if a user input negative number then the condition becomes true and the application or program throws an exception. The C# and Visual Basic provides a keyword throw and Throw respectively which is used to throw an exception when a specified condition becomes true. The following program demonstrates the throw keyword:

Write a program that accepts only positive numbers. If we input negative number then the program produces an exception.
C# Program

```
using System;

namespace ConsoleApplication1
{
class Program
{
static void Main(string[] args)
{
int x;

try
{
x = -1;
```

```
if (x < 0)
{
throw new ArgumentOutOfRangeException("The number cannot be Negative");
}
Console.WriteLine("The Value of X = "+ x);
}

catch(Exception ex)
{
Console.WriteLine(ex.Message);
}
Console.ReadKey();
}
}
}
```

Visual Basic Program

```
Imports System

Module Module1

Sub Main()

Dim x As Integer

Try
x = -1

If x < 0 Then
Throw New ArgumentOutOfRangeException("The number cannot be Negative")
End If

Console.WriteLine("The Value of X = " & x)

Catch ex As Exception
Console.WriteLine(ex.Message())
```

```
End Try

Console.ReadKey()

End Sub
End Module
```

Exception Class

This class represents errors that occur during the execution of an application. It is the base class for all the exceptions. When an error occurs in an application, it reports that error by throwing an exception containing information about the error. The namespace of this class is System. Following is the constructor of this class:

public Exception();

The Exception class provides some important properties which are used to display information about the exceptions that occurs in the application. Following is the details of these properties:

Property	Details
Message	This property is used to return the reason of the error that occurs in the try block.
StackTrace	This property is used to return the exact location where the error occurs. Usually it returns the line number where the error occurs.
HelpLink	This property allows us to provide the help URL for an error that occurs. Usually it is used if we want to provide help about a particular error.

The following table provides some of the predefined exception classes derived from the Sytem.SystemException class:

Exception Class	Description
System.IO.IOException	This class handles all the Input/ output errors.

System.IndexOutOfRangeException	This class handles all the errors generated when a method refers to an array index out of range. For example, if the size of an array is 10 and we are accessing the value of index 11 then it will produce this error.
System. ArrayTypeMismatchException	This class handles all the errors generated when type is mismatched with the array type.
System.NullReferenceException	This class handles all the errors generated from referencing a null object.
System.DivideByZeroException	This class handles all the errors generated when division by zero has occurred.
System.InvalidCastException	This class handles all the errors generated when an invalid or wrong typecasting has occurred.
System.OutOfMemoryException	This class handles all the errors generated when insufficient free memory is not available.
System.StackOverflowException	This class handles all the errors generated when Stack overflow has occurred.

CHAPTER 9

Designing and Building Windows Applications in .NET

CHAPTER CONTENTS

- Windows Applications
- Windows Forms Designer
- Windows Forms
- Control Objects
- Event Handlers
- Properties of Object
- Methods of Object
- Events of Object
- Windows Form Class
- Properties of Windows Form Class
- Method of Windows Form Class
- Events of Windows Form Class
- Control Objects Classes
- Properties of Control Objects Classes
- Methods of Control Objects Classes
- Events of Control Objects Classes
- Windows Applications Designing
- Designing Applications using Visual Studio. NET
- MessageBox Class

Windows Application

Windows application is a software application that runs on a computer system. A Windows application is made up of one or more Windows Forms and one or more Control Objects. A Windows Form is a container that has visual graphical appearance and normally displays on the computer desktop. It is actually the representation of a Window that is used to provide user interface for the development of Windows Forms applications. A Windows Form is a container for the Control Objects that provides different layouts to arrange the Control Objects according to the programmer or developer settings. The Control

Objects are called Windows Forms Control Objects. The Control Objects are graphical objects and they are placed on Windows Forms for different purposes. The Control Objects provide multiple user interfaces and allow a user to interact with the application at multiple points. Each Control Object is an entry point and an execution point for the application. The Windows application provides multiple entry points and multiple execution points for the application unlike Console application because Windows application uses different windows Forms and different Control Objects that provide multiple user interfaces at multiple points of an application. The multiple entry points mean Windows application takes input from the user at multiple points using different Control Objects and display the data or information at the same graphical user interface. The multiple execution points mean Windows application provides multiple execution paths for the application. The Control Objects are used for different purposes such as to allow a user to input data or information to the application using the input devices, to display the data or information, and to arrange Control Objects on Windows Form. Windows application takes input from the user using almost all input devices such as keyboard, mouse, scanner, Barcode reader, and Finger prints reader etc.

Windows applications are event driven applications programming in which the flow of execution of the application is based on different events. Events are the main sources or keys of executions of a Windows application. The Windows application cannot be executed without events. Each event requires an event handler to handle the event. A Windows application is made up of one or more Windows Forms and one or more Control Objects. Each Windows Form and each Control Object of a Windows application provides various procedures called events handlers. Each procedure or event handler is a small part of a Windows application that contains the block of codes or statements. In Windows application the program code is divided among different procedures or events handlers according to different tasks of the block of codes or statements. The block of codes of each task of Windows application is placed in a separate procedure or event handler. The block of codes is always placed inside in the body of the procedure or event handler and when a procedure or event handler is executed then it executes the block of codes written in the body of that procedure or event handler and performs a specific task. A procedure or event handler is a key for the execution of Windows application and each procedure or event handler is an entry point and an execution point for the Windows application. A procedure or event handler requires a calling point or a calling code to become active and executes the block of codes or statements of the Windows application because a procedure or event handler of a Windows application cannot execute automatically without a calling point or calling code. The calling point or calling code of a procedure or event handler is an external source or factor called an event.

Each procedure or event handler requires an event to execute the block of codes or statements of a Windows application. Events are the keys of execution of procedures or events handlers. When an event occurs it informs the application that something has been occurred or changed in the application and calls a particular procedure or event handler and executes the block of codes or statements of the Windows application written in the body of that procedure or event handler. When a procedure or event handler is executed, it executes the block of codes or statements and performs a specific task. Each procedure or event handler has its own purpose and it is executed when a particular event occurs.

In Windows application each procedure or event handler is similar to the main procedure or method of the Console application because in Windows application each procedure contains the block of codes and when a procedure is executed, it executes the block of codes and performs a specific task but the main difference is that when we run the Console application, the compiler always starts execution from the main procedure of the Console application automatically and executes the entire program without any event while in Windows application the procedures cannot be executed automatically because they require events to execute. An event is a signal or an action in Windows application that occurs when a particular external factor, source, or an operation occurs during the Windows application execution. The external factors, sources, or operations are usually performed by the users using the input devices such as keyboard, mouse, barcode readers, and finger print devices etc. They also performed by sensors devices, and timers. The sensors are hardware devices attached to some Windows application for different purposes such as security, checking, matching or comparing objects, and recognition of an object etc. When a user operates a keyboard or a mouse in Windows application, it triggers different events for example, when a user presses any key from the keyboard, the keyboard key Press event occurs similarly, if a user presses the mouse button, the mouse Click event occurs and so on. There are some other factors, sources, or operations involved in Windows applications that triggers different events such as Threads execution, Messages from other application or from the same application, or when a specified condition is satisfied in the application or in Windows application when the Windows Form is loaded into the memory then the form Load event occurs similarly, when the Windows form is resized, the resize event occurs and so on. The execution of the Windows application procedures are related with different events. When an event occurs it informs the application that something has been occurred or changed in the application and calls a particular procedure and performs a specific task.

The procedures in Windows application do not return values to the calling code or calling point because in Windows application the procedures are usually events handlers and the calling codes or calling points of the events handlers are different events. Events are not the application codes but they are external factors or operations performed by the users or any other reasons and they do not have any catching sources to catch the return values of the Windows application procedures or events handlers. The procedure has different types in different programming languages such as routines, subroutines, methods, or functions. The different .NET programming languages use different type of procedures for example, in C# the procedure is called method and in Visual Basic the procedure is called subroutine or function but in case of Windows application the procedure is always a subroutine because in Visual Basic a function always returns a value but an event handler does not returns any value therefore, in Visual Basic the Windows application procedures or events handlers are always subroutines that do not return values.

In Windows application each procedure or event handler has its own unique name. The name of the procedure or event handler is made up of the name of the Control Object followed by an underscore character and the name of the event. Therefore, in Windows application the name of each procedure or event handler contains two parts. The first part of the procedure or event handler name indicates name of the Control Object and the second part of the procedure or event handler name indicates name of the event that occurred. Each procedure or event handler of a Windows application also contains two built-in arguments or parameters. The first argument is sender and the second argument is e. The first argument sender represents the Control Object that triggers or produces the event and the second argument e contains data or information related to the current event that occurs. The type of the first argument sender is always Object and the type of the second argument e depends on the event that occurs. The Control Objects classes provide different events that execute different event handlers of the instances of the Control Objects when we place on a Windows Form. The Microsoft Visual Studio.NET provides the Windows Form Designer to develop Windows applications.

Windows Forms Designer

The Windows Forms designer is a graphical user interface or environment provided by Microsoft Visual Studio.NET that allows us to design the Windows based applications using Windows Forms and different Control Objects. The Windows Forms Designer provides Windows Forms and different types of Control Objects called Windows Forms Control Objects. The Control Objects are the instances of Control Objects Classes and they are placed in a Toolbox that is called Controls Toolbox. A Controls Toolbox is a container that holds the Control Objects in a list of different groups according to the functionality of the Control Objects. The Control Toolbox is normally displayed on the left side of the Windows Forms Designer of Microsoft Visual Studio.NET but we can also access it from the View option of Microsoft Visual Studio.NET main menu. The Control Toolbox contains different types of Control Objects. Each Control Object has its own functionality. The Control Objects are placed on a Windows Form to design a Windows Form according to the application specification. A Control Object is placed on a Windows Form for a particular purpose. The Control Objects are normally placed on the Windows Form by dragging the Control from the Control Toolbox and place it anywhere on the Windows Form. The Control Object can also be added to the Windows Form by double clicking on the Control Object. Each Control Object and each Windows Form provides different events and each event calls a procedure which is called event handler. When we double click on any Control Object, it opens the code editor for a default procedure or event handler of that Control Object and allows us to add the block of codes in the Control Object default procedure or event handler body.

Windows Forms

A Windows Form is a graphical Application Programming Interface (API) provided by Microsoft Visual Studio.NET for different .NET programming languages to develop different visual and graphical user interfaces. The Windows application always starts from a Windows Form. A Windows Form is a rectangular container that has a visual graphical appearance and normally displays on the computer desktop. A Windows Form is actually the representation of a Window and it is used in Windows applications that provide user interface and allow users to interact with the application. The Windows Form takes input or information from the user and displays the output or information to the user on the same interface. The Windows application is made up from one or more Windows Forms. The Windows Forms are actually visual rectangular frames or containers for the Control Objects. The Control Objects are used to design the Windows Forms according to the application specification. The Windows Forms hold Control Objects and provide different layouts to arrange the Control Objects in different formats according to the programmers or developers settings. The area of a Windows Form that holds the Control Objects is called client area or container area of the Windows Form. The Control Objects are graphical controls that are also called Windows Forms Control Objects. The Control Objects are used on the Windows Forms to allow a user to interact with the application. The Control Objects provide different interfaces which allow a user to input data or information to the application, view, or display data or information.

A Windows Form is a class in the .NET Framework and it is defined in the System.Windows.Forms namespace. The Form class represents a Window within an application and it provides different types of Windows Forms such as Single Document Interface (SDI) Windows Forms, Multiple Document Interface (MDI) Windows Forms, and Modal Windows Forms. The modal Windows Forms are special types of Windows Forms that are called Dialog Boxes. A Dialog Box is a special type of a Windows Form in Windows application that allows a user to communicate with the application. It prompts and allows a user to perform a command or sends a response to the application. It asks a question from the user and requires an acknowledgment from the user about a particular task that whether the application processed that particular task or not. It also sends information or progress report to the user and also alerts for the error report when occurs during the application execution or when a user input the wrong or irrelevant information or data to the application.

The Multiple Document Interface (MDI) is the collections of different types of Windows Forms that contain Parent Windows Form and child Windows Forms. The Windows Form class provides different sets of properties, methods, and events that provide different operations or tasks for different purposes. The properties can be set during the program designing time and also can be set during run time of the application. The properties of a Windows Form are used to change the characteristics or state of the Windows Forms such as to change and set the size of the Form, change the Form Title, change the Form background color, change the Form Icon, change the Form style, change the Form border style, change or set the default display location of the Form, change the fore Color of all the Control Objects placed on the Form, change the mouse cursor shape while moving over the Form, change the font style of all the Control Objects placed on the Form and so on.

To use Windows Forms in Windows applications the namespace System. Windows.Forms must be included at the top of the application. Following is the general structure of a Windows Form provided by Microsoft Visual Studio.NET:

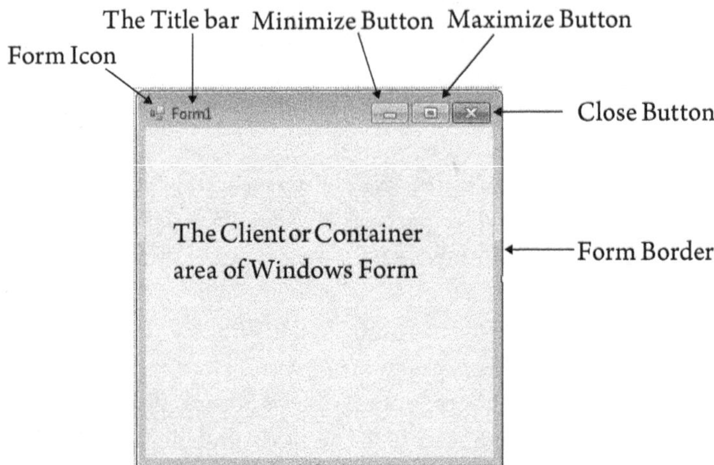

This is the default normal Windows Form of the .NET Framework provided by Visual Studio.NET for Windows applications development. The default name and default title of the Windows Form is always Form1 but we can change and give any user-defined name and title to the Windows Form using its Name and Text properties respectively.

Control Objects

Control Objects are graphical Objects provided by .NET for Windows Forms designing. Control Objects provide different interfaces and allow users to interact with the application. The Control Objects are also called Windows Forms Control Objects because they are used on the Windows Forms. The Windows Forms are containers or interfaces for the Control Objects. The Control Objects are placed on Windows Forms and design a Windows application. Control Objects are placed on a Windows Form for particular purposes and they are placed on a Windows Form to design it according to the application specification. Control Objects provide multiple entry points and multiple execution points for Windows application and allow users to interact with the application at multiple points. There are different types of Control Objects provided by Microsoft .NET Framework. Some of these Control Objects are used on Windows Forms for input and output purposes which allow users to enter data or information to the application and display data or information on the same interfaces, some Control Objects are used to arrange other Control Objects on the surface of a Windows Form which are called Container Control Objects, some Control Objects are used to create Menus, Toolbars, Pop-up Menus, and Task bar on Windows Form, some Control Objects are used to display the Windows standard Modals Dialog Boxes, and some Control Objects are used to provide different services to the users such as Event Log services, Directory entry service, error provider services, Messages Queue services, Processes services, File System Watcher services, Service Controller services, Timer service and so on.

Each Control Object is itself a class. The classes of Control Objects are defined in the System.Windows.Forms namespace. The classes of Control Objects are used to create Control Objects during runtime of an application. Each class of Control Objects provides a constructor that is used to initialize an instance of a Control Object class. The instance of a Control Object class is used to create a new Control Object and place it on a Windows Form during run time of an application using the Windows Form Controls Collection. Each class of Control Objects provides its own set of different properties, methods, and events. When we create a Control Object from its class then the created Control Object uses the properties, methods, and events of its class. The classes of Control Objects are usually used to create Control Objects during run time or execution time of an application.

The instances of Control Objects are also placed in a Toolbox that is called Controls Toolbox. The Controls Toolbox is a small Window that is normally displayed in the left side of Microsoft Visual Studio.NET Windows Forms Designer. The Controls Toolbox can also be accessed from the View option of the main menu of Microsoft Visual Studio.NET Windows Forms Designer. Each Control Object of a Toolbox is the representation of Control Object class. The Controls Toolbox allows us to place Control Objects on Windows Forms during the designing time of an application. When we place a Control Object on a Windows Form, the Windows Forms Designer displays all the properties of that Control Object class in a small Window called Properties Window. The properties Window is normally displayed on the right side of the Windows Forms Designer but it can also be accessed from the View option of the main menu of Visual Studio.NET Windows Forms Designer. The properties of Control Objects are used to perform different operations on the Control Objects for example, to change the Control style, size, background color, background picture, font style, the Control name, the Control title, text color, border style, the Control appearance, the Control icons, the Control Text alignment, the Control visibility, and the Control invisibility and so on.

A Windows Form can be designed by placing the Control Objects either in designing time or runtime of the application. When we write the application code using the Microsoft Visual Studio.NET Windows Form designer then it is called designing time of an application and when we run an application and during the execution time of an application if we place the Control Objects on a Windows Form then it is called runtime of an application. When we design a Windows Form during designing time of an application, we use the Microsoft Visual Studio.NET Windows Form Designer which provides us Windows Forms and Controls Toolbox. The Toolbox provides the instances of Control Objects classes and allows us to place Control Objects on a Windows Form. When we design a Windows Form during runtime of an application, we use the classes of Control Objects. The classes of Control Objects allow us to create Control Objects and place them on a Windows Form.

The Control Objects are categorized in different groups according to the similar functionality of the Control Objects and they are placed in a Toolbox in the form of a list in different groups. Each group of the Control Objects has its own name and each group of the Control Objects is placed in the Controls Toolbox under the name of that group. Following is the details of different groups of Control Objects:

- Common Control Objects
- Containers Control Objects
- Menus and Toolbars Control Objects
- Data Control Objects
- Components Control Object
- Printing Control Objects
- Dialogs Control Objects
- Reporting Control Objects

Common Control Objects

The Common Control Objects are usually used in almost all Windows applications therefore they are called Common Control Objects. The

Microsoft .NET Framework provides various Common Control Objects which are used for different purposes on Windows Forms. These Control Objects are usually used for input and output purposes and allow users to input data to the application and display data on the same interfaces. These Control Objects provides different interfaces to the users for data input and output operations. Following is the list of Common Control Objects provided by .NET Framework:

Button	CheckBox	CheckedListBox
ComboBox	DateTimePicker	Label
LinkLabel	ListBox	ListView
MaskedTextBox	MonthCalendar	NotifyIcon
NumericUpDown	PictureBox	ProgressBar
RadioButton	RichTextBox	TextBox
ToolTip	TreeView	WebBrowser

Containers Control Objects

These Control Objects are containers which allow us to arrange other Control Objects on a Windows Form. The Container Control Objects are usually used when we arrange other Control Objects and make different groups of the Control Objects on a Windows Form. When we place Control Objects on any Container Control Object then it arranges all the Control Objects and makes a group of the Control Objects on a Windows Form. The Microsoft .NET Framework provides different types of Containers Control Objects. Some Containers Control Objects automatically arrange other Control Objects either horizontally or vertically in rows and columns like a table while some Container Control Objects do not arrange other Control Objects automatically but they allow us to arrange the Control Objects on the surface of the Container Control Objects manually. When we place Control Objects on the surface of any Container Control Object, they make a single group on the surface of that Container and share some basic properties of that Container. The Containers Control Objects do not use some properties by itself but they are implemented by other Control Objects placed on the surface of a Container Control Object for example, if we use the Font property of a Container Control Object to change the font then it will be implemented on all the Control Objects placed on the same Container and the Font of all Control Objects will be changed similarly, if we use the ForeColor property of a Container Control Object to change the foreground color then it will change the foreground color of all the Control Objects placed on that Container. Following is the list of Container Control Objects provided by .NET Framework:

FlowLayoutPanel	GroupBox	Panel
SplitContainer	TabControl	TableLayoutPanel

Menus and Toolbars Controls Object

These Control Objects are used to create a Main menu, Pop-up menus, Toolbars, and Taskbar on a Windows Form. Following is the list of Menus and Toolbars Control Objects provided by .NET Framework:

ContextMenuStrip	MenuStrip	StatusStrip
ToolStrip	ToolStripContainer	

Data Control Objects

These Control Objects are used to connect Windows applications to the database. The Data Control Objects provide database connections and allow us to perform different operations on the database. They also provide the data binding services and allow us to bind different Control Objects and connect to the database. Following is the list of Data Control Objects provided by .NET Framework:

BindingNavigator	BindingSource	DataGridView
DataSet		

Components Control Objects

These Control Objects do not have visible interfaces during run time of the application. They are always invisible from the users during run time. The Components Control Objects are used in Windows applications to provide different services such as Events Logs services that allow us to interact with the Microsoft Windows Event Log and perform different operations on it, Errors providers services, access and handle different services and device driver services installed on a computer system, directory services, watch and handle the changes that occurs in a specified folder or a directory, access and handle different processes running in a computer system, Messages Queues services, Serial Port communication services that allow us to read and write data using the serial port of a computer system, the Timer services, the Help provider services, the Background Working services and so on. Following is the list of Components Control Objects provided by .NET Framework:

BackgroundWorker	DirectoryEntry	DirectorySearcher
ErrorProvider	EventLog	FileSystemWatcher
HelpProvider	ImageList	MessageQueue
PerformanceCounter	Process	SerialPort
ServiceController	Timer	

Printing Control Objects

These Control Objects are used in Windows applications to provide the printing services to the Windows applications. The Printing Control Objects allow us to interact with the printers devices using the Windows standard print dialog box and send outputs to the printers installed on a local computer or on a network computer. These Control Objects also provide the page setup Windows standard dialog box and the print preview Windows standard dialog box and allow us to set the page margins, the page orientation, the paper size etc. Following is the list of Printing Control Objects provided by .NET Framework:

PageSetupDialog	PrintDialog	PrintDocument
PrintPreviewControl	PrintPreviewDialog	

Dialog Control Objects

These Control Objects are used in Windows applications to display the Windows standard Modal Dialog Boxes. A Dialog Box is a special type of a Windows Form that allows a user to communicate with the application. It prompts and allows a user to perform a command or sends a response to the application. It asks a question from the user and requires an acknowledgment from the user about a particular task that whether the application processed that particular task or not. It also sends information or progress report to the user and also alerts for the error report when occurs during the application execution or when a user input the wrong or irrelevant data to the application. The Dialog Control Objects provides different Dialog Boxes such as Color Dialog Box, Open File Dialog Box, Save File Dialog Box, Font Dialog Box, and Folder Browser Dialog Box. Following is the list of Dialog Control Objects provided by .NET Framework:

ColorDialog	FolderBrowserDialog	FontDialog
OpenFileDialog	SaveFileDialog	

Reporting Control Objects

These Control Objects provide reporting services to the Windows applications. They provide a visual view for the crystal report to display data or information on the application. They allow us to export or print the report. The Reporting Control Objects provide different properties and methods which are used to perform different operations on the reports such as to set the report format, the export option, and set the print option of a report. Following is the list of Reporting Control Objects provided by .NET Framework:

CrystalReportViewer	CrystalReportDocument

Events Handlers

A Windows application is made up of one or more Windows Forms and one or more Control Objects. The Windows Forms and Control Objects provide various procedures which are called events handlers. An event handler is a small block of codes or statements of the application which is executed to perform a specific task. Each event handler requires an event to execute the block of codes or statements of the application. Events are the keys of execution of events handlers. When an event occurs, it informs the application that something has been occurred or changed in the application and calls a particular event handler and executes the block of codes or statements written in the body of that event handler. Windows application contains a series of different events handlers which are executed in a sequence. The program codes of Windows application is always written in various events handlers. Each event handler has its own purpose and it is related to a particular event. When a particular event occurs, it executes the related event handler.

Events handlers are similar to methods or functions but the main difference is that the methods or functions return values to the calling code or calling point but events handlers do not return values to the calling code or calling point because events handlers are executed by the related events and events are not the application code but they are external factors or operations and they do not have any catching sources to catch the return values of the application.

Each event handler of a Windows application contains two arguments or parameters. The first argument is sender and the second argument is e. The first argument sender represents the Control Object that provides or triggers the event and the second argument e contains data or information related to the current event that occurs. The type of the first argument sender is always Object and the type of the second argument e depends on the event that occurs. The Control Objects classes provide different events that execute different events handlers of the Control Objects.

Properties of an Object

A property of an object is a unit of data about an object or it is an attribute of an object that indicates the object characteristics, states or information. A property of an object takes different values and performs specific operations on object characteristics and change the information of an object according to the value of that property. The Control Objects classes provides different types of properties which perform different operations on the Control Objects such as the Control Object name, title, type, appearance, location on the screen, size, border style, visibility, background color, foreground color, font style, icon of a Control Object, and background picture of a Control Object and so on. The Windows Forms also provide a set of different properties which are used to change the state, or characteristics of a Windows Form such as the Background color of a Windows Form, The Background picture, The Title, the Name of a Windows Form, the Border Style, Appearance, Size, the Default location of a Windows Form on the screen, Icon of a Windows Form and so on. The properties of a Control Object and the properties of a Windows Form can be set during the designing time of Windows application using the Microsoft Visual Studio.NET Designer. The properties can also be set during run time of the application.

Methods of an Object

A method of an object is a procedure that performs different tasks on objects. It takes values as parameters and performs a specific task on an object. The difference between the properties and methods is that the properties of an object are used to change the characteristics, state or appearance of that object while the methods of an object are used to manipulate or to perform some actions on that object. The Control Objects classes provide different types of methods which perform different tasks on the Control Objects. The Windows

Form also provides different types of Methods which perform different tasks on the Windows Form.

Events of an Object

An event of an object is a signal or an action in Windows application that occurs when a particular external factor, source, or an operation occurs. The external factors, sources, or operations are usually performed by the users using the input devices such as keyboard, mouse, barcode readers, and finger print devices etc. The events are also performed by sensors devices, and timers. The sensors are hardware devices attached to some Windows application for different purposes such as security, checking, matching or comparing objects, and recognition of an object etc. When a user operates a keyboard or a mouse, it triggers different events for example, when a user presses any key from the keyboard, the keyboard key Press event occurs similarly, if a user presses the mouse button, the mouse click event occurs and so on. The sensor receives a signal or an input from the environment and responds to the Windows application and executes a particular event handler. There are some other factors, sources, or operations involved in Windows applications that triggers different events such as Threads execution, Messages from other application or from the same application, or when a specified condition is satisfied in the application, or when a Windows Form is loaded into the memory, the form Load event occurs similarly, when a Windows form is resized, the resize event occurs and so on.

Events are the keys of the execution of events handlers. When an event occurs, it informs the application that something has been occurred or changed in the application and calls a particular event handler and executes the block of codes or statements written in the body of that event handler.

Windows Form Class

Windows Form class represents a Windows Form. A Windows Form is used to develop Windows applications. A Windows Form is a visual rectangular container that provides an interface to the users to interact with the application. The Control Objects are placed on the container or client area of Windows Forms and design Windows applications. The Windows Form class is defined in the namespace System.Windows.Forms. A Windows application is made up of one or more Windows Forms and one or more Control Objects. The Windows Form class is used to create a Windows Form dynamically during run time or execution time of the application. To create a Windows Form during run time of an application, an instance of the Windows Form class is declared and initializes it using the constructor of the Windows Form class. The dynamically created Windows Form also allows us to place Control Objects on it dynamically. The dynamically created Windows Forms displays only run time of the application. The Control Objects are placed on the Windows Forms using the Control Objects classes. The Windows Form is also can be added to the application during design time of the application. Following is the general syntax of the Windows Form class constructor:

C# Syntax
public Form()
Visual Basic Syntax
Public Sub New

The default size of a Windows Form is 300 pixels in height and 300 pixels in width. We can change the default size of a Windows Form using the **Size** property. Following is the general syntax to declare and initialize new instance of the Windows Form:

C# Initialization
Form form1 = new Form();
Visual Basic Initialization
Dim form1 As New Form()

In the above declaration **form1** is the name of the new instance of the Windows Form and **Form()** is the constructor of the Windows Form class. The name of the new Windows Form is form1. This is the default name of the Windows Form and we can give any name to the new instance according to the .NET variables naming convention. The default name of the Windows Form is always Form concatenated with a numeric value starting from one for example, Form1, Form2, Form3 and so on. To change the default name of a Windows Form, the Name property of the Windows Form class is used.

Properties of Windows Form Class

Windows Form class provides various properties which are used to change the characteristics, states or appearance of a Windows Form. Following is the list of some basic and important properties of the Windows Form class:

Property	Description
Name	This property of Windows Form class is used to change the default name of a Windows Form and set its new name. The Name property is also used to get the current name of a Windows Form.
Text	This property is used to set or get the title of a Windows Form.
BackColor	This property is used to set or get the background color of a Windows Form.
BackgroundImage	This property is used to get or set the background picture of a Windows Form.
BackgroundImageLayout	This property is used to get or set layout of the background image of a Windows Form. The layout is a position of an image on the surface of the client area or container area of a Windows Form. This property takes five constant values provided by ImageLayout enumeration which provides five different types of layouts for the background image. The constant values are None, Tile, Center, Stretch, and Zoom.
AcceptButton	This property is used to set a command button as an accept button. An accept button is a command button which is activated and clicked automatically when the enter key is pressed from the keyboard.
CancelButton	This property is used to set a command button as a cancel button. A cancel button is a command button which is activated and clicked automatically when the Escape key is pressed from the keyboard.
Cursor	This property is used to get or set the mouse pointer style when the mouse pointer is over the Windows Form.

AutoScroll	This property is used to attach scroll bars automatically to the Windows Form. It takes a Boolean value either True or False.
AutoScrollMargin	This property is used to get or set the auto scroll margin of the Scroll bars.
AutoScrollMinsize	This property is used to get or set the minimum size of the scroll area of a Windows Form.
ControllBox	This property is used to hide or displays the control box of a Windows Form. Each Windows Form has a control box that contains the Form Icon and three buttons that is Minimize button, Maximize button, and close button. This property takes a Boolean value either True or False. If we set the value of this property to True, the control box will be displayed otherwise, the control box will not be displayed.
Font	This property is related with the Windows Form contents or Control Objects which are placed on the Windows Form. It is used to set or change the Font style of the Control Objects or the contents of a Windows Form.
ForeColor	This property is used to get or set the text color of the contents or the Control Objects which are placed on a Windows Form.
FormBorderStyle	This property is used to change the border style of the Windows Form.
Enabled	This property is used to make a Windows Form enabled or disabled.
Location	This property is used to set the location of a Windows Form on the screen coordinates.

MaximumSize	The property is used to set the maximum size of a Windows Form. It takes two integer values. The first value indicates the Form width and the second value indicates the Form height. This property is also used to get the current maximum size.
MinimumSize	This property is used to set the minimum size of a Windows Form. It takes two integer values. The first value indicates the Form width and the second value indicates the form height. This property is also used to get the current minimum size of a Windows Form.
Size	This property is used to set or get the size of a Windows Form.
Visible	This property is used to get or set the visibility of a Windows Form.
SizeGripStylde	This property is used to display the sizing grip for the Windows Form. It takes three values i.e. Auto, Show, and Hide. By default it is Auto for all the Windows Forms that displays the sizing grip when needed.
Padding	This property is used to get or set padding of the Windows Form. Padding is the client area or container area of a Windows Form that keeps the Control Objects. This property takes four integer values and set the padding of a Windows Form. The first value of this property indicates the Left position, the second value indicates the Top position, the third value indicates the Right position, and the fourth value indicates the Bottom position of the Padding.
StartPosition	This property is used to get or set the starting or initial position of the Windows Form when it is displayed on the screen during run time of the application.

WindowsState	This property is used to get or set the state of a Windows Form. The state of a Windows Form means how to display the Windows Form on the screen. It takes three constant values provided by the FormWindowState enumeration. These three constant values are Normal, Minimized, and Maximized.
Icon	This property is used to get or set the Icon of a Windows Form. An Icon is a picture that represents the Windows Form on the computer taskbar.
IsMdiContainer	This property is used to get or set a value that indicates whether a Windows Form is a container for the MDI Child Forms or not. It takes a Boolean value either True or False. Its default value is False that indicates the Form is not a container for the MDI child Forms. If its value is set to True then the Form becomes a container for the MDI child Forms.
MaximizeBox	This property is used to get or set a value that indicates whether the Maximize button of the Form is enabled or disabled. It takes a Boolean value either True or False. Its default value is True that indicates the Maximize button is enabled.
MinimizeBox	This property is used to get or set a value that indicates whether the Minimize button of the Form is enabled or disabled. It takes a Boolean value either True or False. Its default value is True that indicates the Minimize button is enabled.
MainMenuStrip	This property is used to get or set the main Menu for the Windows Form. It takes the MenuStrip control as an input and set main Menu for the Windows Form. The default value of this property is null that indicates no Menu.

ShowIcon	This property is used to display or hide the Icon on the caption bar of the Windows Form. It takes a Boolean value either true or false. If the value of this property is set to True, it displays the Icon otherwise, it hides the Icon.
ShowInTaskbar	This property is used to get or set a value that indicates whether a Form will be displayed on the Windows taskbar or not during run time of the application. It takes a Boolean value either True or False.
AutoSize	This property is used to reset the Windows Form and shrinks or grows the Windows Form to fits its size to all its contents or Control Objects. This property actually shrinks the container area of a Form and fits its size to all its contents or Control Objects. It takes a Boolean value either True or False. By default its value is False that do not resize the Form.
AutoSizeMode	This property is used to get or set type or mode of the auto size of Windows Form. It depends on the AutoSize property and it works only if the value of the AutoSize property is True. This property takes two constant values i.e. GrowOnly and GrowAndShrink.

Methods of Windows Form Class

Windows Form class provides different methods which are used to manipulate and perform different tasks on the Windows Form. Following is the list of some basic and important methods of the Windows Form class:

Method	Description
Activate	This method is used to activate a Windows Form and get the focus.

ActivateMdiChild	This method is used to activate the MDI child Form.
AdjustFormScrollBars	This method is used to adjust the scrollbars on a Windows Form.
BringToFront	This method is used to change the z-order of the Control Objects and bring a specified Control Object on the front of the z-order of Control Objects.
CenterToParent	This method is used to set the position of the child Form within the parent Form and displays a child Form within the center of the parent Form.
CenterToScreen	This method is used to set the position of the Windows Form and displays it on the center of the current screen.
Close	This method is used to close a Windows Form.
Contains	This method is used to indicate whether a specified Control Object is a child of the other Control Object or not.
CreateControls	This method is used to create a Control on a specified Windows Form.
Dispose	This method is used to close a Windows Form without the using of the Close() method and releases all the resources associated to it.
Focus	This method is used to set the input focus to the Control Object.
Refresh	This method is used to refresh the Windows Form.
Validate	This method is used for the validation of the Control Objects.

Events of Windows Form Class

The Windows Form class provides various events which are used to execute codes written in different event handlers. Following is the list of some basic and important Windows Form class events:

Event	Description
Activated	This event occurs when a Windows Form gets the input focus and it becomes active.
Deactivate	This event occurs when a Windows Form lost the input focus and it becomes deactivated.
Move	This event occurs when a Windows Form moves on the screen. It passes an EventArgs to its event handler.
Load	This event occurs when a Windows Form is loaded for the first time. It passes EventArgs to its event handler.
Resize	This event occurs when a Windows Form is resized. When the size of a Windows Form is changed by the mouse, the Resize event occurs. This event passes EventArgs to its event handler.
Shown	This event occurs when a Windows Form is displayed at the first time.
Paint	This event occurs when a Windows Form appears on the screen for the first time or when a Windows Form is redrawn. This event passes a PaintEventArgs to its event handler.
FormClosing	This event occurs when a Windows Form is closing. When we press the close button of a Windows Form or when we press Alt + F4 buttons from the keyboard while when the Windows Form is active and the focus is on it then the FormClosing event occurs and calls the FormClosing event handler and executes the block of statements or codes. The FormClosing event handler is usually used to release the resources allocated to the application. The FormClosing event handler is also used to write the block of codes or statements that cancel the event and prevent the Windows Form from closing. To cancel the event and prevent the Windows Form from closing, the cancel property of the FormClosingEventArgs is set to true in the FormClosing event handler.
FormClosed	This event occurs after a Windows Form has been closed. It always occurs after the FormClosing event.

Layout	This event occurs when a child Control Object changes or repositioned on its parent Control Object or when a parent Control Object repositioned its child Control Objects. This event also occurs when a new Control Object is added to the parent Control Object or when a Control Object is removed from the parent Control Object or when some other changes occurs that effect the layout of the Windows Form. It passes a LayoutEventArgs to the event handler.
Click	This event occurs when a Windows Form is single clicked. It passes an EventArgs to its event handler.
DoubleClick	This event occurs when a Windows Form is double clicked. It passes an EventArgs to its event handler.
Enter	This event occurs when a Windows Form gets the input focus and it becomes active. This event is similar to the Activated event.
Leave	This event occurs when a Windows Form lost the input focus and it becomes no longer active.
Validating	This event occurs when a Windows Form is validating. It occurs after the Leave event. When a Windows Form is deactivated, it triggers the Leave event and calls the Leave event handler. When the Leave event is preceded then the Validating event occurs and calls the Validating event handler. The Validating event passes the CancelEventArgs to the Validating event handler. The Validating event handler allow us to cancel the event by setting the Cancel property of the CancelEventArgs. When Cancel property of the CancelEventArgs is set to true, it cancels the Validating event and the Windows Form does not loss the focus. The Validating event is related with the CausesValidation property of a Windows Form. The CausesValidation property of a Windows Form is used to enabled or disabled the Validating event. If the value of the CausesValidation property of a Windows Form is set to true then that Windows Form triggers the Validating event and if the value of the CausesValidation property is set to false then that Windows Form does not triggers the Validating event.

Validated	This event occurs when a Windows Form has been validated. It occurs after the Validating event is preceded. When the Validated event occurs, it passes an EventArgs to its event handler.
HelpButtonClicked	This event occurs when we click the Help Button of a Windows Form. The Help Button of a Windows Form is displayed on the caption bar of a Windows Form on the left side of the Close button. The Help Button is displayed on the caption bar of a Windows Form if we set the value of the HelpButton property to true.
MdiChildActivate	This event occurs when a MDI child form is activated or closed.
MouseClick	This event occurs when a Windows Form is single clicked by the mouse. It passes the MouseEventArgs to the event handler.
MouseDoubleClick	This event occurs when a Windows Form is double clicked by the mouse. It passes the MouseEventArgs to the event handler.
MouseMove	This event occurs when the mouse pointer is moved over a Windows Form. It passes the MouseEventArgs to its event handler.
MouseHover	This event occurs when the mouse pointer is over a Windows Form and it rests on it for a very small instance of time. It passes the EventArgs to its event handler.

Controls Object Classes

Microsoft .NET Framework provides various types of Control Objects. Each Control Object is a separate class. The Control Objects classes are defined in the namespace System.Windows.Forms. Following is the details of the Control Objects classes:

Button Class

This class of Control Objects represents a Button Control Object. A Button is a square shaped Control Object that contains a title text and a clickable surface.

The title text is the caption of a Button and it is a user-defined text that indicates the description or the purpose of the Button Control Object and the clickable surface of a Button allows us to click on it and perform a particular action. When a Button Control Object is clicked, it pushes inside and then releases. When a Button is clicked, it triggers the Click event and calls event handler associated with the Button Click event and executes the block of statements or code written in the body of that event handler. The Button Control Object is used for different purposes in Windows applications but usually it is used to process or execute a task.

TextBox Class

This class of Control Objects represents a TextBox Control Object. A TextBox Control Object is a square shaped text box which is used to take input text or data from the users and provides text or data to the users in Windows applications. The TextBox Control Object takes any type of text or data such as Alphabetic data, Numeric data, alphanumeric data, Date and Time etc. Therefore, a TextBox Control Object is an Input/output Control Object which is used to take input text or data from the users and display text or data to the users for viewing or editing. The TextBox Control Object also allows us to input or display text or data in the form of password format. A TextBox Control Object normally provides a single row for input and output but it also provides multiple lines that take input from the user and display output using multiple lines. The scroll bars automatically appears when the text or data of the TextBox exceeded the visible area. The TextBox Control Object displays two types of scroll bars i.e. vertically or horizontally or both at the same time. The TextBox Control Object does not allow us to format a portion of the text or data because the format operation of a TextBox always applies to the entire text of the TextBox. The Notepad editor is an example of multiple lines TextBox Control Object. The Microsoft Notepad does not allow us to format a portion of the text but the format operation always applies to the entire text.

RichTextBox Class

This class of Control Objects represents a RichTextBox Control Object. A RichTextBox Control Object is a square shaped text box which is used to take input text or data from the users and provide text or data to the users in Windows applications. The RichTextBox Control Object is similar to the TextBox Control Object but the main difference is that a RichTextBox Control Object is modified format of the TextBox Control Object. The RichTextBox allows us to select text, insert images, change fonts, change colors, load and save richtext formats or plain text formats. The TextBox Control Object does not allow us to select a small portion of the text because the selection option of the TextBox always applies to the entire text or data but a RichTextBox Control Object allows us to select a small portion even select a single or more characters from the entire text or data. A TextBox Control Object does not allow us to format a small portion of the text or data because the format option of the TextBox always applies to the entire text or data. The RichTextBox allows us to format a small portion even a single or more characters from the entire text or data of the RichTextBox. The Microsoft WordPad is an example of the RichTextBox Control Object.

MaskedTextBox Class

This class of Control Objects represents a MaskedTextBox Control Object. A MaskedTextBox Control Object is a square shaped text box that takes input text or data from the users with a specified user-defined format. The functionality of the MaskedTextBox Control Object is similar to the TextBox but the main difference is that the MaskedTextBox takes an input with a specified user-defined format which is called mask. A mask is a specified user-defined format for the input text or data set by the programmer or developer using the Mask property of the MaskedTextBox. The MaskedTextBox Control Object checks the input text or data and accepts only that text or data which matches with the mask otherwise, it rejects the input text or data. The MaskedTextBox Control Object is usually used to input that text or data which is always in a fixed format for example, the Identity Card number, E-mail address, Telephone number, Mobile Number, Registration number, Zip Codes, IBAN number, Dates and Times etc.

CheckBox Class

This class of Control Objects represents a CheckBox Control Object. A CheckBox is a square shaped Control Object that is used to select or deselect an option in the application. A CheckBox contains a title text and a square hole. The title text is a caption that indicates the description or the purpose of a CheckBox and a square hole indicates the status of a CheckBox either it is ON or OFF. A CheckBox Control Object allows us to click inside in the square hole and turns it ON or OFF. When a CheckBox is ON then there is a tick mark inside in the square hole and when it is OFF then there is no tick mark inside in the square hole. When a CheckBox is ON, it means that the option is selected and the compiler executes the code written in the body of its associated event handler and when it is OFF then the option is deselected and the compiler ignores the code written in the body of its associated event handler.

The CheckBox Control Objects are usually used when we have a set of options and we want to select one or more options at a time. To select or turn ON an option, simply click inside in the square hole of a CheckBox Control Object. When the tick mark appears, it means that the CheckBox is selected or ON. When the selected or ON CheckBox is clicked again then it becomes deselected or OFF and the tick mark is disappeared. When the CheckBox is selected or ON, its status is called checked and when it is deselected or OFF then its status is called unchecked.

CheckedListBox Class

This class of Control Objects represents a CheckedListBox Control Object. A CheckedListBox Control Object is similar to the CheckBox Control Object but the main difference is that a CheckBox Control Object is used for a single option but a CheckedListBox Control Object is a list of CheckBox Control Objects and it is used if we have a list of items or options. A CheckedListBox Control Object is a list of items or options where each option of the list has its own CheckBox. The functionality of this Control Object is similar to the CheckBox Control Object but it is the modified form of CheckBox because it is a single Control Object that contains one or more items or options in the form of a list where we can select or turn ON one or more options from the list at the same time while in the case of CheckBox Control Object if we have one or more items or options then we have to place the same numbers of CheckBox Control Objects on the Windows Form for example, if we have two options then we have to place two CheckBox Controls similarly, if we have ten options then we have to place ten CheckBox Control Objects on the Windows Form and so on. Therefore, it is recommended that if we have less or few items or options, the CheckBox Control Objects are used on the Windows Form and if we have more items or options, the CheckedListBox Control Object is used to save the space of the Windows Form.

RadioButton Class

This class of Control Objects represents a RadioButton Control Object. A RadioButton Control Object is a small circular shaped button which is used to select or process a single option at a time from the collection of multiple options in Windows application. A RadioButton contains a title text and a circular hole. The title text is the caption that indicates the description or the purpose of a RadioButton and the circular hole indicate the status of a RadioButton which is either ON or OFF. The RadioButton Control Object allows us to click on the circular hole and turns it ON. When the RadioButton is ON then there is a dot inside in the circular hole of the RadioButton and if it is OFF then there is no dot inside in the circular hole. When a RadioButton becomes ON then we cannot turn it OFF until we turn on another RadioButton Control Object.

The RadioButton Control Objects are usually used when we have a set of options and we need to select or process a single option at a time. When a RadioButton Control Object is ON then its status is called checked and when it is OFF then its status is called unchecked. When the status of a RadioButton is ON then an option is selected and its associated event handler is triggered and the block of code or statements is executed. Therefore, the RadioButton Control Objects are used in the form of groups from which we can select or turn ON a single option at a time. A single RadioButton Control Object is not working properly because a single RadioButton Control Object is always selected or ON and we cannot turn it OFF until we click inside in the circular hole of another RadioButton. When one RadioButton is ON or checked then all the other RadioButton in the same group automatically becomes OFF or unchecked. When we place RadioButton Control Objects on a Windows Form, all the RadioButton automatically make a group. If we want to make two or more groups of the RadioButton Control Objects on a same Windows Form then we place the RadioButton Control Objects inside in the Containers Control Objects such as Panel or TabControl. A Panel and TabControl are Control Objects which are used as containers for other Control Objects. They are used to hold other Control Objects in the form of a group. Each group of the RadioButton Control Objects only can ON or processes a single option at a time and turn OFF the remaining options in the same group.

The RadioButton Control Objects are used for different purposes but usually they are used in different registration forms where we have multiple options and we have to select a single option at a time for example, Gender of a person has two options such as Male or Female. When we fill a registration form then at a time we can only check or turn ON either Male or Female option similarly, if a company has three shifts for its employees then the duty shift of an employee has three options such as Morning shift, Evening shift, and Night shift. If an employee of that company fills the registration form then the employee has three options and the employee have to select only one duty shift option at a time.

ComboBox Class

This class of Control Objects represents a ComboBox Control Object. A ComboBox is a list of items in the form of drop-down. The items list of a ComboBox is normally hidden inside in the ComboBox and when we click on a ComboBox, it displays the list of items in the form of drop-down and allows us to navigate the list of items using the scroll bar of the ComboBox. Each ComboBox Control Object automatically attaches a scroll bar to the list of items when the list of items is increased from its fixed quantity. A ComboBox allows us to select a single item from the list at a time and it does not allow us to select multiple items from the list at the same time. When we select an item from the list of ComboBox, it appears in the textbox of the ComboBox Control Object. A ComboBox Control Object has two parts. The first part of a ComboBox is a textbox that displays the selected item of the list. The textbox also allows us the searching facility to type the name of an item to display. The second part of a ComboBox is a list of items that displays in the form of drop-down. A ComboBox allows us to select a single item at a time.

DateTimePicker Class

This class of Control Objects represents a DateTimePicker Control Object. A DateTimePicker Control Object is used to display the date/time and a monthly calendar. It displays a monthly calendar in the form of a drop-down. It usually displays the current system date and time and the current month and year calendar. This Control Object allows us to select a date or a time or both date and time at the same time and displays it with a specified format. This Control Object provides different formats or verities of Dates and times such as Long format that contains both date and time, Short format that contains only date, Time format that contains only time and Custom that defines a user-defined custom format for the date or time.

Label Class

This class of Control Objects represents a Label Control Object. A Label Control Object is used to display text or any other information on a Windows Form. It displays a static text or information and we cannot change it during run time of the application. The Labels are usually used to provide description or title information to other Control Objects to enable users to operate the Windows Form easily. For example, when a user fills the registration or any other Form, the Labels Control Objects provide the descriptions or title to other Control Objects so that the user can easily understand the purpose of each Control Object on a Windows Form.

LinkLabel Class

This class of Control Objects represents a LinkLabel Control Object. A LinkLabel Control Object is similar to the Label Control Object but the main difference is that it displays a hyperlink. The hyperlink of a LinkLabel Control Object is used to perform different tasks such as to display a Website or any other file associated with the application.

ListBox Class

This class of Control Objects represents a ListBox Control Object. A ListBox is a list of items arranged in the form of lines inside in the ListBox. Each line represents an item of the list. A ListBox Control Object allows us to select one or more items at a time. To select an item from the list, the item is normally clicked. When an item is clicked from the list, it becomes highlighted and a blue color appears on it which indicates the item is selected from the list. By default the ListBox Control Object allows us to select a single item from the list at a time but when we set its SelectionMode property then it allows us to select multiple items from the list at the same time.

ListView Class

This class of Control Objects represents a ListView Control Object. A ListView Control Object is used to display a collection of items in different views. It provides five different views to display the collection of items such as Large Icon, Details, Small Icon, List and Tile.

MonthCalendar Class

This class of Control Objects represents a MonthCalendar Control Object. A MonthCalendar Control Object is used to display a visual graphical monthly calendar on a Windows Form. It displays the monthly calendar of any year according to the user specification. By default the MonthCalendar Control Object displays the system current date monthly calendar. It allows us to select a date of any month and any year. This Control Object provides two navigation buttons which allow us to move the calendar backward and forward directions and change the month.

NumericUpDown Class

This class of Control Objects represents a NumericUpDown Control Object. A NumericUpDown Control Object is used to display a numeric value. The shape of this Control Object is similar to the TextBox Control Object but the main difference is that this Control Object provides two arrow keys Up and Down attached to the right side. The arrow keys allow us to increment or decrement the numeric value by clicking the Up or the Down arrow key. This Control Object is also called Up-Down Control Object. The NumericUpDown Control Object allows us to enter any numeric value from the keyboard or display the default integer value. The default integer value can be set using its two properties i.e. Minimum property and Maximum property. The Minimum property of this Control Object is used to set the initial or starting point of the integer value and the Maximum property of this Control Object is used to set the maximum or the last point of the integer value. This Control Object provides another property that is called Increment property. The Increment property is used to define or set the increment or decrement steps of the integer value. When we click the Up arrow key, it increments the integer value by the step value set in the Increment property and when we click the Down arrow key, it decrements the integer value by the step value set in the Increment property. The NumericUpDown Control Object also allows us to enter the numeric value from the keyboard. The entered numeric value can also be incremented or decremented by the step value set in the Increment property.

The NumericUpDown Control Objects are usually used in Windows applications when we need fixed constant integer values. For example, to control the volume system by clicking the Up and Down arrow keys to increase or decrease the volume similarly, to assign or allocate a specific amount of memory space by clicking the Up and Down arrow keys to increase or decrease the amount of memory space according to the requirement of the user, the number of kids of a person etc.

PictureBox Class

This class of Control Objects represents a PictureBox Control Object. A PictureBox Control Object is a squared box or frame that is used to display an image on the Windows Form. It displays the images of the different formats such as Bitmap, GIF, JPEG, and Icon images. The Image property of this Control Object is used to select an image and display it on the Windows Form.

ToolTip Class

This class of Control Objects represents a ToolTip Control Object. A ToolTip Control Object is used to display a pop-up Windows that contains user-defined information to describe the purpose of the other Control Object. The ToolTip Control Object displays a pop-up Windows when we bring mouse over the Control Object and stop motion of the mouse for some time. This Control Object is used if we want to provide details or descriptions of each other Control Object of a Windows Form and makes the Windows Form user friendly so that a user can easily understand the purpose of each Control Object of a Windows Form.

FlowLayoutPanel Class

This class of Control Objects represents a FlowLayoutPanel Control Object. A FlowLayoutPanel Control Object is a flat container that provides an interface for other Control Objects and allows us to place other Control Objects on its surface. When we place other Control Objects on the FlowLayoutPanel Control Object, it holds all the Control Objects and automatically arranges them in a horizontal or a vertical flow of direction or in the form of rows or columns. This Control Object arranges other Control Objects in different flow of directions either in horizontal flow or in vertical flow. The horizontal flow arranges all the other Control Objects in the form of rows and the vertical flow arranges all the other Control Objects in the form of columns. This Control Object provides the FlowDirection property which is used to set the flow of direction of the other Control Objects. The FlowDirection property takes four constant values and arranges all the other Control Objects in the four flows of directions such as LeftToRight, RightToLeft, TopDown, and BottomUp. The LeftToRight value arranges all the Control Objects from left to the right direction horizontally in the form of rows, the RightToLeft value arranges all the Control Objects from right to the left direction horizontally in the form of rows, the TopDown value arranges all the Control Objects from top to the bottom direction vertically in the form of columns, and the BottomUp value arranges all the Control Objects from bottom to the top direction vertically in the form of columns. The default value of this Control Object is LeftToRight that arranges all the Control Objects from left to the right direction horizontally in the form of rows.

When the FlowLayoutPanel Control Object arranges Control Objects using the horizontal flow of direction, it starts arrangement of the Control Objects from the first row and places Control Objects in the first row. When the first row is completed, it starts the second row and places the Control Objects in the second row and when the second row is completed, it starts the third row and so on, similarly when the FlowLayoutPanel Control Object arranges the Control Objects using the vertical flow of direction, it starts the arrangement of Control Objects from the first column and places Control Objects in the first column. When the first column is completed, it starts the second column and places the Control Objects in the second column and when the second column is completed, it starts the third column and places the Control Objects in third column and so on. When a FlowLayoutPanel Control Object arranged the Control Objects then we cannot disturb their arrangement because it is automatically arrangement of the Control Objects. The FlowLayoutPanel Control Object only allows us to move or switch the arranged Control Objects between the complete rows or complete columns.

GroupBox Class

This class of Control Objects represents a GroupBox Control Object. A GroupBox Control Object is a container like a frame or a box that provides an interface for other Control Objects and allows us to place other Control Objects on its surface. When we place other Control Objects on the GroupBox Control Object, it holds all the Control Objects and makes their group without any automatically arrangement. It displays a frame around the Control Objects and also provides a single title or a caption to the group of the Control Objects that indicates the purpose of the group. The title of the group is optional and we can also skip the title. The GroupBox Control Object cannot arrange the Control Objects automatically like the FlowLayoutPanel Control Object but it only makes a logical group of the Control Objects and provides an optional title or caption to the group.

The GroupBox Control Objects are used for different purposes in Windows applications but usually they are used to make different individual groups of RadioButton Control Objects.

Panel Class

This class of Control Objects represents a Panel Control Object. A Panel Control Object is a container which is used to hold other Control Objects and make their group. The Panel Control Object is similar to the GroupBox Control Object but the only difference is that a Panel Control Object makes a group of other Control Objects and automatically attaches vertical and horizontal scroll bars when its contents or group of Control Objects hides from the visible area of the Panel. The Panel Control Object does not provide a title or caption to the group of Control Objects.

SplitContainer Class

This class of Control Objects represents a SplitContainer Control Object. A SplitContainer is a container that contains two Panels separated by a bar. The SplitContainer allows us to move the bar and increase or decrease the size of each Panel of the SplitContainer. Each Panel of a SplitContainer is similar to the Panel Control Object that is used to hold other Control Objects and makes their group. The SplitContainer attaches the vertical and horizontal scroll bars to both its Panels like Panel Control Object. The SplitContainer also allows us to display or view both the Panels either horizontally or vertically using its Orientation property. The Orientation property of the SplitContainer takes two constant values i.e. Horizontal and Vertical.

TabControl Class

This class of Control Objects represents a TabControl Control Object. The TabControl is a square shaped container which is used to hold other Control Objects and make their multiple groups on the same space of a Windows Form. The TabControl contains multiple pages in which each page is called TabPage. Each TabPage is itself a container which is used to hold other Control Objects and makes their group. The TabPages share the same space on a Windows Form because each TabPage is located on the other TabPage like pages of a book and each TabPage has a Tab button that allows us to click on it and view its contents. The TabControl displays or views a single TabPage at a time and hides the remaining TabPages. When we click on a Tab button, it displays or views the TabPage of that Tab button and hides all the other TabPages.

When we place a TabControl Control Object on a Windows Form, by default it contains only two TabPages with the default titles or captions that is TabPage1 and TabPage2. The TabControl allows us to add or remove TabPages according to the application specification using the Add Tab and Remove Tab options. When we right click on the Tab area of a TabControl, it displays a popup menu from where we can select the Add Tab and Remove Tab options. The Add Tab option is used to add new TabPage to the TabControl and the Remove Tab option is used to remove a TabPage from the TabControl. We can also add and remove TabPages using the TabPages property of the TabControl. When we click on the TabPages property from the properties Toolbox, it opens a small Windows that contains two buttons that is Add and Remove and other different options. When we click on the Add button, it adds new TabPage and when we click on the Remove button, it removes a selected TabPage from the TabControl. We can also add and remove the TabPages dynamically during run time of the application using the TabPages property and its two methods Add and Remove. The Add method of TabPages adds new TabPage to the TabControl and the Remove method of TabPages removes a TabPage from the TabControl. Each TabPage automatically attaches vertical and horizontal scroll bars when contents of a TabPage hide from the visible area of TabPage. If we want to attach scroll bars automatically to a TabPage, we have to set the TabPage AutoScroll property to true. If the value of the AutoScroll property is false then that TabPage does not attach scroll bars automatically.

The TabControl Control Object is usually used to make multiple groups of the Control Objects on the same space or the same location of a Windows Form and save the extra space of a Windows Form. For example, if we have a lot amount of Control Objects and they are not accommodated on a single Windows Form then in such a situation it is a good idea to place all the Control Objects using multiple TabPages of a TabControl and arrange all the Control Objects in different groups on the same space of a Windows Form.

TableLayoutPanel Class

This class of Control Objects represents a TableLayoutPanel Control Object. This Control Object is a grid view panel container that contains multiple rows and columns and it is used to hold other Control Objects and arrange them in rows and columns like a table and make their group. Each cell of a table can hold a single Control Object. When we place other Control Objects on the surface of a TableLayoutPanel, it automatically arranges all the Control Objects in rows and columns and makes their group. When we place a TableLayoutPanel Control Object on a Windows Form, by default it contains only two rows and two columns that can hold only four Control Objects because each cell can hold a single Control Object.

The TableLayoutPanel Control Object allows us to add more rows and more columns to accommodate more Control Objects. It also allows us to remove the existence rows and columns. We can add new rows and new columns to the TableLayoutPanel using the Row and Column options. When we right click on the TableLayoutPanel Control Object then it displays a pop-up menu from where we can select the Row and Column options. To Add new row to the TableLayoutPanel, select the Row option then select the Add option from the pop-up menu similarly, to add new column to the TableLayoutPanel, select the Column option then select the Add option from the pop-up menu. We can remove the existence rows and columns from the TableLayoutPanel on the same way by using the Delete option of Row and Column from the pop-up menu. We can also add and remove rows and columns using the property Window by using the Columns and Rows collections.

ContextMenuStrip Class

This class of Control Objects represents a ContextMenuStrip Control Object. A ContextMenuStrip Control Object is used to create a shortcut menu or pop-up menu for a Windows Form or for other Control Objects placed on a Windows Form. A shortcut menu or pop-up menu displays when we right click on a Windows Form or on other Control Object placed on a Windows Form. A pop-up menu is used to combine different menu items from the main menu of a Windows form to perform quick operations. A pop-up menu does not provide the full functionality of main menu but usually it is used to combine some menu items from the main menu of a Windows Form. The pop-up menus are usually used when we want to perform some specific operations on a Windows Form or on other Control Objects for example, if we want to perform some operations on a text such as Cut, Copy, Paste, and Select all etc then we can use a pop-up menu for quick operation similarly, if we want to perform the Font operations on a text such as to change the Font, change the Font Style, change the Font effects etc then we can use a pop-up menu for quick operation.

If we want to create a pop-up menu for a Windows Form or for other Control Objects placed on a Windows Form, a ContextMenuStrip Control Object is placed on a Windows Form from the Control Toolbox and designs a pop-up menu using its properties. The ContextMenuStrip Control Object provides Items property which is used to add menu items for a pop-up menu. A Windows Form and each Control Object provides ContextMenuStrip Property which is used to attach a pop-up menu to a Windows Form or to other Control Object. To add pop-up menu to a Windows Form or to other Control Object, select the ContextMenuStrip property of a Windows Form or a Control Object and select the name of the target ContextMenuStrip Control Object.

MenuStrip Class

This class of Control Objects represents a MenuStrip Control Object. A MenuStrip Control Object is used to design the main menu of a Windows

Form. This Control Object is used to design the main menu in both Single Document Interfaces (SDI) and in Multiple Document Interfaces (MDI). A menu contains different items which are called Menu Items. Each Menu Item of a main menu triggers event and calls an event handler and executes the program code or a set of statements written in the body of that event handler. To design a main menu of a Windows Form, a MenuStrip Control Object is placed on a Windows Form from the Controls Toolbox and design a main menu using the properties of MenuStrip Control Object. The MenuStrip Control Object provides Items property which is used to add menu items to the main menu. When we click on the Items property of the MenuStrip Control Object, it displays a window that is called Items Collection Editor Window. The Items Collection Editor Window is used to add Menu Items to the main menu. This Window also allows us to set different properties of each menu item. The MenuStrip Control Object allows us to add ComboBox and TextBox as Menu Items. It also allows us to add Separator between the two Menu Items. The Items Collection Editor Window also allows us to add sub Menu Items inside in each Menu Item of a main menu.

We can also add Menu Items to the main menu manually without using the Items Collection Editor Window of Items property. To add Menu Items to the main menu manually, select the MenuStrip Control Object to activate the menu editor and then click on the menu editor. The menu editor is displayed on the top of a Windows Form. When we click on a menu editor, it creates the first Menu Item and prompts for the title or caption of a created Menu Item. The Menu Item requires any user-defined title or caption that describes the purpose of the Menu Item. When we enter a title or caption for the Menu Item then menu editor creates that Menu Item and shifts control to the next Menu Item and prompt for the title or caption of the second Menu Item. When we enter the title or caption for the second Menu Item then it shifts the control to the next Menu Item and so on.

StatusStrip Class

This class of Control Objects represents a StatusStrip Control Object. A StatusStrip Control Object is used to create a status bar on a Windows Form. A status bar is a bar that is normally displayed on the bottom of a Windows Form and it is used to display the status information about an object or about an activity or an event that occurs in the application. The StatusStrip Control Object provides Labels, ProgressBars, DropDownButton and SplitButton which can be placed on a Status bar for different purposes. The Labels are used on a Status bar that displays the status information about an activity or about an event of the application.

The status bar can be created by placing the StatusStrip Control Object on a Windows Form from the Control Toolbox. The StatusStrip Control Object provides Items property which is used to create different items on a status bar. When we click the Items property, it opens the Items Collection Editor Window. The Items Collection Editor Window is used to create Items on a status bar.

ToolStrip Class

This class of Control Objects represents a ToolStrip Control Object. A ToolStrip Control Object is used to create a Toolbar on a Windows Form. A Toolbar is a bar that is usually displayed anywhere on a Windows Form but usually it is displayed on the top of a Windows Form under the main menu. A Toolbar is a graphical user interface container that contains buttons, icons, different Control Objects, and menus etc. These contents of a Toolbar are called items of the Toolbar. A Toolbar allows us to perform different operations on the Windows application. It is actually a shortcut of the main menu items or other commands for quick access and operations. A Toolbar provides a quick access of different Menu Items and other functions and commands of a Windows application. When we click on an item of a Toolbar, it triggers an event and calls an event handler and executes the block of code or statements written in the body of that event handler. The ToolStrip Control Object allows us to create Button, Label, SplitButton, DropDownButton, Separator, ComboBox, TextBox and ProgressBar Control Objects on a Toolbar. A Toolbar can be created by placing a ToolStrip Control Object on a Windows Form from the Control Toolbox. The Toolbar Control Object provides Items property which is used to create different items on a Toolbar. When we click the Items property, it displays the Items Collection Editor Window. The Items Collection Editor Window is used to add different items to the Toolbar. The Items Collection Editor Window also allows us to set different properties of each item of the Toolbar.

Timer Class

This class of Control Objects represents a Timer Control Object. A Timer Control Object is used in Windows applications to execute a task or a block of codes or statements repeatedly after a specified time interval. The Timer

Control Object is used when we want to execute a program or a small part of a program repeatedly after a specified time interval. A time interval is a specified instant or amount of time that creates a gap after each execution of the program or part of the program. A Timer Control Object automatically generates the time interval after a specified instant or amount of time and executes the program or a small part of the program automatically. The Timer Control Object works separately like a thread and it does not disturb the entire program or any other part of the program.

The Timer Control Object provides a property that is called Interval. The Interval property is used to set the time interval for the Timer Control Object. This property takes a time interval in milliseconds so that the time interval for the Timer Control Object is set in the form of millisecond. The Timer Control Object provides another property that is called Enabled property. This property is used to enable and disable the Timer Control Object by setting its Boolean value either true or false. The True value of this property makes a Timer Control Object enabled or functional and the false value of this property makes a Timer Control Object disabled or un-functional. The block of codes or statements or a part of a program is always kept inside in the Tick event handler of a Timer Control Object. When a Timer Control Object generates a time interval, it triggers an event and calls a Tick event handler and executes the block of codes or statements placed in that event handler.

The Timer Control Object is used in Windows applications for different purposes such as to take a backup automatically after some specified interval of time during the execution of database applications, similarly to save the data automatically on the disk after a specified interval of time while we are using documents base applications like MS Word. We also use a Timer Control Object to display any advertisement or a banner repeatedly on a website after a specified interval of time. The Timer Control Object is also used in those applications which are designed for the time management. The Timer Control Object is also used in those applications which are designed to display the updated information to the users after a specified interval of time for example, the flight information system application that displays the updated information to the passengers after some specified interval of time and so on.

FontDialog Class

This class of Control Objects represents a FontDialog Control Object. A FontDialog Control Object is used to display a modal dialog box that contains different Fonts, Font Styles, Font Size, and Font Effects. This dialog box contains only that Fonts installed in the computer system. The FontDialog Control Object allows us to select a specified Font, Font Style, Font Size, and Font Effect from the Font dialog box.

OpenFileDialog Class

This class of Control Objects represents an OpenFileDialog Control Object. An OpenFileDialog Control Object is used to display the Windows modal box that allows us to open a file from the disk by specifying path of that file.

SaveFileDialog Class

This class of Control Objects represents a SaveFileDialog Control Object. A SaveFileDialog Control Object is used to display a Windows modal dialog box that allows us to save a file on the disk.

Properties of Control Objects Classes

The Control Objects classes provide various types of properties that are used to change the characteristics, states, or information of the Control Objects. Each Control Object class provides its own set of properties. Some properties of the Control Objects classes are common and they are used by all the Control Objects but some properties are related to a specific Control Object class. Following is a list of some basic, common and uncommon properties of the Control Objects classes:

Property	Description
BackColor	This property is used to set the background color of a Control Object. It takes Color value as input and change the background color according to the input Color value.
BackgroundImage	This property is used to set the background image of a Control Object. It takes full path of an image as a string value and put that image on the background of a Control Object.

BackgroundImageLayout	This property is related with the BackgroundImage property and it is used to set layout of the background image. The layout is a position of an image on the surface of a Control Object. This property uses the ImageLayout enumeration for the image layout. The ImageLayout enumeration provides five different constant values. Each constant value represents a specific type of layout for the background image. These constant values are None, Tile, Center, Stretch, and Zoom.
Cursor	This property is used to set the mouse pointer style when the mouse pointer is over the Control Object. Microsoft Windows provides different types of mouse pointers. Each mouse pointer is identified by its name. The Cursor property takes the name of a mouse pointer and displays it on the surface of a Control Object when the mouse pointer is over that Control Object. By default it displays the default mouse pointer.
Enabled	This property is used to make a Control Object enabled or disabled. It takes a Boolean value either True or False. The True value makes a Control Object Enabled and the False value makes a Control Object disabled. The Enabled property is common property of all Control Objects classes and approximately all the Control Objects support this property.
	This property is used to set the appearance style of a Control Object. It uses an Enumeration FlatStyle that contains four constant values such as Flat, Popup, Standard, and System. The FlatStyle property takes one constant value of the enumeration at a time

FlatStyle	and change the appearance style of a Control Object according to that constant value. The FlatStyle property is not common to all Control Objects classes. Usually Button, ComboBox, and Label Control Objects support this property.
Font	This property is used to set or change Font of the text displayed by the Control Objects. We can set or change the Font of a Control Object both in the designing time and in runtime of the application. The Font of a Control Object can be changed either by using the Font Dialog or by using different parameters of the Font Property. The Font property can set Font Style, Font size, Font effects, and Font scripts etc.
ForeColor	This property is used to set the fore color or the text color of a Control Object. This property is also used to get or return the current fore color of a Control Object.
Image	This property is used to set an image on the title area of a Button or a Label Control Object.
ImageAlign	This property is used to set the position of the title image on a specified position of the title area of a Button or Label Control Object such as Top Left, Top Center, Top Right, Middle Left, Middle Center, Middle Right, Bottom Left, Bottom Center, and Bottom Right. The ImageAlign property takes one of these constant values and aligns the image.

Text	This property is used to set or get the title of a Control Object. The title of a Control Object is a text displays on a Control Object that briefly introduces or provides a brief description about a Control Object. The default value of this property is the name of a Control Object concatenated with a numeric value starting from one for example, Control1, Control2, and Control3 etc but we can give any user-defined title to a Control Object.
TextAlign	This property is used to set the alignment of the text or title of a Control Object. It is supported by those Control Objects which have Text property. The TextAlign property aligns the text or title on a specified position such as Top Left, Top Center, Top Right, Middle Left, Middle Center, Middle Right, Bottom Left, Bottom Center, and Bottom Right. Some Control Objects such as TextBox, MaskedTextBox etc use the TextAlign property to align the internal Text value on a specified position such as Left, Right, and Center. The RichTextBox Control Object has Text property but it does not support the TextAlign property.
TextImageRelation	This property is used to set the position of the title text and the title image in the title area of a Control Object. It works if a Control Object has a title image. This property uses an enumeration TextImageRelation. This enumeration provides five constant values which are used to set the position of the title text and the title image.

TabIndex	This property is used to set the Tab order of a Control Object within a Windows Form. The Tab order is an order of a Control Object that gets the focus automatically when we press the Tab key from the keyboard. When a Control Object gets a focus then that Control Object can be clicked or operated by using the enter or space bar key. The Tab order is actually an index of integer values that starts from zero and goes onward according to the number of the Control Objects we placed on a Windows Form. When we place a Control Object on a Windows Form, the tab index value automatically assigns to it. The Tab index value starts from zero and goes onward according to the number of Control Objects we placed on a Windows Form. When we place the first Control Object on a Windows Form, the Tab index value zero assigns to it, when we place the second Control Object on a Windows Form, the Tab index value one assigns to it, when we place the third Control Object on a Windows Form, the Tab index value two assigns to it and so on. All Control Objects support the TabIndex property except the Timer, MenuStript, ContextMenuStrip, the Data group, and PictureBox Control Objects.
TabStop	This property is used to exclude or remove a Control Object from the Tab order sequence. This property takes a Boolean value either True or False. When its value is True for a specified Control Object then that Control Object is included in the Tab order sequence and when its value is False for a specified Control Object then that Control Object is not included in the Tab order sequence of the Control Objects.

	This property is used to set the visibility of a Control Object. The visibility of a Control Object means whether a Control Object will be displayed on the Windows Form and visible to the user or not.It takes a Boolean value either True or False.
Visible	The True value of this property makes a Control Object visible to the user and displays it on the Windows Form. The False value of this property makes a Control Object invisible to the user and does not display it on the Windows Form.
Name	This property is used to set the name of a Control Object. Each Control Object has a unique name in a Windows Form. The name of a Control Object uniquely identifies and handles that Control Object on a Windows Form. This property is also used to get or return the current name of a specified Control Object.
Locked	This property is used to lock a Control Object during the design time of an application. It takes a Boolean value either True or false. The True value is used to lock a Control Object and its False value is used to unlock a Control Object.
Modifiers	This property is used to set the access level of a Control Object on a Windows Form. It takes five constant values that are Public, Private, Protected, Friend, and Protected Friend. To set the access level of a Control Object, one of these five constant values is used. This property is used to specify whether validation of a Control Object is performed or not. It takes a Boolean value

CausesValidation	either True or False. The True value of this property indicates that the validation of a Control Object is performed and its false value indicates that the validation of a Control Object is not performed. This property is used and its value is set to true, if we want to use the validation code for a Control Object.
Anchor	This property is used to anchor or attach one or more edges of a Control Object to a Windows Form. Each Control Object has four edges such as Top edge, Left edge, Right edge, and Bottom edge. A Control Object can be anchored or attached to a Windows Form using its one or more edges. When a Control Object is anchored to the Windows Form then its anchored edges remain in the same position or keep the same distance from the corresponding edges of a Windows Form when the Windows Form is resized. This property allows us to anchor a Control Object on a Windows Form using its edges values. This property has four constant values that can be ON or OFF. The constant values are Top, Bottom, Left, and Right.
AutoSize	This property is used to reset a Control Object and shrinks or grows a Control Object to fit its size to its contents. It takes a Boolean value either True or False. By default its value is False that does not resize the Control Object size. When the value of this property is True, it resizes the Control Object and shrinks or grows its size to fit its size to its contents.

AutoSizeMode	This property is used to set the type or mode of the auto size of a Control Object. It depends on the AutoSize property and it works only if the value of the AutoSize property is True. This property takes two constant values that is GrowOnly and GrowAndShrink and provides two different modes for the AutoSize property.
Dock	This property is used to force a Control Object to stick to a certain edge of a Windows Form or other container Control Object. It uses an enumeration that is called DockStyle. The DockStyle enumeration provides six constant values. These constant values are Top, Left, Right, Bottom, None, and Fill.
Location	This property is used to set location of a Control Object on a Windows Form. It takes two integer values in pixels. The first value indicates x-coordinates or horizontal position of a Control Object on a Windows Form and the second value indicates y-coordinates or vertical position of a Control Object on a Windows Form. The Location property is also used to get or return the current location of a Control Object on a Windows Form. It returns the current x-coordinates and y-coordinates of a Control Object in pixels.
Margin	This property is used to set the margin of a Control Object. The margin of a Control Object is a distance between the border of one Control Object and the border of another Control Object or simply it is the distance between the two Control Objects. This property takes four integer values that are Left, Top, Right, and Bottom. The Left

	integer value sets the left side margin, the Top integer value sets the top side margin, the Right integer value sets the right side margin, and the Bottom integer value sets the bottom side margin of a Control Object. This property is also used to get or return the current margin of a Control Object.
MaximumSize	This property is used to set the maximum size of a Control Object. The maximum size of a Control Object means that the maximum width and the maximum height of a Control Object. This property takes two integer values in pixels. The first integer value indicates the maximum width of a Control Object and the second integer value indicates the maximum height of a Control Object. This property is also used to get or return the current maximum size of a Control Object.
MinimumSize	This property is used to set the minimum size of a Control Object. The minimum size of a Control Object means that the minimum width and the minimum height of a Control Object. This property takes two integer values in pixels. The first integer value indicates the minimum width of a Control Object and the second integer value indicates the minimum height of a Control Object. This property is also used to get or return the current minimum size of a Control Object.
Padding	This property is used to set padding of a Control Object on a Windows Form. The Padding of a Control Object is internal area inside in the border of a Control Object. It takes four integer values and set the padding of a Control Object on a Windows Form. The first value indicates the Left position,

	the second value indicates the Top position, the third value indicates the Right position, and the fourth value indicates the Bottom position of a Control Object on a Windows Form. This property is also used to get or return the current padding of a Control Object on a Windows Form.
Size	This property is used to get or set the size of a Control Object on a Windows Form. The size of a Control Object means that the width and height of a Control Object. It sets the Width and Height of a Control Object in pixels. The Size property uses a structure that is called Size structure. The Size structure provides two members i.e. Width and Height. The Width member of the Size structure specifies width or horizontal size of a Control Object and the Height member of the Size structure specifies height or vertical size of a Control Object. The Width and Height members of the Size structure take integer values and set the width and height of a Control Object in pixels.
DataBinding	This property is used to get or set the data binding for the Control Object.
Tag	This property is used to get or set an object that contains data or information about a Control Object. The data or information can be of any type such as string, Boolean, Collection etc. Its default value is null.

Methods of Control Objects Classes

The Control Objects classes provide various methods which are used to perform different tasks or operations on the Control Objects. The methods of Control Objects take input values as parameters and perform different tasks or operations. Each Control Object class provides their own set of different methods but some methods are common methods of all Control Objects classes. Following is the list and details of the common methods of the Control Objects classes:

Methods	Description
BringToFront	This method is used to bring a Control Object to the front of the z-order of the Control Objects on a Windows Form.
SendToBack	This method is used to send a Control Object to the back of the z-order of the Control Objects on a Windows Form.
Contains	This method is used to retrieve a value that indicates whether a specified Control Object is the child of another Control Object or not.
Dispose	This method is used to dispose a Control Object and releases all the resources used by that Control Object.
DoDragDrop	This method is used to start a drag and drop operation on a Control Object.
Focus	This method is used to set the input focus to the Control Object.
GetType	This method is used to get or return the type of the current instance of a Control Object.
Hide	This method is used to hide a Control Object from the user.
PointToClient	This method is used to calculate the location of a specified screen point into client coordinates.
PointToScreen	This method is used to calculate the location of the specified client point into screen coordinates.
Refresh	This method is used to refresh a Control Object.
Show	This method is used to display a Control Object to the user.
SetBounds	This method is used to set the specified bound of a Control Object to the specified location and size.
ToString	This method is used to return a string that represents a specified Control Object.

Events of Control Objects Classes

Control Objects classes provide different events which are used to execute different events handlers of the Control Objects. Each Control Object class provides their own set of Events but most Control Objects classes have common events. Following is the list of some important and common events of the Control Objects classes:

Event	Description
Click	This event occurs when a Control Object is single clicked. It passes an EventArgs to its event handler.
DoubleClick	This event occurs when a Control Object is double clicked. It passes an EventArgs to its event handler.
Enter	This event occurs when a Control Object gets the input focus and it becomes active. This event is similar to the Activated event.
Leave	This event occurs when a Control Object lost the input focus and it becomes inactive.
Validating	This event occurs when a Control Object is validating. It occurs after the Leave event. When a Control Object is deactivated, it triggers the Leave event and calls the Leave event handler. When the Leave event is preceded then the Validating event occurs and calls the Validating event handler.
Validated	This event occurs when a Control Object has been validated. It occurs after the Validating event is preceded. When the Validated event occurs, it passes an EventArgs to its event handler.
Move	This event occurs when a Control Object moves on the screen. It passes an EventArgs to its event handler.
MouseClick	This event occurs when a Control Object is single clicked by the mouse. It passes the MouseEventArgs to the event handler.
MouseDouble Click	This event occurs when a Control Object is double clicked by the mouse. It passes the MouseEventArgs to the event handler.

MouseMove	This event occurs when the mouse pointer is moved over a Control Object. It passes the MouseEventArgs to its event handler.
MouseHover	This event occurs when the mouse pointer is over a Control Object and it rests on it for a very small instance of time. It passes the EventArgs to its event handler.
Layout	This event occurs when a child Control Object changes or repositioned on its parent Control Object or when a parent Control Object repositioned its child Control Objects. This event also occurs when a new Control Object is added to the parent Control Object or when a Control Object is removed from the parent Control Object or when some other changes occurs that effect the layout of a Control Object. It passes a LayoutEventArgs to the event handler.
KeyDown	This event occurs when a Control object has focus and a key is pressed from the keyboard.
KeyPress	This event occurs when a Control Object has focus and a user presses and releases a key from the keyboard.
KeyUp	This event occurs when a Control Object has focus and a key is released.
Resize	This event occurs when a Control Object is resized.
MouseDown	This event occurs when the mouse pointer is over a Control Object and a mouse button is pressed.
MouseUp	This event occurs when the mouse pointer is over a Control Object and a mouse button is released.
MouseEnter	This event occurs when the mouse enters the visible part of a Control Object.
MouseLeave	This event occurs when the mouse leaves the visible part of a Control Object.
TabIndexChanged	This event occurs when the value of the TabIndex property of a Control Object is changed.

TextChanged	This event occurs when the value of the Text property of a Control Object is changed.

Windows Applications Designing

A Windows application contains one or more Windows Forms and one or more Control Objects according to the application specification and requirements. A Windows Form is a visual rectangular container that provides an interface to the Control Objects. The Control Objects are placed on Windows Forms. A Windows Form holds Control Objects and arranges in different layouts. The process of placing Control Objects on a Windows Form is called Windows Form designing. The Control Objects are placed on the client or container area of the Windows Forms. To place Control Objects on a Windows Form during designing time of an application, the GUI (Graphical User Interface) is used. The GUI is applications development interface provided by Microsoft Visual Studio.NET. The GUI provides a visual programming environment that is called Windows Forms Designer. The Windows Forms Designer provides Windows Forms and Control Objects for Windows applications development. The instances of the Control Objects classes are placed in a Toolbox that is called Controls Toolbox. The Controls Toolbox is displayed in the left side of the Visual Studio.NET Windows Forms Designer and it can also be accessed from the View option of the main menu of Visual Studio.NET. Each Control Object of a Controls Toolbox represents a Control Object class. The instances of the Control Objects classes are placed in the Toolbox in the form of a list of different groups according to the same functionality of the Control Objects. Microsoft Visual Studio.NET Windows Forms Designer allows us to place Control Objects on a Windows Form from the Controls Toolbox. To place a Control Object on a Windows Form, a Control Object is simply dragged from the Toolbox and place anywhere on the container or client area of a Windows Form. A Control Object can also be placed on a Windows Form by double clicking a Control Object from the Controls Toolbox. When a Control Object is double clicked from the Controls Toolbox, it automatically places on a Windows Form. When a Control Object is placed on a Windows Form, we can use its properties, methods, and events. Each Control Object has its own default size that appears on a Windows Form with its default size. A Control Object can be resized by using mouse or by using its Size property. When a Control Object is placed on a Windows Form, the properties list of that Control Object is displayed in a small Window that is called properties Window. The properties Window is usually displayed on the right side of the Visual Studio. NET Windows Forms Designer and it can also be accessed from the View option of the main menu of Visual Studio.NET. The properties of Control Objects are used to change the state, or characteristics of the Control Objects.

A Windows Form can also be designed during run time of an application. To place a Control Object on a Windows Form during run time of an application, an instance of that Control Object is declared and it is initialized using the constructor of its class. When an instance of a Control Object class is declared and it is initialized then it is placed on a Windows Form using the Windows Form Controls Collection.

The Windows applications usually contain Multiple Document Interface (MDI) Forms in which one Windows Form is a main Windows Form and all the other Windows Forms are child Windows Forms. The Main Windows Form provides an interface to the child Windows Forms and the child Windows Forms are displayed on it. The Main Windows Form is usually contains Main Menu, Toolbars, and Status bar. The Main Menu contains options or menu items which specify the different tasks or operations of the application. Each menu item performs a specific task of the application. When we click a menu item, it calls a particular event handler and executes the code written in that event handler. The name of each menu item is meaningful and it clearly describes a specific task of the application. For example, if we are designing a database Windows application then a menu item that adds record to the database should have name Add Record, similarly a menu item that deletes record from the database should have name Delete Record, and a menu item that updates record of the database should have name Update Record and so on. A Toolbar is a shortcut of the Main menu that contains the Main Menu items for quick access and operations of the Main Menu items. A Toolbar is usually displayed on a Windows Form either horizontally or vertically at the top of the Windows Form below the Main Menu or at the left side or right side of the Windows Form. A Toolbar has different clickable buttons or icons and allows users to perform specific operations of the Windows application. Each button of the Toolbar indicates the Main Menu specific task. A taskbar is usually displayed on the bottom of the Windows Form. A taskbar is used to display information about the current running process or task of the Windows application. It also displays the icons of the current running applications. A taskbar is also used to display the current date and time.

Designing Applications using Visual Studio.NET

Microsoft Visual Studio.NET is a development tool for different types of software applications designing and development. Microsoft Visual Studio.

NET provides different versions such as Microsoft Visual Studio.NET 2005, 2008, 2010, 2012, 2013, 2015, and Microsoft Visual Studio.NET 2017. The different versions of Microsoft Visual Studio.NET provide the same development environment and approximately the same Control Objects but the latest versions of Microsoft Visual Studio.NET provide more facility as compared to the old versions. Microsoft Visual Studio.NET provides different types of software applications projects such as Console Applications Projects, Windows Forms Applications Projects, ASP.NET Web Applications Projects, Class Library Applications Projects, Silverlight Applications Projects, WPF Applications Projects, WCF Service Applications Projects and so on. Each application project is used to design and develop software applications for particular purposes. The Windows Applications are designed and developed using Microsoft Visual Studio.NET Windows Forms Application Project. To design Windows applications using Microsoft Visual Studio.NET, the following steps should be followed:

1. Open Microsoft Visual Studio.NET Professional.
2. From the File Menu of Visual Studio.NET, select New then select Project.
3. When you select Project, it opens New Project dialog box. The New Project dialog box contains three Panes or columns. The first Pane of the New Project dialog box contains a list of the programming languages provided by Microsoft Visual Studio.NET. The second Pane or the middle Pane of the New Project dialog box displays a list of different Project types. The third Pane of the New Project dialog box displays a brief description about the Project type when you select from the second or middle Pane of the New Project dialog box.
4. Select a programming language you want to use for the application development from the first Pane of the New Project dialog box.
5. When you select a programming language then select Windows Forms Application from the second or middle Pane of the New Project dialog box.
6. After selecting the Windows Forms Application, select a target Framework from the drop-down list which is displayed above the second or middle Pane of the New Project dialog box.
7. Give a name to your new project using the Name text box of the New Project dialog box. The Name text box is displayed under the first Pane of the New Project dialog box. When you do not give any name to your

new project then Microsoft Visual Studio.NET gives a default name to it. The default name is always WindowsApplication1, if it is a first Windows Application project.

8. When you give a name to your project, specify a location where you want to save your project using the Location drop-down list displayed under the Name text box of the New Project dialog box. To specify a location manually, type the location string in the Location text box otherwise, use the Browse button of the New Project dialog box and select a specified location in your computer for your new Windows Application project.
9. Now press the OK button of the New Project dialog box. Following is the screen shot of Microsoft Visual Studio.NET 2013 New Project dialog box:

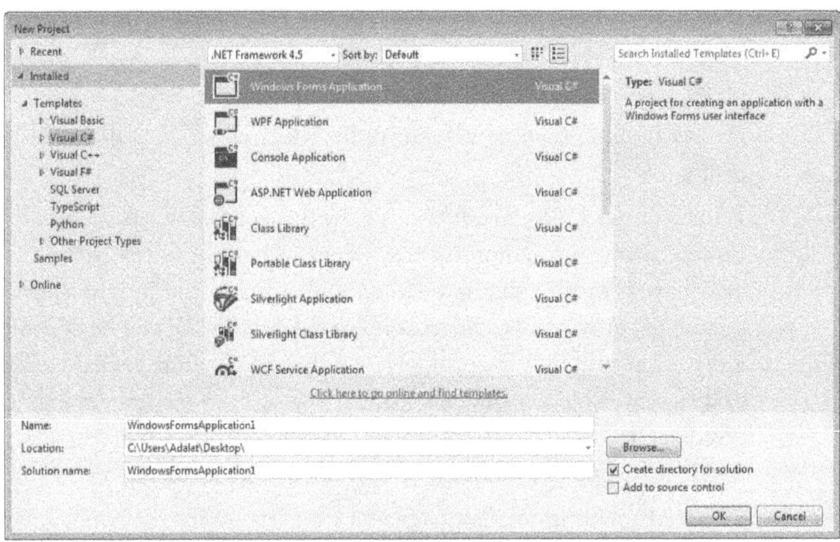

When you press the OK button of the New Project dialog box, a New Windows application Project will be created and the Windows Forms Designer of Microsoft Visual Studio.NET will be opened for the new project of Windows Forms Application. Following is the screen shot of Microsoft Visual Studio. NET Windows Forms Designer:

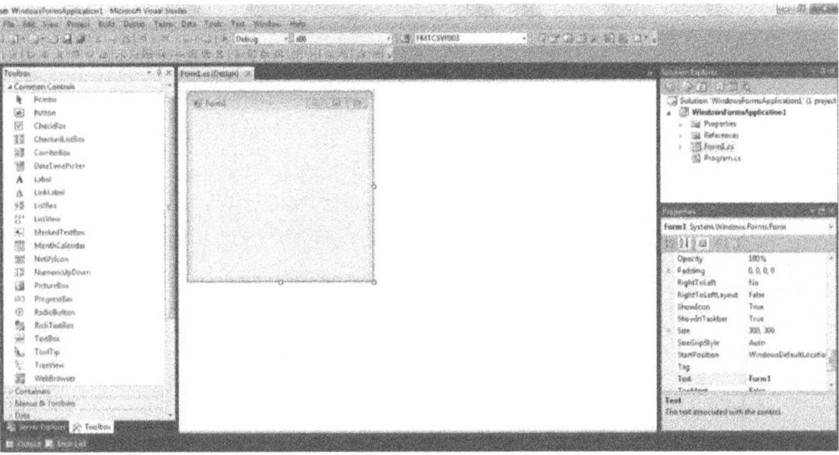

Now you can design your new Windows Forms application using the Windows Forms Designer.

Project # 1

Create a Windows Forms Application project that contains a single Windows Form. The Windows Form contains one Panel Control Object, three Textboxes, three Labels and one Button Control Object. Following is the screen shot of the Windows Form:

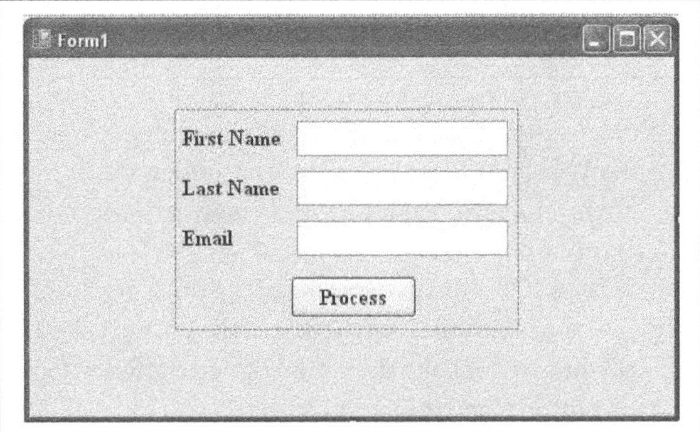

The above Windows Form contains one Panel, three Textboxes, three Labels, and one Button. The Textboxes, Labels and Button are placed inside in the Panel Control Object because Panel Control Object is a container and it is used to hold other Control Objects in the form of a group. The default title of the

Windows Form is Form1. To change the default title of the Windows Form, give new title to it using the Text property of the Windows Form.

Program # 2

Create a Windows Forms Application project that contains a single Windows Form. The Windows Form contains three Textboxes and one Button Control Objects. The first two Textboxes read two numeric values from the keyboard. When we press the Button Control Object, the numeric value of the first textbox i.e. textBox1 and the numeric value of the second textbox i.e. textBox2 are added and the answer is displayed in the third textbox i.e. textBox3. Following is the screen shot of the Windows Form:
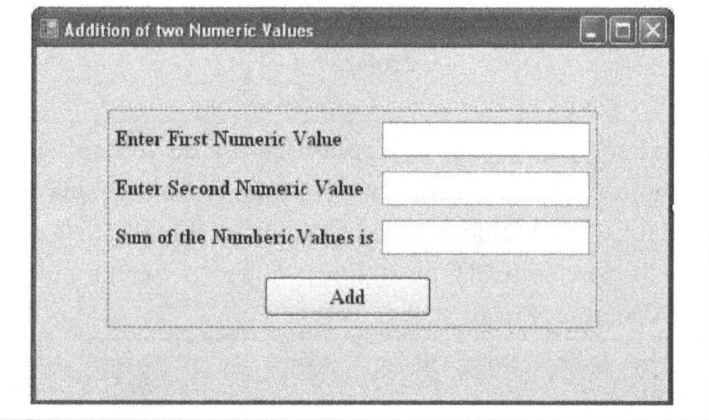

The above Windows Application project contains a single Windows Form. The name of the Windows Form is Form1 and title of the Windows Form is "Addition of two Numeric Values". The Windows Form contains three Textboxes and one Button. The name of the first Textbox is textBox1, the name of the second Textbox is textBox2, the name of the third Textbox is textBox3, the name of the Button is button1, and the title of the Button is Add. To add the numeric values of the textBox1 and the textBox2, add the following code in the click event of the Button Control Object (button1_Click):

```
private void button1_Click(object sender, EventArgs e)
{
Decimal num1, num2;
num1 = Convert.ToDecimal(textBox1.Text);
num2 = Convert.ToDecimal(textBox2.Text);
textBox3.Text = (num1 + num2).ToString();
}
```

MessageBox Class

MessageBox class is used to display a message window which is called dialog box. A dialog box displays a message to the user. The message may be information about a specific task, warning about the wrong operation, or error in the application or wrong entry etc. When a MessageBox displays a message to the user, it interrupts other actions in the application until the user close the MessageBox. A MessageBox can contain text, buttons, and symbols that inform and instruct the user. The Show() method of the MessageBox class is used to display a MessageBox with the specified text, caption, buttons, icon, default button, and help button. The Show() method provides different overloaded forms. Following is the useful and important overloaded forms of the Show() method:

Method	Description
Show(String)	This overloaded form of Show() method is used to display a MessageBox with a specified text message. It takes a String parameter that specifies a text message to display to the user.
Show(String, String)	This overloaded form of Show() method is used to display a MessageBox with a specified text message and a caption or title of the MessageBox. It takes two String parameters. The first parameter specifies the text message to display to the user and the second parameter specifies the caption or title of the MessageBox.

Show(String, String, MessageBoxButtons)	This overloaded form of Show() method is used to display a MessageBox with a specified text, caption, and buttons. It takes three parameters. The first parameter is a String that specifies the text message to display to the user. The second parameter is a String that specifies the caption or title of the MessageBox. The third parameter is MessageBoxButtons that specifies the buttons to display in the MessageBox. The parameter MessageBoxButtons is an enumeration that contains different constant values. Each constant value specifies a single button or a group of buttons to display on the MessageBox. This enumeration provides the following constant values: **AbortRetryIgnore** This constant value displays the Abort, Retry, and Ignore buttons in the MessageBox. **OK** This constant value displays the OK button in the MessageBox. **OKCancel** This constant value displays the OK and Cancel buttons in the MessageBox. **RetryCancel** This constant value displays the Retry and Cancel buttons in the MessageBox. **YesNo** This constant value displays the Yes and No buttons in the MessageBox. **YesNoCancel** This constant value displays the Yes, No, and Cancel buttons in the MessageBox.

Show(String, String, MessageBoxButtons, MessageBoxIcon)	This overloaded form of Show() method is used to display a MessageBox with a specified text, caption, buttons, and icon. It takes four parameters. The first parameter is a String parameter that specifies the text message to display to the user. The second parameter is a String parameter that specifies the caption or title of the MessageBox. The third parameter is MessageBoxButtons that specifies the buttons to display in the MessageBox. The fourth parameter is MessageBoxIcon that specifies which icon to display in the MessageBox. The MessageBoxIcon is an enumeration that contains different constant values. Each constant value indicates an icon to display in the MessageBox. This enumeration contains the following constant values: **Asterisk** This constant value displays a symbol consisting of a lowercase letter i in a circle in a MessageBox. **Error** This constant value displays a symbol consisting of white X in a circle with a red background in a MessageBox. **Exclamation** This constant value displays a symbol consisting of an exclamation point in a triangle with a yellow background in a MessageBox. **Hand** This constant value displays a symbol consisting of a white X in a circle with a red background in a MessageBox.

	Information This constant value displays a symbol consisting of a lowercase letter i in a circle in a MessageBox. **None** This constant value displays no symbols in a MessageBox. **Question** This constant value displays a question mark in a circle in a MessageBox. **Stop** This constant value displays a white X in a circle with a red background in a MessageBox. **Warning** This constant value displays a symbol consisting of an exclamation point in a triangle with a yellow background in a MessageBox.
Show(String, String, MessageBoxButtons, MessageBoxIcon, MessageBoxDefault Button)	This overloaded form of Show() method is used to display a message box with a specified text, caption, buttons, icon, and default button. It takes five parameters. The first parameter is a String parameter that specifies the text message to display to the user. The second parameter is a String parameter that specifies the caption or title of the MessageBox. The third parameter is MessageBoxButtons that specifies the buttons to display in the MessageBox. The fourth parameter is MessageBoxIcon that specifies which icon to display in the MessageBox. The fifth parameter is MessageBoxDefaultButton that specifies the default button for the MessageBox. It is an enumeration that contains three constant values i.e. button1, button2, and button3. The button1 makes the first button of the message box as default button. The button2 makes the second button of the message box as default button. The button3 makes the third button of the message box as default button.

The MessageBox returns DialogResult. The DialogResult is an enumeration that indicates the result of the MessageBox. The result of the MessageBox is the value of a button which is clicked by the user. When a user clicks any button of the MessageBox, it returns the value of that button as DialogResult. The DialogResult enumeration provides the following constant values:

Value	**Description**
Abort	This value is returned from the MessageBox when a user clicks the Abort button.
Cancel	This value is returned from the MessageBox when a user clicks the Cancel button.
Ignore	This value is returned from the MessageBox when a user clicks the Ignore button.
No	This value is returned from the MessageBox when a user clicks the No button.
None	This value is returned from the MessageBox if a MessageBox does not contain buttons.
OK	This value is returned from the MessageBox when a user clicks the OK button.
Retry	This value is returned from the MessageBox when a user clicks the Retry button.
Yes	This value is returned from the MessageBox when a user clicks the Yes button.

MessageBox Program

C# Program

```
//Declare and initialize message and caption variables to pass to the //
MessageBox.Shows() method
string message = "Message to the user";
string caption = "MessageBox Caption";

//Display a simple MessageBox with a message and caption or title
MessageBox.Show(message, caption);

//Display a MessageBox with Yes/No button, Question Mark, and //Icon
```

```
DialogResult res1 = MessageBox.Show(message, caption,
MessageBoxButtons.YesNo,
MessageBoxIcon.Question);

//Display a MessageBox with OK/Cancel button, Information Icon, //and
set the OK button as default button
DialogResult res2 = MessageBox.Show(message, caption,
                              MessageBoxButtons.OKCancel,
                              MessageBoxIcon.Information,
                              MessageBoxDefaultButton.Button1);
if (res2 == DialogResult.OK)
{
MessageBox.Show("You clicked the OK Button");
//Do some Task
}
if (res2 == DialogResult.Cancel)
{
MessageBox.Show("You clicked the Cancel Button");
//Do some Task
}
```

CHAPTER 10

Introduction to Database and Database Management System

CHAPTER CONTENTS

- Database
- Database Management System
- Database Models
- Flat Model
- Relational Model
- Objected Oriented Model
- Relational Database
- Relational Database Management System
- Database Tables
- Primary Key
- Composite Key
- Foreign Key
- Data Integrity
- Entity Integrity
- Referential Integrity
- Domain Integrity
- Database Constraints
- PRIMARY KEY Constraints
- FOREIGN KEY Constraints
- NOT NULL Constraints
- CHECK Constraints
- UNIQUE Constraints
- Target Database
- Structured Query Language
- Data Query Language
- SELECT Statement
- IN Operator
- BETWEEN Operator
- LIKE Operator
- IS NULL Operator

- IS NOT NULL Operator
- Data Manipulation Language
- INSERT Statement
- UPDATE Statement
- DELETE Statement
- Data Definition Language
- CREATE Statement
- Create Database
- Create Table
- Create View
- ALTER Statement
- DROP Statement
- Data Control Language
- GRANT Statement
- REVOKE Statement
- Stored Procedures
- RetrieveStudentsInfo Stored Procedure
- InsertStudentsInfo Stored Procedure

Database

Database is a system that provides an organized mechanism for storing, retrieving, deleting, and updating complex and large information in computer system, or database is the collection of organized data or information that stores permanently in a computer memory and provides a mechanism to perform different operations on the data or information such as insert or store new data in the collection of database data, delete data from the database, update data of the database, and retrieve data from the database. In other words we can say that a database is a structured collection of searchable data or information that stored permanently in a computer memory. A database contains one or more tables called relations. A database stores data or information in various database tables in an organized form. A table is the representation of two dimensional arrays that contains rows and columns. Each table in a database has a unique name and in a single database no two tables can have the same names. Each table in a database has multiple rows and columns. The columns are usually called attributes and rows are called tuples. Each column in a table has a unique name and no two columns in a single table are identical. The value or data of each column is always of the same type. It means a single column only can store the same type data. Each row in a table is always unique that means no two rows in a single table are identical. Each table in a database has a primary key that uniquely identify each row of the table. The primary key is an attribute or column or the combination of two or more columns in a table that restrict the duplicate row if the same row is already exist in the database table.

There are different mechanisms used to organize and manipulate the database data or record. These mechanisms are called database models. A database uses various types of database models for data organization and manipulation. A database model is a theory or specification that determines in which manner or format the data is to be stored, organized, retrieved, and updated in a database system. Each database model defines its own mechanism for the database data organization and manipulation. A software application is used to interact with the database and provides different operation on the data of database is called Database Managements System (DBMS). A DBMS is a software application that enables us to store data in the databases and performs different operations on the data of database.

Database Management System

Database Management System (DBMS) is the collection of software applications that manages databases. The DBMS provides control access to databases and enable us to define, create, update, maintain, and administration of the databases. A DBMS is an interface or a bridge between the users and database that enables multiple users to interact with the database and performs different operations on the data of the database such as insert new data into database, delete data from the database, update the existing data of database, and retrieve data from database. A DBMS is a way of communication between the user and database. When a user input data into database, the DBMS application organizes the user input data, processes it and stores it into database. A DBMS application allows multiple users to access and share the same data of the same database concurrently. There are different types of DBMS software applications used to access databases and perform different operations on the data or record of the databases. The different types of DBMS software applications are Microsoft Access, Microsoft SQL Server, Oracle, Filemaker, Firebird, IBM DB2, Interbase, MySQL, Paradox, Postgre SQL, SQLBase, SQLite, dBase, and Visual FoxPro etc. A DBMS software application has the following five basic important components:

- Hardware
- Software

- Data
- Procedure
- Data Access and Manipulation Language

Hardware

Hardware consists of a set of physical electronic devices such as computers, storage devices, Input/output devices etc. Hardware provides an interface between users and DMBS software application. It is impossible to implement DBMS without hardware devices.

Software

Software is the set of programs used to control and manage overall database. It includes DBMS software itself, the Operating System, the network software being used to share the data among users, and the application programs used to access data.

Data

This component of DBMS is the most important component because databases deal with the data. The DBMS allows us to store data, delete or update date, and retrieve data from the database.

Procedure

A procedure is a set of instructions and rules that enable us to use the DBMS and assists us in the designing and running of the database. It guides the users that operate and manage the database. Procedures refer to the instructions and rules that help to design the database and to use the DBMS.

Data Access and Manipulation Language

This is the most important component of DBMS application that is used to access the database tables and performs different operations on it. The most popular data access language of DBMS is called Structured Query Language (SQL). The SQL is a universal special purpose programming language and it is a part or a component of the DBMS application. Almost all DBMS programs support SQL language. SQL language provides an interface to users to access different tables of database and performs different operations on it such as insert new data or record to the database tables, delete data or record from the database tables, update the existing data or record of the database tables, and retrieve data from one or more database tables.

Database Models

Database model is a theory or specification that determines in which manner or format data is to be stored, organized, retrieved, and updated in a database system. A database model provides a designing and data organizing mechanism to the database system. The database model also provides different statements that perform different operations on the database data. There are different types of database models. Following are some important and popular database models:

- Flat Model
- Relational Model
- Hierarchical Model
- Network Model
- Object Oriented Model
- Dimensional Model

Flat Model

The Flat database model contains a single two-dimensional array that contains rows and columns. This model organizes data in a single two-dimensional array in the form of rows and columns. The rows are called tuples and the columns are called attributes.

Relational Model

According to this model a database consists of a sequence of unordered tables and relationships among the tables. A relational database model organizes the data or information of a database in the form of multiple tables. A table in a relational database model is called a relation and each table in a relational database model contains multiple rows and columns. Each column in a table has a unique name. The column value of a database table is of the same type and each row of a table is always unique. Each table of relational database model has a primary key that uniquely identifies each row of the database table. The primary key is an attribute or column or the combination of two or more columns in a table that restrict the duplicate row if the same row is already exist in the database table. In a relational database model all tables of the database are inter related with each other on the basis of primary keys. This model allows us to work in multiple tables and performs different operations on the data of multiple tables such as insert data, update data, delete data, and retrieve data from one or more tables of the database according to the relationship among different tables of the database. The tables in relational data model can be manipulated using nonprocedural operation called SQL Queries. The SQL query is provided by SQL programming language.

Object Oriented Model

According to this database model the data is stored in database in the form of objects. An object consists of member data and member methods. This database model is used when we have complex data and complex data relationships. The complex data relationship may include many to many objects relationship. The object oriented database model is usually used when we are designing software applications on the basis of CASE (Computer Aided Software Engineering), CAD (Computer Aided Design), and CAM (Computer Aided Manufacture). The object oriented database model is also used to design Multimedia Applications, and general object projects that we change time to time.

Relational Database

Relational Database follows the mechanism of relational database model. A Relational database contains multiple tables that organizes and stores data and makes relationships between the data in different tables. Each table in a relational database is called a relation and each table contains multiple rows and columns. A column in a table is called attribute and a row is called tuple. Each column in a table has a unique name. The column value of a database table is of the same type and each row of a table is always unique. Each table in a relational database model has a primary key that uniquely identifies each row of the table. A primary key is an attribute or column or the combination of two or more columns that uniquely identifies each row of a database table and also creates a relationship between the database tables. The tables in a relational database are related with each other on the basis of primary keys. A software application is used to manage and interact with the relational database and performs different operations on it such as insert new data, delete data, update data, and retrieve data from one or more tables of a relational database. The software application that is used to interact with the relational database and performs different operations on it is called Relational Database Management System (RDBMS).

Relational Database Management System

Relational Database Management System (RDBMS) is a software application based on relational database model that is used to manage relational databases. It provides control access to relational databases and enables us to define, create, update, maintain, and administration of relational databases. The RDBMS application interacts with the relational databases and performs different operations on the data of a relational database such as insert new data, delete data, update data, and retrieve data from one or more tables of a relational database. The most commonly used RDBMS application is SQL programming language. SQL stands for Structured Query Language. It is a special purpose programming language that is used to interact with the relational database and performs different operations on the data or record of the relational database. Relational Database Management System provides different types of Objects called data Objects such as Databases, Tables, Views, Indexes, Users, Roles, and Stored Procedures. The most popular Relational Database Management System software applications are Microsoft Access, Microsoft SQL Server, Microsoft SQL Server Express, Oracle, Firebird, FileMaker Pro, IBM DB2, InterBase, Microsoft Visual FoxPro, MySQL, Postgre SQL, SQLBase, SQLite, Teradata, Panorama, RDM Server, and Openbase etc.

Database Tables

A table is the representation of two dimensional arrays that contains rows and columns. A table organizes the input data in the form of rows and columns. A table in a relational database is also called a relation or an object of the database. Each row in a table is called a record or a tuple and each column in a table is called an attribute. Each column in a table has a unique name and no two columns in a single table can have the same identical names. The column value of a table is of the same type and each row of a table is always unique. Each table in a relational database has a primary key that uniquely identifies each row of the table. A primary key is a column or the combination of two or more columns in a database table that uniquely identifies each row in a table and also creates a data relationship between the two tables of the database. The relationship between the two tables in a database means the data relationship between the two tables in a database. The tables in a relational database are related with each other on the basis of primary keys. Two tables in a relational database will be related with each other if both the tables have a common or a share column. The common or share column between the two tables means the same data type and the same size column and contains the same data. When a column is used in one table as a primary key and that column is used in another table as a foreign key then it forms a parent child relationship between the two tables. The first table in which that column is used as a primary key is called parent table and the second table in which that column is used as a foreign key is called child table. Each table in a database has its own name and no two tables in a single database have the same identical names.

Primary Key

Primary key is a column or combination of two or more columns in a relational database table that uniquely identifies each row in a table. It always checks input data either the input data is already exist or not. If input data is already exists in the table, the primary key generates an error and rejects the input data otherwise, if input data is not already exists in the table, the primary key accept that input data. Primary key ensures that each row in a table is unique and value of the primary key column must not be NULL value. The primary key column does not accept NULL value. When a primary key is made from the combination of two or more columns then it is called composite key. When a primary key is made from the combination of two or more columns, the data of each individual column may be repeated but the corresponding data of the combination of all the columns in a composite key must be unique because in case of multiple columns a primary key is considered the combination of all columns of the composite key. A single column in a composite key cannot uniquely identify each row in a relational database table because a single column in a composite key may have repeated data. The primary key data is usually auto generated but we can also input data to the primary key column. The examples of primary key are, the identity card number of a person, the registration number of a student in a university, the registration number of an employee in an organization, the account number of a person in a bank and so on.

A single table in a relational database can have only one primary key. The primary key can be created in a relational database table at the time of the table creation with the CREATE TABLE statement of SQL and it is also created after the table creation. When a table is created, the primary key can be created with the ALTER TABLE statement of SQL.

Composite Key

When primary key is made from the combination of two or more columns, is called composite key. A composite key is the combination of two or more columns that uniquely identifies each row in a relational database table. The individual column in a composite key can have repeated data but the corresponding data of the combination of all the columns in a composite key must be unique. Therefore, a single column in a composite key cannot uniquely identify each row in a relational database table because a single column in composite key may have repeated data.

Foreign Key

When a column is used as a primary key in one table and that column is used as a non primary key column in other table is called foreign key. A foreign key is a column or combination of columns in a relational database table that matches with the primary key of another table. The primary key and foreign key makes a relationship between the two tables. This relationship between the two tables is called parent child relationship. A table in which a column or combination of columns are used as a primary key is called parent table and a table in which the same identical column or combination of columns are used as a foreign key is called child table. The child table foreign key must reference the parent table primary key. A foreign key column can have repeated data but data of the foreign key column must be matched with the corresponding primary key column of the linked table. A single table in a relational database can have multiple foreign keys and each foreign key can have a different primary key table or parent table. When two tables are related with each other in a relational database using the primary key and foreign key relationship then their data are inter related with each other and we cannot update or delete data of the parent table until we delete that same data from the child table similarly, we cannot add new data or record in a child table unless there is a corresponding data or record in the parent table. When we add new data or record in a child table, the foreign key of the child table first checks the corresponding value in the parent table primary key. If the parent table primary key and the child table foreign key values are identical then database accepts the input data or record otherwise, database rejects the input data or record.

Data Integrity

Data integrity is a fundamental and important mechanism of a Relational Database Management System that defines some important rules and restrictions to control the accuracy and consistency of the database data. When we apply the data integrity rules and restrictions, they ensure the data accuracy and the data consistency when we entered into the database. The data accuracy means accurate data and data consistency means valid data and unique data or non-duplicated data. When we input data into database, the data integrity rules check the data accuracy and the data validity. If the input data is correct and satisfies the data integrity rules, the database accepts that data otherwise, database rejects that input data. The data integrity is actually data validation for database tables. For example, when we insert new data into a table, the data integrity of that table checks the validity of the incoming data either the incoming data is according to the data integrity rules and it satisfies the data integrity rules or not. If the incoming data is according to the data integrity, the database table accepts that data otherwise, the database table rejects that incoming data. The data integrity ensures that each table in a relational database must have a primary key that uniquely identifies each row in a table and no two rows in a single table are identical. The data integrity also makes a relationship between the two tables using a primary key and a foreign key constraints or restrictions and controls the database operations such as delete data or update data of the database tables. The relationship between the two tables is called parent child relationship. If the data of one table is related to the data of another table using a primary key and foreign key and there is a parent child relationship between the two tables then we cannot update or delete the data of the parent table until we update or delete its related data from its child table.

The data integrity is applied or enforced to the database using the database constraints or restrictions. There are the following three main types of data integrity:

- Entity Integrity
- Referential Integrity
- Domain Integrity

Entity Integrity

Entity integrity ensures and enforces that each table in a relational database must have a primary key that uniquely identifies each row in a table and the data of primary key must be unique and not null. When we enter new data in a table, entity integrity checks the input data whether it is already exist in the table or not. If the input data is already exists in the table, the entity integrity rejects the input data and if the input data does not exist in the table, the entity integrity accepts that input data. The entity integrity is implemented or enforced in a database table by adding the primary key constraint.

Referential Integrity

Referential integrity ensures and enforces relationship between the foreign key of one table and the primary key of another table. It prevents us to enter data or record in a foreign key table unless we enter that corresponding data or record in the linked primary key table because each row of a foreign key table references the primary key table. When we enter new data in foreign key table, referential integrity prevents the data entry if the corresponding data does not exist in the primary key table. Referential integrity also prevents the database operations such as delete data or update data of primary key table. For example, we cannot delete data from primary key table unless we delete that corresponding data from its linked foreign key table. Referential integrity is implemented in a relational database table by adding the foreign key constraints.

Domain Integrity

Domain integrity ensures and enforces the validity of data for a specified column. The validity of data means data type, length or size of the data, and null value of a specified column. When we enter data to a database table, domain integrity checks the validity of the input data whether the data type and length of the input data is matched with the data type and length of the target column or not. If the data type or length of the input data does not matched with the specified column data type or length then domain integrity prevents the input data otherwise, domain integrity accepts the input data. Domain integrity also ensures that whether a null value is allowed in a specified column or not. Domain integrity is implemented or enforced in a table by adding a foreign key constraint.

Database Constraints

Database constraints are rules and restrictions used to enforce or implement data integrity into database tables. There are two types of database constraints such as table level constraints and column level constraints. The table level constraints apply to all columns of the table whereas the column level constraints apply to only a specific column in a database table. The constraints can be applied to the table at the time of the table creation and after the table creation. The constraints can be applied to the table at the time of table creation with the CREATE TABLE statement of SQL and when table is created, the constraints can be applied to it with the ALTER TABLE statement of SQL. There are the following five types of database constraints:

- PRIMARY KEY Constraints
- FOREIGN KEY Constraints
- NOT NULL Constraints
- CHECK Constraints
- UNIQUE Constraints

PRIMARY KEY Constraints

The primary key constraint is a column level constraint that ensures each row in a table must be unique and not NULL. When we implement the primary key constraints in a database table then that table does not accept the repeated data. The primary key constraint is used to enforce or implement the entity integrity.

FOREIGN KEY Constraints

The foreign key constraint is a column level constraint that ensures the relationship between the two tables. The relationship between the two tables is possible if we use the primary key column in another table as foreign key. The foreign key constraint is use to enforce or implement the referential integrity.

NOT NULL Constraints

The not null constraint is used to enforce a column in a database table to prevent null value. If we implement the not null constraint on a column of the database table then that column does not accept null value.

CHECK Constraints

This constraint is used to limit the values of one or more columns in a database table. It allows us to perform different checks or conditions on the input data for one or more columns of the table for example, the data range, the data type, and the data size or length for one or more columns. The check constraints always return Boolean values either true or false. When we input data to the table, the check constraints ensure the input data is valid according to different checks and conditions. If the input data is according to the checks and conditions and it returns true value then database table accepts that input data otherwise database table prevents that input data. The check constraint is used to enforce or implement domain integrity.

UNIQUE Constraints

This constraint is also called unique key constraint. It is used to enforce a specified column to prevent duplicate value. When we implement a unique constraint on a column then that specified column does not accept duplicate value. We can use multiple unique constraints in a single table. Unique constraints work same as primary key constraints but the main difference is that a primary key does not accept null value but unique constraint accepts null value. We can define unique constraints multiple times in a single table but we cannot define primary key constraints multiple times in a single table.

Target Database

Throughout this book Microsoft SQL Server database system is used for database programming and the target database is Students database. The Students database is a user-defined database that is designed in SQL Server database system to store data of university students. Therefore, to cover the database programming of this book the Students database must be cleared. The Students database contains the following tables:

- StudentsInfo Table
- StudentsDept Table
- StudentsExams Table

StudentsInfo Table

This table is used to store general information or data of the students. The data of a student contains student registration number, student name, student date of birth, student department, student class code, student contact number, and student email address. This table contains the following columns:

Column Name	Data Type	Length	Description
StdRegNumber	nvarchar	50	This column is used to store the registration number of students. It is a primary key column that uniquely identifies each student because each student in a university has a unique registration number.

StdName	nvarchar	50	This column is used to store the name of students.
StdDoBirth	datetime		This column is used to store the date of birth of students.
StdDeptCode	int		This column is used to store the department code. This column is foreign key column and it is related with the StudentsDept table where this column is primary key that uniquely identifies each department of the university.
StdRegDate	datetime		This column is used to store the registration date of students.
StdContact	nvarchar	14	This column is used to store the contact number of students.
StdEmail	nvarchar	50	This column is used to store the email address of students.

StudentsDept Table

This table contains the data or information about the university departments and it contains the following two columns:

Column Name	Data Type	Length	Description
DeptCode	int		This column is used to store the department code. It is a primary key column that uniquely identifies each department of the university.
DeptName	nvarchar	50	This column is used to store the department name.

StudentsExams Table

This table is used to store data of the student exams. It contains the following columns:

Column Name	Data Type	Length	Description
StdRegNumber	nvarchar	50	This column is used to store the registration number of students. It is foreign key column that is linked with StudentsInfo table where this column is used as primary key column.
ExamType	nvarchar	20	This column is used to store the type of exam.
ExamDate	datetime		This column is used to store the exam date.
MarksObtained	numberic		This column is used to store the obtained marks of students.
StudentPosition	int		This column is used to store the student position.
Percentage	decimal		This column is used to store percentage of students.

Structured Query Language

Structured Query Language (SQL) is a special purpose programming language designed for manipulating data in database tables. It is a nonprocedural programming language that does not provide the ordinary programming structure. This programming language is used to operate and handle data of database tables and performs different operations on it such as insert new data in database tables, delete data from database tables, update data, and retrieve data from database tables. SQL language provides an interface or editor called Query analyzer. Query analyzer is an interface like a text editor that allows us to write different commands of SQL and performs different operations on database tables. The commands of SQL language are called Queries. The SQL commands or Queries can also be executed from Windows application programs. The Windows application programs interact with database and sends request to RDBMS and execute the command or Query of SQL. SQL also allows us to create and delete tables from databases. SQL language is not a case-sensitive language and we can write a Query in both the small and capital letters. SQL language provides various types of statements or commands for database operations. These statements or commands are generally grouped into the following four categories. Each group is considered a separate language:

- Data Query Language
- Data Manipulation Language
- Data Definition Language
- Data Control Language

Data Query Language

Data Query Language (DQL) is used to retrieve data from one or more database tables. It has the following one statement for data retrieving operation:

- SELECT Statement

SELECT Statement

SELECT statement is used to retrieve data from database tables. This statement allows us to select the data of one or more rows and one or more columns from one or more tables or views. When this statement is executed, it returns a specified data in the form of logical table that contains rows and columns called ResultSet. A ResultSet is a logical table of data that contains the result of SQL SELECT statement. It organizes the Query result data in the form of rows and columns like database tables. A ResultSet also contains Meta data that provides columns description. The SELECT statement starts from the keyword SELECT followed by a list of column names and a list of table names of database. The following syntax of SELECT statement is used to retrieve data from one table:

```
SELECT Column-1, Column-2, Column-3,…………, Column-n
FROM Table_Name
WHERE Condition
```

The following syntax is used to retrieve data from multiple tables of database:

```
SELECT Table1.Column1, Table1.Column2, Table1.Column3,
       Table2.Column1, Table2.Column2, Table2.Column3,
       Table-n.Column1,Table-n.Column2,Table- n.Column3,
       Table1.Column-n, Table2.Column-n, Table-n.Column-n
FROM Table1, Table2, Table3, ………………….,Table-n
WHERE Condition
```

SELECT statement contains six parts called clauses. Following are the details of clauses:

- SELECT
- FROM
- WHERE
- ORDER By
- GROUP BY
- HAVING BY

SELECT Clause

This clause specifies a list of columns to be retrieved from one or more database tables. The columns are separated from each other using commas between them. SELECT clause has the following general syntax:

SELECT Column-1, Column-2, Column-3,..............., Column-n

SELECT statement also allows us to retrieve the entire columns from a single table using the asterisk * character instead of using a columns list.

FROM Clause

This clause of SELECT statement specifies a list of tables from which the data to be retrieved. It has the following general syntax:

FROM Table1, Table2, Table3, ...,Table-n

If we retrieve data from more than one table, the tables joining mechanism is used.

WHERE Clause

This clause of SELECT statement specifies a criteria or condition called predicate. A predicate is mathematically logic that contains different mathematical conditions to retrieve specific rows from one or more tables. This clause of SELECT statement works same as conditional statement that matches a specific criterion of the predicate of this clause. The predicate of this clause takes relational operators or relational expressions as a condition or a criterion. Predicate may be single or multiple. If multiple predicates are used, the logical operators AND or OR are used to combine the two or more predicates into a single condition or criterion. The multiple predicates should be enclosed in parenthesis in the form of groups to indicate the order of the estimation or calculation. If parenthesis are not used, the AND operator has stronger priority than the OR operator. The predicate of WHERE clause uses the following operators for condition or criterion:

Operator	**Name**	**Operator**	**Name**
=	Equal Operator	<>	Not Equal Operator
<	Less Operator	>	Greater Operator
<=	Less or Equal	>=	Greater or Equal
IN	IN Operator	BETWEEN	Between Operator
LIKE	Like Operator	IS NOT NULL	Is Not Null
IS NULL	Is Null Operator		

The SQL SELECT statement returns rows of data or records that fulfill the WHERE clause predicates. Following is the general syntax of WHERE clause:

SELECT Columns-list FROM Table-name WHERE Predicates

IN Operator

This operator is used to retrieve the data from a database table on the basis of multiple values of a single column. It is a filter of a column that takes multiple values enclosed in parenthesis. If we retrieve a specific data from a database table according to different values of a specified column, the specified values of a specified column are placed into the IN operator filter. The specified values of a column are enclosed in parenthesis on the right side of IN operator. Following is its general syntax:

```
SELECT Columns1, Column2, Column3, ............, Column-n
FROM Table_name
WHERE Column_name IN (Value1, Value2, Value3,....,Value-n)
```

In the above syntax, the Column_name is the name of a specified column from which the data is to be retrieved. The filter (Value1, Value2, Value3, ..., Value-n) are a list of specified values of the column. When IN operator is used with the WHERE clause, the SELECT statement retrieves data from a table in which the values of the Column_name matches with values of the filter of IN operator. For example, if we retrieve the data of students whose ID number are 23, 56, 78, and 89 then the SQL SELECT statement would be:

SELECT * FROM StudentsInfo WHERE StdRegNumber IN (23, 56, 78, 89)

The above SELECT statement will retrieve four rows of data of four students whose ID numbers are 23, 56, 78, and 89. We can also reverse the functionality of IN operator using the NOT keyword before the IN operator. For example, if we retrieve the data of all students except the data of those students whose ID numbers are 23, 56, 78, and 89 then the SELECT statement will be:

SELECT * FROM StudentsInfo WHERE
StdRegNumber NOT IN (23, 56, 78, 89)

BETWEEN Operator

This operator is used to select a range of data between the two specified values of a specified column. It takes the starting and ending values of the range of data and retrieves the data between the starting and ending range values. The AND keyword is used between the starting value and the ending value of the range. Following is its general syntax:

SELECT Column_list FROM Table_name WHERE Column_name
BETWEEN Value1 AND Value2

In the above SELECT statement, Value1 indicates the starting value and Value2 indicates the ending value of the range of data we retrieve from a table. For example, if we retrieve the data of students whose admission dates are between 1/1/2016 and 1/1/2017 then the following SELECT statement will be used:

SELECT * FROM StudentsInfo WHERE StdRegDate
BETWEEN '1/1/2016' AND '1/1/2017'

LIKE Operator

This operator is used to retrieve the data from a database table when its specified string pattern matches with values of a specified column. It takes a string pattern enclosed in a single quote and searches the same pattern in the values of a specified column. For example, if we don't know the entire value of a column, we can use a single character or pattern of that column value to retrieve the data. We can use any character of a column value in the pattern of LIKE operator such as first character, last character, center character, second last character, second first character, or any other combination of two or more characters etc. Following is the general syntax of LIKE operator:

```
SELECT * FROM TableName WHERE Column_name LIKE Pattern
```

The % sign is used to define the missing letters before and after the pattern. For example, if we retrieve the data of students whose names start from letter 'A' then we can use the LIKE operator as:

```
SELECT * FROM StudentsInfo WHERE StdName LIKE 'A%'
```

The above SELECT statement will retrieve the data of students whose names start from letter A. Similarly, if we retrieve the data of students whose names are ended with the letter 'N' then we can use the LIKE operator as:

```
SELECT * FROM StudentsInfo WHERE StdName LIKE '%N'
```

If we retrieve the data of those students whose names contain a letter 'S' anywhere then we can use the LIKE operator as:

```
SELECT * FROM StudentsInfo WHERE StdName LIKE '%S%'
```

IS NULL Operator

This operator is used to check whether the value of a specified column is null or not. It retrieves the data of rows whose specified column values are null. For example, if we retrieve the data of students who missed the exam and did not get any marks then we can use the IS NULL operator as:

```
SELECT * from StudentsExam WHERE Percentage IS NULL
```

IS NOT NULL Operator

This operator is the reverse of IS NULL operator and it is used to check and ensures that the value of a specified column is not null. It retrieves the data of rows whose specified column values are not null. For example, if we retrieve the data of those students who attended the exam then we can use the IS NOT NULL operator as:

SELECT * from StudentsExam WHERE Percentage IS NOT NULL

ORDER BY Clause

This clause is used to sort the retrieved rows either in ascending or descending form. To sort the retrieved rows on ascending form, the keyword ASC is used, otherwise the keyword DESC is used. The default value of this clause is ASC. Therefore, to sort the retrieved rows on ascending form, the using of ASC is optional. Following is the general syntax of ORDER BY clause:

SELECT * from Table Where Condition ORDER BY ASC or DESC

Data Manipulation Language

Data Manipulation Language (DML) is used to insert, update, and delete data from database tables. It has the following statements:

- INSERT Statement
- UPDATE Statement
- DELETE Statement

INSERT Statement

This statement is used to insert new data or record in database tables. It creates new row in a specified table and insert record in the new created row. This statement always starts from the keyword INSERT followed by INTO keyword. The INTO keyword specifies the target table in which the data or record to be inserted. Following is its general syntax:

```
INSERT INTO Table_name(Column1, Column2, Column3,
                                  ………, Column-n)
VALUES (Value1, Value2, Value3, ……., Value-n)
```

The **Table_name** specifies the name of the target table in which the data to be inserted. The Column1, Column2, Column3, ………, Column-n represent the names of the columns to which the data to be inserted. The Value1, Value2, Value3,………, Value-n represent the values assigned to the corresponding columns. The number of columns and the number of corresponding values must be the same as well as the same type and size.

UPDATE Statement

This statement is used to update the existing record of database tables. It updates the record of one or more rows of a specified table. Following is its general syntax:

UPDATE Table_name SET Column1=Value, Column2=Value,
Column3=Value, ……., Column-n=Value WHERE Predicates

If we skip the WHERE clause, the UPDATE statement updates the entire rows of a specified table.

DELETE Statement

This statement is used to delete records from database tables. It deletes one or more rows from a specified table. Following is its general syntax:

DELETE FROM Table_name WHERE Predicates

If we skip the WHERE clause, the DELETE statement deletes all rows from a specified table.

Data Definition Language

Data Definition Language (DDL) is also called Data Description Language. The statements of this language are used to create, update, and delete data objects. Data objects mean Databases, Tables, Views, Indexes, Users, Roles, and Store Procedures. The DDL has the following three basic statements:

- CREATE Statement
- ALTER Statement
- DROP Statement

CREATE Statement

This statement is used to create new data object for example, new Database, Table, View, Index, User, Role, or Store Procedure. Each object of the Relational Database Management System has its own method but the following syntax is almost common to all the data objects:

CREATE Object_type Object_name

In the above syntax, the Object_type specifies type of the object to be created and Object_name specifies a user-defined name of the object to be created.

Create Database

A Database can be created using a keyword DATABASE that is used as Object_type after the CREATE statement followed by a user-defined name of the database to be created. Following is its general syntax:

```
CREATE DATABASE Database_name
```

Create Table

A table can be created using a keyword TABLE that is used as Object_type after the CREATE statement followed by a user-defined name of the table to be created. Following is its general syntax:

```
CREATE TABLE Table_name
(
Column1 datatype null / not null,
Column2 datatype null / not null,
.....................,
Column-n datatype null / not null
);
```

The **Table_name** indicates the name of the table you want to create. The Column1, Column2,........, Column-n indicates the number of columns you want to create in the table, the datatype indicates the type of the column, and the null / not null indicates either the column default value is null or not null.

Create View

A view can be created using a keyword VIEW which is used as Object_type after the CREATE statement followed by a user-defined name of the view to be created. Following is its general syntax:

```
CREATE VIEW View_name AS
SELECT Column1, Column2, ................, Column-n
FROM Table_name
WHERE Condition
```

The **View_name** indicates a user-defined name of the view you want to create, and Column1, Column2, …………, Column-n is a list of columns used to retrieve data from a specified table for the View.

ALTER Statement

This statement is used to update the existing data object such as Table, View, Index, User, or Role etc. Following is its general syntax:

ALTER Object_type Object_name
…………………………..
Procedure of data object
………………………….

The Objetc_type specifies the type of object and Object_name specifies the name of object to be updated.

DROP Statement

DROP statement is used to delete an existing data object such as Database, Table, Index, View, User, or Store Procedure. The DROP statement deletes a data Object permanently from the Relational Database Management System. Following is its general syntax:

DROP Object_type Object_name

The Object_type specifies the type of data Object and Object_name specifies the name of data object to be deleted. The following syntax of DROP statement is used to delete a specified table:

DROP TABLE Table_name

The Table_name specifies the name of the table to be deleted. The following syntax of DROP statement is used to delete a View:

DROP VIEW View_name

Data Control Language

Data Control Language (DCL) is used to control database access and provides security to database to restrict unauthorized users from database access. The data control language allows us to provide specific privileges to the users of databases. It grants or revokes privileges from the users. The privileges mean access rights, permissions, or authorizations to access the data or information of the database and perform different operations on it such as insert new data in database tables, delete data, update the existing data, and retrieve data from database tables. The data control language controls and provides security to SELECT statement, UPDATE Statement, DELETE Statement, and INSERT Statement to restrict unauthorized users. The data control language has the following two statements:

- GRANT Statement
- REVOKE Statement

GRANT Statement

This statement is used to assign privileges or permissions to a user. It has the following general syntax:

GRANT Previleges_list ON Object_name TO User_name

The Previleges_list specifies a list of privileges to be assigned to a specified user of the database to access the data or information of a specified table of a database specified as Object_name. The Object_name specifies the name of a specified table in a database from which privileges or permissions are to be assigned to a specified user. The User_name specifies the name of a user we assign privileges or permissions. For example, if we want to assign the SELECT statement privilege or permission to a specified user of a database, we can use the GRANT statement as:

GRANT SELECT ON Table_name TO User_name

The above statement assigns the SELECT statement privilege or permission to a specified user of a database to use the SELECT statement in a table specified as Table_name. If we want to assign the INSERT, DELETE and UPDATE privileges or permissions to a specified user of a database then we can use the GRANT statement as

GRANT INSERT, DELETE, UPDATE ON Table_name TO User_name

The above statement assigns the INSERT, DELETE, and UPDATE privileges or permissions to a specified user of a database to use these statements in a table specified as Table_name.

REVOKE Statement

This statement is used to revoke or remove privileges or access permissions from a specified user of a database. The Revoke statement has the following general syntax:

REVOKE Previleges_list ON Object_name FROM User_name

If we want to revoke or remove the DELETE and UPDATE privileges or permissions from a specified user of a database then we can use the REVOKE statement as:

REVOKE DELETE, UPDATE ON Object_name FROM User_name

The above statement removes the DELETE and UPDATE privileges or permissions from a specified user of a database and restricts a user to use the DELETE and UPDATE statements in a database table that is specified as an Object_name.

Stored Procedure

A Stored Procedure is a set of statements or code of SQL which is stored in a relational database management system with a specified name and it is reused again and again from multiple programs such as from remote program, from another Stored Procedure or from command line. A Stored Procedure behaves like a procedure or method that takes input parameters and returns output. Therefore, a Stored Procedure is a prepared set of statements or code of SQL that is stored permanently in a relational database management system for the future use. If a SQL query is using again and again in multiple places or in multiple programs, instead ofhaving to write that query again and again, it is a recommended way to create a Stored Procedure and save that query in it and call it whenever you need. A Stored Procedure can contain SQL statements, Conditional statements and iteration statements etc.

Main Parts of a Stored Procedure

A Stored Procedure contains the following three important parts:

- Input
- Execution
- Output

Input

This part of a Stored Procedure contains input parameters that take input values from the users and provide to the SQL statement for condition or search criteria.

Execution

To execute a Stored Procedure it is invoked or called from a remote program, from another Stored Procedure or from Command line. When a Stored Procedure is invoked and it receives the input parameters then body of the Stored Procedure executes and produces a result or output.

Outputs

When a Stored Procedure is executed successfully then it returns a result. The result of a Stored Procedure is a single value or a result set.

Benefits of Using Stored Procedure

1. Stored Procedures provide security so that the end users cannot access the SQL statements but they just can provide input values to Stored Procedures.
2. A Stored Procedure reduces the time consumption because when we write a single SQL statement again and again in different places then it consumes more time as compared to write a single SQL statement and stored it in a Stored Procedure.
3. A single Stored Procedure can be invoked or called from different places or from multiple programs.
4. When we change or update a single SQL statement in different places or in multiple programs, it consumes more time as compared to change or update the contents of a single Stored Procedure.
5. It is very easy to grant access permission to multiple users for using a Stored Procedure instead of granting access permission to multiple users in case of multiple tables of database.

Create Stored Procedure

To create a Stored Procedure using SQL Server Management Studio follows the following steps:

1. In Object Explorer of SQL Server Management Studio, connect to an instance of Database Engine then expand that instance.

2. Expand Databases, expand your desire database and then expand Programmability.
3. When you expand Programmability, Right-click on Stored Procedures and then click on New Stored Procedure.
4. When you click on the New Stored Procedure option then it create the following format that is the general declaration of the Stored Procedure:

```
SET ANSI_NULLS ON
GO
SET QUOTED_IDENTIFIER ON
GO
-- ===============================================
-- Author:                <Author_Name>
-- Create date:             <Create_Date,>
-- Description:             <Description>
-- ===============================================
CREATE PROCEDURE <Procedure_Name>

-- Add parameters for the stored procedure here

<@Param1 DataType_Name = Default_Value>,
<@Param2 DataType_Name = Default_Value>

AS
BEGIN
SET NOCOUNT ON;

-- Insert statements for procedure here
SELECT<@Param1, sysname, @p1>, <@Param2, sysname, @p2>
END
GO
```

The Author, Create Date, and Description are optional and they indicate the Author name, the Create Date and the Description of a Stored Procedure respectively. The @Param1 and @Param2 indicate parameters of the Stored Procedure. The parameters are variables that take input values from the user and provide to the SQL statement for condition or search criteria. The parameters are declared with a @ sign. The Procedure_Name indicates the name of the Stored Procedure. The name of a Stored Procedure is an identifier that follows the variables naming convention.

RetrieveStudentsInfo Stored Procedure

This Stored Procedure retrieves data or record from the StudentsInfo table. It takes a single input parameter student registration number (StdRegNumber) from the user and retrieves a single row of data of that specified student registration number. Following is its declaration:

```
SET ANSI_NULLS ON
GO
SET QUOTED_IDENTIFIER ON
GO
-- ================================================
-- Author:          Adalat Khan
-- Create date:     11/12/2017
-- Description:     Retrieves record from StudentsInfo
-- ================================================
CREATE PROCEDURE RetrieveStudentsInfo

@StdRegNum nvarchar(MAX)
AS
BEGIN

SET NOCOUNT ON;

SELECT StdRegNumber, StdName, StdDoBirth
from StudentsInfo
where StdRegNumber = @StdRegNum
END
GO
```

In the above Stored Procedure, the RetrieveStudentsInfo is the name of the Stored Procedure, the @StdRegNum is a variable of type nvarchar that takes the input value of the Student Registration Number for the column StdRegNumber and retrieves a single row of data from the StudentsInfo table that matches the input value of the StdRegNumber.

InsertStudentsInfo Stored Procedure

This Stored Procedure inserts record in the StudentsInfo table. It takes four input parameters from the user. The first parameters is a String parameter that takes the student registration number, the second parameter is a String parameter that takes the student name, the third parameter is a DateTime parameter that takes the student date of birth, and the fourth parameter is a String parameter that takes the student email address. Following is its declaration:

```
SET ANSI_NULLS ON
GO
SET QUOTED_IDENTIFIER ON
GO
-- ==============================================
-- Author:         Adalat Khan
-- Create date:    14/11/2017
-- Description:    Insert Data in StudentsInfo Table
-- ==============================================

CREATE PROCEDURE InsertStudentsInfo
@SRegNum nvarchar(50), @SName nvarchar(50),
@SDoBirth datetime, @SEmail nvarchar(50)
AS
BEGIN

SET NOCOUNT ON;

insert into StudentsInfo (StdRegNumber, StdName,
StdDoBirth, StdEmail)
values (@SRegNum,@SName, @SDoBirth, @SEmail)
END
GO
```

In the above Stored Procedure, the InsertStudentsInfo is the name of the Stored Procedure and @SRegNum, @SName, @SDoBirth, @SEmail are input parameters of the Stored Procedure that takes the student registration number, the student name, the student date of birth and the student email address respectively and insert into the database table StudentsInfo.

CHAPTER 11

Database Applications Development in .NET

CHAPTER CONTENTS

- Database Applications
- Designing Database Applications in .NET
- ADO.NET
- DataSet Object
- Internal Architecture of DataSet Object
- DataSet Class
- Constructors of DataSet Class
- Properties of DataSet Class
- DataSetName Property
- Tables Property
- Relations Property
- IsInitialized Property
- Namespace Property
- ExtendedProperties Property
- Methods of DataSet Class
- AcceptChanges Method
- Clear Method
- Clone Method
- Copy Method
- RejectChanges Method
- HasChanges Method
- GetChanges Method
- .NET Framework Data Providers
- .NET Framework Data Provider for SQL Server
- .NET Framework Data Provider for ODBC
- .NET Framework Data Provider for OLEDB
- .NET Framework Data Provider for Oracle
- Core Objects of .NET Framework Data Providers
- Connection Object
- Command Object

- DataReader Object
- DataAdapter Object
- The .NET Framework Data Provider Classes
- SqlConnection Class
- Constructors of SqlConnection Class
- Properties of SqlConnection Class
- ConnectionString Property
- Database Property
- Datasource Property
- WorkstationId Property
- State Property
- ConnectionTimeout Property
- Methods of SqlConnection Class
- Open Method
- Close Method
- Dispose Method
- CreateCommand Method
- Begintransaction Method
- SqlCommand Class
- Constructors of SqlCommand Class
- Properties of SqlCommand Class
- CommandText Property
- CommandType Property
- Connection Property
- CommandTimeout Property
- Parameters Property
- Transaction Property
- Methods of SqlCommand Class
- ExecuteNonQuery Method
- Insert Data Using Stored Procedure
- ExecuteReader Method
- Retrieve Data Using Stored Procedure
- ExecuteScalar Method
- ExecuteXmlReader Method
- BeginExecuteNonQuery Method
- IAsyncResult Interface
- EndExecuteNonQuery Method
- Synchronous Operation

- Asynchronous Operation
- Synchronous and Asynchronous Methods
- BeginExecuteReader Method
- EndExecuteReader Method
- BeginExecuteXmlReader Method
- EndExecuteXmlReader Method
- CreateParameter Method
- Cancel Method
- Clone Method
- Dispose Method
- SqlDataReader Class
- Declaration of SqlDataReader Class
- Properties of SqlDataReader Class
- IsClosed Property
- Connection Property
- FieldCount Property
- HasRows Property
- Methods of SqlDataReader Class
- Read Method
- ReadAsync Method
- GetInt32 Method
- GetString Method
- GetFloat Method
- GetDateTime Method
- GetDecimal Method
- GetDouble Method
- GetValue Method
- GetStream Method
- GetName Method
- Close Method
- Dispose Method
- ToString Method
- SqlDataAdapter Class
- Constructors of SqlDataAdapter Class
- Properties of SqlDataAdapter Class
- SelectCommand Property
- InsertCommand Property
- DeleteCommand Property

- UpdateCommand Property
- Methods of SqlDataAdapter Class
- Fill Method
- DatGridView Class
- Constructors of DataGridView Class
- Properties of DataGridView Class
- Programming Examples of DataGridView
- DataTable Class
- Constructors of DataTable Class
- Properties of DataTable Class
- Methods of DataTable Class
- DataColumn Class
- Constructors of DataColumn Class
- Properties of DataColumn Class
- DataRow Class
- Properties of DataRow Class
- Methods of DataRow Class
- Create a DataTable and Insert Data
- Retrieve Data from DataTable

Database Applications

Database application is a client server application software program designed in computer programming language that permanently stores data or record in the database. It is the combination of application software and a database server. The application software works as front end called client area and database server works as back end called server area of the database application. The application software is directly connected to the database server and provides a visual interface that allows us to access the database data and performs different operations on it such as insert new data in database, delete specific data from database, and update data of the database without using the Database Management System interface directly. The database application also allows us to display data from database according to the input or selected search criteria. The client area is designed using the .NET programming languages such as C# and Visual Basic.NET while the server area of database application uses database such as Microsoft SQL Server, Oracle, and Access database etc. The client area and the server area of database application can be installed on the same computer or on different computers. When the client area and the server area of database application are installed on different computers, the client area of database application uses the local area network to access the server area of the database application.

Designing Database Applications in .NET

The .NET Framework provides an Object Oriented set of software library called ADO.NET that provides two fundamental components such as DataSet Object and .NET Framework Data Provider. The .NET Framework Data Provider provides different types of Data Providers used to establish connections to various types of databases or data sources and provide access to the database data. The .NET Data Provider is a communication link or a bridge between the application software program and the database server that connects the application software program to the database server and provides different functions or operations to perform on the database data.

Furthermore, a database application contains three parts such as application software program, database server, and database driver. The application software program is the first part of database application that is designed in any computer programming language. The second part of database application is the database server. The database server works as back-end and it is called server area of database application. The third part of database application is the database driver. The database driver is used between the application software program and the database server and it establishes a connection between the application software program and the database server. The database driver is actually a communication link or a bridge between the application software program and the database server. Following is the general diagram of the database application program:

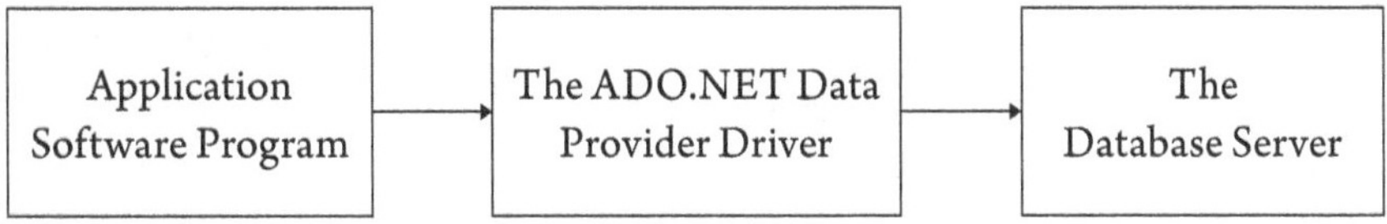

ADO.NET

ADO stands for ActiveX Data Object and .NET means Microsoft .NET Framework. It is a part of the .NET Framework Base Class Library. The ADO. NET is an Object Oriented set of software library that provides access to different data sources. A data source is a database but it can also be a text file, an Excel spreadsheet, or an XML file. ADO.NET provides a communication link or a bridge between the application software and the database server that connects database server to the application software. ADO.NET provides various types of classes used to perform different operations on the data or record of the database system such as retrieve or display data from the database, delete the database data, and update the database data.

ADO.NET handles the database data in disconnected mode. The disconnected mode means, first it establishes a connection to the database and retrieves data from the connected database then close the database connection. When ADO.NET retrieves data from database, it stores the retrieved data in a memory cache and allows us to perform different operations on it in the disconnected mode. When the data is manipulated in disconnected mode then ADO.NET reestablishes or restores a connection to the database and saves or updates the changes in the main database. ADO.NET provides access to various types of databases such as Microsoft SQL Server, Microsoft Access, Oracle, MySQL, FileMaker, dBase, and FoxPro etc. ADO.NET provides two fundamental components such as DataSet Object and .NET Framework Data Provider. Each component of ADO.NET has its own specific function in the database programming. Following is the details of Dataset object and .NET framework Data Provider:

- DataSet Object
- .NET Framework Data Providers

DataSet Object

DataSet object is a container of data that retrieves data from the database and save it in a memory cache in the form of tables that contains rows and columns. The DataSet object retrieves data from one or more tables of database and arranges the retrieved data in the form of rows and columns and store it in a memory cache. The DataSet object also retrieves the relations and constraints of the database tables if data of the retrieved tables are related with each other. Therefore, a DataSet object is made up of the collections of tables, relations, and constraints and it represents the disconnected data of database. The key point of DataSet object is that it retrieves data from the database and stores it in a memory cache and disconnects the database connection and allows us to perform different operations on the disconnected data of DataSet object such as insert new data, delete data, update data, and retrieve or display the data of the DataSet object. When the changes occurred in the data of DataSet object in disconnected mode, the DataSet object reestablishes or restores the database connection and saves or updates the changes in the main database.

DataSet object cannot retrieve data from the database directly but it is used with the conjunction of another object called DataAdapter object. A DataAdapter object works between the database and the DataSet object as a communication link or a bridge that retrieves data from database using SQL command and assigns the retrieved data to the DataSet object. The DataAdapter object uses the Connection object to establish the database connection and uses the SQL Command to retrieves data from the database. When DataAdapter object retrieves data from the database, it assigns the retrieved data to the DataSet object using the Fill method. The Fill method of DataAdapter object fills the DataSet object with the retrieved data of database. When DataSet object received data from the DataAdapter object, it disconnects the database connection and allows us to perform manipulation on the data in disconnected mode. When changes occurred in the data of the DataSet object in disconnected mode, the DataAdapter object then reestablishes the database connection and saves the changes in the main database. Therefore, DataAdapter object is a communication bridge or data traveler between the database and the DataSet object that retrieves data from the database and assigns it to the DataSet object and saves the changes back to the main database.

In .NET Framework each object has a class and each class in .NET Framework provides one or more constructors used to declare objects from the class. A class also provides different properties and methods used to perform different operations on the objects of that class. A DataSet is an object and it can be created or declared from its class. The class name of the DataSet object is DataSet class. The DataSet class provides different constructors used to create or declare DataSet objects.

Internal Architecture of DataSet Object

DataSet object is the collection of tables, relations, and constraints. The tables of DataSet object store data and the relations of DataSet object store relations of the tables. The relation of tables mean data relationship between the two tables if both tables have at least one matching column and they represent the primary key and foreign key relationship. A table of DataSet object is called data table and it is represented by an object DataTable and a relation of DataSet object is called data relation and it is represented by an object DataRelation. The DataTable objects are used to store the data of DataSet object and the DataRelation objects are used to store relations of the tables of DataSet object. Each DataTable object represents one table in a memory cache and each DataRelation object represents a relation between the two DataTable objects.

The DataTable and DataRelation are classes in .NET Framework. When an object of DataTable class is declared, it automatically added into the collection called DataTableCollection and when an object of the DataRelation class is declared, it added into the collection called DataRelationCollection. The DataTableCollection is a collection of DataTable object and the DataRelationCollection is a collection of DataRelation object. The DataTableCollection and the DataRelationCollection are also classes in .NET Framework. We can add a new DataTable object and DataRelation object into DataSet and also can delete a DataTable object and DataRelation object from the DataSet using the DataTableCollection and DataRelationCollection classes. The DataTableCollection and the DataRelationCollection classes provide different properties and methods used to perform different operations on the DataTable objects and DataRelation objects respectively. We can add and delete DataTable objects and DataRelation objects from the DataSet object using the Add and Remove methods of the DataTableCollection class and the DataRelationCollection class respectively.

Each DataTable object contains the collection of rows and columns. A Row of the DataTable object is called data row and it is represented by an object called DataRow object and column of the DataTable object is called data column and it is represented by an object called DataColumn object. Each DataTable object contains one or more DataRow objects and one or more DataColumn objects. The DataRow and DataColumn are classes in .NET Framework. The DataRow objects are declared from DataRow class and they are defined in a collection called DataRowCollection. The DataColumn objects are declared from the DataColumn class and they are defined in a collection called DataColumnCollection. The DataRowCollection and the DataColumnCollection are classes in .NET Framework. The DataRowCollection and DataColumnCollection classes provide different properties and methods used to perform different operations on the DataRow and the DataColumn objects.

When we create a DataTable object, initially it does not have a table schema. A schema means structure of the table such as rows and columns. When we create a DataTable object, we must create the DataColumn and DataRow objects for the created DataTable object then add to the DataSet object. When we add DataColumn objects to the DataTable object, the DataColumn objects become members of the DataColumnCollection similarly, when we add DataRow objects to the DataTable object, the DataRow objects become members of the DataRowCollection.

DataSet Class

DataSet class is an important and main component of ADO.NET. It represents disconnected data of the database. DataSet retrieves data from one or more tables of the database and stores it in a memory cache in the form of tables that contain rows and columns. The DataSet class is defined in the namespace System.Data. Therefore the namespace System.Data is included before using the DataSet object.

Constructors of DataSet Class

DataSet class provides four types of constructors but the following two constructors are commonly used:

- DataSet() Constructor
- DataSet(String) Constructor

DataSet() Constructor

This constructor of DataSet class is used to create objects of DataSet class. It is the default constructor that takes no parameter. Following is its general declaration:

C# Declaration
DataSet dst = new DataSet();
Visual Basic Declaration
Dim dst As DataSet = New DataSet()

In the above declaration, dst indicates a new created object of the DataSet class.

DataSet(String) Constructor

This constructor of DataSet class is used to create an object of the DataSet class with a given string value. The string value represents the name of the DataSet object. Following is its general declaration:

C# Declaration
DataSet dst = new DataSet("String_value");
Visual Basic Declaration
Dim dst As DataSet = New DataSet("String_value")

In the above declaration, dst indicates a new created object of the DataSet class. The String_value is the parameter that represents name of the DataSet object.

Properties of DataSet Class

DataSet class provides the following important properties:

DataSetName	Tables	Relations
IsInitialized	Namespace	ExtendedProperties

DataSetName Property

This property of DataSet class is used to set the name of DataSet object. The name of DataSet object is a user-defined string value that represents a DataSet object. The name can be any string value but it must be according to the variable naming convention. Following is its general declaration:

The C# Declaration
public string DataSetName;
The Visual Basic Declaration
Public Property DataSetName As String

This property of DataSet class is also used to get or return the current name of the DataSet object. It returns a string value that indicates the name of the DataSet object. Following is the programming example of DataSetName property:

C# Example

```
//Declare a DataSet object from DataSet class
DataSet dst = new DataSet();

//Declare a string variable to get the DataSet name
String dstName;

//Set the DataSet object name
dst.DataSetName ="MyDataSet";

//Get the current name of the DataSet object dst
```

```
dstName = dst.DataSetName;

//Display the current name of the DataSet object dst
MessageBox.Show (dstName);
```

Visual Basic Example

```
'Declare a DataSet object from the DataSet class
Dim dst As New DataSet()

'Declare a string variable to get the DataSet name
Dim dstName As String

'Set the DataSet object name
dst.DataSetName = "MyDataSet"

'Get the current name of the DataSet object dst
dstName = dst.DataSetName

'Display the current name of the DataSet object dst
MessageBox.Show(dstName)
```

Tables Property

This property of DataSet class is used to get or return a collection called DataTableCollection. The DataTableCollection is a collection that contains one or more DataTable objects of the DataSet. To get the DataTableCollection from Tables property, an object of the DataTableCollection class is declared and Tables property is assigned to the object of DataTableCollection class. Following is the general declaration of Tables property:

C# Declaration
public DataTableCollection Tables;
Visual Basic Declaration
Public ReadOnly Property Tables As DataTableCollection

The Tables property is read-only property therefore, we cannot set its value manually but it is used to return a collection of DataTable objects. Following is the programming example of Tables property:

C# Example

```
//Declare a DataSet object dst from DataSet class
DataSet dst = new DataSet();

//Declare an instance of the DataTable class
DataTable Table;

//Declare an instance of the DataColumn class
DataColumn Column;

//Declare an instance of the DataRow class
DataRow Row;

//Declare an instance of the DataTableCollection class
DataTableCollection TableCollection;

//Declare a Table Table1
Table = new DataTable("Table1");

//Create a column ID Number from DataColumn class
Column = new DataColumn();
Column.DataType = System.Type.GetType("System.Int32");
Column.ColumnName = "ID Number";
Column.ReadOnly = true;
Column.Unique = true;

//Add the created Column to the DataTable object Table
Table.Columns.Add(Column);

//Create the second Column Name from DataColumn Class
Column = new DataColumn();
Column.DataType = System.Type.GetType("System.String");
Column.ColumnName = "Name";
Column.ReadOnly = false;
Column.Unique = false;

//Add the created column to the DataTable object Table
Table.Columns.Add(Column);
```

```
//Create Row for the DataTable object Table
Row = Table.NewRow();
Row["ID Number"] = "1";
Row["Name"] = "Asad";

//Add the created DataRow object to the DataTable object Table
Table.Rows.Add(Row);

//Add DataTable object Table to DataSet object
dst.Tables.Add(Table);

//Get the collection of DataTables from DataSet object
TableCollection = dst.Tables;

//Count the number of DataTable objects in DataSet object
MessageBox.Show(TableCollection.Count.ToString());
```

Visual Basic Example

```
'Declare a DataSet object dst from DataSet class
Dim dst As New DataSet()

'Declare an instance of the DataTable class
Dim Table As DataTable

'Declare an instance of the DataColumn class
Dim Column As DataColumn

'Declare an instance of the DataRow class
Dim Row As DataRow

'Declare an instance of the DataTableCollection class
Dim TableCollection As DataTableCollection

'Declare a Table Table1
Table = New DataTable("Table1")

'Create a column ID Number from DataColumn class
Column = New DataColumn()
Column.DataType = System.Type.GetType("System.Int32")
```

```
Column.ColumnName = "ID Number"
Column.ReadOnly = True
Column.Unique = True

'Add the created column to the DataTable object Table
Table.Columns.Add(Column)

'Create the second Column from DataColumn class
Column = New DataColumn()
Column.DataType = System.Type.GetType("System.String")
Column.ColumnName = "Name"
Column.ReadOnly = False
Column.Unique = False

'Add the created column to the DataTable object Table
Table.Columns.Add(Column)

'Create Row for the DataTable object Table
Row = Table.NewRow()
Row("ID Number") = "1"
Row("Name") = "Asad"

'Add the created DataRow object to the DataTable object Table
Table.Rows.Add(Row)

'Add DataTable object Table to the DataSet object
dst.Tables.Add(Table)

'Get the collection of DataTables from the DataSet
TableCollection = dst.Tables

'Count the number of DataTable objects in a DataSet object
MessageBox.Show(TableCollection.Count.ToString())
```

Relations Property

This property of DataSet class is used to get or return a collection called DataRelationCollection. The DataRelationCollection is a collection that contains one or more DataRelation objects of the DataSet. Following is the general declaration of this property:

C# Declaration
public DataRelationCollection Relations;
Visual Basic Declaration
Public ReadOnly Property Relations As DataRelationCollection

The Relations property is read-only property therefore, we cannot set its value manually but this property is used to return a collection of the DataRelation objects.

IsInitialized Property

This property of DataSet class is used to check whether the object of DataSet class is initialized or not. It returns a Boolean value either true or false. When the object of DataSet class is initialized, it returns true otherwise, it returns false. Following is the general declaration of this property:

The C# Declaration
public bool IsInitialized;
The Visual Basic Declaration
Public ReadOnly Property IsInitialized As Boolean

The IsInitialized property is read-only property therefore, we cannot set its value manually but this property is used to get the current status of the DataSet object whether the DataSet object is initialized or not. To get the current status of the DataSet object, a Boolean variable is declared and the IsInitialized property is assigned to the declared Boolean variable.

Namespace Property

This property of DataSet class is used to get or set the namespace of the DataSet class.

ExtendedProperties Property

This property of DataSet class is used to get a collection that contains customized information about the users associated with the DataSet class object.

Methods of DataSet Class

The DataSet class provides the following important methods:

AcceptChanges	Clear	Clone
Copy	RejectChanges	HasChanges
GetChanges		

AcceptChanges

This method of DataSet class is used to save the changes that occur in the data of the DataSet object. Following is the general declaration of this method:

C# Declaration
public void AcceptChanges()
Visual Basic Declaration
Public sub AcceptChanges

Following is the programming example of AcceptChanges method:

C# Example

```
//Declare a DataSet object from DataSet class
DataSet dst = new DataSet();

//Call the AcceptChanges() method to save the changes
dst.AcceptChanges();
```

Visual Basic Example

```
'Declare a DataSet object from the DataSet class
Dim dst As DataSet = New DataSet()

'Call the AcceptChanges() method to save the changes
dst.AcceptChanges()
```

Clear Method

This method of DataSet class is used to clear or remove all data from the DataSet object. Following is the general declaration of this method:

C# Declaration
public void Clear()
Visual Basic Declaration
Public sub Clear

Following is the programming example of Clear method:

C# Example

//Declare a DataSet object from the DataSet class
DataSet dst = new DataSet();
 	
//Call the Clear() method to clear the Dataset object
dst.Clear();

Visual Basic Example
'Declare a DataSet object from DataSet class Dim dst As DataSet = New DataSet() 'Call the Clear() method to clear the Dataset object dst.Clear()

Clone Method

This method of DataSet class is used to make a copy of the structure of the DataSet object. It makes a copy of the blank structure of a DataSet object without data. The structure of a DataSet object contains structure of the DataTable objects that contains column names without data, and structure of the DataRelation objects that contains the relationship between the two tables and the table constraints. Following is the general declaration of this method:

C# Declaration
public virtual DataSet Clone()
Visual Basic Declaration
Public Overridable Function Clone As DataSet

Following is the programming example of the Clone method:

C# Example

//Declare a DataSet object from DataSet class
DataSet dst = new DataSet();
 	
//Declare the second DataSet object from DataSet class
DataSet dstClone = new DataSet();
 	
//Call the Clone() method to copy structure of the current DataSet
dstClone = dst.Clone();

Visual Basic Example
'Declare a DataSet object from DataSet class Dim dst As DataSet = New DataSet() 'Declare the second DataSet object from DataSet class Dim dstClone As DataSet = New DataSet() 'Call the Clone() method to copy structure of the current DataSet dstClone = dst.Clone()

In the above programming example, dst is the current DataSet object and dstClone is a new DataSet object that contains structure of the current DataSet object dst without data.

Copy Method

This method of DataSet class is used to make a copy of the DataSet object. It makes a copy of the structure as well as copy of the data. Following is it general declaration:

C# Declaration
public DataSet Copy()
Visual Basic Declaration
Public Function Copy As DataSet

Following is the programming example of Copy method:

C# Example

//Declare a DataSet object from DataSet class
DataSet dst = new DataSet();
 	
//Declare the second DataSet object from DataSet class
DataSet dstCopy = new DataSet();
 	
//Copy the current DataSet object into new DataSet object
dstCopy = dst.Copy();

Visual Basic Example
'Declare a DataSet object from DataSet Class Dim dst As DataSet = New DataSet() 'Declare the second DataSet object from DataSet class Dim dstCopy As DataSet = New DataSet() 'Copy the current DataSet object into new DataSet object dstCopy = dst.Copy()

In the above programming example, dst is the current DataSet object and dstCopy is a new DataSet object that contains copy of the current DataSet object dst.

RejectChanges Method

This method of DataSet class is used to roll back the changes that occurred in the data of DataSet object. When we make changes in the data of a DataSet object, the RejectChanges method allows us to roll back or reject the changes we made in the data of the DataSet object. Following is its general declaration:

C# Declaration
public virtual void RejectChanges()
Visual Basic Declaration
Public Overridable Sub RejectChanges

The RejectChanges method does not return value but it rolls back or rejects the changes that occurred in the data of the DataSet object. Following is the programming example of the RejectChanges method:

C# Example

//Declare a DataSet object from DataSet class
DataSet dst = new DataSet();
 	
//Call RejectChanges() method to cancel changes of the DataSet
dst.RejectChanges();

Visual Basic Example
'Declare a DataSet object from DataSet class Dim dst As DataSet = New DataSet() 'Call RejectChanges() method to cancel changes of the DataSet dst.RejectChanges()

HasChanges Method

This method of DataSet class is used to check whether changes occurred in the data of a DataSet object or not. It returns a Boolean value either true or false. When the data of a DataSet object is changed, it returns true otherwise, it returns false. The changes in the DataSet object means when new data is inserted, the current data is deleted from the DataSet object, or the current data is updated in the DataSet object. Following is the general declaration of this method:

C# Declaration
public bool HasChanges()
Visual Basic Declaration
Public Function HasChanges As Boolean

The HasChanges method is usually used with the decision statement to check whether the changes in the data of DataSet object occurred or not. Following is the programming example of the HasChanges method:

C# Example

//Declare a DataSet object from DataSet class
DataSet dst = new DataSet();
 	
//Declare a Boolean variable b
bool b = dst.HasChanges();
 	
//Check whether changes occurred in the DataSet object or not
if (b == true)
MessageBox.Show("Changes occurred in the DataSet object");
else
MessageBox.Show("Changes did not occurred");

Visual Basic Example

'Declare a DataSet object from DataSet class
Dim dst As DataSet = New DataSet()
 	
'Declare a Boolean variable b
Dim b As Boolean = dst.HasChanges()
 	
'Check whether changes occurred in the DataSet object or not
if b = true Then
MessageBox.Show("Changes occurred in the DataSet object")
else
MessageBox.Show("Changes did not occurred")
End If

GetChanges Method

This method of DataSet class is used to get the changes that occurred in the data of a DataSet object. It returns the affected rows of data of a DataSet object where the changes occurred. This method creates a new DataSet object that contains a copy of all the affected data of the current DataSet object. Following is the general declaration of this method:

C# Declaration
public DataSet GetChanges()

Visual Basic Declaration
Public Function GetChanges As DataSet

Following is the programming example of GetChanges method:

C# Example

//Declare a DataSet object from DataSet class
DataSet dst = new DataSet();
 	
//Declare a DataSet object to get changes from the current DataSet //object
DataSet dstChanges = new DataSet();
 	
//Call the GetChanges() method to get changes from the current //DataSet object
dstChanges = dst.GetChanges();

Visual Basic Example
'Declare a DataSet object from DataSet class Dim dst As DataSet = New DataSet() 'Declare a DataSet object to get changes from the current DataSet 'object Dim dstChanges As DataSet = New DataSet() 'Call the GetChanges() method to get changes from the current 'DataSet object dstChanges = dst.GetChanges()

.NET Framework Data Providers

The .NET Framework provides different types of data Providers used to establish connections to various types of databases or data sources and provide access to the data of databases. The .NET Framework data Provider is a communication link or a bridge between the software application and the database server that connects the application software to the database and provides different functions or operations to perform on the data of the database. The .NET Framework data Provider is a software component of ADO.NET that provides four types of core and fundamental functions or operations such as establish connection to a database, execute Commands against the connected database, retrieve data or result of the Commands from the database, and populate or fill the ADO.NET DataSet object. Each .NET Framework data Provider provides the same four types of core and fundamental functions or operations and each .NET Framework data Provider provides four types of objects. Each object of a .NET Framework data Provider specifies a function or operation of a .NET Framework data Provider. These objects are called core and fundamental objects of .NET framework data provider. Following is the details of these objects:

- Connection Object
- Command Object
- DataReader Object
- DataAdapter Object

The Connection object is used to establish a connection to the database. The Command object is used to execute the Commands against the connected database. The DataReader object is used to retrieve the data or result of the Commands from the database, and the DataAdapter object is used to populate or fill the ADO.NET DataSet object with the retrieved data of the database. The .NET Framework provides different types of Data Providers used to establish connections to various types of databases or data sources and provide access to the data of the databases. There are various types of databases such as Microsoft Access Database, Microsoft SQL Server Database, Oracle Database, Filemaker Database, Firebird Database, IBM DB2 Database, Interbase Database, MySQL Database, Paradox Database, Postgre SQL Database, SQLBase Database, SQLite Database, and Visual FoxPro etc. The .NET Framework provides a universal access to almost all types of databases currently available. The .NET Framework provides two types of access to databases such as direct access and indirect access. The direct access of a database means the .NET Framework accesses and establishes connection to a database without using any external driver or Data Provider. The indirect access to a database means the .NET Framework uses some external drivers or Data Providers to access and establish connection to a database.

The .NET Framework provides direct access only to SQL Server database because the .NET Framework provides a separate Data Provider for the SQL Server database that is used to establish connection to SQL Server database directly and perform different operations on the data of SQL Server database without using any external driver or Data Provider. The .NET Framework uses the ODBC and OLE DB drivers for indirect access to databases. There are also others third party Data providers available which are used to establish connections to databases directly without using any external driver or Data Provider. The .NET Framework provides the following different Data Providers used to establish connections to various databases and perform different operations on the data of databases:

- .NET Framework Data Provider for SQL Server
- .NET Framework Data Provider for ODBC
- .NET Framework Data Provider for OLE DB

.NET Framework Data Provider for SQL Server

This Data Provider of .NET Framework is used to establish a connection to SQL Server database and allow us to access SQL Server Database Management System and perform different operations on the data of SQL Server database such as retrieve data, insert new data in the database, delete data from the database, or update data of the database. To use this Data Provider, the namespace System.Data.SqlClient is included in the application before use.

.NET Framework Data Provider for ODBC

ODBC stands for Open Database Connectivity. It is a Software Application Programming Interface (API) designed by Microsoft Corporation. It is used to establish connections to various types of databases. Therefore, this Data Provider is a universal Data Provider that can establish connections to almost all types of databases currently available. The ODBC Data Provider establishes a database connection using the Driver of that database. Each database has a specific Driver that is usually installed in a computer system. A Driver is a library that implements the functions in the ODBC Data Provider. The ODBC Data Provider establishes a database connection using DSN. A DSN stands for Data Source Name. It is a data structure that contains all information about a specific database connection such as Driver name of the database, name of the database, directory name of the database, and User ID and Password for the data access if required. A DSN is used to establish a database connection through an ODBC driver. When we create a DSN then we use that DSN in the application to connect the application to the database. The DSN name can be called from anywhere or from any block of the application using the .NET Framework Connection object. There are three types of DSN such as User DSN, System DSN, and File DSN. The User DSN is related to a specific single user of the current computer system and it is visible to only a specific user of the current computer system and no other user of the current computer system can use the User DSN of another user. A System DSN is shared among all users of the current computer system and all users of the current computer can use the System DSN. The File DSN is shared among all users who have the same drivers installed.

.NET Framework Data Provider for OLE DB

The OLE DB can also be written as OLEDB and it stands for Linking and Embedding Database. The OLE DB data provider is a Software Application Programming Interface (API) designed by Microsoft Corporation. It is used to establish connections to various types of databases and access their data in a uniform manner. The OLE DB data provider is a successor of the ODBC Data Provider that is designed to extend the features of the ODBC data Provider. The OLE DB data provider supports both the Relational and non-relational databases and it supports various types of databases such as Microsoft Access Database, Microsoft SQL Server Database, Oracle Database, Filemaker Database, Firebird Database, IBM DB2 Database, Interbase Database, MySQL Database, Paradox Database, Postgre SQL Database, SQLBase Database, SQLite Database, and Visual FoxPro etc. The OLE DB data provider supports non-relational databases such as object databases and Excel spreadsheets.

The OLE DB data provider does not support DSN connection. It uses a Connection String to establish connection to the database and access the database data. A Connection String is a string that contains all information about the database. The Connection String is used if we want to establish a database connection without the using of DSN. A Connection String contains different parameters that take different values about the database connection such as name of the driver of database, name of the Server or computer where the database server is installed, name of the target database, and security information such as User name and Password.

Core Objects of .NET Framework Data Providers

The .NET Framework Data Provider is a software component of ADO.NET that provides four types of core and fundamental functions or operations such as establish connection to a database, execute Commands against the connected database, retrieve data or result of the Commands from database or fill the ADO.NET DataSet object. Each .NET Framework Data Provider provides the same four types of core and fundamental functions or operations and each .NET Framework Data Provider provides four types of objects called core and fundamental objects. Following is the details of .NET Framework Data Providers core and fundamental objects:

- Connection Object
- Command Object
- DataReader Object
- DataAdapter Object

Connection Object

This object of data provider establishes a connection to a specified database server. It establishes a connection between the application software and the database server. The Connection object uses a Connection String property to establish connection to the database. A Connection String is a string that contains a set of information requires for the database connection such as name of the server or computer where the database is installed, name of the database, user name and password etc. The Connection String uses all these information as parameters. The base class of the Connection object is called DbConnection class.

Command Object

This object of data provider is used to execute the SQL statements or Stored Procedures against the connected database or data source specified in the Connection object. The Command object works with the Connection object and it requires an instance of the Connection object. To execute the SQL statement or Stored Procedure, first the database connection is established using the Connection object then an instance of the Connection object and SQL statement or Stored Procedure are passed as parameters to the Command Object. The SQL statements are usually select, insert, update, and delete. When the Command Object executes SQL statement or Stored Procedure, it returns a result set. The DataReader object is used to retrieve the result set of the Command Object. The base class of the Command object is called DbCommand class.

DataReader Object

This object of data provider is used to read data from the database. The DataReader object reads data from the database as read-only and forward-only stream of data or a result set and it does not support manipulation of data.

The retrieved data of the DataReader object is read-only and forward-only. The read-only data means it does not allow manipulation and forward-only data means the data is retrieved fast forward-only stream that allow us to read data from the stream in a sequential manner only and it does not allow us to go back or access the previous data. The DataReader object reads one record or one row at a time. When the first row is retrieved, it discards that row and moves control to the next row and reads the second row and on this way the DataReader object reads the last row according to the SQL statement or Stored Procedure. The DataReader object is usually used with the conjunction of a Command object and retrieves the query result of the Command Object. The main difference between DataSet and DataReader object is that a DataSet object retrieves data for manipulation and DataReader object retrieves data as read-only that does not allow manipulation. The DataReader object cannot be created directly but it is created by calling the ExecuteReader method of Command class.

DataAdapter Object

This object of data provider is used to provide a connection between the DataSet object and the database. The DataAdapter object is used with the conjunction of the DataSet object that enables DataSet object to access the data of the database. It is actually a communication link or a bridge between the DataSet object and the database. The DataAdapter object retrieves data from the database and populates or fills the DataSet object with the retrieved data of the database. The DataAdapter object uses a Connection object and establishes connection to the database and uses a Command object and retrieves data from the database using the SQL Commands or Stored Procedure. When it retrieves data from the database, it assigns the retrieved data of the database to the DataSet object and fills the DataSet object with the retrieved data using the fill method. The base class of DataAdapter object is called DbDataAdapter class.

.NET Framework Data Provider Classes

Each data provider of .NET Framework provides different classes used to establish database connections to various databases or data sources and perform different operations on the data of the databases. Following is the details of these classes:

Classes	Description
SqlConnection SqlCommand SqlDataReader SqlDataAdapter	These classes are used to connect to SQL Server database and perform different operations on the data of SQL Server database.
OdBcConnection OdBcCommand OdBcDataReader OdBcDataAdapter	These classes are used to establish database connection using the ODBC Data Provider. They provide access to various types of databases such as Microsoft Access Database, Microsoft SQL Server, Oracle, Filemaker, Firebird, IBM DB2 Database, Interbase Database, MySQL, Paradox, Postgre SQL, SQLBase, SQLite etc.
OleDbConnection OleDbCommand OleDbDataReader OleDbDataAdapter	These classes are used to establish database connection using the OLEDB Data Provider. They provide access to various types of databases such as Microsoft Access Database, Microsoft SQL Server, Oracle, Filemaker, Firebird Database, IBM DB2 Database, Interbase Database, MySQL, Paradox, Postgre SQL, SQLBase, SQLite, Visual FoxPro, and Excel File etc.

SqlConnection Class

SqlConnection class is used to establish connection to SQL Server database. The namespace of this class is System.Data.SqlClient. Therefore, to use this class the namespace System.Data.SqlClient is included before use.

Constructors of SqlConnection Class

Constructor is used to create an object or instance of a class. The SqlConnection class provides the following constructors:

- SqlConnection()
- SqlConnection(String)

SqlConnection() Constructor

This Constructor of SqlConnection class is the default constructor that takes no parameters. It is used to declare an object of SqlConnection class without specifying parameters. Following is its general declaration:

C# Declaration
SqlConnection Con = new SqlConnection();
Visual Basic Declaration
Dim Con As New SqlConnection()

SqlConnection(String) Constructor

This constructor of SqlConnection class takes a String type parameter that specifies a connection String. The connection String is a string that contains all information about the database connection such as name of the Server or Computer where the database is installed, name of the database, the security information such as user name and password of the database etc. Following is its general declaration:

C# Declaration
SqlConnection Con = new SqlConnection(ConnectionString));
Visual Basic Declaration
Dim Con As New SqlConnection(ConnectionString)

Properties of SqlConnection Class

SqlConnection class provides the following important properties:

ConnectionString	Database	Datasource
WorkstationId	State	ConnectionTimeout

ConnectionString Property

ConnectionString is a string that contains a set of information requires for the database connection such as name of the server or computer where the database is installed, name of the target database, the security information such as user name and password of the database, the authentication information about the connection, the information about the connection lifetime, timeout and information about the connection reset. The ConnectionString property uses all these information as parameters. Each parameter of ConnectionString is separated by a semicolon and each parameter takes a single value. The parameter value may either enclosed by a pair of single quotes or double quotes. Following is the list of different parameters of the ConnectionString property:

Parameter	**Description**
Data Source or Server or Address or Addr or Network Address	This parameter indicates the name of the server or computer where the database is installed. This parameter has multiple names such as Data Source, Server, Address, Addr, or Network Address. It takes the name of the local computer or server computer where the database is installed.
Initial Catalog or Database	This parameter specifies the name of the target database. It has two names such as Initial Catalog and Database.
Integrated Security or Trusted Connection	This parameter specifies whether the connection uses windows authentication or not. It takes a Boolean value either true/false or yes/no. If it is set to false then it requires a user name and password and if it is set to true then it uses the Windows current account credentials for the authentication. This parameter also takes a value SSPI that means Security Support Provider Interface. The SSPI is a Microsoft API that is used to provide the integrated security services for authentication. SSPI provides authentication and all the necessary security options to the database connection. The SSPI is actually equivalent to true that provides the Windows current account credentials for the authentication. We can either use true or SSPI.
User ID	This parameter is an optional parameter that specifies a user name of the database account.

Password or Pwd	This parameter specifies the password of a specified user specified in the User ID parameter.
Persist Security Info	This parameter prevents the sensitive information such as passwords from being returned as a part of the connection if the connection is open. It is set to false. Its default value is false.
Connection Timeout or Connect Timeout	This parameter specifies the connection timeout. The connection timeout is a time in seconds to wait for a connection to open. It takes an integer value that specifies the number of seconds to wait for a connection to open. The default duration of connection timeout is 15 seconds and it can also be set to any value. If the system is busy and the connection timeout duration is finished then the connection object generates an error message. If this parameter of Connection String is set to zero then the connection object will wait for the connection until the connection is established.

Following is the programming example of the ConnectionString property of the SqlConnection class:

C# Example

```
//Declare a string variable ConnectionString
string ConnectionString;

//Set the ConnectionString
ConnectionString = "Data Source = DataSource_name; Database =
                    Database_name; Integrated Security = SSPI;";
```

Visual Basic Example

```
'Declare a string variable ConnectionString
Dim ConnectionString As String

'Set the ConnectionString
ConnectionString = "Data Source = DataSource_name; Database =
                    Database_name; Integrated Security = SSPI;"
```

Database Property

This property of SqlConnection class is used to get the name of the current connected database. When the database connection is successfully established and the current status of the connected database is open then the Database property is used to return the name of the current connected database. This property is usually used when an application is connected to multiple databases.

DataSource Property

This property of SqlConnection class is used to get the name of the Data Source. A Data Source is a string value that contains the name of the local computer or server computer in which SQL Server database is installed and the name of the instance of SQL Server database. The name of the computer and the name of the instance of SQL Server database are concatenated with each other using the back slash. This property returns a Data Source name as a string value. The default value of this property is an empty string.

WorkstationId Property

This property of SqlConnection class is used to get the name of the client computer of SQL Server database. The client computer is a computer in which SQL Server database is installed. It returns the name of the client computer as a string value. The default value of this property is an empty string value.

Following is the programming example of Database property, DataSource property, and WorkstationId property of SqlConnection class:

C# Example

```
//Include Namespaces
using System;
using System.Data;
using System.Data.SqlClient;

namespace DatabaseExample
{
class Program
{
static void Main(string[] args)
```

```
{
//Declare an instance of SqlConnection class
SqlConnection con;

//Declare s string variable ConnectionString
string ConnectionString;

ConnectionString =
        "Data Source=localhost\\MSSQLSERVER2014;" +
        "Initial Catalog=Students;" +
        "User ID=adalat khan;Password=Std123";

con=new SqlConnection(ConnectionString);
con.Open();

Console.WriteLine("Database Name = " + con.Database);
Console.WriteLine("Data Source Name = " + con.DataSource);
Console.WriteLine("Computer Name = " + con.WorkstationId);

Console.ReadKey();
}
}
}
```

Visual Basic Example

```
'Include Namespaces
Imports System.Data
Imports System.Data.SqlClient

Module Module1

Sub Main()

'Declare an instance of SqlConnection class
Dim con As SqlConnection

'Declare s string variable ConnectionString
Dim ConnectionString As String
```

```
'Set ConnectionString for SqlConnection class object con
ConnectionString =
            "Data Source=localhost\MSSQLSERVER2014;" &
            "Initial Catalog=Students;" &
            "User ID=adalat khan;Password=Std123"

con = New SqlConnection(ConnectionString)
con.Open()

Console.WriteLine("Database Name = " & con.Database)
Console.WriteLine("Data Source Name = " & con.DataSource)
Console.WriteLine("Computer Name = " & con.WorkstationId)

Console.ReadKey()
End Sub
End Module
```

State Property

This property of SqlConnection class is used to get the most current state of the SqlConnection class object. This property returns a ConnectionState enumeration that indicates the current state of the SqlConnection class object. The ConnectionState enumeration contains different fixed values that indicate different states of the SqlConnection class object. Following is the details of the ConnectionState enumeration fixed values:

State Value	Description
Closed	This value of ConnectionState enumeration indicates that the SqlConnection class object is currently closed.
Open	This value of ConnectionState enumeration indicates that the SqlConnection class object is currently open.
Connecting	This value of ConnectionState enumeration indicates that the SqlConnection class object is currently connecting to the database.
Executing	This value of ConnectionState enumeration indicates that the SqlConnection class object is currently executing the SQL Commands.

Fetching	This value of ConnectionState enumeration indicates that the SqlConnection class object is currently retrieving data from the database.
Broken	This value of ConnectionState enumeration indicates that the connection of SqlConnection class object is currently Broken from the database.

Following is the programming example of the State property of SqlConnection class:

C# Example

```
//Include the Namespaces
using System;
using System.Data;
using System.Data.SqlClient;

namespace DatabaseExample
{
class Program
{
static void Main(string[] args)
{
//Declare an instance of SqlConnection class
SqlConnection con;

//Declare s string variable ConnectionString
string ConnectionString;

ConnectionString =
"Data Source=localhost\\MSSQLSERVER2014;" +
"Initial Catalog=Students;" +
"User ID=adalat khan;Password=Std123";

con=new SqlConnection(ConnectionString);
con.Open();

//Check the connection Status
if (con.State == ConnectionState.Closed)
```

```
Console.WriteLine("The Connection is Closed");
else
if (con.State == ConnectionState.Open)
Console.WriteLine("The Connection is Open");
Console.ReadKey();
}
}
}
```

Visual Basic Example

```
'Include the Namespaces
Imports System.Data
Imports System.Data.SqlClient

Module Module1

Sub Main()
'Declare an instance of SqlConnection class
Dim con As SqlConnection
'Declare s string variable ConnectionString
Dim ConnectionString As String

ConnectionString =
"Data Source=localhost\MSSQLSERVER2014;" &
"Initial Catalog=Students;" &
"User ID=adalat khan;Password=Std123"

con = New SqlConnection(ConnectionString)
con.Open()

If con.State = ConnectionState.Closed Then
Console.WriteLine("The Connection is Closed")
ElseIf con.State = ConnectionState.Open Then
Console.WriteLine("The Connection is Open")
End If
Console.ReadKey()
End Sub
End Module
```

ConnectionTimeout Property

This property of SqlConnection class is used to get the amount of time in seconds that indicates how long a connection object will wait for a database connection to establish before terminating an attempt and generates an error. This property actually returns the connection timeout value that is set in the Connection Timeout parameter of the Connection String. Following is its general declaration:

C# Declaration
public override int ConnectionTimeout
Visual Basic Declaration
Public Overrides ReadOnly Property ConnectionTimeout As Integer

The following declaration of Connection String uses the Connection Timeout parameter:

C# Declaration
string ConnectionString; ConnectionString = "Data Source = DataSource_name; Database = Database_name; Integrated Security = SSPI; Connection Timeout = 30;";
Visual Basic Declaration
Dim ConnectionString As String ConnectionString = "Data Source = DataSource_name; Database = Database_name; Integrated Security = SSPI; Connection Timeout = 30;"

Methods of SqlConnection Class

SqlConnection class provides the following methods:

- Open Method
- Close Method
- Dispose Method
- CreateCommand Method
- Begintransaction Method

Open Method

This method of SqlConnection class is used to open the database connection after setting the ConnectionString property. Following is its general declaration:

C# Declaration
public override void Open()
Visual Basic Declaration
Public Overrides Sub Open

Following is the programming example of Open method:

C# Programming Example

```
//Declare an instance of SqlConnection class
SqlConnection Con;

//Declare a string variable ConnectionString
string ConnectionString;

//Set the ConnectionString property of SqlConnection class
ConnectionString = "Data Source = DataSource_name; Database =
Database_name; Integrated Security = SSPI;";
Con = new SqlConnection(ConnectionString);

//Call the Open method to open the database connection
Con.Open();
```

Visual Basic Programming Example

```
Dim Con As SqlConnection
Dim ConnectionString As String
Dim Timeout As Integer

ConnectionString = "Data Source = DataSource_name; Database =
Database_name; Integrated Security = SSPI;"
Con = New SqlConnection(ConnectionString)
Con.Open()
```

Close Method

This method of SqlConnection class is used to close the open connection of database that is established by the Open method of SqlConnection class.

Dispose Method

This method of SqlConnection class is used to release all the resources used by the connection object.

CreateCommand Method

This method of SqlConnection class is used to create SqlCommand object for SqlConnection object. The CreateCommand method returns an object of the SqlCommand. Therefore, to get the return value of this method an object of the SqlCommand is declared.

BeginTransaction Method

This method of SqlConnection class is used to start the database transaction.

SqlCommand Class

SqlCommand class is used to execute SQL statements or Stored Procedures against the SQL Server database and performs different operations on the data of database such as insert data, delete data, update data, or retrieve data from the database.

Constructors of SqlCommand Class

SqlCommand class provides the following constructors used to declare instances of the SqlCommand class:

- SqlCommand()
- SqlCommand(String)
- SqlCommand(String, SqlConnection)
- SqlCommand(String, SqlConnection, SqlTransaction)

SqlCommand() Constructor

This is the default constructor of SqlCommand class that takes no parameters. This constructor is used to declare an object of the SqlCommand class without specifying any parameter value.

SqlCommand(String)

This constructor of SqlCommand class takes a single parameter. The parameter of this constructor is a String variable that takes SQL statement. This constructor is used to declare an object by specifying SQL text query. Following is the general syntax of this constructor to declare an object:

C# Declaration
string Str = "select * from table"; SqlCommand Cmd = new SqlCommand(Str);
Visual Basic Declaration
Dim Str As String = "select * from table" Dim Cmd As New SqlCommand(Str)

In the above declaration, Str is a string variable that holds the SQL statement or query string and Cmd is a user-defined name of the object of SqlCommand class.

SqlCommand(String, SqlConnnection)

This Constructor of SqlCommand class takes two parameters. The first parameter is a string variable that takes SQL statement and second parameter takes an object of the SqlConnection class. This constructor is used to declare an object of the SqlCommand class by specifying the SQL statement and SqlConnection class object. Following is the general syntax to declare an object of the SqlCommand class using this Constructor:

C# Declaration
string Str = "select * from Table"; String ConnectionString; ConnectionString = "Data Source = DataSource_name; Database = Database_name; Integrated Security = SSPI;"

SqlConnection Con = new SqlConnection(ConnectionString)); SqlCommand Cmd = new SqlCommand(Str, Con);
Visual Basic Declaration
Dim Str As String = "select * from Table" Dim ConnectionString As String ConnectionString = "Data Source = DataSource_name; Database = Database_name; Integrated Security = SSPI;" Dim Con As New SqlConnection(ConnectionString) Dim Cmd as New SqlCommand(Str, Con)

SqlCommand(String, SqlConnection, SqlTransaction)

This constructor of SqlCommand class takes three parameters. The first parameter is a string variable that takes SQL statement. The second parameter takes an object of the SqlConnection class and third parameter takes an object of the SqlTransaction cass. Following is the general syntax to declare an object of the SqlCommand class using this Constructor:

C# Declaration
string Str = "select * from Table"; String ConnectionString;
ConnectionString = "Data Source = DataSource_name; Database = Database_name; Integrated Security = SSPI;"; SqlConnection Con = new SqlConnection(ConnectionString)); SqlTransaction Trans; SqlCommand Cmd = new SqlCommand(Str, Con, Trans);
Visual Basic Declaration
Dim Str As String = "select * from Table" Dim ConnectionString As String ConnectionString = "Data Source = DataSource_name; Database = Database_name; Integrated Security = SSPI;" Dim Con As New SqlConnection(ConnectionString) Dim Trans as SqlTransaction Dim Cmd as New SqlCommand(Str, Con, Trans)

Properties of SqlCClass

SqlCommand class provides the following important properties:

CommandText	CommandType	Connection
CommandTimeout	Parameters	Transaction

CommandText Property

This property of SqlCommand class is used to specify the SQL query, Stored Procedure or a database table to execute against the SQL Server database.

CommandType Property

This property of SqlCommand class is used to specify the type of the command to be executed against the SQL Server database. The CommandType property is usually used with the conjunction of the CommandText property and it is the explanation of CommandText property that explains the value of the CommandText property. The CommandText property takes three types of values such as SQL query, Stored Procedures, and name of a database table. The CommandText property takes one value at a time and executes against the SQL Server database. The CommandType property is used to explain what the current value of the CommandText property is. The CommandType property takes the following three constant values:

- CommandType.Text
- CommandType.StoredProcedure
- CommandType.TableDirect

The CommandType property takes the constant value CommandType.Text if the CommandText property is using the SQL query, the CommandType property takes the constant value CommandType.StoredProcedure if the CommandText property is using the Stored Procedure, and the CommandType property takes the constant value CommandType.TableDirect if the CommandText property is using the database table directly.

Connection Property

This property of SqlCommand class is used to set the current connection object of SqlConnection class. The object of SqlCommand class requires an object of the SqlConnection class to establish a connection to the database and executes the SQL query or Stored Procedure against the connected database. The Connection property of SqlCommand class is used if we declare an object of the SqlCommand class using the first two constructors because the first two constructors of SqlCommand class do not take the connection object as parameter. The last two constructors of SqlCommand class take an object of the SqlConnection class therefore, the Connection property does not use in the case of last two constructors of SqlCommand class.

CommandTimeout Property

This property of SqlCommand class is used to get or set the command timeout. The command timeout is the amount of time in seconds that indicates how long an object of the SqlCommand class will wait for a command to execute before terminating an attempt and generates an error. The default value of this property is 30 seconds and it can also be set manually.

Following is the programming example that demonstrates the CommandText property, the CommandType property, the Connection property, and the CommandTimeout property of SqlCommand class:

C# Example

```
using System;
using System.Data;
using System.Data.SqlClient;

namespace DatabaseExample
{
class Program
{
static void Main(string[] args)
{
SqlConnection con;
SqlCommand cmd;
String ConnectionString;


ConnectionString =
        "Data Source=localhost\\MSSQLSERVER2014;" +
```

```
            "Initial Catalog=Students;" +
            "User ID=adalat khan;Password=Std123";

con=new SqlConnection(ConnectionString);
cmd = new SqlCommand();
cmd.CommandText = "select * from Table";
cmd.CommandType = CommandType.Text;
cmd.CommandTimeout = 15;
cmd.Connection = con;
con.Open();

Console.WriteLine(cmd.CommandText);
Console.WriteLine(cmd.CommandTimeout);
Console.WriteLine(cmd.Connection);

Console.ReadKey();
}
}
}
```

Visual Basic Example

```
Imports System.Data
Imports System.Data.SqlClient

Module Module1

Sub Main()
Dim con As SqlConnection
Dim cmd As SqlCommand
Dim ConnectionString As String

ConnectionString =
            "Data Source=localhost\MSSQLSERVER2014;" &
            "Initial Catalog=Students;" &
            "User ID=adalat khan;Password=Std123"

con = New SqlConnection(ConnectionString)
cmd = New SqlCommand()
cmd.CommandText = "select * from Table"
```

```
cmd.CommandType = CommandType.Text
cmd.CommandTimeout = 15
cmd.Connection = con
con.Open()

Console.WriteLine(cmd.CommandText)
Console.WriteLine(cmd.CommandTimeout)
Console.WriteLine(cmd.Connection)
Console.ReadKey()
End Sub
End Module
```

Parameters Property

This property of SqlCommand class is used to get the collection SqlParameterCollection and adds the SQL parameters to it. The SqlParameterCollection represents a collection of parameters associated with the SqlCommand class. The Parameters property of SqlCommand class specifies a collection of parameters for the SQL query. The SQL query allows us to specify parameters for the columns of database tables and provide values to the parameters during run-time. This type of SQL query is called parameterized query. A parameterized query is a query in which placeholders are used for parameters and the parameter values are supplied at execution time of the application. Therefore, a parameterized query is also called dynamic query. Consider the following SQL query:

```
Query = "select * from StudentsInfo
                    where StdName = '" & "Asad" & "'"
```

The above query performs a search operation and retrieves StdName from the StudentsInfo table whose name is Asad. This query is a static query that always performs the same operation because the input value is fixed and it does not allow us to change the input value during run-time of the application similarly, consider the following SQL query:

```
Query = "insert into StudentsInfo
            (StdRegNumber, StdName, StdDoBirth) values
    ('" & "001" & "', '" & "Sahil Khan" & "', '" & "1/1/1990" & "')"
```

The above query performs the insertion operation that inserts data or record in the StudentsInfo table. It inserts the values of three fields or columns such as StdRegNumber, StdName, and StdDoBirth. The corresponding input values of the three columns are 001, Sahil Khan, and 1/1/1990 respectively. This is also a static query and it does not allow us to change the input values during runtime of the application. Each column input value of the static query requires a pair of double quotes and a pair of single quotes along with the AND (&) operator. This type of input is complicated and ambiguous. To reduce this complication and make the query dynamic, the parameterized query is used. Following is the declaration of the parameterized query:

```
Query = "insert into StudentsInfo
                (StdRegNumber,StdName,StdDoBirth) values
                (@RegNum,@SName,@DoBirth)";

SqlCommand cmd;
cmd.Parameters.AddWithValue("@RegNum", textbox1.text);
cmd.Parameters.AddWithValue("@SName", textbox2.text);
cmd.Parameters.AddWithValue("@DoBirth", textbox3.text);
```

The above query is parameterized dynamic query that takes the columns input values during run-time of the application. In the above query, the @RegNum, @SName, and @DoBirth are parameters that take the input values and assign to the columns StdRegNumber, StdName, and StdDoBirth respectively. The parameter is defined with @ character. The parameterized query can also be defined as:

```
Query = "insert into StudentsInfo
                (StdRegNumber,StdName,StdDoBirth) values
                (@RegNum,@SName,@DoBirth)";

cmd.Parameters.Add("@RegNum",SqlDbType.NVarChar).Value =
                                                textbox1.text;
cmd.Parameters.Add("@SName", SqlDbType.NVarChar).Value =
                                                textbox2.text;
cmd.Parameters.Add("@DoBirth",SqlDbType.DateTime).Value=
                                                textbox3.text;
```

OR

```
SqlParameter param1 = cmd.Parameters.Add(
                        "@RegNum", SqlDbType.NVarChar);
                        param1.Value = textbox1.text;
SqlParameter param2 = cmd.Parameters.Add(
                        "@Sname", SqlDbType.NVarChar);
                        param2.Value = textbox2.text;
SqlParameter param3 = cmd.Parameters.Add(
                        "@DoBirth", SqlDbType.NVarChar);
                        param3.Value = textbox3.text;
```

Add Method

This is a method of SqlParameterCollection class and it is used to add parameters to the collection. It is an overloaded member method of the SqlParameterCollection class that provides different overloaded forms. Each overloaded form of this method takes different parameters. Following is the general declaration of the commonly used overloaded forms of Add method:

C# Declaration

```
public SqlParameter Add(
            string parameterName, SqlDbType sqlDbType
                  )

public SqlParameter Add(
            string parameterName, SqlDbType sqlDbType, int size
                  )
```

Visual Basic Declaration

```
Public Function Add (
            parameterName As String, sqlDbType As SqlDbType
                )
```

```
Public Function Add (
            parameterName As String, sqlDbType As SqlDbType,
            size As Integer
                ) As SqlParameter
```

The first declaration takes two parameters and the second declaration takes three parameters. The first two parameters are common in both the declarations. The first parameter is a string value that specifies the parameter name. The second parameter is SqlDbType parameter that specifies the type of the target column to which the value is provided and the third parameter is an integer parameter that specifies the length or size of the target column.

AddWithValue Method

This is the method of SqlParameterCollection class and it is used to add parameters to the collection. It works same as Add method but the main difference is that the AddWithValue method does not requires the column type and size. This method is usually used if we do not know the column type and column size. Following is its general declaration:

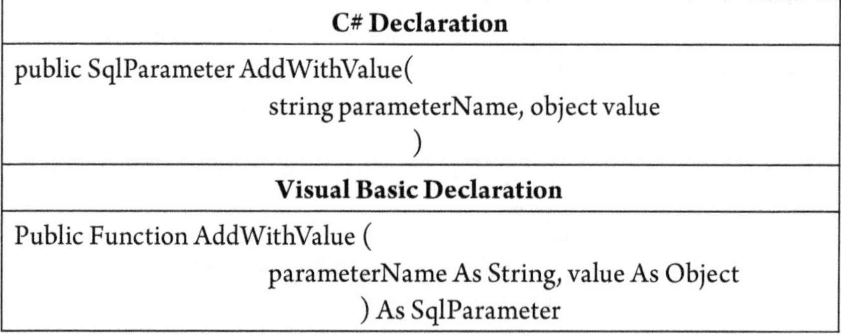

C# Declaration
public SqlParameter AddWithValue(string parameterName, object value)
Visual Basic Declaration
Public Function AddWithValue (parameterName As String, value As Object) As SqlParameter

In the above declaration, the first parameter is a string parameter that specifies the name of the parameter and the second parameter is an object type parameter that specifies the value of the parameter.

Transaction Property

This property of SqlCommand class is used to get or set the transaction within which the SqlCommand executes. When we perform an operation on the database and the operation either successfully completed or failed then this type of operation is called transaction. For example, add new record to the database, delete record from the database, or update record of the database.

Methods of SqlCommand Class

The SqlCommand class provides the following methods:

ExecuteNonQuery	ExecuteReader
ExecuteScalar	ExecuteXmlReader
BeginExecuteNonQuery	EndExecuteNonQuery
BeginExecuteReader	EndExecuteReader
BeginExecuteXmlReader	EndExecuteXmlReader
CreateParameter	Cancel
Clone	Dispose
Equals	ResetCommandTimeout
CreateObjRef	GetType
GetHashCode	ToString

ExecuteNonQuery Method

This method of SqlCommand class is used to execute the SQL statements or Stored Procedures. It is used to execute the INSERT, DELETE, UPDATE, CREATE, and SET statements of the SQL. The ExecuteNonQuery method cannot execute the SELECT statement of SQL and it cannot retrieve data or records from the database. Therefore, this method is used to insert new data or record in the database, delete data from the database, or update data of the database. The ExecuteNonQuery method is also used to create a database object by executing the CREATE statement such as Tables, Stored Procedures, Views etc. Following is its general declaration:

C# Declaration
public abstract int ExecuteNonQuery();
Visual Basic Declaration
Public Override Function ExecuteNonQuery As Integer

The ExecuteNonQuery method returns an integer value that specifies the number of rows inserted, deleted, or updated in the database. Following is the programming example of ExecuteNonQuery method:

C# Program

```
using System;
using System.Data;
using System.Data.SqlClient;

namespace DatabaseExample
{
class Program
{
static void Main(string[] args)
{
SqlConnection con;
SqlCommand cmd;
String ConnectionString, Query;

ConnectionString =
                    "Data Source=localhost\\MSSQLSERVER2014;" +
                    "Initial Catalog=Students;" +
                    "User ID=adalat khan;Password=Std123";

con=new SqlConnection(ConnectionString);

//SQL query to insert record in the Database
Query = "insert into StudentsInfo
(StdRegNumber,StdName,StdDoBirth,StdDeptCode) values
(@RegNum,@SName,@DoBirth,@DeptCode)";

cmd = new SqlCommand(Query, con);
cmd.CommandType = CommandType.Text;
cmd.Parameters.AddWithValue("@RegNum", "001");
cmd.Parameters.AddWithValue("@SName", "Sajad Khan");
cmd.Parameters.AddWithValue("@DoBirth", "01/03/1991");
cmd.Parameters.AddWithValue("@DeptCode", "001");
con.Open();
int result = cmd.ExecuteNonQuery();
con.Close();

if(result!=0)
```

```
Console.WriteLine("The Data has been Saved in the Database");

Console.ReadKey();
}
}
}
```

Visual Basic Program

```
Imports System.Data
Imports System.Data.SqlClient

Module Module1

Sub Main()
Dim con As SqlConnection
Dim cmd As SqlCommand
Dim ConnectionString, Query As String

ConnectionString =
                    "Data Source=localhost\MSSQLSERVER2014;" &
                    "Initial Catalog=Students;" &
                    "User ID=adalat khan;Password=Std123"

con = New SqlConnection(ConnectionString)

//SQL query to insert record in the Database
Query = "insert into StudentsInfo
(StdRegNumber,StdName,StdDoBirth,StdDeptCode) values
(@RegNum,@SName,@DoBirth,@DeptCode)"

cmd = New SqlCommand(Query, con)
cmd.CommandType = CommandType.Text
cmd.Parameters.AddWithValue("@RegNum", "001")
cmd.Parameters.AddWithValue("@SName", "Sajad Khan")
cmd.Parameters.AddWithValue("@DoBirth", "01/03/1991")
cmd.Parameters.AddWithValue("@DeptCode", "001")
con.Open()
Dim result As Integer = cmd.ExecuteNonQuery()
con.Close()
```

```
If result <> 0 Then
Console.WriteLine("The Data has been Saved in the Database")
End If

Console.ReadKey()
End Sub

End Module
```

The above program inserts data or record in the StudentsInfo table. It inserts a single record or row at a time.

Insert Data Using Stored Procedure

In this program we will use a Stored Procedure InsertStudentsInfo which is created in SQL Server. This Stored Procedure inserts data or record of students in the StudentsInfo table. For more details about this Stored Procedure please go to chapter # 10 and reads the topic InsertStudentsInfo Stored Procedure. The following program inserts data or record in the StudentsInfo table using the Stored Procedure InsertStudentsInfo.

Write a program that inserts data or record in the database using Stored Procedure.

C# Program

```
using System;
using System.Data;
using System.Data.SqlClient;

namespace DatabaseExample
{
class Program
{
static void Main(string[] args)
{
SqlConnection con;
String ConnectionString, Query;

ConnectionString =
```

```
                "Data Source=localhost\\MSSQLSERVER2014;" +
                "Initial Catalog=Students;" +
                "User ID=adalat khan;Password=Std123";

//Establish the database connection
con = new SqlConnection(ConnectionString);

//Open the database connection
con.Open();

Query = "InsertStudentsInfo"; //Stored Procedure Name
SqlCommand cmd = new SqlCommand(Query,con);
cmd.CommandType = CommandType.StoredProcedure;

//Provide the input Parameter values to the Stored Procedure
//InsertStudentsInfo to insert record into the database table
//StudentsInfo
String StudentRegNumber = "099";
String StudentName = "Shahid";
DateTime StudentDoBirth = new DateTime(1999,1,1);
String StudentEmail = "shahid@gmail.com";

cmd.Parameters.Add("@SRegNum", SqlDbType.NVarChar);
cmd.Parameters["@SRegNum"].Value = StudentRegNumber;

cmd.Parameters.Add("@SName", SqlDbType.NVarChar);
cmd.Parameters["@SName"].Value = StudentName;

cmd.Parameters.Add("@SDoBirth", SqlDbType.NVarChar);
cmd.Parameters["@SDoBirth"].Value = StudentDoBirth;

cmd.Parameters.Add("@SEmail", SqlDbType.NVarChar);
cmd.Parameters["@SEmail"].Value = StudentEmail;

cmd.ExecuteNonQuery();

//Close the Command and Connection Objects
cmd.Dispose();
```

```
con.Close();

Console.ReadKey();
}
}
}
```

Visual Basic Program

```
Imports System.Data
Imports System.Data.SqlClient

Module Module1

Sub Main()
Dim con As SqlConnection
Dim ConnectionString, Query As String

ConnectionString =
                    "Data Source=localhost\MSSQLSERVER2014;" &
                    "Initial Catalog=Students;" &
                    "User ID=adalat khan;Password=Std123"

'Establish the Database connection
con = New SqlConnection(ConnectionString)

'Open the database connection
con.Open()

Query = "InsertStudentsInfo" 'Stored Procedure Name
Dim cmd As SqlCommand = New SqlCommand(Query, con)
cmd.CommandType = CommandType.StoredProcedure

'Provide the input Parameters value to the Stored Procedure
'InsertStudentsInfo to insert record into the database table
'StudentsInfo
Dim StudentRegNumber As String = "099"
Dim StudentName As String = "Shahid"
Dim StudentDoBirth As Date = New Date(1999, 1, 1)
Dim StudentEmail As String = "shahid@gmail.com"
```

```
cmd.Parameters.Add("@SRegNum", SqlDbType.NVarChar)
cmd.Parameters("@SRegNum").Value = StudentRegNumber
cmd.Parameters.Add("@SName", SqlDbType.NVarChar)
cmd.Parameters("@SName").Value = StudentName

cmd.Parameters.Add("@SDoBirth", SqlDbType.NVarChar)
cmd.Parameters("@SDoBirth").Value = StudentDoBirth

cmd.Parameters.Add("@SEmail", SqlDbType.NVarChar)
cmd.Parameters("@SEmail").Value = StudentEmail

cmd.ExecuteNonQuery()

'Close the Command and Connection Objects
cmd.Dispose()
con.Close()

Console.ReadKey()
End Sub
End Module
```

ExecuteReader Method

This method of SqlCommand class is used to read or retrieve data from the database. It executes the SELECT statement of SQL or Stored Procedure and read or retrieves data from the database according to the SELECT statement or Stored Procedure. It reads or retrieves a Read-Only display of data from the database and it does not allow us to edit or update the data of the database. The ExecuteReader method only executes the SELECT statement and it does not support the INSERT, DELETE, and UPDATE statements of the SQL. When it executed the SELECT statement of the SQL, it returns an object of the SqlDataReader class. The object of the SqlDataReader class contains the data of the database retrieved by the ExecuteReader method according to the SELECT statement of the SQL or Stored Procedure. The retrieved data of the ExecuteReader method is then access from the SqlDataReader class object using its Read() method. The object of the SqlDataReader class allows us to read a single row or single record at a time. The data of the SqlDataReader object is a read-only and forward-only stream of data. The read-only stream of data means the data of the SqlDataReader object is a read only and we cannot manipulate it and the forward-only stream of data means when we retrieve one row or one record from the SqlDataReader object then we cannot go back to the previous row or previous record of the SqlDataReader object. Following is the general declaration of the ExecuteReader method:

C# Declaration
public SqlDataReader ExecuteReader();
Visual Basic Declaration
Public Function ExecuteReader As SqlDataReader

The ExecuteReader method returns an object of the SqlDataReader class. To get the return value of the ExecuteReader method, an object of the SqlDataReader class is declared and the ExecuteReader method is assigned to the declared object of the SqlDataReader class.

Write a program that displays data from the database using the SqlDataReader class object.

C# Program

```
//Include the Namespaces
using System;
using System.Data;
using System.Data.SqlClient;

namespace DatabaseExample
{
class Program
{
static void Main(string[] args)
{
SqlConnection con;
SqlCommand cmd;
String ConnectionString, Query;

ConnectionString =
                    "Data Source=localhost\\MSSQLSERVER2014;" +
                    "Initial Catalog=Students;" +
                    "User ID=adalat khan;Password=Std123";
```

```
//Establish the database connection
con = new SqlConnection(ConnectionString);

Query = "select StdRegNumber, StdName from StudentsInfo";

//Execute the SqlCommand
cmd = new SqlCommand(Query, con);

//Open the database connection
con.Open();

//Read data from the database using the SqlDataReader object
SqlDataReader Reader = cmd.ExecuteReader();
while (Reader.Read())
{
Console.Write("Reg Number = " + Reader.GetString(0));
Console.Write("Name = " + Reader.GetString(1));
Console.WriteLine();
}

//Close the connection, command and SqlDataReader object
Reader.Close();
cmd.Dispose();
con.Close();

Console.ReadKey();
}
}
}
```

Visual Basic Program

```
'Include the Namespaces
Imports System.Data
Imports System.Data.SqlClient

Module Module1
```

```
Sub Main()
Dim con As SqlConnection
Dim cmd As SqlCommand
Dim ConnectionString, Query As String

ConnectionString =
                    "Data Source=localhost\MSSQLSERVER2014;" &
                    "Initial Catalog=Students;" &
                    "User ID=adalat khan;Password=Std123"


'Establish the Database connection
con = New SqlConnection(ConnectionString)

Query = "select StdRegNumber, StdName from StudentsInfo"

'Execute the SqlCommand
cmd = New SqlCommand(Query, con)

'Open the database connection
con.Open()

'Read data from the database using the SqlDataReader object
Dim Reader As SqlDataReader = cmd.ExecuteReader()
While (Reader.Read())
Console.Write("Reg Number = " + Reader.GetString(0))
Console.Write("Name = " + Reader.GetString(1))
Console.WriteLine()
End While

'Close the Database connection and SqlDataReader object
Reader.Close()
cmd.Dispose()
con.Close()

Console.ReadKey()
End Sub
End Module
```

In the above program the Reader is an object and the GetString() is a method of the SqlDataReader class. The SqlDataReader class is covered in this chapter under the topic SqlDataReader class.

Retrieve Data Using Stored Procedure

In this program we will use a Stored Procedure RetrieveStudentsInfo which is created in SQL Server. This Stored Procedure takes a single String parameter Student Registration Number and displays a single row of that specified student registration number. For more details about this Stored Procedure please go to chapter # 10 and reads the topic RetrieveStudentsInfo Stored Procedure. The following program displays data from the database using the Stored Procedure RetrieveStudentsInfo.

Write a program that displays data from the database using Stored Procedure.
C# Program

```
using System;
using System.Data;
using System.Data.SqlClient;

namespace DatabaseExample
{
class Program
{
static void Main(string[] args)
{
SqlConnection con;
String ConnectionString;

ConnectionString =
                "Data Source=localhost\\MSSQLSERVER2014;" +
                "Initial Catalog=Students;" +
                "User ID=adalat khan;Password=Std123";

//Establish the database connection
con = new SqlConnection(ConnectionString);

SqlCommand cmd = new SqlCommand();
```

```
cmd.CommandText = "RetrieveStudentsInfo";
cmd.CommandType = CommandType.StoredProcedure;
cmd.Connection = con;

//Pass Parameter to the Stored Procedure RetrieveStudentsInfo
//for search criteria to search a specified Student record
String StudentRegistrationNumber = "001";
cmd.Parameters.Add("@StdRegNum", SqlDbType.NVarChar);
cmd.Parameters["@StdRegNum"].Value =
                              StudentRegistrationNumber;

//Open the database connection
con.Open();

//Read data from Stored Procedure using SqlDataReader object
SqlDataReader Reader = cmd.ExecuteReader();
while (Reader.Read())
{
Console.WriteLine("Reg Number = " + Reader.GetString(0));
Console.WriteLine("Name = " + Reader.GetString(1));
Console.WriteLine("Date of Birth = " + Reader.GetDateTime(2));
}

//Close the connection, command and SqlDataReader object
Reader.Close();
cmd.Dispose();
con.Close();

Console.ReadKey();
}
}
}
```

Visual Basic Program

```
Imports System.Data
Imports System.Data.SqlClient

Module Module1
```

```
Sub Main()
Dim con As SqlConnection
Dim ConnectionString As String

ConnectionString =
                    "Data Source=localhost\MSSQLSERVER2014;" &
                    "Initial Catalog=Students;" &
                    "User ID=adalat khan;Password=Std123"

'Establish the Database connection
con = New SqlConnection(ConnectionString)

Dim cmd As SqlCommand = New SqlCommand()
cmd.CommandText = "RetrieveStudentsInfo"
cmd.CommandType = CommandType.StoredProcedure
cmd.Connection = con

'Pass Parameter to the Stored Procedure RetrieveStudentsInfo
'for search criteria to search a specified Student record
Dim StudentRegistrationNumber As String = "001"
cmd.Parameters.Add("@StdRegNum", SqlDbType.NVarChar)
cmd.Parameters("@StdRegNum").Value = StudentRegistrationNumber

'Open the database connection
con.Open()

'Read data from the database using the SqlDataReader object
Dim Reader As SqlDataReader = cmd.ExecuteReader()
While (Reader.Read())
Console.WriteLine("Reg Number = " + Reader.GetString(0))
Console.WriteLine("Name = " + Reader.GetString(1))
Console.WriteLine("Date of Birth = " + Reader.GetDateTime(2))
End While

'Close the connection, command and SqlDataReader object
Reader.Close()
cmd.Dispose()
```

```
con.Close()

Console.ReadKey()
End Sub
End Module
```

ExecuteScalar Method

This method is used to retrieve a single value from the database. It is usually used to calculate the aggregate value of the specific data or record of the database. This method executes the SELECT statement of the SQL or Stored Procedure and retrieves the aggregate or single value according to the SQL query or stored procedure. Therefore, the ExecuteScalar method is used if we want to find the average value of the specific data or record of the database, to find the sum of the specific data or record, to find the maximum or minimum value of the specific data or record, and to count specific data or record of the database etc. When ExecuteScalar method is executed, it returns the result of the SELECT statement or Stored Procedure in the form of an object. The returned object contains result of the ExecuteScalar method. The result of the ExecuteScalar method is then get from the object by casting the object according to the type of the retrieved data. Following is the general declaration of the ExecuteScalar method:

C# Declaration
public override object ExecuteScalar();
Visual Basic Declaration
Public Overrides Function ExecuteScalar As Object

Following is the programming example of the ExecuteScalar method of SqlCommand class:

Write a program that counts the total number of records in a database table using the ExecuteScalar method.
C# Program

```
//Include the Namespaces
using System;
using System.Data;
```

```
using System.Data.SqlClient;

namespace DatabaseExample
{
class Program
{
static void Main(string[] args)
{
SqlConnection con;
SqlCommand cmd;
String ConnectionString, Query;

ConnectionString =
                    "Data Source=localhost\\MSSQLSERVER2014;" +
                    "Initial Catalog=Students;" +
                    "User ID=adalat khan;Password=Std123";

//Establish the database connection
con = new SqlConnection(ConnectionString);
Query = "select count (*) from StudentsInfo";
cmd = new SqlCommand(Query, con);

//Open the database connection
con.Open();

//Count records in a database table
int count = (int) cmd.ExecuteScalar();
con.Close();
Console.WriteLine("The total number of records = " + count);

Console.ReadKey();
}
}
}
```

Visual Basic Program

```
'Include the Namespaces
Imports System.Data
Imports System.Data.SqlClient
```

```
Module Module1

Sub Main()
Dim con As SqlConnection
Dim cmd As SqlCommand
Dim ConnectionString, Query As String

ConnectionString =
                    "Data Source=localhost\MSSQLSERVER2014;" &
                    "Initial Catalog=Students;" &
                    "User ID=adalat khan;Password=Std123"

'Establish the Database connection
con = New SqlConnection(ConnectionString)

Query = "select count(*) from StudentsInfo"
'Execute the SqlCommand
cmd = New SqlCommand(Query, con)

'Open the database connection
con.Open()

'Count records in a database table
Dim count As Integer = Convert.ToInt32(cmd.ExecuteScalar())
con.Close()
Console.WriteLine("The total number of records = " & count)

Console.ReadKey()
End Sub
End Module
```

ExecuteXmlReader Method

This method of SqlCommand class is used to read or retrieve data from the database. It works same as ExecuteReader method but the main difference is that when ExecuteXmlReader method executes the SELECT statement or Stored Procedure, it returns an object of the XmlReader class. The object of the XmlReader class contains the data of the database retrieved by the ExecuteXmlReader method according to the SELECT statement of the SQL or

Stored Procedure. The retrieved data of the ExecuteXmlReader method is then access from the XmlReader class object. Following is the general declaration of the ExecuteXmlReader method:

C# Declaration
public XmlReader ExecuteXmlReader();
Visual Basic Declaration
Public Function ExecuteXmlReader As XmlReader

BeginExecuteNonQuery Method

This method is used to execute the SQL statements or Stored Procedure. It is used to execute the INSERT, DELETE, UPDATE, CREATE, and SET statements of the SQL or Stored Procedure. This method works same as ExecuteNonQuery method but the main difference is that the BeginExecuteNonQuery method is an asynchronous method that executes asynchronously. Asynchronous execution is an execution of a process or a task that starts execution and does not interrupt another process or task currently running but it runs concurrently with other running process or task. When BeginExecuteNonQuery method starts the execution of SQL statement or stored procedure, it does not interrupt another process or task currently executing but it executes concurrently with other running process or task. An asynchronous process needs the terminating statement to terminate or finish the asynchronous process therefore, the BeginExecuteNonQuery method requires the EndExecuteNonQuery method to terminate or finish the current asynchronous process of the BeginExecuteNonQuery method. When the EndExecuteNonQuery method terminates execution of the BeginExecuteNonQuery method then it returns an interface IAsyncResult. Following is the general declaration of the BeginExecuteNonQuery method:

C# Declaration
public IAsyncResult BeginExecuteNonQuery ();
Visual Basic Declaration
Public Function BeginExecuteNonQuery () As IAsyncResult

IAsyncResult

The IAsyncResult is an interface that represents the status of the asynchronous execution of the method either the method is executed successfully or not. This interface is implemented to the asynchronous nature methods. Each asynchronous method returns the IAsyncResult interface. The object of this interface is also passed to the method that finishes or terminates the asynchronous operation. The object of the IAsyncResult represents status of the asynchronous operation either the operation is completed successfully or not. The IAsyncResult interface provides the following properties:

Property	Description
AsyncState	This property is used to get an object that contains information about an asynchronous operation.
AsyncWaitHandle	This property is used to get a Wait Handle. The Wait Handle is used to wait for an asynchronous operation to complete.
CompletedSyncronously	This property is used to check whether the asynchronous operation is completed synchronously or not. It returns true if the operation is completed otherwise, it returns false.
IsCompleted	This property is used to check whether the asynchronous operation is completed successfully or not. If the operation is completed successfully, it returns true otherwise it returns false.

EndExecuteNonQuery Method

This method is used to finish the asynchronous execution of the BeginExecuteNonQuery method. The EndExecuteNonQuery method takes an object of the IAsyncResult interface as an input parameter and returns an integer value. Following is the general declaration of this method:

C# Declaration
Public int EndExecuteNonQuery (IAsyncResult asyncResult);

Visual Basic Declaration
Public Function EndExecuteNonQuery (asyncResult As IAsyncResult) As Integer

Synchronous Operation

When a task or an operation is currently executing and during execution of the current task or operation if another task or operation starts execution then the current task or operation interrupts and stops the execution and the new task or operation starts the execution. When the new task or operation is completed successfully then the interrupted task or operation again starts its execution. Therefore, a synchronous operation allows us to execute a single operation or task at a time.

Asynchronous Operation

When a task or an operation is currently executing and during execution of the current task or operation if a new task or operation starts execution then the current task or operation does not interrupt and continue its execution without waiting to complete the new task or operation. Therefore, an asynchronous task or operation allows us to execute multiple tasks or operations at the same time concurrently.

Synchronous and Asynchronous Methods

When a program is executing and during the execution if it calls a synchronous procedure or method, the program execution is interrupted and the program control transfers to the synchronous method and waits for the method to complete. When the Synchronous method is completed successfully then the program control returns back to the calling point and starts the remaining program execution while when a program is executing and during the execution if it calls an asynchronous method, it does not interrupt the program execution. The calling program and asynchronous method both can run concurrently without any interruption. Furthermore, an asynchronous method is a method that can run concurrently with the other methods or processes without any interruption.

BeginExecuteReader Method

This method is an asynchronous method that is used to start the asynchronous execution of SQL statement or stored procedure and retrieve data from the database. The BeginExecuteReader method works same as ExecuteReader method but the main difference is that the BeginExecuteReader method is an asynchronous method and it executes asynchronously. The EndExecuteReader method is used to finish the asynchronous execution of the BeginExecuteReader method. When this method is executed successfully then it returns the IAsyncResult interface. Following is the general declaration of BeginExecuteReader method:

C# Declaration
public IAsyncResult BeginExecuteReader();
Visual Basic Declaration
Public Function BeginExecuteReader As IAsyncResult

EndExecuteReader Method

This method is used to finish the asynchronous execution of the BeginExecuteReader method. This method takes an object of the IAsyncResult interface as an input parameter and returns an object of the SqlDataReader class. The SqlDataReader class provides forward only stream of rows of data from the database. Following is the general declaration of the EndExecuteReader method:

C# Declaration
public SqlDataReader EndExecuteReader (IAsyncResult asyncResult);
Visual Basic Declaration
Public Function EndExecuteReader (asyncResult as IAsyncResult) As SqlDataReader

BeginExecuteXmlReader Method

This method is an asynchronous method that is used to start the asynchronous execution of SQL statement or stored procedure. This method works same as ExecuteXmlReader method but the main difference is that the BeginExecuteXmlReader method is an asynchronous method that executes asynchronously. Following is the general declaration of the BeginExecuteXmlReader method:

C# Declaration
public IAsyncResult BeginExecuteXmlReader();
Visual Basic Declaration
Public Function BeginExecuteXmlReader As IAsyncResult

EndExecuteXmlReader Method

This method is used to finish the asynchronous execution of the BeginExecuteXmlReadermethod. This method takes an object of the IAsyncResult interface as an input parameter and returns an object of the XmlReader class. Following is the general declaration of the EndExecuteXmlReader method:

C# Declaration
public XmlReader EndExecuteXmlReader (IAsyncResult asyncResult);
Visual Basic Declaration
Public Function EndExecuteXmlReader (asyncResult as IAsyncResult) As XmlReader

Following is the programming example of BeginExecuteReader and EndExecuteReader methods:

C# Program

```
using System;
using System.Data;
using System.Data.SqlClient;

namespace DatabaseExample
{
class Program
{
static void Main(string[] args)
{
```

```
SqlConnection con;
SqlCommand com;
String ConnectionString;
ConnectionString=
                    "Data Source=localhost\\MSSQLSERVER2014;" +
                    "Initial Catalog=Students;" +
                    "User ID=adalat khan;Password=Std123";

con=new SqlConnection(ConnectionString);
con.Open();

String Query = "select StdRegNumber,StdName,StdDoBirth
                from StudentsInfo";

com = new SqlCommand(Query, con);

IAsyncResult result = com.BeginExecuteReader();
SqlDataReader DataReader = com.EndExecuteReader(result);
try
{
while (DataReader.Read())
{
Console.WriteLine(DataReader.GetString(0));
Console.WriteLine(DataReader.GetString(1));
Console.WriteLine(DataReader.GetDateTime(2));
}
}
finally
{
DataReader.Close();
con.Close();
}
Console.ReadKey();
}
}
}
```

CreateParameter Method

This method of SqlCommand class is used to create a new instance of the SqlParameter object. Following is its general declaration:

C# Declaration
public SqlParameter CreateParameter ()
Visual Basic Declaration
Public Function CreateParameter As SqlParameter

Cancel Method

This method of SqlCommand is used to cancel the execution of SqlCommand object.

Clone Method

This method of SqlCommand is used to make a copy of the current SqlCommand object.

Dispose Method

This method of SqlCommand class is used to release all the resources allocated to the object of SqlCommand class.

SqlDataReader Class

This class is used to read data from SQL Server database. It executes the SELECT statement of SQL or Stored Procedure and read or retrieves data from the database according to the SELECT statement or Stored Procedure. It reads or retrieves a Read-Only and forward-only stream of data from the database. The read-only stream of data means the data is read only and we cannot delete or update the retrieved data. The forward-only stream of data means the retrieved data of this class is in a sequential manner and it does not allow us to go back or access the previous data. This class only executes the SELECT statement and it does not support the INSERT, DELETE, and UPDATE statements of the SQL. The SqlDataReader class is placed in a namespace System.Data.SqlClient. Therefore, to use this class in the application, the namespace System.Data.SqlClient is included in the application before use.

Declaration of SqlDataReader Object

An object of a class is usually declared from the constructor of that class but unlike other classes the SqlDataReader class does not allow us to declare its objects from the constructor of this class. The SqlDataReader class is associated with the SqlCommand class and the objects of this class can be declared by executing the ExecuteReader method of the SqlCommand class. When the ExecuteReader method of SqlCommand class is executed then it returns an object of the SqlDataReader class. To get the return value of the ExecuteReader method, an instance of the SqlDataReader class is declared and the ExecuteReader method is assigned to the declared instance of the SqlDataReader class. Following is the general declaration of the SqlDataReader class object by executing the ExecuteReader method of the SqlCommand class:

C# Declaration
SqlCommand Cmd; SqlDataReader Reader; Reader = Cmd.ExecuteReader();
Visual Basic Declaration
Dim Cmd As SqlCommand Dim Reader As SqlDataReader Reader = Cmd.ExecuteReader()

When the ExecuteReader method of SqlCommand class returns an object of the SqlDataReader class, it contains the data of database retrieved by the SqlCommand object.

Properties of SqlDataReader Class

The SqlDataReader class provides the following properties:

IsClosed	Connection	FieldCount	HasRows

IsClosed Property

This property of SqlDataReader class is used to check the current status of SqlDataReader object whether it is closed or not. This property returns a

Boolean value either true or false. If the object of this class is closed, it returns true otherwise, it returns false. Following is its general declaration:

C# Declaration
public override bool IsClosed
Visual Basic Declaration
Public Overrides ReadOnly Property IsClosed As Boolean

Following is the programming example of IsClosed property:

Write a program that checks the current status of SqlDataReader object whether it is closed or not.
C# Program

```
using System.Data;
using System.Data.SqlClient;

SqlConnection Con;
SqlCommand Cmd;
SqlDataReader Reader;
bool Status;

String ConnectionString, Query;

ConnectionString=
                "Data Source=localhost\\MSSQLSERVER2014;" +
                "Initial Catalog=Students;" +
                "User ID=adalat khan;Password=Std123";

Query="select * from StudentsInfo";

Con = new SqlConnection(ConnectionString);
Cmd = new SqlCommand(Query, Con);
Con.Open();

//Read data from the database using SqlDataReader class
Reader = Cmd.ExecuteReader();

//Assign the current status of SqlDataReader object to the Boolean //variable
```

```
Status = Reader.IsClosed;
if(Status==true)
MessageBox.Show("The SqlDataReader object is closed");
else
MessageBox.Show("The SqlDataReader object is open");

Con.Close()
```

Visual Basic Program

```
Imports System.Data
Imports System.Data.SqlClient

Dim Con As SqlConnection()
Dim Cmd As SqlCommand()
Dim Reader As SqlDataReader
Dim Status As Boolean

Dim ConnectionString As String, Query As String

ConnectionString=
                    "Data Source=localhost\MSSQLSERVER2014;" &
                    "Initial Catalog=Students;" &
                    "User ID=adalat khan;Password=Std123"

Query="select * from StudentsInfo"

Con = new SqlConnection(ConnectionString)
Cmd = new SqlCommand(Query, Con)
Con.Open()

'Read data from the database using the SqlDataReader
Reader = Cmd.ExecuteReader()

'Assign the current status of SqlDataReader object to the Boolean //variable
Status = Reader.IsClosed
If Status = True Then
MessageBox.Show("The SqlDataReader object is closed")
else
```

```
MessageBox.Show("The SqlDataReader object is open")
End If

Con.Close();
```

Connection Property

This property of SqlDataReader class is used to get the current SqlConnection object associated with the SqlDataReader object. Each SqlDataReader object uses SqlConnection object to establish a connection to the database and reads data or records from the connected database.

FieldCount Property

This property of SqlDataReader class is used to count the number of columns in the current retrieved rows. When SqlDataReader object retrieves data from the database, the FieldCount property is used to count the number of columns in the current retrieved rows and returns an integer value that indicates the number of columns in the retrieved rows.

HasRows Property

This property of SqlDataReader class is used to check whether the object of SqlDataReader contains one or more rows of data. This property returns a Boolean value either true or false. If the object of SqlDataReader contains one or more rows of data then it returns true otherwise, it returns false.

Methods of SqlDataReader Class

The SqlDataReader class provides the following methods:

Read	ReadAsync	GetInt32	GetString
GetFloat	GetDateTime	GetDecimal	GetDouble
GetValue	GetStream	GetName	Close
Dispose	ToString		

Read Method

This method is used to read data from the object of SqlDataReader class. It reads a complete row at a time. The default position of this method is prior to the first row of data and starts reading from the first row of SqlDataReader object. When it reads one complete row, it moves control to the next row and reads the second row and on this way this method reads the entire rows of data one by one. The Read method reads the rows of data according to the SQL statement provided to the SqlCommand object. The Read method returns a Boolean value either true or false. When it reads the next row, it returns true and if the next row does not exist, it returns false. When it returns false then it stops the reading of data. The Read method is usually used with the iteration statement to read the data or record from the object of SqlDataReader class. When the Read method reads a row from the object of SqlDataReader class, it returns a true value that is used as the condition of the iteration statement or loop and the loop executes and when the Read method returns false then loop terminates.

ReadAsync Method

This method is used to read data from the object of SqlDataReader class. It reads a complete row at a time. This method works same as Read method but the main difference is that the ReadAsync method reads data from the object of SqlDataReader class asynchronously.

GetInt32 Method

This method of SqlDataReader class is used to retrieve the value of the specified column as a 32-bit signed integer. When the Read method reads a row of data or record from the object of SqlDataReader class, the GetInt32 method retrieves the specified integer column from the retrieved row of data or record of the Read method. The GetInt32 method takes an integer value as parameter that specifies the column index position of the SQL SELECT command or Stored Procedure and returns the value of that specified column as a 32-bit signed integer value. The SQL SELECT command or Stored Procedure contains number of columns or fields. Each column has its own index number that is used to access the column. The column index is an integer value that always starts from 0. The index 0 specifies the first column of the SQL SELECT command or Stored Procedure, the index 1 specifies the second column of the SQL SELECT command or Stored Procedure and so on. Following is its general declaration:

C# Declaration
Public override int GetInt32(int i)
Visual Basic Declaration
Public Overrides Function GetInt32(i As Integer) As Integer

GetString Method

This method of SqlDataReader class is used to retrieve the value of the specified column as a String. It takes an integer value as parameter that specifies the column index position of the SQL SELECT command or Stored Procedure and returns the value of that specified column as a String value.

GetFloat Method

This method of SqlDataReader class is used to retrieve the value of the specified column as a single-precision floating point number. It takes an integer value as parameter that specifies the column index position of the SQL SELECT command or Stored Procedure and returns the value of that specified column as a single-precision floating point number.

GetDateTime Method

This method of SqlDataReader class is used to retrieve the value of the specified column as a DateTime object. It takes an integer value as parameter that specifies the column index position of the SQL SELECT command or Stored Procedure and returns the value of that specified column as a DateTime object. The date time object contains the date and time.

Write a program that displays the values of the Integer column, the String column and the DateTime column of the SQL SELECT command.

C# Program

```
using System;
using System.Data;
using System.Data.SqlClient;

namespace DatabaseExample
{
```

```
class Program
{
static void Main(string[] args)
{
SqlConnection con;
SqlCommand cmd;
String ConnectionString, Query;

ConnectionString =
                "Data Source=localhost\\MSSQLSERVER2014;" +
                "Initial Catalog=Students;" +
                "User ID=adalat khan;Password=Std123";

//Establish the database connection

con = new SqlConnection(ConnectionString);
con.Open();
Query = "select StdName,StdDoBirth,StdDeptCode
        from StudentsInfo";

cmd = new SqlCommand(Query, con);
SqlDataReader Reader = cmd.ExecuteReader();

while (Reader.Read())
{
//Display the String value of the Column StdName
Console.WriteLine("Student Name ="+ Reader.GetString(0));

//Display the DateTime value of the Column StdDoBirth
Console.WriteLine("Birth Date ="+ Reader.GetDateTime(1));

//Display the integer value of the column StdDeptCode
Console.WriteLine("Department Code ="+ Reader.GetInt32(2));
}
Reader.Close();
con.Close();

Console.ReadKey();
```

```
}
}
}
```

Visual Basic Program

```
Imports System.Data
Imports System.Data.SqlClient

Module Module1

Sub Main()
Dim con As SqlConnection
Dim cmd As SqlCommand
Dim ConnectionString, Query As String

ConnectionString =
                    "Data Source=localhost\MSSQLSERVER2014;" &
                    "Initial Catalog=Students;" &
                    "User ID=adalat khan;Password=Std123"

Query = "select StdName,StdDoBirth,StdDeptCode
          from StudentsInfo"

con = New SqlConnection(ConnectionString)
cmd = New SqlCommand(Query, con)
con.Open()

Dim Reader As SqlDataReader = cmd.ExecuteReader()

While Reader.Read()

'Display the String value of the Column StdName
Console.WriteLine("Student Name = " & Reader.GetString(0))

'Display the DateTime value of the Column StdDoBirth
Console.WriteLine("Birth Date = " & Reader.GetDateTime(1))

'Display the integer value of the column StdDeptCode
```

```
Console.WriteLine("Department Code = " & Reader.GetInt32(2))
End While

Reader.Close()
con.Close()

Console.ReadKey()
End Sub
End Module
```

GetDecimal Method

This method of SqlDataReader class is used to retrieve the value of the specified column as a fixed-position numeric value. It takes an integer value as parameter that specifies the column index position of the SQL SELECT command or Stored Procedure and returns the value of that specified column as a fixed-position numeric value.

GetDlouble Method

This method of SqlDataReader class is used to retrieve the value of the specified column as a double-precision floating point number. It takes an integer value as parameter that specifies the column index position of the SQL SELECT command or Stored Procedure and returns the value of that specified column as a double-precision floating point number.

GetValue Method

This method of SqlDataReader class is used to retrieve the value of the specified column in the form of object. It takes an integer value as parameter that specifies the column index position of the SQL SELECT command or Stored Procedure and returns the value of that specified column in the form of object.

GetStream Method

This method of SqlDataReader class is used to retrieve the binary data, image data, varbinary data, user defined types data, and variant types data from the specified column. A variant is a special data type that can contain any kind of data except fixed-length string data. A variant can also contain the special values such as Empty, Error, Nothing, and Null. The GetStream method takes an integer value as a parameter that specifies the column index position of the SQL SELECT command or Stored Procedure and retrieves the data of that specified column as an object of the Stream class.

GetName Method

This method of SqlDataReader class is used to get the name of a specified column of the SQL SELECT command or Stored Procedure as a String. It takes an integer value as a parameter that specifies the column index position of the SQL SELECT command or Stored Procedure and returns the name of that specified column as a String.

Close Method

This method is used to close the current open object of the SqlDataReader class.

Dispose Method

This method is used to release all the resources allocated to the object of SqlDataReader class.

ToString Method

This method of SqlDataReader class is used to return a string that represents the current object. This method is usually used to convert an object to a string value.

Write a program that displays the column names of the SQL SELECT command.
C# Program

```
using System;
using System.Data;
using System.Data.SqlClient;

namespace DatabaseExample
{
class Program
```

```
{
static void Main(string[] args)
{
SqlConnection con;
SqlCommand cmd;
String ConnectionString;
ConnectionString =
                "Data Source=localhost\\MSSQLSERVER2014;" +
                "Initial Catalog=Students;" +
                "User ID=adalat khan;Password=Std123";

con =new SqlConnection(ConnectionString);
con.Open();

String Query = "select StdRegNumber,StdName,StdDoBirth
                from StudentsInfo";

cmd = new SqlCommand(Query, con);
SqlDataReader DataReader = cmd.ExecuteReader();

//Display the column names
Console.WriteLine(DataReader.GetName(0));
Console.WriteLine(DataReader.GetName(1));
Console.WriteLine(DataReader.GetName(2));

DataReader.Close();
con.Close();

Console.ReadKey();
}
}
}
```

Visual Basic Program

```
Imports System.Data
Imports System.Data.SqlClient

Module Module1
```

```
Sub Main()
Dim con As SqlConnection
Dim cmd As SqlCommand
Dim ConnectionString, Query As String

ConnectionString =
                    "Data Source=localhost\MSSQLSERVER2014;" &
                    "Initial Catalog=Students;" &
                    "User ID=adalat khan;Password=Std123"

Query = "select StdRegNumber,StdName,StdDoBirth from
            StudentsInfo"

con = New SqlConnection(ConnectionString)
cmd = New SqlCommand(Query, con)
con.Open()

Dim DataReader As SqlDataReader = cmd.ExecuteReader()

'Display the column names
Console.WriteLine(DataReader.GetName(0))
Console.WriteLine(DataReader.GetName(1))
Console.WriteLine(DataReader.GetName(2))

DataReader.Close()
con.Close()

Console.ReadKey()
End Sub
End Module
```

SqlDataAdapter Class

SqlDataAdapter class is used to provide a connection between the DataSet object and the SQL Server database. The SqlDataAdapter class is a communication link or a bridge between the DataSet object and the SQL Server database with the help of SqlConnection class object. The SqlDataAdapter object uses the object of SqlConnection class to establish a connection to the database and uses the SQL command to retrieve data from the connected database. When the object of SqlDataAdapter retrieves data from the SQL Server database, it assigns the retrieved data to the DataSet object using the Fill method. The Fill method of SqlDataAdapter class fills the DataSet object with the retrieved data of database. When DataSet object received data from the SqlDataAdapter object, it disconnects the database connection and allows us to perform manipulation on the data in disconnected mode. When changes occurred in the data of the DataSet object in disconnected mode, the SqlDataAdapter object then reestablishes the database connection and saves the changes in the main database. Therefore, SqlDataAdapter object is a communication bridge or data traveler between the database and the DataSet object that retrieves data from the database and assigns it to the DataSet object and saves the changes back to the main database. The SqlDataAdapter class is placed in the System.Data.SqlClient namespace. To use the SqlDataAdapter class in the application the namespace System.Data.SqlClient must be included in the application before use. This class cannot be inherited.

Constructors of SqlDataAdapter Class

The SqlDataAdapter class provides the following constructors used to declare objects of SqlDataAdapter class:

- SqlDataAdapter()
- SqlDataAdapter(SqlCommand)
- SqlDataAdapter(String, SqlConnection)
- SqlDataAdapter(String, String)

SqlDataAdapter()

This is a default constructor of the SqlDataAdapter class that takes no parameters. It is used to declare objects of the SqlDataAdapter class without specifying any parameters. Following is its general declaration:

C# Declaration
SqlDataAdapter Adapter = new SqlDataAdapter();
Visual Basic Declaration
Dim Adapter As SqlDataAdapter = New SqlDataAdapter

In the above declaration, the Adapter is a user-defined name of the declared object of SqlDataAdapter class.

SqlDataAdapter(SqlCommand)

This Constructor of SqlDataAdapter class takes one parameter. The parameter of this constructor is an object of the SqlCommand class that specifies the SQL statement or Stored Procedure. Following is its general declaration:

C# Declaration
SqlDataAdapter Adapter = new SqlDataAdapter(SqlCommand);
Visual Basic Declaration
Dim Adapter As SqlDataAdapter = New SqlDataAdapter(SqlCommand)

SqlDataAdapter(String, SqlConnection)

This constructor of SqlDataAdapter class takes two parameters. The first parameter is a string variable that specifies the SQL command or Stored Procedure and the second parameter is an object of the SqlConnection class that specifies the active connection of database. Following is its declaration:

C# Declaration

```
String ConnectionString;
ConnectionString =
                "Data Source=localhost\\MSSQLSERVER2014;" +
                "Initial Catalog=Students;" +
                "User ID=adalat khan;Password=Std123";

//Establish Connection to the Database
SqlConnection Con = new SqlConnection(ConnectionString);

//Execute the SQL Query
string sql = "select * from Table";

//Declare the object of SqlDataAdapter
SqlDataAdapter Adapter = new SqlDataAdapter(sql, Con);
```

Visual Basic Declaration
Dim ConnectionString As String ConnectionString = "Data Source=localhost\MSSQLSERVER2014;" & "Initial Catalog=Students;" & "User ID=adalat khan;Password=Std123" 'Establish Connection to the Database SqlConnection Con = new SqlConnection(ConnectionString) 'Execute the SQL Query string sql = "select * from Table" Dim Adapter As SqlDataAdapter = New SqlDataAdapter(sql, Con)

SqlDataAdapter(String, String)

This Constructor of SqlDataAdapter class takes two String type parameters. The first parameter specifies the SQL statement or Stored Procedure and the second parameter specifies a Connection String. Following is its declaration:

C# Declaration
String ConnectionString; ConnectionString = "Data Source=localhost\\MSSQLSERVER2014;" + "Initial Catalog=Students;" + "User ID=adalat khan;Password=Std123"; //Execute the SQL Query string sql = "select * from Table"; SqlDataAdapter Adapter; Adapter = new SqlDataAdapter(sql, ConnectionString);
Visual Basic Declaration
Dim ConnectionString As String; ConnectionString = "Data Source=localhost\MSSQLSERVER2014;" &

```
                    "Initial Catalog=Students;" &
                    "User ID=adalat khan;Password=Std123"

Dim sql As String = "select * from Table"

Dim Adapter as SqlDataAdapter
Adapter = New SqlDataAdapter(sql, ConnectionString)
```

Properties of SqlDataAdapter Class

SqlDataAdapter class provides the following important properties:

- SelectCommand Property
- InsertCommand Property
- DeleteCommand Property
- UpdateCommand Property

SelectCommand Property

This property of SqlDataAdapter class is a Command object that is used to select or retrieve data from the database and populates or fills the DataSet object with the result of the SQL SELECT query. Following is the programming example of this property:

C# Example

```
SqlConnection con;
SqlDataAdapter Adapter = new SqlDataAdapter();
DataSet dst = new DataSet();
String ConnectionString, query;
ConnectionString =
                "Data Source=localhost\\MSSQLSERVER2014;" +
                "Initial Catalog=Students;" +
                "User ID=adalat khan;Password=Std123";

con = new SqlConnection(ConnectionString);
query = "select * from StudentsInfo";
con.Open();
```

```
Adapter.SelectCommand = new SqlCommand(query, con);
Adapter.Fill(dst);
con.Close();
```

Visual Basic Example

```
Dim con As SqlConnection
Dim ConnectionString, query As String
Dim dst As DataSet = New DataSet()
Dim adapter As SqlDataAdapter = New SqlDataAdapter()

ConnectionString =
                "Data Source=localhost\MSSQLSERVER2014;" &
                "Initial Catalog=Students;" &
                "User ID=adalat khan;Password=Std123"

con = New SqlConnection(ConnectionString)
query = "select * from StudentsInfo"
con.Open()
adapter.SelectCommand = New SqlCommand(query, con)
adapter.Fill(dst)
con.Close()
```

InsertCommand Property

This property of SqlDataAdapter class is used to insert data or record in the database. The InsertCommand property sets the SQL command or Stored Procedure and inserts data or record in the database according to the modification made in the DataSet object. When the SqlDataAdapter object populates or fills the DataSet object with the retrieved data of the database, it disconnects the database connection and DataSet object allows us to perform manipulation in the data of the DataSet object in disconnected mode. When modification occurred in the data of the DataSet object, the SqlDataAdapter reconnects the database and saves the changes that occurred in the DataSet object in disconnected mode. Therefore, when new data or record is inserted in the DataSet object in disconnected mode, the SqlDataAdapter object reconnects the database connection and inserts the records into the database or saves the changes that occurred in the DataSet object using the InsertCommand property. Following is the programming example of InsertCommand property:

C# Example

SqlConnection con;
SqlDataAdapter adapter = new SqlDataAdapter();
 	
String ConnectionString =
"Data Source=localhost\\\\MSSQLSERVER2014;" +
"Initial Catalog=Students;" +
"User ID=adalat khan;Password=Std123";
 	
con = new SqlConnection(ConnectionString);
 	
String query = "insert into StudentsInfo" +
"(StdRegNumber,StdName,StdDoBirth) values" +
"('002','Shakeel','03/07/1993')";
con.Open();
adapter.InsertCommand = new SqlCommand(query, con);
adapter.InsertCommand.ExecuteNonQuery();
con.Close();

Visual Basic Example
Dim con As SqlConnection Dim ConnectionString, query As String Dim adapter As SqlDataAdapter = New SqlDataAdapter() ConnectionString = "Data Source=localhost\MSSQLSERVER2014;" & "Initial Catalog=Students;" & "User ID=adalat khan;Password=Std123" con = New SqlConnection(ConnectionString) query = "insert into StudentsInfo" & "(StdRegNumber,StdName,StdDoBirth) values" & "('002','Shakeel','03/07/1993')" con.Open() adapter.InsertCommand = New SqlCommand(query, con) adapter.InsertCommand.ExecuteNonQuery() con.Close()

DeleteCommand Property

This property of SqlDataAdapter class is used to delete data or record from the database. The DeleteCommand property sets the SQL command or Stored Procedure and deletes data or records from the database according to the modifications made in the DataSet object. When data or record is deleted from the DataSet object in disconnected mode, the SqlDataAdapter object reconnects the database connection and deletes records from the database or saves the changes that occurred in the DataSet object using the DeleteCommand property. Following is the programming example of DeleteCommand property:

C# Example

```
SqlConnection con;
SqlDataAdapter adapter = new SqlDataAdapter();

String ConnectionString =
                "Data Source=localhost\\MSSQLSERVER2014;" +
                "Initial Catalog=Students;" +
                "User ID=adalat khan;Password=Std123";

con = new SqlConnection(ConnectionString);

String query = "delete from StudentsInfo" +
              "where StdRegNumber = '002'";
con.Open();
adapter.DeleteCommand = new SqlCommand(query, con);
adapter.DeleteCommand.ExecuteNonQuery();
con.Close();
```

Visual Basic Example

```
Dim con As SqlConnection
Dim ConnectionString, query As String

Dim adapter As SqlDataAdapter = New SqlDataAdapter()

ConnectionString =
                "Data Source=localhost\MSSQLSERVER2014;" &
                "Initial Catalog=Students;" &
                "User ID=adalat khan;Password=Std123"
```

```
con = New SqlConnection(ConnectionString)

query = "delete from StudentsInfo where StdRegNumber = '002'"
con.Open()
adapter.DeleteCommand = New SqlCommand(query, con)
adapter.DeleteCommand.ExecuteNonQuery()
con.Close()
```

UpdateCommand Property

This property of SqlDataAdapter class is used to save the changes permanently in the database that occurs in a DataSet object in disconnected mode. This property sets the SQL command or Stored Procedure and updates the data or records in the database according to the modifications that occurred in the DataSet object in disconnected mode. Following is the programming example of UpdateCommand property:

C# Example

```
SqlConnection con;
SqlDataAdapter adapter = new SqlDataAdapter();

String ConnectionString =
                    "Data Source=localhost\\MSSQLSERVER2014;" +
                    "Initial Catalog=Students;" +
                    "User ID=adalat khan;Password=Std123";

con = new SqlConnection(ConnectionString);

String query = "update StudentsInfo set StdName = 'Shahid'" +
                "where StdRegNumber = '001'";
con.Open();
adapter.UpdateCommand = new SqlCommand(query, con);
adapter.UpdateCommand.ExecuteNonQuery();
con.Close();
```

Visual Basic Example

```
Dim con As SqlConnection
Dim ConnectionString, query As String
```

```
Dim adapter As SqlDataAdapter = New SqlDataAdapter()

ConnectionString =
                    "Data Source=localhost\MSSQLSERVER2014;" &
                    "Initial Catalog=Students;" &
                    "User ID=adalat khan;Password=Std123"

con = New SqlConnection(ConnectionString)

query = "update StudentsInfo set StdName='Shahid' where
         StdRegNumber = '001'"
con.Open()
adapter.UpdateCommand = New SqlCommand(query, con)
adapter.UpdateCommand.ExecuteNonQuery()
con.Close()
```

Methods of SqlDataAdapter Class

SqlDataAdapter class provides the following methods:

Fill Method

This method of SqlDataAdapter class is used to populate or fill the DataSet object with the retrieved data of the database. The object of SqlDataAdapter class uses the object of SqlConnection class and establishes a connection to the database and uses the SQL command or Stored Procedure and retrieves data from the connected database. When the object of SqlDataAdapter class retrieves data from the database, the Fill method populates or fills the DataSet object with the retrieved data. The Fill method is an overloaded member method of the SqlDataAdapter class and it provides the following overloaded forms:

- Fill(DataSet)
- Fill(DataTable)
- Fill(DataSet, String)
- Fill(Int32, Int32, DataTable[])
- Fill(DataSet, Int32, Int32, String)

Fill(DataSet)

This overloaded form of Fill method is used to populate or fill the DataSet object with the retrieved data of the database. It takes an object of the DataSet class as parameter that specifies the target DataSet object to be filled with the retrieved data of the database. Following is its general declaration:

C# Declaration
Public override int Fill(DataSet dst)
Visual Basic Declaration
Public Override Function Fill(dst As DataSet) As Integer

It returns an integer value that specifies the number of data rows added to the DataSet object.

Fill(DataTable)

This overloaded form of Fill method is used to fill the object of DataTable class with the retrieved data of the database. It takes an object of the DataTable class that specifies the target DataTable object to be filled with the retrieved data of the database. Following is its general declaration:

C# Declaration
Public int Fill(DataTable DTable)
Visual Basic Declaration
Public Function Fill(DTable As DataTable) As Integer

It returns an integer value that specifies the number of data rows added to the object of DataTable class.

Fill(DataSet, String)

This overloaded form of Fill method is used to fill the DataSet object with the data of a specified table of the database. It takes two parameters. The first parameter is an object of the DataSet class that specifies the target DataSet object to be filled with the data of the specified table of database and the second parameter is a String parameter that specifies the table of the database. Following is its general declaration:

C# Declaration
Public int Fill(DataSet dst, String Table)
Visual Basic Declaration
Public Function Fill(dst As DatSet, Table As String) As Integer

It returns an integer value that specifies the number of data rows added to the DataSet object.

Fill(Int32, Int32, DataTable[])

This overloaded form of Fill method is used to fill the DataTable object with the retrieved data of the database. It takes three parameters. The first parameter is an integer variable of type Int32 that specifies the starting position of the record to be retrieved from the database, the second parameter is also an integer variable of type Int32 that specifies the ending position or the maximum number of records to be retrieved from the database, and the third parameter is a DataTable that species the DataTable object to be filled with the retrieved data of the database. Following is its general declaration:

C# Declaration

```
public int Fill(
        int startRecord,
        int maxRecords,
        params DataTable[] dataTables
       )
```

Visual Basic Example

```
Public Function Fill (
            startRecord As Integer,
            maxRecords As Integer,
            ParamArray dataTables As DataTable()
            ) As Integer
```

Fill(DataSet, Int32, Int32, String)

This overloaded form of Fill method is used to fill the DasetSet object with the retrieved data of the database. It takes four parameters. The first parameter is an object of the DataSet class that specifies a DataSet object to be filled with the retrieved data of the database, the second parameter is an integer variable of type Int32 that specifies the starting position of the record to be retrieved from the database, the third parameter is also an integer variable of type Int32 that specifies the ending position or the maximum number of records to be retrieved from the database, and the fourth parameter is a String variable that specifies the table of the database from which the data is to be retrieved. Following is its general declaration:

C# Declaration
public int Fill(DataSet dataSet, int startRecord, int maxRecords, string Table)
Visual Basic Declaration
Public Function Fill (dataSet As DataSet, startRecord As Integer,
maxRecords As Integer, Table As String) As Integer

DataGridView Class

This class is used to display the retrieved data or record of the database in a grid view manner. A grid is a series of vertical and horizontal lines that intersect each other and create a two dimensional table that contains rows and columns. The horizontal lines indicate rows of the DataGridView and the vertical lines indicate columns of the DataGridView. Each row represents a single record and each column represents a single attribute of a record. Therefore, an object of the DataGridView class is used to display the retrieved data of the database in the form of rows and columns like a two dimensional table. A row of the DataGridView object is the collection of columns that contains different attributes of a record. Each attribute of a record is displayed in a square box of the DataGridView object. Each square box of the DataGridView object is called a cell. A cell is a small space that is made up of the intersection of horizontal and vertical lines or the intersection of rows and columns of the DataGridView object. Each cell of the DataGridView object is like a square that has four borders. The DataGridView class is also used to display data from the collections such as the elements of an array etc. To display the array elements using DataGridView class, an object of DataGridView class is declared and the array is bind using the DataSource property of the DataGridView class.

The DataGridView class displays data as read-only as well as in editable form. The read-only form displays the data or record and it does not allow modification of the data and the editable form displays the data and also allows us manipulation of the displayed data such as insert new row of data, delete rows from the displayed data and update the displayed data of the DataGridView object. The DataGridView class provides different properties used to perform different operations on the objects of DataGridView class. The DataGridView class allows us to customize the rows and columns and also allows us to customize each cell of the DataGridView object by using different properties of DataGridView class. The properties of DataGridView class perform different operations such as to change or set the background style, the background color, the text or foreground color, and the border style of each cell of an object of the DataGridView class.

The DataGridView class is declared in the System.Windows.Forms namespace. Therefore, to use the DataGridView class in the application, the namespace System.Windows.Forms must be included in the application before use. The object of DataGridView class can be used in an application in two ways such as using the DataGridView class or directly from the Control Toolbox of the Windows Forms Designer. The object of the DataGridView class is already placed in the Control Toolbox of the Windows Forms Designer. To use an object of the DataGridView class directly from the Control Toolbox, the DataGridView object is placed to the Window Form. To use the DataGridView object dynamically or during run time of the application, the constructor of the DataGridView class is used to declare object of the DataGridView class.

Constructor of DataGridView Class

DataGridView class provides the following one constructor that is used to declare objects of the DataGridView class:

- DataGridView() Constructor

DataGridView() Constructor

This constructor of DataGridView class is used to declare objects of the DataGridView class. Following is its general declaration:

C# Declaration
DataGridView dgvDisplay = new DataGridView();
Visual Basic Declaration
Dim dgvDisplay As New DataGridView()

In the above declaration, the dgvDisplay is a user-defined name of an object of the DataGridView class.

Properties of DataGridView Class

DataGridView class provides the following different properties:

AllowUserToAddRows	AllowUserToDeleteRows
AllowUserToOrderColumns	AllowUserToResizeColumns
AllowUserToResizeRows	AlternatingRowsDefaultCellStyle
AutoSizeColumnsMode	AutoSizeRowsMode
BackColor	BackgroundColor
BackgroundImage	Bottom
Bounds	CellBorderStyle
ClientRectangle	ClientSize
ClipboardCopyMode	ColumnCount
ColumnHeadersBorderStyle	ColumnHeadersDefaultCellStyle
ColumnHeadersHeight	ColumnHeadersHeightSizeMode
ColumnHeadersVisible	Columns
CompanyName	DataMember
DataSource	DefaultCellStyle
DefaultCursor	DisplayRectangle
Font	FontHeight
ForeColor	GridColor

Height	HorizontalScrollBar
HorizontalScrollingOffset	Item(Int32, Int32)
Item(String, Int32)	Left
Location	Margin
MaximumSize	MinimumSize
MultiSelect	ReadOnly
Right	RightToLeft
RowCount	RowHeadersBorderStyle
RowHeadersVisible	RowHeadersWidth
Row	ScrollBars
SelectedCells	SelectedColumns
SelectedRows	SelectionMode
Size	SortedColumn
SortOrder	Top

AllowUserToAddRows Property

This property of DataGridView class allows us to add new rows of data to the DataGridView object. It takes a Boolean value either true or false. If its value is set to true, the user can insert or add new rows to the DataGridView object and if its value is set to false, the user cannot insert or add new rows to the DataGridView object. The default value of this property is true. This property is a read/write property and it returns a Boolean value either true or false. The return value of this property indicates its current status. To get the current status of this property, a Boolean variable is declared and the property is assigned to the declared Boolean variable.

AllowUserToDeleteRows Property

This property of DataGridView class allows us to delete rows from the DataGridView object. It takes a Boolean value either true or false. If its value is set to true, the user can delete rows from the DataGridView object and if its value is set to false, the user cannot delete rows from the DataGridView object. The default value of this property is true. This property is a read/write property and it returns a Boolean value either true or false. The return value of this property indicates its current status. To get the current status of this property, a Boolean variable is declared and the property is assigned to the declared Boolean variable.

AllowUserToOrderColumns Property

This property of DataGridView class is used to reposition the columns or changes a column position of the DataGridView object by dragging a column header to a new position. This property allows a user to drag a column from the column header and places it on another location of the DataGridView object using mouse. This property takes a Boolean value either true or false. If the value of this property is set to true, the users can reposition the columns and if its value is set to false, the users cannot reposition the columns. The default value of this property is true. This property is a read/write property and it returns a Boolean value either true or false.

AutoSizeColumnsMode Property

This property of DataGridView class is used to set the auto size mode of the columns width of DataGridView object. When this property is set, it automatically adjusts the columns width of the DataGridView object and fits its contents according to the value assigned to this property. The AutoSizeColumnsMode property uses an enumeration called DataGridViewAutoSizeColumnsMode. This enumeration contains different fixed values used to set the auto size mode of the columns width of DataGridView object. The AutoSizeColumnsMode property uses a single value of the enumeration at a time and sets the columns width according to that fixed value of the enumeration. The default value of this property is None that does not adjust the columns width of the DataGridView object by default. Following is the list of values of the enumeration DataGridViewAutoSizeColumnsMode:

Value	Description
AllCells	This value of the enumeration is used to adjust the columns width and fit the contents of all cells in the columns of the DataGridView object, including the header cells.

AllCellsExceptHeader	This value of the enumeration is used to adjust the columns width and fit the contents of all cells in the columns except the header cells of the DataGridView object.
DisplayedCells	This value of the enumeration is used to adjust the columns width and fit the contents of all cells in the columns including header cells that are in rows currently displayed onscreen.
DisplayedCellsExceptHeader	This value of the enumeration is used to adjust the column widths and fit the contents of all cells in the columns excluding the header cells that are in rows currently displayed onscreen.
ColumnHeader	This value of the enumeration is used to adjust the columns width and fit the contents of the header cells in the columns of the DataGridView object. This value does not fit the contents of the non header cells in the columns of the DataGridView object.
Fill	This value of the enumeration is used to adjust the columns width and fit the contents of all cells in the columns of the DataGridView object according to the display area of the DataGridView object.
None	This value of the enumeration is used to disable the auto columns size of the DataGridView object.

AutoSizeRowsMode Property

This property of DataGridView class is used to set the auto size mode of the rows height of DataGridView object. When this property is set, it automatically adjusts the rows height of the DataGridView object and fits the contents of the rows according to the value assigned to this property. The AutoSizeRowsMode property uses an enumeration called DataGridViewAutoSizeRowsMode enumeration. This enumeration contains different fixed values for the auto size mode of the rows height of DataGridView object. This property uses a single value of the enumeration DataGridViewAutoSizeRowsMode at a time and set the rows height of the DataGridView object according to that fixed value of the enumeration. The default value of this property is None that does not set the rows height of the DataGridView object. Following is the list of values of the enumeration DataGridViewAutoSizeRowsMode:

Value	Description
AllCells	This value of the enumeration is used to adjust the rows height and fit the contents of all cells in the rows of DataGridView, including header cells.
AllCellsExceptHeaders	This value of the enumeration is used to adjust the rows height and fit the contents of all cells in the rows of DataGridView except the header cells.
DisplayedCells	This value of the enumeration is used to adjust the rows height and fit the contents of all cells in the rows of DataGridView including header cells that are in rows currently displayed onscreen.
DisplayedCellsExceptHeaders	This value of the enumeration is used to adjust the rows height and fit the contents of all cells in the rows of DataGridView excluding the header cells that are in rows currently displayed onscreen.
DisplayedHeaders	This value of the enumeration is used to adjust the rows height of DataGridView and fit the contents of the row headers currently displayed onscreen.
AllHeaders	This value of the enumeration is used to adjust the rows height of the DataGridView and fit the contents of the row header.

None	This value of the enumeration is used to disable the auto adjustment of the rows height. This is the default value of the DataGridView.

AllowUserToResizeColumns Property

This property of DataGridView class is used to resize the columns width of the DataGridView object. It takes a Boolean value either true or false. If the value of this property is set to true, the users can resize the columns width and if its value is set to false, the users cannot resize the columns width of the DataGridView object. The default value of this property is true. This property depends on the AutoSizeColumnsMode property and it works only if the AutoSizeColumnsMode property is set to None value of the enumeration DataGridViewAutoSizeColumnsMode.

AllowUserToResizeRows Property

This property of DataGridView class is used to resize the rows height of the DataGridView object. It takes a Boolean value either true or false. If the value of this property is set to true, the users can resize the rows height and if its value is set to false, the users cannot resize the rows height of the DataGridView object. The default value of this property is true. This property depends on the AutoSizeRowsMode property and it works only if the AutoSizeRowsMode property is set to None value of the DataGridViewAutoSizeRowsMode enumeration.

BackgroundColor Property

This property of DataGridView class is used to set the background color of the DataGridView object. It sets the background color of the non container area of the DataGridView object. The non container area of the DataGridView object is an area where the data does not display.

BorderStyle Property

This property of DataGridView class is used to set the style of the outer or external border of the DataGridView object. The BorderStyle property uses an enumeration called BorderStyle enumeration. This enumeration contains three fixed values for the outer border style of the DataGridView object. The BorderStyle property uses a single value of the BorderStyle enumeration at a time and sets the outer or external border style of the DataGridView object. Following is the list of the fixed values of BorderStyle enumeration:

Value	Description
FixedSingle	This value of the BorderStyle enumeration is used to set a single line border for the DataGridView object.
Fixed3D	This value of the BorderStyle enumeration is used to set a three dimensional border for the DataGridView object.
None	This value of the BorderStyle enumeration is used to set no borders for the DataGridView object.

CellBorderStyle Property

This property of DataGridView class is used to set the border style of all the cells of DataGridView object. A cell is a small space that is made up of the intersection of horizontal and vertical lines or the intersection of rows and columns of the DataGridView object. Each cell of the DataGridView object is like a square that has four borders and each cell contains data. The CellBorderStyle property uses an enumeration called DataGridViewCellBorderStyle enumeration. This enumeration contains different fixed values for the border style of the cells of DataGridView object. The CellBorderStyle property uses a single value of the DataGridViewCellBorderStyle enumeration at a time and sets the cells borders style of the DataGridView object. The DataGridViewCellBorderStyle enumeration contains the following fixed values:

Value	Description
Custom	This value of the enumeration is used to customize the cells border style of the DataGridView object.
Single	This value of the enumeration is used to set a single line border style for all the cells of the DataGridView object.
Raised	This value of the enumeration is used to set a three dimensional raised border style for all the cells of the DataGridView object.
Sunken	This value of the enumeration is used to set a three dimensional sunken border style for all the cells of the DataGridView object.

None	This value of the enumeration is used to set no border style for the DataGridView object.
SingleVertical	This value of the enumeration is used to set a single line border style for all the cells of the DataGridView object vertically.
RaisedVertical	This value of the enumeration is used to set a three dimensional border style for all the cells of the DataGridView object vertically.
SunkenVertical	This value of the enumeration is used to set a three dimensional sunken border style for all the cells of the DataGridView object vertically.
SingleHorizontal	This value of the enumeration is used to set a single line border style for all the cells of the DataGridView object horizontally.
RaisedHorizontal	This value of the enumeration is used to set a three dimensional raised border style for all the cells of the DataGridView object horizontally.
SunkenHorizontal	This value of the enumeration is used to set a three dimensional sunken border style for all the cells of the DataGridView object horizontally.

GridColor Property

This property of DataGridView class is used to set the color of the cells border of the DtaGridView object. The GridColor property depends on the CellBorderStyle property of the DataGridView class and it works only if value of the CellBorderStyle property is set to Single line border style of the cells. The GridColor property is also ignored when the visual styles are enabled for the application.

RowHeadersVisible Property

This property of DataGridView class is used to display and hide the row header of the DataGridView object. The row header is a column that contains header for each row of the DataGridView object. The row header column is displayed at the beginning of the columns list of the DataGridView object. The RowHeadersVisible property takes a Boolean value either true or false. If its value is set to true, it displays the row header column and if its value is set to false, it hides the row header column of the DataGridView object. The default value of this property is true.

RowHeadersBorderStyle Property

This property of DataGridView class is used to set the border style of the row header column of the DataGridView object. This property takes an enumeration called DataGridViewHeaderBorderStyle enumeration. This enumeration contains different fixed values for the border style of the row header. Following is the list of fixed values of the DataGridViewHeaderBorderStyle enumeration:

Value	Description
Custom	This value of the enumeration is used to customize the border style of row header of the DataGridView object.
Single	This value of the enumeration is used to set a single line border style for the row header of the DataGridView object.
Raised	This value of the enumeration is used to set a three-dimensional raised border style for the row header of the DataGridView object.
Sunken	This value of the enumeration is used to set a three-dimensional sunken border style for the row header of the DataGridView object.
None	This value of the enumeration is used to remove borders from the row header of the DataGridView object.

RowHeadersWidth Property

This property of DataGridView class is used to set width of the row header of the DataGridView object. It takes an integer positive value and sets width of the row header in the form of pixels.

ColumnHeadersVisible Property

This property of DataGridView class is used to display and hides the column header of the DataGridView object. The column header is a row that is displayed at the top of the DataGridView object and it contains description or name of each column of the DataGridView object. This property takes a Boolean value either true or false. If the value of this property is set to true, it displays the column header row and if the value of this property is set to false, it hides the column header row of the DataGridView object. The default value of this property is true.

ColumnHeadersHeight Property

This property of DataGridView class is used to set the height of the column header row of the DataGridView object. It takes an integer positive value and sets the height of the column header row in the form of pixels.

ColumnHeadersBorderStyle Property

This property of DataGridView class is used to set the border style of the column header row of the DataGridView object. It takes an enumeration called DataGridViewHeaderBorderStyle enumeration. This enumeration contains different fixed values for the border style of the column header row. The ColumnHeadersBorderStyle property uses one of the fixed values of the DataGridViewHeaderBorderStyle enumeration at a time and sets the border style of the column header row of the DataGridView object. Following is the list of the fixed values of DataGridViewHeaderBorderStyle enumeration:

Value	Description
Custom	This value of the enumeration is used to customize the border style of the columns header row of the DataGridView object.
Single	This value of the enumeration is used to set a single line border style for the columns header row of the DataGridView object.
Raised	This value of the enumeration is used to set a three-dimensional raised border style for the columns header row of the DataGridView object.
Sunken	This value of the enumeration is used to set a three-dimensional sunken border style for the columns header row of the DataGridView object.
None	This value of the enumeration is used to remove borders from the columns header row of the DataGridView object.

The following programming example demonstrates the above properties of the DataGridView class:

C# Example

//Set the current status of this property to false
DataGridView.AllowUserToAddRows = false;
 	
//Set the AllowUserToDeleteRows property to false
DataGridView.AllowUserToDeleteRows = false;
 	
//Set the AllowUserToOrderColumns property to false
DataGridView. AllowUserToOrderColumns = false;
 	
//Set the AutoSizeColumnsMode property to AllCells
DataGridView.AutoSizeColumnsMode =
DataGridViewAutoSizeColumnsMode.AllCells;
 	
//Set the AutoSizeRowsMode property to AllCells DataGridView.
AutoSizeRowsMode = DataGridViewAutoSizeRowsMode.AllCells;
 	
//Set the AlloUserToResizeColumns property to false
DataGridView. AllowUserToResizeColumns = false;
 	
//Set the AlloUserToResizeRows property to false
DataGridView. AllowUserToResizeRows = false;
 	
//Set the Background color of the DataGridView object
DataGridView. BackgroundColor = Color.Black;
 	
//Set the BorderStyle property to a single line border style value
DataGridView.BorderStyle = BorderStyle.FixedSingle;
 	
//Set the CellBorderStyle property to a single line border style
DataGridView. CellBorderStyle = DataGridViewCellBorderStyle.Single;
 	
//Set the GridColor property to Red Color
DataGridView.GridColor = Color.Red;
 	
//Set the RowHeadersVisible property to true

```
DataGridView.RowHeadersVisible = true;

//Set the RowHeadersWidth property to 100 pixels
DataGridView.RowHeadersWidth = 100;

//Set the ColumnHeadersBorderStyle property to a single line //border
DataGridView.ColumnHeadersBorderStyle =
DataGridViewHeaderBorderStyle.Single;
```

Visual Basic Example

```
'Set the current status of this property to false
DataGridView.AllowUserToAddRows = False

'Set the AllowUserToDeleteRows property to false
DataGridView.AllowUserToDeleteRows = False

'Set the AllowUserToOrderColumns property to false
DataGridView. AllowUserToOrderColumns = False

'Set the AutoSizeRowsMode property to AllCells DataGridView.
AutoSizeRowsMode = DataGridViewAutoSizeRowsMode.AllCells

'Set the AutoSizeColumnsMode property to AllCells
DataGridView.AutoSizeColumnsMode =
DataGridViewAutoSizeColumnsMode.AllCells

'Set the AlloUserToResizeColumns property to false
DataGridView. AllowUserToResizeColumns = False

'Set the AlloUserToResizeRows property to false
DataGridView. AllowUserToResizeRows = False

'Set the Background color of the DataGridView object
DataGridView. BackgroundColor = Color.Black

'Set the BorderStyle property to a single line border style value
DataGridView.BorderStyle = BorderStyle.FixedSingle
```

```
'Set the CellBorderStyle property to a single line border style
DataGridView.CellBorderStyle = DataGridViewCellBorderStyle.Single

'Set the GridColor property to Red Color
DataGridView.GridColor = Color.Red

'Set the RowHeadersVisible property to true
DataGridView.RowHeadersVisible = True

'Set the RowHeadersWidth property to 100 pixels
DataGridView.RowHeadersWidth = 100

'Set the ColumnHeadersBorderStyle property to a single line
'border
DataGridView.ColumnHeadersBorderStyle =
DataGridViewHeaderBorderStyle.Single
```

ColumnCount Property

This property of DataGridView class is used to count the number of columns displayed in the DataGridView object. It returns an integer value that indicates the total number of columns displayed in the DataGridView object.

RowCount Property

This property of DataGridView class is used to count the number of rows displayed in the DataGridView object. It returns an integer value that indicates the total number of rows displayed in the DataGridView object.

Columns Property

This property of DataGridView class is used to get or return a collection DataGridViewColumnCollection that contains all columns of the DataGridView object. This collection is a class that provides different properties and methods and allows users to perform different operations on the columns collection such as adds new column to the columns collection, delete columns from the columns collection, and count the number of columns in the columns collection, and clear the columns collection of the DataGridView object.

Row Property

This property of DataGridView class is used to get or return a collection DataGridViewRowCollection that contains all rows of the DataGridView object. This collection is a class that provides different properties and methods and allows users to perform different operations on the rows collection such as adds new rows to the rows collection, delete rows from the rows collection, count the number of rows in the rows collection, and clear the rows collection of the DataGridView object.

Following is the programming example of the Columns and Rows properties:

C# Example

//Set the number of columns to be added to the DataGridView
//object
DataGridView.ColumnCount = 3;
 	
//Add three columns to the DataGridView object using the
//Columns Collection
DataGridView.Columns[0].Name = "Column1";
DataGridView.Columns[1].Name = "Column2";
DataGridView.Columns[2].Name = "Column3";
 	
//Add five rows to the DataGridView object using the Rows //Collection
DataGridView.Rows.Add("Row1.Column1","Row1.Column2", "Row1.Column3");
DataGridView.Rows.Add("Row2.Column1", "Row2.Column2", "Row2.Column3");
DataGridView.Rows.Add("Row3.Column1", "Row3.Column2", "Row3.Column3");
DataGridView.Rows.Add("Row4.Column1", "Row4.Column2", "Row4.Column3");
DataGridView.Rows.Add("Row5.Column5", "Row5.Column2", "Row5.Column3");

Visual Basic Example

'Set the number of columns to be add to add to the DataGridView //object
DataGridView.ColumnCount = 3
 	
'Add three columns to the DataGridView object using the

```
//Columns Collection
DataGridView.Columns(0).Name = "Column1"
DataGridView.Columns(1).Name = "Column2"
DataGridView.Columns(2).Name = "Column3"

'Add five rows to the DataGridView Object using the Rows 'Collection
DataGridView.Rows.Add("Row1.Column1", "Row1.Column2", "Row1.
Column3")
DataGridView.Rows.Add("Row2.Column1", "Row2.Column2", "Row2.
Column3")
DataGridView.Rows.Add("Row3.Column1", "Row3.Column2", "Row3.
Column3")
DataGridView.Rows.Add("Row4.Column1", "Row4.Column2", "Row4.
Column3")
DataGridView.Rows.Add("Row5.Column5", "Row5.Column2", "Row5.
Column3")
```

ScrollBars Property

This property of DataGridView class is used to set scrollbars to the DataGridView object. This property uses an enumeration called ScrollBars enumeration. The ScrollBars enumeration provides four fixed values. Following is the list of the fixed values of ScrollBars enumeration:

Value	Description
None	This value of the enumeration is used to display no scroll bars or it hides the scroll bars of the DataGridView object.
Horizontal	This value of the enumeration is used to display the Horizontal scroll bar of the DataGridView object.
Vertical	This value of the enumeration is used to display the vertical scroll bar of the DataGridView object.
Both	This value of the enumeration is used to display both vertical and horizontal scrollbars of the DataGridView object.

Following is the programming example of ScrollBars property:

C# Example

//Set the horizontal scroll bar of the DataGridView object
DataGridView.ScrollBars = ScrollBars.Horizontal;

Visual Basic Example
'Set the horizontal scroll bar of the DataGridView object DataGridView.ScrollBars = ScrollBars.Horizontal

DataSource Property

This property of DataGridView class is used to set an object that contains data for the DataGridView object to display. The DataSource object can contain data of the database or data of the collections and the possible DataSource object may be a DataSet, a DataTable, a DataView, or an array. The DataSource property takes a single data object at a time.

DataMember Property

This property of DataGridView class is used to set the name of the table or the list in the DataSource object. This property is used when the DataSource object contains multiple tables or multiple lists. It does not use in the case of a single table or a single list.

Font Property

This property of DataGridView class is used to set font of the text of DataGridView object. The Font property is used to set the text face, the text style, and the text size.

ForeColor Property

This property of DataGridView class is used to set the foreground color of the text of DataGridView object. It uses the Color enumeration that represents ARGB. The ARGB means alpha, red, green, and blue. The Color enumeration provides different properties. Each property of the Color enumeration represents a color.

SelectionMode Property

This property of DataGridView class is used to define the selection mode of the DataGridView object. The selection mode means how to select data of the DataGridView object. This property defines different types of selection modes such as to select one or more individual cells, one or more complete rows, and one or more columns of the DataGridView object. The SelectionMode property uses an enumeration that is called DataGridViewSelectionMode. This enumeration provides five fixed values. Each fixed value defines a selection mode. The SelectionMode property uses a single value of the DataGridViewSelectionMode enumeration at a time and sets the selection mode of the DataGridView object. Following is the list of fixed values of the DataGridViewSelectionMode enumeration:

Value	Description
CellSelect	This value of the enumeration allows users to select one or more individual cells of the DataGridView object.
FullRowSelect	This value of the enumeration allows users to select one or more complete rows of the DataGridView object.
FullColumnSelect	This value of the enumeration allows users to select one or more complete columns of the DataGridView object.
RowHeaderSelect	This value of the enumeration allows users to select row header of the DataGridView object.
ColumnHeaderSelect	This value of the enumeration allows users to select the column header of the DataGridView object.

MultiSelect Property

This property of DataGridView class allows the multiple selections of DataGridView object. The multiple selections allow us to select one or more cells, one or more rows and one or more columns of the DataGridView object at the same time. The MultiSelect property takes a Boolean value either true or false. When its value is set to true, it allows the multiple selections and if its value is set to false, it does not allow the multiple selections of DataGridView object.

SelectedCells Property

This property of DataGridView class is used to get a collection that contains all the selected cells of the DataGridView object. When a cell is selected from the DataGridView object, it automatically adds to the collection that is called DataGridViewSelectedCellCollection. This collection is a class that provides different properties and methods and allows us to perform different operations such as count the total number of selected cells, returns a cell of a specified index, and returns a list of the elements from the collection. Following is the programming example of SelectedCells property:

C# Example

//Declare an instance of the DataGridViewSellectedCellCollection //class
DataGridViewSelectedCellCollection SltdCells;
 	
//Get the collection of selected cells from DataGridView object
SltdCells =DataGridView.SelectedCells;
 	
//Display the selected cells from the DataGridView object
MessageBox.Show(SltdCells.Count.ToString());

Visual Basic Example
'Declare an instance of the DataGridViewSellectedCellCollection 'class Dim SltdCells As DataGridViewSelectedCellCollection 'Get the collection of selected cells from the DataGridView object SltdCells = DataGridView.SelectedCells 'Display the selected cells from the DataGridView object MessageBox.Show(SltdCells.Count.ToString())

SelectedRows Property

This property of DataGridView class is used to get a collection that contains all the selected rows of the DataGridView object. When a row is selected from the DataGridView object, it automatically adds to the collection that is called DataGridViewSelectedRowCollection. The DataGridViewSelectedRowCollection is a class that provides different properties and methods and allows us to perform different operations such as count the total number of selected rows, gets or returns a row at a specified index, and returns a list of the elements from the collection. The SelectedRows property depends on the SelectionMode property of the DataGridView class.

To get the number of rows from the selected rows collection, the SelectionMode property must be set to FullRowSelect, or RowHeaderSelect value of the DataGridViewSelectionMode enumeration. Following is the programming example of SelectedRows property:

C# Example

```
//Declare an instance of the DataGridViewSellectedRowCollection //class
DataGridViewSelectedRowCollection SltdRows;

//Set the SelectionMode property to FullRowSelect value
DataGridView.SelectionMode =
                    DataGridViewSelectionMode.FullRowSelect ;

//Get collection of the selected rows from DataGridView object
SltdRows =DataGridView.SelectedRows;

//Display the selected rows of the DataGridView object
MessageBox.Show(SltdRows.Count.ToString());
```

Visual Basic Example

```
'Declare an instance of the DataGridViewSellectedRowCollection 'class
Dim SltdRows As DataGridViewSelectedRowCollection

'Set the SelectionMode property to FullRowSelect value
DataGridView.SelectionMode =
                    DataGridViewSelectionMode.FullRowSelect

'Get collection of the selected rows from DataGridView object
SltdRows = DataGridView.SelectedRows

'Display the selected rows of the DataGridView object
MessageBox.Show(SltdRows.Count.ToString())
```

SelectedColumns Property

This property of DataGridView class is used to get a collection that contains all the selected columns of the DataGridView object. When a column is selected from the DataGridView, it automatically adds to the collection called DataGridViewSelectedColumnCollection. This collection is a class that provides different properties and methods and allows us to perform different operations such as count the total number of selected columns, get a column at a specified index, and get a list of the elements from the collection. This property depends on the SelectionMode property of the DataGridView class. To get the total number of selected columns from the columns collection, the SelectionMode property must be set to the FullColumnSelect or ColumnHeaderSelect value of the DataGridViewSelectionMode enumeration.

Programming Examples of DataGridView

Create a new Windows Forms application project from Visual Studio.NET. Place a Command Button and a DataGridView control object from the Visual Studio Tools Box. Double click on Command Button and place the following code in the click event of Command Button.

DataSet Program

Write a program that displays data from database into DataGridView using DataSet object
C# Program

```
private void button1_Click(object sender, EventArgs e)
{
SqlConnection con;
SqlDataAdapter Adapter;
DataSet dst = new DataSet();
String ConnectionString, query;
ConnectionString =
                "Data Source=localhost\\MSSQLSERVER2014;" +
                "Initial Catalog=Students;" +
                "User ID=adalat khan;Password=Std123";

con = new SqlConnection(ConnectionString);
query = "select * from StudentsInfo";
con.Open();
Adapter = new SqlDataAdapter(query, con);
Adapter.Fill(dst);
dataGridView1.DataSource = dst.Tables[0];
con.Close();
}
```

Visual Basic Program
Private Sub Button1_Click(sender As Object, e As EventArgs) Handles Button1.Click Dim con As SqlConnection Dim ConnectionString, query As String Dim dst As DataSet = New DataSet() Dim adapter As SqlDataAdapter = New SqlDataAdapter() ConnectionString = "Data Source=localhost\MSSQLSERVER2014;" & "Initial Catalog=Students;" & "User ID=adalat khan;Password=Std123" con = New SqlConnection(ConnectionString) query = "select * from StudentsInfo" con.Open() adapter = New SqlDataAdapter(query, con) adapter.Fill(dst) DataGridView1.DataSource = dst.Tables(0) con.Close() End Sub

DataTable Program

Write a program that displays data from database into DataGridView using DataTable object
C# Program
private void button1_Click(object sender, EventArgs e) { SqlConnection con; SqlDataAdapter Adapter; DataTable dt = new DataTable(); String ConnectionString, query; ConnectionString = "Data Source=localhost\\MSSQLSERVER2014;" +

```
                    "Initial Catalog=Students;" +
                    "User ID=adalat khan;Password=Std123";

con = new SqlConnection(ConnectionString);
query = "select * from StudentsInfo";
con.Open();
Adapter = new SqlDataAdapter(query, con);
Adapter.Fill(dt);
dataGridView1.DataSource = dt;
con.Close();
}
```

Visual Basic Program

```
Private Sub Button1_Click(sender As Object, e As EventArgs) Handles
Button1.Click

Dim con As SqlConnection
Dim ConnectionString, query As String
Dim dt As DataTable = New DataTable()
Dim adapter As SqlDataAdapter = New SqlDataAdapter()

ConnectionString =
                    "Data Source=localhost\MSSQLSERVER2014;" &
                    "Initial Catalog=Students;" &
                    "User ID=adalat khan;Password=Std123"

con = New SqlConnection(ConnectionString)
query = "select * from StudentsInfo"
con.Open()
adapter = New SqlDataAdapter(query, con)
adapter.Fill(dt)
DataGridView1.DataSource = dt
con.Close()
End Sub
```

DataTable Class

DataTable class represents a single table of in-memory. In-Memory is a database management system that uses the computer main Random Access Memory (RAM) as a data store. The computer main Random Access Memory has higher access speed as compared to the speed of a hard desk and the data of the Random Access Memory can be accessed very easily. A DataTable is the collection of columns and rows. A column of DataTable is called DataColumn and a row of DataTable is called DataRow. The DataColumn and DataRow are classes and they provide different properties and methods. A DataTable object cannot be used for data until the schema is defined for it. The schema can be defined by adding the DataColumn objects and setting the constraints of each column. Constraints handle and maintain the data integrity by limiting the data that can be placed in the column. To add a column to the DataTable object, an object of DataColumn class is declared and then adds to the object of DataTable using the Columns property of DataTable class. The columns in a DataTable are represented in a collection DataColumnCollection and rows in a DataTable are represented in a collection DataRowCollection. The DataTable class is declared in the namespace System.Data. Therefore, to use the DataTable class, the namespace System.data must be imported in the application before use.

Constructors of DataTable Class

Constructors of DataTable class are used to declare objects of DataTable. Each object of DataTable class represents a table. Following are the different constructors of DataTable class:

- DataTable() Constructor
- DataTable(String) Constructor
- DataTable(String, String) Constructor

DataTable() Constructor

This is a default constructor of the DataTable class that does not take parameters. This constructor is used to declare objects of DataTable class without parameters. Following is its general declaration:

C# Declaration
DataTable table = new DataTable();
Visual Basic Declaration
Dim table As New DataTable

DataTable(String) Constructor

This constructor takes a String parameter that specifies the name of the DataTable object or table name. The table name or name of the DataTable object is a user defined name or an identifier. Following is its general declaration:

C# Declaration
public DataTable(string tableName); DataTable table = new DataTable("Table1");
Visual Basic Declaration
Public Sub New (tableName As String) Dim table As DataTable = New DataTable("Table1")

DataTable(String, String) Constructor

This constructor takes two String parameters. The first parameter specifies the name of the DataTable object or table name and second parameter specifies the namespace for the XML representation of the data stored in the DataTable. Following is its general declaration:

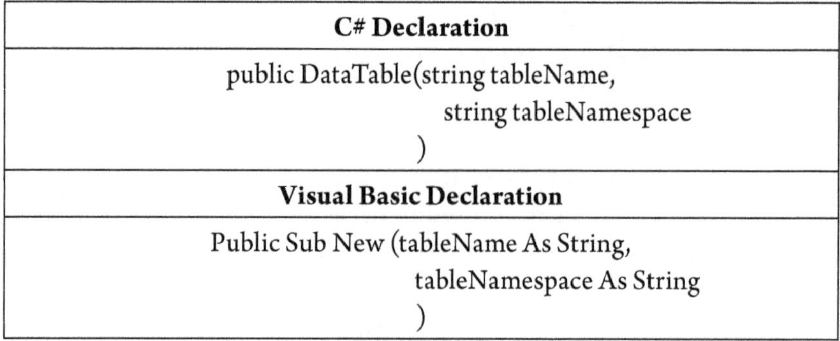

C# Declaration
public DataTable(string tableName, string tableNamespace)
Visual Basic Declaration
Public Sub New (tableName As String, tableNamespace As String)

Properties of DataTable Class

DataTable class provides the following important properties:

Name	Description
TableName	This property is used to set the name of a DataTable object. It takes a String value that specifies the name of a DataTable object to be created. This property is a read/write property and it is also used to get the name of a current object of DataTable.
Columns	This property is used to get the columns collection of a DataTable object. The columns collection is a class that is called DataColumnCollection class. The object of this class contains all the columns of a DataTable object. If a DataTable object does not contain columns, the columns collection will be an empty collection.

Rows	This property is used to get the rows collection of a DataTable object. The rows collection is a class that is called DataRowCollection class. The object of this class contains all the current rows of a DataTable object. If a DataTable object does not contain rows, the rows collection will be an empty collection. The following example retrieves each value of each row of a DataTable object using the Columns and Rows properties:
	foreach(DataRow row in table.Rows)
	
	{
	foreach(DataColumn column in table.Columns)
	{
	Console.WriteLine(row[column]);
	}
	}

ChildRelation	This property is used to get the collection of child relations of a DataTable object. The collection of child relations is a class that is called DataRelationCollection class. The object of this class contains all the child relations of a DataTable object.

ParentRelation	This property is used to get the collection of parent relations of a DataTable object. The collection of parent relations is a class that is called DataRelationCollection class. The object of this class contains the parent relations of a DataTable object.
Constraints	This property is used to get the collection of constraints of a DataTable object. The collection of constraints is a class that is called ConstraintCollection class. The object of this class contains the constraints of a DataTable object.

PrimaryKey	This property is used to set the primary key for a DataTable object. It takes an array of DataColumn objects that contains one or more DataColumn objects for primary key. Following is the declaration to set the primary key for a DataTable object:
	
	//Set three DataColumn objects as Primary //Key.
	DataTable table = new DataTable();
	DataColumn[] keys = new DataColumn[3];
	DataColumn column;
	
	The above declaration declares a DataTable object and an array of DataColumn objects that contains there DataColumn objects. The PrimaryKey property is a read/write property and it is also used to get the current primary key of a DataTable object. To get the current primary key columns from a DataTable object, an array of DataColumn is declared and the PrimaryKey property is assigned to it. Following is the general declaration to get the primary key columns from a DataTable object:
	
	DataTable table = new DataTable();
	DataColumn[] columns;
	columns = table.PrimaryKey;

Namespace	This property is used to set the namespace for the XML representation of the data stored in a DataTable. It is a read/write property and it is also used to get the namespace.
MinimumCapacity	This property is used to set the initial starting size of a DataTable object. It is a read/write property and it is also used to get the initial starting size value of a DataTable object.
DataSet	This property is used to get the DataSet object belongs to the current DataTable object.
IsInitialized	This property is used to get a value that indicates whether the DataTable object is initialized or not. It gets a Boolean value either true or false. The true value indicates that the DataTable object is initialized and false value indicates that the DataTable object is not initialized.

Methods of DataTable Class

DataTable class provides various methods but the following methods are important:

Method	Description
AcceptChanges	This method is used to commit all the changes made in the DataTable object. When this method is called, all the modifications are stopped and commits all the changes.
Clear	This method is used to delete all the data of a DataTable object.
Clone	This method is used to create a clone of a DataTable. It creates a new DataTable object with the same schema of the current DataTable. The Clone method only creates the table structure but it does not copy the data of the current DataTable to the new DataTable.

Copy	This method is used to copy a DataTable. It creates a new DataTable with the same structure of the current DataTable. It also copies data from the current DataTable to the new DataTable.
NewRow	This method is used to create a new row. A new row is created by declaring an instance of the DataRow class and assigns the NewRow method to it. When a new row is declared and data is assigned to it then it is added to the DataTable object by using the Rows.Add method. Following is its general declaration: DataTable table = new DataTable(); DataRow Row1 = table.NewRow(); Row1["Column-Name-1"] = "Value-1"; Row1["Column-Name-2"] = "Value-1"; Row1["Column-Name-3"] = "Value-1"; Row1["Column-Name-n"] = "Value-n"; table.Rows.Add(Row1);
RejectChanges	This method is used to reject or roll back all the changed that have made after calling the AcceptChanges method last time.
Reset	This method is used to reset the state of a DataTable. It resets the DataTable to its original state and deletes all the rows and columns structure.
	Select() method is used to get rows from a DataTable. It is used either with parameters or without parameters. When it is used without parameters, it retrieves all the DataRow and when it is used with parameter, it retrieves specified number of DataRow objects according to a condition in the expression parameter. The parameterized Select() method takes a String expression as parameter that contains a condition or criteria and retrieves DataRow objects according to the condition. The String expression is SQL like

Select	String that contains condition or criteria. When Select() method retrieves DataRow objects, it returns an array of DataRow that contains all the retrieved DataRow objects of a DataTable. The Select() method is an overloaded member method of the DataTable class that provides different overloaded forms. Following is the general declaration of the different overloaded forms of Select method:
	
	//First Overloaded Form of Select Method:
	DataTable table = new DataTable();
	DataRow[] rows = table.Select();
	
	//Second Overloaded Form of Select Method:
	DataTable table = new DataTable();
	string expression;
	expression = "Column_Name<Condition>";
	DataRow[] rows
	rows = table.Select(expression);
	
	//Third Overloaded form of Select Method:
	DataTable table = new DataTable();
	expression = "Column_Name<Condition>";
	string sortOrder = "Column_Name<Order>";
	DataRow[] rows;
	rows = table.Select(expression, sortOrder);
	
	The first overloaded form of Select method does not take parameters and it retrieves all the DataRow objects from a DataTable object. The second overloaded form takes a single String parameter that specifies an expression as a condition. The third overloaded form of Select method takes two String parameters, the first parameter specifies an expression and the second parameter specifies the sort order. The sort order parameter contains a column name and value of the sort order either ASC or DESC.

DataColumn Class

DataColumn class is used to create the columns of a DataTable object. The columns of a DataTable are represented in a collection DataColumnCollection. Each DataColumn object represents a single column of the DataTable. When a DataColumn object is created in a DataTable, it automatically added to the DataColumnCollection. The DataColumn class is declared in a namespace System.Data.

Constructors of DataColumn Class

DataColumn class provides the following constructors used to declare objects of the DataColumn class:

- DataColumn() Constructor
- DataColumn(String) Constructor
- DataColumn(String, Type) Constructor

DataColumn() Constructor

This constructor is a default constructor of the DataColumn class that is used to declare objects of the DataColumn class without parameters. Following is its general declaration:

C# Declaration
DataColumn column = new DataColumn();
Visual Basic Declaration
Dim column As DataColumn = New DataColumn()

DataColumn(String) Constructor

This constructor takes a single String parameter that specifies the column name to be created. Following is its general declaration:

C# Declaration
DataColumn column = new DataColumn("Name");
Visual Basic Declaration
Dim column As DataColumn = New DataColumn("Name")

DataColumn(String, Type) Constructor

This constructor takes two parameters. The first parameter is a String parameter that specifies the column name and the second parameter is a Type parameter that specifies the DataType of the column to be created. Following is its general declaration:

C# Declaration
System.Type ColumnType DataColumn column ColumnType = System.Type.GetType("System.Int32"); column = new DataColumn("Name", ColumnType);
Visual Basic Declaration
Dim ColumnType As System.Type Dim column As DataColumn ColumnType = System.Type.GetType("System.Int32") column = New DataColumn("Name", ColumnType)

Properties of DataColumn Class

DataColumn class provides the following important properties:

Property	Description
AllowDBNull	This property is used to set a value that indicates whether the column can store a null value or not. It takes a Boolean value either true or false. If its value is set to true, the column can store null values and if its value is set to false, the column cannot store null values. This property is a read/write property and it is also used to get its current value.
AutoIncrement	This property is used to set a value that indicates whether the column automatically increments value of the column for new rows added to the table or not. It takes a Boolean value either true or false. If its value is set to true, it increments the column value and if its value is set to false, it cannot increments the column value. The default value of this property is false that means the column is not auto incremented by default.

	This property is a read/write property and it is also used to get its current value.
AutoIncrementSeed	This property is used to set the starting value of a column to be created. It is used with the conjunction of the AutoIncrement property and it works only if the AutoIncrement property is set to true. The default value of this property is 0. This property is a read/write property and it is also used to get the current starting value of the column.
AutoIncrementStep	This property is used to set a steep value for a column. A steep value is a long value by which the column is auto incremented when a new row is inserted in the table. This property is used with the conjunction of the AutoIncrement property and it works only if the AutoIncrement property is set to true. If this property is not set, the default steep value is 1. This property is a read/write property and it is also used to get the current step value of a column.
Caption	This property is used to set a caption of the column to be created. A caption is a String value that specifies the purpose of the column. This property is a read/write property and it is also used to get the current caption of the column.
ColumnMapping	This property is used to set the MappingType of the column to be created. The MappingType is an enumeration that specifies how the column is mapped. This property is a read/write property and it is also used to get the current mapping value of the column.
ColumnName	This property is used to set the name of the column to be created. The name of a column is a String value that identifies a column in a table. If this property is not set then by default it uses the caption value as a column name. This property is a read/write property and it is also used to get the current name of the column.

DataType	This property is used to set the data type of the column to be created. The data type specifies the type of the value to be stored in the column. This property is a read/write property and it is also used to get the current data type of the column.
DefaultValue	This property is used to set the default value of the column to be created.
Expression	This property is used to set the expression for a column. An expression is a String value that is used as condition to filter rows, calculate the values in a column, or create an aggregate column.
MaxLength	This property is used to set the maximum length of a String type column. It takes an integer value that specifies the number of characters as a column length. This property is a read/write property and it is also used to get the current length of a column.
ReadOnly	This property is used to set a value that indicates either the column is read only or not. It takes a Boolean value either true or false. If its value is set to true, the column will be read only and if its value is set to false, the column will not be read only. The default value of this property is false.
Unique	This property is used to set a value that indicates whether the column is a unique column or not. It takes a Boolean value either true or false. If its value is set to true, the column will be a unique column and if its value is set to false, the column will not be unique. The default value of this property is false that means the column is not unique by default.

DataRow Class

DataRow class is used to create rows of a DataTable. The rows are created to insert data or record into the DataTable. A single record is stored in a single row. Each DataRow object represents a single row of a DataTable. The rows of a DataTable are represented in a collection that is called DataRowCollection. When a DataRow object is declared in a DataTable, it automatically added to the collection

DataRowCollection. The DataRow class is declared in a namespace System.Data. Following is the general syntax to declare objects of the DataRow class:

C# Syntax
protected internal DataRow(DataRowBuilder builder)
Visual Basic Syntax
Protected Friend Sub New (builder As DataRowBuilder)

Properties of DataRow Class

DataRow class provides the following important properties:

Property	Description
Item	This property represents a single value or an item of a row. It is an overloaded member method of the DataRow class that provides different overloaded forms.
ItemArray	This property represents all the items or values of a row.
RowState	This property indicates the current state of a row.
Table	This property returns the DataTable with the current created row.

Methods of DataRow class

DataRow class provides the following important methods:

Method	Description
AcceptChanges	This method is used to commit all the changes that occur in the current DataRow object.
BeginEdit	This method is used to start an edit operation on a DataRow object.
CancelEdit	This method is used to cancel the current edit operation on a DataRow object.
Delete	This method is used to delete a DataRow.

EndEdit	This method is used to terminate or end the current edit operation on a DataRow object.
GetChildRows	This method is used to return child rows of a DataRow object. It returns an array of DataRow objects that represents the child rows. This method is an overloaded member method of the DataRow class that provides different overloaded forms.
GetParentRows	This method is used to return the parent row of the current DataRow object.
RejectsChanges	This method is used to reject all the changes that are accepted last time by executing the method AcceptChanges.

Create a DataTable and Insert Data

To create a DataTable, an object is declared from the DataTable class then the schema is defined for the created object using the DataColumn class. When the schema is defined, the DataTable is ready to insert data or record. The data or record is inserted into the DataTable using the DataRow class. Following is a code to create a DataTable and insert data or record in it:

```
//Declare a DataTable object
DataTable StudentsInfo = new DataTable();

//Declare a DataColumn Variable
DataColumn dtColumn;

//Create the First Column
dtColumn = new DataColumn();
dtColumn.DataType = System.Type.GetType("System.String");
dtColumn.ColumnName = "StdRegNumber";
dtColumn.Caption = "Student Registration Number";
dtColumn.ReadOnly = true;
dtColumn.Unique = true;

//Add the First Column StdRegNumber to the table StudentsInfo
StudentsInfo.Columns.Add(dtColumn);
```

```
/Create the Second Column
dtColumn = new DataColumn();
dtColumn.DataType = System.Type.GetType("System.String");
dtColumn.ColumnName = "StdName";
dtColumn.Caption = "Student Name";
dtColumn.AutoIncrement = false;
dtColumn.ReadOnly = false;
dtColumn.Unique = false;

//Add the Second Column StdName to the table StudentsInfo
StudentsInfo.Columns.Add(dtColumn);

//Create the Third Column
dtColumn = new DataColumn();
dtColumn.DataType = System.Type.GetType("System.DateTime");
dtColumn.ColumnName = "StdDoBirth";
dtColumn.Caption = "Date of Birth";
dtColumn.ReadOnly = false;
dtColumn.Unique = false;

//Add the Third Column StdDoBirth to the table StudentsInfo
StudentsInfo.Columns.Add(dtColumn);

//Make the StdRegNumber column as a Primary Key Column
DataColumn[] PrimaryKeyColumns = new DataColumn[1];
PrimaryKeyColumns[0] = StudentsInfo.Columns["StdRegNumber"];
StudentsInfo.PrimaryKey = PrimaryKeyColumns;

//Declare a DataSet Object
DataSet dst = new DataSet();

//Add the StudentsInfo table to the Dataset Object
dst.Tables.Add(StudentsInfo);

//Insert Data or Record into the table StudentsInfo

//Declare the First Row of StudentsInfo table
DataRow FirstRow = StudentsInfo.NewRow();
```

```
/FirstRow["StdRegNumber"] = "Std001";
FirstRow["StdName"] = "Ishtiyaq Ali";
DateTime BirthDate1 = new DateTime(2003, 05, 19);
FirstRow["StdDoBirth"] = BirthDate1;
StudentsInfo.Rows.Add(FirstRow);

//Declare the Second Row of StudentsInfo table
DataRow SecondRow = StudentsInfo.NewRow();
SecondRow["StdRegNumber"] = "Std002";
SecondRow["StdName"] = "Latif Khan";
DateTime BirthDate2 = new DateTime(2005, 07, 11);
SecondRow["StdDoBirth"] = BirthDate2;
StudentsInfo.Rows.Add(SecondRow);

//Declare the Third Row of StudentsInfo table
DataRow ThirdRow = StudentsInfo.NewRow();
ThirdRow["StdRegNumber"] = "Std003";
ThirdRow["StdName"] = "Saim Ali";
DateTime BirthDate3 = new DateTime(2009, 09, 05);
ThirdRow["StdDoBirth"] = BirthDate3;
StudentsInfo.Rows.Add(ThirdRow);

//Bind the Dataset object to the DataGridView object
dataGridView1.DataSource = dst.Tables[0];
```

Retrieve Data from DataTable

Select() method of DataTable class is used to retrieve data from DataTable. It retrieves data from each DataColumn object of a DataRow. Select() method is used either without parameters or with parameters. When it is used without parameters, it retrieves all DataRow objects of a DataTable and when it is used with parameter, it retrieves specified number of DataRow objects according to the expression parameter. The following program retrieves data from a DataTable using the parameterized and parameter-less Select() method:

```
using System;
using System.Data;
using System.Data.SqlClient;

namespace ConsoleApplication1
{
class Program
{
static void Main(string[] args)
{
//Declare a DataTable object
DataTable StudentsInfo = new DataTable();

//Declare a DataColumn Variable
DataColumn dtColumn;

//Create the First Column
dtColumn = new DataColumn();
dtColumn.DataType = System.Type.GetType("System.String");
dtColumn.ColumnName = "StdRegNumber";
dtColumn.Caption = "Student Registration Number";
dtColumn.ReadOnly = true;
dtColumn.Unique = true;

//Add the First Column StdRegNumber to the table StudentsInfo
StudentsInfo.Columns.Add(dtColumn);

//Create the Second Column
dtColumn = new DataColumn();
dtColumn.DataType = System.Type.GetType("System.String");
dtColumn.ColumnName = "StdName";
dtColumn.Caption = "Student Name";
dtColumn.AutoIncrement = false;
dtColumn.ReadOnly = false;
dtColumn.Unique = false;

//Add the Second Column StdName to the table StudentsInfo
```

```
StudentsInfo.Columns.Add(dtColumn);

//Create the Third Column
dtColumn = new DataColumn();
dtColumn.DataType = System.Type.GetType("System.DateTime");
dtColumn.ColumnName = "StdDoBirth";
dtColumn.Caption = "Date of Birth";
dtColumn.ReadOnly = false;
dtColumn.Unique = false;

//Add the Third Column StdDoBirth to the table StudentsInfo
StudentsInfo.Columns.Add(dtColumn);

//Make the StdRegNumber column as a Primary Key Column
DataColumn[] PrimaryKeyColumns = new DataColumn[1];
PrimaryKeyColumns[0] = StudentsInfo.Columns["StdRegNumber"];
StudentsInfo.PrimaryKey = PrimaryKeyColumns;

//Declare a DataSet Object
DataSet dst = new DataSet();

//Add the StudentsInfo table to the Dataset Object
dst.Tables.Add(StudentsInfo);

//Insert Data or Record into the table StudentsInfo

//Declare the First Row of StudentsInfo table
DataRow FirstRow = StudentsInfo.NewRow();
FirstRow["StdRegNumber"] = "Std001";
FirstRow["StdName"] = "Ishtiyaq Ali";
DateTime BirthDate1 = new DateTime(2003, 05, 19);
FirstRow["StdDoBirth"] = BirthDate1;
StudentsInfo.Rows.Add(FirstRow);

//Declare the Second Row of StudentsInfo table
DataRow SecondRow = StudentsInfo.NewRow();
SecondRow["StdRegNumber"] = "Std002";
```

```
SecondRow["StdName"] = "Latif Khan";
DateTime BirthDate2 = new DateTime(2005, 07, 11);
SecondRow["StdDoBirth"] = BirthDate2;
StudentsInfo.Rows.Add(SecondRow);

//Declare the Third Row of StudentsInfo table
DataRow ThirdRow = StudentsInfo.NewRow();
ThirdRow["StdRegNumber"] = "Std003";
ThirdRow["StdName"] = "Saim Ali";
DateTime BirthDate3 = new DateTime(2009, 09, 05);
ThirdRow["StdDoBirth"] = BirthDate3;
StudentsInfo.Rows.Add(ThirdRow);

//Retrieve the data or record of all Students from StudentsInfo //Table
DataRow[] allrows = StudentsInfo.Select();

//A loop that retrieves all the values of rows from the DataRow //Array
for (int i = 0; i < allrows.Length; i++)
{
Console.Write("Reg Number = " + allrows[i]["StdRegNumber"]);
Console.Write(" ");
Console.Write("Name = " + allrows[i]["StdName"]);
Console.Write(" ");
Console.WriteLine("DoBirth = " + allrows[i]["StdDoBirth"]);
}

//Retrieve a specified Student data or record using the //StdRegNumber
column
Console.WriteLine("Retrieve Student Record By StdRegNumber");

String expressionByRegNum = "StdRegNumber = 'Std002'";
DataRow[] rowsByRegNum;
rowsByRegNum = StudentsInfo.Select(expressionByRegNum);

//A loop that retrieves all the values of rows from the DataRow //Array
for (int i = 0; i < rowsByRegNum.Length; i++)
```

```
{
Console.Write("Reg Number = " +
rowsByRegNum[i]["StdRegNumber"]);
Console.Write(" ");
Console.Write("Name = " + rowsByRegNum[i]["StdName"]);
Console.Write(" ");
Console.WriteLine("DoBirth = " +
rowsByRegNum[i]["StdDoBirth"]);
}

//Retrieve a specified Student data or record using the StdDoBirth //column
Console.WriteLine("Retrieve Student Record By DoBirth");

DataRow[] rowsByDoBirth;
rowsByDoBirth=StudentsInfo.Select("StdDoBirth= '9/5/2009'");

//A loop that retrieves all the values of rows from the DataRow //Array
for (int i = 0; i < rowsByDoBirth.Length; i++)
{
Console.Write("Reg Number = " +
rowsByDoBirth[i]["StdRegNumber"]);
Console.Write(" ");
Console.Write("Name = " + rowsByDoBirth[i]["StdName"]);
Console.Write(" ");
Console.WriteLine("DoBirth = " +
rowsByDoBirth[i]["StdDoBirth"]);
}

Console.ReadKey();
}
}
}
```

CHAPTER 12

Delegates, Anonymous Methods and Lambda Expression

CHAPTER CONTENTS

Delegates

Delegate is a reference type and a type safe function pointer that references methods using their memory addresses and invoke them dynamically during run time of the program. A delegate has a specified set of parameters and a return type like a method and it invokes a method that has the matching parameters and return type. It means that the parameters and return type of a delegate must be the same as the parameters and the return type of a method it references to. An instance of a delegate takes a method as a parameter and references it using its memory address. To invoke a method using a delegate, first a custom delegate reference type is defined using the delegate keyword and its parameters list and a return type is declared according to the target method then an instance is declared from it and it is instantiated by assigning the target method to it as parameter. When a method is assigned as parameter to an instance of the delegate reference type, it stores the memory address of that method and invokes it dynamically during runtime of the program. An instance of the delegate invokes either a static method associated with a class or an instance method associated with an object. A delegate reference type is similar to other reference types but the main difference is that other reference types hold the references or the memory addresses of variables and a delegate reference type holds the reference or the memory address of a method like a function pointer in C++ programming language.

A delegate is similar to the function pointers in C++ programming language. The function pointer of C++ programming language is a pointer variable that points to a function using its memory address. To invoke a function using a function pointer, we simply assign the memory address of the method to the function pointer variable and invoke it using its memory address. A function pointer variable in C++ is a pointer variable but its declaration is similar to the function declaration that has the matching parameters list and a return type with the parameters list and the return type of the function that points to it. Therefore, a function pointer variable in C++ programming invokes a function that has the matching parameters and a return type. The main difference between the C++ function pointers and the delegates is that the C++ function pointer holds only the memory address of a function and it does not carry any additional information such as the number of parameters used by the function, the types of the parameters, and the return type of the function while a delegate holds the memory address of a method and carry all the information associated with the method we want to invoke and also can access any variable visible to the enclosing scope. The delegates are actually the .NET implementation of functions pointers and they are object-oriented, type safe and secure unlike C++ functions pointers. Therefore, we can say that delegates are the .NET reference objects which can be used to invoke methods of matching signatures and return type. A delegate invokes a method synchronously and asynchronously and it can also be used to define callback methods. A callback method is a user-defined method that is used to process the result of an asynchronous operation in a separate thread.

Invoke Methods using Delegates

To invoke a method using a delegate, we must follow the following three steps:

1. Declaration of Delegate Type
2. Instantiation of Delegate Instances
3. Invocation of Method

Declaration of Delegate Type

The declaration of delegate defines a custom delegate reference type using a keyword delegate. A delegate reference type has a specified set of parameters and a return type according to the method it references to. A delegate reference type can be declared within the scope of a namespace or within the scope of a class. We cannot declare a delegate as a data member of a class and we cannot declare it as a local variable within the scope of a method because the declaration of a delegate is actually a new type definition and types can be defined only within the scope of a namespace and within the scope of a class. We cannot define any type within the scope of a method. Following is the general syntax to define a delegate reference type:

C# Syntax
[Modifiers] delegate ReturnType DelegateName([ParameterList]);
Visual Basic.NET Syntax
[Modifiers] Delegate Function DelegateName([ParameterList]) As ReturnType

The declaration of a delegate type usually has five parts such as modifiers, the delegate keyword, return type, the delegate name, and a list of parameters. The first part of a delegate declaration is [Modifiers] that indicates an access modifier. The access modifiers are keywords used to specify the declared accessibility of a member or a data type. The main and important access modifiers are public, protected, private, and internal modifiers. The second part of the delegate declaration is a delegate keyword. A delegate keyword is a reserved word provided by the .NET Framework that is used to declare a delegate reference type. The third part of the delegate declaration is ReturnType that indicates the return type of the delegate reference type. The return type of the delegate reference type must be the same as the return type of the method we want to invoke. The fourth part of the delegate declaration is the DelegateName that indicates a user-defined name of the delegate reference type we want to declare. The user-defined name of a delegate reference type must follow the variables and methods naming convention of the .NET Framework. The fifth part of the delegate declaration is [ParameterList] that indicates the number of parameters of a delegate reference type. The parameters list of the delegate reference type must be the same as the parameters list of the method we want to invoke.

Instantiation of Delegate Instances

The instantiation of a delegate instance is a process in which an instance of a delegate is referenced or associated with a method that has the matching parameters and a return type. A method can be referenced or associated with an instance of a delegate by assigning that method to it as parameter. When a custom delegate reference type is defined using the delegate keyword and its parameters list and a return type is declared according to the target method then an instance is declared from it and it is instantiated by assigning the target method to it as parameter. When the method is assigned as a parameter to an instance of the delegate, it stores the memory address of that method and the method is referenced or associated to it. Following is the general syntax to declare and instantiate an instance of a delegate reference type:

C# Syntax

//Declare an instance of the Delegate reference type
DelegateName instanceName;
 	
//Instantiate an instance of the Delegate reference type
instanceName = new DelegateName(MethodName)

Visual Basic.NET Syntax
'Declare an instance of the Delegate reference type Dim instanceName As DelegateName 'Instantiate an instance of the Delegate reference type instanceName = New DelegateName(AddressOf MethodName)

The above declaration declares and instantiates an instance of the delegate reference type. The name of the declared instance is instanceName. The DelegateName indicates the name of the delegate reference type from which we declare an instance instanceName. The new keyword is used to instantiate the instance of the delegate reference type. The MethodName indicates the name of the method we want to invoke.

Invocation of Methods

When a method is referenced or associated with an instance of the delegate then this is the last step in which a method is invoked by calling the associated instance of the delegate and assign values to its parameters, if the referenced or associated method takes parameters. Following is the general syntax to invoke a method using the referenced or associated delegate instance:

C# Syntax
ReturnType instanceName(ParametersList);
Visual Basic.NET Syntax
ReturnType instanceName(ParametersList)

In the above declaration, the ReturnType represents the return type of the referenced or associated method, the instanceName represents the name of the delegate instance, and the ParametersList represents the number of parameters of the referenced or associated method.

Types of Delegates

The delegates are categorized into the following two types:

- Single Cast Delegates
- Multicast Delegates

Single Cast Delegates

A single cast delegate is a type of delegate that references to a single method at a time. A single cast delegate holds the reference or the memory address of a single method that has the matching parameters and a return type. Following is an example of a single cast delegate type definition:

C# Example of Delegate type definition
public delegate int myDelegate(int x);
Visual Basic Example of Delegate type definition
Public Delegate Function myDelegate(x As Integer) As Integer

The above declaration defines a delegate reference type myDelegate. The myDelegate is a user-defined name of the delegate reference type that takes a single integer parameter and returns an integer value. Therefore, the myDelegate reference type references and invokes a method that takes a single integer parameter and returns an integer value.

Program # 1

Write a program that invokes a simple static method using a delegate and displays a message in the method body. The method has no parameters list and no return type.
C# Program

```
using System;
namespace ProgramNamespace
{
//Define a Delegate type that has no parameters list and no return //type
public delegate void dlgMessage();

public class MainProgramClass
{
static void Main(string[] args)
{
//Declare an instance of the delegate reference type dlgMessage
dlgMessage instDelegate;

//Instantiate the delegate instance instDelegate by assigning a //method
instDelegate = new dlgMessage(displayMessage);

//Invoke the method displayMessage() using the delegate instance //
instDelegate

instDelegate();

Console.WriteLine("Press any key to exit program");
Console.ReadKey();
}

//Declare a method that has no parameters and no return type and //display
a message

public static void displayMessage()
{
Console.WriteLine("Welcome to the .NET Delegates");
}
}
}
```

Visual Basic Program
Imports System Namespace ProgramNamespace 'Define a Delegate type that has no parameters list and no return 'type
Public Delegate Sub dlgMessage() Public Class MainProgramClass 'Declare a method that has no parameters and no return type and 'display a message Public Shared Sub displayMessage() Console.WriteLine("Welcome to the .NET Delegates") End Sub Public Shared Sub Main() 'Declare an instance of the delegate reference type dlgMessage Dim instDelegate As dlgMessage 'Instantiate the delegate instance instDelegate by assigning a 'method instDelegate = New dlgMessage(AddressOf displayMessage) 'Invoke the method displayMessage() using the delegate instance 'instDelegate instDelegate() Console.WriteLine("Press any key to exit program") Console.ReadKey() End Sub End Class End Namespace

Program # 2

Write a program that invokes a non static method of a class using a delegate. The method has no parameters list and it returns a string message to its calling point.
C# Program

```
using System;
namespace MainProgramNamespace
{
//Define a Delegate type that has no parameters list and returns a //string
public delegate string dlgMessage();

//Declare a class that contains a single non-static method. The //method has
no parameters list and returns a string message to its //calling point

public class MyMethodClass
{
//Declare a non-static method that has no parameters list and //returns a
string message to its calling point

public string displayMessage()
{
return "Welcome to the .NET Delegates";
}
}

public class MainProgramClass
{
static void Main(string[] args)
{
//Declare an instance of the class MyMethodClass
MyMethodClass obj = new MyMethodClass();

//Declare an instance of the delegate reference type dlgMessage
dlgMessage instDelegate;

//Instantiate the delegate instance instDelegate by assigning the //non static
method displayMessage() of the class MyClass
```

```
instDelegate = new dlgMessage(obj.displayMessage);

//Invoke the method displayMessage() using the delegate instance //
instDelegate and declare a string variable that holds the return //value of
the displayMessage() method

string msg = instDelegate();

//Display the message
Console.WriteLine(msg);

Console.WriteLine("Press any key to exit program");
Console.ReadKey();
}
}
}
```

Visual Basic Program

```
Imports System
Namespace MainProgramNamespace

'Define a Delegate type that has no parameters list and returns a 'string
Public Delegate Function dlgMessage() As String

'Declare a class that contains a single non-static method. The 'method has no
parameters list and returns a string message to its 'calling point

Public Class MyMethodClass

'Declare a non-static method that has no parameters list and returns 'a string
message to its calling point

Public Function displayMessage() As String
Return "Welcome to the .NET Delegates"
End Function
End Class

Public Class MainProgramClass
Public Shared Sub Main()
```

```
'Declare an instance of the class MyMethodClass
Dim obj As New MyMethodClass()

'Declare an instance of the delegate reference type dlgMessage
Dim instDelegate As dlgMessage

'Instantiate the delegate instance instDelegate by assigning the non-'static
method displayMessage() of the class MyMethodClass

instDelegate = New dlgMessage(AddressOf obj.displayMessage)

'Invoke the method displayMessage() using the delegate instance
'instDelegate and declare a string variable that holds the return 'value of the
displayMessage() method

Dim msg As String = instDelegate()

'Display the message
Console.WriteLine(msg)

Console.WriteLine("Press any key to exit program")
Console.ReadKey()
End Sub
End Class
End Namespace
```

When the above program executes, it displays a message "Welcome to the .NET Delegates". The program contains a delegate reference type dlgMessage and a method displayMessage. The delegate reference type dlgMessage is a parameter-less delegate reference type that does not take any parameter and its return type is string that returns a string value. The method displayMessage is a parameter-less user-defined method we defined in a separate class MyMethodClass. The user-defined method displayMessage returns a message "Welcome to the .NET Delegates". The parameter and the return type of the delegate dlgMessage and the parameter and the return type of the method displayMessage are the same because both the method and delegate reference type do not take any parameter and both have a string return type. In the main method of the program, we also declared an instance of the delegate reference type. The name of the delegate reference type instance is instDelegate. The instance instDelegate is used and invokes the method displayMessage that returns a string message "Welcome to the .NET Delegates".

Program # 3

Write a program that invokes a non-static method of a class using a delegate. The method takes two integer parameters and returns their sum to its calling point.
C# Program

```
using System;
namespace ProgramNamespace
{
//Define a Delegate reference type that takes two integer //parameters and
returns an integer value

public delegate int calculateTwoValues(int x, int y);

//Declare a class that contains a single non-static method. The //method has
two integer parameters and returns their sum to its //calling point

public class MyMethodClass
{
//Declare a non-static method that takes two integer parameters //and
returns their sum to its calling point

public int addValues(int x, int y)
{
return (x + y);
}
}
public class MainProgramClass
{
static void Main(string[] args)
{
//Declare an instance of the class MyMethodClass
MyMethodClass obj = new MyMethodClass();
```

```
//Declare an instance of the delegate reference type
calculateTwoValues instDelegate;

//Instantiate the delegate instance instDelegate by assigning the //non-static
method addValues() of the class MyMethodClass

instDelegate = new calculateTwoValues(obj.addValues);

//Invoke the method addValues() using the delegate instance //instDelegate
and declare an integer variable that holds the return //value of the addValues()
method

int sumValue = instDelegate(10, 20);

//Display the result of the addValues() method
Console.WriteLine(sumValue);

Console.WriteLine("Press any key to exit program");
Console.ReadKey();
}
}
}
```

Visual Basic Program

```
Imports System
Namespace ProgramNamespace

'Define a Delegate reference type that takes two integer parameters 'and
returns an integer value

Public Delegate Function calculateTwoValues(x As Integer, y As Integer)
As Integer

'Declare a class that contains a single non-static method. The 'method has
two integer parameters and returns their sum to its 'calling point

Public Class MyMethodClass
```

```
'Declare a non-static method that takes two integer parameters and 'returns their sum to its calling point

Public Function addValues(x As Integer, y As Integer) As Integer
Return (x + y)
End Function
End Class

Public Class MainProgramClass

Public Shared Sub Main()

'Declare an instance of the class MyMethodClass
Dim obj As New MyMethodClass()

'Declare an instance of the delegate reference type
Dim instDelegate As calculateTwoValues

'Instantiate the delegate instance instDelegate by assigning the non-'static method addValues() of the class MyMethodClass

instDelegate = New calculateTwoValues(AddressOf obj.addValues)

'Invoke the method addValues() using the delegate instance 'instDelegate and declare an integer variable that holds the return 'value of the addValues() method

Dim sumValue As Integer = instDelegate(10, 20)

'Display the result of the addValues() method
Console.WriteLine(sumValue)

Console.WriteLine("Press any key to exit program")
Console.ReadKey()
End Sub
End Class
End Namespace
```

When the above program executes, then it displays the sum of two integer values and displays the result. The program contains a delegate reference type calculateTwoValues and a method addValues we defined in a separate class MyMethodClass. The delegate reference type calculateTwoValues takes two integer parameters and return an integer value. The method addValues also takes two integer parameters and returns an integer value. The parameters and the return type of the delegate calculateTwoValues and the parameters and the return type of the method addValues are same because both the method and the delegate reference type take two integer parameters and return an integer value. In the main method of the program, we declared an instance of the delegate reference type. The name of the delegate reference type instance is instDelegate. The instance instDelegate instance passed two integer values from the main method of the program and invokes the method addValues. The method addValues calculates the sum of the two received values and returns the result back to the main method of the program. In the main method of the program, we declared an integer variable that stores the result of the method.

Multicast Delegates

A multicast delegate is a type of the delegate that references and invokes multiple methods at the same time. An instance of the multicast delegate reference type holds the references or the memory addresses of multiple methods which have the same parameters lists and the same return types as the parameters list and the return type of that of the delegate reference type. It means that the methods we want to invoke by using multicast delegate must have matching parameters and return types with the delegate reference type. The declaration of a multicast delegate and a single cast delegate is the same but the main difference is that an instance of a single cast delegate reference type references and invokes a single method at a time whereas an instance of a multicast delegate reference type reference and invokes multiple methods at the same time. The multicast delegate reference type is derived from the MulticastDelegate class that represents a multicast delegate type. The multicast delegate provides two operators i.e. += operator and -= operator which are used to add and remove the reference of a method respectively to the instance of the multicast delegate reference type. The multicast delegate holds the reference of a methods with a += operator and removes the reference of a method with -= operator. Following is an example of a multicast delegate type definition:

C# Delegate Type Definition
public delegate void myDelegate(int x);

Visual Basic Delegate Type Definition
Public Delegate Sub myDelegate(x As Integer)

The above declaration defines a delegate type myDelegate. The myDelegate is a user-defined name of the delegate that takes a single integer parameter and its return type is void that does not return any value. The above delegate myDelegate is a multicast delegate type that references and invokes multiple methods at the same time.

Write a program that invokes multiple methods using a multicast delegate.

Hints: Declare three methods in a class and invoke these methods using a delegate from the main method of the program. The methods take two integer parameters and they do not return any value. The first method takes two integer values and calculates their sum. The second method takes two integer values and calculates their subtraction and the third method takes two integer values and calculates their multiplication.

C# Program

```
using System;
namespace ProgramNamespace
{
//Define a Multicast delegate reference type that takes two integer
//parameters
public delegate void calculateTwoValues(int x, int y);

//Declare a class that contains three user-defined methods
public class MyMethodClass
{
public void AddValues(int x, int y)
{
Console.WriteLine("The sum of two values is");
Console.WriteLine(x + y);
}

public void SubtractValues(int x, int y)
{
Console.WriteLine("The subtraction of two values is");
```

```
Console.WriteLine(x - y);
}

public void MultiplyValues(int x, int y)
{
Console.WriteLine("The multiplication of two values is");
Console.WriteLine(x * y);
}
}

public class MainProgramClass
{
public static void Main()
{
//Declare an instance of the class MyMethodClass
MyMethodClass obj = new MyMethodClass();

//Declare an instance of the delegate reference type
calculateTwoValues instDelegate;

//Instantiate the multicast Delegate using multiple methods
instDelegate += new calculateTwoValues(obj.AddValues);
instDelegate += new calculateTwoValues(obj.SubtractValues);
instDelegate += new calculateTwoValues(obj.MultiplyValues);

//Invoke the multiple methods using the instance of the multicast
//delegate and pass two integer values to all methods

instDelegate(5, 2);

Console.WriteLine("Press any key to exit program");
Console.ReadKey();
}
}
}
```

Visual Basic Program
'In Visual Basic we cannot use the += operator, but there is a static 'method that produce the same result.

```
'In the following C# code:
instDelegate += new calculateTwoValues(obj.AddValues);
instDelegate += new calculateTwoValues(obj.SubtractValues);
instDelegate += new calculateTwoValues(obj.MultiplyValues);

'could be translate into:
instDelegate = CType(calculateTwoValues.Combine(
{
New calculateTwoValues(AddressOf obj.AddValues),
New calculateTwoValues(AddressOf obj.SubtractValues),
New calculateTwoValues(AddressOf obj.MultiplyValues)}),
calculateTwoValues)

'Furthermore, in VB there is the implicit casting through a delegate 'and the
AddressOf operator. Then all calls like this:

Dim instDelegate As calculateTwoValues
instDelegate = New calculateTwoValues(AddressOf obj.addValues)

'could be directly:
Dim instDelegate As calculateTwoValues = AddressOf obj.addValues

'Then, the multicast could be:
instDelegate = CType(calculateTwoValues.Combine(
New calculateTwoValues()
{
AddressOf obj.AddValues, AddressOf obj.SubtractValues, AddressOf obj.
MultiplyValues}), calculateTwoValues)
```

AsyncCallback Delegate

AsyncCallback delegate is used to invoke a method when a corresponding asynchronous operation completes. This delegate is usually used to process the result of an asynchronous operation and checks the status of the asynchronous operation whether the corresponding asynchronous operation has successfully completed or not. The AsyncCallback delegate is also used if we want to perform some post operations when a corresponding asynchronous operation successfully completes. The AsyncCallback delegate is referenced or associated with a method known as callback method. The callback method is a user-defined method in which we put some piece of codes about the post operation of asynchronous operation and we want to execute that code in a separate thread when a corresponding asynchronous operation completes for example, if we want to process the result of an asynchronous operation, if we want to release the resources used by the corresponding asynchronous operation, or if we want to perform some other tasks etc. When an asynchronous operation successfully completed then the AsyncCallback delegate takes the result of that asynchronous operation as a parameter and invokes the referenced or associated callback method. The AsyncCallback delegate references a callback method using its memory address.

When an asynchronous operation successfully completed, it returns an instance of the IAsyncResult interface. The IAsyncResult interface represents the status of an asynchronous operation. The AsyncCallback delegate takes instance of the IAsyncResult interface as a parameter and invokes the referenced or associated callback method. The parameters and return type of the AsyncCallback delegate must be the same as the parameters and return type of the callback method. It means that the AsyncCallback delegate only can invoke a callback method that has the matching parameters and return type. The return value of the AsyncCallback delegate is always void and it does not return any value. Following is the general declaration of the AsyncCallback delegate:

C# Declaration
public delegate void AsyncCallback(IAsyncResult asResult)
Visual Basic.NET Declaration
Public Delegate Sub AsyncCallback (asResult As IAsyncResult)

The above declaration declares the AsyncCallback delegate. The **asResult** is an instance of the IAsyncResult interface that shows the status of the asynchronous operation.

Callback Method

Callback method is a user-defined method that contains a piece of program codes and it is referenced or associated with the AsyncCallback delegate. The callback method executes when a corresponding asynchronous operation completes. When a corresponding asynchronous operation is completed successfully, the AsyncCallback delegate takes the callback method as a parameter and executes it in a separate thread parallel to the main thread of the program. The callback method is usually used to put some piece of the program code about the post operation of an asynchronous operation that is executed in a separate thread when a corresponding asynchronous operation completes for example, if we want to process the result of an asynchronous operation to check whether the corresponding asynchronous operation has completed successfully or not, if we want to release the resources used by the corresponding asynchronous operation, or if we want to perform some other tasks etc. When an asynchronous operation is completed successfully, the AsyncCallback delegate takes the callback method as a parameter and executes its codes in a separate thread. The callback method takes the result of the corresponding asynchronous operation i.e. an instance of the IAsyncResult interface as a parameter. The IAsyncResult interface represents the status of an asynchronous operation.

Action Delegate

Action delegate is a type of the delegate that is used to reference or associate methods and invokes them directly at run time of the program. It is a reference type that allows us to declare its instances and reference or associate methods and invoke them directly without explicitly defining a custom delegate reference type. The Action delegate has a specified set of parameters like a method and it invokes a method that has the matching parameters with it. It means that the parameters and return type of the Action delegate must be the same as the parameters and return type of the method it references to. The return type of the Action delegate is always void and it does not return any value. Therefore, an Action delegate invokes a method that has the matching parameters and void return type. To reference and invoke a method using an Action delegate, an instance of the Action delegate is declared using the Action keyword and references or associates it with the target method to be invoked by assigning that method to it as a parameter. When a method is assigned to an instance of the Action delegate as a parameter, the instance of the Action delegate stores its memory address and the method is referenced or associated with it. The referenced method can be invoked by simply calling the associated instance of the Action delegate and provide values to its parameters if the referenced method takes parameters otherwise, the parameters list of the instance of the Action delegate should be left blank.

The Action delegate is not a generalized delegate but it is a limited delegate reference type that is bounded to some specific number of parameters. Microsoft initially defined a single parameter Action delegate in .NET Framework 2.0 and it is further extended through different versions of the .NET

Framework. The .NET Framework 3.0 provides four Action delegates such as zero parameter, two parameters, three parameters, and four parameters Action delegates. The .NET Framework 4.0 provides a series of Action delegates that take parameters from 0 to 16. The zero parameter Action delegate is a parameter-less Action delegate that does not take any parameter and it is used to reference and invoke parameter-less methods. The parameterized Action delegates take parameters from 1 to 16 and they are used to reference and invoke the parameterized methods which have the matching parameters with the delegates for example, a single parameter Action delegate can reference and invoke a method that has the same type of single parameter, a two parameters Action delegate can reference and invoke a method that has the same types of two parameters and so on.

The parameters of the Action delegates are generic type parameters that take any type of values and they are represented by T followed by numeric values starting from 1 to 16. For example, a single parameter Action delegate is represented as Action<T>, a two parameters Action delegate is represented as Action<T1, T2>, a three parameters Action delegate is represented as Action<T1, T2, T3>, and a 16 parameters Action delegate is represented as Action<T1, T2, T3,----------,T16)>. Following is the general syntax to declare a parameter-less Action delegate:

C# Syntax
public delegate void Action()
Visual Basic.NET Syntax
Public Delegate Sub Action

The above declaration declares a parameter-less Action delegate. The parameter-less Action delegate invokes a method that has no parameters and does not return a value. Following is the general syntaxes to declare parameterized Action delegates:

C# Syntax

//The Declaration of Action delegate that takes a single parameter
public delegate void Action<in T>(T arg)
 	
//The Declaration of Action delegate that takes two parameters

```
public delegate void Action<in T1, in T2>
                                        (
                                        T1 arg1,
                                        T2 arg2
                                        )

//The Declaration of Action delegate that takes three parameters
public delegate void Action<in T1, in T2, in T3>
                                        (
                                        T1 arg1,
                                        T2 arg2,
                                        T3 arg3
                                        )

//The Declaration of Action delegate that takes 16 parameters
public delegate void Action<in T1, in T2, in T3, in T4,--, in T16>
                                        (
                                        T1 arg1,
                                        T2 arg2,
                                        T3 arg3,
                                        T4 arg4,
                                        ----------
                                        ----------
                                        ----------
                                        T16 arg16
                                        )
```

Visual Basic Syntax

```
The Declaration of Action delegate that takes a single parameter
Public Delegate Sub Action(Of In T) (arg As T)

'The Declaration of Action delegate that takes two parameters
Public Delegate Sub Action(Of In T1, In T2)
                                        (
                                        arg1 As T1,
                                        arg2 As T2
                                        )
```

```
'The Declaration of Action delegate that takes three parameters
Public Delegate Sub Action(Of In T1, In T2, In T3)
                          (
                          arg1 As T1,
                          arg2 As T2,
                          arg3 As T3
                          )

'The Declaration of Action delegate that takes 16 parameters
'Public Delegate Sub Action(Of In T1, In T2, In T3, In T4,------,
In T16)
                          (
                          arg1 As T1,
                          arg2 As T2,
                          arg3 As T3,
                          arg4 As T4
                          -------------
                          -------------
                          -------------
                          arg16 As T16
                          )
```

In the above declaration of the Action delegates, the **in** or **In** represents the input parameters of the referenced methods, the T represents the type of the input parameter of a single parameter referenced or associated method, the arg represents the actual parameter of a single parameter referenced or associated method, the values from T1 to T16 represent the type of the input parameters of the referenced or associated methods that take more than one parameter, and the values from arg1 to arg16 represent the actual parameters of the referenced or associated methods that take more than one parameter. The type of a parameter is general type parameter and it takes any type of values such as int, float, double, long double, string etc. T1 represents the type of the first parameter of a referenced method, T2 represents the type of the second parameter of a referenced method, T3 represents the type of the third parameter of a referenced method, and T16 represents the type of the sixteenth parameter of a referenced method. The arg1 represents the first parameter, arg2 represents the second parameter, and arg16 represents the sixteenth parameter of a referenced or associated method.

Invoke Methods using Action Delegate

A parameter-less Action delegate is used to invoke a parameter-less method and a parameterized Action delegate is used to invoke a parameterized method. To invoke a method using an Action delegate we must follow the following three steps:

- Declaration of Action Delegate Instance
- Instantiation of Action Delegate Instance
- Invocation of Methods

Declaration of Action Delegate Instance

To invoke a method using an Action delegate, an instance of the Action delegate is declared using a keyword Action. The declaration of the Action delegate instance is the same as the declaration of a variable but the main difference is that a variable is a value type that holds a value and an instance of the Action delegate is a reference type that references or holds the memory address of a method. Following is the general syntax to declare an instance of the Action delegate:

C# Syntax

//Declare an instance of the parameter-less Action delegate
 	
Action [instanceName];
 	
// Declare an instance of the parameterized Action delegate
 	
Action<[ParametersList]> [instanceName];

Visual Basic Syntax

The above declarations declare instances of the Action delegate. The first declaration declares an instance of the parameter-less Action delegate which is used to reference or associate a parameter-less method. The second declaration declares an instance of the parameterized Action delegate which is used to reference or associate a parameterized method. The [**instanceName**] indicates a user-defined name of an instance of the Action delegate to be declared. We can give any name to an instance of the Action delegate but it must follow the variables naming convention. The [**ParametersList**] indicates a list of parameters that takes parameters from 1 to 16. To invoke a method that has a single parameter, an instance of the Action delegate is declared that takes a single parameter of the same type similarly, to invoke a method that has two parameters, an instance of the Action delegate is declared that takes two parameters of the same type, to invoke a method that has 16 parameters, an instance of the Action delegate is declared that takes 16 parameters of the same types.

Instantiation of Action Delegate Instance

An instance of the Action delegate is instantiated by assigning a method to it as parameter. When an instance of the Action delegate is declared, it is instantiated by assigning a target method to it as parameter. The instance of the Action delegate stores the memory address of the assigned method and the method is referenced or associated with it. Following is the general syntax to instantiate an instance of the Action delegate:

C# Syntax
//Instantiate an instance of the Action delegate by assigning a //method to it [instanceName] = [methodName];
Visual Basic Syntax
'Instantiate an instance of the Action delegate by assigning a 'method to it [instanceName] = [methodName]

In the above declaration, the [**instanceName**] indicates the name of an instance of the Action delegate and the [**methodName**] indicates the name of a method we want to invoke using the Action delegate.

Invocation of Method

When an instance of the Action delegate is instantiated by assigning a specified method, it stores the memory address of that method and the method is referenced or associated with it. To invoke a referenced or associated method we simply call the instance of Action delegate and provide values to its parameters if the referenced or associated method takes parameters. Following is the general syntax to invoke an associated or referenced method using the instance of Action delegate:

C# Syntax

//Invoke an associated or referenced parameter-less method using //the instance of the Action delegate
 	
instanceName();
 	
//Invoke an associated or referenced parameterized method using //the instance of the Action delegate
 	
instanceName([ParametersList]);

Visual Basic Syntax
'Invoke an associated or referenced parameter-less method using 'the instance of the Action delegate instanceName() 'Invoke an associated or referenced parameterized method using 'the instance of the Action delegate instanceName([ParametersList]);

In the above declaration, the **instanceName** indicates the name of an instance of the Action delegate and the [**ParametersList**] indicates the number of parameters of the referenced or associated method.

Program # 1

Write a program that invokes a parameter-less method using a parameter-less Action delegate and displays a message on the screen.
C# Program
using System; namespace MainProgramNamespace { class MainProgramClass { static void Main(string[] args)

```
{
//Declare an instance of the parameter-less Action delegate
Action instActionDelegate;

//Instantiate the instance of Action delegate by assigning a method
instActionDelegate = displayMessage;

//Invoke the assigned or referenced method
instActionDelegate();

Console.WriteLine("Press any key to exit program");
Console.ReadKey();
}
static void displayMessage()
{
Console.WriteLine("Welcome to the Action Delegate");
}
}
}
```

Visual Basic Program

```
Namespace MainProgramNamespace

Class MainProgramClass

Public Shared Sub displayMessage()
Console.WriteLine("Welcome to the Action Delegate")
End Sub

Public Shared Sub Main()

'Declare an instance of the parameter-less Action delegate
Dim instActionDelegate As Action

'Instantiate the instance of Action delegate by assigning a method
instActionDelegate = AddressOf displayMessage

'Invoke the assigned or referenced method
instActionDelegate()
```

```
Console.WriteLine("Press any key to exit program")
Console.ReadKey()
End Sub
End Class
End Namespace
```

Program # 2

Write a program that invokes a parameter-less anonymous method using a parameter-less Action delegate.
C# Program

```
using System;

namespace MainProgramNamespace
{
class MainProgramClass
{
static void Main(string[] args)
{
//Declare an instance of the Action Delegate
Action instActionDelegate;

//Instantiate the instance of Action delegate by assigning an //anonymous
method
instActionDelegate = delegate()
{
Console.WriteLine("Welcome to the Action Delegate");
};

//Invoke the assigned or referenced anonymous method
instActionDelegate();

Console.WriteLine("Press any key to exit program");
Console.ReadKey();
}
}
}
```

Visual Basic Program

```
Namespace MainProgramNamespace

Class MainProgramClass

Public Shared Sub Main()

'Declare an instance of the Action delegate
Dim instActionDelegate As Action

'Instantiate the instance of Action delegate by assigning an 'anonymous
method

instActionDelegate = Sub()
Console.WriteLine("Welcome to the Action Delegate")
End Sub


'Invoke the assigned or referenced anonymous method
instActionDelegate()

Console.WriteLine("Press any key to exit program")
Console.ReadKey()
End Sub
End Class
End Namespace
```

Program # 3

Write a program that invokes a parameter-less anonymous method using a parameter-less Action delegate. The anonymous method is written using the Lambda Expression.

C# Program

```
using System;

namespace MainProgramNamespace
{
class MainProgramClass
```

```
{
static void Main(string[] args)
{
//Declare an instance of the Action Delegate
Action instActionDelegate;

//Instantiate the instance of Action delegate by assigning an //anonymous method. The anonymous method is written in the //form of a Lambda expression

instActionDelegate = () =>
{
Console.WriteLine("Welcome to the Action Delegate");
};

//Invoke the assigned or referenced anonymous method
instActionDelegate();

Console.WriteLine("Press any key to exit program");
Console.ReadKey();
}
}
}
```

Visual Basic Program

```
Namespace MainProgramNamespace

Class MainProgramClass

Public Shared Sub Main()

'Declare an instance of the Action Delegate
Dim instActionDelegate As Action

'Instantiate the instance of Action delegate by assigning an 'anonymous method. The anonymous method is written in the 'form of a Lambda expression
```

```
instActionDelegate = Function()
Console.WriteLine("Welcome to the Action Delegate")
End Function

'Invoke the assigned or referenced anonymous method
instActionDelegate()

Console.WriteLine("Press any key to exit program")
Console.ReadKey()
End Sub
End Class
End Namespace
```

Program # 4

Write a program that invokes a method using the Action delegate. The method takes a single integer parameter.
C# Program

```
using System;

namespace MainProgramNamespace
{
class MainProgramClass
{
static void Main(string[] args)
{
//Declare an instance of the Action Delegate that takes a single //integer
parameter

Action<int> instActionDelegate;

//Instantiate the instance of Action delegate by assigning a method
instActionDelegate = displayValue;

//Invoke the assigned or referenced method
```

```
instActionDelegate(5);

Console.WriteLine("Press any key to exit program");
Console.ReadKey();
}
static void displayValue(int x)
{
Console.WriteLine("The value received from calling point");
Console.WriteLine(x);
}
}
}
```

Program # 5

Write a program that invokes an anonymous method using the Action delegate. The anonymous method takes a single integer parameter.
C# Program

```
using System;

namespace MainProgramNamespace
{
class MainProgramClass
{
static void Main(string[] args)
{
//Declare an instance of the Action Delegate that takes a single //integer
parameter

Action<int> instActionDelegate;

//Instantiate the instance of Action delegate by assigning an //anonymous
method


instActionDelegate = delegate(int x)
{
```

```
Console.WriteLine("The value received from calling point");
Console.WriteLine(x);
};

//Invoke the assigned or referenced anonymous method
instActionDelegate(5);

Console.WriteLine("Press any key to exit program");
Console.ReadKey();
}
}
}
```

Visual Basic Program

```
Namespace MainProgramNamespace

Class MainProgramClass

Public Shared Sub Main()

'Declare an instance of the Action Delegate that takes a single 'integer parameter

Dim instActionDelegate As Action(Of Integer)

'Instantiate the instance of Action delegate by assigning an 'anonymous method

instActionDelegate = Sub(x As Integer)
Console.WriteLine("The value received from calling point")
Console.WriteLine(x)
End Sub

'Invoke the assigned or referenced anonymous method
instActionDelegate(5)

Console.WriteLine("Press any key to exit program")
Console.ReadKey()
```

```
End Sub
End Class
End Namespace
```

Program # 6

Write a program that invokes a method using the Action delegate. The method takes two float values as parameters and displays their sum.

C# Program

```
using System;

namespace MainProgramNamespace
{
class MainProgramClass
{
static void Main(string[] args)
{
//Declare an instance of the Action Delegate that takes two float //parameters

Action<float, float> instActionDelegate;

//Instantiate the instance of Action delegate by assigning a named //method
addTwoValues()

instActionDelegate = addTwoValues;

//Invoke the assigned or referenced method using the instance of //Action
delegate

instActionDelegate(2.5f, 3.5f);

Console.WriteLine("Press any key to exit program");
Console.ReadKey();
}
static void addTwoValues(float a, float b)
{
```

```
Console.WriteLine("The sum of two values = " + (a + b));
}
}
}
```

The above program adds two float values and displays their result. The program uses a method addTwoValues() that takes two float values as parameters and it is invoked by the instance of Action delegate instActionDelegate.

Program # 7

Write a program that invokes an anonymous method using the Action delegate. The anonymous method takes two float values as parameters and displays their sum.
C# Program

```
using System;

namespace MainProgramNamespace
{
class MainProgramClass
{
static void Main(string[] args)
{
//Declare an instance of the Action Delegate that takes two float //
parameters

Action<float, float> instActionDelegate;

//Instantiate the instance of Action delegate by assigning an //anonymous
method

instActionDelegate = delegate(float a, float b)
{
Console.WriteLine("The sum of two values = " + (a + b));
};

//Invoke the assigned or referenced anonymous method
```

instActionDelegate(2.5f, 3.5f);
 	
Console.WriteLine("Press any key to exit program");
Console.ReadKey();
}
}
}

Visual Basic Program
Namespace MainProgramNamespace Class MainProgramClass Public Shared Sub Main() 'Declare an instance of the Action Delegate that takes two float 'parameters Dim instActionDelegate As Action(Of Single, Single) 'Instantiate the instance of Action delegate by assigning an 'anonymous method instActionDelegate = Sub(a As Single, b As Single) Console.WriteLine("The sum of two values = " & (a + b)) End Sub   'Invoke the assigned or referenced anonymous method instActionDelegate(2.5F, 3.5F) Console.WriteLine("Press any key to exit program") Console.ReadKey() End Sub End Class End Namespace

Program # 8

Write a program that invokes an anonymous method using the Action delegate. The anonymous method takes two float values as parameters and displays their sum. The anonymous method is written in the form of a Lambda Expression.
C# Program

```
using System;

namespace MainProgramNamespace
{
class MainProgramClass
{
static void Main(string[] args)
{
//Declare an instance of the Action Delegate that takes two float //
parameters

Action<float, float> instActionDelegate;

//Instantiate the instance of Action delegate by assigning an //anonymous
method. The anonymous method is written in the //form of a Lambda
Expression that takes two float parameters

instActionDelegate = (a, b) =>
{
Console.WriteLine("The sum of two values = " + (a + b));
};

//Invoke the assigned or referenced anonymous method and pass //two
float values to it

instActionDelegate(2.5f, 3.5f);

Console.WriteLine("Press any key to exit program");
Console.ReadKey();
}
}
}
```

Visual Basic Program
Namespace MainProgramNamespace Class MainProgramClass Public Shared Sub Main() 'Declare an instance of the Action Delegate that takes two float 'parameters Dim instActionDelegate As Action(Of Single, Single) 'Instantiate the instance of Action delegate by assigning an 'anonymous method. The anonymous method is written in the 'form of a Lambda Expression that takes two float parameters instActionDelegate = Function(a, b) Console.WriteLine("The sum of two values = " & (a + b)) End Function 'Invoke the assigned or referenced anonymous method and pass 'two float values to it instActionDelegate(2.5F, 3.5F) Console.WriteLine("Press any key to exit program") Console.ReadKey() End Sub End Class End Namespace

The above program adds two float values and displays their result. The program uses an anonymous method in the form of a Lambda Expression that takes two float parameters and it is invoked by an Action delegate.

Program # 9

Write a program that adds 16 integer values and displays their result using the Action delegate and a Lambda Expression.

C# Program

```
using System;

namespace MainProgramNamespace
{
class MainProgramClass
{
static void Main(string[] args)
{
//Declare an instance of the Action Delegate that takes 16 integer //
parameters

Action<int,int,int,int,int,int,int,int,int,int,int,int,int,int,int,int>
instActionDelegate;

//Instantiate the instance of Action delegate by assigning an //anonymous
method. The anonymous method is written in the form of a Lambda
Expression that takes 16 integer values as //parameters

instActionDelegate = (a, b, d, e, f, g, h, i, j, k, l,m, n,o,p,q) =>
{
Console.WriteLine("The sum of 16 values = " + (a + b + d + e + f + g + h + i
+ j + k + l + m + n + o + p + q));
};

//Invoke the assigned or referenced anonymous method and pass //16
integer values to it
instActionDelegate(1, 2, 3, 4, 5, 6, 7, 8, 9, 3, 4, 5, 6, 6, 3, 8);

Console.WriteLine("Prress any key to exit program");
Console.ReadKey();
}
}
}
```

Func Delegate

Func delegate is used to reference a method and invokes it directly without explicitly declaring a custom delegate reference type. It has a specified set of parameters and it always returns a value. A Func delegate references and invokes a method which has the same or matching parameters and the same or matching return type. Func delegate is similar to the Action delegate but the main difference is that an Action delegate does not return value and its return type is always void whereas a Func delegate always returns a value and its return type is the same as the referenced method. Therefore, a Func delegate invokes a method that has the same or matching parameters and the same or matching return type. The Func delegates are defined in the .NET Framework starting from version 2.0 and it is further extended through different versions of the .NET Framework. The .NET Framework 4.0 defines parameterized Func delegate from single parameter to maximum 16 parameters.

To reference and invoke a method using a Func delegate, an instance of the Func delegate is declared using the Func keyword and assigned the target method to it as parameter. When a method is passed as a parameter to the Func delegate, the Func delegate stores its memory address and the method is referenced to it. The referenced method can be invoked by simply calling the associated instance of the Func delegate and provide values to its parameters if the referenced method takes parameters otherwise, the input parameters list of the Func delegate would be blank. The parameters of Func delegate are generic type parameters and they take any type of values depend on the referenced method.

Func delegate is a fixed and limited delegate reference type which is bounded to some specific number of parameters. Microsoft .NET provides a series of fixed Func delegates in the System namespace which are used to invoke both parameter-less and parameterized methods maximum up to 16 parameters. The return type of the Func delegate is defined inside in the parameters list of the Func delegate as out parameter. The parameterized Func delegate takes input parameters from 1 to 16 parameters and also contains an out parameter that indicates the return value of the Func delegate. Therefore, if a method takes no parameters, the referenced Func delegate will take no input parameters and will take only the output parameter that indicates the return value, if a method takes a single parameter, the referenced delegate will take one input parameter that matched the parameters of the referenced method and one output parameter that indicates the return value, if a method takes two parameters, the referenced Func delegate will take two input parameters that matched the parameters of the referenced method and one output parameter that indicates the return value, if a method takes three parameters, the referenced Func delegate will take three input parameters that matched the parameters of the referenced method and one output parameter that indicates the return value of the Func delegate and so on. Following is the general syntax to declare a parameter-less Func delegate:

C# Syntax
public delegate TResult Func<out TResult>()
Visual Basic Syntax
Public Delegate Function Func(Of Out TResult) As TResult

The above declaration declares a parameter-less Func delegate. The parameter-less Func delegate invokes a method that has no parameters but returns a value. The keyword **out** represents the output parameter and **TResult** represents the return type of the referenced method. Following is the general syntax to declare parameterized Func delegate that take more than one parameters:

C# Syntax

```
//The declaration of a single parameter Func delegate
public delegate TResult Func<in T, out TResult>(T arg)

//The declaration of two parameters Func delegate
public delegate TResult Func<in T1, in T2, out TResult>
                        (
                        T1 arg1,
                        T2 arg2
                        )

//The declaration of three parameters Func delegate
public delegate TResult Func<in T1, in T2, in T3, out TResult>
                        (
                        T1 arg1,
                        T2 arg2,
                        T3 arg3
                        )

//The declaration of 16 parameters Func delegate
public delegate TResult Func <in T1, in T2, in T3, in T4,--------,
in T16, out TResult>
                        (
                        T1 arg1,
```

```
T2 arg2,
T3 arg3,
T4 arg4,
----------
----------
----------
T16 arg16
)
```

Visual Basic Syntax

```
'The declaration of a single parameter Func delegate
Public Delegate Function Func(Of In T, Out TResult) (arg As T)
As TResult

'The declaration of two parameters Func delegate
Public Delegate Sub Action(Of In T1, In T2, Out TResult)
        (
        arg1 As T1,
        arg2 As T2
        )

'The declaration of three parameters Func delegate
Public Delegate Sub Action(Of In T1, In T2, In T3, Out TResult)
        (
        arg1 As T1,
        arg2 As T2,
        arg3 As T3
        )

'The declaration of 16 parameters Func delegate
Public Delegate Sub Action(Of In T1, In T2, In T3, In T4,-----,
In T16, Out TResult)
        (
        arg1 As T1,
        arg2 As T2,
        arg3 As T3,
        arg4 As T4
        )
```

In the above declaration of Func delegate, the **in** or **In** represents the input parameters of the referenced methods, the T represents the type of the input parameter of a single parameter referenced or associated method, the arg represents the actual parameter of a single parameter referenced or associated method, the values from T1 to T16 represent the type of the input parameters of the referenced or associated methods that take more than one parameter, and the values from arg1 to arg16 represent the actual parameters of the referenced or associated methods that take more than one parameter. The type of a parameter is general type parameter and it takes any type of values such as int, float, double, long double, string etc. T1 represents the type of the first parameter of a referenced method, T2 represents the type of the second parameter of a referenced method, T3 represents the type of the third parameter of a referenced method, and T16 represents the type of the sixteenth parameter of a referenced method. The arg1 represents the first parameter, arg2 represents the second parameter, and arg16 represents the sixteenth parameter of a referenced or associated method. The **TResult** is an out parameter that represents the return value of the referenced method.

Program # 1

Write a program that invokes a parameter-less method using a parameter-less Func delegate. When the method invokes then it returns a string message to the calling point.

C# Program

```
using System;

namespace MainProgramNamespace
{
class MainProgramClass
{
static void Main(string[] args)
{
//Declare an instance of the parameter-less Func delegate that //returns a
string value

Func<string> instFuncDelegate;

//Instantiate the instance of Func delegate by assigning a method //that
returns a string value
```

```
instFuncDelegate = displayMessage;

//Invoke the assigned or referenced method and declare a string //variable
to catch the returned string value of the method

string msg = instFuncDelegate();

//Display the returned Messsage
Console.WriteLine(msg);

Console.WriteLine("Press any key to exit program");
Console.ReadKey();
}
static string displayMessage()
{
return "Welcome to the Func Delegate";
}
}
}
```

Visual Basic Program

```
Namespace MainProgramNamespace

Class MainProgramClass

Public Shared Function displayMessage() As String
Return "Welcome to the Func Delegate"
End Function

Public Shared Sub Main()

'Declare an instance of the parameter-less Func delegate that 'returns a string
value

Dim instFuncDelegate As Func(Of String)

'Instantiate the instance of Func delegate by assigning a method 'that returns
a string value
```

```
instFuncDelegate = AddressOf displayMessage

'Invoke the assigned or referenced method and declare a string 'variable to catch the returned string value of the method

Dim msg As String = instFuncDelegate()

'Display the returned Messsage
Console.WriteLine(msg)

Console.WriteLine("Press any key to exit program")
Console.ReadKey()
End Sub

End Class
End Namespace
```

Program # 2

Write a program that invokes a parameter-less anonymous method using a parameter-less Func delegate. When the anonymous method invokes then it returns a string message to the calling point.
C# Program

```
using System;

namespace MainProgramNamespace
{
class MainProgramClass
{
static void Main(string[] args)
{
//Declare an instance of the parameter-less Func delegate that //returns a string value

Func<string> instFuncDelegate;

//Instantiate the instance of Func delegate by assigning an //anonymous method that returns a string value
```

```
instFuncDelegate = delegate()
{
return "Welcome to the Func Delegate";
};

//Invoke the assigned or referenced anonymous method and //declare a string variable to catch the return string value of the //anonymous method

string msg = instFuncDelegate();

//Display the returned Messsage
Console.WriteLine(msg);

Console.WriteLine("Press any key to exit program");
Console.ReadKey();
}
}
}
```

Visual Basic Program

```
Namespace MainProgramNamespace

Class MainProgramClass

Public Shared Sub Main()

'Declare an instance of the parameter-less Func delegate that 'returns a string value

Dim instFuncDelegate As Func(Of String)

'Instantiate the instance of Func delegate by assigning an 'anonymous method that returns a string value

instFuncDelegate = Function() "Welcome to the Func Delegate"

'Invoke the assigned or referenced anonymous method and 'declare a string variable to catch the return string value of the 'anonymous method
```

```
Dim msg As String = instFuncDelegate()

'Display the returned Messsage
Console.WriteLine(msg)

Console.WriteLine("Press any key to exit program")
Console.ReadKey()
End Sub
End Class
End Namespace
```

Program # 3

Write a program that invokes a parameter-less anonymous method using a parameter-less Func delegate. When the anonymous method invokes then it returns a string message to the calling point. The anonymous method is written in the form of a Lambda Expression.

C# Program

```
using System;

namespace MainProgramNamespace
{
class MainProgramClass
{
static void Main(string[] args)
{
//Declare an instance of the parameter-less Func Delegate that //returns a string value

Func<string> instFuncDelegate;

//Instantiate the instance of the Func delegate by assigning an //anonymous method that returns a string value. The anonymous //method is written in the form of a Lambda Expression

instFuncDelegate = () =>
```

```
{
return "Welcome to the Func Delegate";
};

//Invoke the assigned or referenced anonymous method and //declare a string variable to catch the return string value of the //anonymous method

string msg = instFuncDelegate();

//Display the returned Messsage
Console.WriteLine(msg);

Console.WriteLine("Press any key to exit program");
Console.ReadKey();
}
}
}
```

Visual Basic Program

```
Namespace MainProgramNamespace

Class MainProgramClass

Public Shared Sub Main()

'Declare an instance of the parameter-less Func delegate that 'returns a string value

Dim instFuncDelegate As Func(Of String)

'Instantiate the instance of the Func delegate by assigning an 'anonymous method that returns a string value. The anonymous 'method is written in the form of a Lambda Expression

instFuncDelegate = Function()
Return "Welcome to the Func Delegate"
End Function
```

```
'Invoke the assigned or referenced anonymous method and 'declare a string variable to catch the return string value of the 'anonymous method

Dim msg As String = instFuncDelegate()

'Display the returned Messsage
Console.WriteLine(msg)

Console.WriteLine("Press any key to exit program")
Console.ReadKey()
End Sub
End Class
End Namespace
```

Program # 4

Write a program that invokes a method using the Func delegate. The method takes two float values as parameters and returns their sum to the calling point.

C# Program

```
using System;

namespace MainProgramNamespace
{
class MainProgramClass
{
static void Main(string[] args)
{
//Declare an instance of the Func delegate that takes two float //parameters and returns a float value

Func<float, float, float> instFuncDelegate;

//Instantiate the instance of the Func delegate by assigning a //named method addTwoValues() that takes two float values as //parameters and returns a float value to the calling point

instFuncDelegate = addTwoValues;
```

```
//Invoke the assigned or referenced method using the instance of //the Func delegate and pass two float values to it and declare a //float variable to catch the returned value of the method

float result = instFuncDelegate(2.5f, 3.5f);

//Display the returned result of the method

Console.WriteLine("The sum of two values = " + result);
Console.WriteLine("Press any key to exit program");
Console.ReadKey();
}
static float addTwoValues(float a, float b)
{
return a + b;
}
}
}
```

The above program adds two float values and displays their result. The program uses a named method addTwoValues() that takes two float values as parameters and it is invoked by the instance of Func delegate instFuncDelegate.

Program # 5

Write a program that invokes an anonymous method using the Func delegate. The anonymous method takes two float values as parameters and returns their sum to the calling point.
C# Program

```
using System;

namespace MainProgramNamespace
{
class MainProgramClass
{
static void Main(string[] args)
{
//Declare an instance of the Func Delegate that takes two float //parameters and returns a float value
```

```
Func<float, float, float> instFuncDelegate;

//Instantiate the instance of the Func delegate by assigning an //anonymous method that takes two float values as parameters and //return a float value to the caling point

instFuncDelegate = delegate(float a, float b)
{
return a + b;
};

//Invoke the assigned or referenced anonymous method using the //instance of the Func delegate and pass two float values to it and //declare a float variable to catch the returned value of the //anonymous method

float result = instFuncDelegate(2.5f, 3.5f);

//Display the returned result of the anonymous method

Console.WriteLine("The sum of two values = " + result);

Console.WriteLine("Press any key to exit program");
Console.ReadKey();
}
}
}
```

Visual Basic Program

```
Namespace MainProgramNamespace

Class MainProgramClass

Public Shared Sub Main()

'Declare an instance of the Func Delegate that takes two float 'parameters and returns a float value

Dim instFuncDelegate As Func(Of Single, Single, Single)
```

```
'Instantiate the instance of the Func delegate by assigning an 'anonymous
method that takes two float values as parameters and 'return a float value to
the calling point

instFuncDelegate = Function(a As Single, b As Single)
Return a + b
End Function


'Invoke the assigned or referenced anonymous method using the 'instance of
the Func delegate and pass two float values to it and 'declare a float variable
to catch the returned value of the 'anonymous method

Dim result As Single = instFuncDelegate(2.5F, 3.5F)

'Display the returned result of the anonymous method

Console.WriteLine("The sum of two values = " & result)

Console.WriteLine("Press any key to exit program")
Console.ReadKey()
End Sub
End Class
End Namespace
```

Program # 6

Write a program that invokes an anonymous method using the Func delegate. The anonymous method takes two float values as parameters and returns their sum to the calling point. The anonymous method is written in the form of a Lambda Expression.
C# Program

```
using System;

namespace MainProgramNamespace
{
class MainProgramClass
{
static void Main(string[] args)
```

```
{
//Declare an instance of the Func Delegate that takes two float //parameters and returns a float value

Func<float, float, float> instFuncDelegate;

//Instantiate the instance of the Func delegate by assigning an //anonymous method that takes two float values as parameters and //return a float value to the caling point. The anonymous method //is written in the form of a Lambda Expression

instFuncDelegate = (a, b) =>
{
return a + b;
};

//Invoke the assigned or referenced anonymous method using the //instance of the Func delegate and pass two float values to it and //declare a float variable to catch the returned value of the //anonymous method

float result = instFuncDelegate(2.5f, 3.5f);

//Display the returned result of the anonymous method

Console.WriteLine("The sum of two values = " + result);

Console.WriteLine("Press any key to exit program");
Console.ReadKey();
}
}
}
```

Visual Basic Program

```
Namespace MainProgramNamespace

Class MainProgramClass

Public Shared Sub Main()
```

```
'Declare an instance of the Func Delegate that takes two float 'parameters and returns a float value

Dim instFuncDelegate As Func(Of Single, Single, Single)

'Instantiate the instance of the Func delegate by assigning an 'anonymous method that takes two float values as parameters and 'return a float value to the calling point. The anonymous method is 'written in the form of a Lambda Expression

instFuncDelegate = Function(a, b)
Return a + b
End Function

'Invoke the assigned or referenced anonymous method using the 'instance of the Func delegate and pass two float values to it and 'declare a float variable to catch the returned value of the 'anonymous method

Dim result As Single = instFuncDelegate(2.5F, 3.5F)

'Display the returned result of the anonymous method

Console.WriteLine("The sum of two values = " & result)

Console.WriteLine("Press any key to exit program")
Console.ReadKey()
End Sub
End Class
End Namespace
```

Anonymous Method

Anonymous method is an unnamed method that contains only body without a name or identifier and it is invoked by the delegates. An anonymous method is referenced or associated with a delegate and it cannot be invoked explicitly or directly without the using of delegate. The body of anonymous method is surrounded by curly braces and it contains the inline code. The anonymous method is used when we have a small task or operation and we want to perform it inline. An anonymous method is similar to a named method but the main difference is that a named method has a specified name, an access modifier, a return type, a parameters list that contains zero or more parameters, and a body that contains a block of code whereas an anonymous method is an unnamed method that has no name or identifier, no access modifier, and no return type and its declaration always starts from the keyword delegate followed by the parameters list and the method body. The parameters list of an anonymous method may contain zero or more parameters and they are surrounded by small braces. An anonymous method does not need to specify its return type but it allows us to return a value using the return statement. A named method can be invoked directly or explicitly by simply calling its name while an anonymous method cannot be invoked directly or explicitly like a named method but it can be invoked implicitly using a delegate. To invoke an anonymous method, an instance of the delegate is declared and the anonymous method is referenced or associated with it. When an anonymous method is referenced or associated with an instance of the delegate then it is invoked by calling that instance and pass values to its parameters if it takes parameters. An anonymous method can be referenced or associated with an instance of the delegate by assigning the anonymous method to it as a parameter. When an anonymous method is assigned to an instance of the delegate as a parameter, the instance of the delegate stores its memory address and the method is referenced or associated with it.

A delegate can reference and invoke an anonymous method that has the matching parameters with it. It means that the parameters of the delegate and the parameters of the referenced or associated anonymous method must be the same. For example, if an anonymous method does not take any parameter then it can be referenced and invoked by an instance of a delegate that does not take any parameter similarly, if an anonymous method takes a single integer parameter, then we must declare an instance of the delegate that takes a single integer parameter and so on. Following is the general syntax to declare a parameter-less anonymous method:

C# Declaration Syntax
instDelegate = delegate() {-Body of the anonymous method-}; Or

instDelegate = delegate()
{
[-Body of the anonymous Method-]
};

Visual Basic Declaration Syntax
instDelegate = Sub() [-Body of the anonymous method-] Or instDelegate = Sub() ------------------------- [-Body of the Anonymous Method-] ------------------------- End Sub

In the above declaration, the instDelegate is an instance of the parameter-less delegate that does not take any parameter and it references a parameter-less anonymous method. The [-Body of the Anonymous Method-] indicates the body of the anonymous method that contains the inline code. Following is the general syntax to declare a parameterized anonymous method that takes the specified number of parameters:

C# Declaration Syntax

instDelegate = delegate(ParametersList) {[-Body of Method-]};
 	
Or
 	
instDelegate = delegate(ParametersList)
{
[-Body of Method-]
};

Visual Basic Declaration Syntax
instDelegate = Sub(ParametersList) [-Body of Method-] Or instDelegate = Sub(ParametersList)

```
-----------------------------------------
[-Body of Method-]
-----------------------------------------
End Sub
```

In the above declaration, the instDelegate is an instance of the parameterized delegate that takes one or more parameters according to the method it references and invokes for example, if the anonymous method takes a single integer parameter, then it must take a single integer parameter, similarly if an anonymous method takes one integer and one float parameter then it must take one integer and one float parameters and so on. The ParametersList indicates a list of parameters of the anonymous method that contains one or more parameters. The [-Body of Method-] indicates the body of the anonymous method that contains the inline code.

Program # 1

Write a program that displays a message on the screen using a parameter-less anonymous method.
C# Program

```
using System;

namespace ProgramNamespace
{
//Define a delegate reference type that references or associates a //parameter-less anonymous method which have no parameters and //does not return value

delegate void MyDelegate();

public class MainProgramClass
{
public static void Main()
{
//Declare an instance of the delegate MyDelegate reference type
MyDelegate instDelegate;
```

```
//Reference or associate the parameter-less anonymous method //with the instance of the delegate instDelegate by assigning the //anonymous method to it as parameter using a single line //assignment

instDelegate = delegate() {Console.WriteLine("Hello");};

//We can also reference or associate the anonymous method with //the instance of the delegate instDelegate by assigning the //anonymous method to it as parameter using the multiple lines //assignment

instDelegate = delegate()
{
Console.WriteLine("Hello");

};

//Invoke the anonymous method that displays a message on the //screen

instDelegate();

Console.WriteLine("Press any key to exit ");
Console.ReadKey();
}
}
}
```

Visual Basic Program

```
Imports System
Namespace ProgramNamespace

'Define a Delegate reference type that references or associates a 'parameter-less anonymous method which have no parameters and 'does not return value

Delegate Sub MyDelegate()

Public Class MainProgramClass
```

```
Public Shared Sub Main()

'Declare an instance of the delegate MyDelegate reference type
Dim instDelegate As MyDelegate

'Reference or associate the parameter-less anonymous method with 'the instance of the delegate instDelegate by assigning the 'anonymous method to it as a parameter using a single line 'assignment

instDelegate = Sub() Console.WriteLine("Hello")

'We can also reference or associate the anonymous method with the 'instance of the delegate instDelegate by assigning the anonymous 'method to it as parameter using the multiple lines assignment

instDelegate = Sub()
Console.WriteLine("Hello")
End Sub

'Invoke the anonymous method that displays a message on the 'screen

instDelegate()

Console.WriteLine("Press any key to exit ")
Console.ReadKey()

End Sub
End Class
End Namespace
```

The above program displays Hello on the screen using an anonymous method. In the program, we defined a delegate reference type MyDelegate that has no parameters and does not return value. In the main method of the program, we declared an instance instDelegate of the delegate reference type MyDelegate and it is instantiated by assigning an anonymous method that has no parameters and does not return any value. The instance instDelegate of MyDelegate reference type is then used and invoke the referenced anonymous method.

Program # 2

Write a program that adds two integer values using an anonymous method. The anonymous method takes two integer parameters and returns their sum to the calling point.
C# Program

```
using System;

namespace ProgramNamespace
{
//Define a Delegate reference type that references or associates an //
anonymous method having two integer parameters and return an //integer
value

delegate int MyDelegate(int x, int y);

public class MainProgramClass
{
public static void Main()
{
//Declare an instance of the delegate MyDelegate reference type
MyDelegate instDelegate;

//Reference or associate the parameterized anonymous method //with the
instance of the delegate instDelegate by assigning the //anonymous method
to it as parameter using a single line //assignment

instDelegate = delegate(int x, int y) {return x + y;};

//We can also reference or associate the anonymous method with //the
instance of the delegate instDelegate by assigning the //anonymous method
to it as parameter using multiple lines //assignment

instDelegate = delegate(int x, int y)
{
return x + y;
```

```
};

//Invoke the anonymous method and pass two integer values to it //and declare an integer variable to store the result of the //anonymous method

int result = instDelegate(2, 3);

//Display the result of the anonymous method
Console.WriteLine("The sum of two values = " + result);
Console.WriteLine("Press any key to exit ");
Console.ReadKey();
}
}
}
```

Visual Basic Program

```
Imports System
Namespace ProgramNamespace

'Define a Delegate reference type that references or associates an 'anonymous method having two integer parameters and return an 'integer value

Delegate Function MyDelegate(x As Integer, y As Integer) As Integer

Public Class MainProgramClass

Public Shared Sub Main()

'Declare an instance of the delegate MyDelegate reference type
Dim instDelegate As MyDelegate

'Reference or associate the parameterized anonymous method with 'the instance of the delegate instDelegate by assigning the 'anonymous method to it as parameter using a single line 'assignment

instDelegate = Function(x As Integer, y As Integer) x + y
```

```
'We can also reference or associate the anonymous method with the 'instance of the delegate instDelegate by assigning the anonymous 'method to it as parameter using multiple lines assignment

instDelegate = Function(x As Integer, y As Integer)
Return (x + y)
End Function

'Invoke the anonymous method and pass two integer values to it 'and declare an integer variable to store the result of the anonymous 'method

Dim result As Integer = instDelegate(2, 3)

'Display the result of the anonymous method
Console.WriteLine("The sum of two values = " & result)

Console.WriteLine("Press any key to exit ")
Console.ReadKey()

End Sub
End Class
End Namespace
```

Lambda Expression

Lambda expression is a simplified form of an anonymous method that is used to write an anonymous method without its declaration in the form of an expression. It divides an anonymous method into two parts and makes an expression by placing an operator called Lambda operator. The declaration of an anonymous method always starts from a keyword delegate followed by a parameters list and its body. The parameters list of an anonymous method may contain zero or more parameters and each parameter requires its data type specification for example, if an anonymous method takes one or more parameters then we must specify the data type of each parameter. A Lambda Expression reduces a keyword delegate and the data type specifications of the parameters and it allows us to write an anonymous method without the using of the keyword delegate and the data type specifications of its parameters. The Lambda Expression allows us an option to declare all the input parameters of an anonymous method with their data type specifications or simply provide the names of the input parameters without their data type specifications. The compiler automatically manages the data types of the input parameters from the usage. A Lambda expression contains two parts separated by an operator called Lambda Operator. The Lambda operator is the combination of an equal operator and a greater than operator and it is represented as =>. The Lambda operator is placed between the two parts of the Lambda Expression in which the left side part of the Lambda Expression indicates the input parameters list of the anonymous method surrounded by small braces and the right side part of the Lambda Expression indicates the body of the anonymous method. The body of an anonymous method may contain a single or multiple statements. If body of an anonymous method contains a single statement, then usually it is written on the same line with the Lambda operator and if body of an anonymous method contains multiple statements, then it is surrounded by the curly braces {} just like an anonymous method.

To write an anonymous method using a Lambda Expression, it divides the anonymous method into two parts such as a parameters list and body of the anonymous method. The left side part of the Lambda Expression takes the input parameters of an anonymous method without its parameters data type specifications. It just takes the names of the input parameters and there is no need to specify their data types because the compiler automatically inferred the data types of the input parameters from the usage. The right side part of the Lambda Expression takes the body of the anonymous method. The Lambda Expression is introduced in C# 3.0. Following is the general syntax to declare a Lambda Expression:

```
([InputParametersList]) => {[BodyOfAnonymousMethod]};
```

The above syntax is a general syntax of a Lambda Expression that writes an anonymous method in two parts and makes an expression. The left side part of the Lambda Expression is ([InputParametersList]) that indicates the number of input parameters of an anonymous method, the sign => indicates the Lambda operator, and the right side part of the Lambda Expression is [BodyOfAnonymousMethod] that indicates the body of an anonymous method. If body of an anonymous method contains more than one statement, then the body is surrounded by curly braces and the above syntax can be written as:

```
([InputParametersList]) => {[BodyOfAnonymousMethod]};

Or

([InputParametersList]) =>
{
BodyOfAnonymousMethod
};
```

Benefits of using Lambda Expression

The Lambda Expression is a best choice to use it in the program to reduce the block of code and makes it easier and understandable. It reduces the complexity of an anonymous method and makes it simplify and shorter. A Lambda Expression reduces the delegate keyword from the declaration of an anonymous method and the data type specifications of its parameters. The main use of a Lambda Expression is to access the LINQ. If we want to access LINQ in our program code, the Lambda Expression is a best choice to access the LINQ.

Write a program that displays a message on the screen using a parameter-less anonymous method. The anonymous method uses a Lambda Expression.
C# Program

```
using System;

namespace ProgramNamespace
{
//Define a delegate reference type that references or associates a //parameter-less anonymous method in the form of a Lambda //Expression which have no parameters and does not return value

delegate void MyDelegate();

public class MainProgramClass
{
public static void Main()
{
//Declare an instance of the delegate MyDelegate reference type
```

```
MyDelegate instDelegate;

//Reference the Lambda Expression with the instance of the //delegate instDelegate

instDelegate = () => {Console.WriteLine("Hello");};

//Invoke the Lambda Expression using the instance of the delegate
instDelegate();

Console.WriteLine("Press any key to exit ");
Console.ReadKey();
}
}
}
```

CHAPTER 13

Collections in .NET

CHAPTER CONTENTS

- Collections
- IEnumerable Interface
- IEnumerable<T> Interface
- ICollection Interface
- IList Interface
- IDictionary Interface
- Non-generic Collections
- ArrayList
- SortedList
- DictionaryEntry Structure
- Stack
- Queue
- Hashtable
- Generic Collections
- List<T>
- SortedList<TKey,TValue>
- KeyValuePair<TKey, TValue> Structure
- Dictionary<TKey, TValue>
- Stack<T>

Collections

A Collection is a data structure which is used to store data in different forms such as in the form of List, Stack, Queue, ArrayList, SortedList, HashTable, BitArray, generic List, generic Stack, generic Queue, Dictionary, generic SortedList, and generic Queue etc. Each form of a Collection is a separate class that allows us to declare objects and store data in a collection. Each collection stores data temporary in the computer memory. There are two types of collections in the .NET i.e. non-generic collections and generic collections. The non-generic collections are defined in the System.Collections namespace and generic collections are defined in the System.Collections.Generic namespace. Each collection class provides properties and methods to perform different operations on the data. The main difference between the non-generic and generic collections is that the non-generic collections store data of different data types at the same time such as int, float, double, and string etc and they store all the elements as object type whereas the generic collections store data of the same data type at the same time. Generic collections are faster than non-generic collections because the type casting (Boxing) is happen in case of non generic collections. Boxing is a process of converting in which a value type is converted into an object type. Generic collections were introduced in .NET framework 2.0. Each collection class implements the IEnumerable interface therefore, values can be accessed from the collections using the **foreach** loop.

IEnumerable Interface

IEnumerable is a base interface for all the non-generic collections that can be enumerated. The IEnumerable interface is defined in the namespace System.Collections. The IEnumerable interface defines a single method GetEnumerator. The GetEnumerator method is used to return an object of the IEnumerator interface that iterates through a collection. The IEnumerator is the base interface for all the non-generic enumerators. The object of IEnumerator interface can be used with foreach statement to read data in the collection. The IEnumerator interface defines two methods and one property. The methods are Reset() method and MoveNext() method and the property is Current property. The Reset() method is used to set the position of the IEnumerator before the first element of the collection. The MoveNext() method is used to move the IEnumerator to the next element of the collection. The Current property is used to get the current element of the collection. The object of IEnumerator retrieves data as a read-only stream of data that does not allow modification. To get data from a collection, initially, the IEnumerator object is positioned before the first element in the collection or the Reset() method is used to bring the IEnumerator position before the first element in the collection then the MoveNext() method is used to advance or move the IEnumerator to the first element of the collection and the Current property is used to get the current element of the collection and then the MoveNext() method is used to move the IEnumerator to the next element of the collection and on this way the entire elements of the collection are retrieved.

IEnumerable<T> Interface

It is a base interface for all the generic collections defined in the namespace System.Collections.Generic such as List<T>, Queue<T>, Stack<T>,

LinkedList<T>, Dictionary<T>, SortedList<T>, HashSet<T> etc. The IEnumerable<T> interface inherited from the IEnumerable interface. Therefore a type which implements the IEnumerable<T> interface will also implement members of the IEnumerable interface. The IEnumerable<T> interface defines a single method GetEnumerator which returns an object of the IEnumerator<T> interface. The IEnumerator<T> is the base interface for all the generic enumerators. The object of IEnumerator<T> interface can be used with foreach statement to read data in the collection. The IEnumerator<T> interface defines a single property and three methods. The property is Current property and methods are Reset() method, MoveNext() method, and Dispose() Method. The Current property is used to get the element in the collection at the current position of the enumerator.

ICollection Interface

This interface defines the size, enumerators, and synchronization methods for non-generic collections. It is inherited from IEnumerable interface. The ICollection interface is the base interface for classes in the System.Collections namespace. A class which implements ICollection interface will also implements IEnumerable interface, therefore any class that implements the ICollection interface can also be enumerated using the foreach statement.

Properties of ICollection

The ICollection interface defines the following properties:

Property	Description
Count	This property is used to get or count the number of elements of the ICollection. It returns an integer value that indicates the number of elements contained in the ICollection.
IsSynchronized	This property is used to get a value that indicates whether access to the ICollection is synchronized or not. It returns true if access to the ICollection is synchronized otherwise, it returns false.
SyncRoot	This property is used to get an object that can be used to synchronize access to the ICollection.

Methods of ICollection

The ICollection interface defines the following methods:

Method	Description
CopyTo(Array, Int32)	This method is used to copy the elements of the ICollection into an Array starting at a specified array index. It takes two parameters. The first parameter is Array type parameter that specifies the destination array to which elements are to be copied from the ICollection. The second parameter is an integer parameter that specifies the index position in the destination array at which the copying operation begins.
GetEnumerator()	This method is inherited from the IEnumerable interface.

IList Interface

The IList interface represents a non-generic collection of objects from which the elements can be accessed or retrieved using their index positions. It is inherited from ICollection, and IEnumerable interfaces.

Properties of IList Interface

The IList interface inherited the properties of ICollection interface and also defines the following properties:

Property	Description
IsFixedSize	This property is used to get a value that indicates whether the IList has a fixed size or not. It returns a Boolean value either true or false. If the IList has a fixed size, it returns true otherwise, it returns false.
IsReadOnly	This property is used to get a value that indicates whether the IList is read-only or not. It returns a Boolean value either true or false. If the IList is read only, it returns true otherwise, it returns false.

Item[Int32]	This property is used to get or set the element at the specified index position of the IList. It takes an integer parameter that specifies the index position of the element to get or set.
Count	Inherited from ICollection interface.
IsSynchronized	Inherited from ICollection interface.
SynRoot	Inherited from ICollection interface.

Methods of IList

The IList interface inherited the methods of ICollection, and IEnumerable interfaces and also defines the following methods:

Methods	Description
Add(Object)	This method is used to add an element to the IList. It takes a single parameter of object type that specifies any type of element to be added into the IList such as int, float, double string etc. When an element is added into the IList, it returns an integer value that indicates the index position of the inserted element. If the element is not added into the IList, it returns -1.
Clear()	This method is used to remove all items from the IList.
Contains(Object)	This method is used to determine whether the IList contains a specific element or not. It takes an element as parameter and searched the entire IList for that element. If the element is found in the IList, it returns true otherwise, it returns false.
IndexOf(Object)	This method is used to find the index position of a specific element in the IList. It takes an element as parameter and searched the entire IList for that element. If the element is found, it returns the index position of that element otherwise, it returns -1.

Insert(Int32, Object)	This method is used to insert a new element into the IList at a specified index position. It takes two parameters. The first parameter is an integer value that specifies the index position of the IList where the element is to be inserted. The second parameter is an object type parameter that specifies an element to be inserted in the IList.
Remove(Object)	This method is used to remove the first occurrence of a specific element from the IList. It takes a single parameter of object type that specifies the element to be removed from the IList.
RemoveAt(Int32)	This method is used to remove an element from the IList at the specified index position. It takes an integer value that specifies the index position of the element to be removed from the IList.
CopyTo(Array, Int32)	Inherited from ICollection interface.
GetEnumerator()	Inherited from IEnumerable interface.

IDictionary Interface

This interface represents a non-generic collection that is based on key-value pairs. The key-value pairs mean a collection that stores data in such a way that each entry in a collection contains a Key and a value. The keys and values in a collection can be of any data type but in a single collection all the keys must have the same data type. Each key in a collection is unique and cannot be duplicated because each key uniquely identifies the value. The key in a collection must not be null whereas the value can be null or duplicated. The IDictionary interface is inherited from the ICollection, and IEnumerable interfaces. The IDictionary interface is the base interface for all non-generic collections based on key-value pairs. The IDictionary interface inherited the properties and methods of the ICollection and IEnumerable interfaces.

Non-Generic Collections

The non-generic collections are used to store data of different data types. Each non-generic collection stores data of different data types in the form of object therefore, to retrieve elements from a non-generic collection, each element needs to cast it to the appropriate type or use the implicit type *var* keyword. Each non-generic collection is a class in .NET framework. The non-generic collections classes are defined in the namespace System.Collections. The base interface of all non-generic collections is IEnumerable interface. Following is a list of non-generic collections:

- ArrayList
- SortedList
- Stack
- Queue
- Hashtable

ArrayList

ArrayList is used to store data of any data type like an array. It stores each element in the form of object. It is similar to an ordinary array but the main difference is that a single ordinary array can store the same data type elements whereas a single ArrayList can store the elements of multiple data types such as int, float, char, double, and string etc at the same time. An ArrayList does not need to specify its size or limit but it automatically grows its size according to the number of elements inserted. The ArrayList class implements the IList, ICollection, and IEnumerable interfaces therefore, it inherits the properties and methods of these interfaces.

Properties of ArrayList

ArrayList provides the following important properties:

Property	Description
Capacity	This property is used to get or set the capacity or size of the ArrayList. The capacity or size indicates the number of elements that the ArrayList can contain.
Count	This property is used to get the number of elements or count the number of elements of the ArrayList.
IsFixedSize	This property is used to get a value that indicates whether the ArrayList has a fixed size or not.
IsReadOnly	This property is used to get a value that indicates whether the ArrayList is read-only or not.

Item[Int32]	This property is used to get or set an element at a specified index position. It takes an integer parameter that specifies the index position of the element to get or set.

Methods of ArrayList

ArrayList provides the following important methods:

Method	Description
Add() AddRange()	The Add() method is used to add a single element at the end of an ArrayList and AddRange() method is used to add a range of elements from a specified collection into an ArrayList.
Insert() InsertRange()	The Insert() method is used to insert a single element at a specified index position in an ArrayList and InsertRange() method is used to insert a range of elements from a specified ArrayList collection into the target ArrayList collection starting from a specified index position of the ArrayList.
Remove() RemoveRange()	The Remove() method is used to remove a specified element from an ArrayList. It takes a single parameter of type object that specifies the element to be removed from the ArrayList. The RemoveRange() method is used to remove a range of elements from an ArrayList. It takes two integer parameters. The first parameter specifies the index position from where the remove operation starts and second parameter specifies the number of elements to be removed from the ArrayList.
RemoveAt()	This method is used to remove an element at a specified index position from an ArrayList. It takes a single integer parameter that specifies the index position in an ArrayList from where the element is to be removed.
Sort()	This method is used to sort the entire elements of an ArrayList.

Reverse()	This method is used to reverse the order of the entire elements of an ArrayList.
Contains	This method is used to check whether a specified element exists in an ArrayList or not. It returns true if a specified element exist, otherwise it returns false.
Clear	This method is used to remove all the elements from an ArrayList.
CopyTo	This method is used to copy all the elements or a range of elements from an ArrayList into an ordinary array compatible to ArrayList.
GetRange	This method is used to return specified number of elements starting from a specified index position from an ArrayList.
IndexOf	This method is used to search a specified element in an ArrayList. It returns the index position of a specified element if found in the ArrayList. It returns -1, if a specified element did not find in the ArrayList.
ToArray	This method is used to convert an ArrayList into an ordinary array compatible to ArrayList.

Declaration and Initialization of ArrayList

To create ArrayList, an object is declared from the ArrayList class and it is initialized by the new keyword. Following is the declaration and initialization syntax of the ArrayList:

C# Syntax
ArrayList arryList1 = new ArrayList();
Visual Basic Syntax
Dim arrayList1 As ArrayList arryList1 = new ArrayList()

Adding values to ArrayList

To add values to ArrayList, an object of the ArrayList is declared from the ArrayList class and it is initialized by the new keyword. The values can be added to an object of the ArrayList by the following two ways:

- Adding Values Syntax
- Object Initializer Syntax

Adding Values Syntax

In this syntax elements are assigned to an object of the ArrayList using built-in methods of the ArrayList class such as Add() method, AddRange() method, Insert() method, or InsertRange() method. Following is an example of the ArrayList initialization using the Add() method syntax:

```
//C# Initialization and values assignment
ArrayList arryList1 = new ArrayList();
arryList1.Add(1);
arryList1.Add(99);
arryList1.Add("Hello C#");
arryList1.Add(3.2f);
arryList1.Add(5678);
```

```
'Visual Basic Initialization and values assignment
Dim arrayList1 As ArrayList = New ArrayList()
arrayList1.Add(1)
arrayList1.Add(99)
arrayList1.Add("Hello C#")
arrayList1.Add(3.2F)
arrayList1.Add(5678)
```

Object Initializer Syntax

In this syntax, elements are assigned to an object of the ArrayList directly without using any built-in methods of the ArrayList class. In this syntax all the elements are enclosed within curly braces and they are separated from each other by using commas between them. Following is an example of the Object Initializer Syntax:

```
//C# Initialization and values assignment
ArrayList arrayList1 = new ArrayList() {1, 99, "Hello", 3.2f, 5678};
```

```
'Visual Basic Initialization and values assignment
Dim arrayList1 As ArrayList
arrayList1 = New ArrayList() From {1, 99, "Hello", 3.2f, 5678}
```

Accessing ArrayList Elements

The ArrayList elements are accessed using the index value of each element. Each element in an ArrayList has an index position. The index position is zero-based index which always starts from zero. The first element of an ArrayList has index position 0, the second element of an ArrayList has index position 1, and the third element of an ArrayList has index position 2 and so on.

The following example access elements from the ArrayList:

```
ArrayList arryList1 = new ArrayList();
arryList1.Add(1);
arryList1.Add(99);
arryList1.Add("Hello C#");
arryList1.Add(3.2f);
arryList1.Add(5678);

//Access individual elements from the ArrayList using index of the //ArrayList
ArrayList arryList1 = new ArrayList();
int firstElement = (int) myArryList[0]; //It returns 1
int secondElement = (int) myArryList[1]; //It returns 99
string thirdElement = (string) myArryList[2]; //It returns Hello C#
float fourthElement = (float) myArryList[3]; //It returns 3.2
double fourthElement = (double) myArryList[4]; //It returns 5678

//Access individual elements from the ArrayList using index of the //ArrayList
and the implicit type var keyword
var firstElement = myArryList[0]; //It returns 1
var secondElement = myArryList[1]; //It returns 99
var thirdElement = myArryList[2]; //It returns Hello C#
var fourthElement = myArryList[3]; //It returns 3.2
var fourthElement = myArryList[4]; //It returns 5678

//Access elements from an ArrayList using foreach loop to iterate an //ArrayList
ArrayList myArryList = new ArrayList();
arryList1.Add(1);
arryList1.Add(99);
arryList1.Add("Hello C#");
arryList1.Add(3.2f);
arryList1.Add(5678);
```

```
foreach (var v in myArryList)
Console.WriteLine(v);

//The elements of an ArrayList can also be accessed using for loop
for(int i = 0 ; i<ArryList1.Count; i++)
Console.WriteLine(ArryList1[i]);
```

Program # 1

Write a program that inserts data into an ArrayList using the addRange() method.
C# Program

```
using System;
using System.Collections;

namespace ConsoleApplication1
{
class Program
{
static void Main(string[] args)
{
ArrayList arrayList1 = new ArrayList();
arrayList1.Add(1);
arrayList1.Add(2);

ArrayList arrayList2 = new ArrayList();
arrayList2.Add(3);
arrayList2.Add(4);
arrayList2.Add(5);

arrayList2.InsertRange(0, arrayList1);

foreach (var value in arrayList2)

Console.WriteLine(value);

Console.ReadKey();
}
}
}
```

Visual Basic Program
Imports System Imports System.Collections Module Module1 Sub Main() Dim arrayList1 As ArrayList = New ArrayList() arrayList1.Add(1) arrayList1.Add(2) Dim arrayList2 As ArrayList = New ArrayList() arrayList2.Add(3) arrayList2.Add(4) arrayList2.Add(5) arrayList2.InsertRange(0, arrayList1) For Each value In arrayList2 Console.WriteLine(value) Next Console.ReadKey() End Sub End Module

The above program inserts the values of arrayList1 into arrayList2 starting from index position 0. It shifts the values of arrayList2 to the next index positions. The values of arrayList2 will be shifted after index position 1 and they will start from index position 2 because arrayList1 contains two elements and they are inserted in index position 0 and 1.

Program # 2

Write a program that removes an element using Remove() and RemoveAt() methods.

C# Program

ArrayList arrayList1 = new ArrayList();
arrayList1.Add(1);
arrayList1.Add(2);
arrayList1.Add("Hello");
arrayList1.Add(3.2);
arrayList1.Add('c');
 	
//Remove the element "Hello" from ArrayList
arrayList1.Remove("Hello");
 	
//Remove the element from ArrayList at index position 1
arrayList1.RemoveAt(1);
 	
foreach (var value in arrayList1)
Console.WriteLine(value);

Visual Basic Program
Dim arrayList1 As ArrayList = New ArrayList() arrayList1.Add(1) arrayList1.Add(2) arrayList1.Add("Hello") arrayList1.Add(3.2) arrayList1.Add("c") 'Remove the element "Hello" from ArrayList arrayList1.Remove("Hello") 'Remove the element from ArrayList at index position 1 arrayList1.RemoveAt(1) For Each value In arrayList1 Console.WriteLine(value) Next

The above program uses two methods Remove() and RemoveAt(). The Remove() method removes the "Hello" element and RemoveAt() method removes the element at index position 1 therefore, the program would display the output {1, 3.2, c}.

Program # 3

Write a program that removes a range of elements from an ArrayList using RemoveRange() method.
C# Program

ArrayList arrayList1 = new ArrayList();
arrayList1.Add(1);
arrayList1.Add(2);
arrayList1.Add("Hello");
arrayList1.Add(3.2);
arrayList1.Add('c');
 	
//Remove three elements starting from index position 0
arrayList1.RemoveRange(0,3);
 	
foreach(var value in arrayList1)
Console.WriteLine(value);

SortedList

SortedList is a collection that is used to store data in key-value pairs. The key-value pairs mean SortedList stores data in such a way that each entry in a SortedList contains a Key and a value. The keys and values in a SortedList can be of any data type but in a single SortedList all the keys must have the same data type. Each key in a SortedList is unique and cannot be duplicated because each key uniquely identifies the value. The key in a SortedList must not be null whereas the value can be null or duplicated. Therefore, to add an element into a SortedList, two values must be provided, one for the Key and another for the value to be stored in the SortedList collection. The SortedList automatically sorts all the values in ascending order according to the Key. Since SortedList store any type of values therefore, to access values from the SortedList, each value needs to be casted to appropriate data type. SortedList also allows us to access each element using index position of the element. The SortedList internally maintains two arrays of type object, one for the keys and another for the values therefore, SortedList sorts the elements every time when we add new elements or when we delete elements. The SortedList class implements IDictionary, ICollection, and IEnumerable interfaces, therefore values from SortedList can be accessed both by the keys and index position of the elements.

Properties of SortedList

SortedList provides the following important properties:

Property	Description
Capacity	This property is used to get or set the capacity or size of the SortedList. The capacity or size indicates the number of elements that the SortedList can contain.
Count	This property is used to count or get the number of elements contained in the SortedList.
IsFixedSize	This property is used to get a value that indicates whether the SortedList has a fixed size or not.
IsReadOnly	This property is used to get a value that indicates whether the SortedList is read-only or not.
Item[Object]	This property is used to get or set the element at the specified key in the SortedList. It takes an object type parameter that specifies a key associated with the value to get or set.
Keys	This property is used to get a list of keys of a SortedList.
Values	This property is used to get a list of values of a SortedList.

Methods of SortedList

SortedList provides the following important methods:

Method	Description
Add(object key, object value)	This method is used to add an element with the specified key and value into a SortedList. It takes two object type parameters. The first parameter indicates the key and the second parameter indicates the value to add to the SortedList.
Remove(object key)	This method is used to remove an element with the specified key from a SortedList. It takes an object type parameter that specifies the key of the element to remove from the SortedList.

RemoveAt(int index)	This method is used to remove an element at the specified index position from a SortedList. It takes an integer parameter that indicates the index position of the element to remove from the SortedList.
GetKey(int index)	This method is used to return a specified key from a SortedList at a specified index position. It takes an integer parameter that specifies the index position of the key to be returned.
Contains(object key)	This method is used to check whether a specified key exists in a SortedList or not. It takes an object type parameter that specifies a key to check in the SortedList. It returns a Boolean value either true or false. If the specified key exists in the SortedList, it returns true otherwise, it returns false.
ContainsKey(object key)	This method is used to determine whether the specified key exists in the SortedList or not. It takes a specified key as parameter and returns a Boolean value either true or false. If the specified key exists in the SortedList, it returns true otherwise, it returns false. This method takes a single object parameter that specifies the key to be searched in the SortedList.
ContainsValue(object value)	This method is used to determine whether the specified value exists in the SortedList or not. It takes a specified value as parameter and returns a Boolean value either true or false. If the specified value exists in the SortedList, it returns true otherwise it returns false.
GetByIndex(int index)	This method is used to get a value at a specified index position from a SortedList. It takes an integer parameter that specifies the index position of the value to be returned from the SortedList.
Clear()	This method is used to remove all the elements from a SortedList.

IndexOfKey(object key)	This method is used to return an index position of a specified key which is stored in internal array. It takes an object parameter that specifies a key to be searched in internal array.
IndexOfValue(object value)	This method is used to return an index position of a specified value which is stored in internal array. It takes an object parameter that specifies a value to be searched in internal array.

Program # 1

Write a program that retrieves values from a SortedList using individual key of each value, using for loop, and foreach loop.

C# Program

```
using System;
using System.Collections;

namespace ConsoleApplication1
{
class Program
{
static void Main(string[] args)
{
SortedList sortedList1 = new SortedList();
sortedList1.Add("k1", 99);
sortedList1.Add("k2", 3.2f);
sortedList1.Add("k3", "Hello");
sortedList1.Add("k4", 'C');
sortedList1.Add("k5", 996799.999);

//Access values of SortedList using Key of each value
int first = (int) sortedList1["k1"];
float second = (float) sortedList1["k2"];
string third = (string) sortedList1["k3"];
char fourth = (char) sortedList1["k4"];
double fifth = (double) sortedList1["k5"];

Console.WriteLine(first);
```

```
Console.WriteLine(second);
Console.WriteLine(third);
Console.WriteLine(fourth);
Console.WriteLine(fifth);

//Access values of SortedList using for loop
for (int i = 0; i < sortedList1.Count; i++)
{
Console.WriteLine("key: {0}, value: {1}",
sortedList1.GetKey(i), sortedList1.GetByIndex(i));
}

//Access values of SortedList using foreach loop
foreach (DictionaryEntry r in sortedList1)
Console.WriteLine("key: {0}, value: {1}", r.Key, r.Value);

Console.ReadKey();
}
}
}
```

DictionaryEntry Structure

DictionaryEntry structure defines a dictionary key-value pair that can be set or retrieved. The foreach statement requires the type of each element in the collection. Since each element of the IDictionary is a key-value pair and the element type is not the type of the key or the type of the value but the element type is DictionaryEntry. To access values from SortedList using foreach loop, the type of the element would be DictionaryEntry rather than type of the key or value. The DictionaryEntry has two properties i.e. Key property and Value property. The Key property is used to get or set the key in the key-value pairs and the Value property is used to get or set the value in the key-value pairs.

Program # 2

Write a program that removes elements from SortedList using Remove() and RemoveAt() methods.

C# Program

//Declare and Initialize SortedList
SortedList sortedList1 = new SortedList();\
sortedList1.Add("k1", 99);
sortedList1.Add("k2", 3.2f);
sortedList1.Add("k3", "Hello");
sortedList1.Add("k4", 'C');
sortedList1.Add("k5", 996799.999);
 	
//Remove element from SortedList whose key is 'k1'
sortedList1.Remove("k1");
 	
//Remove element from SortedList at index position 2
sortedList1.RemoveAt(2);
 	
foreach (DictionaryEntry kvp in sortedList1)
Console.WriteLine("key: {0}, value: {1}", kvp.Key, kvp.Value);

Stack

Stack is a collection that stores elements in such a way that the last inserted element is retrieved or removed first and the first inserted element is retrieved or removed last. A Stack is a single sided collection which inserts and remove elements from one side therefore, the mechanism of Stack is called LIFO (Last in First Out) or FILO (First in Last Out). It means that the last inserted element will be retrieved or removed first. The current index position of a Stack is called top position. When an element is inserted in a Stack, the top position is incremented by 1 and when an element is removed from a Stack, the top position is decremented by 1 so, a Stack has a single side for insertion and deletion of elements. C# language provides both non-generic and generic Stack. Stack class implements ICollection and IEnumerable interfaces. A Stack can contain null values as well as duplicate values.

Properties of Stack

Stack provides the following important properties:

Property	Description
Count	This property is used to count the number of elements in a Stack.

Methods of Stack

Stack provides the following important methods:

Method	Description
Push	This method is used to insert an element at the top position of a Stack. It inserts an element and increases the top position of the Stack by 1. It uses an increment operator to increment the top position.
Pop	This method is used to remove an element from the top position of a Stack. It removes an element from the top position of the Stack and decreases the top position by 1. It uses decrement operator to decrement the top position.
Peek	This method is used to return element from the top position of a Stack. It only returns the element of the top position and does not modify the Stack.
Contains	This method is used to check whether an element exist in a Stack or not.
Clear	This method is used to remove all elements from a Stack.

Program # 1

Write a program that inserts elements in a Stack.

C# Program

```
//Declare a Stack
Stack stack1 = new Stack();

//Insert elements in the Stack
stack1.Push(1);
stack1.Push(2);
stack1.Push(3);
stack1.Push("Hello");
stack1.Push(4);
stack1.Push(5);
stack1.Push(null);
```

```
//Retrieve elements from the Stack
foreach (var item in stack1)
Console.WriteLine(item);

//Retrieve the current element from the top position of the Stack using //
peek() method
Console.WriteLine("Peek Element {0}", stack1.Peek());
```

Visual Basic Program

```
'Declare a Stack
Dim stack1 As Stack = New Stack()

'Insert elements in the Stack
stack1.Push(1)
stack1.Push(2)
stack1.Push(3)
stack1.Push("Hello")
stack1.Push(4)
stack1.Push(5)
stack1.Push(Nothing)

'Retrieve elements from the Stack
For Each item In stack1
Console.WriteLine(item)
Next

'Retrieve the current element from the top position of the Stack 'using peek()
method
Console.WriteLine("Peek Element {0}", stack1.Peek())
```

Program # 2

Write a program that removes elements from a Stack.

C# Program

```
Stack stack1 = new Stack();
stack1.Push(1);
stack1.Push(2);
stack1.Push(3);
```

```
stack1.Push(4);
stack1.Push(5);

//Count the total number of elements of the Stack
Console.WriteLine("Number of elements = "+ stack1.Count);

//Remove an element from the top position of the Stack
stack1.Pop();

//Remove the entire elements from the Stack
while (stack1.Count > 0)
Console.WriteLine(stack1.Pop());

//Count the total number of elements of the Stack
Console.WriteLine("Number of elements = "+ stack1.Count);
```

Visual Basic Program

```
Dim stack1 As Stack = New Stack()
stack1.Push(1)
stack1.Push(2)
stack1.Push(3)
stack1.Push(4)
stack1.Push(5)

'Count the total number of elements of the Stack
Console.WriteLine("Number of elements = " & stack1.Count)
'Remove an element from the top position of the Stack
stack1.Pop()

'Remove the entire elements from the Stack
While stack1.Count > 0
Console.WriteLine(stack1.Pop())
End While

'Count the total number of elements of the Stack
Console.WriteLine("Number of elements = " & stack1.Count)
```

Program # 3

Write a program that checks an element whether it exists in the Stack or not.
C# Program

```
//Check an element whether it exists in the Stack or not
Stack stack1 = new Stack();
stack1.Push(1);
stack1.Push(2);
stack1.Push(3);
stack1.Push(4);
stack1.Push(5);

Console.WriteLine(stack1.Contains(3)); //It returns true
Console.WriteLine(stack1.Contains(9)); //It returns false
```

Queue

Queue is a collection that stores elements in the form of FIFO (First in First Out). FIFO means, the first inserted element will be retrieved or removed first and the last inserted element will be retrieved or removed last. It is a two ended collection that inserts elements in one end and removes elements from another end. The insertion end is called Enqueue and the retrieval or removal end is called Dequeue. Queue can contain null as well as duplicate elements. Queue implements the ICollection and IEnumerable interfaces.

Properties of Queue

Queue provides the following important properties:

Property	Description
Count	This property is used to count the total number of elements of a Queue.

Methods of Queue

Queue provides the following important methods:

Method	Description
Enqueue	This method is used to add an element into the Queue.

Dequeue	This method is used to remove an element from the beginning of the Queue.
Peek	This method is used to return the first element from the Queue.
Contains	This method is used to check whether an element exists in the Queue or not
Clear	This method is used to remove all the elements from the Queue.
TrimToSize	This method is used to set the capacity of the queue to the actual number of elements in the Queue.

Program # 1

Write a program that inserts and remove elements from a Queue.

C# Program

```
//Declare a Queue
Queue queue1 = new Queue();

//Insert elements into the Queue
queue1.Enqueue(1);
queue1.Enqueue(2);
queue1.Enqueue(3);
queue1.Enqueue(4);
queue1.Enqueue(5);

//Retrieve and remove elements from the Queue
Console.WriteLine("Total Elements = " + queue1.Count);

while (queue1.Count > 0)
Console.WriteLine(queue1.Dequeue());

Console.WriteLine("Total Elements = " + queue1.Count);
```

Visual Basic Program

```
'Declare a Queue
Dim queue1 As Queue = New Queue()
```

```
'Insert elements into the Queue
queue1.Enqueue(1)
queue1.Enqueue(2)
queue1.Enqueue(3)
queue1.Enqueue(4)
queue1.Enqueue(5)

'Retrieve and remove elements from the Queue
Console.WriteLine("Total Elements = " & queue1.Count)

While (queue1.Count > 0)
Console.WriteLine(queue1.Dequeue())
End While

Console.WriteLine("Total Elements = " & queue1.Count)
```

Hashtable

Hashtable is a collection that stores elements in the form of key-value pairs and they are organized on the bases of hash code of the key. The key-value pairs mean Hashtable stores data in such a way that each entry in a Hashtable contains a Key and a value. The keys and values in a Hashtable can be of any data type but in a single Hashtable all the keys must have the same data type. Each key in a Hashtable is unique and cannot be duplicated because each key uniquely identifies the value. The key in a Hashtable must not be null whereas the value can be null or duplicated. Therefore, to add an element into a Hashtable, two values must be provided, one for the Key and another for the value to be stored in the Hashtable collection. The Hashtable is defined in the namespace System.Collections. Hashtable implements the IDictionary, ICollection, and IEnumerable interfaces. Hashtable retrieves an item by comparing the hash code of keys so the performance of a Hashtable is slower than the Dictionary collection. Hashtable uses the default hash code provider which is object.GetHashCode() but we can also use the user-defined hash code. The DictionaryEntry is used with the foreach statement to iterate the Hashtable.

Properties of Hashtable

HashTable provides the following important properties:

Property	Description
Count	This property is used to get the total number of key-value pairs in the Hashtable.
Item	This property is used to get or set the value associated with the specified key.
Keys	This property is used to get an ICollection of keys of the Hashtable.
Values	This property is used to get an ICollection of values of the Hashtable.

Methods of Hashtable

HashtTable provides the following important methods:

Methods	Description
Add	This method is used to add an element with a key-value pair into the Hashtable.
Remove	This method is used to remove an element from the Hashtable.
Clear	This method is used to remove all the elements from the Hashtable.
Contains	This method is used to check whether the Hashtable contains a specific key or not. It returns true, if a specified key exists in the Hashtable otherwise, it returns false.
ContainsKey	This method is used to check whether the Hashtable contains a specific key or not. It returns true, if a specified key exists in the Hashtable otherwise, it returns false.
ContainsValue	This method is used to check whether the Hashtable contains a specified value or not. It returns true, if a specified value exists in the Hashtable otherwise, it returns false.
GetHash	This method is used to return the hash code for the specified key.

Program

Write a program that stores Keys and Values in a Hashtable
C# Program

```
//Declare Hashtable
Hashtable Hashtable1 = new Hashtable();

//Initialize Hashtable
Hashtable1.Add(1, "C#");
Hashtable1.Add(2, "Java");
Hashtable1.Add(3, "Visual Basic");
Hashtable1.Add(4, "Android");
Hashtable1.Add(5, null);

//The Hashtable can also be initialized using the object Initializer //syntax
Hashtable Hashtable1 = new Hashtable()
{
{1, "C#"},
{2, "Java"},
{3, "Visual Basic"},
{4, "Android"},
{5, null}
};

//Retrieve Keys and Values from the Hashtable
foreach (DictionaryEntry item in Hashtable1)
Console.WriteLine("key:{0}, value:{1}",item.Key, item.Value);
```

Visual Basic Program

```
'Declare Hashtable
Dim Hashtable1 As Hashtable = New Hashtable()

'Initialize Hashtable
Hashtable1.Add(1, "C#")
Hashtable1.Add(2, "Java")
Hashtable1.Add(3, "Visual Basic")
Hashtable1.Add(4, "Android")
Hashtable1.Add(5, Nothing)
```

```
'The Hashtable can also be initialized using the object Initializer
'syntax
Dim Hashtable1 As Hashtable = New Hashtable() From {
{1, "C#"},
{2, "Java"},
{3, "Visual Basic"},
{4, "Android"},
{5, Nothing}
}

For Each item As DictionaryEntry In Hashtable1
Console.WriteLine("key:{0}, value:{1}", item.Key, item.Value)
Next
```

Generic Collections

Generic collections are used to store elements of a specified data types. A single generic collection can store elements of a single data type and it needs to specify its data type at the time of the declaration. If a generic collection is declared as integer, it stores only integer data, if a generic collection is declared as float, it stores only float data, and if a generic collection is declared as string, it stores only string data etc. Generic collections are defined in the namespace System.Collections.Generic. Following is the details of the important generic collections:

- List<T>
- SortedList<TKey,TValue>
- Dictionary<TKey, TValue>
- Stack<T>

List<T>

List<T> is a generic collection which is used to store data of a specific data type like array. It is same as array but the main difference is that a List<T> does not need to specify its size but it automatically grows its size according to the number of elements inserted. The List<T> can store null values and also duplicate values.

Declaration and Initialization of List<T>

List<T> can be declared and initialized by the following two ways:

C# Syntax
List<int> List1 = new List<int>(); //or IList<int> List1 = new List<int>();
Visual Basic Syntax
Dim List1 As List(Of Integer) = New List(Of Integer)() 'or Dim List1 As IList(Of Integer) = New List(Of Integer)()

In the above example, the first statement uses List<T> type variable whereas the second statement uses IList<T> type variable to initialize the List. The IList<T> is an interface and List<T> is a class so, List<T> class is the concrete implementation of the IList<T> interface. In object-oriented programming it is advisable to program to interface rather than real class because interface is more general than a class therefore, use IList<T> type variable to create an object of List<T> because List<T> includes more helper methods than IList<T> interface.

Properties of List<T>

List<T> provides the following important properties:

Property	Description
Items	This property is used to get or set an element at the specified index.
Count	This property is used to count the total number of elements of a List<T>.

Methods of List<T>

List<T> provides the following important methods:

Method	Description
Add	This method is used to add an element at the end of a List<T>.
AddRange	This method is used to add a range of elements from the specified collection at the end of a List<T>.
BinarySearch	This method is used to search for the element and returns its index position.
Clear	This method is used to remove all the elements from a List<T>.
Contains	This method is used to check whether the specified element exists in a List<T> or not.
Find	This method is used to find the first element based on the specified predicate function.
Foreach	This method is used to iterate through a List<T>.
Insert	This method is used to insert an element at the specified index in a List<T>.
InsertRange	This method is used to insert elements of another collection at the specified index.
Remove	This method is used to remove the first occurrence of the specified element.
RemoveAt	This method is used to remove the element at the specified index.
RemoveRange	This method is used to remove all the elements that match with the supplied predicate function.
Sort	This method is used to sort all the elements.
TrimExcess	This method is used to set the capacity to the actual number of elements.
TrueForAll	This method is used to determine whether every element in a List<T> matches the conditions defined by the specified predicate or not.

Add values to List<T>

Values can be added to List<T> by the following ways:

C# Program

//Declare and initialize an Integer List
IList<int> integerList = new List<int>();
 	
//Add elements in the List
integerList.Add(1);
integerList.Add(2);
integerList.Add(3);
integerList.Add(4);
integerList.Add(5);
 	
//Declare a string List and add string elements to it
IList<string> stringList = new List<string>();
stringList.Add("C#");
stringList.Add("Visual Basic");
stringList.Add("Java");
stringList.Add("C");
stringList.Add(null);
 	
//Declare a List of type Class
IList<Student> studentList = new List<Student>();
studentList.Add(new Student());
studentList.Add(new Student());
studentList.Add(new Student());
 	
A List can also be initialized using object Initializer syntax:
 	
IList<int> integerList = new List<int>(){1, 2, 3, 4, 5};
 	
//or
 	
IList<Student> studentList = new List<Student>()
{
new Student(){StdID=1, StdName="Mohsin"},
new Student(){StdID=2, StdName="Mohib"},

```
new Student(){StdID=3, StdName="Marwan"},
new Student(){StdID=3, StdName="Muniba"},
new Student(){StdID=4, StdName="Sara"}
};
```

Visual Basic Program

```
'Declare and initialize an Integer List
Dim integerList As IList(Of Integer) = New List(Of Integer)()

'Add elements in the List
integerList.Add(1)
integerList.Add(2)
integerList.Add(3)
integerList.Add(4)
integerList.Add(5)

'Declare a string List and add string elements to it
Dim stringList As IList(Of String) = New List(Of String)()
stringList.Add("C#")
stringList.Add("Visual Basic")
stringList.Add("Java")
stringList.Add("C")
stringList.Add(Nothing)
```

A List can also be initialized using object Initializer syntax:

```
Dim integerList As IList(Of Integer) = New List(Of Integer)()
{1, 2, 3, 4, 5};

'or

Dim studentList As IList(Of Student) = New List(Of Student)() From
{
New Student() With {.StdID = 1, .StdName = "Mohsin"},
New Student() With {.StdID = 2, .StdName = "Mohib"},
New Student() With {.StdID = 3, .StdName = "Marwan"},
New Student() With {.StdID = 3, .StdName = "Muniba"},
New Student() With {.StdID = 4, .StdName = "Sara"}
}
```

Accessing Elements from List<T>

Elements from a List<T>can be accessed by the following ways:

C# Program

//Declare an integer List
IList<int> integerList = new List<int>() {1, 2, 3, 4, 5};
 	
//Retrieve elements from the List using foreach loop
foreach (var element in integerList)
Console.WriteLine(element);
 	
//We can also access individual element from a List by using index //of an element
 	
IList<int> integerList = new List<int>() {1, 2, 3, 4, 5};
 	
int element1= integerList[0]; //It returns 1
int element2= integerList[1]; //It returns 2
int element3= integerList[2]; //It returns 3
int element4= integerList[3]; //It returns 4
int element5= integerList[4]; //It returns 5

Visual Basic Program
'Declare an integer List Dim integerList As IList(Of Integer) = New List(Of Integer)() From {1, 2, 3, 4, 5} 'Retrieve elements from the List using For Each loop For Each element In integerList Console.WriteLine(element) Next 'We can also access individual element from a List by using index 'of an element Dim integerList As IList(Of Integer) = New List(Of Integer)() From {1, 2, 3, 4, 5}

```
Dim element1 As Integer = integerList(0) 'It returns 1
Dim element2 As Integer = integerList(1) 'It returns 2
Dim element3 As Integer = integerList(2) 'It returns 3
Dim element4 As Integer = integerList(3) 'It returns 4
Dim element5 As Integer = integerList(4) 'It returns 5
```

Program

Write a program that counts the total number of element of a List using Count property.

C# Program

```
List<int> integerList = new List<int>() {1, 2, 3, 4, 5};

Console.Write("Total elements = " + integerList.Count);
```

Visual Basic Program

```
Dim integerList As List(Of Integer) = New List(Of Integer)

integerList.Add(1)
integerList.Add(2)
integerList.Add(3)
integerList.Add(4)
integerList.Add(5)

Console.Write("Total elements = " & integerList.Count)
```

Program

Write a program that removes specified elements using Remove() and RemoveAt() method from a List.

C# Program

```
List<int> integerList = new List<int>() {1, 2, 3, 4, 5};

integerList.Remove(1); //It removes value 1 from the list

integerList.RemoveAt(2); //It removes value at index position 2
```

```
foreach (var element in integerList)
Console.WriteLine(element);
```

SortedList<TKey, TValue>

SortedList<TKey, TValue> is a generic SortedList that is used to store data in key-value pairs. The key-value pairs mean it stores data in such a way that each entry in a generic SortedList contains a Key and a value. The keys and values in a generic SortedList can be of any data type but in a single SortedList all the keys must have the same data type. Each key in a SortedList is unique and cannot be duplicated because each key uniquely identifies the value. The key in a SortedList must not be null whereas the value can be null or duplicated. Therefore, to add an element into a SortedList, two values must be provided, one for the Key and another for the value. The generic SortedList automatically sorts all the elements in ascending order according to the Key based on associated IComparer<T>. The generic SortedList is represented as SortedList<TKey, TValue> where TKey represents the type of the key and TValue represents the type of the value.

Declaration of SortedList<TKey, TValue>

The generic SortedList can be declared from the generic SortedList class SortedList<TKey, TValue> and it is initialized by the new keyword. The type for the key and type for the value is also specified. Following is the declaration and initialization of the generic SortedList:

C# Syntax
SortedList<int, string> sortedList1 = new SortedList<int, string>();
Visual Basic Syntax
Dim sortedList1 As SortedList(Of Integer, String) = New SortedList(Of Integer, String)()

In the above declaration, sortedList1 represents an object of the SortedList that stores string values and integer keys.

Properties of SortedList<TKey, TValue>

Generic SortedList provides the following important properties:

Property	Description
Capacity	This property is used to get or set the number of elements that the SortedList can store.
Count	This property is used to get the total number of elements of the SortedList.
Item	This property is used to get or set the element with the specified key of the SortedList.
Keys	This property is used to get the list of keys of the SortedList.
Values	This property is used to get the list of values of the SortedList.

Methods of SortedList<TKey, TValue>

Generic SortedList provides the following important methods:

Method	Description
Add(TKey, TValue)	This method is used to add key-value pairs into SortedList. It takes two parameters. The first parameter specifies the key and the second parameter specifies the value to be stored in the collection.
Remove(TKey)	This method is used to remove element with the specified key. It takes a specified key of the value as parameter to be removed from the SortedList.
RemoveAt(int)	This method is used to remove element at the specified index. It takes the index position of the element to be removed from the SortedList.
ContainsKey(TKey)	This method is used to check whether the specified key exists in the SortedList or not. It takes a key as parameter and returns a Boolean value either true or false. If the specified key exists in the SortedList, it returns true otherwise, it returns false.

ContainsValue(TValue)	This method is used to check whether the specified value exists in the SortedList or not. It takes a value as parameter and returns a Boolean value either true or false. If the specified value exists in the SortedList, it returns true otherwise, it returns false.
Clear()	This method is used to remove all the elements from the SortedList.
IndexOfKey(TKey)	This method is used to return an index of a specified key stored in internal array of SortedList.
IndexOfValue(TValue)	This method is used to return an index of a specified value stored in internal array of SortedList.

Program

Write a program that adds and retrieve elements from a generic SortedList.

C# Program

```
using System;
using System.Collections.Generic;

namespace ConsoleApplication1
{
class Program
{
static void Main(string[] args)
{
//Declare a generic SortedList that has integer keys and string //values
SortedList<int, string> sortedList1 = new SortedList<int, string>();

//Add elements to SortedList
sortedList1.Add(1, "C");
sortedList1.Add(2, "C++");
sortedList1.Add(3, "C#");
sortedList1.Add(4, "Visual Basic");
sortedList1.Add(5, "Java");
```

```
//Access values from SortedList using Keys
Console.WriteLine(sortedList1[1]);
Console.WriteLine(sortedList1[2]);
Console.WriteLine(sortedList1[3]);
Console.WriteLine(sortedList1[4]);
Console.WriteLine(sortedList1[5]);

//Access values from SortedList using for Loop
for (int i = 0; i < sortedList1.Count; i++)
{
Console.WriteLine("key: {0}, value: {1}", sortedList1.Keys[i], sortedList1.
Values[i]);
}

//Access values from SortedList using foreach Loop
foreach (KeyValuePair<int, string> kv in sortedList1)
Console.WriteLine("key: {0}, value: {1}", kv.Key, kv.Value);

Console.ReadKey();
}
}
}
```

Visual Basic Program

```
Imports System
Imports System.Collections.Generic

Module Module1

Sub Main()

'Declare a generic SortedList that has integer keys and string values
Dim sortedList1 As SortedList(Of Integer, String) = New SortedList(Of
Integer, String)()

'Add elements to SortedList
sortedList1.Add(1, "C")
sortedList1.Add(2, "C++")
sortedList1.Add(3, "C#")
```

```
sortedList1.Add(4, "Visual Basic")
sortedList1.Add(5, "Java")

'Access values from SortedList using Keys
Console.WriteLine(sortedList1(1))
Console.WriteLine(sortedList1(2))
Console.WriteLine(sortedList1(3))
Console.WriteLine(sortedList1(4))
Console.WriteLine(sortedList1(5))

'Access values from SortedList using for Loop
For i As Integer = 0 To sortedList1.Count - 1
Console.WriteLine("key: {0}, value: {1}", sortedList1.Keys(i), sortedList1.
Values(i))
Next

'Access values from SortedList using For Each Loop
For Each kv As KeyValuePair(Of Integer, String) In sortedList1
Console.WriteLine("key: {0}, value: {1}", kv.Key, kv.Value)
Next

Console.ReadKey()

End Sub
End Module
```

KeyValuePair<TKey, TValue> Structure

This structure defines a key-value pair that can be set or retrieved. It provides two properties i.e. Key and Value. The Key property is used to get the key from key-value pair and Value property is used to get value from the key-value pair. The foreach statement returns an object of the type of the elements in the collection. Each element of the generic SortedList is based on IDictionary<TKey, TValue> and the element type is not the type of the key or the type of the value but the element type is KeyValuePair<TKey, TValue>. This structure is defined in the namespace System.Collections.Generic.

Dictionary<TKey, TValue>

Dictionary is a generic collection that is used to store data in key-value pairs. It is represented as Dictionary<TKey, TValue>. The TKey specifies the type of the key and TValue specifies the type of the value. The key must be unique and value can be null or duplicated.

Declaration of Dictionary<TKey, TValue>

A Dictionary can be declared from the IDictionary<Tkey, TValue> interface or from the Dictionary<TKey, Tvalue> class. Following is the declaration and initialization of Dictionary:

C# Syntax
IDictionary<int, string> dict1 = new Dictionary<int, string>(); or Dictionary<int, string> dict1 = new Dictionary<int, string>();
Visual Basic Syntax
Dim dict1 As IDictionary(Of Integer, String) = New Dictionary(Of Integer, String)() or Dim dict1 As Dictionary(Of Integer, String) = New Dictionary(Of Integer, String)()

In the above declaration, dict1 specifies the name of the dictionary object, the type of the key and type of the value are also specified. In the above declaration, the type of the key is int and type of the value is string. It is recommended to program to the interface rather than to the class therefore, use IDictionary<TKey, TValue> rather than Dictionary<TKey, TValue>.

Properties of Dictionary<TKey, TValue>

Dictionary provides the following important properties:

Property	Description
Count	This property is used to get the total number of elements of the Dictionary collection.

Item	This property is used to get or set the element with the specified key in the Dictionary collection.
Keys	This property is used to get the list of keys of the Dictionary collection.
Values	This property is used to get the list of values of the Dictionary collection.

Methods of Dictionary<TKey, TValue>

Dictionary provides the following important methods:

Method	Description
Add(T)	This method is used to add an item to the Dictionary collection.
Add(TKey, TValue)	This method is used to add key-value pairs in the Dictionary collection.
void Remove(T item)	This method is used to remove the first occurrence of the specified item from the Dictionary collection.
Remove(TKey)	This method is used to remove the element with the specified key from the Dictionary collection.
Clear()	This method is used to remove all the elements from Dictionary collection.

Adding values to Dictionary<Tkey, TValue>

A Dictionary can be declared and initialized by the following ways:

C# Program

```
//Declare and initialize a Dictionary object
IDictionary<int, string> dict1 = new Dictionary<int, string>();

//Initialize Dictionary object by using Add() method
dict1.Add(1,"C++");
dict1.Add(2,"C#");
dict1.Add(3,"Visual Basic");
```

```
//Dictionary can also be initialized using collection Initializer //syntax as:

IDictionary<int, string> dict1 = new Dictionary<int, string>()
                                    {
                                        {1,"One"},
                                        {2, "Two"},
                                        {3,"Three"}
                                    };
```

Visual Basic Program

```
'Declare and initialize a Dictionary object
Dim dict1 As IDictionary(Of Integer, String) = New Dictionary(Of Integer,
String)()

'Initialize Dictionary object by using Add() method
dict1.Add(1, "C++")
dict1.Add(2, "C#")
dict1.Add(3, "Visual Basic")

'Dictionary can also be initialized using collection Initializer syntax 'as:

Dim dict1 As IDictionary(Of Integer, String) = New Dictionary(Of Integer,
String)() From
                                    {
                                        {1, "One"},
                                        {2, "Two"},
                                        {3, "Three"}
                                    }
```

Accessing elements of Dictionary<TKey, TValue>

Elements from Dictionary collection can be accessed by the following different ways:

C# Program

```
//Declare a Dictionary object
IDictionary<int, string> dict1 = new Dictionary<int, string>();

//Initialize Dictionary object by using Add() method
```

```
dict1.Add(1, "C++");
dict1.Add(2, "C#");
dict1.Add(3, "Visual Basic");

//Access elements of Dictionary using foreach Loop
foreach (KeyValuePair<int, string> item in dict1)
{
Console.WriteLine("Key: {0}, Value: {1}", item.Key, item.Value);
}

//Access individual elements from Dictionary collection using keys
Console.WriteLine(dict1[1]);
Console.WriteLine(dict1[2]);
Console.WriteLine(dict1[3]);
```

Visual Basic Program

```
'Declare a Dictionary object
Dim dict1 As IDictionary(Of Integer, String) = New Dictionary(Of Integer,
String)()

'Initialize Dictionary object by using Add() method
dict1.Add(1, "C++")
dict1.Add(2, "C#")
dict1.Add(3, "Visual Basic")

'Access elements of Dictionary using For Each Loop
For Each item As KeyValuePair(Of Integer, String) In dict1
Console.WriteLine("Key: {0}, Value: {1}", item.Key, item.Value)
Next

'Access individual elements from Dictionary collection using keys
Console.WriteLine(dict1(1))
Console.WriteLine(dict1(2))
Console.WriteLine(dict1(3))
```

Stack<T>

Stack<T> is a generic collection that stores elements in such a way that the last inserted element is retrieved or removed first and the first inserted element is retrieved or removed last. A Stack is a single sided collection which inserts and remove elements from one side therefore, the mechanism of Stack is called LIFO (Last in First Out) or FILO (First in Last Out). It means that the last inserted element will be retrieved or removed first. The current index position of a Stack is called top position. When an element is inserted in a Stack, the top position is incremented by 1 and when an element is removed from a Stack, the top position is decremented by 1 so, a Stack has a single side for insertion and deletion of elements. Stack class implements ICollection, IEnumerable, and IEnumerable<T> interfaces. A Stack can contain null values as well as duplicate values. The generic Stack is represented as Stack<T>. The parameter T specifies the type of the Stack. The generic Stack<T> is defined in the namespace System.Collections.Generic.

Properties of Stack<T>

The generic Stack<T> provides the following important properties:

Property	Description
Count	This property is used to count the number of elements in a Stack<T>.

Methods of Stack<T>

The generic Stack<T> provides the following important methods:

Method	Description
Push(T)	This method is used to insert an element at the top position of a Stack<T>. It inserts an element and increases the top position of the Stack<T> by 1. It uses an increment operator to increment the top position.
Pop	This method is used to remove and return an element from the top position of a Stack<T>. It removes an element from the top position of the Stack<T> and decrease the top position by 1. It uses the decrement operator to decrement the top position.
Peek	This method is used to return element from the top position of a Stack<T>. It only returns the element of the top position and does not modify the Stack<T>.

Contains(T)	This method is used to check whether an element exist in a Stack<T> or not.
Clear	This method is used to remove all elements from a Stack<T>.

Program # 1

Write a program that inserts elements in a Stack<T>.

C# Program

```
//Declare an integer Stack<T>
Stack<int> stack1 = new Stack<int>();

//Insert elements in the Stack
stack1.Push(1);
stack1.Push(2);
stack1.Push(3);
stack1.Push(70);
stack1.Push(99);

//Retrieve elements from the Stack<T> using foreach loop
foreach (var item in stack1)
Console.WriteLine(item);

//Retrieve the current element from the top position of the Stack using //
peek() method
Console.WriteLine("Peek Element {0}", stack1.Peek());
```

Visual Basic Program

```
'Declare an integer Stack<T>
Dim stack1 As Stack(Of Integer) = New Stack(Of Integer)()

'Insert elements in the Stack
stack1.Push(1)
stack1.Push(2)
stack1.Push(3)
stack1.Push(70)
stack1.Push(99)

'Retrieve elements from the Stack<T> using foreach loop
```

```
For Each item In stack1
Console.WriteLine(item)
Next

'Retrieve the current element from the top position of the Stack 'using peek()
method
Console.WriteLine("Peek Element {0}", stack1.Peek())
```

Program # 2

Write a program that removes elements from a Stack.
C# Program

```
Stack<int> stack1 = new Stack<int>();
stack1.Push(1);
stack1.Push(2);
stack1.Push(3);
stack1.Push(4);
stack1.Push(5);

//Count the total number of elements of the Stack
Console.WriteLine("Number of elements = " + stack1.Count);

//Remove an element from the top position of the Stack
stack1.Pop();

//Remove the entire elements from the Stack
while (stack1.Count > 0)
Console.WriteLine(stack1.Pop());

//Count the total number of elements of the Stack
Console.WriteLine("Number of elements = " + stack1.Count);
```

Visual Basic Program

```
Dim stack1 As Stack(Of Integer) = New Stack(Of Integer)()
stack1.Push(1)
stack1.Push(2)
stack1.Push(3)
stack1.Push(4)
```

```
stack1.Push(5)

'Count the total number of elements of the Stack
Console.WriteLine("Number of elements = " & stack1.Count)

'Remove an element from the top position of the Stack
stack1.Pop()

'Remove the entire elements from the Stack
While stack1.Count > 0
Console.WriteLine(stack1.Pop())
End While
'Count the total number of elements of the Stack
Console.WriteLine("Number of elements = " & stack1.Count)
```

Program # 3

Write a program that checks an element whether it exists in the Stack or not.

C# Program

```
//Check an element whether it exists in the Stack or not
Stack<int> stack1 = new Stack<int>();
stack1.Push(1);
stack1.Push(2);
stack1.Push(3);
stack1.Push(4);
stack1.Push(5);

Console.WriteLine(stack1.Contains(3)); //It returns true
Console.WriteLine(stack1.Contains(9)); //It returns false
```

CHAPTER 14

LINQ in .NET

CHAPTER CONTENTS

- LINQ
- IEnumerable Interface
- IEnumerable<T> Interface
- IQueryable Interface
- LINQ Syntax
- Query Expression Syntax
- Lambda Method Syntax
- The var Keyword
- LINQ Query Operators
- Filtering Operators
- Projecting Operators
- Joining Operators
- Ordering Operators
- Grouping Operators
- Conversions Operators
- Sets Operators
- Aggregation Operators
- Quantifiers Operators
- Generation Operators
- Elements Operators
- DataContext Class
- Constructors of DataContext Class
- Properties of DataContext Class
- Connection Property
- Mapping Property
- Log Property
- Methods of DataContext Class
- DatabaseExists Method
- DeleteDatabae Method
- ExecuteCommand Method
- ExecuteQuery Method
- GetTable Method

- GetChangeSet Method
- SubmitChanges Method
- LINQ to SQL
- Difference between LINQ to SQL and Entity Framework
- Programming Examples of LINQ to SQL
- InsertOnSubmit() Method
- InsertAllOnSubmit() Method
- LINQ to Dataset

LINQ

LINQ stands for Language Integrated Query. It is a data querying methodology that provides general purpose query capabilities to the .NET programming languages with similar syntax to SQL query. LINQ provides query capability to multiple data sources such as LINQ query to databases, LINQ query to XML documents and LINQ query to in-memory objects such as arrays, lists, generic list and other collection types. LINQ is the collection of extension methods for classes that implements IEnumerable and IQueryable interfaces, therefore the LINQ query is applicable to any object that implements the IEnumerable or IQueryable interface. LINQ provides a set of general purpose standard query operators used to perform different operations such as filter operation, groups operation, join operation, sorting operation, traversal operation, and projection operation on the elements of the collections or sequences. A collection or sequence is an object whose type implements IEnumerable<T> interface or IQueryable<T> interface. The IEnumerable<T> is a generic collection which is a base interface for the generic collections in the namespace System.Collections. Generic such as List<T>, LinkedList<T>, Queue<T>, Dictionary<T>, SortedList<T>, HashSet<T> etc. The <T> indicates type of the collection. The IEnumerable<T> is inherited from the base interface IEnumerable and IQueryable<T> is inherited from the base interface IQueryable. The LINQ is a structured query syntax built in C# and VB.NET that can be used to retrieve data from different data sources and from the collection of objects. When LINQ query is executed, it returns a new generic collection either IEnumerable<T> or IQueryable<T>, objects, or simple types. When LINQ query is used with the in-memory objects or with XML, it returns IEnumerable<T> collection and when LINQ query is used with the database then it returns the IQueryable<T> collection. Therefore, an object of IEnumerable<T> or IQueryable<T> interface is declared to receive the result of the LINQ query.

IEnumerable Interface

IEnumerable is a base interface for all the non-generic collections that can be enumerated. The IEnumerable interface is defined in the namespace System.Collections. The IEnumerable interface defines a single method GetEnumerator. The GetEnumerator method is used to return an object of the IEnumerator interface that iterates through a collection. The IEnumerator is the base interface for all the non-generic enumerators. The object of IEnumerator interface can be used with for-each statement to read data in the collection. The IEnumerator interface defines two methods and a one property. The methods are Reset() method and MoveNext() method and the property is Current property. The Reset() method is used to set the position of the IEnumerator before the first element of the collection. The MoveNext() method is used to move the IEnumerator to the next element of the collection. The Current property is used to get the current element of the collection. The object of IEnumerator retrieves data as a read-only stream of data that does not allow modification. To get data from a collection, initially, the IEnumerator object is positioned before the first element in the collection or the Reset() method is used to bring the IEnumerator position before the first element in the collection then the MoveNext() method is used to advance or move the IEnumerator to the first element of the collection and the Current property is used to get the current element of the collection and then the MoveNext() method is used to move the IEnumerator to the next element of the collection and on this way the entire elements of the collection are retrieved.

IEnumerable<T> Interface

It is a base interface for all the generic collections defined in the namespace System.Collections.Generic such as List<T>, Queue<T>, Stack<T>, LinkedList<T>, Dictionary<T>, SortedList<T>, HashSet<T> etc. The IEnumerable<T> interface inherited from the IEnumerable interface. Therefore a type which implements the IEnumerable<T> interface will also implement members of the IEnumerable interface. The IEnumerable<T> interface defines a single method GetEnumerator which returns an object of the IEnumerator<T> interface. The IEnumerator<T> is the base interface for all the generic enumerators. The object of IEnumerator<T> interface can be used with for-each statement to read data in the collection. The IEnumerator<T> interface defines a single property and three methods. The property is Current property and methods are Reset() method, MoveNext() method, and Dispose() Method. The Current property is used to get the element in the collection at the current position of the enumerator.

IQueryable Interface

IQueryable interface is used to evaluate queries against a specific data source in which the type of the data is not specified. IQueryable interface inherits IEnumerable interface and it returns IEnumerator interface that iterates through a collection. The IQueryable interface works same as IEnumerable interface but the main difference is that IEnumerable interface provides a great functionality and achieves a good efficiency in case of disconnected or in-memory data sources or databases while IQueryable interface provides a great functionality and achieve a good efficiency in case of connected data sources or databases such as SQL etc. Therefore, if we work in in-memory data collections, the IEnumerable interface is the best choice and if we work in connected data sources or databases, the IQueryable interface is the best choice.

The IQueryable interface provides a single method GetEnumerator() and three properties such as ElementType, Expression, and Provider. The GetEnumerator() method is used to return the IEnumerator interface that iterates through a collection. The ElementType property is used to get the type of the elements. The elements are returned when the expression tree of the current instance of IQueryable is executed. The Expression property is used to get the expression tree associated with the instance of the IQueryable interface. The Provider property is used to get the query provider associated with the current data source.

Extension Method

An Extension method is a method that enables us to add new methods to the existing types without creating a new derived type and without modification of the original type. Extension method is a static method and it can be defined in the existing static class. The first parameter of an Extension method is defined with the "this" keyword which specifies the type that the method operates on and the data type of the first parameter is the data type that is used to extend the method. It means that the first parameter of an Extension method can be any type of variable but it is preceded with the keyword "this". An Extension method can be called using the instance method syntax and it can be called using the same type of the type of its first parameter that is preceded with the "this" keyword. For example, if the first parameter of an Extension method is defined as integer, it can be called with the integer type similarly, if the first parameter of an Extension method is defined as a String, it can be called with the String type etc.

Following is an example of Extension method for integer data type which returns a string value. The Method name is "EvenNumber" that takes an integer value and checks whether the input value is even or odd. If the value is even, the method returns a string "even" and if a value is odd, the method returns a string "odd":

C# Program

```
using System;

namespace ExtensionMethodExample
{
public static class ExtensionMethodExample
{
public static String EvenNumber(this int num)
{
if (num % 2 == 0)
return "Even";
else
return "Odd";
}
}
class Program
{
static void Main(string[] args)
{
int n;
String result;
n = 99;
result = n.EvenNumber();
Console.WriteLine(result);

//We can also call an Extension method by using the value instead //of variable
```

```
result = 99.EvenNumber();
Console.WriteLine(result);

Console.ReadKey();
}
}
}
```

LINQ Syntax

LINQ provides the following two general syntaxes:

- Query Expression Syntax
- Lambda Method Syntax

Query Expression Syntax

The Query Expression syntax is also called Query syntax. It starts with a From clause followed by a range variable and a collection from which we need to retrieve the data. The collection is either an IEnumerable<T> or IQueryable<T> collection. The structure of From clause is similar to foreach loop. After the From clause, the Where clause is used followed by an expression that performs filter operations. The expression of Where clause contains the LINQ Query filtering operators to filter the data. After the expression of Where clause, the select or group by clause is used followed by an expression to prepare the query result or the number of fields to be retrieved from the collection. The LINQ Query Expression syntax always starts with the From clause followed by a range variable and ends with the select or group by clause. Following is the general syntax of LINQ Query Expression:

```
<Query-Result> = From <Range-Variable> in <Collection>
where <Expression> select or group by <Fields>
```

The <Query-Result> specifies the LINQ query variable that stores the LINQ query commands. The <Query-Result> is a generic collection either IEnumerable<T> or IQueryable<T>, objects, or simple types. The <Range-Variable> specifies a range variable of a collection, the <Collection> specifies a generic collection either IEnumerable<T> or IEQueryable<T> from which the data is to be retrieved, the "where" specifies Where clause which is used for the predicate or condition, the <Expression> specifies the filter operators of LINQ standard Query Operators to filter the data. The filters operators are used either in the form of SQL expression or using Lambda expression. The <Fields> specifies the number of fields to be retrieved from the collection or it may also be an expression that prepares the query result. To access the standard LINQ Query Operators, the namespace System.Query must be imported in the application or program.

Execution of LINQ Query Expression

The LINQ query expression cannot be executed directly but it needs an iterator to iterate the LINQ query variable. The foreach is usually used to iterate the LINQ query variable and retrieve the elements from the collection.

The following programming examples explain the LINQ query expression syntax:

Program # 1

Write a program that retrieves even numbers and a range of values from an integer array using LINQ query expression.
C# Program

```
using System;
using System.Linq;
namespace ConsoleApplication1
{
class Program
{
static void Main(string[] args)
{

//Declare an integer array
int[] IntArray = new int[] {3, 5, 7, 8, 9, 11, 16, 19, 23, 26};

//LINQ Query to retrieve Even numbers from array
var EvenNum = from n in IntArray
              where n % 2 == 0 select n;
```

```
foreach (var numbers in EvenNum)
{
Console.WriteLine(numbers);
}

//LINQ Query to retrieve a range of values from array
var NumRange = from n in IntArray
                  where (n > 8 && n < 23) select n;

foreach (var numbers in NumRange)
{
Console.WriteLine(numbers);
}
Console.ReadKey();
}
}
}
```

Visual Basic Program

```
Module Module1
Sub Main()

'Declare an integer array
Dim IntArray As Integer() = {3, 5, 7, 8, 9, 11, 16, 19, 23, 26}

'LINQ Query to retrieve Even numbers from array
Dim EvenNum As IEnumerable(Of Integer) = From n In IntArray
                                          Where n Mod 2 = 0
                                          Select n

For Each numbers In EvenNum
Console.WriteLine(numbers)
Next

'LINQ Query to retrieve a range of values from array
Dim NumRange As IEnumerable(Of Integer) = From n In IntArray
                                  Where (n > 8 And n < 23) Select n

For Each numbers In NumRange
```

```
Console.WriteLine(numbers)
Next

Console.ReadKey()
End Sub
End Module
```

Program # 2

Write a program that retrieves different variety of elements from a String array.

C# Program

```
//Declare a String array
string[] StringArray = {
                        "one", "two", "three", "four", "five",
                        "six", "seven", "eight", "nine", "ten"
};

//Retrieve those elements whose length are equal to four characters
IEnumerable<string> strLength = from str in StringArray
                                where str.Length == 4
                                select str;

foreach (var str in strLength)
{
Console.WriteLine(str);
}

//Retrieve those elements whose contain character i
IEnumerable<string> strContains = from str in StringArray
where str.Contains("i")
select str;

foreach (var str in strContains)
{
Console.WriteLine(str);
}
```

Visual Basic Program

```
'Declare a String array
Dim StringArray As String() = {
                        "one", "two", "three", "four", "five",
                        "six", "seven", "eight", "nine", "ten"
}

'Retrieve those elements whose length are equal to four characters
Dim strLength As IEnumerable(Of String) =
                                        From str In StringArray
                                        Where str.Length = 4
                                        Select str
For Each s In strLength
Console.WriteLine(s)
Next

'Retrieve those elements whose contain character i
Dim strContains As IEnumerable(Of String) =
From str In StringArray
Where str.Contains("i")
Select str
For Each s In strContains
Console.WriteLine(s)
Next
```

LINQ Method Syntax

Method syntax is also known as fluent syntax. The LINQ Method syntax uses extension methods for writing LINQ queries. LINQ provides various Extension methods such as where(), select(), orderby(), sum(), average() etc. Extension methods are defined in the namespace System.Linq and they implement IEnumerable<T> or IQueryable<T> interface. Each extension method of LINQ takes a Lambda expression as a predicate function as parameter.

The following programming examples explain the LINQ method syntax:

Program # 1

Write a program that retrieves even numbers and a range of values from an integer array using LINQ method syntax.
C# Program

```
//Include namespaces
using System.Linq;
using System.Collections.Generic;

//Declare an Integer Array
int[] IntArray = new int[] {3, 5, 7, 8, 9, 11, 16, 19, 23, 26};

//LINQ Query to retrieve Even numbers from array
IEnumerable<int> EvenNum = IntArray.Where(n => n % 2 == 0);

foreach (var numbers in EvenNum)
{
Console.WriteLine(numbers);
}

//LINQ Query to retrieve a range of values from array
IEnumerable<int> RangeNum =
                                IntArray.Where(n => n > 8 && n < 23);

foreach (var numbers in RangeNum)
{
Console.WriteLine(numbers);
}
```

Visual Basic Program

```
'Include namespaces
Imports System.Collections.Generic

'Declare an Integer Array
Dim IntArray As Integer() = {3, 5, 7, 8, 9, 11, 16, 19, 23, 26}

'LINQ Query to retrieve Even numbers from array
```

```
Dim EvenNum As IEnumerable(Of Integer) =
                        IntArray.Where(Function(n) n Mod 2 = 0)

For Each number In EvenNum
'Console.WriteLine(number)
Next

'LINQ Query to retrieve a range of values from array
Dim RangeNum As IEnumerable(Of Integer) =
                   IntArray.Where(Function(n) n > 8 And n < 23)

For Each number In RangeNum
Console.WriteLine(number)
Next
```

Program # 2

Write a program that retrieves different variety of elements from a String array using LINQ Method syntax.

C# Program

```
//Include namespaces
using System.Linq;
using System.Collections.Generic;

//Declare a String Array
string[] StringArray = {
"one", "two", "three", "four", "five",
"six", "seven", "eight", "nine", "ten"
};

//Retrieve those elements whose length are equal to four characters
var strLength = StringArray.Where(str => str.Length == 4);

foreach (var str in strLength)
{
Console.WriteLine(str);
}
```

```
//Retrieve those elements whose contain character i
var strContains = StringArray.Where(str =>str.Contains("i"));

foreach (var str in strContains)
{
Console.WriteLine(str);
}
```

Visual Basic Program

```
'Include namespaces
Imports System.Collections.Generics;

'Declare a String Array
Dim StringArray As String() = {
"one", "two", "three", "four", "five",
"six", "seven", "eight", "nine", "ten"
}

'Retrieve those elements whose length are equal to four characters
Dim strLength As IEnumerable(Of String) =
StringArray.Where(Function(str) str.Length = 4)

For Each s In strLength

Console.WriteLine(s)
Next

'Retrieve those elements whose contain character i
Dim strContains As IEnumerable(Of String) =
StringArray.Where(Function(str) str.Contains("i"))

For Each s In strContains
Console.WriteLine(s)
Next
```

The var Keyword

The var keyword is used to declare an anonymous data type variable that can be initialized by any type of value. The data type of a var variable is unknown and it is decided by the compiler during run time of the program. A var variable needs to initialize at the time of declaration. The compiler infers or assumes the data type of a var type variable from the value assigned to it. For example, if a var type variable is initialized with an integer value, the compiler decides the data type of that variable as integer data type, similarly if a var type variable is initialized with a String value then the compiler decides the data type of that variable as String data type etc. If a var variable is not initialized, the compiler generates an error. Therefore, a var variable must be initialized at the time of the declaration. Consider the following variables declaration:

```
var n = 21; //Assigned an integer value
var str = "Hello"; //Assigned a string value
var bol = false; //Assigned a Boolean value
```

The compiler assumes the data types of the above variables from their values and they are identical to the following declaration:

```
int n = 21;
string str = "Hello";
bool bol = false;
```

LINQ Query Operators

LINQ standard query operators are the methods which allow us to write LINQ query. They are defined as extension methods in the Enumerable and Queryable static classes and placed in the namespace System.Linq. The LINQ query operators provide the query capabilities to perform different operations such as filter operation, groups operation, joins operation, sorting operation, traversal operation, and projection operation on the elements of the collections or sequences whose type implements IEnumerable<T> or IQueryable<T> interface. The LINQ standard query operators can be categorized into the following types:

- Filtering Operators
- Projecting Operators
- Joining Operators
- Ordering Operators
- Grouping Operators
- Conversions Operators
- Sets Operators

- Aggregation Operators
- Quantifiers Operators
- Generation Operators
- Elements Operators

Filtering Operators

Filtering operators are used with the condition to select elements from the collection. They select those elements from the collection if a specified condition is satisfied. Following is the details of filtering operators:

Filtering Operators	Description
Where	This operator is used to filter elements of a collection based on the predicate function or condition. It uses a specified condition and returns elements from a collection based on the predicate function or condition.
OfType	This operator is used to filter a collection based on the data type of the elements. It takes a data type name as a parameter and selects those elements from a collection that have matching data type. For example, if we have a general list in which we have multiple data type elements, the OfType operator is used to filter the list and retrieves elements on the basis of data types.

Programming Example

Write a program that retrieves elements from a general list on the basis of data type of the list elements.
C# Program

```
using System;
using System.Linq;
using System.Collections.Generic;

namespace ConsoleApplication1
{
public class Employee
```

```
{
public int EmployeeID {get; set;}
public string EmployeeName {get; set;}
}
class Program
{
static void Main(string[] args)
{
IList<object> list = new List<object>();
list.Add(13);
list.Add(7);
list.Add(3.5d);
list.Add("C# Programming");
list.Add("Linq Example");
list.Add(new Employee()
{
EmployeeID = 001,
EmployeeName = "Naveed Alam",
});

//LINQ Query to retrieve Integer elements from the list
var intElements = from i in list.OfType<int>() select i;

foreach (var element in intElements)
{
Console.WriteLine(element);
}

//LINQ Query to retrieve double elements from the list
var objElements = from s in list.OfType<double>() select s;

foreach (var element in objElements)
{
Console.WriteLine(element);
}

//LINQ Query to retrieve string elements from the list
var stringElements = from s in list.OfType<string>() select s;
```

```
foreach (var element in stringElements)
{
Console.WriteLine(element);
}

//LINQ Query to retrieve Employee type elements from the list
var empElements = from s in list.OfType<Employee>()
                  select s.EmployeeName;

foreach (var element in empElements)
{
Console.WriteLine(element);
}
Console.ReadKey();
}
}
}
```

Sorting Operators

Sorting Operators are used to sort or order the elements in a collection either in ascending or descending order. Following is the details of Sorting operators:

Sorting Operators	Description
OrderBy	This operator is used to sort the elements in ascending order.
OrderByDescending	This operator is used to sort the elements in descending order.
ThenBy	This operator is used to sort the elements again in ascending order. It is used after the OrdrBy or OrderByDescending operators and performs the sorting operation again in ascending order. The ThenBy operator is usually used if we want to perform the sorting operation using multiple fields for example, if we want to perform the sorting operation using the ID field and then we want to perform the sorting operation using the Name filed etc.

ThenByDescending	This operator is used to sort the elements again in descending order. It is used after the OrderBy or OrderByDescending operators and performs the sorting operation again in descending order. It works same as ThenBy operator but the main difference is that it performs the sorting operation again in descending order.

The following programs explain the LINQ Sorting operators in details:

Program # 1

Write a program that sorts an integer array in ascending and descending orders.
C# Program

```
//Include namespace
using System.Linq;

//Declare an Integer Array
int[] intArray = new int[] {3, 5, 11, 7, 8, 26, 19, 9, 23, 16};

//LINQ Query to sort the array list in Ascending order
var sortResultAsc = from s in intArray
                    orderby s
                    select s;

Console.WriteLine("Ascending Order:");
foreach (var numbers in sortResultAsc)
Console.WriteLine(numbers);

//LINQ Query to sort the array list in Descending order
var sortResultDes = from s in intArray
                    orderby s descending
                    select s;

Console.WriteLine("Descending Order:");
foreach (var numbers in sortResultDes)
Console.WriteLine(numbers);
```

Visual Basic Program

``'Include namespace
Imports System.Collections.Generic
 	
Dim intArray As Integer() = {3, 5, 11, 7, 8, 26, 19, 9, 23, 16}
 	
'LINQ Query to sort the array list in Ascending order
Dim sortResultAsc As IEnumerable(Of Integer) =
                                        From s In intArray
                                        Order By s Select s
 	
Console.WriteLine("Ascending Order:")
For Each numbers In sortResultAsc
Console.WriteLine(numbers)
Next
 	
'LINQ Query to sort the array list in Descending order
Dim sortResultDes As IEnumerable(Of Integer) =
                                        From s In intArray
                                        Order By s Descending
                                        Select s
 	
Console.WriteLine("Descending Order:")
For Each numbers In sortResultDes
Console.WriteLine(numbers)
Next```

Program # 2

Write a program that sorts the employees name in a general list in ascending and descending orders.
C# Program
using System; using System.Linq; using System.Collections.Generic; namespace ConsoleApplication1

```
{
public class Employee
{
public int EmployeeID {get; set;}
public string EmployeeName {get; set;}
}

public class Program
{
public static void Main()
{

//Employee Collection
IList<Employee> EmployeeList = new List<Employee>()
{
new Employee() {
EmployeeID = 1, EmployeeName = "Zahir Shah"},
new Employee() {
EmployeeID = 2, EmployeeName = "Bilal Khan"},
new Employee() {
EmployeeID = 3, EmployeeName = "Fawad Khan"},
new Employee() {
EmployeeID = 4, EmployeeName = "Imad Khan"},
new Employee() {
EmployeeID = 5, EmployeeName = "Hassan Khan"}
};

//LINQ Query to sort the Employees name in Ascending order
var ascendingResult = from s in EmployeeList
                      orderby s.EmployeeName
                      select s;

//LINQ Query to sort the Employees name in Descending order
var descendingResult = from s in EmployeeList
                      orderby s.EmployeeName descending
                      select s;

Console.WriteLine("Ascending Order:");
```

```
foreach (var std in ascendingResult)
Console.WriteLine(std.EmployeeName);

Console.WriteLine("Descending Order:");
foreach (var std in descendingResult)
Console.WriteLine(std.EmployeeName);

Console.ReadKey();
}
}
}
```

Visual Basic Program

```
Imports System.Linq
Imports System.Collections.Generic

Module Module1

Public Class Employee
Public Property EmployeeID As Integer
Public Property EmployeeName As String
End Class

Sub Main()

Dim EmployeeList As IList(Of Employee) = New List(Of _
Employee)() From
{New Employee() With {
.EmployeeID = 1, .EmployeeName = "Zahir Shah"},
New Employee() With {
.EmployeeID = 2, .EmployeeName = "Bilal Khan"},
New Employee() With {
.EmployeeID = 3, .EmployeeName = "Fawad Khan"},
New Employee() With {
.EmployeeID = 4, .EmployeeName = "Imad Khan"},
New Employee() With
{.EmployeeID = 5, .EmployeeName = "Hassan Khan"}}
```

```
'LINQ Query to sort the Employees name in Ascending order
Dim ascendingResult = From s In EmployeeList
                      Order By s.EmployeeName Select s

'LINQ Query to sort the Employees name in Descending order
Dim descendingResult = From s In EmployeeList
                      Order By s.EmployeeName
                      Descending Select s

Console.WriteLine("Ascending Order:")
For Each std In ascendingResult
Console.WriteLine(std.EmployeeName)
Next

Console.WriteLine("Descending Order:")
For Each std In descendingResult
Console.WriteLine(std.EmployeeName)
Next

Console.ReadKey()
End Sub
End Module
```

Set Operators

Set operators are used to find Union, Intersection, Missing elements between the two collections. They are also used to remove the duplicate elements from a collection. Following is the details of the Set operators:

Set Operators	Description
Distinct	This operator is used to remove duplicate elements from a collection.
Except	This operator is used to return those elements from one collection which are not present in the second collection.

Intersect	This operator is used to find the intersection between the two collections. Intersection means the same or common elements between the two collections.
Union	This operator is used to find the union between the two collections. Union means unique elements of both the collections.

The following program explains the Distinct, Except, Intersect, and Union operators:

C# Program

```
//Include namespaces
using System.Linq;
using System.Collections.Generic;

//Declare two Integer Arrays
int[] List1 = {2, 4, 6, 8, 10, 12, 14, 17, 8, 3};
int[] List2 = {3, 6, 9, 12, 15, 8, 17, 19, 4};

//LINQ Query to find Union between List1 and List2
IEnumerable<int> unionResult = List1.Union(List2);

Console.WriteLine("Union of List1 and List2:");
foreach(var numbers in unionResult)
Console.WriteLine(numbers);

//LINQ Query to find Intersection between List1 and List2
IEnumerable<int> intersectResult = List1.Intersect(List2);

Console.WriteLine("Intersection of List1 and List2:");
foreach(var numbers in intersectResult)
Console.WriteLine(numbers);

//LINQ Query to remove Duplicate values from List1
IEnumerable<int> distinctResult =
                                    (from n in List1 select n).Distinct();
```

```
Console.WriteLine("Values of List1 without Duplication:");
foreach(var numbers in distinctResult)
Console.WriteLine(numbers);

//LINQ Query to retrieve those values from List1 which are not //present
in List2
IEnumerable<int> exceptResult = List1.Except(List2);

Console.WriteLine("Values from List1 which are not in List2:");
foreach(var numbers in exceptResult)
Console.WriteLine(numbers);
```

Visual Basic Program

```
'Include namespaces
Imports System.Linq
Imports System.Collections.Generic

'Declare two Integer Arrays
Dim List1 As Integer() = {2, 3, 4, 6, 8, 10, 12, 14, 17, 8, 3}
Dim List2 As Integer() = {3, 6, 9, 12, 15, 8, 17, 19, 4}

'LINQ Query to find Union between List1 and List2
Dim unionResult As IEnumerable(Of Integer) = List1.Union(List2)

Console.WriteLine("Union of List1 and List2:")
For Each numbers In unionResult
Console.WriteLine(numbers)
Next

'LINQ Query to find Intersection between List1 and List2
Dim intersectResult As IEnumerable(Of Integer) =
                                        List1.Intersect(List2)

Console.WriteLine("Intersection of List1 and List2:")
For Each numbers In intersectResult
Console.WriteLine(numbers)
Next
```

```
'LINQ Query to remove Duplicate values from List1
Dim distinctResult As IEnumerable(Of Integer) =
                                   (From n In List1 Select n).Distinct()

Console.WriteLine("Values of List1 without Duplication:")
For Each numbers In distinctResult
Console.WriteLine(numbers)
Next

'LINQ Query to retrieve those values from List1 which are not 'present in
List2
Dim ExceptResult As IEnumerable(Of Integer) =
                                             List1.Except(List2)

Console.WriteLine("Values from List1 which are not in List2:")
For Each numbers In ExceptResult
Console.WriteLine(numbers)
Next
```

Quantifier Operators

Quantifier operators are used in conditional statements and return true or false according to the specified condition. A quantifier operator returns true if a specified condition becomes true and it returns false if the condition becomes false. Following is the list of quantifier operators:

Quantifier Operators	Description
All	This operator is used to return true when all the elements of a collection satisfies a condition. If all elements of a collection do not satisfy a condition, it returns false.
Any	This operator is used to return true if any single element in a collection satisfy a condition. If no element in a collection satisfy a condition, it returns false.
Contains	This operator is used to return true when a collection contains a matching element of the condition else it returns false.

The following program explains the quantifier operators All, Any and Contains:

C# Program

```
using System.Linq;

int[] intArray = {2, 4, 6, 8, 10, 12, 14, 17, 8, 3};

//LINQ Query to check whether all the elements of array are Even
bool areAllElementsEven = intArray.All(i => i % 2 == 0);

//LINQ Query to check whether any element of array is Odd
bool IsAnyElementOdd = intArray.Any(i => i % 2 != 0);

//LINQ Query to check whether the array contain element 10
bool IsContainElementTen = intArray.Contains(10);
```

```
Console.WriteLine("All Even = " + areAllElementsEven);
Console.WriteLine("Any Odd = " + IsAnyElementOdd);
Console.WriteLine("Is Contain 10 = " + IsContainElementTen);
```

Visual Basic Program

```
Dim intArray As Integer() = {2, 4, 6, 8, 10, 12, 14, 17, 8, 3}

'LINQ Query to check whether all the elements of array are Even
Dim areAllElementsEven As Boolean =
intArray.All(Function(i) i Mod 2 = 0)

'LINQ Query to check whether any element of array is Odd
Dim IsAnyElementOdd As Boolean =
intArray.Any(Function(i) i Mod 2 <> 0)

'LINQ Query to check whether the array contain element 10
Dim IsContainElementTen As Boolean = intArray.Contains(10)

Console.WriteLine("All Even = " &
areAllElementsEven.ToString())
Console.WriteLine("Any Odd =" & IsAnyElementOdd.ToString())
Console.WriteLine("Is Contain 10 = " &
IsContainElementTen.ToString())
```

Projection Operators

Projection operators are used to change the result of a query into a new defined form. Following is a list of Projection operators:

Projection Operators	Description
Select	This operator is used to select value from a collection.
SelectMany	This operator is used to select values from a collection of collection. The collection of collection means nested collection.

Partitioning Operators

Partitioning operators are used to filter and return elements from a collection based on the index positions of elements or by a condition. These operators are also used for paging implementation. Following is a list of partitioning operators:

Partitioning Operators	Description
Take	This operator is used to return elements from a collection up to a specified index position. It starts from starting index position of a collection and retrieves elements until a specified index position is reached. When a specified index position is reached, it stops the process. For example, if we have a collection {3, 5, 8, 7, 11, 16} and we want to return elements from starting index position to index position 2 then the target index position will be 3 and it will be specified to the parameter of the Take operator as Take(3). The Take(3) will return elements from index position 0 to index position 2 and will skip elements from index position 3 to the last element of the collection. The resultant elements will be {3, 5, 8}.
TakeWhile	This operator is used to return those elements that satisfy a specified condition. For example, if we have a collection {3, 5, 8, 7, 11, 16} and we want to return all those elements which are less than 8 then the condition will be TakeWhile(n => n < 8). It will return the elements {3, 5}.

Skip	This operator is used to return elements from a specified index position of a collection. For example, if we have a collection {3, 5, 8, 7, 11, 16} and we want to retrieve elements from element 7 to element 16, the target index position will be 3 because element 7 is located on index position 3. The target index position 3 is passed to the parameter of the Skip operator as Skip(3). The Skip(3) will return elements from index position 3 to the end of the collection and will skip elements from index position 0 to index position 2. The resultant elements will be {7, 11, 16}.
SkipWhile	This operator is used to skip those elements that satisfy a specified condition.

The following program demonstrates the partitioning operators Take, TakeWhile, Skip, and SkipWhile in details:

C# Program

```
using System.Collections.Generic;
using System.Linq;

//Declare an Integer Array
int[] IntegerNumbers = {3, 5, 8, 7, 11, 16};

//This LINQ Query only returns the elements 3, 5
var result = IntegerNumbers.TakeWhile(n => n < 8);

foreach (var numbers in result)
{
Console.WriteLine(numbers);
}

//This LINQ Query skips the elements less than 8 such as 3 and 5 using the condition SkipWhile(n => n < 8) and will return elements from 8 to 15 because the TakeWhile condition is less than 16 so 16 will also be skipped. The returned elements will be 8, 7, 11

var result1 = IntegerNumbers.SkipWhile(n => n < 8)
```

```
                    .TakeWhile(n => n < 16);

foreach (var numbers in result1)
{
Console.WriteLine(numbers);
}

//This LINQ Query returns elements 3, 5, 8
var result2 = IntegerNumbers.Take(3);

foreach (var numbers in result2)
{
Console.WriteLine(numbers);
}

//This LINQ Query returns elements from index position 3 to the //end of
the sequence and will return elements 7, 11, 16

var result3 = IntegerNumbers.Skip(3);

foreach (var numbers in result3)
{
Console.WriteLine(numbers);
}
```

Join Operators

Join operators are used to join two collections into one collection like SQL joining. They join two collections on the basis of matched keys and return a single collection. Following is the details of Join operators:

Join Operators	Description
Join	This operator is used to join two collections based on matching keys and return a single collection.
GroupJoin	This operator is used to join two collections based on matching keys. It returns a group of collections.

Following is the general syntax of LINQ joining query:

from ... in outerCollection
join ... in innerCollection
on outerKey equals innerKey
select ...

The following programs show how to join two collections on the basis of common key or attribute:

Program # 1

Write a program that joins two lists in which one list is Employees general list and another list is the employees Departments.
C# Program

```
using System;
using System.Linq;
using System.Collections.Generic;

namespace ConsoleApplication1
{
public class Employee
{
public int EmpID {get; set;}
public string EmpName {get; set;}
public int Age {get; set;}
public int DeptID {get; set;}
}

public class Department
{
public int DeptID {get; set;}
public string DeptName {get; set;}
}
public class Program
{
public static void Main()
{
```

```
//The Employees Collection
IList<Employee> EmployeesList = new List<Employee>()
{
new Employee() {
EmpID = 1, EmpName = "Mohsin Shah", Age = 19, DeptID = 1},
new Employee() {
EmpID = 2, EmpName = "Mohib Shah", Age = 16, DeptID = 1},
new Employee() {
EmpID = 3, EmpName = "Hassan Shah", Age = 16, DeptID = 2},
new Employee() {
EmpID = 4, EmpName = "Moniba Khan", Age = 11, DeptID = 3},
new Employee() {
EmpID = 5, EmpName = "Sara Khan", Age = 6, DeptID = 3}
};

//The Departments Collection
IList<Department> DepartmentsList = new List<Department>()
{
new Department(){DeptID = 1, DeptName="Engineering"},
new Department(){DeptID = 2, DeptName="Mathematics"},
new Department(){DeptID = 3, DeptName = "Medical"}
};

//LINQ Query to join Employee and Department Collection
var innerJoin = from emp in EmployeesList          //Outer Collection
join dept in DepartmentsList                       //Inner Collection
on emp.DeptID equals dept.DeptID                   //Key Selector
select new
{
//Result Selector
EmployeeName = emp.EmpName,
DepartmentName = dept.DeptName
};

foreach (var j in innerJoin)
{
```

```
Console.WriteLine("{0} - {1}", j.EmployeeName,
                               j.DepartmentName);
}

Console.ReadKey();
}
}
}
```

Program # 2

Write a program that joins two string lists and retrieves the common elements between them using the LINQ method syntax.
C# Program

```
//Include namespaces
using System.Linq;
using System.Collections.Generic;

//Declare a String List
IList<string> collection1 = new List<string>()
{
"Pakistan",
"China",
"Germany",
"Saudi Arabia"
};

IList<string> collection2 = new List<string>()
{
"Saudi Arabia",
"Germany",
"France",
"Austria"
};

var innerJoin = collection1.Join(// Outer Collection
collection2, //Inner Collection
str1 => str1, //Outer Key
```

```
str2 => str2, //Inner Key
(str1, str2) => str1);

foreach (var j in innerJoin)
{
Console.WriteLine("{0} ", j);
}
```

Grouping Operators

Grouping operators are used to group the elements of a collection based on some specific keys like SQL Group By clause. When a grouping operator grouped the elements of a collection on the basis of common key, it returns each group of elements in a collection that represents an object of IGrouping<TKey, TElement> interface. The IGrouping<TKey, TElement> interface represents a collection of objects that have a common key. The TKey is the type of the key of the IGrouping<TKey, TElement> and the TElement is the type of the value of the IGrouping<TKey, TElement>. Following is the details of grouping operators:

Grouping Operators	**Description**
GroupBy	This operator is used to group the elements of a collection based on a specific key and returns each group of elements in a
	collection that represents an object of the IGrouping<TKey, TElement> interface.
ToLookup	This operator is used to group the elements of a collection based on a specific key and returns each group of elements in a collection that represents an object of the IGrouping<TKey, TElement> interface. The ToLookup operator is the same as GroupBy operator but the main difference is that the processing of ToLookup operators is faster than GroupBy. Therefore, to use a collection of huge data, the ToLookup operator is used.

The following programming examples show how to group the elements of a collection on the basis of specific keys:

Program # 1

Write a program that group the elements of an integer array on the basis of even and odd and returns two sub collections which contains even and odd elements respectively.
C# Program

```
using System.Linq;

//Declare an Integer Array
int[] intArray = {1, 2, 3, 4, 5, 6, 7, 8, 9};

var query = intArray.GroupBy(i => i % 2);

foreach (IGrouping<int, int> group in query)
{
Console.WriteLine("Key:{0}", group.Key);
foreach (int number in group)
{
Console.WriteLine(number);
}
}
```

Visual Basic Program

```
Imports System.Collections.Generic

'Declare an Integer Array
Dim intArray As Integer() = {1, 2, 3, 4, 5, 6, 7, 8, 9}

Dim query = intArray.GroupBy(Function(i) i Mod 2)

For Each group As IGrouping(Of Integer, Integer) In query
Console.WriteLine("Key:{0}", group.Key)
For Each number As Integer In group
Console.WriteLine(number)
Next
Next
```

The above program produced grouped Key values of 0 and 1 because the module value is 2 similarly, if the module value is 3 then it will produce the grouped key values of 0, 1, 2, and so on.

Program # 2

Write a program that group the Students List by Department name and count the total number of students in each department.
C# Program

```
using System;
using System.Linq;
using System.Collections.Generic;

namespace ConsoleApplication1
{
class Students
{
public string Name{get; set;}
public string Gender {get; set;}
public string Department {get; set;}
}
class Program
{
static void Main(string[] args)
{
List<Students> StudentsList = new List<Students>()
{
new Students() {
Name = "Mohsin", Gender = "M", Department = "Engineering"},
new Students() {
Name = "Hassan", Gender = "M", Department = "Physics"},
new Students() {
Name = "Shakoor", Gender = "M", Department = "IT"},
new Students() {
Name = "Naveed", Gender = "M", Department = "Physics"},
new Students() {
Name = "Salman", Gender = "M", Department = "IT"},
new Students() {
```

```
Name = "Muniba Khan", Gender = "F", Department = "Medical"},
new Students() {
Name = "Sara Khan", Gender = "F", Department = "Medical"},
new Students() {
Name = "Neelam", Gender = "F", Department = "Mathematics"},
new Students() {
Name = "Saeed Khan", Gender = "M", Department = "Chemistry"},
new Students() {
Name = "Kashif", Gender = "M", Department = "Chemistry"}
};

//LINQ Query to group the Students List by Department name and //count the total number of students in each department using the //LINQ Query Expression
var result = from students in StudentsList
group students by students.Department;

Console.WriteLine("LINQ Query Expression");
foreach (var std in result)
{
Console.WriteLine(std.Key + " = " + std.Count());
}

//LINQ Query to group the Students List by Department name and //count the total number of students in each department using the //LINQ Query Method
var result1 = StudentsList.GroupBy(d => d.Department);

Console.WriteLine("LINQ Query Method");
foreach (var std1 in result1)
{
Console.WriteLine(std1.Key + " ---- " + std1.Count());
}

//LINQ Query to group the Students List by Department name and // count the total number of students in each department and also //retrieve the students name in each department using the LINQ//Query Expression
var result2 = from students in StudentsList
```

```
group students by students.Department;

Console.WriteLine("Department Name and Students List");
foreach (var std2 in result2)
{
Console.WriteLine(std2.Key + " ---- " + std2.Count());
foreach (var s in std2)
{
Console.WriteLine(s.Name);
}
}
Console.ReadKey();
}
}
}
```

Sequencing Operators

Sequencing operators are used to create a new sequence of value. Following is the details of sequencing operators:

Sequencing Operators	Description
DefaultIfEmpty	This operator is used to return a default blank sequence. It is usually used for adding default element if source sequence or collection is empty.
Empty	This operator is used to return an empty sequence.
Range	This operator is used to return a range of numeric numbers. For example, we need a new sequence starting from 1 to 10.
Repeat	This operator is used to returns a sequence of repeating same value at specific number of times. For example, we need five elements of value "Default" in a collection.

Equality Operators

The equality operators provide a single operator which is used to compare collections or sequences. Following is the details of this operator:

Equality Operators	Description
SequenceEqual	This operator is used to compare two collections or sequences and return true if they are equals.

Element Operators

These operators are used to find an element at a specific index in the collection. Following is the details of Element operators:

Element Operators	Description
ElementAt	This operator is used to return an element at a specific index of a collection.
ElementAtOrDefault	This operator is used to return an element at a specific index of a collection. If the required element did not find, it returns a blank result.
First	This operator is used to return the first element of a collection or the first element that satisfy a condition.
FirstOrDefault	This operator is used to return the first element of a collection or the first element that satisfy a condition. If the collection is empty or no element matches the condition, it returns a default value.
Last	This operator is used to return the last element of a collection or the last element that satisfy a condition.
LastOrDefault	This operator is used to return the last element of a collection or the last element that satisfy a condition. If a collection is empty or no element matches the condition, it returns a default value.
Single	This operator is used to return a single element of a collection. It works only if a collection is a single element collection. If a collection has more than one element, it returns an exception.

SingleOrDefault	This operator is used to return a single element of a collection or an element that satisfy a condition. If a collection is empty or no element matches the condition, it returns a default value.

The following program uses the FirstOrDefault, First, Last, ElementAt operators:

C# Program

```
using System.Linq;

//Declare an empty string array collection
string[] emptyArray = {};

//Declare a non empty string array collection
string[] notEmptyArray = {"Mohsin", "Hassan", "Moniba"};

var result = emptyArray.FirstOrDefault();
Console.WriteLine("Null Result = " + result);

result = notEmptyArray.First();
Console.WriteLine("First Elemnt = " + result);

result = notEmptyArray.Last();
Console.WriteLine("Last Element = " + result);

result = notEmptyArray.ElementAt(1);
Console.WriteLine("Element at Index 1 = " + result);

//LINQ Query to return the first element that starts with a specified //
character specified with the StartWith method
result = notEmptyArray.First(s => s.StartsWith("M"));
Console.WriteLine("First Elemnt with First Character = " + result);
```

Conversion Operators

These operators are used to convert elements of a collection to another data types. Following is the details of Conversion operators:

Conversion Operators	Description
AsEnumerable	This operator is used to return a new collection of IEnumerable<T>. It is usually used to make a queryable collection into an in-memory collection.
AsQueryable	This operator is used to return a new collection of IQueryable<T>.
Cast	This operator is used to cast the element to a specific type.
ToArray	This operator is used to return a new collection of an array[] type.
ToDictionary	This operator is used to return a new collection of generic Dictionary<Key,Value> type.
ToList	This operator is used to return a new collection of generic List type.

Concatenation Operators

This operators group provides a single operator which is used to create new collection based on the two collections. Following is the details of this operator:

Concatenation Operators	Description
Concat	This operator is used to concatenate two collections and returns a new collection by joining all the elements of both the collections.

Program # 1

Write a program that concatenates two string array collections and returns a single array collection that contains the elements of both the collections.
C# Program

```
using System.Linq;

//Declare two String Arrays
string[] array1 = {"Mohsin", "Mohib", "Hassan", "Zia"};
```

```
string[] array2 = {"Moniba", "Sara", "Anood", "Mohib"};

//LINQ Query to concatenate the elements of Array1 and array2
var newArray = array1.Concat(array2).OrderBy(s => s);

foreach (var e in newArray)
Console.WriteLine(e);
```

Visual Basic Program

```
Imports System.Linq

'Declare two String Arrays
Dim array1 As String() = {"Mohsin", "Mohib", "Hassan", "Zia"}
Dim array2 As String() = {"Moniba", "Sara", "Anood", "Mohib"}

'LINQ Query to concatenate the elements of Array1 and array2
Dim newArray = array1.Concat(array2).OrderBy(Function(s) s)

For Each e In newArray
Console.WriteLine(e)
Next
```

Aggregation Operators

Aggregation operators are used to find the computational values such as sum, average, count, max and min. Following is the details of Aggregation operators:

Aggregation Operators	Description
Average	This operator is used to find the average value of all elements of a collection.
Count	This operator is used to count the number of elements of a collection.
LongCount	This operator is used to count the number of elements of a huge collection. It returns a long data type and it is used when a collection has more than int.Max elements.
Max	This operator is used to find the maximum value of a collection.

Min	This operator is used to find the minimum value of a collection.
Sum	This operator is used to find the sum of the elements of a collection.
Aggregate	This operator is used to perform the custom aggregation operation on a collection.

Program # 1

Write a program that finds the sum of the elements, the Minimum value, the Maximum value, and Average value of an integer array.
C# Program

```
using System.Linq;

//Declare an Integer Array
int[] intArray = {1, 3, 4, 2, 6, 5, 7, 8, 9, 11};

//LINQ Query to find Sum of the elements of array
var sumValue = intArray.Sum(s => s);
Console.WriteLine("Sum of Array Elements = " + sumValue);

//LINQ Query to find the Minimum value of array
var minValue = intArray.Min(s => s);
Console.WriteLine("Minimum value of Array = " + minValue);

//LINQ Query to find the Maximum value of array
var maxValue = intArray.Max(s => s);
Console.WriteLine("Maximum value of Array = " + maxValue);

//LINQ Query to find the Average value of array
var averageValue = intArray.Average(s => s);
Console.WriteLine("Average value of Array = " + averageValue);
```

DataContext Class

DataContext class is used to communicate with the database in LINQ. It equivalent to the SqlConnection that establishes a connection to the database and performs different operations such as submits and retrieves objects to database, converts objects to SQL queries, and SQL queries to objects. It takes a connection string and opens a database according to the provided connection string. The namespace of the DataContext class is System.Data.Linq. The DataContext class provides the following constructors:

- DataContext(DbConnection)
- DataContext(DbConnection, MappingSource)
- DataContext(String)
- DataContext(String, MappingSource)

DataContext(DbConnection)

This constructor is used to declare and initialize a new instance of the DataContext class. It takes a single parameter DbConnection that represents the Connection String of the target database.

DataContext(DbConnection, MappingSource)

This constructor is used to declare and initialize a new instance of the DataContext class. It takes two parameters. The first parameter is DbConnection that represents the Connection String of the target database, and the second parameter is MappingSource that represents a source for mapping information.

DataContext(String)

This constructor is used to declare and initialize a new instance of the DataContext class. It takes a single parameter String that represents a File name, a Server name, or a Connection String. The File name is the name of a file where a SQL Server Express database resides, the Server name is the name of a server where a database is installed, and the Connection String is a connection string of the target database.

DataContext(String, MappingSource)

This constructor is used to declare and initialize a new instance of the DataContext class. It takes two parameters. The first parameter is a String parameter that represents a File name, a Server name, or a Connection String. The File name is the name of a file where a SQL Server Express database resides, the Server name is the name of a server where a database is installed, and the Connection String is a connection string of the target database, and the second parameter is a MappingSource parameter that represents a source for the mapping information.

Properties of DataContext Class

The DataContext class provides the following important properties:

- Connection Property
- Mapping Property
- Log Property

Connection Property

This property of DataContext class is used to get the current connection used by the .NET framework. Following is its general declaration:

C# Declaration
public DbConnection Connection {get;}
Visual Basic Declaration
Public ReadOnly Property Connection As DbConnection

Mapping Property

This property of DataContext class is used to get the MetaModel on which the mapping is based. The MetaModel is an abstraction that represents the mapping between a database and domain objects.

Log Property

This property is used to get or set the destination to write the SQL query or command.

Methods of DataContext Class

DataContext class provides the following important methods:

- DatabaseExists Method
- DeleteDatabae Method
- ExecuteCommand Method
- ExecuteQuery Method
- GetTable Method
- GetChangeSet Method
- SubmitChanges Method

DatabaseExists Method

This method of DataContext class is used to determine whether the associated or connected database exists or not. It returns a Boolean value either true or false. If the associated or connected database exist, it returns true, and if the associated or connected database does not exist then it returns false.

DeleteDatabase Method

This method of DataContext class is used to delete the associated database.

ExecuteCommand Method

This method of DataContext class is used to execute the SQL command directly on the associated or connected database. It is usually used to insert records in the database, delete or update specific records of the database. The ExecuteCommand method takes two parameters. The first parameter is a string parameter that specifies the SQL command to be executed, and the second parameter is an array of type object that is called array of parameters. The array of parameters contains a list of parameters to be passed to the SQL command. Following is its general declaration:

C# Declaration
public int ExecuteCommand(string command, params object[] parameters)
Visual Basic Declaration
Public Function ExecuteCommand(command As String, ParamArray parameters As Object()) As Integer

When the ExecuteCommand method is executed, it returns an integer value that specifies the number of rows modified by the executed command.

ExecuteQuery Method

This method of DataContext class is used to execute the SQL queries directly on the associated database. It provides the following two overloaded forms:

- ExecuteQuery(Type, String, Object[])
- ExecuteQuery<TResult>(String, Object[])

ExecuteQuery(Type, String, Object[])

This overloaded form of ExecuteQuery method is used to execute SQL queries directly on the database. It takes three parameters. The first parameter is System.Type parameter that specifies the type of the IEnumerable<T> to be returned. The second parameter is a String type parameter that specifies the SQL query to be executed. The third parameter is Object type array that is called array of parameters. The array of parameters contains a list of parameters to be passed to the SQL command. Following is its general declaration:

C# Declaration
public IEnumerable ExecuteQuery(Type elementType, string query, params object[] parameters)
Visual Basic Declaration
Public Function ExecuteQuery (elementType As Type, query As String, ParamArray parameters As Object()) As IEnumerable

When this overloaded form of ExecuteQuery method is executed, it returns the IEnumerable<T> collection of objects.

ExecuteQuery<TResult>(String, Object[])

This overloaded form of ExecuteQuery method is used to execute SQL queries directly on the database and returns objects. It takes two parameters. The first parameter is a String parameter that specifies the SQL query to be executed and the second parameter is an array of object type that is called array of parameters. The array of parameters contains a list of parameters to be passed to the SQL command. Following is its general declaration:

C# Declaration
public IEnumerable<TResult> ExecuteQuery<TResult>(string query, params object[] parameters)
Visual Basic Declaration
Public Function ExecuteQuery(Of TResult) (query As String, ParamArray parameters As Object()) As IEnumerable(Of TResult)

When this overloaded form of ExecuteQuery method is executed, it returns the IEnumerable<TResult> collection of objects

GetTable Method

This method of DataContext class is used to return a collection of objects of a particular type where the type is defined by the type parameter or by the TEntity parameter. The GetTable method takes a single parameter that defines the type of the objects to be returned. It provides the following two overloaded forms:

- GetTable(Type)
- GetTable<TEntity>()

GetTable(Type)

This overloaded form of the GetTable method takes a Type parameter that specifies the type of the objects to be returned. Following is its general declaration:

C# Declaration
public ITable GetTable(Type type)
Visual Basic Declaration
Public Function GetTable (type As Type) As ITable

The parameter Type specifies the type of the objects to be returned. When it is executed, it returns a collection of objects defined by the Type parameter.

GetTable<TEntity>()

This overloaded form of the GetTable method takes the TEntity parameter that specifies the type of the objects to be returned. When we created a DataContext class then the GetTable<TEntity>() method is used to get a specified table or a list of tables which are linked to the current DataContext class. Following is its general declaration:

C# Declaration
public Table<TEntity> GetTable<TEntity>()
Visual Basic Declaration
Public Function GetTable(Of TEntity) As Table(Of TEntity)

The parameter TEntity specifies the type of the objects to be returned. When it is executed, it returns a collection of objects defined by the TEntity parameter.

GetChangeSet Method

This method of DataContext class is used to get the modified objects tracked by DataContext. It returns ChangeSet. Following is its general declaration:

C# Declaration
public ChangeSet GetChangeSet()
Visual Basic Declaration
Public Function GetChangeSet As ChangeSet

SubmitChanges Method

This method of DataContext class is used to wrap up all of the changes and calculate the set of modified objects to be inserted, updated, or deleted, and executes specified commands to submit the changes to the database.

The following programs demonstrate the DatabaseExists method and ExecuteCommand method of the DataContext class:

Program # 1

Write a program that checks whether a specified database exists or not using the DatabaseExists method of DataContext class.
C# Program

```
using System;
using System.Data.Linq;

namespace ConsoleApplication1
{
class Program
{
static void Main(string[] args)
{

//Declare a string variable ConnectionString
string ConnectionString;

ConnectionString =
                "Data Source=localhost\\MSSQLSERVER2014;" +
                "Initial Catalog=Students;" +
                "User ID=adalat khan;Password=Std123";

//Declare an object of the DataContext class and open database
DataContext context = new DataContext(ConnectionString);

bool dbExist = context.DatabaseExists();
if (dbExist == true)
{
Console.WriteLine("Database Exist");
}
else
{
Console.WriteLine("Database does not Exist");
}
Console.ReadKey(true);
}
}
}
```

Program # 2

Write a program that deletes a specific record from the database using the ExecuteCommand method of DataContext class.
C# Program

```
using System;
using System.Data.Linq;

namespace ConsoleApplication1
{
class Program
{
static void Main(string[] args)
{
//Declare a string variable ConnectionString
string ConnectionString;

ConnectionString =
                    "Data Source=localhost\\MSSQLSERVER2014;" +
                    "Initial Catalog=Students;" +
                    "User ID=adalat khan;Password=Std123";

//Declare an object of the DataContext class and open database
DataContext context = new DataContext(ConnectionString);

//Execute the ExecuteCommand method and delete record of a //student
who's Registration number is 5
int result = context.ExecuteCommand("DELETE from StudentsInfo
WHERE StdRegNumber = {0}", 5);

Console.WriteLine("The number of rows deleted = " + result);

Console.ReadKey();
}
}
}
```

Visual Basic Program
Imports System Imports System.Data.Linq Module Module1 Sub Main() Dim ConnectionString As String ConnectionString = "Data Source=localhost\MSSQLSERVER2014;" & "Initial Catalog=Students;" & "User ID=adalat khan;Password=Std123" 'Declare an object of the DataContext class and open database Dim context As DataContext = New DataContext(ConnectionString) 'Execute the ExecuteCommand method and delete record of a 'student who's Registration number is 5 Dim result As Integer = context.ExecuteCommand("DELETE from StudentsInfo WHERE StdRegNumber = {0}", 5) Console.WriteLine("The number of rows deleted = " & result) Console.ReadKey() End Sub End Module

LINQ to SQL

LINQ to SQL is a mapping between the Relational Database Schema and Objects. The relational data can be manipulated using LINQ by its mapped objects. When an object is linked to relational data, it receives attributes of the relational data. The mapping is done by translating the relational database schemas into object definitions and this can be done automatically by using the LINQ to SQL Tools in Visual Studio which is called Object Relational Designer (O/R Designer). The Object Relational Designer is an editor which is used to create the LINQ to SQL mapping. The Object Relational Designer has two panels. The Left side panel is the designer panel where we can drag and drop the required tables from the Server explorer and the right side panel is used to perform advanced configurations like mapping to stored procedures or functions from the database. Following are the basic steps to add LINQ to SQL:

1. Open a new project.
2. Add a new database connection using the Server Explorer.
3. From Server Explorer, right click on Data Connections and click e Add Connection option. Following is the snapshot of the Server Explorer:

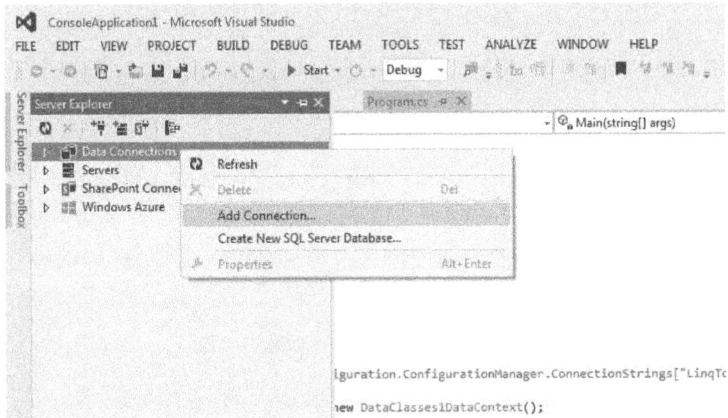

4. From Add Connection window, select the Server name where the SQL server is installed or enter the complete path of the target SQL server instance name in the Server Name text box.
5. Now select the target database name from the Select or enter a database name dropdown list and click Ok. Following is the snapshot of the Add Connection window:

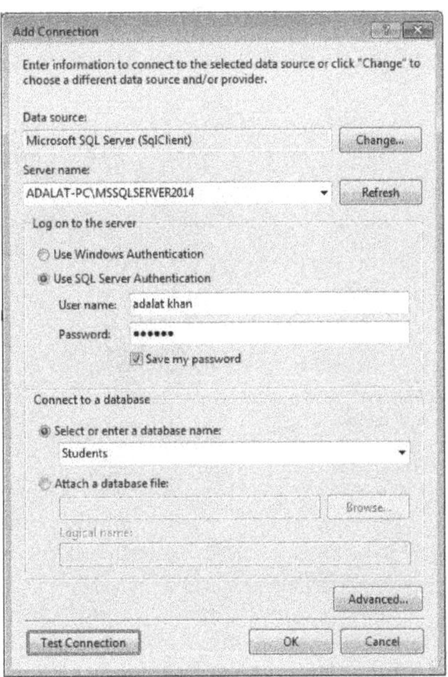

6. Now to add LINQ to SQL, Right click on the project name from the Solution Explorer and click the Add option then click the New Item option. Following is the snapshot of the Add New Item window:

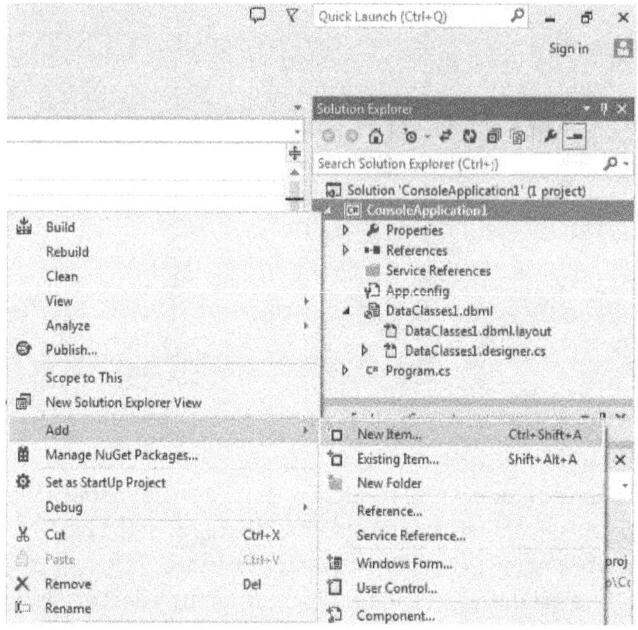

7. Now from Add New Item window, click on LINQ to SQL classes. The default name of the LINQ to SQL classes is DataClasses1.dbml. We can also change the default name to any other name. Following is the snapshot:

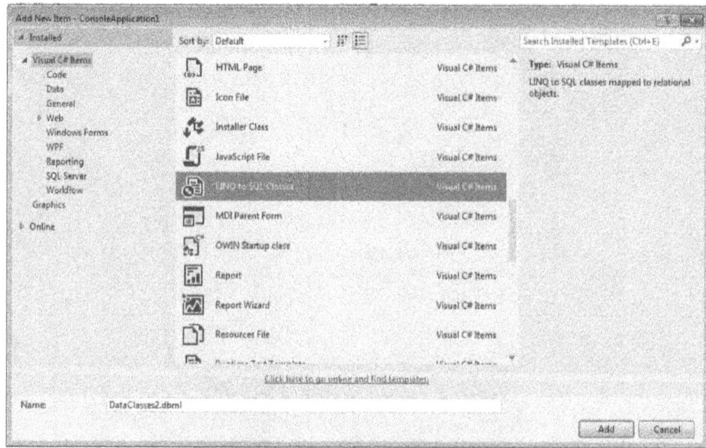

8. Now select the required tables from the server Explorer and drag into the DataClasses1.dbml left side panel
9. The LINQ to SQL classes (DataClasses1.dbml) has a toolbox which we can use to set the associations or relationships between the tables.
10. When the LINQ to SQL Classes is created and the required tables are added then it creates a DataContext DataClasses1DataContext. The DataClasses1DataContext is the default name of the DataContext and it depends on the name of the DataClasses1.dbml. Following is the snapshot of the DataClasses1DataContext.dbml:

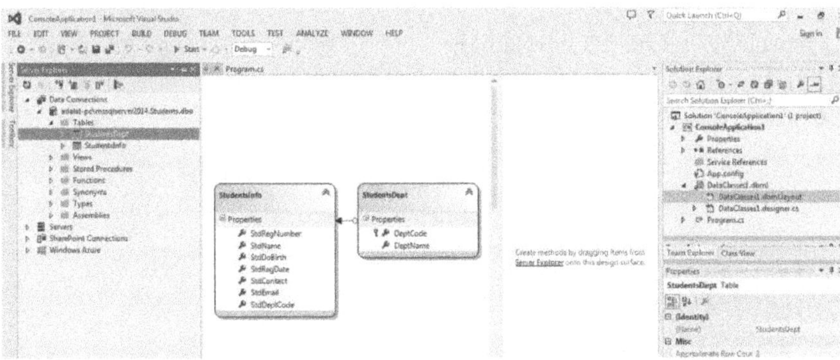

11. Now LINQ to SQL is ready to use. Just declare an object from the created DataContext DataClasses1DataContext and performs LINQ query on this object.

Programming Examples of LINQ to SQL

The following programming examples explain LINQ to SQL and demonstrate how to display the Data Model of the .dbml, how to display data from the database using LINQ to SQL and how to manipulate the database data.

Program # 1

Write a program that retrieves the tables list of the DataContext .dbml class.
C# Program

```
using System;
using System.Linq;

namespace ConsoleApplication1
```

```
{
class Program
{
static void Main(string[] args)
{
DataClasses1DataContext dbcontext = new
                                        DataClasses1DataContext();
var dtm = dbcontext.Mapping;
foreach (var t in dtm.GetTables())
{
Console.WriteLine(t.TableName);
}
Console.ReadKey();
}
}
}
```

Program # 2

Write a program that retrieves data from a database table using LINQ to SQL.
C# Program

```
using System;
using System.Data.Linq;
using System.Linq;

namespace ConsoleApplication1
{
class Program
{
static void Main(string[] args)
{
//Declare an object of the DataContext
DataClasses1DataContext dbContext = new
                                        DataClasses1DataContext();

//Retrieve data from StudentsInfo table
var result = from d in dbContext.GetTable<StudentsInfo>()
          select d;
```

```
foreach (var std in result)
{
Console.WriteLine("Student ID = " + std.StdRegNumber);
Console.WriteLine("Student Name = " + std.StdName);
Console.WriteLine("Student Date of Birth = " + std.StdDoBirth);
}
Console.ReadKey();
}
}
}
```

Visual Basic Program

```
Imports System
Imports System.Data.Linq

Module Module1

Sub Main()

'Declare an object of the DataContext
Dim dbContext As DataClasses1DataContext = New
                                        DataClasses1DataContext()

'Retrieve data from StudentsInfo table
Dim result = From d In dbContext.GetTable(Of StudentsInfo)()
          Select d

For Each std In result
Console.WriteLine("Student ID = " & std.StdRegNumber)
Console.WriteLine("Student Name = " & std.StdName)
Console.WriteLine("Student Date of Birth = " & std.StdDoBirth)
Next

Console.ReadKey()

End Sub
End Module
```

Program # 3

<table>
<tr><td>Write a program that inserts new data into a database table using LINQ to SQL.</td></tr>
<tr><td align="center">C# Program</td></tr>
<tr><td>

```
using System.Linq;

DataClasses1DataContext dbContext = new
                                        DataClasses1DataContext();

//Declare an object from the StudentsInfo Table and assign values //to its
attributes
StudentsInfo obj = new StudentsInfo();
obj.StdRegNumber = "008";
obj.StdName = "Hassan Shah";
DateTime dob = new DateTime(1991, 11, 09);
obj.StdDoBirth = dob;

try
{
//Insert new student into StudentsInfo table
dbContext.GetTable<StudentsInfo>().InsertOnSubmit(obj);

//Save changes to the Database
dbContext.SubmitChanges();

Console.WriteLine("The record has been inserted");
}

catch(Exception e)
{
Console.WriteLine(e.Message);
}
```

</td></tr>
<tr><td align="center">Visual Basic Program</td></tr>
<tr><td>

```
Imports System.Linq

Dim dbContext As DataClasses1DataContext = New
```

</td></tr>
</table>

```
                                        DataClasses1DataContext()

'Declare an object from the StudentsInfo Table and assign values to 'its
attributes
Dim obj As StudentsInfo = New StudentsInfo()
obj.StdRegNumber = "008"
obj.StdName = "Hassan Shah"
Dim dob As DateTime = New DateTime(1991, 11, 9)
obj.StdDoBirth = dob

Try
'Insert new student record into StudentsInfo table
dbContext.GetTable(Of StudentsInfo)().InsertOnSubmit(obj)

'Save changes to the Database
dbContext.SubmitChanges()

Console.WriteLine("The record has been inserted")

Catch e As System.Data.SqlClient.SqlException
Console.WriteLine("The Record already Exist")

End Try
```

InsertOnSubmit() Method

This method is used to add record or entity to the current table of the database. It is used with the conjunction of the SubmitChanges() method of DataContext class. The SubmitChanges() method submit and save the inserted record or entity of the InsertOnSubmit() method.

InsertAllOnSubmit() Method

This method is used to add more records or entities to the current table of the database. If we want to insert more than one record then we need to create a list for all the entities and call this method only one time. This method is also used with the conjunction of the SubmitChanges() method.

Program # 4

Write a program that inserts more than one record into a database table using LINQ to SQL.
C# Program

```
using System;
using System.Linq;
using System.Collections.Generic;

namespace ConsoleApplication1
{
class Program
{
static void Main(string[] args)
{

DataClasses1DataContext dbContext = new

DataClasses1DataContext();

//Declae a List of type StudentsInfo table to insert more records into //the StudentsInfo table
List<StudentsInfo> newStd = new List<StudentsInfo>();

newStd.Add(new StudentsInfo()
{StdRegNumber = "1", StdName = "Shahid", StdDoBirth = Convert.ToDateTime("01/01/1993")});
newStd.Add(new StudentsInfo()
{StdRegNumber = "2", StdName = "Moniba Khan", StdDoBirth = Convert.ToDateTime("07/15/2006")});
newStd.Add(new StudentsInfo()
{StdRegNumber = "3", StdName = "Sara Khan", StdDoBirth = Convert.ToDateTime("05/25/2011")});
newStd.Add(new StudentsInfo()
{StdRegNumber = "4", StdName = "Mohib Shah", StdDoBirth = Convert.ToDateTime("11/09/2001")});
newStd.Add(new StudentsInfo()
```

```
{StdRegNumber = "5", StdName = "Mohsin Shah", StdDoBirth = Convert.
ToDateTime("04/11/1998")}});

try
{
//Insert all Students into StudentsInfo table
dbContext.GetTable<StudentsInfo>().InsertAllOnSubmit(newStd);

//Save changes into the database
dbContext.SubmitChanges();
Console.WriteLine("The record has been inserted");
}
catch (Exception e)
{
Console.WriteLine(e.Message);
}
Console.ReadKey();
}
}
}
```

Program # 5

Write a program that deletes a single specified record from the database table using LINQ to SQL
C# Program

```
using System.Linq;

DataClasses1DataContext dbContext = new
                                DataClasses1DataContext();
try
{
//LINQ query to retrieve a specified student record using the //Student
Registration Number
StudentsInfo std = dbContext.GetTable<StudentsInfo>().
                Single(d => d.StdRegNumber == "1");

//Delete the retrieved student record from the StudentsInfo table
```

```
dbContext.GetTable<StudentsInfo>().DeleteOnSubmit(std);

//Save changes into the database
dbContext.SubmitChanges();

Console.WriteLine("The record has been Deleted");
}
catch (Exception e)
{
Console.WriteLine(e.Message);
}
```

Visual Basic Program

```
Imports System.Linq

Dim dbContext As DataClasses1DataContext = New
DataClasses1DataContext()

Try
'LINQ query to retrieve a specified student record using the Student
'Registration Number
Dim std As StudentsInfo = dbContext.GetTable(Of StudentsInfo)().
                          Single(Function(d) d.StdRegNumber = "1")

'Delete the retrieved student record from the StudentsInfo table
dbContext.GetTable(Of StudentsInfo)().DeleteOnSubmit(std)

'Save changes into the database
dbContext.SubmitChanges()

Console.WriteLine("The record has been Deleted")

Catch e As System.InvalidOperationException
Console.WriteLine("The record does not Exist")

End Try
```

Program # 6

Write a program that deletes multiple records from a database table using LINQ to SQL.
C# Program

```
using System.Linq;
using System.Collections.Generic;

DataClasses1DataContext dbContext = new
                                    DataClasses1DataContext();
try
{
//Declare a List and add the target Students Registration Numbers //into the List we want to Delete
List<string> list1 = new List<string>();
list1.Add("1");
list1.Add("2");
list1.Add("3");
list1.Add("4");
list1.Add("5");

//LINQ query to retrieve the selected Students record from the // StudentsInfo table selected in the List<string> list1 to delete
var result = from d in dbContext.GetTable<StudentsInfo>()
          where list1.Contains(d.StdRegNumber)
          select d;

//Delete the selected Students record from the StudentsInfo table //selected in the List<string> list1
dbContext.GetTable<StudentsInfo>().DeleteAllOnSubmit(result);

//Save changes into the database
dbContext.SubmitChanges();

Console.WriteLine("The record has been Deleted");
}

catch (Exception e)
```

```
{
Console.WriteLine(e.Message);
}
```

Visual Basic Program

```
Imports System.Linq
Imports System.Collections.Generic

Dim dbContext As DataClasses1DataContext = New
DataClasses1DataContext()

Try
'Declare a List and add the target Students Registration Numbers 'into the
List we want to Delete
Dim list1 As List(Of String) = New List(Of String)

list1.Add("1")
list1.Add("2")
list1.Add("3")
list1.Add("4")
list1.Add("5")

'LINQ query to retrieve the selected Students record from the 'StudentsInfo
table selected in the List<string> list1 to delete
Dim result = From d In dbContext.GetTable(Of StudentsInfo)()
             Where list1.Contains(d.StdRegNumber)
             Select d

'Delete the selected Students record from the StudentsInfo table 'selected
in the List<String> list1
dbContext.GetTable(Of StudentsInfo)().DeleteAllOnSubmit(result)

'Save changes into the database
dbContext.SubmitChanges()

Console.WriteLine("The record has been Deleted")
```

```
Catch e As System.InvalidOperationException
Console.WriteLine("The record does not Exist")

End Try
```

Program # 7

Write a program that updates a specified record in a database table using LINQ to SQL.

C# Program

```
using System.Linq;

DataClasses1DataContext dbContext = new
                                        DataClasses1DataContext();
try
{
//LINQ query to retrieve a specified record of a student we want to //update
using the student Registration Number
StudentsInfo std = dbContext.GetTable<StudentsInfo>().
Single(d => d.StdRegNumber == "1");

//Set new data for the attributes of the selected student record
std.StdName = "Shahid Khan";
std.StdDoBirth = Convert.ToDateTime("01/01/1995");

//Save changes into the database
dbContext.SubmitChanges();
Console.WriteLine("The record has been Updated");
}
catch (Exception e)
{
Console.WriteLine(e.Message);
}
```

Visual Basic Program

```
Imports System.Linq

Dim dbContext As DataClasses1DataContext = New
```

```
DataClasses1DataContext()

Try
'LINQ query to retrieve a specified record of a student we want to 'update
using the student Registration Number
Dim std As StudentsInfo = dbContext.GetTable(Of StudentsInfo)().
Single(Function(d) d.StdRegNumber = "1")

'Set new data for the attributes of the selected student record
std.StdName = "Shahid Khan"
std.StdDoBirth = Convert.ToDateTime("01/01/1995")

'Save changes into the database
dbContext.SubmitChanges()
Console.WriteLine("The record has been Updated")

Catch e As System.InvalidOperationException
Console.WriteLine("The record does not exist")

End Try
```

LINQ to Dataset

To handle Dataset using LINQ, first a connection to the database is established and then the Dataset object is filled with the data from the database and LINQ query is used to handle the data. The following program demonstrates how to retrieve data from a Dataset object using LINQ query:

C# Program

```
using System;
using System.Data;
using System.Data.SqlClient;
using System.Linq;

namespace ConsoleApplication1
{
class Program
{
static void Main(string[] args)
{
```

```
String conStr;

//Connection String
conStr = "Data Source=localhost\\MSSQLSERVER2014;" +
                         "Initial Catalog=Students;" +
                         "User ID=adalat khan;Password=Std123";

string sql = "Select * from StudentsInfo";

//Create the DataAdapter object to retrieve data from the database
SqlDataAdapter dtAdapter = new SqlDataAdapter(sql, conStr);

//Create the Table Mappings
dtAdapter.TableMappings.Add("Table", "StudentsInfo");

//Create and fill the DataSet object
DataSet dst = new DataSet();
dtAdapter.Fill(dst);

DataTable stdInfo = dst.Tables["StudentsInfo"];

var result = from d in stdInfo.AsEnumerable()
select new
{
stdID = d.Field<string>("StdRegNumber"),
stdName = d.Field<string>("StdName"),
dob = d.Field<DateTime>("StdDoBirth")
};

foreach (var r in result)
{
Console.WriteLine("Student ID = " + r.stdID);
Console.WriteLine("Name = " + r.stdName);
Console.WriteLine("Birth Date = " + r.dob);
}

Console.WriteLine("\nPress any key to continue.");
Console.ReadKey();
}
}
}
```

Visual Basic Program
Imports System Imports System.Data Imports System.Data.SqlClient Imports System.Linq Module Module1 Sub Main() Dim ConStr As String 'Connection String ConStr = "Data Source=localhost\MSSQLSERVER2014;" & "Initial Catalog=Students;" & "User ID=adalat khan;Password=Std123" Dim sql As String = "Select * from StudentsInfo" 'Create the DataAdapter object to retrieve data from the database Dim dtAdapter As SqlDataAdapter dtAdapter = New SqlDataAdapter(sql, ConStr) 'Create the Table Mappings dtAdapter.TableMappings.Add("Table", "StudentsInfo") 'Create and fill the DataSet object Dim dst As DataSet = New DataSet() dtAdapter.Fill(dst) Dim stdInfo As DataTable = dst.Tables("StudentsInfo") Dim result = From d In stdInfo.AsEnumerable() Select New With { .stdID = d.Field(Of String)("StdRegNumber"), .stdName = d.Field(Of String)("StdName"), .dob = d.Field(Of DateTime)("StdDoBirth")}

```
For Each r In result
Console.WriteLine("Student ID = " & r.stdID)
Console.WriteLine("Name = " & r.stdName)
Console.WriteLine("Birth Date = " & r.dob)
Next

Console.WriteLine(vbLf & "Press any key to continue")
Console.ReadKey()

End Sub
End Module
```

Difference between LINQ to SQL and Entity Framework

LINQ to SQL and Entity Framework both provide mapping between databases and .NET classes but the main difference is that LINQ to SQL supports only SQL Server database and allow us to access and modify SQL Server database by using LINQ syntax and Entity Framework supports various Relational Databases Management Systems such as SQL Server, Oracle, DB2 and MySQL etc. Following is a list that describes the difference between LINQ to SQL and Entity Framework:

LINQ to SQL	Entity Framework
It supports and provides access to only SQL Server database.	It supports and provides access to various databases management systems such as SQL Server, Oracle, DB2, MYSQL etc.
It generates a .dbml file to maintain the selected tables of the database and the relationship between them.	It generates an .edmx file, .csdl file, .msl file and .ssdl file to maintain the selected tables and the relationship between then.
It is simple to use and it does not support complex type.	It is complex to use and it provides support to complex type.
It cannot generate database from model.	It can generate database from model.

It allows only one to one mapping between the entity classes and the relational tables, views.	It allows one-to-one, one-to-many and many-to-many mapping between the entity classes and the relational tables, views.
It uses DataContext class to perform query to data.	It uses ObjectContext class, and DbContext class to perform query to data.

CHAPTER 15

Streams and Files handling in .NET

CHAPTER CONTENTS

- Streams
- Stream Class
- FileStream Class
- Constructors of FileStream Class
- Properties of FileStream Class
- Methods of FileStream Class
- FileMode Enumearion
- FileAccess Enumeration
- FileShare Enumeration
- StreamWriter Class
- Methods of StreamWriter Class
- StreamReader Class
- Methods of StreamReader Class
- File Class
- Methods of File Class
- FileInfo Class
- Properties of FileInfo Class
- Methods of FileInfo Class
- XDocument Class
- Properties of XDocument Class

Streams

Stream is a source or an object that is used to transfer data from one point to another point or read-write data from external sources of the application memory. The external sources of the application may be physical files of the disk such as text files, XML files, Images, audio/video files, and TCP/IP sockets etc. The .NET framework provides a set of classes that can be used to write data to or read data from physical files of the disk and data from TCP/IP sockets. The .NET Stream classes are defined in the System.IO namespace. The Stream classes are categorized into three different types such as byte

Streams classes, character Streams classes, and binary Streams classes. The byte streams classes are used to read data from the stream or write data to the stream as bytes. The character streams classes are used to deal with the data of the stream as characters. The binary streams classes are used to deal with the data of the stream as binary data. Following is the details of the .NET framework Stream classes:

Classes Type	Classes List	Description
Byte Streams Classes	Stream Class FileStream Class MemoryStream Class BufferedStream Class NetworkStream Class PipeStream Class CryptoStream Class	These classes are used to write data to the stream and read data from the stream as bytes.
Character Streams Classes	TextReader Class TextWriter Class StreamReader Class StreamWriter Class StringReader Class StringWriter Class	These classes are used to write data to the stream and read data from the stream as characters.
Binary Stream Classes	BinaryReader Class BinaryWriter Class	These classes are used to write data to the stream and read data from the stream as binary data.

Stream Class

The Stream class is an abstract class that provides standard methods to transfer data from one point to another point or read/write data from different files and other sources. The Stream class read or writes data in the form of bytes. It is defined in the System.IO namespace. The Stream class is the base class of all the Stream classes in the .NET framework that read or writes data from different sources in bytes.

FileStream Class

FileStream class provides a stream for the files to read data from, write data to, open a file or closes a file on a file system. It supports both synchronous and asynchronous read and write operations. This class is derived from the Stream class. The FileStream class is used to read data from and write data such as bytes, characters, strings, and other data-type data to a file. The FileStream class is defined in the namespace System.IO therefore, to use FileStream class in the application or program, the namespace System.IO must be imported.

Constructors of FileStream Class

FileStream class provides the following important constructors to initialize instances or objects of the FileStream class:

Constructor	Description
FileStream(String, FileMode)	This constructor is used to initialize a new instance or object of the FileStream class. It takes two parameters. The first parameter is a string parameter that specifies the file path and second parameter is FileMode parameter that specifies the mode of the file. The FileMode is a buit-in enumeration that specifies the file mode. This constructor takes one of the FileMode enumeration value at a time and set the file mode.
FileStream(String, FileMode, FileAccess)	This constructor is used to initialize a new object of the FileStream class. It takes three parameters. The first parameter is a string parameter that specifies the file path, the second parameter is a FileMode parameter that specifies the file mode, and the third parameter is the FileAccess parameter that specifies the file access permission. The FileAccess is a built-in enumeration that provides different constant member values to specify different access permissions of a file.

FileStream(String, FileMode, FileAccess, FileShare)	This constructor is used to initialize a new object of the FileStream class. It takes four parameters. The first parameter is a string parameter that specifies the file path, the second parameter is the FileMode parameter that specifies the file mode, the third parameter is the FileAccess parameter that specifies the file access permission, and the fourth parameter is FileShare parameter that controls the file sharing among multiple accesses. The FileShare is a built-in enumeration that provides different constant member values to control the sharing of a file among multiple accesses.
FileStream(String, FileMode, FileAccess, FileShare, Int32)	This constructor is used to initialize a new object of the FileStream class. It takes five parameters. The first parameter is a string parameter that specifies the file path, the second parameter is FileMode parameter, the third parameter is FileAccess parameter, the fourth parameter is
	FileShare parameter, and the fifth parameter is an integer parameter that specifies the buffer size.
FileStream(String, FileMode, FileAccess, FileShare, Int32, Boolean)	This constructor is used to initialize a new object of the FileStream class with the specified path, creation mode, read-write, sharing permission, buffer size, and synchronous or asynchronous state.
FileStream(SafeFileHandle, FileAccess)	This constructor is used to initialize a new object of the FileStream class for the specified file handle with the specified read-write permission. It takes two parameters. The first parameter specifies the file handle and the second parameter specifies the file access permission.

FileStream(SafeFileHandle, FileAccess, Int32)	This constructor is used to initialize a new object of the FileStream class for the specified file handle with the specified read-write permission and buffer size.
FileStream(SafeFileHandle, FileAccess, Int32, Boolean)	This constructor is used to initialize a new object of the FileStream class for the specified file handle with the specified read-write permission, buffer size, and synchronous or asynchronous state.

Properties of FileStream Class

The FileStream class provides the following important properties:

Property	Description
Length	This property is used to get the length of the stream in bytes. It returns a long value that represents the length of the stream in bytes.
Name	This property is used to get the name of the FileStream.
Position	This property is used to get or set the current position of the stream.
ReadTimeOut	This property is used to get or set a value in milliseconds that determines the timeout of the stream before read.
WriteTimeOut	This property is used to get or set a value in milliseconds that determines the timeout of the stream before write.
CanRead	This property is used to determine whether the current stream is readable or not. If the current stream is readable or read-only, it returns true otherwise, it returns false.
CanWrite	This property is used to determine whether the current stream is writable or not. If the current stream is writable, it returns true otherwise, it returns false.
IsAsync	This property is used to determine whether the current FileStream is opened asynchronously or synchronously. It returns true if the current FileStream is opened asynchronously otherwise, it returns false.

Methods of FileStream Class

FileStream class provides the following important methods:

Method	Description
CopyTo(Stream)	This method is used to copy bytes from the current stream and writes them to another stream.
Close	This method is used to close the current stream and releases resources associated with the current stream.
ReadByte()	This method is used to read a byte from the file and shifts or advances the read position to the next byte of the stream. It returns an integer value that indicates a byte. If end of the stream reached then it returns -1.
Read(Byte[], Int32, Int32)	This method is used to read a block of bytes from the stream and writes them into a given buffer. It takes there parameters. The first parameter is byte array that specifies a buffer in which the bytes are written from the stream. The second parameter is integer parameter that specifies the byte offset in buffer or array at which to begin storing the data reads from the stream. The second parameter actually gives the offset of the byte in array (the buffer index) at which to begin reading. The third parameter is an integer parameter that specifies the length of the file or the maximum number of bytes to be read from the stream into byte array. This method returns an integer value that specifies the total number of bytes read from the stream into byte array or buffer. It returns zero if the end of the stream is reached.
WriteByte(Byte)	This method is used to write a byte to the current position of the file stream. It takes a single parameter of type byte that specifies a value in byte to write to the stream.
Write(Byte[], Int32, Int32)	This method is used to write a block of bytes to the file stream. It takes three parameters. The first parameter is array type parameter that specifies the buffer containing data to write to the stream. The

	second parameter specifies the zero-based byte offset in buffer or array at which to begin copying bytes to the stream. The third parameter is integer parameter that specifies the length of the byte array or the maximum number of bytes to be written to the file.
SetLength	This method is used to set the length of the current stream to the given value.

FileMode Enumeration

This enumeration provides different member values used to specify how the operating system should open a file. Each member value of this enumeration has different specification for the file to open. Following is the details of the member values of FileMode enumeration:

Member	Description
Append	This constant value is used to open a file and seeks to the end of the file. If the file does not exist, it creates a new file. This constant value is usually used if we write text to the end of the file.
Create	This constant value is used to create a new file. If the file already exists, it will be overwritten.
CreateNew	This constant value is used to create a new file. If the specified file already exists, it thrown IOException.
Open	This constant value is used to open an existing file. If the file does not exist, it thrown the exception FileNotFoundException.
OpenOrCreate	This constant value is used to open or create a file. If the specified file already exists, it open that file otherwise, it creates new file.
Truncate	This constant value is used to open an existing file. When the file is opened, it is truncated so that its size is zero bytes.

FileAccess Enumeration

This enumeration provides different constant member values used to specify access permission to the file such as read, write, or read/write access permission. Following is the details of the member values of the FileAccess enumeration:

Member	Description
Read	This constant value is used to allow read access permission to the file.
ReadWrite	This constant value is used to allow both the read and write access permission to the file.
Write	This constant value is used to allow write access permission to the file.

FileShare Enumeration

This enumeration provides different constant member values used to control the kind of access other FileStream objects can have to the same file. If a single file is used by multiple processes then this enumeration is used to control the access of that file among multiple processes for example, two or more process can read data from the same file simultaneously or not. Following is the details of the member values of the FileShare enumeration:

Member	Description
Delete	This constant value is used to allow consequent deleting of a file.
None	This constant value is used to decline sharing of the current file. If the FileShare value is none and the file is already opened and if any request comes for the current file to open, the request will fail until the file is closed.
Read	This constant value is used to allow consequent opening of the file for reading.
ReadWrite	This constant value is used to allow consequent opening of the file for reading or writing.
Write	This constant value is used to allow consequent opening of the file for writing.

Program # 1

Write a program that creates a text file and writes some text to it using the Write() method of the FileStream class.
C# Program

```
using System.IO;
using System.IO;

//Specify the path to create a text file and writes data to it
string filePath = "D:\\TestFile.txt";

//Create a text file and writes some text to it
FileStream fs = new FileStream(filePath, FileMode.Append, FileAccess.
Write);

//Declare a byte array to store the target text
byte[] byteArray = new byte[100];

//Declare a String variable that holds the target text
String myString = "This text will store in the file";

//Convert the String into byte and store in byte array
byteArray = System.Text.Encoding.UTF8.GetBytes(myString);

//Write the text of byte array in the text file
fs.Write(byteArray, 0, byteArray.Length);

//Close the file stream
fs.Close();
Console.WriteLine("The Text has been saved in the file");
```

Visual Basic Program

```
Imports System.IO
Imports System.Text

'Specify the path to create a text file and writes data to it
Dim filePath As String = "D:\TestFile.txt"
```

```
'Create a text file and writes some text to it
Dim fs As FileStream = New FileStream(filePath, FileMode.Append,
FileAccess.Write)

'Declare a byte array to store the target text
Dim byteArray As Byte() = New Byte(100) {}

'Declare a String variable that holds the target text
Dim myString As String = "This text will store in the file"

'Convert the String into byte and store in byte array
byteArray = System.Text.Encoding.UTF8.GetBytes(myString)

'Write the text of byte array into the text file
fs.Write(byteArray, 0, byteArray.Length)

'Close the file stream
fs.Close()
Console.WriteLine("The Text has been saved in the file")
```

To specify the file path in C#, double back slashes are used in the path string such as C:\\MyDir\\MyFile. To specify the file path in Visual Basic, single slash is used in the path string such as C:\MyDir\MyFile.

Program # 2

Write a program that reads data from a text file using the Read() method of the FileStream class.

C# Program

```
//Specify the target file path to read data
string filePath = "D:\\TestFile.txt";

FileStream fs = new FileStream(filePath,
FileMode.Open, FileAccess.Read);

//Get the file length
int length = (int)fs.Length;
```

```
//Create a bytes array
byte[] bytesArray = new byte[length];

//A variable to store the length of the file or the total number of //bytes of the file
int totalBytesOfFile = (int)fs.Length;

//Reads the bytes from the file into byte array
fs.Read(bytesArray, 0, totalBytesOfFile);

//Convert the byte array into String
string data = Encoding.UTF8.GetString(bytesArray, 0, bytesArray.Length);

Console.WriteLine(data);
```

Visual Basic Program

```
Dim filePath As String = "D:\TestFile.txt"
Dim fs As FileStream = New FileStream(filePath, FileMode.Open, FileAccess.Read)

Dim length As Integer = CInt(fs.Length)
Dim bytesArray As Byte() = New Byte(length - 1) {}
Dim totalBytesOfFile As Integer = CInt(fs.Length)

fs.Read(bytesArray, 0, totalBytesOfFile)

Dim data As String = Encoding.UTF8.GetString(bytesArray, 0, bytesArray.Length)
Console.WriteLine(data)
```

Program # 3

Write a program that counts the total number of bytes read from the stream into byte array.

C# Program

```
//Specify the target file path to read data
string filePath = "D:\\TestFile.txt";
```

```
FileStream fs = new FileStream(filePath,
FileMode.Open, FileAccess.Read);

//Get the file length
int length = (int)fs.Length;

//Create a bytes array
byte[] bytesArray = new byte[length];

//A variable to store the length of the file or the total number of //bytes of
the file
int totalBytesOfFile = (int)fs.Length;

//A variable to store the return value of the Read() method
int countBytes = 0;

while (totalBytesOfFile > 0)
{
countBytes = fs.Read(bytesArray, 0, totalBytesOfFile);

totalBytesOfFile -= countBytes;

//Break when the end of the file is reached
if (countBytes == 0)
break;
}

Console.WriteLine("Total Bytes read = " + countBytes);
```

StreamWriter Class

StreamWriter class is used to write data to the text file. It writes characters to a stream in a particular encoding. The default encoding of this class is UTF-8 encoding. The StreamWriter class is derived from the TextWriter class. The StreamWriter class is defined in the namespace System.IO therefore, to use this class in the application or program, the namespace System.IO must be imported.

Methods of StreamWriter Class

The StreamWriter class provides the following important and useful method:

Member	Description
Close()	This method is used to close the current StreamWriter object and releases the resources associated to it.
Write()	This method is used to write data to a text stream without a newline.
WriteLine()	This method is used to write data to a text stream with a newline.

StreamReader Class

StreamReader class is used to read data from text files. This class reads characters from a byte stream in a particular encoding. The default encoding of the StreamReader class is UTF-8 encoding. The StreamReader class is designed for character input in a particular encoding. This class is derived from the abstract class TextReader. The StreamReader class is defined in the namespace System.IO therefore, to use this class in the application or program, the namespace System.IO must be imported.

Methods of StreamReader Class

The StreamReader class provides the following important and useful methods:

Member	Description
Close()	This method is used to close the current StreamReader object and releases all the resources associated to it.
Read()	This method is used to read the next character from the input stream and advances or shifts the position to the next character. The Read() method returns integer value that specifies the ASCII code of the read character. If end of the stream is reached then it returns -1.

Read(Char[], Int32, Int32)	This method is used to read a block of characters from the current stream into a buffer beginning at the specified index position. It takes three parameters. The first parameter is a character array that specifies a buffer in which the characters are written from the stream. The second parameter is integer parameter that specifies the index of the buffer at which to begin writing. The third parameter is an integer parameter that specifies the length of the file or the maximum number of characters to be read from the stream into character array. This method returns an integer value that specifies the total number of characters read from the stream into character array or buffer. It returns zero if the end of the stream is reached.
ReadLine()	This method is used to read a single line of characters from the current stream and returns it as a string. It returns -1 if the end of the input stream is reached. To read all lines from the stream, the ReadLine() method is used with iteration statement.
ReadToEnd()	This method is used to read all characters from the current position to the end of the stream and returns the data as a single string.
Peek()	This method is used to read the next available character without using. It returns an integer value that specifies the ASCII code of the next available character. It returns -1 if the end of the stream is reached or if there is no characters in the stream.

Program # 1

Write a program that opens a text file, write data to and reads data from it using the FileStream, StreamWriter and StreamReader classes.
C# Program

```
using System.IO;
using System.Text;

//Specify the path to open the specified file
string filePath = "D:\\TestFile.txt";

//Write data to a file using the FileStream and StreamWriter classes
using (FileStream fs = new FileStream(filePath, FileMode.Open, FileAccess.
Write))
{
//Declare a StreamWriter object to write data to the file
using (StreamWriter swriter = new StreamWriter(fs))
{
swriter.WriteLine("This is my first Line");
swriter.WriteLine("This is my second Line");
swriter.WriteLine("This is my third Line");
}

fs.Close();
}

//Read data from a file using the FileStream and StreamReader //classes
using (FileStream fs1 = new FileStream(filePath, FileMode.Open,
FileAccess.Read))
{
//Declare a StreamReader object to read data from the file
using (StreamReader sreader = new StreamReader(fs1))
{
string data = sreader.ReadToEnd();
Console.WriteLine(data);
}

fs1.Close();
}
```

Visual Basic Program
Imports System.IO Imports System.Text 'Specify the path to open the specified file Dim filePath As String = "D:\TestFile.txt" 'Write data to a file using the FileStream and StreamWriter classes Using fs As FileStream = New FileStream(filePath, FileMode.Open, FileAccess.Write) 'Declare a StreamWriter object to write data to the file Using swriter As StreamWriter = New StreamWriter(fs) swriter.WriteLine("This is my first Line") swriter.WriteLine("This is my second Line") swriter.WriteLine("This is my third Line") End Using fs.Close() End Using 'Read data from a file using the FileStream and StreamReader 'classes Using fs1 As FileStream = New FileStream(filePath, FileMode.Open, FileAccess.Read) 'Declare a StreamReader object to read data from the file Using sreader As StreamReader = New StreamReader(fs1) Dim data As String = sreader.ReadToEnd() Console.WriteLine(data) End Using fs1.Close() End Using

Program # 2

Write a program that opens a text file, write data to and reads data from it using the StreamWriter and StreamReader classes without using the FileStream class.
C# Program

```
using System.IO;
using System.Text;

//Specify the path to open the specified file
string filePath = "D:\\TestFile.txt";

//Declare a StreamWriter object to write data to the file
using (StreamWriter swriter = new StreamWriter(filePath))
{
swriter.WriteLine("This is my first Line");
swriter.WriteLine("This is my second Line");
swriter.WriteLine("This is my third Line");
}

//Declare a StreamReader object to read data from the file
using (StreamReader sreader = new StreamReader(filePath))
{
string data = sreader.ReadToEnd();
Console.WriteLine(data);
}
```

Visual Basic Program

```
'Specify the path to open the specified file
Dim filePath As String = "D:\TestFile.txt"

'Declare a StreamWriter object to write data to the file
Using swriter As StreamWriter = New StreamWriter(filePath)
swriter.WriteLine("This is my first Line")
swriter.WriteLine("This is my second Line")
swriter.WriteLine("This is my third Line")
End Using

'Declare a StreamReader object to read data from the file
```

```
Using sreader As StreamReader = New StreamReader(filePath)
Dim data As String = sreader.ReadToEnd()
Console.WriteLine(data)
End Using
```

File Class

File class is a static class that is used to perform different operations on a single physical file of the disk such as open a file from the disk, create a new file on the disk, makes a copy of an existing file, delete a file from the disk, move a file from one location to another location on the disk, get or set the file creation date, get or set the file access date etc. This class performs operations on a single file at a time. The main advantage of the File class is that it provides less code operations as compared to other classes. The File class is defined in the System.IO namespace therefore, to use File class in the application or program the namespace System.IO must be included in the application.

Methods of File Class

The File class provides the following important methods:

Method	Description
AppendAllLines	This method is used to open a file and appends lines to a file and then closes the file. If the specified file does not exist, it creates a new file and writes the specified lines to the newly created file then closes the file.
AppendAllText	This method is used to open a file and appends the specified string to the file and then closes the file. If the specified file does not exist, it creates a new file and writes the specified string to the newly created file then closes the file.
AppendText	This method is used to create a StreamWriter that appends UTF-8 encoded text to a file. If the specified file does not exist, it creates a new file.

ReadAllBytes	This method is used to open a binary file and reads its contents into a byte array then closes the file. It takes a string parameter that specifies the full path of the file from which data is to be read into byte array. The return type of this method is byte array that contains the contents of the binary file.
ReadAllLines	This method is used to open a text file and reads all the lines of the file into a string array and then closes the file. This method provides two overloaded forms. The first overloaded form of this method takes a single parameter of string type that specifies the full path of the file from which the lines are to be read into a string array. The second overloaded form of this method takes two parameters. The first parameter is a string parameter that specifies the full path of the file from which the lines are to be read into a string array and the second parameter is encoding that is applied to the contents of the file. The return value of the ReadAllLines() method is a string array that contains all the lines of the specified file.
ReadAllText	This method is used to open a text file and reads all the lines of the file into a string then closes the file. It provides two overloaded forms. The first overloaded form of this method takes a single parameter of string type that specifies the full path of the text file from which the lines are to be read into a string. The second overloaded form of this method takes two parameters. The first parameter is a string parameter that specifies the full path of the text file from which the lines are to be read into a string and the second parameter is encoding that is applied to the contents of the file. The return type of the ReadAllText() method is a string that contains all the lines of the file.

ReadLines	This method is used to open a file and reads all the lines of a file into a string collection then closes the file. It provides two overloaded forms. The first overloaded form of this method takes a single parameter of string type that specifies the full path of the text file from which the lines are to be read into a string collection. The second overloaded form of this method takes two parameters. The first parameter is a string parameter that specifies the full path of the text file from which the lines are to be read into a string collection and the second parameter is encoding that is applied to the contents of the file. The return type of the ReadLine() method is an IEnumerable string collection that contains all the lines of the file.
WriteAllBytes	This method is used to write the specified byte array to the file. If the specified file does not exist, it creates a new file and writes the byte array into the newly created file. This method takes two parameters. The first parameter is a string parameter that specifies the full path of the file to write the byte array and the second parameter is byte array that specifies the byte array to write to the file.
WriteAllLines	This method is used to write the specified lines to a file. If the specified file does not exist, it creates a new file and writes the specified lines to the newly created file. This method takes two parameters. The first parameter of this method is string parameter that specifies the full path of the file to write all the lines and the second parameter is a string collection IEnumerable<string> that specifies lines to write to the file.
WriteAllText	This method is used to write specified string text to a file. If the specified file does not exist, it creates a new file and writes the string text into the newly created file.

Copy	This method is used to make a copy of a specified file. It takes two string parameters. The first parameter specifies the full path of a file to make its copy and the second parameter specifies the destination full path where the new copy of the file is to be placed. The Copy() method also allows us to provide a new name to the file in the destination location. If the same name file exists in the destination location then the Copy() method produces an IOException.
Create	This method is used to create a new file on the specified path. If the specified file already exists then it overwrites the file. It returns a FileStream object that provides read-write access to the file specified in the path.
CreateText	This method is used to create or open a file for writing UTF-8 encoded text.
Decrypt	This method is used to decrypt a file that was encrypted by the current account using the Encrypt method.
Delete	This method is used to delete a specified file. It takes a string parameter that specifies the file path.
Encrypt	This method is used to encrypt a file.
Exists	This method is used to determine whether the specified file exists or not. It returns a Boolean value either true or false. If the specified file exists, it returns true otherwise, it returns false.
Move	This method is used to move a specified file to a new location on the disk. It takes two string parameters. The first parameter specifies the full path of the source file and the second parameter specifies the destination full path where the file is to be transferred. The Move() method also allows us to provide a new name to the file in the destination path.

Open	This method is used to open a file in the specified FileMode. The Open() method provides three overloaded forms. The first overloaded form takes a single parameter FileMode that specifies the file mode. The second overloaded form of Open() method takes two parameters. The first parameter is FileMode parameter that specifies the file mode and the second parameter is FileAccess parameter that provides the file access permission for example, the file is opened as Read only, Write only, or ReadWrite. The third overloaded form of Open() method takes three parameters. The first parameter is FileMode parameter, the second parameter is FileAccess parameter, and the third parameter is FileShare parameter. When Open() method opens a specified file, it returns a FileStream object with the specified mode, access permission, and sharing options.
OpenRead	This method is used to return a read-only FileStream object from an existing file with the FileShare mode set to Read. The FileStream object is then used to read data from the file.
OpenText	This method is used to return a StreamReader object from an existing file with UTF-8 encoding that reads text from an existing text file.
OpenWrite	This method is used to return a write-only FileStream object from an existing file. If the specified file does not exist, it creates a new file and returns a write-only FileStream object. The FileStream object is then used to write text to the specified file. This method sets FileShare to none.
Replace	This method is used to replace the contents of a specified file with the contents of another file and then deletes the original file.
GetLastAccessTime	This method is used to return the date and time of the specified file or directory that was last accessed. It takes a string parameter that specifies the full path of the file or directory and returns a DateTime object that represents the last access date and time.

Program # 1

<table>
<tr><td>Write a program that checks whether a specified file exists on the disk or not.</td></tr>
<tr><td>C# Program</td></tr>
<tr><td>string filePath = “D:\\TestFile.txt”;
bool isExists = File.Exists(filePath);
if (isExists == true)
Console.WriteLine(“The specified file exists”);
else
Console.WriteLine(“The specified file does not exist”);</td></tr>
<tr><td>Visual Basic Program</td></tr>
<tr><td>Dim filePath As String = “D:\TestFile.txt”
Dim isExists As Boolean = File.Exists(filePath)
If isExists = True Then
Console.WriteLine(“The specified file exists”)
Else</td></tr>
<tr><td>Console.WriteLine(“The specified file does not exist”)
End If</td></tr>
</table>

Program # 2

<table>
<tr><td>Write a program that deletes a specified file from the disk.</td></tr>
<tr><td>C# Program</td></tr>
<tr><td>string filePath = “D:\\TestFile.txt”;
if(File.Exists(filePath))
File.Delete(filePath);
else
Console.WriteLine(“The specified file does not exist”);</td></tr>
<tr><td>Visual Basic Program</td></tr>
<tr><td>Dim filePath As String = “D:\TestFile.txt”
If File.Exists(filePath) Then
File.Delete(filePath)
Else
Console.WriteLine(“The specified file does not exist”)
End If</td></tr>
</table>

Program # 3

Write a program that moves a file from one place to another place on the disk.
C# Program
string sourcePath = "D:\\\\TestFile.txt"; string destinationPath = "D:\\\\New Folder\\\\TestFile.txt"; File.Move(sourcePath, destinationPath);
Visual Basic Program
Dim sourcePath As String = "D:\\TestFile.txt" Dim destinationPath As String = "D:\\New Folder\\TestFile.txt" File.Move(sourcePath, destinationPath)

Program # 4

Write a program that makes a copy of a specified file.
C# Program
string sourcePath = "D:\\\\TestFile.txt"; string destinationPath = "D:\\\\New Folder\\\\TestFile.txt"; File.Copy(sourcePath, destinationPath);
Visual Basic Program
Dim sourcePath As String = "D:\\TestFile.txt" Dim destinationPath As String = "D:\\New Folder\\TestFile.txt" File.Copy(sourcePath, destinationPath)

Program # 5

Write a program that opens a file and returns StreamReader object and reads data from the file.
C# Program
string filePath = "D:\\\\TestFile.txt"; StreamReader sr = File.OpenText(filePath); string data = sr.ReadToEnd(); Console.WriteLine(data);
Visual Basic Program
Dim filePath As String = "D:\\TestFile.txt"

```
Dim sr As StreamReader = File.OpenText(filePath)
Dim data As String = sr.ReadToEnd()
Console.WriteLine(data)
```

Program # 6

Write a program that returns the last accessed time and last write time of a file.
C# Program
string filePath = "D:\\TestFile.txt"; DateTime lastTime = File.GetLastAccessTime(filePath); DateTime lstWrtTime = File.GetLastWriteTime(filePath); Console.WriteLine("Lsst Accesed Time =" + lastTime.ToString()); Console.WriteLine("Last Write Time =" + lstWrtTime.ToString());

Program # 7

Write a program that appends text to a specified file using the AppendAllText() method.
C# Program
string filePath = "D:\\TestFile.txt"; File.AppendAllText(filePath, "This Text will be appended");
Visual Basic Program
Dim filePath As String = "D:\TestFile.txt" File.AppendAllText(filePath, "This Text will be appended")

Program # 8

Write a program that reads a file into byte array.
C# Program
string filePath = "D:\\TestFile.txt"; byte[] fileToByteArray = File.ReadAllBytes(filePath);
Visual Basic Program
Dim filePath As String = "D:\TestFile.txt" Dim fileToByteArray As Byte() = File.ReadAllBytes(filePath)

FileInfo Class

FileInfo class is used to perform different operations on physical files of the disk such as open a file from the disk, create a new file on the disk, makes a copy of an existing file, delete a file from the disk, move a file from one location to another location of the disk, find the last accessed date and time of a file etc. The FileInfo class provides the same functionality as the static File class but the main difference is that the FileInfo class is used in both single and multiple files. The FileInfo class can provide multiple operations on files at the same time. The StreamReader and StreamWriter classes are used with the FileInfo class for writing or reading data from physical files. The FileInfo class is defined in the System.IO namespace therefore, to use this class the namespace System. IO must be imported in the application.

Properties of FileInfo Class

The FileInfo class provides the following important properties:

Property	Description
Directory	This property is used to get an instance of the parent directory of the file.
DirectoryName	This property is used to get the directory full path of the file.
Exists	This property is used to get a value that indicates whether a file exists or not. If the file exists it returns true otherwise, it returns false.
Extension	This property is used to get the extension part of the file. It returns a string that contains the extension including the period (.) character.
FullName	This property is used to get the full path of the directory or file.
IsReadOnly	This property is used to get or set a value that indicates whether the file is read-only or not. If the file is read-only, it returns true otherwise, it returns false.
LastAccessTime	This property is used to get or set the last accessed time of the current file or directory.

LastWriteTime	This property is used to get or set the last written time of the current file or directory.
Length	This property is used to get the size of the current file in bytes.
Name	This property is used to get the name of the current file.

Methods of FileInfo Class

The FileInfo class provides the following important methods:

Method	Description
AppendText	This method is used to create a StreamWriter object that is used to append text to the file accessed by the current instance of the FileInfo class. If the specified file does not exist, it creates a new file and returns a StreamWriter object.
CopyTo	This method is used to make a copy of a specified file to a new location on the disk. If the same file already exists on the destination location then it produces an IOException. This method also allows us to provide new name to the file to make a copy with a new name.
Create	This method is used to create a file. It returns a FileStream object that represents the created file. The Create() method granted full read-write access to the new file by default for all users.
CreateText	This method is used to create a StreamWriter object that is used to write text to the specified file accessed by the current instance of the FileInfo class. The CreateText() method granted full read-write access to the file by default. This method overwrites the existing text of the file.
Decrypt	This method is used to decrypt a specified file that was encrypted by the current account using the Encrypt method.

Delete	This method is used to delete a specified file.
Encrypt	This method is used to encrypt a specified file.
GetAccessControl	This method is used to get a FileSecurity object that encapsulates the access control list (ACL) entries for a specified file.
MoveTo	This method is used to move a specified file to a new location. If the same file already exists in the destination path, it produces an IOException. This method also allows us to provide new name to the file to move it with the new name.
Open	This method is used to open a file in the specified FileMode. The Open() method provides three overloaded forms. The first overloaded form takes a single parameter FileMode that specifies the file mode. The second overloaded form of Open() method takes two parameters. The first parameter is FileMode parameter that specifies the file mode and the second parameter is FileAccess parameter that provides the file access permission for example, the file is opened as Read only, Write only, or ReadWrite. The third overloaded form of Open() method takes three parameters. The first parameter is FileMode parameter, the second parameter is FileAccess parameter, and the third parameter is FileShare parameter. When Open() method opens a specified file, it returns a FileStream object with the specified mode, access permission, and sharing options.
OpenRead	This method is used to return a read-only FileStream object from an existing file with the FileShare mode set to Read. The FileStream object is then used to read data from the file.
OpenText	This method is used to return a StreamReader object from an existing file with the UTF-8 encoding that reads text from an existing text file.

OpenWrite	This method is used to return a write-only FileStream object from an existing file. If the specified file does not exist, it creates a new file and returns a write-only FileStream object. The FileStream object is then used to write text to the specified file. This method sets FileShare to none.
Replace	This method is used to replace the contents of a specified file with the file of the current FileInfo object. When it replaces the content of the file then it deletes the original file.

Program # 1

Write a program that creates a StreamWriter object to write new text to the file.

C# Program

```
string filePath = "D:\\TestFile.txt";
FileInfo fi = new FileInfo(filePath);
StreamWriter str = fi.CreateText();
str.WriteLine("Welcome");
str.WriteLine("to");
str.WriteLine("C# Programming");
Console.WriteLine("The Text has been Saved in the File");
str.Close();
```

Visual Basic Program

```
Dim filePath As String = "D:\TestFile.txt"
Dim fi As FileInfo = New FileInfo(filePath)
Dim str As StreamWriter = fi.CreateText()
str.WriteLine("Welcome")
str.WriteLine("to")
str.WriteLine("C# Programming")
Console.WriteLine("The Text has been Saved in the File")
str.Close()
```

Program # 2

Write a program that deletes a file from the disk.
C# Program

string filePath = "D:\\\\TestFile.txt";
FileInfo fi = new FileInfo(filePath);
if (fi.Exists)
{
fi.Delete();
Console.WriteLine("The File has been Deleted");
}

Program # 3

Write a program that creates a StreamWriter object to append new text to the file.
C# Program

string filePath = "D:\\\\TestFile.txt";
FileInfo fi = new FileInfo(filePath);
using(StreamWriter sw = fi.AppendText())
{
sw.WriteLine("Welcome");
sw.WriteLine("to");

sw.WriteLine("C# Programming");
sw.Close();
Console.WriteLine("The Text has been appended to the File");
}

Visual Basic Program
Dim filePath As String = "D:\TestFile.txt" Dim fi As FileInfo = New FileInfo(filePath) Using sw As StreamWriter = fi.AppendText() sw.WriteLine("Welcome") sw.WriteLine("to") sw.WriteLine("C# Programming") sw.Close() Console.WriteLine("The Text has been appended to the File") End Using

Program # 4

Write a program that moves a specified file from its current location to a new location on the disk.
C# Program
string filePath = "D:\\TestFile.txt"; string filePath2 = "D:\\New Folder\\TestFile.txt"; FileInfo fi1 = new FileInfo(filePath); FileInfo fi2 = new FileInfo(filePath2); fi1.MoveTo(filePath2); Console.WriteLine("{0} was moved to {1}.", filePath, filePath2);

Program # 5

Write a program that makes a copy of a specified file to another location on the disk.
C# Program
string filePath = "D:\\TestFile.txt";
string filePath2 = "D:\\New Folder\\TestFile.txt"; FileInfo fi1 = new FileInfo(filePath); FileInfo fi2 = new FileInfo(filePath2); fi1.CopyTo(filePath2); Console.WriteLine("{0} was copied to {1}.", filePath, filePath2);

Program # 6

Write a program that creates a StreamReader object to read data from a file.
C# Program
string filePath = "D:\\TestFile.txt"; FileInfo fi = new FileInfo(filePath); StreamReader sr = fi.OpenText(); string data = sr.ReadToEnd(); Console.WriteLine(data);
Visual Basic Program
Dim filePath As String = "D:\TestFile.txt" Dim fi As FileInfo = New FileInfo(filePath)

```
Dim sr As StreamReader = fi.OpenText()
Dim data As String = sr.ReadToEnd()
Console.WriteLine(data)
```

Program # 7

Write a program that creates a StreamReader object to read data from a file using the FileStream object.

C# Program

```
string filePath = "D:\\TestFile.txt";
FileInfo fi = new FileInfo(filePath);

//Open or Create a file for Read
FileStream fs = fi.Open(FileMode.OpenOrCreate, FileAccess.Read);

//Create StreamReader object to read data from the file
StreamReader sr = new StreamReader(fs);
string data = sr.ReadToEnd();
Console.WriteLine(data);

//Close FileStream and StreamReader objects
sr.Close();
fs.Close();
```

Program # 8

Write a program that creates a StreamWriter object to write data to a file using the FileStream object.

C# Program

```
string filePath = "D:\\TestFile.txt";
FileInfo fi = new FileInfo(filePath);

//Open or create a file for Write
FileStream fs = fi.Open(FileMode.OpenOrCreate, FileAccess.Write);

//Create a StreamWriter object to write data to the file
StreamWriter sw = new StreamWriter(fs);
```

```
sw.WriteLine("Welcome");
sw.WriteLine("to");
sw.WriteLine("C# Programming");
sw.Close();

//Close FileStream and StreamWriter objects
sw.Close();
fs.Close();
```

Program # 9

Write a program that reads an image file into byte array.
C# Program

```
string filePath = "D:\\Picture1.jpg";
FileInfo fi = new FileInfo(filePath);

//Declare a byte array to save the data
byte[] data = new byte[filePath.Length];

//Create a FileStream object to read image file
FileStream fs = fi.OpenRead();
fs.Read(data, 0, data.Length);
Console.WriteLine("The Image File has been read in byte Array");
fs.Close();
```

Visual Basic Program

```
Dim filePath As String = "D:\TestFile.txt"
Dim fi As FileInfo = New FileInfo(filePath)

'Declare a byte array to save the data
Dim data As Byte() = New Byte(filePath.Length) {}

'Create a FileStream object to read image file
Dim fs As FileStream = fi.OpenRead()
fs.Read(data, 0, data.Length)
Console.WriteLine("The Image File has been read in byte Array")
fs.Close()
```

XDocument Class

This class represents an XML document and it is used to read or write xml files. The XDocument class is defined in the namespace System.Xml.Ling therefore, to use this class in the application, the namespace System.Xml.Ling must be imported in the application.

Properties of XDocument Class

Following is the list of important and useful properties of XDocument class:

Name	Description
BaseUri	This property is used to get the base URI for the current or this XObject.
Declaration	This property is used to get or set the XML declaration for the current document.
Document	This property is used to get the XDocument for the current XObject.
DocumentType	This property is used to get the Document Type Definition (DTD) for the current document.
FirstNode	This property is used to get the first child node of the current node.
LastNode	This property is used to get the last child node of the current node.
NextNode	This property is used to get the next sibling node of the current node.
NodeType	This property is used to get the node type for the current node.
Parent	This property is used to get the parent XElement of the current XObject.
PreviousNode	This property is used to get the previous sibling node of the current node.
Root	This property is used to get the root element of the XML Tree for the current document.

CHAPTER 16

Web Technologies in .NET

CHAPTER CONTENTS	
	➢ Websites ➢ Web Pages ➢ World Wide Web ➢ Website Domain ➢ Web Server ➢ Web Browser ➢ Uniform Resource Locator ➢ Localhost ➢ Hypertext Transfer Protocol ➢ Request Methods of HTTP ➢ Hypertext Transfer Protocol Secure ➢ Types of Websites ➢ Scripting ➢ Client-side Scripting ➢ Server-side Scripting ➢ Scripting Programming Languages ➢ Markup Languages ➢ Tags ➢ Hyper Text Markup Language ➢ Web Application

Website

A Website is the collection of Web Pages related with each other in a systematic way and all the Web Pages are grouped into a single entity called Web Domain or Website Domain. A Web Domain or Website Domain is a fully qualified name of a Website that identifies and represents a Website over the internet. The Website Domain is also called Host Name, Domain Name or simply Domain. A Website is a container or a central location that contains a single Web page or a set of Web pages and the whole Website is represented by a single fully qualified name which is called Website Domain or simply Domain. A Web page is a file or document that is also called World Wide Web (WWW) and it is usually written in a plain text combine with the formatting instructions of Hypertext Markup Language such as HTML, and XHTML that supports links to other documents as well as graphics, audio, and video files. Each Web Page has its own unique Uniform Resource Locator (URL) that is called Web Address. The URL or Web Address is used to access a specified Web Page of a Website over the internet using the Web Browser. A Web Browser is a software application that displays Web Pages, images, videos, and text by using a Uniform Resource Locator (URL). A URL is a formatted text string used by Web browsers, email clients and other software to identify a network resource on the Internet. The network resources are files that can be plain Web pages, text documents or files, graphics, videos, multimedia, or some other programs file etc. If we want to access a specified Web Page of a Website, we use the URL of that specified Web Page. Each Website has a default Web Page that is called main Web Page. The main Web Page is actually the starting page of a Website. When we access a Website without specifying the URL of any Web Page then the default or main Web Page of that Website is displayed. In a single Website all the Web Pages are interrelated with each other through hyperlinks and they allow users to navigate the full Website. The user can go from one Web Page to another Web Page by clicking the links on the Web Pages. A Website is also written as Web site or simply site.

Websites can be developed for various purposes and tasks such as Personal Websites which are developed for personal profile or for personal information, Commercial Websites which are developed for business and e-commerce, Government Websites which are developed for government organizations, Educational Websites which are developed for universities, colleges, schools and for other educational institutions, Search Engine Websites which are developed for searching various items, products, services and other information etc over the internet.

Web Pages

A Web Page is a file or document that is also called World Wide Web (WWW) and it is usually written in a plain text combine with the formatting instructions of Hypertext Markup Language such as HTML, and XHTML that supports links to other documents as well as graphics, audio, and video files. This means we can jump from one Web Page document or file to another Web Page document or file by simply clicking on the links. A Web Page also contains hyperlinks to other related Web Pages and downloadable files, source documents, definitions and other Web resources. Each Web Page has a unique Uniform Resource Locator (URL) that is called Web Address. The URLs or Web Addresses organize the Web Pages into a hierarchy and they are interrelated with each other that provide full navigation to the user. The URL or Web Address of a Web Page is used to access that Web Page. If we want to access a specified Web Page of a Website then we give the URL or Web Address of that specified Web Page to the Web Browser. The Web Browser then displays the requested Web Page to the user.

World Wide Web

The World Wide Web abbreviated as WWW or W3 is a Web Page document or file written in a plain text combine with the formatting instructions of Hypertext Markup Language such as HTML, and XHTML that supports links to other documents as well as graphics, audio, and video files. The World Wide Web or a Web Page has a unique Uniform Resource Locator (URL). The Uniform Resource Locator (URL) is a formatted text string used by web browsers, email clients and other software to identify a network resource on the Internet. The network resources are files that can be plain Web pages, text documents or files, graphics, multimedia, videos, or some other program files. The URL is also called Web Address that is used to locate a Web resource on the internet. If we want to access a Web Page, we use the URL or Web Address of that specified Web Page over the internet using the web browser. When it finds a Web resource, the web browser displays that Web resource on the screen. The URL or Web Address organizes the World Wide Web or Web Page into a hierarchy in a central location that is called Website and it is represented by a single fully qualified name that is called Website Domain or simply Domain. The World Wide Web or a Web Page also contains hyperlinks to other related Web Pages and downloadable files, source documents, definitions and other Web resources.

Website Domain

A website Domain is a name or a label of a website that uniquely identifies a website over the internet. A website Domain is also called website host. A website Domain or host is a fully qualified name that provides a unique address to a website and it uniquely identifies and represents a website over the internet. When we designed a website, we register a unique name for our website to uniquely identify it over the internet. The website Domain or host is used in the URL to identify a particular web page. A website Domain or host provides several IP addresses to be linked to the same website Domain or host and they are assigned to the web pages. The website Domain or host also consists of many parts or levels and they are separated by periods or dots. A website is actually a container or a central location that contains a single web Page or a set of web Pages. Each web page has its own unique URL and the entire website is represented by a single fully qualified name that is called website Domain, web Domain, or host. The website Domain or host organizes the web pages of a website in a hierarchy under a single entity.

Web Server

A Web server is a software application that uses the client/server model and Hypertext Transfer Protocol (HTTP). A Web Server delivers Web pages to the users in response to the HTTP requests from remote browser. When a user sends a request for a particular Web page, the web server delivers that Web page to the client using the web browser. The communication between the user and the web server takes place using the Hyper Text Transfer Protocol (HTTP). Each Web page of a Website has its own unique name that is called Uniform Resource Locator (URL) or Web address. The URL or Web Address is used to locate or access a specified Web Page over the internet. If we want to access a specified Web Page, we put the Web Address or URL of that specified Web Page into the address bar of the web browser. The web browser sends the URL request to the web server. The web server locates the requested Web Page over the internet. If the requested Web Page is found then web server delivers that Web Page to the web browser where it is displayed to the user. The primary purpose of the web server is to delivers Websites. A single web server may support multiple Websites, or a single Website may be hosted on several linked or mirrored web servers. Any computer can be turned into a web server by installing server software and connecting the computer to the Internet. There are many web server software applications available that can be installed in computer system to turn the computer as a web server. Following are some important and most useful web server Software:

- Internet Information Services
- Apache

Internet Information Services

Internet Information Services (IIS) is a group of Internet servers (including a Web or Hypertext Transfer Protocol server and a File Transfer Protocol server) with additional capabilities for Microsoft's Windows NT and Windows Server operating systems. Microsoft includes a set of programs for building and administering Web sites and support for writing Web-based applications that access database. Internet Information Services is used to make our computer a web server. If we want to have a web server for developing dynamic website or we want to publish website on our own server then we install the IIS. IIS takes request from the user and executes the required files and sends result back to the user. IIS server also provides the services of SMTP (Simple Mail Transfer Protocol). We can send emails using SMTP. IIS is used on windows plate form. For other plate form there are different web servers are used for example, Apache Web Server is used for Linux etc.

Apache

Apache is an open source web server developed and maintained by Apache Software Foundation. Apache web server is the alternative of Internet Information Services or IIS but the main difference is that Apache web server is free and it runs on multiple platforms such as Windows operating system, UNIX Operating System, Apples Operating System X, and Linux Operating System while IIS only runs on Windows Operating System.

Web Browser

A Web Browser is a software application used to locate or retrieve, present, and navigate information resources on the World Wide Web. The information resources may be Web pages, images, videos, audios, or other files or pieces of contents. The information resource is identified by a Uniform Resource Locator (URL). The primary purpose of web browser is to retrieve information resources from the web server and display to the user. The web browser provides a communication link between the user and the web server. The web browser also allows users to navigate Web pages by simply clicking on the series of links. A Web Page contains hyperlinks to other related Web Pages and downloadable files, source documents, definitions and other Web resources. If we want to access and display information resources such as Web pages etc, we give the URL or Web address of that specified Web page to the address bar of the web browser. The web browser then sends HTTP request to the web server for that specified Web page. If a specified Web page is found then web server sends it to the web browser. The web browser then displays that Web page to the user. The most powerful and most useful web browsers software applications are Internet Explorer, Google Chrome, Mozilla Firefox, Opera, and Safari etc. The first web browser was invented in 1990 by Sir Tim Berners-Lee. It was called World Wide Web and was later renamed Nexus. The first commonly available web browser with a graphical user interface was Erwise. The development of Erwise was initiated by Robert Cailliau.

Uniform Resource Locator

Uniform Resource Locator (URL) is a formatted text string used by Web browsers, email clients and other software to identify a network resource on the Internet. The network resources are files that can be plain Web pages, text documents or files, graphics, multimedia, videos, or some other program files. A URL is also called Web Address that is used to locate a Web resource on the internet. When it finds a Web resource, the web browser displays it on the screen. The Web resource may be a World Wide Web or a Web Page file or document, graphics, audio, video, multimedia, and other program file. If we want to access a specified Web Page of a Website, we give the URL of that Web Page to the address bar of the Web Browser. When the Web Page is found then Web Browser displays that Web Page on the screen. A URL string consists of the following three parts:

- URI Scheme
- Domain Name
- File or Resource Location

The URI stands for Uniform Resource Identifier and it is the top level of the Uniform Resource Identifier (URI) naming structure. The URI Scheme is actually a protocol that defines how the resource will be obtained. The URI Scheme examples are HTTP, HTTPS, FTP, and File etc. The second part of the URL is Domain Name. The Domain Name is also called Host Name. The Domain Name or Host Name is fully qualified name of a Website that provides a unique address to the Website and it uniquely identifies and represents a Website over the internet. A Domain Name consists of many parts or levels and they are separated by periods (dots). The right most part or level is called top level Domain for example, in the Website www.Google.com, the .com is the top level Domain. The third part or level of the Domain Name is File or Resource Location that specifies the full path of a resource.

Localhost

A localhost is a hostname in computer networking that refers to the local computer or current computer we are using. The localhost is used in communicating with the loopback network interface. The loopback network interface is a virtual network interface that enables a local machine or computer to communicate with itself. Each local machine or computer in a computer network is a localhost and each localhost is always designated as IP address 127.0.0.1. The IP address 127.0.0.1 is called loopback address. The loopback address does not send information to the computer network but it always routes back all the sending information to the local computer from which we send. The IP address 127.0.0.1 is designated for the software loopback interface of a machine and it is not physically connected to a computer network because the loopback network interface is actually a virtual network interface that has no connectivity tool but it is just a software application or functionality of a network system that communicate with itself. The loopback address i.e. 127.0.0.1 is used to communicate with the local computer instead of computer network and all the messages sent to 127.0.0.1 do not get delivered to the computer network but the machine or computer adapter intercepts all the sending messages and returns them to the sending machine or computer.

The loopback address is usually used for testing and configuration purposes and it is actually a test mechanism of network adapters. The loopback address allows us to test a lot of services, devices, and functionality of various processes such as to test the functionality of a network card and TCP/IP stack either they are installed into the local computer or not similarly, to test the web server for web hosting, to test and debug the physical connection problem, to start the web server of a local computer, to block access to a particular website, to stop access to the internet. If we use loopback address 127.0.0.1 in the connections LAN settings option then we cannot access internet.

Hypertext Transfer Protocol

Hypertext Transfer Protocol (HTTP) is a software application layer protocol that works between the web browser and web server. The HTTP establishes a communication link between the web browser and web server that sends and receives or transfers information across the internet using the Uniform Resource Locator (URL). The HTTP serves as a request and response protocol between the web browser and web server. A web browser acts as a client and a web server acts as a server. When we enter a URL in the address bar of the web browser, the web browser submits an HTTP request message to the web server. The web server then responses to the web browser and provides the requested resources such as HTML files or other contents or information and also provides the status information about the request. The HTTP is an application layer network protocol built on the top of the TCP/IP Suit of protocol and it provides communication link and exchanges information between the web browser and web server using the request and response messages. The web browser sends HTTP request to the web server for a particular network resource. The web server response and sends the requested network resource to the web browser. Therefore, the Hypertext Transfer Protocol (HTTP) is also called request/ response protocol because it sends request for a particular network resource and also response when web server finds that network resource and sends to the web browser. The HTTP uses the TCP port 80 by default and it also uses the alternate TCP ports such as 8080 and 8008. The HTTP protocol automatically displays in the address bar when we put the URL of any Web page. The HTTP always displays at starting of the URL and it is separated from the URL by using the double slashes and a full colon between the HTTP and the URL. The HTTP provides different methods for sending and receiving messages between the web browser and web server. The HTTP provides a separate method to each message type.

Request Methods of HTTP

HTTP provides different methods used to send and receive information between the Web Browser and Web Server. Following is the details of HTTP request methods:

HTTP Method	Description
GET	This method is used to get or retrieve data or information from the Web Server. It retrieves only data or information from the Web Server and it does not perform any other task. The HTTP uses the GET method when a user or client sends a request to the Web Server for a resource for example, when a user sends a request for a Webpage or other resource then the Web Server sends the requested Webpage or other resource to the user.
HEAD	This method is used when a user or client is requesting some information about a resource but not requesting the resource itself. For example, when a user or client want to retrieve the Meta information or data written in the response header but does not want to retrieve the entire contents of a resource.

POST	This method is used when a user or client sends information or data to the Web Server for example, when a user fills an online form such as login form or any other registration form and submits it to the server.
PUT	This method is used when a user or client sends a replacement document or uploads a new document to the Web Server under the URL request.
DELETE	This method is used when a user or client want to delete a document from the Web Server identified by the URL request.
TRACE	This method is used when a user or client is asking the available proxies or intermediate servers changing the request to announce them.
OPTIONS	This method is used when a user or client wants to determine other available methods to retrieve or process a document on the Web Server.
CONNECT	This method is used when a client wants to establish a transparent connection to a remote host, usually to facilitate the SSL encrypted communication (HTTPS) through an HTTP proxy.
PATCH	This method is used to perform a partial modification to a resource. The PATCH method requests that a set of changes described in the request entity be applied to the resource identified by the Request-URI.

Hypertext Transfer Protocol Secure

Hypertext Transfer Protocol Secure is shortly called HTTPS. HTTPS is a software application protocol that works between the web browser and web server using the Uniform Resource Locator (URL). The HTTPS establishes a communication link between the web browser and web server that sends and receives or transfers information across the internet in more secure way. HTTPS is similar to HTTP but the main difference is that HTTPS is the secure version of HTTP and it exchanges or transfers information in more secure way. The main feature of HTTPS is that it encrypts the data before sends to the web server. HTTPS first encrypts the data then sends it to the web server. When HTTPS encrypts data then the data converts into some other form and no unauthorized person can read the encrypted information or data. The HTTPS is slower than HTTP because HTTPS encrypts the data or information and then send it in a secure way. HTTPS is used in case of secure Websites that requires login and sensitive information such as an online bank Website etc. HTTPS ensures the secure online ecommerce transactions. HTTPS uses the TCP port 443 to transfer information. When a user connects to a Website through HTTPS, the Website encrypts the session with a Digital Certificate using the Secure Socket Layer (SSL) protocol. The Secure Socket Layer (SSL) is a standard security protocol that uses a cryptographic system and encrypts data or information with two keys such as public key and private key. The public key is shared and known to everyone and the private key is secret and only known to the recipient of the message. When a SSL Digital Certificate is installed on a Website then the users can see a padlock icon at the bottom area of the navigator. When an Extended Validation Certificate is installed on a Website, the users with the latest version of Firefox, Internet Explorer or Opera see the green address bar at the URL area of the navigator. When the Website is secure and using the HTTPS protocol, the web browser always displays a padlock icon to indicate that the Website is secure and it also displays https:// in the address bar.

Secure Socket Layer

Secure Sockets Layer (SSL) is a standard security protocol technology that ensures the secure communication between the web server and web browser. The SSL uses cryptography system that creates an encrypted link between a web server and a web browser and it ensures that all the data passed between the web server and web browser remains secure and private and unauthorized users cannot access and read the data or information. The SSL is usually used by secure Websites and provides full security protection to online transactions and other sensitive information such as secure the online credit card transaction, secure the social security numbers, secure the login credentials information, secure the connection between an email client such as Microsoft Outlook and an email server such as Microsoft Exchange, secure the transfer of files over https and FTP(s) services, secure the intranet based traffic such as internal networks, file sharing, extranets, database connections, and other sensitive information to be transmitted securely. The SSL uses a cryptography system that encrypts the data or information before sending to the web server and establishes an encrypted link between the web server and web browser. When SSL encrypts the data or information using the cryptography system and successfully established an encrypted link between the web server and web browser then the data or information is send to the web server. The SSL encrypts the data or information using the two keys such as public key and private key. The public key is shared and known to everyone and the private key is secret and only known to the recipient of the message. When a Website is secure and using the SSL protocol technology then the web browser always displays a padlock icon to indicate that the Website is secure and it also displays https:// in the address bar instead of http://. We can use the SSL security protocol technology for any Website we want to make it more secure for online transaction and e-commerce. The SSL security protocol technology can be configured and activated for a Website using the SSL certificate. When we want to configure and activate the SSL security protocol technology for a Website, the web server requires the SSL certificate. The SSL certificate is issued by a certificate issuing authority that is called Certificate Authority (CA). When we get the SSL certificate from CA then we install it on the web server. When we install the SSL certificate on the web server then our Website become secure and can use the SSL security protocol technology.

Secure Socket Layer Certificate

Secure Socket Layer (SSL) Certificate is a Digital Certificate issued by a certificate issuing authority that is called Certificate Authority (CA). The SSL Digital Certificate provides us authentication to use the SSL security protocol technology for a Website. A SSL Digital Certificate is an electronic file that uniquely identifies people and other resources over the internet and enables security for a Website. The SSL Digital Certificate contains a variety of information about the owner of the certificate and also contains information about the certificate, and certificate issuing authority such as the name of the owner who want to get the certificate or name of the company, email address, contact address and location, the URL information that uses the SSL Digital Certificate, the owner's public key information, the validation period of the certificate, the serial number, and information about the Certificate Authority (CA). The SSL Digital Certificate is based on public key cryptography that uses a pair of keys such as a public key and a private key for encryption and decryption of data and information over the internet. These keys work together to establish an encrypted connection between the web server and the web browser. If we want to configure and activate the SSL security protocol technology for our Website then we must have to get the SSL Digital Certificate and install it on the web server. To get an SSL Digital Certificate we must create a Certificate Signing Request (CSR) data file on our web server. When we create a Certificate Signing Request (CSR) data file, the web server prompt and ask to provide information about our Website and company or a person for example, the Website URL, the company or owner information i.e. the company name and location or the owner name who want to get the SSL Digital Certificate. When we provide all these information then the web server creates two cryptographic keys such as a Private Key and a Public Key. The private key is private and secure and the Public Key does not need to be secret and is placed into a Certificate Signing Request (CSR) data file. The private key is only known to the receiver of the message and the public key is shared and known to everyone. The Certificate Signing Request (CSR) data file is send to the SSL Certificate Authority (CA) for issuing certificate. The CA uses the CSR data file and keeps all the detailed records about the owner or receiver of the SSL Digital Certificate and issues Digital Certificate on the basis of Certificate Signing Request (CSR) data file. There are various certificates authorities who provide the SSL Digital Certificates and charge for their services. Every Certificate Authority has different products, prices, SSL certificate features, and levels of customer satisfaction etc. Every Certificate Authority (CA) provides a Certification Practice Statement (CPS) that defines the procedures used to verify applications. When a Certificate Authority (CA) verifies an application then issues Digital Certificate to the verified applicant. When we receive a Digital Certificate from a Certificate Authority (CA), we install it on our web server. When we installed the Digital Certificate on our web server, it activates the padlock and the https protocol over port 443 and allows secure connections from a web server to a web browser.

Types of Websites

A Website is developed for a specific purpose and task such as for personal profile or personal information, for business and e-commerce, for government organizations and e-governments, for education and training, for files and data sharing, and for searching various items, products, services, and other information. Following are some types of Websites according to various purposes and tasks:

- Personal Websites
- Commercial Websites
- Educational Websites
- Government Websites
- Search Engine Websites
- Files and Data Sharing Websites

Personal Websites

A personal Website is developed by individual that contain information about a personal profile and other information related to the personal life of a person such as position, education, family, culture, and personal feelings etc. The personal Websites are also called blogs and they can also used to share and publish personal posts such as Articles, personal and family pictures, videos, stories, achievements, goals, conferences, future planning, and other personal relations etc.

Commercial Websites

Commercial Websites are designed for commercial use such as for online business and e-commerce. The commercial Websites allow us to do securely business over the internet and they offer to buy various items, products or services from various sellers of the world over the internet. Some commercial Websites also allow us to sale and purchase items, products, or services over the internet. The commercial Websites are also used for online advertisements that advertise banners and other information about products, items, business, and other organizations. The commercial Websites which offer online business or e-commerce are called virtual stores or electronic stores. There are various Websites which offer online business and e-commerce and allow us to sale and purchase various items, products, and services over the internet such as Amazon.com, eBay.com, Alibaba.com, Zappos.com, Business.com, DHgate.com, and Groupon.com etc are the best Websites for online shopping.

Educational Websites

Educational Websites are developed for education and training and usually they are related with schools, colleges, universities, and other training centers and institutions etc. Educational Websites provides complete details about the courses, the schedules, and about the faculty. Educational Websites also provides online prospectus and registration forms and allow us to apply to the course online by filling the online registration form. Some Educational organizations also developed such Websites that offers online education system. The online education system provides a unique ID and password to each registered student and allows the registered students to read and watch the online lectures, submit their assignments, and conduct the examination online. There are various educational Websites that offers online education system. The best educational Website is the virtual university Website i.e. http://www.vu.edu.pk.

Government Websites

Government Websites are developed to provide government information and data over the internet to facilitate citizens and also provide quick response to the queries of the citizens. The government Websites also called e-government or online government. There are different kinds of government Websites such as a Website that deals the ID's and Passport system and it provides information about the national identity card and passport, similarly the federal government Websites, the provincial government Website or the state government Website provides information about government jobs and allow citizens to apply to the job online by filling the online form. The various ministries of government also developed their Websites that allow citizens to communicate directly with any ministry of government and also send their feedback.

Search Engine Websites

Search Engine Websites are developed by a company or an individual that provides the searching facility to the users. A search engine Website searches and locates various files, documents, items, products, services, Web pages, Websites, videos, audios, multimedia, and all other types of files over the internet in the response of the user input keyword or query and return results to the user. A search engine Website takes input keyword or query from a user and searches or locate various other Websites and matches the user input keyword or query with the contents of the various Websites over the internet. If the user input keyword or query matches with the contents of any Website, the search engine returns the complete information and links of the matched Websites to the user. If the user input keyword or query matches with the contents of more Websites then search engine Websites creates an index and displays the returned information and links in a list in the form of index. The search engine Websites are designed in such a way that they can accept any types of input text, keyword or query due to the strong intelligent system and sensitivity. The search engines automatically correct the spelling of some input text, keyword, or query if a user did some spelling mistakes in the input text, keyword, or query because search engines have strong sense and intelligent system. If a search engine sometime cannot correct the spelling of the input text, keyword, or query then it provides suggestions about our input text, keyword, or query and displays some words or text that are very close to our input text, keyword or query. The most powerful and the most useful search engine Websites are Google.com, Bing.com, Yahoo.com, Yippy.com, Ask.com, Aol.com, Wow.com, Info.com, Mywebsearch.com, Dogpile.com, Webcrawler.com, Webopedia.com, Mahalo.

com, Duckduckgo.com, Gigablast.com, Thatlive.com, Wikipedia.org, Mamma.com, Excite.com etc.

Files and Data Sharing Websites

The files and data sharing Websites offers cloud storage, file synchronization, and client software. The files and data sharing Websites provide storage space to each user by creating an account and allow users to store their personal files, pictures, audios, videos, and other files in their storage space. When we store files and data to any files and data sharing Website, it allows us to access our files and data anywhere in the world. The files and data sharing Websites provide synchronization facility that synchronizes the files and data in a computer from which we want to access our files and data. The main feature of a files and data sharing Website is that it creates a special folder on each computer from which we want to access our files and data and then it synchronizes all our stored files and data in that folder so that it appears to be the same folder with the same contents regardless of which computer is used to view it. If we want to use our stored files and data then first we share a link with the computer from which we want to access. When we share a link then the files and data sharing Website synchronize our stored files and data in that computer and we get the updated files and data. When we update our files and data in one computer, it automatically synchronizes and updates in all the connected computers we shared with the links. The most powerful and most useful files and data sharing Websites are Dropbox.com, Copy.com, Mediafire.com, 4shared.com, SkyDrive.com, iCloud.com, Box.com, Uploaded.net, Sendspace.com, Depositfiles.com, Rapidshare.com, Mega.co.nz, and Filecrop.com etc. The files and data sharing Websites actually installed a Desktop software application on each connected computer and create a folder in all the connected computers. The files and data sharing Websites synchronize the files and data using the installed desktop application software.

Scripting

A script is a piece of codes that contains a list of commands or sequence of instructions or a script is a program that contains a list of commands or instructions in a sequence and it is usually interpreted or carried out by another program or scripting engine rather than by the computer processor. A script is written in any scripting programming language and it is used to automate processes and create Web pages. Each script represents a text document or file that contains commands or instructions in a sequence written in any scripting programming language and usually it is opened and edited by using text editor. A script always interprets and executes directly without the compilation and linking process and it executes quickly as compare to the coding of other programming languages such as C, C++, Java etc because script does not require any compilation and linking process but it interprets by another program or a scripting engine. The process of writing a piece of codes or a program in a scripting programming language is called scripting. The scripting is also called programming because it is a process in which we write a piece of codes or a program in a scripting programming language. Scripting is used to design and develop Websites and Web applications. The scripting process is divided into two types such as client side scripting and server-side scripting. The client-side scripting is also called client-side programming and server-side scripting is also called server-side programming. Following is the details of the client side scripting and server-side scripting:

Client-side Scripting

Client-side scripting is used to design the outside or front end interface of a Website or Web application for example a client side scripting is used to create Web pages and embed or create various controls, forms, hyperlinks, pictures, icons, borders, tables, lists of items, user interfaces, colors, shapes, signs etc on Web pages and creates the entire outside or front end infrastructure of Websites. The client side scripting is executed by the web browser and provides visual interfaces to the users that allow users to click on the links, navigate the Website, and go from one Web page to another Web page etc. The client-side scripting actually creates visual interfaces and enables users to send requests to the server and retrieve data or information and other services from the server. The client-side scripting also validates the user input data and response to the user if a user enters invalid data in any field of a Web page form. The client-side scripting can be written in HTML, CSS, JavaScript, VBScript, Ajax, JQuery etc.

Server-side Scripting

Server-side scripting is used to design the internal or back end of a Website or Web application such as user logins, user rights, privileges, privacy, and provides other services such as to store the user data or information in the database and provides data or information to the user according to the user query, provides online secure transactions and e-commerce facility etc. The server-side scripting is executed by the web server and provides services to the users. The server-side scripting establishes the database connection and provides a unique ID to each user. When a user fills an online form on a Website and press the submit button, the server-side scripting stores the user data into the database and provides an acknowledgment to the user that the data has been successfully sent to the server. The server-side scripting can be written in various server-side scripting programming languages such as ASP, ASP.NET, JSP, PHP, Perl CGI, Python, Ruby, ActiveVFP, ColdFusion etc.

Scripting Programming Languages

A scripting programming language is a high level programming language that allows us to write scripts to automate processes and create or develop Web pages. A scripting programming language is designed in such a way that it does not execute the script or a piece of codes directly by the processor but it always integrating and communicating with other programming language and interprets the script or piece of codes by using another programming language. The scripting programming languages are always used with the conjunction of other programming languages to interpret or carried out the codes or scripts of the scripting programming languages. A scripting programming language always interprets at run time that uses a separate program to read the code and interpret it. The scripting programming languages are used to design and develop Web pages. There are various types of scripting programming languages such as JavaScript, VBScript, PHP, Perl, Python, Ruby, ASP, ASP. NET, JSP, Cold Fusion, ActiveVFP, and Tcl etc.

Markup Languages

A Markup Language is a computer language that is used to define, process, present, and annotate text, structure and arrange data, defines various objects and user interfaces within text files or documents and displays them on a web browser. The Markup Languages use a special type of rules or instructions that are called tags. A tag is a set of rules and instructions of a Markup Language that takes one or more attributes and performs a specific operation such as to display the formatted text or data using different text formats, colors, size, and styles, structure and arrange data, define and embed various objects such as graphics, animations, tables, borders, charts, pictures, audio/video files, flash animation files, and defines other various Control Objects to provide visual interfaces to users such as web Forms, Textboxes, Buttons, Radio Buttons, Check Boxes, Labels, Combo Boxes, and List Boxes etc. The tags of a Markup Language take one or more attributes that provide values to the tags. If we provide values to the tags, we usually assign them by assignment operator and enclosed each value of an attribute by double quotes. The Markup Languages also provide various formatting tags and use Cascading Style Sheet to format texts and layouts. The Markup Languages display text files or documents in web browsers and perform tasks according to the values of the tags used in the documents. The Markup Languages do not compile their codes by the compiler directly but all Markup Languages interprets their codes by other software application such as web browser. A web browser displays the contents of a Markup Language text file or document according to the instructions or tags used in the text file or document. The Markup Languages are used to develop websites by designing one or more web pages and joining them with each other using hyperlinks. There are various types of Markup Languages but the most important and very popular Markup Languages are HTML (Hyper Text Markup Language), XHTML (Extensible Hyper Text Markup Language), XML (Extensible Markup Language), and CFML (ColdFusion Markup Language) etc.

Tags

A tag is a set of rules and instructions of a Markup Language that takes one or more attributes and performs a specific operation such as to display the formatted text or data using different text formats, colors, size, and styles, structure and arrange data, define and embed various objects such as graphics, animations, tables, borders, charts, pictures, audio/video files, flash animation files, and defines other various Control Objects to provide visual interfaces to users such as Web Forms, Textboxes, Buttons, Radio Buttons, Check Boxes, Labels, Combo Boxes, and List Boxes etc within text files or documents and displays them on a web browser.

A tag is written within left and right angular brackets as <tag>. The enclosed characters or a set of rules and instructions are not visible when a document is displayed on a web browser but they are rules and instructions for the computer to perform a specific operation and achieve a task. There are two types of tags in Markup Languages such as single tags and pair tags. The single tags are used individually and they do not have ending tags while pair tags are designed to be used in pairs. Each pair tags contain starting tag and ending tag and text is enclosed within the starting tag and the ending tag as <starting-tag>---text---</ending-tag>. The starting tag is the starting point of the text and ending tag is the ending point of the text. The ending tag always uses a slash / that indicates the ending tag and tells to the web browser that the enclosed text should be displayed to the user. The tags of a Markup Language take one or more attributes that provide values to the tags. If we provide values to the tags, we usually assign them by assignment operator and enclosed each value of an attribute by double quotes. The value of a tag may be a numeric value, name of a color or RGB color numeric value, or it may be a constant value usually enclosed within double quotes.

Hyper Text Markup Language

Hyper Text Markup Language is a markup language that is shortly called HTML. It is originally designed by Tim Berners-Lee in 1990. The HTML is used to design HTML documents called Web pages and displays text and other information in a web browser. Each web page is actually a HTML file that contains plain text. The extension of HTML file is .html or .htm. The Hyper Text Markup Language allows us to design a series of HTML documents or web pages which are linked together by using hyperlinks. A hyperlink is a special type of clickable link provided by HTML that is used to go from one web page to another web page. Each HTML file or web page is made up of many HTML tags. The Hyper Text Markup Language provides a set of keywords called HTML tags. An HTML tag is a set of rules and instructions or an HTML tag is a coding instruction embedded in the HTML document that is used to perform a specific operation. The Hyper Text Markup Language is developed in many versions such as HTML version 2.0, HTML version 3.0, HTML version 3.2, HTML version 4.0, HTML version 4.01, and HTML version 5. The most recent version of HTML is version 5 that is written as HTML5 and it was released in January 2008.

Web Application

A web application is a software application that is usually part of a website and runs on a web browser. A web application is also an independent software application that runs without a web browser and performs a specific task like a desktop software applications. A web application that is part of a website is usually works within a website and runs on a web browser while a web application that works without a website is usually installed in a local user computer or a mobile device and runs without a web browser and behaves like a desktop software application. A web application works on the basis of client/server architecture and it is developed by the combination of server-side and client-side scripting or programming. The client-side scripting design the outside or external structure of a web application while server-side scripting design the back end or internal part of the web application such as to establish the database connection, provides services to the user, sends the user data or information to the database and retrieves data or information from the database according to the user query. The server-side scripting is performed by using the server-side scripting languages such as ASP, ASP.NET, PHP, ColdFusion etc and client-side scripting is performed by using the client-side scripting languages or markup languages such as HTML, DHTML, JavaScript, VBScript etc. The Google Apps, Microsoft Office Live, Skype, WebEx, WebOffice, Webmail, online auctions, Wikis, online retail sales, and many other are the examples of Web Application.

CHAPTER 17

The Basic Fundamentals and Requirements of ASP.NET

CHAPTER CONTENTS

- The Structure of ASP.NET Page
- Directives
- Page Directive
- Master Directive
- Control Directive
- Register Directive
- Reference Directive
- PreviousPageType Directive
- OutputCache Directive
- Import Directive
- Implements Directive
- Assembly Directive
- MasterType Directive
- Application Directive
- Code Declaration Blocks
- The ASP.NET Controls
- The Code Render Blocks
- Server-side Comments
- Server-side Include Directives
- The AP.NET Views
- View Engine
- ASPX View Engine
- Razor View Engine
- Comparison of ASPX and Razor View Engines
- Master Pages
- Content Pages
- ContentPlaceHolder Controls
- Content Controls
- MIME types in ASP.NET

- HTML Controls
- HTML Server Controls
- ASP.NET Web Server Controls
- ASP.NET Validation Server Controls
- RequiredFieldValidator
- RangeValidator
- CompareValidator
- RegularExpressionValidator
- CustomValidator
- ValidationSummary
- Repeater Control

The Structure of ASP.NET Page

ASP.NET is a framework of the .NET technology that provides an interface in the form of blank pages called web pages and allows developers or programmers to use a page and design it using the programming code of any .NET programming language and execute it on the server. ASP.NET supports both the Visual C# and Visual Basic.NET programming languages of the .NET technology for the code writing. A single programming language either Visual C# or Visual Basic.NET is selected for the code writing. The ASP.NET web page does not support multiple programming languages at a time. The default programming language of the ASP.NET page is Visual Basic. NET. If we want to set Visual C# language as the default language for the ASP. NET page, we use a directive at the top of the page. The ASP.NET framework defines a specific structure for a page that must be followed at the time of a page designing. To design a Web page we must follow the structure and rules of the ASP.NET framework. ASP.NET defines the following elements for the structure of a page:

1. Directives
2. Code Declaration Blocks
3. The ASP.NET Controls
4. The Code Render Blocks
5. Server-side Comments
6. Server-side Include Directives

Directives

A directive is a command or an instruction for the compiler that specifies some settings to control and manage how an ASP.NET Web page is compiled and processed. The directive settings are used by the compiler when the page is compiled. The ASP.NET Directives are also called page directives. ASP.NET provides various types of directives used for different settings such as to set the programming language we are using for the web page coding, to import namespaces in the web page, to import external files into the web page, to register custom controls etc. The directive is usually used at the top of the web page but it can also be used anywhere within the web page. A directive may take one or more attributes and it is enclosed within the block **<%@.....Directive Name..... %>**. A directive begin with the characters <%@ and end with the characters %>. Following is the general syntax of using a directive in ASP.NET web page:

```
<%@ Directive_Name attribute = Value [attribute = Value] %>
```

ASP.NET provides various types of directives. Following is the details of the ASP.NET directives:

- Page Directive
- Master Directive
- Control Directive
- Register Directive
- Reference Directive
- PreviousPageType Directive
- OutputCache Directive
- Import Directive
- Implements Directive
- Assembly Directive
- MasterType Directive
- Application Directive

Page Directive

The Page Directive is used to define the page related attributes used by the ASP. NET page parser and compiler. The page related attributes are used to specify a programming language and other general settings for the web page. The ASP. NET web pages can be written in different programming languages therefore, we must specify the programming language for each web page. Each ASP.NET page uses a single programming language at a time. The Page directive specifies settings for the web page that affect the entire ASP.NET web page. The Page directive is included using special delimiters. The page directive can also be used to enable tracing and debugging for a page. Following is the general syntax to use the page directive in ASP.NET web page:

<%@page attribute = “value”[attribute = “value”]%>
Or
<%@ attribute = “value”[attribute = “value”]%>

The above both declarations of the Page directive are equivalent. In the first declaration the keyword Page is optional and we may eliminate it. The Page directive provides various types of attributes that take different values and set specific actions for the ASP.NET web page. The Page directive provides the following different attributes:

Attribute	Description
Title	This attribute is used to set the title of the web page. It takes a string value that indicates the page title.
Language	ASP.NET uses a single programming language for a single page at a time. To use a programming language for a page, we must set that programming language before use. This attribute is used to set the programming language to be used for the page coding. It takes the name of any programming language supported by the .NET technology such as Visual Basic, C#, or Jscript. The name of the programming language is enclosed in double quits and it is assigned to the Language attribute using the assignment operator. Following is its general syntax: <%@ Language=”Language_Name” %>

AutoEventWireup	This attribute indicates For every page there is an automatic way to bind the events to methods in the same .aspx file or in code behind. The default value is true. It indicates whether events of the page are autowired or not. It takes a Boolean value either true or false. When its value is set to true then the events autowiring is enabled otherwise, the events autowiring is disabled.
CodeFile	This attribute specifies a file with which the page is associated.
CodeBehind	This attribute specifies the name of the compiled file that contains the class associated with the page. This attribute is used for Web application projects. It does not use for website project.
Culture	This attribute specifies the culture settings for the page. It takes different values for the culture settings. If we set its value to auto, the page automatically detects culture.
UICulture	This attribute specifies the UI culture settings for the page. It takes any value of the UI culture.
ValidateRequest	This attribute indicates whether request validation should occur or not. It takes a Boolean value either true or false. If we set its value to true, the request validation checks all the input data against a hard-coded list of potentially dangerous values. If a proper match occurs then an HttpRequestValidationException class is thrown. The default value of this attribute is true.
Theme Attribute	This attribute is used to specify the theme for the page. This is a new feature available in ASP. NET 2.0 or later versions.

SmartNavigation	This attribute is used to indicate the smart navigation feature of the page. It takes a Boolean value either true or false. If we set its value to true, it returns the postback to the current position of the page. The default value of this attribute is false.
MasterPageFile	This attribute is used to specify the location of the MasterPage file to be used with the current ASP.NET page.
EnableViewState	This attribute is used to indicate whether the view state is maintained across the page requests or not. It takes a Boolean value either true or false. The true value of this attribute indicates that the view state is maintained and the false value of this attribute indicates that the view state is not maintained. The default value of this attribute is true.
EnableSessionState	This attribute defines the session-state requirements for the page. It takes a Boolean value either true or false. If the value of this attribute is true, it enables the session state and if the value of this attribute is false, it does not enable the session state. The default value of this attribute is true.
EnableEventValidation	This attribute enables validation of events in postback and callback scenarios. The value of this attribute is true if events are being validated otherwise, its value is false. The default value of this attribute is true. All event-driven controls in ASP.NET use this feature by default.
ErrorPage	This attribute is used to specify a target URL for redirection if an unhandled page exception occurs. For example, this attribute is used if you want to redirect another page that contains the error information.

Inherits	This attribute is used to specify a code-behind class for the page to inherit. This can be any class derived from the Page class. This attribute is used with the CodeFile attribute, which contains the path to the source file for the code-behind class. The Inherits attribute is case-sensitive when using C# as the page language, and case-insensitive when using Visual Basic as the page language. If this attribute does not contain a namespace then the ASP.NET checks whether the ClassName attribute contains a namespace or not. If the ClassName attribute contains a namespace then the ASP.NET attempts to load the class referenced in the Inherits attribute using the namespace of the ClassName attribute. The Inherits attribute and the ClassName attribute both uses the same namespace.
Debug	This attribute is used to indicate whether the page should be compiled with the debug symbols or not.

There are also some other attributes which are rarely used such as Buffer, CodePage, ClassName, EnableSessionState, Description, EnableTheming, EnableViewStateMac, TraceMode, WarningLevel etc. Following is an example of the Page directive:

```
<%@ Title="My Page" Language="C#" AutoEventWireup="true" CodeFile=
"Sample.aspx.cs" Inherits="Sample" %>
```

Master Directive

The Master Directive is similar to the Page Directive but the main difference is that the master directive is used only for Master pages that have .master extension. The Master directive has the following few attributes:

- Language
- AutoEventWireup
- CodeFile

- Title
- MasterPageFile
- EnableViewState
- Inherits

Following is an example of the Master directive:

```
<%@ Master Language="C#" AutoEventWireup="true"
CodeFile="WebMaster.master.cs" Inherits="WebMaster" %>
```

Control Directive

This directive is associated with the user controls and it is used only when we build user controls. It helps us to define the properties to be inherited by the user control. These values are assigned to the user control as the page is parsed and compiled. The Control directive provides the following attributes:

- Language
- AutoEventWireup
- CodeFile
- MasterPageFile
- EnableViewState
- Inherits
- Debug
- src

Register Directive

This directive is used to register user controls on the pages. When we create a user control and we want to use it on the web page then first we have to register it using this directive so that the control can be accessed by the web page. The Register directive associates aliases with namespaces and class names for notation in custom server control syntax. When we drag and drop a user control onto the .aspx pages, the Visual Studio automatically creates a Register directive at the top of the page. This directive provides the following attributes:

Attribute	Description
Assembly	This attribute indicates the assembly we are associating with the TagPrefix.

Namespace	This attribute indicates the namespace to relate with the TagPrefix.
Src	This attribute specifies the location of the user control we want to use on the web page.
TagName	This attribute is a name used to refer a user control uniquely by its name.
TagPrefix	This attribute is used to specify a unique namespace for the user control.

Following is an example of Register Directive:

<%@ Register TagName=" UserControl 1" TagPrefix="UC1" Src="~\usercontrol\usercontrol1.ascx" %>

For the above directive following would be the user control:

<UC1:UserControl1 runat="server"/>

Reference Directive

This directive is used to reference another ASP.NET page or another user control with the current ASP.NET page or the current control. It declares that the referenced ASP.NET page or user control should be complied along with the current ASP.NET page or the current user control. This directive provides the following attributes:

Attribute	Description
Control	This attribute specifies an external user control that ASP.NET should dynamically compile and link to the current page at run time.
Page	This attribute specifies an external page that ASP.NET should dynamically compile and link to the current page at run time.
VirutalPath	This attribute specifies the location of the page or user control from which the active page will be referenced.

Following is the example of Reference directive:

```
<%@ Reference VirutalPath="YourReferencePage.ascx" %>
```

For example:

```
<%@Reference VirtualPayh="~/UserControl1.ascx"%>
```

PreviousPageType Directive

The PreviousPageType is used to achieve the cross-page posting concept between the ASP.NET pages. This directive contains the following two attributes:

Attribute	Description
TagName	This attribute sets the name of the derived class from which the postback will occur.
VirutalPath	This attribute sets the location of the posting page from which the postback will occur.

Following is the example of PreviousPageType directive:

```
<%@ PreviousPageType VirtualPath="~/PreviousPageName.aspx" %>
```

OutputCache Directive

This directive is used to control the output caching policies of the ASP.NET page or user control. This directive provides the following attributes:

Attribute	Description
Duration	This attribute is used to specify the duration of time in seconds that the page or user control is cached.
Location	This attribute is used to specify the location to store the output cache. It takes an enumeration that contains different constant values. Each constant value of the enumeration indicates a location where the output cache is to be stored. The constant values of the enumeration are Any, Client, Downstream, Server, ServerAndClient,

	and None. The Location attribute takes a single constant value of the enumeration at a time.
VaryByParam	This attribute is used to specify a semi-colon separated list of strings to vary the output cache.
VaryByControl	This attribute is used to specify a semi-colon separated list of strings to vary the output cache of a user Control.
VaryByCustom	This attribute is used to specify the custom output caching requirements.
VaryByHeader	This attribute is used to specify a semi-colon separated list of HTTP headers to vary the output cache.

Following is the example of OutputCache directive:

<%@ OutputCache Duration="60" Location="Server" VaryByParam= "None"%>

Turn Off & On the Output Cache

To turn off the output cache for an ASP.NET Web page at the client location and at the proxy location, we set the Location attribute value and the VaryByParam attribute value to none in the OutputCache directive. The following example shows how to turn off the Output Cache for an ASP.NET page at the client location and at the proxy location:

<%@ OutputCache Location="None" VaryByParam="None" %>

Import Directive

This directive is used to import the namespaces in the ASP.NET pages. To use any class or interface in the ASP.NET page, we must import the namespace of that class or interface in the ASP.NET page using the Import directive. This directive has a single attribute that takes the name of the namespace to be imported. When we open a new project of the ASP.NET, by default it imports only some namespaces automatically. If we want to use a class that is not a member of one of the default namespace then we must explicitly import the namespace of that class or we must use the fully qualified name of that class if we do not want to import its namespace. For example, suppose we want to send an email from an ASP.NET page using the Send method of the SmtpMail class. The SmtpMail class is contained in the System.Web.Mail namespace.

This is not one of the default namespaces imported into an ASP.NET page therefore, the namespace of the SmtpMail class is imported in the ASP.NET page using the Import directive. The following examples show how to imports the namespace in the ASP.NET pages:

```
<%@Import Namespace="System.Data"%>
<%@ Import namespace="System.Data.SqlClient" %>
```

Implements Directive

This directive gets the ASP.NET page to implement a specified .NET framework interface. It has a single attribute Interface that helps to specify the .NET Framework interface. When the ASP.NET page or user control implements an interface, it has direct access to all its events, methods and properties. Following is the example of this directive:

```
<%@ Implements Interface="System.Web.UI.IValidator" %>
```

Assembly Directive

This directive is used to make the ASP.NET page aware of external components. It provides the following two attributes:

Attribute	Description
Name	This attribute enables us to specify the name of an assembly we want to attach to the page. It takes the name of the file without extension.
src	This attribute represents the name of a source code file.

The following example shows how to specify an assembly:

```
<%@Assembly Name="MyAssembly"%>
<%@Assembly src="MYAssembly.cs">
```

MasterType Directive

This directive connects a class name to the ASP.NET page for getting strongly typed references or members contained in the specified Master Page. This directive provides attributes such as Typename and virtualpath. The Typename attribute sets the name of the derived class from which to get the strongly typed or reference members and virtualpath attribute sets the location of the page from which these are retrieved. The following example shows how to set this directive:

```
<%@MasterType VirtualPath="/MasterPage1.master"%>
```

Application Directive

This directive defines application-specific attributes. It is provided at the top of the global.aspx file. This directive provides two attributes that are Description and Language. The Description attribute specifies the text description of the application. The Language attribute specifies the programming language used in the code blocks. Following is the general syntax of this attribute:

```
<%@ Application Language="C#" %>
<%@ Page Trace="True" %>
```

Debug Directive

This directive is used to enable runtime error messages to be displayed on a page. To display errors in ASP.NET page we must include the following directive:

```
<%@ Page Debug="True" %>
```

Code Declaration Blocks

The code declaration block contains the program code that expresses our views or logic. In this section of the ASP.NET page any programming language of the .NET technology is used to write our view or logic in the form of coding. The Code Declaration Block usually contains Variables, Constant values, Decision Statements, Iteration Statements, Subroutines, Functions or Methods, Arrays, and other statements of the programming language according to the view or logic. The Code Declaration Block is enclosed within the <script> and </script> tags. It starts with the <script> and ends with the </script>. Following is the general syntax to declare the Code Declaration Block in ASP.NET page:

```
<script>
-------------------------------
Program Code Here
-------------------------------
</script>
```

The <script> tag provides the following important attributes:

Attribute	Description
Language	This attribute is used to specify a programming language we want to use for the program code in the ASP.NET page. It takes the name of the programming language supported by ASP.NET such as C#, Visual Basic, and Jscript etc. The name of the programming language is enclosed in double quotes and assigns it to the Language attribute using the
	assignment operator. If the programming language is not specified by this attribute then the ASP.NET page use the default programming language which is defined by the page directive <%@ Page Language %>. If no programming language is specified in the ASP.NET page, the default programming language is Visual Basic.
Type	This attribute is used to specify the scripting language we want to use for the program code in the ASP.NET page. It specifies the MIME type of the script. The JavaScript supported MIME types are text/javascript, text/ecmascript, application/javascript, and application/ecmascript. If we do not specify this attribute then the script is treated as JavaScript. <script Type="Media_Type">

Writing Code of ASP.NET

ASP.NET is a part of Microsoft .NET technology that uses the .NET framework for code writing, compilation and execution. The ASP.NET application codes can be written in any of the following languages:

- Visual Basic.NET
- C#.NET

The Code Render Blocks

The Code Render Block is used to execute the code within the HTML or text content of the ASP.NET page. There are two types of code such as inline code and inline expressions. The inline code are enclosed within <% -----Code here----- %> and the inline expressions are enclosed within <%= Expression here %>. The inline expressions actually display the value of a variable or method.

The Server-side Comments

This directive is used to add Server-side comments to the ASP.NET pages. The Server-side comments are placed within <%-- Comments here --%> block. The Server-side comments starts with the <%-- and ends with the --%>. The Server-side comments are usually added to a page for the documentation purposes. We cannot see the contents of the Server-side comment tags unlike the normal HTML comment tags by using the View Source command on the Web browser. The Server-side comments can also be useful when we are debugging an ASP.NET page. We can temporarily remove both ASP.NET controls and code render blocks from a page by surrounding these elements with server-side comments.

Server-side Include Directives

This directive is used to include external files in ASP.NET pages or the contents of one ASP.NET file into another ASP.NET file. For example, if we have fixed contents such as footers, headers, functions etc then we create these contents in one ASP.NET page and include this file into another ASP.NET page whenever we need these contents. The Server-side Include directive defines the following two syntaxes to include the contents of one ASP.NET file into another ASP.NET file:

```
<! -- #include file="FileName.aspx" -->
<! -- #include virtual="/DirectoryName/FileName.aspx" -->
```

The first syntax takes the name of a file we want to include into an ASP.NET page. The second syntax uses the attribute virtual that takes the full path of the file we want to include into an ASP.NET page. The full path of a file includes the virtual directory path and the file name.

Declaring Variables in ASP.NET

ASP.NET does not have built-in data types to declare variables but it uses the variables of a programming language that is used in the ASP.NET page for example, if we use Visual Basic.NET in the ASP.NET page then ASP.NET will use the Visual Basic.NET built-in data types for variables declaration similarly, if we use visual C# in the ASP.NET page then ASP.NET will use the visual C# built-in data types for variables declaration. ASP.NET provides two mechanisms for variables declarations such as implicit variables declaration and explicit variables declaration. The implicit declaration of variables is very simple and it does not require the type specification of a variable to be declared. When we declare a variable implicitly, the type of that variable automatically declares as object and it takes any type of value such as integer, float, double, string, object etc and the explicit declaration of a variable requires the type specification of a variable to be declared. The implicit declaration of variables is not a good programming practice because they have serious drawbacks as compared to explicit variables. Following are some technical differences between implicit and explicit variables declaration:

Implicit Variables	Explicit Variables
The implicit variables are general type variables and they do not require the type specification at the time of declaration.	The explicit type variables require the type specification at the time of declaration.
An implicit variable can take any type of value for example, if a variable is declared as implicit type, it takes any type of value such as integer, float, double, character, string etc.	An explicit variable can take a single type value for example, if a variable is declared as integer, it will take an integer value, if a variable is declared as float, it will take float value etc.
An implicit variable cannot be declared before use or without initialization.	An explicit variable can be declared before use and with or without initialization.
The implicit type variable is declared using the keyword var. The var keyword declares a variable of type object that takes any type of value such as integer, float, double, character, string etc.	The explicit type variables can be declared in ASP.NET using the type specification that is each variable is declared with its type such as int, float, double, string etc.

The ASP.NET Views

A View is usually a file of ASP.NET that contains the combine code of HTML and one of the programming languages supported by ASP.NET such as Visual

Basic.NET, Visual C#.NET etc. A View represents the user interface and it contains all the user interactions.

View Engine

A view engine is ASP.NET programming markup syntax used to add server-based code to the ASP.NET web pages and create dynamic and interactive web pages using different programming languages. The View engine works between the user view and a browser and it is responsible for creating HTML from the user views and delivers the valid HTML output to the browser. A view engine provides a basic syntax for writing the user view. Each view engine has its own syntax for writing the user view. The View engine works with the ASP.NET MVC. The default view engines of the ASP.NET are ASPX and Razor view engines. The ASPX view engine works with all versions of the ASP.NET MVC while Razor view engine works with the ASP.NET MVC 3 and later versions. There are also various kinds of third party view engines available for the ASP.NET MVC which can be downloaded from the nuget packages. Following are some common view engines:

- ASPX
- Razor
- Spark
- NHaml
- NDJango
- Sharp
- Tiles
- String Template
- SharpDOM

ASPX View Engine

The ASPX view engine is the default view engine of the ASP.NET which uses the classic ASP syntax. This view engine is also called Web Form view engine because the syntax of ASPX view engine is same as the syntax of the ASP.NET Web Forms. According to the ASPX view engine, the code block always enclosed in <% ……… %> block. The code bloc of this view engine starts with the <% and ends with the %>. The file extension of the ASPX view engine is .aspx which is the default extension of the ASP.NET file.

Razor View Engine

The Razor view engine is an advanced and a simple-syntax view engine of the ASP.NET which is used to create dynamic web pages with the C# or Visual Basic .NET programming languages. The Razor view engine works with the ASP.NET MVC and it supports both the C# and Visual Basic .NET view files. The Razor view engine was released for Microsoft Visual Studio 2010 in January 2011and it was released as part of the ASP.NET MVC 3 and the Microsoft WebMatrix tool set. The Razor view engine works with the ASP.NET MVC 3 and later versions and it is the default view engine of the ASP.NET MVC 3 and MVC 4. The Razor view engine defines separate syntaxes for the code blocks of C# and Visual Basic.NET view files. The Razor view engine is part of the Visual Studio.NET 2010 and later versions and its namespace is System.Web.Razor. To use the Razor view engine in Microsoft Visual Studio.NET, the namespace System.Web.Razor must be imported at the top of the program. The Razor view engine defines the following fundamental rules for the code blocks of C# and Visual Basic.NET view files:

- The Razor code block always starts with @ sign. The @ sign is always used as a prefix to the code block of both the C# and Visual Basic.NET view files. The Razor code block is enclosed in braces {...} in C# programming language and enclosed in Code……End Code in Visual Basic.NET. The Razor code block for Visual Basic.NET starts with @Code statement and always ends with the End Code statement. Following are the general syntaxes of the Razor view engine for the code blocks of C# and Visual Basic.NET programming languages:

Razor Code Block for C#	Razor Code Block for VB.NET

@{
…………………………
The Code Block here
……………………………
}
	@Code
	…………………………
	The Code Block here
	……………………………
	End Code

- The namespace of the Razor view engine is System.Web.Razor. Therefore, to use the Razor view engine in Visual Studio.NET, the namespace System.Web.Razor must be imported at the top of the program.

- The file extension of the Razor view engine for the C# programming language is .cshtml and for VB.NET programming language is .vbhtml.
- The variables name, functions, and expressions always start with @ sign.
- The comments are placed in a block @* ………. *@.

Comparison of ASPX and Razor View Engines

Following are the main differences between the ASPX and Razor view engines:

Razor View Engine	**ASPX View Engine**
The Razor view engine is an advanced and simple syntax based view engine that was introduced for Visual Studio.NET 2010 in January, 2011 with ASP.NET MVC3.	The ASPX view engine is the default view engine of the ASP.NET MVC and it has the same syntax as the syntax of the ASP.NET Web Forms.
The namespace of the Razor view engine is System.Web.Razor.	The namespace of the ASPX view engine is System.Web.Mvc. WebFormViewEngine.
The file extension of the Razor view engine for the C# programming language is .cshtml and for VB.NET programming language is .vbhtml.	The file extensions of the ASPX view engine for the user view file is .aspx, the file extension for the partial views and editor templates is .ascx, and the file extension for the layout/ master pages is .master.
Razor view engine has new and advanced syntax that are compact, expressive and reduces typing.	The ASPX view Engine has the same syntax like the ASP.NET Web Forms uses for the .aspx pages.
The Razor syntax is easy to learn and much clean than the ASPX syntax. The Razor syntax uses the @ symbol to make the code like as: @Html.ActionLink("Login", "Login")	The ASPX view engine syntax is mixed with the html and it makes the code like as: <% Html.ActionLink("Login", "Login") %>

By default, the Razor view engine prevents the XSS attacks (Cross-Site Scripting Attacks) means it encodes the script or html tags like <,> before rendering to view.	The ASPX view engine does not prevent XSS attacks (Cross-Site Scripting Attacks) means any script saved in the database will be fired while rendering the page.
The Razor engine is little bit slow as compared to the ASPX view engine.	The ASPX view engine is faster than the Razor view Engine.
The Razor view engine does not support the design mode in visual studio and we cannot see the page look and feel in design mode.	Web Form engine support design mode in visual studio and we can see the page look and feel without running the application.

Master Pages

A master page is an ASP.NET file that contains static text, HTML elements such as lists, tables, images, forms, headers, footers, labels etc, and server controls such as ASP.NET controls. A master page provides predefined layout. The extension of a master page is .master. The master page is a feature that allows us to define the common structure and interface markup elements for the ASP.NET Web application such as headers, footers, style definitions, or navigation bars. A master page can serve as a template for one or more Web Forms and it can be shared by any of the pages in Website or Web application. Each .aspx Web Form only needs to define the content unique to itself and this content will plug into specified areas of the Master Page layout. A master page contains ContentPlaceHolder controls which are used to bind the Content pages with the master page. The master page is identified by a @ Master directive. Following is the general syntax of master page:

```
<%@ Master Language="C#" CodeFile="Site.
master.cs" Inherits="SiteMaster" %>
```

The @ Master directive contains attributes such as Language, CodeFile, and Inherits. The Language attribute specifies the programming language which is used for the code writing such as C# or Visual Basic etc, the CodeFile attribute specifies the code behind file that contains the programming code, and Inherits attribute specifies the base class of the master pages.

Content Pages

The Content pages are separate pages which are defined for the ContentPlaceHolder controls of a master page. The Content pages are defined according to the application specification and requirement. Each Content page contains contents of the application. The extension of a Content page is .aspx. To link or associate a Content page with the master page, the MasterPageFile attribute of Page directive is used and provide the name of the target master page. The following Page directive link or associate the Site.master page to the Content page:

```
<% @ Page Language="C#" MasterPageFile = "~/
Site.master" Title="Content Page"%>
```

In a Content page, we create the content by adding Content controls and link or associate them to the ContentPlaceHolder controls of the master page. Each Content control of a Content page requires a ContentPlaceHolder control in a master page for example, if a master page contains two ContentPlaceHolder controls called Main ContentPlaceHolder and Footer ContentPlaceHolder control then in a Content page, we must create two Content controls, one Content control for the Main ContentPlaceHolder control and another Content control for the Footer ContentPlaceHolder control of the master page.

ContentPlaceHolder Controls

A ContentPlaceHolder control is used in master pages to define a region in a Master Page and renders all text, markup, and server controls from an associated Content control of a Content page. For example, if we want to display text, markup, and server controls etc on a specific region of a master page, we define a ContentPlaceHolder control on that specific region and link or associate it with the Content control of a Content page. The ContentPlaceHolder control is defined anywhere in the header section or in body section of a master page. A master page can contain one or more ContentPlaceHolder controls. Each ContentPlaceHolder control provides ID property that is used to identify a ContentPlaceHolder control in a master page. The ID of each ContentPlaceHolder control is unique and no two ContentPlaceHolder controls can have the same ID. The ID of a ContentPlaceHolder control is used to link or associate a Content control of a Content page.

Content Controls

A Content control is used on the Content page to display text, markup, and server controls in the created region of the linked or associated ContentPlaceHolder control of a master page. A Content page contains one or more Content controls which are used to link or associate ContentPlaceHolder controls of a master page. A Content control provides ContentPlaceHolderID property which is used to link or associate a ContentPlaceHolder control of a master page. To link or associate a ContentPlaceHolder control of a master page with a Content page, the ID of a ContentPlaceHolder control is assigned to the ContentPlaceHolderID property of that Content page to be associated. In a content page everything is inside the Content controls except script blocks for server code. If anything (except script blocks) is outside the Content controls, it will produce an error. If a Content page has three sections such as Header section, Main section, and Footer section then a master page will have three ContentPlaceHolder controls, one for the Header section to display the contents of the Header section, one for the Main section to display the contents of the Main section, and one for the Footer section to display the contents of the Footer section. Following is a Content page that contains three sections:

Content Page

```
<%-- This is the Page Directive --%>
<%@ Page Title="Info" Language="C#" MasterPageFile="~/MasterPage"
CodeBehind="Info.aspx.cs" Inherits="ApplicationName.Info" %>

<%-- Header Section --%>
<asp:Content ID ="Header" ContentPlaceHolderID="HeaderContent"
runat="server">
------------------------------------------------
This is Header section of a Content Page
------------------------------------------------
</asp:Content>

<%-- Main Section --%>
<asp:Content ID="Body" ContentPlaceHolderID="MainContent"
runat="server">
```

```
--------------------------------------------------
This is Body or Main section of a Content Page
--------------------------------------------------
</asp:Content>
<%-- Footer Section --%>
<asp:Content ID="Footer" ContentPlaceHolderID="FooterContent"
runat="server">
--------------------------------------------------
This is Footer section of a Content Page
--------------------------------------------------
</asp:Content>
```

The name of the preceding Content page is Info and it contains three sections, the first section is for the Header contents, the second section is for the Body or Main contents, and the third section is for the Footer section. It uses the master page and the code behind file Info.aspx.cs. The Page directive binds the content page to the master page using the MasterPageFile attribute. Following is the master page designed for the preceding Content page:

Master Page

```
<%@ Master Language="C#" CodeFile="Site.master.cs" Inherits=
"SiteMaster" %>

<!DOCTYPE html>

<head runat="server">
<title><%: Page.Title %> - My ASP.NET Application</title>
</head>

<body>
<form runat="server">
<div>
<asp:ContentPlaceHolder ID ="HeaderContent" runat ="server">

</asp:ContentPlaceHolder>
</div>

<div>
```

```
<asp:ContentPlaceHolder ID="MainContent" runat="server">

</asp:ContentPlaceHolder>
</div>

<div>
<asp:ContentPlaceHolder ID="FooterContent" runat="server">

</asp:ContentPlaceHolder>
</div>

</form>
</body>
</html>
```

The preceding master page contains three sections that are Header section, Body or Main section, and Footer section.

MIME types in ASP.NET

MIME stands for Multi-purpose Internet Mail Extensions. It is also called media types. The MIME types identify the type of a piece of data or file we send or receive over the internet. It classifies the data in different types such as text data, images, video, xml, or JSON data etc. The MIME type defines a standard constant value for each type of data which are used to identify the type of the data over the internet. The MIME types or media types allows the mail client or Web browser to send and receive files like text files, spreadsheets, audio, video, xml, and images files through Internet mail. A MIME type consists of two string parts separated by a slash (/). The first part of a MIME type specifies the type of the data or the media type and the second part specifies the sub type of the data. The type refers to a logical grouping of many MIME types that are closely related to each other and the sub type is specific to one file type within the type for example, we have different types of data such as text data, images, and videos data etc. If we consider the images then we know that within the images data there are different types of images such as jpg, jpeg, bmp, png, and gif etc similarly, if we consider video data then we know that there are different types of videos such as avi, flv, wmv, mov, mp4, and mpeg etc therefore, the first part of a MIME type indicates the type of the data whether the data is text data, images data, xml data, or video data and the second part of a MIME type specifies the internal type or category inside the type of a data. For example, the MIME type for png image is image/png. In the MIME type image/png, the first part (image) specifies that the data is in images format and the second part (png) specifies that the images data is a png image. The MIME types work same as the file extensions in windows operating system where we know the type of a file from its extension similarly, from MIME types we can determine the type of the data send or receive over the internet. The data is categorized into the following types. Each type of data further contains sub types and each sub type has a MIME type or MIME constant value. Following is the list of some useful MIME types:

Type	Description	Subtypes
Text	This type represents any file that contains text data. The text files are basically human readable files.	text/plain text/html text/xml text/css text/javascript
Image	This type represents images files. There are various types of images such as bitmap images, jpg or jpeg images, png images, gif images etc.	image/bmp image/png image/gif image/jpeg image/gif image/webp image/x-icon
Audio	This type represents audio files. There are different types of audios such as mp3 audio, avi audio, mpeg audio, wav audio etc.	audio/wav audio/mpeg3 audio/x-wav video/avi audio/midi audio/mpeg audio/webm audio/ogg
Video	This type represents video files. There are different types of videos such as mp3 video, mp4 video, mpeg video etc.	video/msvideo video/mpeg video/webm, video/ogg

Application	This type represents different applications files such as xml files, word files, excel files, word perfect files, zip files, xhtml files, json files, and pdf files etc.	application/xml application/msword application/excel application/ wordperfect application/zip application/xhtml application/rss+xml application/json application/pdf

When an HTTP message contains an entity-body, the Content-Type header specifies the format of the message body. This tells the receiver how to parse the contents of the message body. For example, if an HTTP response contains a PNG image then the response might have the following headers:

- HTTP/1.1 200 OK
- Content-Length: 95267
- Content-Type: image/png

A request message contains a header that is called Accept header. The Accept header specifies the type of the media that a client wants. When a client sends a request message to the server for a specified server response, the Accept header tells the server about the type of the media that the requested client wants from the server. For example:

Accept: text/html,application/xhtml+xml,application/xml

The preceding header of the requested message tells the server that the client either wants HTML, XHTML, or XML. The media type determines how Web API serializes and de-serializes the HTTP message body. The Web API has built-in support for XML, JSON, and BSON data. We can support the additional media types by writing a media type formatter. The Media type formatters are the component responsible for serializing model data so that it can be sent to the client. A media formatter is a class that is used to read/write a CLR object from/to the body of the HTTP request/response.

HTML Controls

HTML controls are the native elements of the web browser provided by HTML language. These controls are not part of the .NET framework but they are the HTML elements used in web pages. The HTML controls are not server side controls and they are not available in the web server but they only can be accessed in HTML pages.

HTML Server Controls

HTML server controls are the HTML controls but they are available in the server. The HTML elements in ASP.NET pages are by default treated as text and they are not available in the server. To make an HTML element programmable and access it in the server, the runat="server" attribute is added to it. When a runat="server" attribute is added to an HTML element, it becomes a server control and it can be accessed in the server. Each element or server control in ASP.NET web page has id attribute which is used to identify a server control or element on the ASP.NET web page. No two server controls have the same id attribute in a single ASP.NET web page. The id reference can be used to manipulate the server control at run time. All HTML server controls must be within a <form> tag with the runat="server" attribute. The runat="server" attribute indicates that the form is processed on the server. It also indicates that the enclosed control can be accessed by the server scripts.

ASP.NET Web Server Controls

The ASP.NET Web Server controls are objects placed on ASP.NET web pages for input and output data. A Web Server control provides interface to the user to interact with the application and read or write the data. The Web Server controls are special ASP.NET tags understood by the server. The tag of ASP.NET Server Control starts with the <asp: followed by the object name for example, to create a textbox control, the ASP.NET tag is <asp:TextBox similarly, to create a button control the ASP.NET tag is <asp:Button. Each ASP.NET server control requires two attributes, one is ID attribute and another is runat="server" attribute. Each ASP.NET Server control has a unique ID. The ID attribute is used to uniquely identity the ASP.NET Server control on the ASP.NET web page and access it programmatically from the server side. The runat="server" attribute makes the control as server control and allows us to access a control from the server side. The ASP.NET server control tag can be self closed by having a forward slash (/) before the ending tag or have a closing

tag. Following is the general syntax to create ASP.NET Web Server control on an ASP.NET web page:

```
<asp:Control_name ID=”Control_Id” runat=”server” />
```

Or

```
<asp:Control_name ID=”Control_Id” runat=”server”>
</asp:Control_name>
```

In the preceding syntax, the Control_name specifies ASP.NET server control such as Button, TextBox, Label, CheckBox, CheckBoxList, Panel, Calendar, DropDownList, RadioButton etc. The Control_Id specifies the ID of an ASP.NET server control that uniquely identifies the control on an ASP.NET web page. Following is the example of some ASP.NET server controls:

TextBox Control Example:

```
<asp:TextBox ID=”textbox1” runat=”server” />
```

Or

```
<asp:TextBox ID=”textbox1” runat=”server” ></asp:TextBox>
```

Button Control Example:

```
<asp:Button ID=”textbox1” runat=”server” />
```

DropDownList Control Example:

```
<asp:DropDownList id=”countries” runat=”server”>
        <asp:ListItem Text=”Select” Value=””/>
        <asp:ListItem Text=”Visual C#” Value=”Visual C#”/>
        <asp:ListItem Text=”VB.NET” Value=”VB.NET”/>
        <asp:ListItem Text=”SQL Server” Value=”SQL Server”/>
</asp:DropDownList>
```

ASP.NET Validation Server Controls

Validation Server Controls are used to validate the user input on the ASP.NET web pages. The validation Server Controls defined some rules or conditions for the user input and when a user input the data on an ASP.NET web page, the validation server control checks the input according to the rules or conditions. If the input value of a user matches or satisfy the validation condition, the input passes to the server for processing and if the input value of a user does not match or satisfy the validation condition, it displays an error message to the user. Validation is an important part of an ASP.NET web application to check the user input so that the invalid or unauthorized data do not get stored. Each validation control performs a specific type of validation for example, validation of integer numbers, validation for telephone or mobile numbers, validation for email addresses, validation for date formats, validation for a specific value or a range of values etc. A web form may also contain some important fields to be filled by the user therefore, validation for the necessary fields are very important. By default, the page validation is performed when a Button control, ImageButton control, or LinkButton control is clicked. If we want to prevent the default validation of these controls, we can prevent it by setting the CausesValidation property of these controls to false.

The validation controls are usually linked or tied to the input controls to check the user's input or selected value for the linked or tied control. The input controls are TextBox control, CheckBox control, CheckBoxList, DropDownList, and RadioButton control etc. Each validation control provides ControlToValidate property which is used to link or tie an input control with the validation control. A single validation control validates only one input control but multiple validation controls can be linked or tied to a single input control. The validation process of a linked or tied control is only performed when its CauseValidation property is set to true. When the value of the CauseValidation property is set to true, we can also use the ValidationGroup property to specify the name of the validation group for which the Button control causes validation. ASP.NET provides the following validation controls:

- RequiredFieldValidator
- RangeValidator
- CompareValidator
- RegularExpressionValidator
- CustomValidator
- ValidationSummary

RequiredFieldValidator Control

RequiredFieldValidator control is used to check the user input data for a particular control. It checks whether a user has entered the input for a particular control or not. If the user did not enter data in a particular control, it displays the error message. This validation control is usually linked or tied to a textbox control to force input into the textbox and prevent the textbox to store the empty data.

Properties of RequiredFieldValidator Control

The RequiredFieldValidator control has the following important properties:

Property	Description
ControlToValidate	This property is used to link an input control to the RequiredFieldValidator control for validation. It takes the ID of the input control to validate.
Text	This property is used to display error message when the validation fails.
Display	This property is used to set how the error message contained in the Text property is displayed. It actually sets the behavior of the error message. It takes three constant values to set the behavior of the error message. The constant values are Static, Dynamic, and None. The default constant value is Static. The None constant value hides the error message.
EnableClientScript	This property is used to specify whether the client-side validation is enabled or not. It takes a Boolean value either true or false. The true value means the client-side validation is enabled and the false value means the client-side validation is disabled.
Enabled	It takes a Boolean value that specifies whether the validation control is enabled or not.
ErrorMessage	This property is used to define an error message to display when the validation fails. When the Text property is set, the ErrorMessage property does not display the error message but it displays the error message in the ValidationSummary control.
ForeColor	This property is used to set the foreground color of the control.
ID	It is a unique ID that uniquely identifies the control on the page.
InitialValue	This property is used to specify the initial value for the input control. The default value of this property is "".

IsValid	This property is used to determine that whether the linked control specified by the ControlToValidate is determined to be valid or not. If the validation is succeeded, its value is true otherwise, its value is false.
BackColor	This property is used to change background color of the RequiredFieldValidator control.

Following is the general syntax of the RequiredFieldValidator control:

```
<asp:RequiredFieldValidator ID="Id-name" runat="server"
    ControlToValidate ="Control-name"
    ErrorMessage="Error message"
</asp:RequiredFieldValidator>
```

In the preceding syntax, the **Control-name** indicates a server control which is linked or tied with the RequiredFieldValidator control for validation.

Following is the programming example of the RequiredFieldValidator control that validates a textbox control and enforces a user to input value into the textbox control:

```
<asp:TextBox ID="TextBox1" runat="server"></asp:TextBox>

<asp:RequiredFieldValidator ID="TextBoxValidator" runat="server"
    ControlToValidate="TextBox1"
    ErrorMessage="The field is required">
</asp:RequiredFieldValidator>

<asp:Button ID="Button1" runat="server" Text="Check TextBox" />
```

The preceding example contains one TextBox control, one Button control, and one RequiredFieldValidator control. The TextBox control is linked with the RequiredFieldValidator control to check the user input for the TextBox control. If a user does not enter any value into the TextBox control, the RequiredFieldValidator control displays an error message that "The field is required".

RangeValidator Control

RangeValidator control is used to define a range of value for a particular server control. The range of value means the minimum and maximum limit for the input value. The RangeValidator control defines the minimum and maximum limit for a particular input control to restrict a value that does not satisfy or match the defined range. If a user input a value which is not in the defined range, it displays an error message. Therefore, the RangeValidator control defines a range of value for a particular server control and enforces a user to input value within the defined range. The RangeValidator control has the following important properties:

Property	Description
ControlToValidate	This property is used to link an input control to the RangeValidator control for validation. It takes the ID of the input control to validate.
Type	This property is used to define the type of the data for the linked or tied server control so that the control has only to accept the defined type value. The available values for the Type property are Currency, Date, Double, Integer, and String.
MinimumValue	This property is used to specify the minimum value of the range.
MaximumValue	This property is used to specify the maximum value of the range.
Text	This property is used to display error message when the validation fails.
Display	This property is used to set how the error message contained in the Text property is displayed.
ErrorMessage	This property is used to define an error message to display when the validation fails.
ID	It is a unique ID that uniquely identifies the control on the page.

Following is the general syntax of the RangeValidator control:

```
<asp:RangeValidator ID="Id-name" runat="server"
    ControlToValidate="Control-name"
```

```
    ErrorMessage="Error Message"
    MinimumValue="Minimum-value"
    MaximumValue="Maximum-value"
    Type="Integer">
</asp:RangeValidator>
```

In the preceding syntax, the **Control-name** indicates a server control which is linked or tied with the RangeValidator control for validation. Following is the programming example of the RangeValidator control:

```
<asp:TextBox ID="TextBox1" runat="server"></asp:TextBox>
<p>
<asp:RangeValidator ControlToValidate="TextBox1" runat="server"
    ID="TextBoxRange" Type="Integer"
    MinimumValue="1" MaximumValue="100"
    Text="The value must be from 1 to 100" />
</p>
<asp:Button ID="Button1" runat="server" Text="Check TextBox" />
```

The preceding example contains one TextBox control, one Button control, and one RangeValidator control. The TextBox control is linked with the RangeValidator control to check the user input for the TextBox. The RangeValidator control defines a range of integer values from 1 to 100. If a user input value which is not in the defined range, the RangeValidator control displays an error message that “The value must be from 1 to 100.

CompareValidator Control

CompareValidator control is used to compare a value of one control with a value of another control or with a fixed value. This validation control provides the following important properties:

Properties	Description
Type	This property is used to define the type of the data for the linked or tied server control so that the control has only to accept the defined type value. The available values for the Type property are Currency, Date, Double, Integer, and String

ControlToCompare	This property is used to link an input control to the CompareValidator control in order to compare its value with the value of another input control that is linked to the CompareValidator control using the ControlToValidate property.
ValueToCompare	This property specifies the constant value to compare it with the value of the input control which is linked to the CompareValidator control using the ControlToValidate property.
ControlToValidate	This property is used to link an input control to the CompareValidator control. It takes ID of the input control to validate.
Operator	This property specifies the comparison operator. The available operators are Equal operator, NotEqual operator, GreaterThan operator, GreaterThanEqual, LessThan, LessThanEqual, and DataTypeCheck.
ID	It is a unique ID that uniquely identifies the control on the page.
ErrorMessage	This property is used to define an error message to display when the validation fails.
Text	This property is used to display error message when the validation fails.
Display	This property is used to set how the error message contained in the Text property is displayed.

Following is the general syntax of the CompareValidator control:

```
<asp:CompareValidator ID="Id-name" runat="server"
    ControlToValidate="Control-name"
    ControlToCompare="Second-control-name"
    ErrorMessage="Error Message">
</asp:CompareValidator>
```

Following is a programming example of the CompareValidator control:

```
<asp:TextBox ID="TextBox1" runat="server" /><br />
```

```
<asp:TextBox ID="TextBox2" runat="server" />
<p>
<asp:CompareValidator ID="CompareTwoValues" runat="server"
ControlToValidate="TextBox1"
ControlToCompare="TextBox2"
type="Integer" Operator="LessThan"
ErrorMessage="The first value must be less than the second value">
</asp:CompareValidator>
</p>
<asp:Button ID="Button1" runat="server" Text="Compare" />
```

The preceding example contains two TextBox controls, one Button control, and one CompareValidator control. The TextBox controls are linked with the CompareValidator control using its properties. The first TextBox control is linked with the CompareValidator control using the ControlToValidate property and the second TextBox control is linked with the CompareValidator using the ControlToCompare property. The Operator property is using the LessThan operator and the input value type is Integer. The LessThan operator compares the input value of the first TextBox control with the input value of the second TextBox control. The input value of the first TextBox that is TextBox1 must be less than the input value of the second TextBox that is textBox2. If the input value of the first TextBox is greater than the input value of the second TextBox, the CompareValidator control displays an error message that "The first value must be less than the second value".

The following programming example compares two dates that is start date and end date. The end date is always greater or equal to the start date. If the end date is less than the start date, the CompareValidator control displays an error message:

```
<div>
From Date: <asp:TextBox ID="txtFromDate" runat="server" TextMode=
"Date"></asp:TextBox>
</div>
<div>
To Date: <asp:TextBox ID="txtToDate" runat="server" TextMode=
"Date"></asp:TextBox>
```

```
<asp:CompareValidator ID="DateCompare" runat="server"
ControlToValidate="txtFromDate"
ControlToCompare="txtToDate"
ErrorMessage="From Date must be less than To Date"
Operator="LessThanEqual" Type="Date">
</asp:CompareValidator>
</div>
<div>
<asp:Button ID="Button1" runat="server" Text="Check Date" />
</div>
```

The preceding programming example contains two TextBox controls, one Button control, and one CompareValidator control. The first TextBox control txtFromDate takes the start date and the second TextBox control txtToDate takes the end date from a user. The CompareValidator control compares the input date value of the txtFromDate with the input date value of the txtToDate. If the input date value of the txtFromDate is less or equal to the input date value of the txtToDate, the CompareValidator control passes the entries of both the TextBox controls otherwise, if the input date value of the txtToDate control is less than the input date value of the txtFromDate control, the CompareValidator control displays an error message that "From Date must be less than To Date".

RegularExpressionValidator Control

RegularExpressionValidator control is used to validate the input text by matching against a pattern of a regular expression. A regular expression is a sequence of characters that define a search pattern which is used to match characters combination within a longer piece of text. To search a text, sub string, or a group of characters within a longer text using the regular expression pattern, the regular expression is set in the ValidationExpression property of the RegularExpressionValidator control. The RegularExpressionValidator control is usually used to validate the complex expressions. These expressions may be phone number, email address, zip code etc. If we do not find our desired regular expression, we can also create our custom regular expression.

Properties of RegularExpressionValidator Control

The RegularExpressionValidator control provides the following important properties:

Property	Description
ControlToValidate	This property is used to link or tie an input control to the RegularExpressionValidator control for validation. It takes ID of the input control to validate.
EnableClientScript	It takes a Boolean value that specifies whether the client-side validation is enabled or not.
Enabled	It is a Boolean value that specifies whether the validation control is enabled or not.
ErrorMessage	This property is used to define an error message to display when the validation fails.
ForeColor	This property is used to set the foreground color of the RegularExpressionValidator control.
BackColor	This property is used to set the background color of the RegularExpressionValidator control.
ID	It is a unique ID that uniquely identifies the control on the page.
IsValid	It is a Boolean value that indicates whether the control specified by ControlToValidate is determined to be valid or not.
Runat	This property is used to specify that the control is a server control.
Text	This property is used to display error message when the validation fails.
Display	This property is used to set how the error message contained in the Text property is displayed.
ValidationExpression	This property is used to specify the regular expression used to validate the input control.

Following is the general syntax of the RegularExpressionValidator Control:

```
<asp:RegularExpressionValidator ID="Id-name" runat="server"
    ControlToValidate="Control-name"
    ValidationExpression="Regular-Expression">
    ErrorMessage="Error Message"
</asp:RegularExpressionValidator>
```

In the preceding syntax, the **Control-name** specifies the name of the input control, and the **Regular-Expression** specifies the Regular Expression pattern which is used to search it within an input value of a user. If the input value of a user is according to the pattern, the value will be accepted otherwise, the ErrorMessage property will display the error message.

Escape Characters of Regular Expression

The following escape characters are the commonly used syntax constructs for regular expressions:

Escape Character	Description
\b	It matches a backspace character.
\t	It matches a tab character.
\r	It matches a carriage return.
\v	It matches a vertical tab.
\f	It matches a form feed.
\n	It matches a new line.
\e	It matches Escape character.

Character Classes of Regular Expression

A character class is used to define a set of characters. When a set of characters is defined, any single character of the defined set can occur or match in an input string. A character class defines a single character or a range of characters for example, a set of characters "asdb" consider individual characters such as "a", "s", "d", and "b". The range of characters can be defined by specifying the first character followed by a hyphen character (-) and the last character. If we define more than one character range, they are concatenated. The range of lowercase letters can be defined as a-z. The range a-z means the lowercase letters from "a" to "z" similarly, the range of uppercase letters is A-Z. The range A-Z means the uppercase letters from "A" to "Z", the range of numeric numbers from 0 to 9 is 0-9. The character classes are also called metacharacters. Following is the list of character classes:

Character Class	Description
.	It matches any character except \n. If it is placed within the bracket expressions, it matches a literal dot. For example, a.c matches "abc" but [a.c] matches only "a", ".", or "c".
[---]	It matches any single character in the set. It matches a single character that is contained within the brackets. For example, the bracket expression or the pattern [abc] matches "a", "b", or "c". The pattern [a-z] specifies lowercase single letter from "a" to "z". The pattern [0-9] specifies a single digit from 0 to 9 and the pattern [abcw-z] specifies the letters "a", "b", "c", "w", "x", "y", or "z" and it can also be written as [a-cw-z].
[^---]	This is a negative character class that excludes or negates any single character in the set. It matches a single character that is not contained within the brackets. For example, [^abc] excludes a, b, or c and matches any character other than "a", "b", or "c". The bracket expression [^a-z] excludes lowercase letters from "a" to "z" and matches any single character that is not a lowercase letter from "a" to "z".
(---)	It defines a group.
\w	It matches the word characters. The word characters include alphanumeric characters such as lowercase and uppercase letters in the range a-z and A-Z, numeric digits in the range 0-9, and an underscore character. Therefore, this character class matches any alphabetic character lowercase and uppercase letters in the range A-Z or a-z, any numeric digit from 0-9, and an underscore character. For example, the pattern [a-zA-Z0-9_] is equivalent to the pattern [\w].

\W	It matches any non-word character. The non-word characters include characters other than alphanumeric characters such as lowercase and uppercase letters in the range a-z and A-Z, numeric digits in the range 0-9, and an underscore character (_). This character class is equivalent to the pattern [^a-zA-Z0-9_].
\s	It matches whitespace characters such as space, tab, new line etc.
\S	It matches any non-whitespace character.
\d	It matches any decimal character.
\D	It matches any non-decimal character.
^	It matches the beginning of the string.
$	It matches the end of the string.

Quantifiers of Regular Expression

A quantifier is used to specify the number of times a character can appear in a string. Following is the list of quantifiers:

Quantifier	Description
*	This quantifier indicates zero or more occurrences of the preceding element. For example, the pattern ab*c matches "ac", "abc", "abbc", "abbbc", and so on. In this example the preceding element of the "*" quantifier is "b" therefore, the element "b" will occur zero or more times and the remaining elements "a" and "c" must occur only one time.
+	This quantifier indicates one or more occurrences of the preceding element. The preceding element of this quantifier must occur at least one time and optionally can occur more than one times. For example, the pattern ab+c matches "abc", "abbc", "abbbc", and so on. In this example the preceding element of the "+" quantifier is "b" therefore, the element "b" must occur at least one time and optionally can occur more than one times. The

	elements "a" and "c" must occur only one time. The pattern [a-z]+ matches a string that contains lowercase letters from "a" to "z" in which a single letter can occur one or more times similarly the pattern [a-zA-Z]+ matches a string that contains lowercase letters, uppercase letters or the combination of both lowercase and uppercase and in the string a single character may occur one or more times for example, Aaaa, aBEdZ, aAabbBBb, ccCCcdefGH, asdFGhhh, yYYtttRrr, etc.
?	This quantifier indicates zero or one occurrences of the preceding element. For example, the pattern abcd?e matches both "abce" and "abcde". In this example, the preceding element of "?" quantifier is "d" therefore, the element "d" will occur zero or one time and all the other elements must occur only one time. The pattern [a-z]? matches a blank entry or a single lowercase character from "a" to "z".
{x}	This quantifier matches the preceding item exactly x amount of times. For example, the pattern a{2} matches "aa", the pattern a{5} matches "aaaaa", the pattern [0-9]{2} matches an integer numeric value that contains two digits such as 00, 01, 11, 12, 54, 89, 99 etc. The pattern [a-z]{2} matches a string that contains any combination of two lowercase letters from a to z similarly, the pattern [a-zA-Z]{2} matches a string that contains two letters of both the combination of lowercase and uppercase from a to z or from A to Z.
{x,}	This quantifier matches the preceding element x number of times or more times. The preceding element of {x,} must occur at least x number of times or more than x number of times for example, the pattern abc{2,} matches abcc, abccc, abcccc, abccccc and so on. In this example the preceding element of {2} is "c" therefore, the element "c" must occur at least two times or more than two times.

{x,y}	The pattern [a-z]{2,} matches a string that contains at least two lowercase letters or more than two lowercase letters but cannot contain less than two lowercase letters. This quantifier matches the preceding element at least x number of times but not more than y number of times. In this quantifier x indicates the minimum number of times to repeat the preceding element and y indicates the maximum number of times to repeat the preceding element. For example, the pattern abc{2,5} matches abcc, abccc, abcccc, abccccc. In this example, the preceding element of the {2,5} is "c" therefore, the element "c" must occurs at least two times or more than two times but not more than five times because the maximum limit is 5. The pattern [a-z]{2,5} matches a string that contains at least two lowercase letters or more than two lowercase letters but cannot contain more than five lowercase letters. This quantifier is usually used if we want to fix the minimum and maximum number of characters of a value for example, to fix the minimum and maximum number of characters for a password to enforce a user to enter a password not less than the fixed minimum number of characters and not more than the fixed maximum number of characters.

Syntax of Regular Expression Pattern

A pattern of regular expression is defined between the two character signs caret ^ sign and dollar $ sign. The caret sign indicates the beginning of the pattern and the dollar sign indicates the end of the pattern. The caret sign and the dollar sign are not searched in the input value but the pattern between these two signs are searched or matched in the input string. For example, the pattern ^abs$ searches or matches only abs.

The following programming example, validate a TextBox control for a four digit fixed number:

```
<asp:TextBox ID="txtNumber" runat="server" />
<asp:RegularExpressionValidator ID="rexpNumber" runat="server"
    ControlToValidate="txtNumber"
    ValidationExpression="^[0-9]{4}$"
    ErrorMessage="Please enter a 4 digit number!">
</asp:RegularExpressionValidator>
```

Following is the list of Regular Expression validation for some commonly used input values:

Field	Expression	Description
Name	^[a-zA-Z''-'\s]{1,40}$	This expression pattern validates a name. According to this expression pattern a name can contain at least one character and maximum
		40 characters but it cannot exceed from 40 characters. The name can contain small letters, capital letters, single quote, and spaces.
E-mail	^[\w-\.]{1,}\@([\da-zA-Z-] {1,}\.){1,}[\da-zA-Z-]{2,6}$ Or "\w+([-+.]\w+)*@\w+([-.]\ w+)*\.\w+([-.]\w+)*"	This pattern validates an e-mail address. For example, someone@example.com
Password	^.*(?=.{8,})(?=.*[\d]) (?=.*[\W]).*$	This expression pattern validates a strong password. According to this expression pattern the password must contains at least eight characters and it must contains at least one digit and at least one special character.

Currency	^(-)?\d+(\.\d\d)?$	This expression pattern validates currency amount negative or positive.

CustomValidator

The CustomValidator control is used if we need to perform more complex validation logic for a particular input control and the other validation controls do not satisfy our requirements for example, if we want to define our own validation logic which is not provided by the other validation controls such as to validate check boxes controls or radio button controls etc. The CustomValidator control allows us to write application specific custom validation routines for both the client side and server side validation. The validation routine is a function or event handler which is executed to perform the validation logic. The client side validation is accomplished using the ClientValidationFunction property of the CustomValidator control. The client side routine is a function which is written in a scripting language such as JavaScript or VBScript. When a user input value to the input control, the associated CustomValidator control executes the function or event handler and performs the validation. If the user's input is not according to the validation setting, the ErrorMessage property of the CustomValidator control displays the error message. The server side validation routine is an event handler which is called from the ServerValidate event of the CustomValidator control. The server side validation routine is written either in C# or in Visual Basic.NET. Following is the general syntax of the client side function and the server side event handler of the CustomValidator control:

Syntax of Client Side Function (JavaScript)

function Function-Name(Sender, args)
{
Validation-Logic;
}

Syntax of Server Side Event Handler

protected void CustomValidator1_ServerValidate(object source, ServerValidateEventArgs args)
{
Validation-Logic;
}

Properties of CustomValidator Control

The CustomValidator control provides the following important properties:

Property	Description
ClientValidationFunction	This property is used to specify the name of the client-side validation function to be executed. The client side validation function is defined in the <script> tag.
ControlToValidate	This property is used to specify the input control to validate. It takes the ID of an input control to validate.
Display	This property is used to set how the error message contained in the Text property is displayed.
EnableClientScript	It is a Boolean value that specifies whether the client-side validation is enabled or not.
Enabled	It is a Boolean value that specifies whether the validation control is enabled or not.
ErrorMessage	This property is used to define an error message to display when the custom validation is failed.
ForeColor	This property is used to define the foreground color of the control.
ID	This property is used to define a unique id for the CustomValidator control to identify it in the page.
IsValid	This property is used to determine that whether the linked control specified by the ControlToValidate is determined to be valid or not. If the validation is succeeded, its value is true otherwise, its value is false.
Text	This property is used to display error message when the validation fails.

ValidateEmptyText	This property is used to enable the blank or empty control validation. By default the CustomValidator control does not perform the validation operation on an empty control but when we enable a control using this property, the control also validates in empty mode. This property takes a Boolean value either true or false. The true value enable the control validation in empty mode and the false value disable the control to validate in empty mode.

Methods of CustomValidator Control

The CustomValidator control provides the following important methods:

Methods	Description
OnServerValidate	This method raised the ServerValidate event that called an event handler and execute the validation logic.
Validate	This method performs validation and updates the IsValid property.

The following programming example checks the length of the password. If the password length is less than 8 characters, it displays error message otherwise, it accepts the password:

Client Side Validation Example

HTML Code:
(Place this code in the Default.aspx or any other .aspx page)

```
<asp:TextBox ID="txtPassword" runat="server"></asp:TextBox>

<asp:CustomValidator ID ="CustomValidator1"
runat="server" ValidateEmptyText="true"
ControltoValidate="txtPassword"
clientValidationFunction="ValidateLength" ForeColor="Red"
ErrorMessage="Password cannot be less than 8 characters">
```

```
</asp:CustomValidator>

<asp:Button ID="Button1" runat="server" text="Password" />

JavaScript Code:
<script type="text/javascript">
function ValidateLength(Sender, args)
{
if (args.Value.length < 8)
return args.IsValid = false;
else
return args.IsValid = true;
}
</script>
```

Server Side Validation Example

```
HTML Code:
(Place this code in the Default.aspx or any other .aspx page)

<asp:TextBox ID="txtPassword" runat="server"></asp:TextBox>

<asp:CustomValidator ID ="CustomerValidator1"
runat="server" ValidateEmptyText="true"
ControltoValidate="txtPassword"
OnServerValidate ="CustomerValidator1_ServerValidate"
ForeColor="Red"
ErrorMessage="Password cannot be less than 8 characters">
</asp:CustomValidator>

<asp:Button ID="Button1" runat="server" text="Password" />

Server Side Code:
(Place this code in the Default.aspx.cs or any other .aspx.cs page)

protected void CustomerValidator1_ServerValidate(object source,
ServerValidateEventArgs args)
{
if (args.Value.Length < 8)
```

```
args.IsValid = false;
else
args.IsValid = true;
}
```

ValidationSummary Control

The ValidationSummary control is used to summarize the error messages from all the validation controls on a web page and display the summary in a single location. It displays the error message of each validation control which is specified by the ErrorMessage property of each validation control. The summary can be displayed as a list, a bulleted list, or a single paragraph, based on the value of the DisplayMode property. If the ErrorMessage property of the validation control is not set, no error message is displayed for that validation control. This control has the following important properties:

Property	Description
ShowSummary	This property is used to show the error messages in a specified format.
ShowMessageBox	This property is used to show the error messages in a separate window.
DisplayMode	This property is used to display the summary in different modes. It provides three different modes that are SingleParagraph, BulletList, and List.
ID	This property specifies a unique id for the control.
EnableClientScript	This property is used to enable or disable the client script. It takes a Boolean value either true or false.
HeaderText	This property is used to specify a custom title in the heading section of the summary.

Following is the general syntax of the ValidationSummary control:

```
<asp:ValidationSummary ID="ValidationSummary1" runat="server"
    DisplayMode = "BulletList"
    ShowSummary = "true"
    HeaderText="Title">
</asp:ValidationSummary>
```

Repeater Control

The Repeater Web server control is a data-bound container control that is used to display data from the data sources. It displays data as data items in table format. The repeater control creates a custom list and displays the data from a data source in the form of list. The data source may be data tables, databases, xml files, collections etc. The Repeater control works as a loop statement that starts the data reading operation from the first record of a data source and displays records one by one by repeating the operation until the last record has read and display in a custom list. The custom list is a user defined list and it may be HTML tags such as <li>, <ul>, <div>, or <table>. The Repeater control has a DataSource property that is used to set the DataSource of this control to any ICollection, IEnumerable, or IListSource instance. When the DataSource property of the Repeater control is set, the data from one of these types of data sources can be bound to the Repeater control using its DataBind() method. A Repeater control is same as GridView control but the main difference is that a Repeater control does not have predefined features like paging, sorting of record, and data editing. The Repeater control is added to the web page from the Toolbox of Visual Studio. The Repeater control is placed in the Toolbox under the Data option. A Repeater control has the following five templates:

1. <HeaderTemplate>
2. <AlternatingItemTemplate>
3. <Itemtemplate>
4. <SeperatorTemplate>
5. <FooterTemplate>

<HeaderTemplate>

This template is the header text which is used to display Header text for a Data Source collection. It displays only once at the first time.

<AlternatingItemTemplate>

This template is used to change the background color or style of the alternating items in a Data Source collection. The alternating item is actually a data row so, this template basically change the background color or style of the alternate row of the record.

<Itemtemplate>

This is the main template which is used to display the data from the data tables, databases, xml files, and collections.

<SeperatorTemplate>

This template is used to specify a separator element after each item to separate each item in the collection. It is usually HTML separator tag such as <br> or <hr>.

<FooterTemplate>

This template is the footer text which is used to display a footer element for the Data Source collection.

Programming Example of Repeater Control

Open a new empty project of ASP.NET Web application and add a Web Form to it. Give a name to the Web Form. Suppose the name of the Web Form is RepeaterControl. Now open the aspx file RepeaterControl.aspx and put the following code:

```
<%@ Page Language="C#" AutoEventWireup="true" CodeBehind="Repeater
Control.aspx.cs" Inherits="MyWebApplication.RepeaterControl" %>

<!DOCTYPE html>

<html xmlns="http://www.w3.org/1999/xhtml">
<head runat="server">
<title>Repeater Control Example</title>

<%-- Style Sheet definition for the Repeater Control Header --%>
<style>
.header {
background-color:#0094ff;
color:#ffffff;
width:100%;
}
.alternativeitem {
background-color:#808080;
color:#ffffff;
```

```
width:100%;
}
</style>
</head>
<body>
<form id="form1" runat="server">
<div>
<asp:Repeater runat="server" ID="rptStudentRecord">
<HeaderTemplate>
<table border="1">
<tr class="header">
<th>
<b>Registration Number</b>
</th>
<th>
<b>Name</b>
</th>
<th>
<b>Birth Date</b>
</th>
</tr>
</HeaderTemplate>
<ItemTemplate>
<tr>
<td>
<%# Eval("StdRegNumber") %>
</td>
<td>
<%# Eval("StdName") %>
</td>
<td>
<%# Eval("StdDoBirth") %>
</td>
</tr>
</ItemTemplate>
<AlternatingItemTemplate>
<tr class="alternativeitem">
<td>
<%# Eval("StdRegNumber") %>
```

```
</td>
<td>
<%# Eval("StdName") %>
</td>
<td>
<%# Eval("StdDoBirth") %>
</td>
</tr>
</AlternatingItemTemplate>
<FooterTemplate>
<tr>
<td colspan="4">
<b>Footer Section</b>
</td>
</tr>
</table>
</FooterTemplate>
</asp:Repeater>
</div>
</form>
</body>
</html>
```

Following is the code of RepeaterControl.aspx.cs file:

```
using System;
using System.Configuration;
using System.Data;
using System.Data.SqlClient;
using System.Web.UI;

namespace MyWebApplication
{
public partial class RepeaterControl : System.Web.UI.Page
{
protected void Page_Load(object sender, EventArgs e)
{
if (!Page.IsPostBack)
{
GetStudentsRecord();
```

```
}
}
public void GetStudentsRecord()
{
string constr = ConfigurationManager.ConnectionStrings["constring"].
ConnectionString;
string sql = "select * from StudentsInfo";
using (SqlConnection con = new SqlConnection(constr))
{
using (SqlCommand cmd = new SqlCommand(sql, con))
{
using (SqlDataAdapter adapter = new SqlDataAdapter(cmd))
{
DataTable dt = new DataTable();
adapter.Fill(dt);
rptStudentRecord.DataSource = dt;
rptStudentRecord.DataBind();
}
}
}
}
}
}
```

Following is the Connection String in the Web.Config file:

```
<connectionStrings>
<add name="conString" connectionString="Data Source=localhost\MSSQL
SERVER2014;Initial Catalog=Students;User ID=adalat khan;Password=
MybookDb" providerName="System.Data.SqlClient" />
</connectionStrings>
```

The above program establishes a connection to the Students database and retrieves data from the StudentsInfo table then displays the retrieved data using the Repeater container control. The Repeater control displays the entire data retrieved using the SQL query.

CHAPTER 18

Websites and Web Applications Development in ASP.NET

CHAPTER CONTENTS

- ASP.NET
- Development Models of ASP.NET
- Web Pages Model
- Web Application Model
- Model View Controller Model
- The Development Tools of ASP.NET
- Microsoft WebMatrix
- Visual Web Developer
- Microsoft Visual Studio.NET
- Website and Web Application Project
- ASP.NET Websites and Web Applications Development using Visual Studio.NET
- ASP.NET Website Project
- ASP.NET Web Application Project
- The Structure of ASP.NET Web Application
- Adding files and folders to ASP.NET Web Application
- Add Controls to ASP.NET Web Form
- Database Connection in ASP.NET Web Application
- Designing Web Applications using ASP.NET MVC 5
- Folders and Files Structure of MVC 5 Web Application
- Adding Layout to pages
- System.Web.Mvc Namespace
- Controller Class
- Action Methods
- Routing in MVC
- ActionResult Class
- ActionResult Return Type
- ViewResult Class
- Create a Controller

- ➢ Create a View
- ➢ Connect Database to MVC Application using Entity Framework
- ➢ HTML Helpers

ASP.NET

ASP.NET is a server-side Web development application technology or Framework designed for the development of dynamic and interactive Websites, Web Applications, and Web Services in the .NET environment using HTML, CSS, and scripting languages either JavaScript or VBScript. It was developed by Microsoft Corporation and was first released in January 2002 with version 1.0 of the .NET Framework. ASP.NET is actually the successor of Microsoft Active Server Pages (ASP) technology. Microsoft Active Server Pages (ASP) is also known as classic ASP and it was first introduced in 1998 as the Microsoft's first server side scripting engine. The classic ASP is a technology that enables scripts in web pages which are executed by the Internet Server. ASP allows us to develop dynamic and interactive Websites. ASP pages have the file extension .asp and they are normally written in VBScript.

ASP.NET is a technology that works on the .NET Framework and it contains all the Web related functionalities. ASP.NET is a built-in part of Microsoft .NET Framework and it allows us to take full advantage of the features of the Common Language Runtime such as type safety, inheritance, language interoperability, and versioning of the .NET Framework. ASP.NET allows us to access classes of the .NET Framework for the building of ASP.NET Web applications using programming languages of the .NET Framework such as C# and Visual Basic. NET. The .NET Framework made an object-oriented hierarchy therefore, ASP. NET has an object oriented programming approach. Each ASP.NET page and each element in an ASP.NET page is treated as an object and run on the server.

The ASP.NET pages have the extension .aspx and they are normally written in C# or in Visual Basic.NET. The user controls in ASP.NET can be written in different languages. A Web Application of ASP.NET contains one or more pages and when a user sends a request for an ASP.NET page, the IIS delegates the processing of the page to the ASP.NET Runtime System. The ASP.NET Runtime System transforms the .aspx page into an instance of a class which inherits from the base class page of the .NET Framework. An ASP.NET page gets compiled into an intermediate language by the .NET Common Language

Runtime-compliant compiler and then a JIT compiler turns the intermediate code to the native machine code and then that machine code is eventually run on the processor and then returns result to the browser as plain HTML. The ASP.NET pages load much faster than the classic ASP pages because the ASP.NET code is run straight from the processor while the classic ASP uses the embedded VBScript or JScript that continuously interpreted and cached.

Development Models of ASP.NET

A Development Model is a process or methodology that is selected for the development of software applications. It provides a complete structure or methodology to the software application to be designed. It also specifies various stages of the software application and the order in which it is carried out. The Development Model is selected for the development of software application according to the nature of the software to be developed. ASP.NET supports the following three development models:

- Web Pages Model
- Web Application Model
- Model View Controller Model

Web Pages Model

Web Pages Model is the simplest programming development model for the building of ASP.NET Web pages. It is a lightweight and Razor syntax based development model that has no drag and drop server controls, server events and state management techniques and usually it is a single page model like classic ASP and PHP. This model provides an easy way to combine the HTML code, CSS, JavaScript and server code. The Microsoft WebMatrix Tool is used to design and built the ASP.NET Web Pages applications.

Web Application Model

Web Application Model of ASP.NET is a Web development model based on ASP.NET Web Forms. The ASP.NET Web Application Model provides Web Forms and different Control Objects. The ASP.NET Web pages are officially called Web Forms. The Web Forms are similar to the Window Forms and they are the main building blocks for Web application development. A Web Form contains various Control Objects according to the nature of the Web Form. The Control Objects are used to design the Web Forms. The Control Objects provide different user interfaces for different operations such as for input/ output the data of Web application etc. A user fills Control Objects of a Web Form and presses the submit button to send data to the Web Server. The Server processes the input of the user actions and triggers the reactions. The browser submits a Web Form to the Web Server and Server returns a full markup page or HTML page in response. The Web Forms are contained in files with an extension .aspx. These files typically contain static HTML markup as well as markup defining server-side Web Controls and User Controls. The dynamic code which runs on the server can be placed in a page within a block <% ------ %> which is similar to other Web development technologies such as PHP, JSP, and ASP. The Microsoft Visual Studio and Microsoft Visual Web Developer Tools are used to design and build the ASP.NET Web Forms applications.

Model View Controller Model

The Model View Controller (MVC) of ASP.NET is an open source lightweight and test-driving framework designed by Microsoft that contains three components Model, View, and Controller. The MVC provides the Model, View, Controller pattern and it allows software developers to build a Web application as a composition of three parts or components such as Model, View and Controller. The MVC model works on the basis of three tiers architecture. The MVC model has no drag and drop server controls, server events and state management techniques. The Microsoft Visual Studio and Microsoft Visual Web Developer Tools are used to design and build the ASP.NET MVC applications. Following is the details of the three layers or three parts of the ASP.NET MVC programming model:

Model

The Model component of MVC application represents the state of a particular data part or data portion of the application and it usually interacts with the file, database, and the Web service etc. The Model part of the MVC application handles the application logic for the application data. It usually stores and retrieves data from the database. It contains all of the application business logic, validation logic, and database access logic. If we want to access the database, we can create our database classes in the Modal folder of the application.

View

The View component of MVC application represents the user interface and it contains all the user interactions. The View component accepts information from the Controller component and delivers a user interface to display that information. The View component of MVC application handles the display operations such as to display the data and information. It provides a visual shape to the Model for example, when Model retrieves data then View provides a visual shape to that data and responses back to the browser. The View component of MVC provides Graphical User Interface (GUI) and application-specific entry forms or interactive windows to the user that sends data to the user and receives input from the user using the GUI interface such as web Forms and Control objects such as textboxes, checkboxes, radio buttons, combo boxes, and command buttons etc. This part of the MVC application is also called Presentation Layer because it physically represents data and other information to the user. Since this part of the application is related to the user directly therefore, if it is designed well, user friendly, validated for data entry, comprehensive, and responsive, the whole application will be attractive for the users and will more beneficial and efficient. If this part of the application is designed poorly, the whole software application will be unprofessional and will not attractive for the users.

Controller

The Controller component of MVC works between the Model and the View components and it is responsible for controlling the application logic and flow of the application execution. The Controller handles any incoming URL request. When we send a request to MVC application, a controller handles our request and returns response to that request. The Controller accepts input from the users and converts it to commands then sends to the View component where it is displayed in the user interface. The Controller also sends commands to the Model to update the state of the Model for example, editing a document etc. The Controller accepts input from the user using the View component of MVC and sends to the Modal component for processing and logical operations then sends response back to the requested user using View. The Controller uses the basic logic of MVC application and processes the commands, make logical decision and evaluations for example, if a user sends data, the Controller decides which Model to use in order to process the user input. The MVC application contains one or more Controllers and each Controller in MVC is a class that contains different methods. The methods of a Controller are called action methods. Each action method returns action result.

Different Versions of ASP.NET MVC

The MVC programming model of ASP.NET has different versions such as MVC1, MVC2, MVC3, MVC4, MVC5, and MVC6 etc. Each version of MVC has its own programming templates. The MVC was released on March, 2009 that runs on the .NET Framework 3.5 with Visual Studio 2008 and Visual Studio 2008 SP1. The MVC2 was released on March, 2010 that runs on the .NET Framework 3.5 with Visual Studio 2008 and Visual Studio 2010. The MVC3 was released on January, 2011 that runs on the .NET Framework 4.0 with Visual Studio 2010. The MVC3 pattern supports different View Engines. The Razor View Engine is the default View Engine of MVC3 pattern. The MVC4 was released on August, 2012 that runs on the .NET Frameworks 4.0 and 4.5 with Visual Studio 2010 SP1 and Visual Studio 2012. The MVC4 pattern supports different View Engines. The Razor View Engine is the Default View Engine of the MVC4 pattern. The MVC4 provides various programming templates for the designing of Web applications such as Empty, Basic, Internet Application, Intranet Application, Mobile Application, and Web API. The MVC5 was released on October, 2013 that runs on the .NET Framework 4.5 and 4.5.1 with Visual Studio 2013.

The Development Tools of ASP.NET

A development tool is a readymade or a built-in software application which is used by the developers to create other software applications. The software Development Tool provides a visual interface and other features to the developer to write, compile, debug and maintain the software application code. The various Development Tools are used to build the ASP.NET Web applications. Following are some important and most useful Development Tools of ASP.NET:

- Microsoft WebMatrix
- Visual Web Developer
- Microsoft Visual Studio.NET

Microsoft WebMatrix

Microsoft WebMatrix is a free, fast and lightweight set of Web development tool for building Web applications. The Microsoft Corporation developed WebMatrix development tool for the purpose of providing Web developers with coding, customization, and publishing capabilities all in one place. The

WebMatrix development tool enables developers to quickly install and publish open-source applications or built-in templates to create, customize, publish and maintain their Websites. The Microsoft WebMatrix Development tool contains many individual component tools or parts that work together and create a complete Web development environment. The individual tools or parts of the Microsoft WebMatrix Development tool include a Web server, Database engines, Deployment Tool, Search Engine Optimization (SEO) Tool and various programming languages or Server-side scripting languages. The Microsoft WebMatrix provides full support for the using of ASP.NET, PHP, Node.js and HTML5. The WebMatrix Development Tool can be free downloaded from Microsoft Website.

Visual Web Developer

Visual Web Developer is a freeware Development Tool for the development of ASP.NET Web applications. It allows the developers to develop the dynamic Web applications with a streamlined development environment in a very easy way. The Microsoft Visual Web Developer provides a great set of tools, wizards, more than 60 reusable controls, and hundreds of reusable code snippets to reduce the time and effort needed to create an attractive professional Web application. The Visual Web Developer gives the developers the ability to visually design the Website through the using of toolbox, property window, login controls, Web part controls, navigation controls, document outline, master page, and table designer. There is a set of controls dialogs and wizards to help the developers in communicating with a certain database or data source. The Visual Web Developer also provides some tools to simplify the debugging process. Microsoft Visual Web Developer provides a set of tools such as the versatile HTML and CSS editing tools that are paired with the ASP.NET to allow developers to quickly build Web applications.

Microsoft Visual Studio.NET

Microsoft Visual Studio.NET is an Integrated Development Environment (IDE) designed by Microsoft Corporation. It provides a complete set of development tools to develop console applications, Window forms applications, ASP.NET Web applications, Web Services applications etc. Microsoft Visual Studio.NET is used to write the native code and managed code supported by Microsoft Windows. Microsoft Visual Studio .NET is designed for the .NET framework. The .NET framework provides different features for Microsoft Visual Studio.NET, for example the Common Language

Runtime (CLR), The Common Language Infrastructure (CLI), the .NET Framework Class library that contains a huge amount of classes, interfaces, delegates, enumeration, structures, and value types. Microsoft Visual Studio. NET provides different types of programming languages to work and run on the same visual environment and access the same resources of the .NET Framework. These programming languages are Visual C#, Visual Basic.NET, Visual C++.NET, ASP.NET. The .NET Framework also provides multiple language interoperability. The multiple language interoperability means each language of the Microsoft Visual Studio.NET can use the programming codes written in other language. The programming languages of Visual Studio.NET use the same common .NET Framework Class Library and designed different applications using the common Integrated Development Environment (IDE).

Website and Web Application Project

The .NET Framework provides an interface for many programming languages to work on the same interface and to use the common .NET Framework Class Library. The .NET Framework also allows the developers to write an application in one .NET Framework programming language and convert it into another .NET Framework programming language code. Each programming language of the .NET Framework provides its own building structure and a methodology for the development of applications. The development process of an application in the .NET programming languages is called a project. A project is a planning, organizing, methodology and a process for the development of an application.

ASP.NET Websites and Web Applications Development using Visual Studio.NET

The ASP.NET Websites and Web applications are designed using Microsoft Visual Studio.NET. ASP.NET is a platform for the development and running of Websites and Web applications on a Web server. ASP.NET is a part of the .NET Framework and it provides access to all of the features of the .NET Framework for example, we can create ASP.NET Websites and Web applications using any .NET programming language such as Visual Basic.NET, Visual C#.NET, Managed Extensions for C++ similarly, we can use the .NET Framework debugging facilities, we can store, retrieve, and manipulate data using ADO. NET, we can access operating system services using the .NET Framework classes, and so on. The ASP.NET Websites and Web applications always run on a Web server configured with Microsoft Internet Information Services (IIS). When we are using Microsoft Visual Studio.NET, we do not need to use or work directly with IIS because we can handle and use IIS directly from Visual Studio.NET using the ASP.NET classes. Microsoft Visual Studio.NET handles file management tasks such as creating IIS Websites and Web applications when needed and providing techniques to deploy the Websites and Web applications to IIS.

Microsoft Visual Studio.NET is a best Tool for the development of ASP.NET Websites and Web applications because it makes the application development much faster, easier, and more reliable. Microsoft Visual Studio.NET provides different facilities to the programmers or developers such as Visual Designers for the Web pages with drag-and-drop controls and HTML code views with the syntax checking and highlighting, it provides the integrated compilation and debugging facility, it provides the Project management facilities for creating and managing Website and Web application files including deployment to local or remote servers, it also provides the code-aware editors that include statement completion, syntax checking, and other IntelliSense features.

ASP.NET Website Project

To design a Website using one of the .NET Framework programming languages, a new project is created using Microsoft Visual Studio.NET. A new Project of ASP.NET Website can be created using Microsoft Visual Studio.NET 2015 by using the following steps:

1. Open Microsoft Visual Studio.NET 2015.
2. From the File menu of Microsoft Visual Studio.NET, select New then select Web Site. It displays New Web Site dialog box.
3. The New Web Site dialog box contains three pans that are left side pane, middle pane, and right side pane. From the left side pane, under the Installed Templates, select your desired programming language such as C# or Visual Basic then from the middle pane select ASP.NET Web Forms Site.
4. In the Web location box, select File System then enter the name of the folder where you want to keep your Web site.
5. Now click the OK button of the New Web Site dialog box. After these steps, a new Web Site project will be opened.

When you create a new Website Project using Microsoft Visual Studio.NET, it creates a folder for the new Website Project and saves the Project in the created folder. Microsoft Visual Studio.NET also creates the necessary files and folders on the server, sets the appropriate security settings on them, and creates the IIS application. The ASP.NET Website Project folder contains different sub folders and files. Microsoft Visual Studio.NET automatically creates the Solution and displays it in the Solution Explorer Window. Following is the snapshot of the Solution Explorer Window of a Website project:

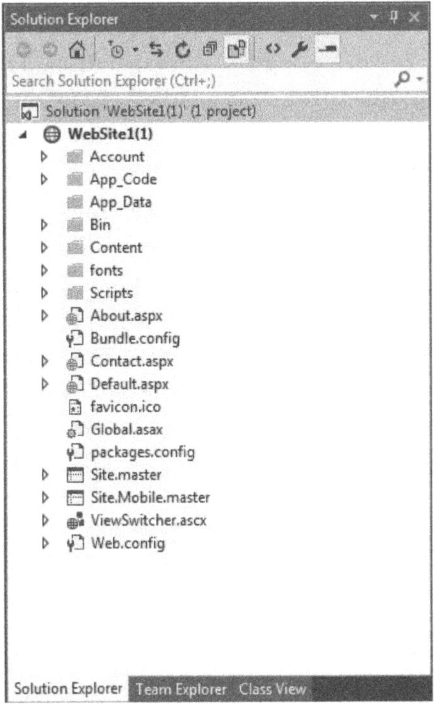

ASP.NET Web Application Project

To design a Web application using one of the .NET Framework programming languages, a new project is created using Microsoft Visual Studio.NET. A new Project of ASP.NET Web application can be created using Microsoft Visual Studio.NET 2015 by using the following steps:

3. Open Microsoft Visual Studio.NET 2015.
4. From **File** menu select **New** then click on the **Project** option**.** The Project option displays the **New Project** dialog box. The New Project dialog

box contains three pans or columns. The Left side pan displays the list of Microsoft Visual Studio.NET Programming languages and other templates, the middle or the center Pan displays a list of available Projects types of the selected Programming language and the right side Pan displays a brief description of the selected project type.

5. From the left side Pane of the New Project dialog box, select the programming language either Visual C# or Visual Basic then from the middle or center Pane of the New Project dialog box, select ASP.NET Web Application. Now give a name to your project using the Name textbox and select a location from your system where you want to keep your project folder using the Browse button. The Name textbox is located below the left and the middle Panes of the New Project dialog box and the Browse button is located below the right side Pane of the New Project dialog box.
6. Now press the OK button of the New Project dialog box. When you press the OK button of the New Project dialog box, the New ASP.NET Project window is displayed that contains different templates for the ASP.NET Web Application project such as Empty, Web Forms, MVC, Web API etc. Now select Web Forms and uncheck the checkbox of the Microsoft Azure that is Host in the cloud. Now click the OK button. When you click the OK button, the new project is created. Following is the snapshot of Microsoft Visual Studio.NET 2015 New Project dialog box:

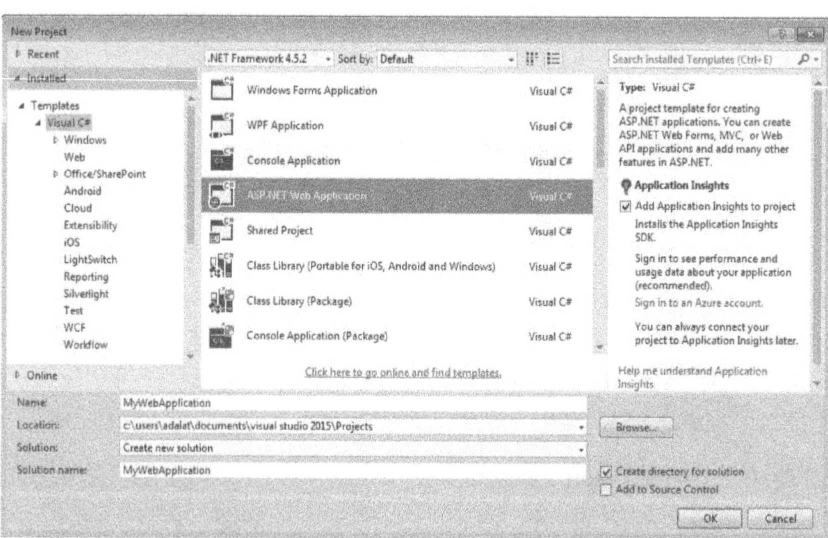

When we create a new Web application Project using Microsoft Visual Studio.NET, it creates a folder for the new Web application Project and saves the Project in the created folder. Microsoft Visual Studio.NET also creates the necessary files and folders on the server, sets the appropriate security settings on them, and creates the IIS application. The ASP.NET Web application Project folder contains different sub folders and files. Microsoft Visual Studio.NET automatically creates the Solution and displays it in the Solution Explorer Window. Following is the snapshot of the Solution Explorer Window:

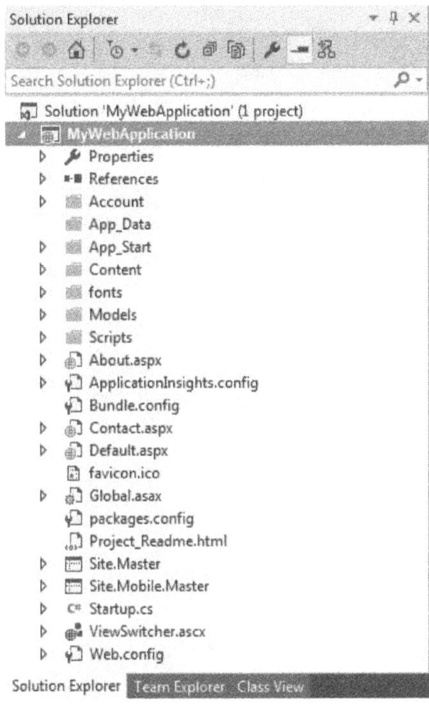

The Structure of ASP.NET Web Application Project

When we create a new project of ASP.NET Web application using Microsoft Visual Studio.NET, it automatically creates some default files and folders for the development and building of Web application. The default files and folders contain all the Web content files or Web pages such as .aspx and HTML files, the Source files, Assemblies files such as .dll and .exe files, the Data Source files (.mdb files), References, and other files such as Images and Configuration files. The default folders and files are contained in a Solution and they make up the complete structure of ASP.NET Web application. The default folders and files create the default structure of ASP.NET Web application but we can also define our own structure by adding more folders and files. The default structure of folders and files make it easier to work with ASP.NET Web application. If we do not want to create our own structure, we can easily use the default structure of ASP.NET Web application project to save our time. If we do not want to use the default structure, we can create our own structure of ASP.NET Web application by adding new folders and files that is more suitable for our ASP.NET Web application. Microsoft Visual Studio.NET creates a single project file for the entire ASP.NET Web application project that stores information about the project such as the list of files and folders that are included in the project and references of other projects. The extension of the project file depends on the programming language which is used for the development of ASP.NET Web application. If we used Visual C# programming language, the project file extension will be .csproj and if we used Visual Basic, the project file extension will be .vbproj. The ASP.NET Web application project creates different folders and files by default and displays them in Solution Explorer Window. Following is the list of important files and folders of ASP.NET Web application project:

1. Properties
2. References
3. Account
4. App_Data
5. Scripts
6. Content
7. About.aspx
8. Default.aspx
9. Global.aspx
10. Site.Master
11. Web.config

Properties

The Properties file of ASP.NET Web application project provides the general configuration settings and general information about the Web application project. The properties file contains different Tabs that provide various configuration settings and general information about the Web application project. Each Tab of the Properties file opens a separate page that contains configuration settings and information about a specific task. To access the Properties of Web application project, select the Project node in Solution Explorer then on the Project menu click Properties. When we click Properties of the project, it opens Properties Window. The Properties file provides the following Tabs:

Properties Tab	Description
Application	The Application Tab of the Properties file contains basic information about the project such as Assembly Name of the project, the Default Namespace of the project, the Target Framework used by the project, the Output Type of the Project, information about the Icon and Manifest of the project. To access the Application Tab of the Properties file, select a project node in Solution Explorer then on the application Project menu click Properties. When the Project Designer appears then click the Application Tab.
Build	The Build Tab contains the general configuration settings of the project such as the Conditional Compilation Symbol, the Target Platform, the Errors and Warnings, and configuration settings about the target location where we want to build our new Application project.
Web	The Web Tab of the project Properties contains the configuration settings that allow us to specify Start Action, Server settings, and Debugging properties for Web pages. Using this tab we can specify how Visual Studio interprets the command to test a Web page when we select Start Debugging or Start Without Debugging on the Debug menu.
Package/ Publish Web	The Package/Publish Web Tab contains the configuration settings about the deployment of application project that allow us to deploy Web application to Web Servers. When we create an ASP.NET Web application project or an ASP.NET Website project in Visual Studio.NET then we usually deploy the project to a Web server where other users can access our application. The deployment usually involves copying the application files from one server

	to another, include or exclude generated debug symbol, include or exclude files from the App_Data folder, include or exclude all the databases configured in Package/Publish SQL Tab of the project properties, the Web deployment settings such as location where the package will be created, the IIS Website/ application name to use on the destination server, the password information used to encrypt secure IIS settings.
Package/ Publish SQL	The Package/Publish SQL Tab contains configuration settings about the deployment of the application project that allow us to deploy the databases for application project. When we configure database publishing using the Package/Publish SQL Tab then only the initial deployment of a database is specified. We have to configure incremental deployment of database updates manually by creating custom SQL scripts. The Package/Publish SQL Tab is used only when we cannot configure database deployment in the publish profile.
Silverlight Applications	The Silverlight Applications Tab allows us to add a Silverlight application to the ASP.NET Web application project. If you have a Silverlight application and you want to add it to the ASP.NET Web application project, select the Silverlight Applications Tab and select your Silverlight application project. If you don't have a Silverlight application project then you can create a new Silverlight application project and add it to the solution of your Web Application project. To create a new Silverlight application project, click the Add button from the Silverlight Applications Tab. When you click the Add button, the Add Silverlight Application window is opened. Now give a name to the Silverlight application in the Name textbox, select the location of the Silverlight application where you want to store the Silverlight application project using the Browse button and then click the Add button.

Build Events	The Build Events Tab allows us to specify the pre-build and post-build events to the application project. The Built Events are commands that run before the build starts or after the build finishes of the application. The Build Events are executed only if the build successfully reaches those points in the build process. When a project is built, the pre-build events are added to a file PreBuildEvent.bat and the post-build events are added to a file PostBuildEvent.bat. If we want to ensure error checking then we add our own error-checking commands to the build steps.
Resources	The Resources Tab provides information about the resources used by the application. If the application currently does not use any resources, it allows us to add new resources to the application project. The Resources Tab also allows us to edit or remove resources from the application project.
Settings	The Settings Tab specifies the settings of the application project. The Application settings enable us to store and retrieve property settings and other information for the application dynamically. They also enable us to maintain custom application and user preferences on a client computer.
Reference Paths	The Reference Paths Tab allows us to specify the folder path for assembly references used by the application project. When we reference an assembly in our application project then Visual Studio first searches for the assembly in the application project directory. If we use an assembly not located in the project directory, we can specify its location using the Reference Paths Tab.
Signing	The Signing Tab is a very important Tab because it is responsible for the security of the application project. The Signing Tab allows us to sign the application project and deployment manifests and also to sign the assembly. The Signing of the application project improves the security of our Web application. The Signing an assembly with a strong name makes it more

	difficult for attackers to introduce malicious code into our Web application. A strong name consists of the assembly identity, the assembly simple text name, the assembly version number, the culture information, a public key, and a digital signature. It is generated from an assembly file using the corresponding private key. The Visual Studio can assign strong names to an assembly. Assemblies with the same strong name are expected to be identical. We can ensure that a name is globally unique by signing an assembly with a strong name.

References

The References file contains reference contract files (.wsdl files), schemas (.xsd files), and discovery document files such as .disco and .discomap files that allow us to create a Web reference for use in a Web application.

Account

This is a folder that is created by default when we create a new project of ASP.NET Web application. This folder contains source files .aspx that defines Web Forms. The Account folder provides the main Login Web Form, and Registration Web Form.

App_Data

The App_Data folder is responsible to store the data sources we used in our ASP.NET Web application. This folder usually contains application data files including .mdf database files, XML files, and other data store files.

Content

This folder contains a cascading style sheet file that is Site.css and bootstrap files such as bootstrap.css, and bootstrap.min.css. The style sheet file extension is .css that indicates Cascading Style Sheet. The Cascading Style Sheet is a style sheet language that provides different styles and formatting for documents written in markup language. The Site.css file is created automatically in this folder when a new project of ASP.NET MVC Web application is created. The Site.css file provides different colors, margin settings, behavior, font style, font size, headings, paragraphs, layouts, padding settings, background color, text transformation, text decoration, font variant, borders styles and setting, line height, and some other formats for ASP.NET MVC Web application.

About.aspx

The About.aspx is a source file of ASP.NET Web application that is created automatically when a new project of ASP.NET Web application is created. The About.aspx file contains the HTML and ASP.NET code that defines the Web Form. The Default.aspx file is created according to the programming language used in the ASP.NET Web application project. If we are using Visual C# programming language, the file name will be About.aspx.cs and if we are using the Visual Basic.NET programming language then the file name will be About. aspx.vb. The About.aspx source file is usually used to include information or brief summary about the Web application we are building.

Default.aspx

The Default.aspx is a source file of ASP.NET Web Application that is created automatically when a new project of ASP.NET Web application is created. This file contains Web Control Objects, Presentation, Business logic, HTML and ASP.NET code that defines the Web Form. The Default.aspx file is created according to the programming language used in the ASP.NET Web application project. If Visual C# programming language is used, the file name is Default. aspx.cs and if Visual Basic.NET programming language is used, the file name is Default.aspx.vb. When we run ASP.NET Web application, by default the Default.aspx file is executed and it displays a Web Form that contains some default text. The default page is actually a home page of the Web application that is automatically displayed when a user navigate our Website without specifying a particular page.

Global.asax

This is a global file for the entire ASP.NET Web application project that represents the ASP.NET Web application project Global class and contains methods or event handlers that run at various points in the Web application. The methods or events handlers of the Global.asax file are automatically created when a new project of the ASP.NET Web application is created. The Global. asax is an optional file that allows us to execute codes using the methods or events handlers. The methods or events handlers of the Global.asax handle the application and the application sessions. The Global.asax file is responsible to execute the code for responding to application-level events raised by ASP.NET or by HttpModules. The Global.asax file resides in the root directory of the ASP.NET Web application. When an ASP.NET Web application is running then during run time the Global.asax file is parsed and compiled into a dynamically generated .NET Framework class derived from the HttpApplication base class. The Global.asax file contains the following methods or events handlers:

Event Handler	Description
Application_Start	This method or event handler triggers when the Web application starts first time. This event handler usually executes the code that runs on the Web application startup for example, if we want to display a user-defined message or other information when the Web application starts first time.
Application_End	This method or event handler triggers when the Web application ends or time out. This event handler usually executes the code that indicates or informs the user that the Web application is ended or time out etc. This event handler is also used if we want to perform some cleaning operation when the Web application ended or time out for example, if we want to release the resources, kills or deactivate the variables, and terminates or finishes the database connections etc.
Application_Error	This method or event handler triggers when an unhandled error occurs within the Web application. This event handler is used if we want to display a user-defined message whenever an error occurs in the Web application.
Session_Start	This method or event handler triggers when a user session is started in the application.
Sesscion_End	This method or event handler triggers when a user session end or time out.

Site.Master

The Site.Master file of ASP.NET Web application is called Master Page. A Master Page is an ASP.NET file with the extension .master that holds the layout and standard behavior for the entire ASP.NET Web application. A Master Page of the ASP.NET Web application can contain static text, HTML elements and ASP Server Controls. The master page is a feature that allows us to define the common structure and interface markup elements for the ASP.NET Web application such as headers, footers, style definitions, or navigation bars. A master page can serve as a template for one or more Web Forms and it can be shared by any of the pages in Web application. Each .aspx Web Form only needs to define the content unique to itself and this content will plug into specified areas of the Master Page layout. The master page defines placeholders for content pages. The resultant page is a combination or merge of the master page and the content page. A Content page is a web page which is associated to a Master Page. A Content Page contains only markup and controls inside Content controls and it cannot have any top-level content. Any Content Page can use controls that specifically override content placeholder sections in the Master Page. When we create a Master Page, it is a template for the Web application. When we are not using Master Pages, we create the initial template for the Web application then we copy and paste that template for each and every page.

Web.config

The Web.config is an XML text file that contains configuration settings for ASP.NET Web application. The configuration settings of the Web.config file are used to configure the ASP.NET Web application. The ASP.NET Web application Web.config file allows us to establish the project specific settings for security, compilation options, user authentication, debugging, tracing, connection strings, and for error handling etc. The configuration settings affect all the Web applications on a server, a single application, individual pages, or it affect individual folders in a Web application. The ASP.NET configuration data is always stored in XML text files, each named Web.config. The Web.config files can appear in multiple directories in the ASP.NET Web applications. Each Web.config file applies configuration settings to its own directory and to all the child directories below it. If the application contains child directories, it can define a Web.config file for each folder. The scope of each configuration file is determined in a hierarchical top-down manner. Each configuration file contains nested XML tags and sub tags with attributes that specify the configuration settings. The configuration information resides between the <configuration> and the </configuration> root XML tags. The Microsoft Visual Studio.NET generates a default Web.config file for each ASP.NET Web application because the Web.config file helps in the application debugging process and without the Web.config file an application cannot be debugged.

Adding files and folders to ASP.NET Web Application

The ASP.NET Web application project allows us to add new and existing Items or files to the ASP.NET Web application. The ASP.NET Web application project also allows us to add new standard folders to the ASP.NET Web application. The new and existing Items or files and standard folders can be added to the ASP.NET Web application by using the following steps:

1. In the Solution Explorer Window, right-click on the ASP.NET Web application project name, then click **Add** and select the desired item or file. If you want to add a new item or file to the Web application then select the **New Item** option. The **New Item** option displays the **Add New Item** window that contains different types of items. If you want to add an existing item or file to the Web application then select the **Existing Item** option and if you want to add a standard folder to the Web application then in the Solution Explorer Window, right-click on the ASP.NET Web application project name, click Add and then select **New Folder** option. Following is the snapshot of the **Add New Item** window:

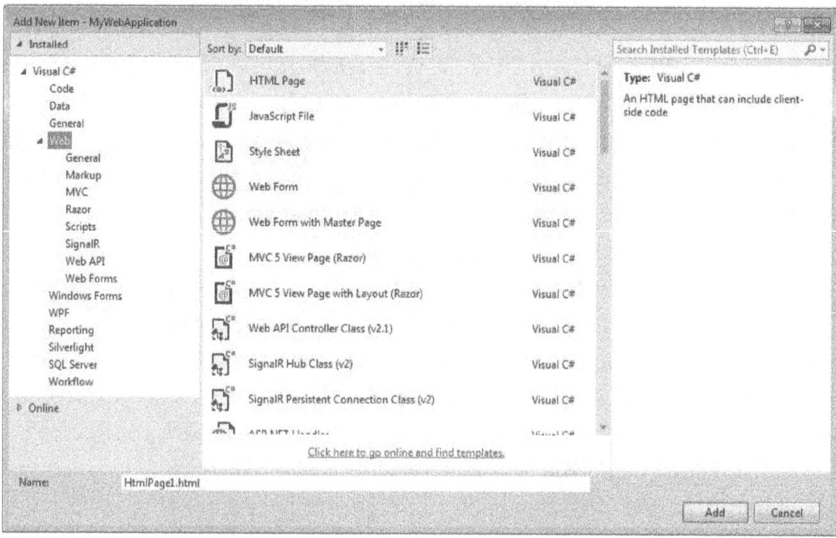

From the **Add New Item** window you can select different types of new items such as HTML page, JavaScript file, Style Sheet, Web Form, Web Form with Master Page, Web Forms User Control, Web Service (ASMX), WCF Service, Web Configuration File, Typescript file etc. When you select your desired new item from the **Add New Item** window then give a name to the new item and then click the Add button.

Add Controls to ASP.NET Web Form

Controls are graphical objects provided by .NET framework for Web Forms designing. Controls provide different interfaces and allow users to interact with the application. The Controls are also called Web Forms controls because they are used on the Web Forms. The Web Forms are containers or interfaces for the Controls. The Controls are placed on the Web Forms and design Websites or Web applications. Controls are placed on a Web Form for particular purposes and they are placed on a Web Form to design it according to the application specification. There are different types of controls provided by Microsoft .NET Framework. Some of these controls are used on Web Forms for input and output purposes which allow users to enter data or information to the application and display data or information on the same interfaces, some controls are used to arrange other controls on the surface of a Web Form which are called Container controls, some controls are used to create Menus, SiteMapPath, and TreeView on a Web Form.

The instances of Controls are placed in a Toolbox that is called Controls Toolbox. The Controls Toolbox is a small Window that is normally displayed in the left side of Microsoft Visual Studio.NET Web Forms Designer. The Controls Toolbox can also be accessed from the View option of the main menu of Microsoft Visual Studio.NET Web Forms Designer. The Controls Toolbox allows us to place Control Objects on Web Forms during the designing time of an application. There are different ways to add controls to the ASP.NET Web Form such as using Toolbox, using HTML code, and dynamically adding controls to the Web Form using programming code. To add controls to the Web Form using the Toolbox, switch the ASP.NET Web Form to the design mode and drag a control on mouse from the Toolbox and drop it into the Web Form. To add controls to the ASP.NET Web Form using the HTML code, a standard ASP.NET tag is used for each control. Each ASP.NET tag starts from the <asp prefix word followed by the name of a control. The name of the control is concatenated with the prefix <asp using the full colon between them. Following is the general syntax of the ASP.NET standard control:

```
<asp:Control-name ID= "Control-Id" runat ="Server"/>
```

The **Control-name** specifies a control such as Button control, TextBox, DropDownList, CheckBox, CheckBoxList control etc. The ID is an attribute of each control that uniquely identifies a control on a Web Form. For example, to create a button control, the following standard ASP.NET tag is used:

```
<asp:Button ID = "Id" runat = "Server" Text = "Button Caption" />
```

Database Connection in ASP.NET Web Application

To connect database to the ASP.NET Web application project and perform different operations on it such as add new record into the database, update the existing record of the database, and search a particular record in the database etc, follow the following steps:

1. Open a new project of ASP.NET Web application and give a name to it. Suppose the name of the project is DatabaseConnection.
2. Now add a new Web Form with Master Page using the **Add New Item window** and give a name to it. Suppose the name of the new Web Form is RegistrationForm.
3. Now open the RegistrationForm.aspx and put the following html code in the BodyContent section of the page to design the registration form:

```
<asp:Content ID="BodyContent" ContentPlaceHolderID="MainContent"
runat="server">
<table>
<tr><td>Registration Number</td><td>
<asp:TextBox ID="txtRegNum" runat="server"></asp:TextBox>
</td></tr>
<tr><td>Name</td><td>
<asp:TextBox ID="txtName" runat="server"></asp:TextBox>
</td></tr>
<tr><td>Date of Birth</td><td>
<asp:TextBox ID="txtBirth" runat="server"></asp:TextBox>
</td></tr><tr><td></td>
<td>
<asp:Button ID="btnSave" runat="server" Text="Save" />
<asp:Button ID="btnUpdate" runat="server" Text="Update"/>
</td></tr>
</table>
</asp:Content>
```

The above html code designs the following registration form:

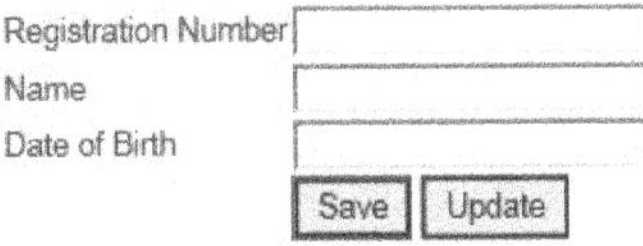

Now switch to the design mode of the RegistrationForm and double click on the button to generate the click event of the button. The status bar of the page contains three options that are Design, Split, and Source. Click the Design option to switch the form to the design mode. The event can also be generated by adding the event attribute to the button. To generate the click event of the button, add OnClick event attribute to the <asp:Button> tag and put the equal sign on the front of the OnClick event as <asp:Button ID="btnSave" runat= "Server" OnClick=. When you put the equal sign, the Visual Studio displays a small popup window that displays a message <Create New Event>. Click this message and generate the click event of the button. Following is the click event handlings of the Save and Update buttons:

```
//The Click event handling of the Save button
protected void btnSave_Click(object sender, EventArgs e)
    {

    }

//The click event handling of the Update button
protected void btnUpdate_Click(object sender, EventArgs e)
    {

    }
```

Now establish the SQL database connection and insert record into the database table. To establish the SQL database connection, open the Web.Config file and place the connection string in the Web.Config file. The connection string is placed within the <connectionString> element using the <add> element. The <connectionString> element is placed within the <configuration> element. The connection string is also can be placed in the RegistrationForm.aspx.cs file directly but it is a good practice to place the connection string in the Web. config file within the <configuration> element. Following is the connection string of the SQL server database in the Web.Config file:

```
<connectionStrings>
<add name="conString" connectionString="Data Source=localhost\MSSQL SERVER2014;Initial Catalog=Students;User ID=adalat khan;Password= Isfront1" providerName="System.Data.SqlClient" />
</connectionStrings>
```

The preceding connection string establishes a connection to the SQL server database. In SQL server database we already created a database Students. The Students database is discussed in chapter number 10 in more details. Please check chapter number 10 of this book for more details about the Students database. You can create a database of any name and any structure but follow these steps and implement your own database. Now open the RegistrationForm.aspx.cs file and include the following namespaces at the top of the program in the directives section:

```
using System.Data;
using System.Data.SqlClient;
using System.Configuration;
```

To insert new data into the database table, put the following code in the click event of the Save button btnSave_Click:

```
//Retrieve Connection String from the Web.Config file
string constring = ConfigurationManager.ConnectionStrings["constring"].
ConnectionString;

//Declare an instance of the new connection
SqlConnection con = new SqlConnection(constring);
con.Open();

//SQL Query to insert record from the textbox controls into the //database
table
string sqlquery = "insert into StudentsInfo (StdRegNumber, StdName,
StdDoBirth) values (@RegNum, @Name, @Birth)";
SqlCommand cmd = new SqlCommand(sqlquery, con);
cmd.Parameters.Add("@RegNum", SqlDbType.NVarChar).Value = txtReg
Num.Text;
cmd.Parameters.Add("@Name", SqlDbType.NVarChar).Value = txtName.
Text;
cmd.Parameters.Add("@Birth", SqlDbType.Date).Value = txtDoBirth.Text;
```

```
cmd.ExecuteNonQuery();
cmd.Dispose();
con.Close();
```

To update a particular record, put the following code in the click event of the update button btnUpdate_Click:

```
string constring = ConfigurationManager.ConnectionStrings["constring"].
ConnectionString;
SqlConnection con = new SqlConnection(constring);
con.Open();
string sqlquery = "update StudentsInfo set StdName = @Name, StdDoBirth =
@Birth where StdRegNumber = @RegNum";
SqlCommand cmd = new SqlCommand(sqlquery, con);
cmd.Parameters.Add("@RegNum", SqlDbType.NVarChar).Value = txtReg
Num.Text;
cmd.Parameters.Add("@Name", SqlDbType.NVarChar).Value = txtName.
Text;
cmd.Parameters.Add("@Birth", SqlDbType.Date).Value = txtDoBirth.Text;
cmd.ExecuteNonQuery();
cmd.Dispose();
con.Close();
```

Designing Web Applications using ASP.NET MVC 5

MVC Web application provides different versions such as MVC1, MVC2, MVC3, MVC4, and MVC5 etc. Each version of MVC has its own programming templates. The MVC5 programming model runs on the .NET Framework 4.5 or later version. To design the ASP.NET MVC 5 Web application using Microsoft Visual Studio.NET 2015, follow the following steps:

10. Open Microsoft Visual Studio.NET 2015 Enterprise Edition.
11. From the File Menu of Visual Studio.NET, select New then select Project.
12. When we select Project, it opens the New Project dialog box. The New Project dialog box contains three Panes or columns. The first Pane of the New Project dialog box contains a list of programming languages provided by Microsoft Visual Studio.NET. The second Pane or the middle Pane of the New Project dialog box displays a list of different

Project types of a particular Programming Language. The third pane displays a brief description of the selected project type.

13. Now select a programming language you want to use for the ASP.NET MVC 5 Web Application from the first Pane of the New Project dialog box.
14. After selecting a programming language, select ASP.NET Web Application from the second Pane of the New Project dialog box.
15. After selecting the ASP.NET Web Application, select a target Framework for the application development from the drop-down list that is displayed above the second Pane of the New Project dialog box. It should be noted that using Microsoft Visual Studio.NET 2015, the MVC Web application template is available in the .NET Framework 4.5 and later versions therefore, to open a new project of ASP.NET MVC Web application, always select the .NET Framework 4.5 or later version.
16. Now give a name to your new ASP.NET Web Application project using the Name text box of the New Project dialog box. The Name text box is displayed under the first Pane of the New Project dialog box.
17. After given a name to your ASP.NET MVC Web Application project, now specify a location where you want to save your project using the Location drop-down list displayed under the Name text box of the New Project dialog box. To specify a location manually, just type the location string in the Location text box otherwise, use the Browse button of the New Project dialog box and select a specified location for your new MVC Web application project.
18. Now give a name to the solution of the project using the Solution Name text box. The Solution Name text box is displayed under the Solution drop-down list. If you do not want to give a name to the solution, Microsoft Visual Studio.NET by default uses the project name as a solution name.
19. Now press the OK button of the New Project dialog box. When you press the Ok button, a new window is displayed that contains different types of project templates such as Empty, Web Forms, MVC, Web API, Single Page Application etc. Select MVC template and press the Ok button.

Folders and Files Structure of MVC 5 Web Application

When a new project of ASP.NET MVC 5 Web application is created, the default folders and files are created. The default folders and files contain all the Web content files or Web pages such as ASP.NET and HTML files, Source files, Assemblies files such as .dll and .exe files, Data Source files (.mdb files), References, and other files such as Images and Configuration files. The default folders and files are contained in the Solution and they make up the complete structure of ASP.NET MVC Web application. The default folders and files create the default structure of the ASP.NET MVC Web application but we can also define our own structure by adding more folders and files. The default structure of folders and files make it easier to work with the ASP.NET MVC Web application. Microsoft Visual Studio.NET creates a single project file for the entire ASP.NET MVC Web application project that stores information about the project such as the list of files and folders that are included in the project and any other references which reference other projects. The extension of the project file depends on the programming language that is used for the development of ASP.NET MVC Web application. If the C# programming language is used, the project file extension will be .csproj and if the Visual Basic programming language is used, the project file extension will be .vbproj. The ASP.NET MVC Web application creates the following folders and files by default and displays them in the Solution Explorer window. Following is the snapshot of the project explorer window of MVC Web application:

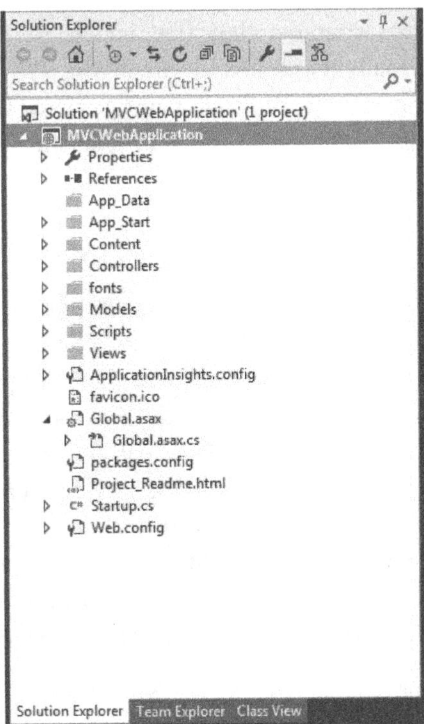

Properties

The Properties file of ASP.NET MVC Web application project provides the general configuration settings and general information about the Web application project. The properties file contains different Tabs that provide various configuration settings and general information about the MVC Web application project.

References

The References file of ASP.NET MVC project contains all the references associated to the ASP.NET MVC project such as Assemblies, DDL dependencies, Namespaces etc.

App_Data Folder

The App_Data folder is responsible to store the data sources we used in our ASP.NET Web application. This folder usually contains application data files including .mdf database files, XML files, and other data store files.

App_Start Folder

The App_Start folder contains class files which are executed when the application starts. Usually these class file are config files like AuthConfig.cs, BundleConfig.cs, FilterConfig.cs, RouteConfig.cs etc. The RouteConfig.cs class file contains the default format of the url that should be supplied in the browser to navigate to a specified page.

Content Folder

This folder contains a cascading style sheet file that is Site.css and bootstrap files such as bootstrap.css, and bootstrap.min.css. The style sheet file extension is .css that indicates Cascading Style Sheet. The Cascading Style Sheet is a style sheet language that provides different styles and formatting for documents written in markup language. The Site.css file is created automatically in this folder when a new project of ASP.NET MVC Web application is created. The Site.css file provides different colors, margin settings, behavior, font style, font size, headings, paragraphs, layouts, padding settings, background color, text transformation, text decoration, font variant, borders styles and setting, line height, and some other formats for ASP.NET MVC Web application.

Controllers Folder

The Controllers folder is responsible for the user interactions such as processing the user incoming requests, handling the input data, saving the input data, and sending a response back to the user. The Controllers folder contains two different files **AccountControler.cs**, and **HomeController.cs**. The file AccountControler.cs handles the user account information such as the user name and password, change password, new user registration, and user authentication. The HomeController.cs file is responsible to handle the user general inputs and responses such as the user contact information, telephone information, and index information.

Fonts Folder

This folder contains the custom font files for the ASP.NET MVC Web application project.

Models Folder

The Models folder contains Models of the application that handles the application logic and data. Each Model in the Models folder contains one or more classes that represent the application Models. Each class represents a single Model of the application. Models hold and manipulate the application data. When we create a new project of ASP.NET MVC, it creates a file **AccountModels.cs** automatically that contains models for the application security such as RegisterModel class that handles the user registration, LogOnModel that handles the user logon, and ChangePasswordModel that handles the user password change.

Scripts Folder

This folder stores the JavaScript files of the MVC application. By default Visual Studio.NET and Visual Web Developer fills this folder with the standard MVC, Ajax, and jQuery files.

Views Folder

The Views folder contains the HTML files for the application to display the output to the users. It is basically a user interface that allows users to interact with the application and send or receive information to and from the application. The Views folder contains one folder for each controller. The View folder contains different subfolders and files. Following is the list of these folders and files:

File / Folder	Description
Account Folder	The Account folder contains various pages related to the user accounts such as create a new user account, manage the user accounts, the user local login account, reset the user password, change the user password, and register external login.
Home Folder	The Home folder contains three main important html pages that are About.cshtml, Contact.cshtml, and Index.cshtml, The page About.cshtml is used to provide additional information. The Contact.cshtml page is used to provide the contact information such as residential address, email address, and telephone number etc. The Index.cshtml page is used to provide the index information. This is the default index file and it is created automatically when we create the ASP.NET MVC project. This file contains some default contents or information and it allows us to put our own contents or information in this file.
Shared Folder	The Shared folder is used to store views shared between controllers such as master pages and layout pages. The Shared folder contains three main files such as _Layout.cshtml file, _LoginPartial.cshtml file, and Error.cshtml file. The first file _Layout.cshtml represents the layout of each page in the application. This file contains a default code for the layout of pages but we can also add our own code for the layout of the pages. The second file _LoginPartial.cshtml is associated with the user's authentications. The third file Error.cshtml is associated with the errors when occurs in the application. This file allows us to define our own error messages.
_ViewStart.cshtml File	The _ViewStart file is located in the View folder and it contains the following content: @{

	Layout = "~/Views/Shared/_Layout.cshtml"; } This code is automatically added to all views displayed by the application. If we remove this file, we must add this line to all views.

Global.asax

This is a global file for the entire MVC Web application project that represents the Global class of MVC web application and contains methods or event handlers that run at various points in the application. The Global.asax is an optional file that allows us to execute codes using the methods or events handlers. The methods or events handlers of the Global.asax handle the application and the application sessions. The methods or events handlers of the Global. asax file are Application_BeginRequest, application_start, application_error, session_start, session_end etc. The Global.asax file is responsible to execute the code for responding to application-level events raised by ASP.NET or HttpModules.

Web.config

The Web.config is an XML file that contains configuration settings for the ASP.NET MVC Web application. This file allows us to establish the MVC Web application project specific settings for security, compilation options, user authentication, debugging, tracing, connection strings, and for error handling etc. The configuration settings affect all the Web applications on a server, a single application, individual pages, or it affect individual folders in a Web application.

packages.config File

The Packages.config file is managed by NuGet to keep track of what packages and versions we have installed in the application.

Adding Layout to pages

When we create a new project of ASP.NET MVC web application, its pages have the default layout. We can change the default layout of the pages using our own layout. To change the default layout of the pages, the new layout style is placed in the file _Layout.cshtml that is located inside the Shared folder and Shared folder is located inside the View folder.

System.Web.Mvc Namespace

The System.Web.Mvc namespace contains classes and interfaces that supports ASP.NET MVC framework for designing Web applications. The classes of this namespace represent Controllers, Controller factories, Action Results, Views, Partial View, Model Binders etc.

Controller Class

The Controller class represents a Controller in MVC application. A Controller is responsible for controlling the application logic and flow of the application execution. The Controller handles any incoming URL request. When we send a request to MVC application, a Controller handles our request and returns response to that request. The Controller accepts input from the users and converts it to commands then sends to the View component where it is displayed in the user interface. The Controller accepts input from the user using the View and sends to the Modal for processing and logical operations then sends response back to the requested user using View. The Controller class provides methods which perform different actions and return different action results back to the requests. The Action methods are triggered when we enter a particular URL address in the browser address bar. The Controller class is derived from the base class System.Web.Mvc.Controller. The name of a Controller class must end with the word "Controller". We can give any name to a Controller class but our name must end with the word Controller for example, a Home controller can be named as HomeController similarly, the customers controller can be named as CustomersController etc.

Action Methods

Action methods are defined in the Controllers which perform different actions according to the input requests and return responses back to the input requests. Each controller has one or more action methods and each action method is triggered and performs a particular action. The action methods have mapping with the user interactions such as when a user enters a URL into the browser, when a user clicks a particular link, or when a user submits a form then each of these user interactions triggers a particular action method. Each URL in MVC application is associated with a particular action method. A URL in MVC application contains Controller name and action method name. When a user inputs a URL into the browser, the MVC application uses routing rules to parse the URL and determines the requested Controller and the requested action method. The Controller then handles the user request and triggers the requested action method. An Action method works as ordinary method but the main difference is that an action method must be public, it cannot be private or static, an action method cannot be overloaded and it always returns ActionResult. Every Controller has default Index action method and its route is by default configured in the RouteConfig class. The RouteConfig class is placed inside the App_Start folder of MVC application. By default when we enter a URL, always the Index action method is triggered. We can define routes for the action methods of each Controller using the RouteConfig class.

Routing in MVC

Routing is a pattern system that maps the incoming browser requests to a particular MVC action method defined in a specified Controller. The Routing system in MVC uses a route table that contains the URL patterns. When a user sends a URL request in the web browser, the URL is mapped according to the MVC route table and triggers a particular action method that match the incoming URL. Each URL is associated with an action method. An ASP.NET web application contains different .aspx pages. Each URL in web application is associated with a single page of .aspx and when a user sends a URL request in the browser, the associated .aspx page is return back to the browser similarly, a MVC application contains different Controllers and each Controller contains one or more action methods. An action method contains a specific code and when it is executed then it performs a specific task. In MVC application each URL is associated with the action method. When a user sends a URL request to a MVC application, the MVC application maps the incoming URL request using the route table and triggers a particular action method. In MVC application the RouteConfig.cs is a class file which is used as a route table. The RouteConfig.cs file is used for adding the routing rules for the Controllers and action methods. The RouteConfig.cs file is located in the App_Start folder of MVC application and it is registered in the Global.asax file inside the Application_Start() method or event handler using the RegisterRoutes() method of the RouteConfig class. When a MVC application first starts, the Application_Start() method or event handler is called. When the Application_Start() method is started, it triggers the RegisterRoutes() method of the RouteConfig class. The RegisterRoutes() method creates the route table for the input URL routings.

Routing is a good approach that defines a user friendly URL which helps a user in searches a particular content of the application. The routing technique is also helpful in Search Engine Optimization (SEO). When we create a MVC application project, by default the Home Controller and Index action method is set in the route table therefore, when a user starts the application, by default the Index action method of the Home Controller is triggered. Following is the default route configuration of the Index action method:

```
public class RouteConfig
{
public static void RegisterRoutes(RouteCollection routes)
{
routes.IgnoreRoute("{resource}.axd/{*pathInfo}");

routes.MapRoute(
name: "Default",
url: "{controller}/{action}/{id}",
defaults: new {
            controller = "Home",
            action = "Index",
            id = UrlParameter.Optional
}
);
}
}
```

The above code is in the RouteConfig.cs file which is located in the App_Start folder of MVC application. The first line of the above code is the class name RouteConfig. The second line of the code is RegisterRoutes() method which creates the route table. The RegisterRoutes() method takes a single parameter of the class RouteCollection that defines a collection of routes for the MVC application. The RegisterRoutes() method triggers two extension methods IgnoreRoute() and MapRoute(). The IgnoreRoute() method is used to ignore files we do not want users to access those files. The MapRoute() method contains three parameters. The first parameter is the name which is used to provide the name of the route, the second parameter is url which is used to provide the url pattern we want to set, and the third parameter is default which is used to set the Controller name, the action method name, and the ID of the action method's parameter. The ID is an optional parameter which can be omitted. The url attribute of the MapRoute() method usually takes three values such as the Controller name, the action method name and the ID value of the action method but we can skip each part of these three values.

According to the MVC routing a URL contains three parts. The first part is a Controller name, the second part is the action method name and the third part is the parameter ID such as /Controller/Action/ID. The default route table contains a single route named Default. The Default route maps the first part of a URL to a Controller name, the second part of a URL to a controller action method, and the third part of a URL to a parameter ID. The default Controller is Home Controller and the default action method is Index() method. For example, consider the following URL:

http://MySiteName.com/Home/Index/77

In the above URL, Home is the name of the Controller, Index is the name of the action method, and 77 is the ID parameter of the action method. Therefore, the above URL will execute the following code:

http://MySiteName.com/Home/Index(77)

The Default route includes defaults for all the three parameters. If we do not supply a controller, the default Controller Home will be executed, if we do not supply an action method, the default action method Index() will be executed, and if we do not supply an ID, the ID parameter will be default to an empty string. We can set any Controller as the default Controller and any action method of the Controller as the default action method. If a user does not supply the Controller name, the default Controller will be executed and if a user does not supply an action method, the default action method will be executed. If a user enter only the site name without specifying the Controller name, the action method name and the ID value, the default Controller and the default action method will be executed which are defined in the MVC routing in the RouteConfig.cs file. Now consider the following routing:

```
routes.MapRoute(
name: “Default”,
url: “{controller}/{action}/{id}”,
defaults: new {
            controller = “Account”,
            action = “Register”,
            id = UrlParameter.Optional
            }
);
```

According to the above routing pattern, the default Controller is Account Controller and the default action method is Register() method. When a user enter the site name in the web browser's address bar without specifying the Controller name and the action method name then the Register() action method of the AccountController will be executed because we set the Account Controller and the Register() action method as default controller and default action method.

ActionResult Class

ActionResult is an abstract class that represents the result of an action method or the return type of an action method. It is the base class of all the action results. This class is inherited from the System.Object and it provides a single method ExecuteResult. Following is its general declaration:

```
public abstract class ActionResult
```

A common action result is obtained by calling the View method. When the View method is triggered, it returns an instance of the ViewResult class. The ViewResult class is derived from the ActionResult class. In that case, the return type of the action method is ActionResult. An instance of the ViewResult class is returned as shown below:

```
public ActionResult Index()
{
return View();          //This is a ViewResult class
}
```

In the above example, Index method is an action method that returns the ActionResult using the View() method. The View() method is defined in the Controller base class, which returns the appropriate ActionResult. The above code means that we are returning an object of the ViewResult class. The ViewResult class is derived from the ActionResult class so due to polymorphism, this object is automatically type casted to its parent class type ActionResult. When an action returns a ViewResult, HTML is returned to the browser. The ActionResult class provides a single method ExecuteResult. The ExecuteResult method enables processing of the result of an action method by a custom type that inherits from the ActionResult class. Following is the general declaration of the ExecuteResult method:

```
public abstract void ExecuteResult(ControllerContext context)
```

ActionResult Return Type

The action methods return an instance of a class which is derived from the ActionResult class. The ActionResult class is the base class of all the action results. There are different types of action results returned by the action methods according to the task that the action method performs. There are the following different types of action results which can be sent to the end user:

Action Result	Action Method	Description
ViewResult	View	This result type handles HTML and markup and it renders a view as a Web page.
PartialViewResult	PartialView	This result type is used to render a partial view, which defines a section of a view that can be rendered inside another view.
RedirectResult	Redirect	This result type performs an HTTP redirection to a specified URL.
RedirectTo RouteResult	RedirectToAction RedirectToRoute	This result type redirects to another action method.
ContentResult	Content	This result type represents a text result or a user-defined content type.
JsonResult	Json	This result type serializes a given object to JSON format and returns a serialized JSON object.
JavaScriptResult	JavaScript	This result type returns a script that can be executed on the client.

FileResult	File	This result type returns a file.
EmptyResult	(None)	This result type returns an empty result.

The above return types are separate classes. Each class is inherited from the ActionResult class.

ViewResult Class

This class represents an ActionResult that is used to render a view to the response. This class contains methods for finding the view to render and for executing the result. The ViewResult class also contains properties that identify the view to render, the name of the view, the name of the master view, view data, temporary data, and a collection for view engines for the application.

Create a Controller

To create a new Controller in an ASP.NET MVC application, follow the following steps:

1. Create a new project of ASP.NET MVC 5 web application.
2. Now right click on the Controller folder of the ASP.NET MVC web application project, click Add then click on the Controller option. When we click on the Controller option, it opens the Add Scaffold window. The Add Scaffold window contains different templates for the new Controller that are MVC 5 Controller empty, MVC 5 Controller with read/write actions, MVC 5 Controller with views using entity framework, Web API 2 Controller empty etc. Select MVC 5 Controller empty template and click on the Add button. When we click on the Add button, a small dialog opens that ask for the Controller name, give any name to the Controller and click on the Add button. The Controller name must ends with the word Controller. When we click the Add button, a new Controller is added to our ASP.NET MVC 5 project. Following is the default code of the new Controller:

```
namespace MVCWebApplication.Controllers
{
public class CustomersController : Controller
```

```
{
// GET: Customers
public ActionResult Index()
{
return View();
}
}
}
```

The name of our new Controller is CustomersController. As we see that the new Controller is derived from the base class Controller. Every Controller in MVC must derive from the Controller class. The Controller CustomersController contains an action method Index that returns an object of the ActionResult class. The Index method is the default action method of a Controller class. When we create a new Controller in ASP.NET MVC project, a new folder is created automatically inside the View folder with the same name of the Controller name for example, if we create a Controller Customers then the Customers folder will be created automatically inside the View folder.

Create a View

A View is a component of MVC application that provides user interactions. A View contains graphical user interface objects and data forms. It takes data from the user and sends to the Controller and takes data from the Controller and displays it to the users using the graphical user interface objects. The View component of MVC application is a separate folder in MVC project Folders and Files list and all the views of the application are stored in this folder. Each Controller has its own folder inside the View folder with the same name as the Controller name. When a Controller is created, it automatically creates the same name folder in the View folder of the application. To create a View for a Controller, follow the following steps:

1. Inside the View folder of MVC application, right click on the same name folder of a Controller for which you want to create view and click on the Add option then click on the View option. When we click on the View option, the Add View window is displayed that ask for the View name and View template.
2. Now give a name to the View and select the Empty template for the View and click on the Add button. When we click on the Add button, the View will be created.

Connect Database to MVC Application using Entity Framework

To connect database to MVC application using Entity Framework, the following three components must be added to MVC application:

- Database Model
- Database Controller
- Database View

Database Model

To add database Model to MVC application follow the following steps:

1. In the Solution Explorer window of Visual studio, right click on the MVC project name, select the Add option then select the New Item option. The New Item option opens the Add New Item window. The Add New Item window contains three panes that are left side pane, middle or center pane and right side pane. From the left pane select Visual C# and from the middle pane select ADO.NET Entity Data Model and give a name to it using the name text box which is located below the middle pane of the Add New Item window then press the Add button. Suppose the name of the ADO.NET Entity Data Model is StudentsModel. Its default name is Model1. Following is its snapshot:

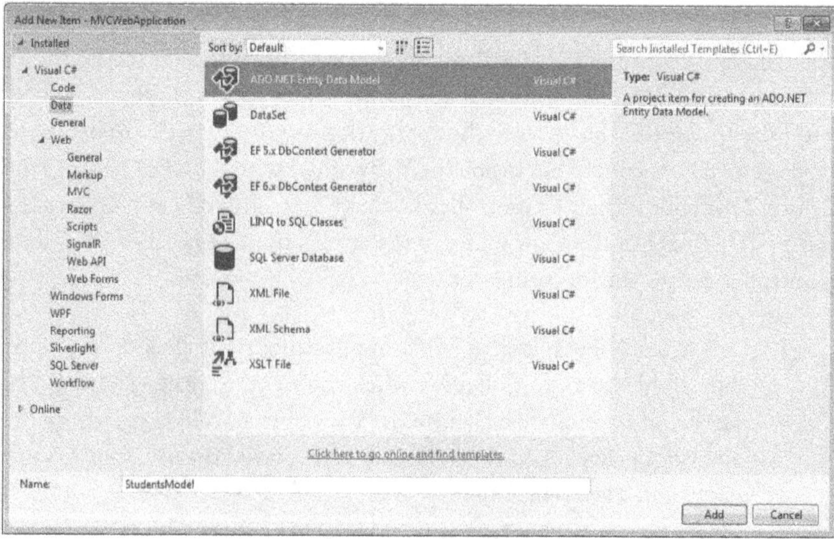

2. When we press the Add button, it displays the Entity Data Model Wizard window that contains different model contents that are EF Designer from database, Empty EF Designer model, Empty Code First model, Code First from database. Select EF Designer from database option and click the Next Button. Following is its snapshot:

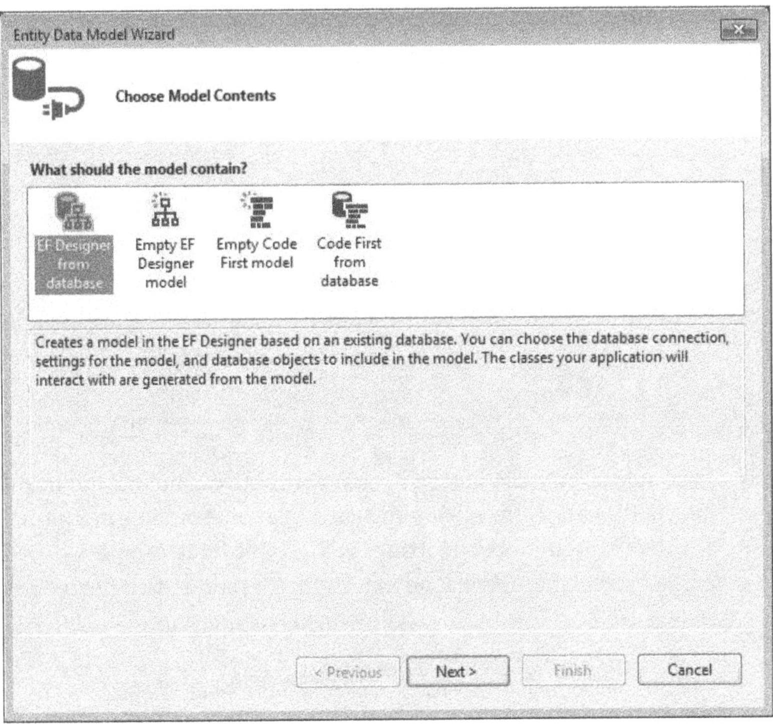

3. When we click the Next button, it opens another window from where to choose the Data Connection. To choose the Data Connection, click the New Connection button. The New Connection button opens the Connection Properties window. From the Connection Properties window, enter the Server computer name where the SQL Server database is installed and the instance of the SQL Server database using the Server name textbox. Now from the Authentication drop-down control select the SQL Server Authentication and put the user name and password in the User name and Password textboxes respectively and then select the desired database from the Select or enter a database name drop-down list. When you select the database then press the Ok button. Following is its snapshot:

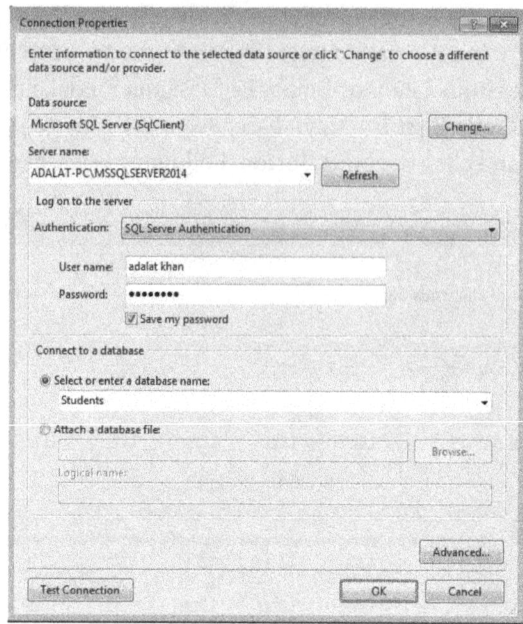

4. Now select the radio button option entitled Yes, include the sensitive data in the connection string and enter the context name in the textbox entitled Save connection settings in Web.Config as. Suppose the name of the context is StudentsContext. When you entered the context name then press the Next button. Following is its snapshot:

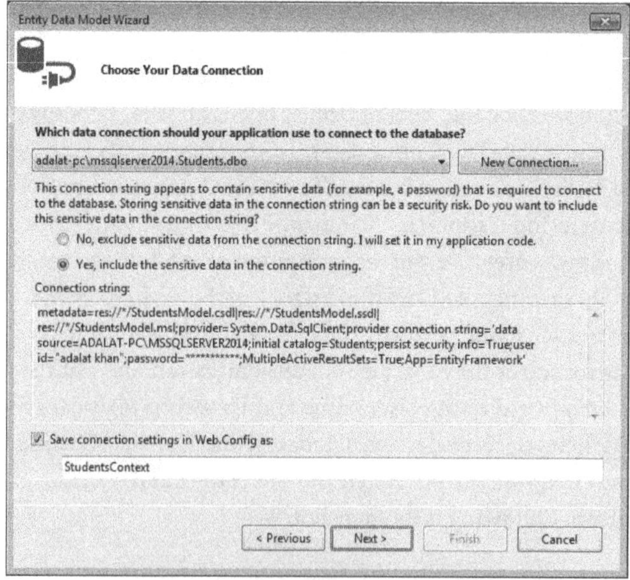

5. When we press the Next button, it opens another window from which we can include tables from the database. This window displays three types of database objects that are Tables, Views, and Stored Procedures. Each type of object has a check box option. Now click the check box option of the Tables, make it checked and select the desired tables to add to the project. Now enter the name of the Model Namespace using the Model Namespace textbox. Suppose the name of the Model Namespace is StudentsModel. When you entered name of the Model Namespace then press the Finish button. Following is its snapshot:

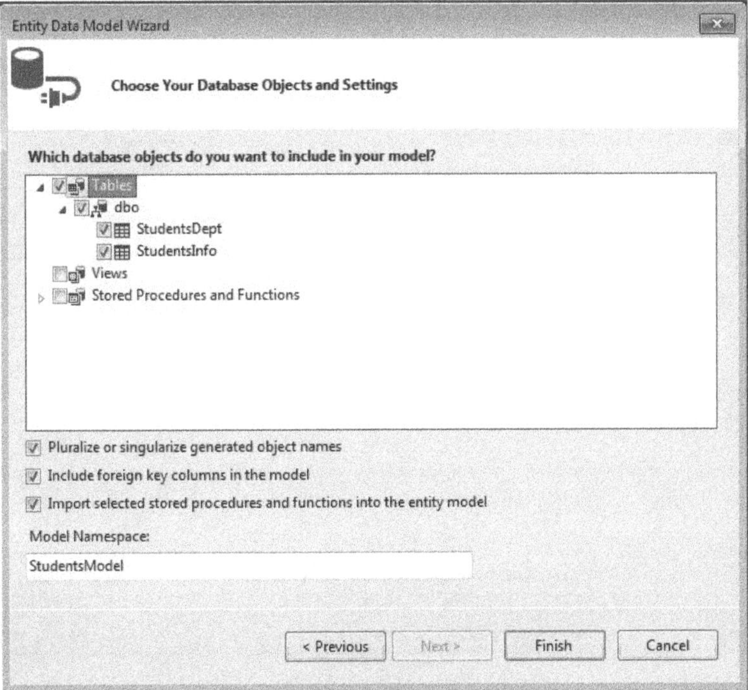

We added two tables StudentsDept and StudentsInfo of Students database. The Students database is discussed in chapter number 10. When we press the Finish button, a new file StudentsModel.edmx is added to the MVC project. The name of the .edmx file is the name we entered in the Model Namespace textbox. The .edmx is an XML file that defines the schema for data model. The .edmx file contains different classes. It contains a separate class for each database table we selected during the connection wizard.

Database Controller

To add a database Controller follows the following steps:

1. Right click on the Controller folder of ASP.NET MVC web application project, click Add then click the Controller option. The Controller option opens the Add Scaffold window. The Add Scaffold window contains different templates for the new Controller that are MVC5 Controller empty, MVC5 Controller with read/write actions, MVC5 Controller with views using entity framework, Web API 2 Controller empty etc. Following is the snapshot of the Add Scaffold window of Controller:

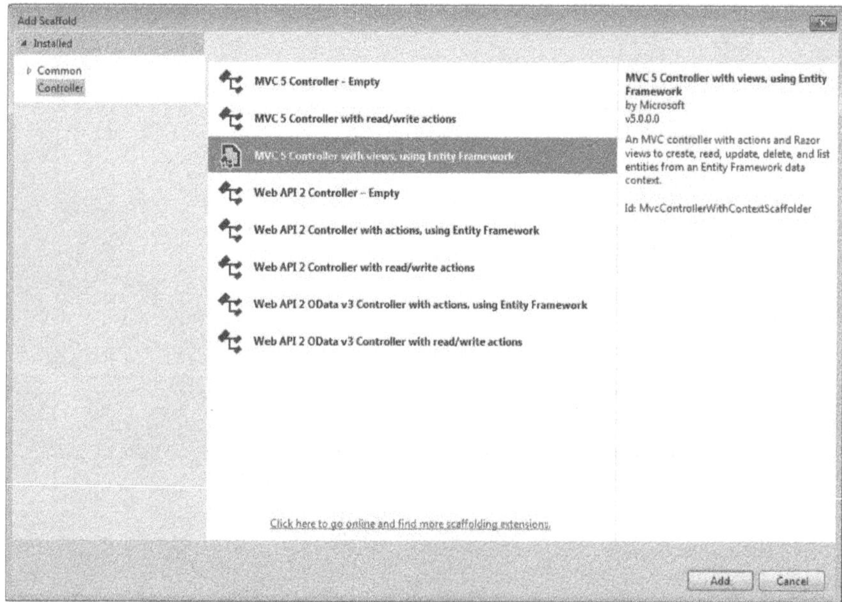

2. Now from the Add Scaffold window select MVC5 Controller with views, using Entity Framework and press the Add button. The Add button opens the Add Controller window. The Add Controller window contains two dropdown lists to select Modal class and Data Context class for the Controller. Each Controller needs a Modal and a Data Context classes. From the first dropdown list select the Modal class and from the second dropdown list select the Data Context class. The Modal class is usually a database table from which you want to retrieve or add data.

3. Now give name to the Controller using the Controller name textbox of the Add Controller window and click the Add button. The Controller name always ends with the word Controller. Suppose the name of the Controller is StudentsController. Following is the snapshot of the Add Controller window:

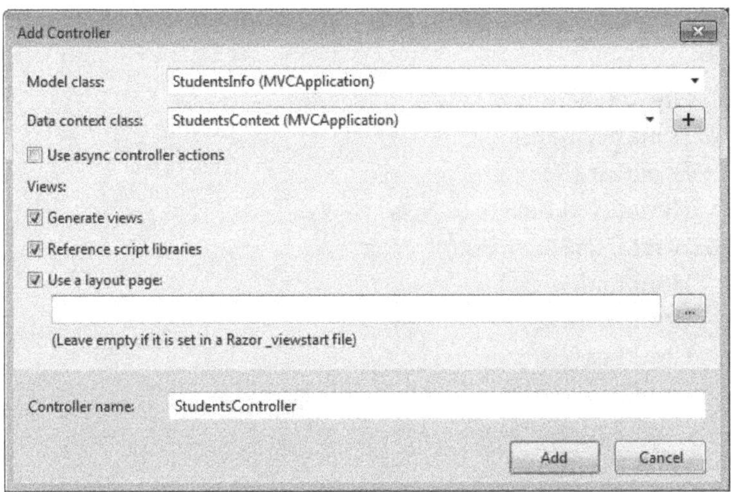

When we click the Add button, a new Controller StudentsController is added to our ASP.NET MVC web application project. The new Controller StudentsController contains different actions such as Index, Create, Details, Edit, and Delete. Each action returns ActionResult.

Database View

When we create a Controller by selecting the option MVC5 Controller with views, using Entity Framework of the Add Scaffold window, it automatically creates the Views. For each action of the Controller a separate View is created. A view is a C# or Visual Basic and HTML page that provides visual interface to the user. The file extension of a View is cshtml in C# and .vbhtml in Visual Basic. A View takes input data from the user and sends to the Controller and receives result from the Controller and displays it to the user using different Form Controls.

HTML Helpers

HTML helpers allow us to Render HTML code in our View. An HTML helper is just a method that returns a string. The string can represent any type of content that we want. For example, we can use HTML Helpers to render standard HTML tags like HTML <input> and <img> tags. We also can use HTML Helpers to render more complex content such as a tab strip or an HTML table of database data. The HTML helpers are similar to ASP.NET Web Form controls. Just like web form controls in ASP.NET, the HTML helpers are used to modify HTML. The ASP.NET MVC framework includes the following set of standard HTML Helpers:

- Html.ActionLink()
- Html.BeginForm()
- Html.Label()
- Html.CheckBox()
- Html.DropDownList()
- Html.EndForm()
- Html.Hidden()
- Html.ListBox()
- Html.Password()
- Html.RadioButton()
- Html.TextArea()
- Html.TextBox()

HTML Links

The MVC application uses HTML.ActionLink() helper to render an HTML link. The Html.ActionLink() is used to create a link on a View page and links a Controller's action method. Following is its general syntax:

Razor Syntax
@Html.ActionLink("Link-Text", "Action", "Controller")
ASP Syntax
<%=Html.ActionLink("Link-Text", "Action", "Controller")%>

In the preceding syntax, the Html.ActionLink takes three parameters. The first parameter indicates the link title text, the second parameter indicates the Action method name and the third parameter indicates the Controller name. Consider the following example of Html.ActionLink:

@Html.ActionLink("Click here", "About", "Home")

This ActionLink calls the About action method of the Home Controller and renders the following HTML code:

```
<a href="/Home/About">Click here</a>
```

We can also pass values to a controller's action method. For example, we can pass the id of a database record to a database edit action:

```
@Html.ActionLink("Edit Record", "Edit", new {Id=187})
```

HTML Form Elements

To create HTML Form elements, we can use BeginForm() and EndForm() helpers. The BeginForm helper implements the IDisposable interface and it is used with the **using** keyword. The BeginForm helper provides different overloaded forms. Following is its syntax with no parameters:

```
@using (Html.BeginForm())
{

}
```

TextBox

The Html.TextBox Helper method is used to render a textbox in the view. The Html.TextBox helper method takes different parameters such as class, textbox name, placeholder, type etc. Following is its syntax:

```
@Html.TextBox("txtName")
```

The txtName indicates the name of the textbox.

TextArea

The Html.TextArea helper is used to render the <textarea> element in the view.

RadioButton

The Html.RadioButton helper is used to render the radio button in the view. This helper method takes three parameters that is name of the control, value and Boolean value for selecting the value initially either the RadioButton is checked or unchecked. Following is its syntax:

@Html.RadioButton("rdbName","TitleText", bool value)

The first parameter indicates the name of the RadioButton, the second parameter is the title text of the RadioButton, and third parameter is the Boolean value either true or false. The true value indicates that the RadioButton is checked and the false value indicates that the RadioButton is unchecked.

CheckBox

The Html.CheckBox helper method is used to render a checkbox in the view. The CheckBox helper method takes two parameters. The first parameter is a string that indicates the CheckBox name and the second parameter is a Boolean value either true or false that indicates either the CheckBox value is selected or not. Following is its syntax:

@Html.CheckBox("chkName", bool value)

The first parameter indicates the checkbox name and the second parameter indicates the Boolean value either true or false. The true value indicates that the CheckBox is checked or selected.

DropDownList

The Html.DropDownList helper method is used to render a drop down list in the view.

CHAPTER 19

Web Services in .NET

CHAPTER CONTENTS
Web Services Components of Web Services SOAP UDDI WSDL Basic Architecture of Web Service Create ASP.NET Web Service Project Consume Web Service in ASP.NET Web Application Include Web Service Reference in Web Application [WebMethod] BufferResponse CacheDuration Description EnableSession MessageName

Web Services

A web service is an XML-based information exchange system that creates direct interaction between the two applications over the internet or network in order to exchange data or information. It enables us to communicate and exchange data or information between the two different applications created in the same or different languages over the internet or network for example, if we use multiple software systems and we need to transfer data from one application to another application then a web service is a best source to accomplish this task. The software system that sends requests for data is called a service requester whereas the software system that would process the request and provide the data is called a service provider. A web service works between all types of applications software and it does not matter if both the service requester software and service provider software are written in different programming languages because web services use XML files for data exchange and most software applications however, interpret XML tags.

A Web service accomplishes the applications interactions and data communication among various applications by using a combination of open protocols and standards such as XML, SOAP, WSDL, and UDDI. The XML is an XML file used to tag the data, the SOAP stands for Simple Object Access Protocol. The SOAP is an XML based protocol that is used for sending and receiving messages between the applications without confronting interoperability issues, the WSDL stands for Web Services Description Language and it is used for describing the services available and UDDI stands for Universal Description Discovery and Integration. The UDDI is an XML-based standard that lists what services are available. The web service file extension is asmx.

Components of Web Services

There are the following three major components of a Web Service:

- SOAP
- UDDI
- WSDL

SOAP

SOAP stands for Simple Object Access Protocol. It is a communication protocol that is responsible to allow communication and messages transfer between the two different applications of the same or different platform and the same or different programming languages. The SOAP protocol is language independent and platform independent that sends and receives messages between the different applications without facing the interoperability issues. The SOAP communication is carried out through HTTP. A SOAP message is an ordinary XML document that contains the following elements:

- <Envelope> Element
- <Header> Element
- <Body> Element
- <Fault> Element

The <Envelope> element is the root element of the SOAP message that defines the XML document as a SOAP message. It defines the start and end of the message. It actually defines the SOAP message structure. The <Envelope> element is the mandatory element of the SOAP message. The <Header>

element is an optional element of the SOAP message that contains the header information. The header may contain the routing data which is basically the information which tells the XML document to which client it needs to be sent to. The <Header> element is defined inside the <Envelope> element before the <Body> element. The <Body> element is the main element of the SOAP message that contains the actual message. The <Body> element is defined inside the <Envelope> element after the <Header> element. The <Fault> element is an optional element that contains information about errors that occurs while processing the message. The <Fault> element is defined inside the <Body> element. Following is the general skeleton of a SOAP message:

```
<?xml version="1.0"?>
<soap:Envelope
xmlns:soap="http://www.w3.org/2003/05/soap-envelope/"
soap:encodingStyle="http://www.w3.org/2003/05/soap-encoding">

<soap:Header>
...
</soap:Header>

<soap:Body>
...
<soap:Fault>
<-- The Fault element is an optional element and it is used only if a fault occurs in web service.
-->
</soap:Fault>
</soap:Body>

</soap:Envelope>
```

UDDI

UDDI stands for Universal Description Discovery and Integration. The UDDI is an XML-based standard that lists what services are available. The UDDI uses WSDL to describe interfaces to web services. It can communicate via SOAP, CORBA, and Java RMI Protocol.

WSDL

WSDL stands for Web Service Description Language. It is a standard that describes the availability of service. It enables a web service to tell to the clients that what messages it accepts and which results it will return. The WSDL is written in XML and it is used in the combination with the SOAP and XML schema to provide web services over the internet.

Basic Architecture of Web Service

A Web Service is a web application that follows code-behind architecture such as the ASP.NET web pages but it does not have a user interface. A Web Service application is basically a class containing methods that are exposed over the Web using simple messaging protocol stacks. The methods of a Web Service are called web methods. Each web method is represented by the [WebMethod] attribute. The Web Service methods are similar to the ordinary methods but the main difference is that a web service method can be accessed by the way of a web browser. A Web Service application is used by other applications called clients applications. To consume a Web Service application, a separate client application is created in any programming language. A client application invokes a Web Service application over HTTP using a web method. When we create a Web Service application using ASP.NET, the following files are automatically created:

File	Description
.asmx	The .asmx file is the ASP.NET Web Service source file that stands for Active Server Method file. It is similar to .ASPX files but the main difference is that the .asmx file does not have graphical user interface and it is the end point for AP.NET Web Services. The .asmx file moves data and performs other actions behind the scenes. It displays the Web Service methods in a list and allows user to invoke the Web Service methods. The .asmx file placed the required Web Services directive at the top of this file to create association between the URL address of the Web Service and its implementation. The .asmx file is used to add Web Services logic to the methods visible by the client application and it acts as the base URL for clients calling the XML web service.

code-behind	When we create an ASP.NET Web Service application, a code-behind file is generated with a language-specific extension. For example, if the Visual C# language is used for the ASP.NET Web Service project then a code behind file is created with the .cs extension and if the Visual Basic language is used for the ASP.NET Web Server project then a code behind file is created with the .vb extension. The .cs or .vb file is the code behind file that contains the Web Service logic. This file contains a class which is inherited from the System.Web.Services.WebService class. The Web Service methods are defined in the class of the .cs or .vb file. Each method of the Web Service is represented by [WebMethod] attribute. The [WebMethod] attribute is placed prior to the method name. The Web Service method is used to define the Web Service logic or a task
.wsdl	This file is generated when we add a Web Service application to a client application. This file describes the Web Services interface available to the client.

Create ASP.NET Web Service Project

To create a Web Service application, first create a Website then add a Web Service file to the Website. A Website can be created using Microsoft Visual Studio or Microsoft Visual Web Developer. To create a Website using Microsoft Visual Studio.NET, a new project of ASP.NET Website can be created using Microsoft Visual Studio.NET 2015 by using the following steps:

6. Open Microsoft Visual Studio.NET.
7. From the File menu of Microsoft Visual Studio.NET, select New then select Web Site. It will display New Web Site dialog box.
8. The New Web Site dialog box contains three pans that are left side pane, middle pane, and right side pane. From the left side pane, under the Installed Templates, select your desired programming language such as C# or Visual Basic then from the middle pane select ASP.NET Empty Web Site.
9. In the Web location box, select File System then enter the name of the folder where you want to keep your Web site.
1. Now click on the OK button of the New Web Site dialog box. After these steps, an empty Web Site project will be opened.
2. Now add a Web Service file to the Web Site project. To add a Web Service

file to the Web Site, right click on the Project Name from the Solution Explorer and select Add then select the Add New Item option. When you select the Add New Item option, it opens the Add New Item window.

3. The Add New Item window contains three pans that are left side pane, middle pane and right side pane. From the middle pane of the Add New Item window, select the Web Service file and under the name textbox enter the name for the Web Service file and then press the Add button of the Add New Item window. The name of the Web Service file should be any valid name. The extension of the Web Service file is .asmx. When the Web Service file is added to the Web Site project then two files are automatically added to the Web Site project. The extension of the one file is .cs and the extension of the second file is .asmx. Suppose the name of the Web Service file is WebServiceCalculation then two files are automatically added to the Web Site project. The name of the first file is WebServiceCalculation.cs and the name of the second file is WebServiceCalculation.asmx. These two files are created automatically in the App_Code folder.

Following is the default code of the WebServiceCalculation.cs file:

ASP.NET C# Web Service

```
using System.Web.Services;

[WebService(Namespace = "http://tempuri.org/")]
[WebServiceBinding(ConformsTo = WsiProfiles.BasicProfile1_1)]
public class WebServiceCalculation : WebService
{
public WebServiceCalculation()
{
//Uncomment the following line if using designed components
//InitializeComponent();
}

[WebMethod]
public string HelloWorld()
{
return "Hello World";
}
}
```

The default Web Service contains a single method and when it is invoked using the Web Browser, it displays a string message Hello World. We can change the code of this method according to our task or functionality and we can also create more Web Service methods according to the number of tasks or functionality. For example if we want to create a Web Service for calculation purpose to add and subtract two integer values then we will create two Web Service methods one method to perform addition and another method to perform subtraction. To create a Web Service that performs addition and subtraction of two integer values, the above code of the WebServiceCalculation.cs file will be replaced as follows:

ASP.NET C# Web Service

```
using System.Web.Services;

[WebService(Namespace = "http://tempuri.org/")]
[WebServiceBinding(ConformsTo = WsiProfiles.BasicProfile1_1)]
public class WebServiceCalculation : WebService
{
public WebServiceCalculation()
{
//Uncomment the following line if using designed components
//InitializeComponent();
}

[WebMethod]
public int AddTwoValues(int x, int y)
{
return x + y;
}

[WebMethod]
public int SubtractTwoValues(int x, int y)
{
return x - y;
}
}
```

The above Web Service application contains two web service methods in which one method calculate the sum of two integer values and second method calculate subtraction of the two integer values. Now the Web Service Server application is ready to use. When the above Web Service application is run, the .asmx file lists the name of the two Web Service methods in the Web Browser. To use a Web Service, a client application is created and it is reference with the Web Service application using the Add Web reference to the website.

Consume Web Service in ASP.NET Web Application

To consume a Web Service application in ASP.NET Web Application, follow the following steps:

1. Open a new empty project of ASP.NET Web Application.
2. Now go to the Solution Explorer, right click on the project name and press the **Add** option then select **Service Reference**. The **Service Reference** opens the Add Service Reference window.
3. Now from the Add Service Reference window, press the **Advanced** button. The **Advanced** button of the Add Service Reference window opens the Service Reference Settings window.
4. Now from the Service Reference Settings window, press the **Add Web Reference** button. The **Add Web Reference** button opens the Add Web Reference window that contains a URL textbox. Now copy the URL of the .asmx file of the Web Service application and put this URL in the URL textbox of the Add Web Reference window and press the Go button.
5. When we press the Go button, the Web Service is displayed in the browser of the Add Web Reference window and the Web Service file .asmx is displayed in the browser of the Add Web Reference window then in the **Web reference name** textbox, a default name is displayed for the Web Service that is usually the name of the localhost. We can give any name to the **Web reference name**.
6. Change the **Web reference name** from the localhost to any other name suppose ReferenceWebService and then press the **Add Reference** button. The **Add Reference** button creates a Proxy at the client side. The **Web reference name** is used as a directive in the client application and it must be included in the client application. We can also use a fully qualified name of the Web Service application main class. The Web Service reference automatically added to the Web Application under the Web references folder.
7. Now add a new Web Form to the Web application and give a meaningful name to it. Suppose the name of the new Web Form is

ConsumeWebServiceForm. Now create three textboxes controls and two command button controls on the ConsumeWebServiceForm. The first two textboxes control will read two integer values from the user and the third textbox control is used to display the result of the Web Service method. The first button control is used to send values of the first two textbox control to the AddTwoValues Web Service method and the second button control is used to send the values of the first two textbox controls to the SubtractTwoValues Web Service method.

Include Web Service Reference in Web Application

When the Web Service reference is added to the ASP.NET Web Application, the Web reference name is included in it in the directive section of the Web application. When the Web reference name is included in the ASP.NET Web Application, the Web Service class is visible to use its member methods. The member methods of the Web Service class are Web Service methods. To use Web Service methods, in the client application of ASP.NET Web application, an object of the Web Service class is declared and it is used to invoke the Web Service methods. Following is the general syntax to include the Web reference name in the ASP.NET Web application:

```
using ASP.NET Web Application Name.Web reference name;
```

Now open the Web Form ConsumeWebServiceForm.aspx of the ConsumeWebService Web application in design view and create three textboxes controls and two button controls or put the following code:

The design code of the Web Form ConsumeWebServiceForm.aspx
<html xmlns="http://www.w3.org/1999/xhtml"> <head runat="server"> <title></title> </head> <body> <form id="form1" runat="server"> <div> <asp:TextBox ID="TextBox1" runat="server"></asp:TextBox> <asp:TextBox ID="TextBox2" runat="server"></asp:TextBox> <asp:TextBox ID="TextBox3" runat="server"></asp:TextBox>

```
<asp:Button ID="Button1" runat="server" Text="Add Values"
OnClick="Button1_Click" />
<asp:Button ID="Button2" runat="server" Text="Subtract Values"
OnClick="Button2_Click" />
</div>
</form>
</body>
</html>
```

Now open the code behind file ConsumeWebServiceForm.aspx.cs of the Web Form ConsumeWebServiceForm.aspx and put the following code:

Code of the code behind file ConsumeWebServiceForm.aspx.cs of the ConsumeWebService Web application.

```
using System;
using ConsumeWebService.ReferenceWebService;

namespace ConsumeWebService
{
public partial class ConsumeWebServiceForm : System.Web.UI.Page
{
//Declare an object from the class of Web Service
WebServiceCalculation obj = new WebServiceCalculation();

protected void Page_Load(object sender, EventArgs e)
{

}

protected void Button1_Click(object sender, EventArgs e)
{
int x, y, Result;

x = Convert.ToInt32(TextBox1.Text);
y = Convert.ToInt32(TextBox2.Text);
Result = obj.AddTwoValues(x, y);
TextBox3.Text = Result.ToString();
}
```

```
protected void Button2_Click(object sender, EventArgs e)
{
int x, y, Result;

x = Convert.ToInt32(TextBox1.Text);
y = Convert.ToInt32(TextBox2.Text);
Result = obj.SubtractTwoValues(x, y);
TextBox3.Text = Result.ToString();
}
}
}
```

[WebMethod]

It is an attribute that is used in the Web Service applications to mark a method as an XML web service method. When a method is marked as an XML web service method then that method can be exposed in the client application. We cannot access any method of a web service application in a client application without the [WebMethod] attribute. The [WebMethod] attribute is usually used to a Public method of the web service application. We can also use the properties of this attribute to further configure the behavior of the XML Web service method. The ASP.NET makes it possible to map traditional methods to Web Service operations through the [WebMethod] attribute. The [WebMethod] supports a number of properties that control the behavior of the methods. The fully qualified name of the [WebMethod] is System.Web.Services.WebMethod. The [WebMethod] attribute provides the following properties:

- BufferResponse
- CacheDuration
- Description
- EnableSession
- MessageName

BufferResponse

This property of the WebMethod attribute enables buffering of responses for an XML Web service method. It takes a Boolean value either true or false. When we set it to true then ASP.NET buffers the entire response before sending it down to the client. The buffering is very efficient and helps improve performance by minimizing communication between the worker process and the IIS process. When we set it to false then ASP.NET buffers the response in chunks of 16KB. If we do not want the entire contents of the response in memory at once then we set this property to false. The default value of this property is true.

CacheDuration

ASP.NET has built-in support for caching the data on the server. Web Services can use the caching support of ASP.NET to cache the result of a web method. The CacheDuration property takes an integer value that indicates the number of seconds that the web method response will remain in the cache. The default value is 0, which means the server doesn't cache the response. When we enable caching, the server holds responses in memory for the cache duration, so we must use caution if we expect responses to be large or if we expect requests to vary widely. Following is the general syntax of the CacheDuration property:

```
[WebMethod(CacheDuration = 20)]
```

In the above declaration we assign 20 to CacheDuration that means the server will hold the response in memory for 20 seconds.

Description

This property is used to specify a description for the web service method. Following is the general syntax of Description:

```
[WebMethod(Description = "Description")]
```

EnableSession

This property of the WebMethod attribute enables session state for an XML Web service method. It takes a Boolean value either true or false. When we set its value to true, the XML Web service can access the session state collection directly from HttpContext.Current.Session.

MessageName

This property of the WebMethod attribute enables the XML Web service to uniquely identify overloaded methods using an alias.

About The Author

The author of this Book **Mr. Adalat Khan** is a resident of Koza Bandai district Swat Khyber Pakhtunkhwa Pakistan. He has passed his Intermediate (F.Sc Pre Engineering) from Government **Jehanzeb College** Saidu Sharif Swat and his Bachelor Degree **"Bachelor of Computer Sciences (BCS)"** from **CECOS** University of IT and Emerging Sciences Peshawar Pakistan and Master Degree **"Master of Information Technology (MIT)"** from **GOMAL** University Dera Ismail Khan Pakistan. The author has extensive experience in C/C++, Visual C++, Visual C++.NET, Visual Basic, Visual Basic.NET, Visual C#.NET, ASP.NET, SQL Server Database, Java, Java Script, VB Script, Web APIs, XML, HTML5, CSS3, Bootstrap etc.

Note for the Readers:
This book contains several logical programs. If you face any problem or ambiguity about any program or any step, you can send your questions directly to the author by using the following Email address:

Email Address:
adalatkn@gmail.com

Suggestions and Comments
If there is any error or technical mistakes anywhere in this book please feel free to send your suggestions and comments by using the above email address.

www.ingramcontent.com/pod-product-compliance
Lightning Source LLC
LaVergne TN
LVHW040916080326
832904LV00042B/313/J

* 9 7 8 1 9 8 4 5 0 1 5 3 0 *